CW00558426

Mesolithic Scotland and its Neighbours

This volume is dedicated to

John M. Coles MA ScD PhD FSA FBA Hon FSA Scot

Mesolithic Scotland
and its
Neighbours

The Early Holocene Prehistory of Scotland,
its British and Irish Context,
and some Northern European Perspectives

Edited by
ALAN SAVILLE

Edinburgh 2004
SOCIETY OF ANTIQUARIES OF SCOTLAND

Published in 2004 by the Society of Antiquaries of Scotland
Editor: Alan Saville

Society of Antiquaries of Scotland, Royal Museum of Scotland,
Chambers Street, Edinburgh EH1 1JF
Tel: 0131 247 4115
Fax: 0131 247 4163
Email: administration@socantscot.org
Website: www.socantscot.org

British Library Cataloguing-in-Publication Data
A catalogue record for this book is available from the British Library

ISBN 0 903903 28 8

The Society gratefully acknowledges grant-aid towards the publication of this volume from:

HISTORIC SCOTLAND

CBA
COUNCIL FOR BRITISH
ARCHAEOLOGY

Typeset in Times by Waverley Typesetters, Galashiels
Design and production by Lawrie Law and Alison Rae
Manufactured in Great Britain by The Bath Press, Bath

Contents

SECTION 1: INTRODUCTION

SECTION 2: SCOTLAND, THE SETTING

SECTION 3: SCOTLAND, THE ARCHAEOLOGY

SECTION 4: BRITAIN AND IRELAND

SECTION 5: NORTHERN EUROPE

List of Figures

List of Tables

Preface

This volume is the outcome of a conference held at the Royal Museum in Edinburgh on 5–7 November 1999, organized by the Society of Antiquaries of Scotland. As Research Convener for the Society at the time I felt it important that the Society should be promoting major international conferences on particular phases or aspects of Scotland's past, seen non-parochially in a wider UK and European perspective. Following my own research orientation, but also with the thought that such a conference might become the first of a chronologically themed series, I proposed Scotland's very earliest prehistory as the topic. The Society's officers and committees embraced my suggestion, initially with some scepticism ('a whole weekend on the Mesolithic?'), but subsequently with enthusiasm as preparations developed over the course of eighteen months under the overview of the Society's Director, Fionna Ashmore, who was a strong supporter from the very start. The Prehistoric Society and the National Museums of Scotland joined with the Society of Antiquaries of Scotland as co-hosts of the conference, and it became clear there was considerable interest from potential speakers and delegates.

One of my intentions in choosing the topic was to raise the profile of Mesolithic studies in Scotland by demonstrating that this is an exciting, lively, and significant area of research. To this end it seemed important to ensure there was time for open discussion following each session at the conference, and I have included these discussions in this publication to give a true flavour of the entertaining and stimulating – frank but friendly! – interchange of views which took place.

Another firm intention was that, while the focus was Mesolithic Scotland, the conference should not be restricted in coverage or attitude. It was important to set what was known of this period in Scotland within the context of the rest of the UK and Ireland, and to expand horizons by looking at aspects of Mesolithic archaeology of particular potential relevance in other parts of northern Europe. This ambition was realized by talks which covered aspects of the Mesolithic in virtually the whole of the British Isles (England, Scotland, Wales, and the Isle of Man), Denmark, Ireland, Norway, Poland,

and Sweden. Equally I felt it essential when looking at the Scottish evidence to ensure that the physical and biological environment in which Mesolithic people found themselves in Scotland was fully explored, rather than just the conventional archaeology.

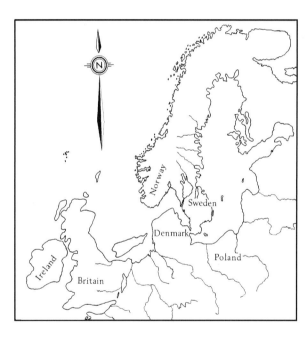

An approximation of the extent of northern Europe early in the Holocene, with the names of the countries represented in this volume superimposed.

It was gratifying that the conference attracted a large audience, including many amateur enthusiasts and Fellows of the Society with a special interest in, or just a vague curiosity about, the Mesolithic period. Very many of the most important Mesolithic discoveries throughout Europe have been made in the first instance by amateurs and Scotland is no exception in this regard, so it was particularly pleasing to have Reg Candow, the discoverer of the Morton site (Candow 1989), as an enthusiastic participant in the conference. Reg's subsequent death while this publication was in preparation is a matter of deep regret.

Clearly it is important that Mesolithic research is not undertaken within an academic vacuum but produces information which is communicated to the wider public. Recent fieldwork projects in Scotland, such as the Southern Hebrides Mesolithic Project (Mithen 2000), the Scotland's First Settlers Project (Hardy & Wickham-Jones 2002; 2003), and the Manor Valley Project (Cowie 2000) have done just that, in some cases involving local people directly in practical Mesolithic research. Also the state heritage organization, Historic Scotland, has sponsored two imaginative series of popular archaeology books, each of which has included highly successful volumes on the Mesolithic period (Finlayson 1998; Wickham-Jones 1994). The material presented in the present volume is inevitably for the most part at a specialist level, but it does provide a rich quarry of up-to-date information which can, and I hope will, be disseminated further by others.

The complete programme of the actual conference is given below (page xv). It was immensely gratifying to be able to assemble in one forum so many of the major specialists in this field and my very sincere thanks go to all the speakers for their willing participation. The only talk listed which was not actually delivered at the conference was that by Dr Andrew Kitchener, who was unfortunately taken ill on the weekend. All the talks, including that of Dr Kitchener, have been turned into papers for this volume with the exception of two – those by Clive Bonsall (see Bonsall et al. 2002a & 2002b; Parker et al. 2002) and Dr Tony Pollard (see Pollard 2000). In the publication the papers are presented in a different sequence to that in which the talks were given at the conference, and an introductory chapter has been added to provide background for the papers which follow. Talks as presented during the conference were of necessity quite brief, and in the written versions all have been expanded, some very considerably and sometimes with a recast emphasis and with additional collaborators.

For me, while the conference itself was a hugely enjoyable, adrenalin-fueled occasion, the editing process to produce this volume has been an experience of an altogether different nature! What seemed such a straightforward, simple undertaking in the abstract, became in the reality a struggle to fulfil in competition with other unforeseen commitments and complications. To those contributors who were exemplary in the rapidity and quality of presentation of their submissions (and re-submissions), I apologize for the lapse of time involved. In fact all contributors were given the option of updating their papers in 2003 and much new material and many new references have been added. Patrick Ashmore in particular has very helpfully updated the listing and analysis of radiocarbon dates in his contributions. No

publication can be entirely up-to-the-moment of course, and the recent exciting discoveries of Mesolithic 'houses' at East Barns, Dunbar, East Lothian, and Howick, Northumberland (Denison 2003; Gooder 2003; Waddington 2003), are a reminder that the database is ever-growing and changing in character. Nevertheless, I believe this volume represents a very significant collection of papers which together form a coherent compendium of information on the Mesolithic period in Scotland, the rest of the UK, and well beyond.

This volume is respectfully dedicated to John Coles, in recognition of his many contributions to Scottish archaeology, but in particular his work at, and publication of, the site at Morton in Fife, which kick-started the modern era of Mesolithic studies in Scotland (Coles 1971).

ALAN SAVILLE
Marchmont, Edinburgh
December 2003

References

Bonsall, C., Anderson, D.E. and Macklin, M.G. 2002a. The Mesolithic–Neolithic transition in western Scotland and its European context. *Documenta Prehistorica* **29**, 1–19.

Bonsall, C., Macklin, M.G., Anderson, D.E. and Payton, R.W. 2002b. Climate change and the adoption of agriculture in north-west Europe. *European Journal of Archaeology* **5**(1), 9–23.

Candow, R. 1989. *Prehistoric Morton*. Dundee: privately printed.

Coles, J.M. 1971. The early settlement of Scotland: excavations at Morton, Fife. *Proceedings of the Prehistoric Society* **37**(2), 284–366.

Cowie, T. (ed.). 2000. *'A Winsome Grace Peculiarly its Own': An Introduction to the Archaeology of the Manor Valley.* Peebles: Peeblesshire Archaeological Society.

Denison, S. 2003. Mesolithic houses in both Scotland and the North East. *British Archaeology* **69** (March 2003), 7.

Finlayson, B. 1998. *Wild Harvesters: the First People in Scotland*. Edinburgh: Canongate Books/Historic Scotland.

Gooder, J. 2003. Excavating the oldest house in Scotland: East Barns, Dunbar, East Lothian. *Scottish Archaeological News* **42** (Summer 2003), 1–2.

Hardy, K. and Wickham-Jones, C. 2002. Scotland's First Settlers: the Mesolithic seascape of the Inner Sound, Skye, and its contribution to the early prehistory of Scotland. *Antiquity* **76**, 825–33.

Hardy, K. and Wickham-Jones, C.R. 2003. Scotland's First Settlers: an investigation into settlement, territoriality and mobility during the Mesolithic in the Inner Sound, Scotland, first results. *In* L Larsson *et al.* (eds), *Mesolithic on the Move: Papers Presented at the Sixth International*

Conference on the Mesolithic in Europe, Stockholm 2000, 369–81. Oxford: Oxbow Books.

Mithen, S. (ed.). 2000. *Hunter-Gatherer Landscape Archaeology: The Southern Hebrides Mesolithic Project 1988–98. Vols. 1–2*. Cambridge: McDonald Institute Monograph.

Parker, A.G., Goudie, A.S., Anderson, D.E., Robinson, M.A. and Bonsall, C. 2002. A review of the mid-Holocene elm decline in the British Isles. *Progress in Physical Geography* **26**(1), 1–45.

Pollard, T. 2000. Risga and the Mesolithic occupation of Scottish islands. *In* R. Young (ed.), *Mesolithic Lifeways: Current Research from Britain and Ireland*, 143–52. Leicester: University of Leicester (Leicester Archaeology Monograph **7**).

Waddington, C. 2003. A Mesolithic settlement at Howick. *Archaeology in Northumberland 2002–2003*, 19–20.

Wickham-Jones, C.R. 1994. *Scotland's First Settlers*. London: Batsford/Historic Scotland.

Note on the presentation of radiocarbon determinations

It will be seen that, following current convention for Palaeolithic/Mesolithic archaeology, and for Quaternary studies in general, most of the contributors to this volume use 'dates' in the form of radiocarbon (^{14}C) years BP (before present = before AD 1950). Radiocarbon determinations are often cited in the text in abbreviated form using the uncalibrated centrum (prefaced by '*c.*' for *circa*) to indicate this is both an abstraction and a 'shorthand' for an age range which may extend for several centuries either side of that figure. The inherent problems of using radiocarbon years are described by Ashmore (this volume, Chapter 6), and calibration into calendar years of all the Scottish determinations is very helpfully provided by him (Chapter 7). It is important that readers appreciate the significance and limitations of the BP convention, but at the moment there is no generally accepted alternative to this form of chronological presentation.

Where the laboratory numbers of determinations are included, they use the conventional abbreviations to identify laboratories (e.g. OxA = Oxford Radiocarbon Accelerator Unit, Research Laboratory for Archaeology and the History of Art, Oxford University).

Note on places

In most cases site names and locations have been reproduced in the form in which individual contributors submitted them, with or without more specific geographic indicators, though where necessary the references cited should provide clarification. For Scotland the position is complicated by the move in 1975 from Counties to Regions and Districts, which were in turn replaced in 1996 by the current Council Areas. Where practical the current Council Area designations have been used, but some older, in many ways more informative locators – such as Wester Ross – have been retained. In the text the name of the Inner Hebridean island of Rùm is standardized thus, following the current Gaelicized usage of the Ordnance Survey, rather than the Anglicized version of 'Rhum', which was in general use during the 1980s–90s when the Mesolithic site at Kinloch on Rùm was excavated, published, and publicized.

Acknowledgements

My foremost debt in preparing this volume is to my wife, Annette Carruthers, who has not only helped directly with sound editorial advice, proof-reading, and the loan of her computer, but who has cheerfully accepted the disruption to life and home during its extended gestation. The main burden of the practical organization of the conference which led to these proceedings fell to Fionna Ashmore, Director of the Society of Antiquaries of Scotland, and without her imaginative and efficient administration and belief in the enterprise neither the conference nor this volume could have succeeded.

The input in the final stages by Alison Rae, the Society's Publications Production Manager, has been invaluable. Morvern Hardie, the Society's Administrative Assistant, helped by Fionna Ashmore, undertook the initial transcription of the tapes of the conference discussion sessions, which were originally recorded by Chris Dawson and Grant Macrae. I am grateful to all the conference participants for agreeing to the proceedings being recorded for publication. Kevin Hicks undertook the dust-jacket design and Duncan Anderson helped with various photographic problems.

Thanks are due to the Council for British Archaeology and Historic Scotland for financial support towards this publication, and to the National Museums of Scotland for much help in kind during its preparation.

Conference Programme

Friday 5 November 1999

Welcome by Mark Jones, Director, National Museums of Scotland, and by Professor Michael Lynch, President, Society of Antiquaries of Scotland

Keynote opening address by the President of the Prehistoric Society,
Professor Paul Mellars: *The Mesolithic period in Scotland within Europe: retrospect and prospect.*

Saturday 6 November 1999

Dr Torben Bjarke Ballin: *The Mesolithic period in southern Norway: material culture and chronology.*

Professor Lars Larsson: *The Mesolithic period in southern Scandinavia: with special reference to burials and cemeteries.*

Professor Søren Andersen: *The Mesolithic period in southern Scandinavia: with special reference to shell middens.*

Dr Zofia Sulgostowska: *The Polish Mesolithic as seen from the perspective of peat-bog sites.*

Professor Peter Woodman: *Ireland, settling the periphery: the Mesolithic of an Atlantic island.*

Elizabeth A. Walker: *Wales during the Mesolithic period: results from recent research.*

Dr Sinéad B. McCartan: *The Mesolithic in the Isle of Man: an island perspective.*

Dr Nick Barton: *The Mesolithic period in England: an overview of the current position.*

Sunday 7 November 1999

Professor Colin Ballantyne: *After the ice: paraglacial and postglacial evolution of the physical landscape of Scotland: 20ka to 5ka BP.*

Dr Richard Tipping: *Vegetation structure and change in early Holocene Scotland.*

Dr Andrew Kitchener: *Missing mammals from Mesolithic middens: a comparison of the fossil and archaeological records.*

Professor Kevin Edwards: *Palaeoecology in the Scottish Mesolithic: new work, new thoughts.*

Patrick Ashmore: *Dating the Mesolithic period in Scotland.*

Alan Saville: *Scotland: the Mesolithic material culture.*

Caroline R. Wickham-Jones: *Structural evidence in the Scottish Mesolithic.*

Dr Tony Pollard: *Catching the tide: Mesolithic maritimism reconsidered.*

Dr Bill Finlayson: *The use of stone tools in Mesolithic Scotland: function, value, decision-making, and landscapes.*

Clive Bonsall: *The Mesolithic/Neolithic transition in western Scotland.*

Keynote closing address by Professor Steven Mithen: *The Mesolithic experience in Scotland.*

List of Contributors

Søren H. Andersen
Moesgård Museum, DK-8270 Højbjerg, Denmark

Patrick Ashmore
Historic Scotland, Longmore House, Salisbury Place, Edinburgh EH9 1SH, Scotland

Colin K. Ballantyne
School of Geography and Geosciences, University of St Andrews, Fife KY16 9AL, Scotland

Torben Bjarke Ballin
Lithic Research, Banknock Cottage, Denny, Stirlingshire FK6 5NA, Scotland

Nick Barton
Institute of Archaeology, 36 Beaumont Street, Oxford OX1 2PG, England

László Bartosiewicz
Institute of Archaeological Sciences, Lorand Eötvös University, H-1088 Budapest, Muzeum krt 4/B, Hungary

Clive Bonsall
Department of Archaeology, University of Edinburgh, Old High School, Infirmary Street, Edinburgh EH1 1LT, Scotland

Andrew David
English Heritage, Fort Cumberland, Fort Cumberland Road, Eastney, Portsmouth PO4 9LD, England

Kevin J. Edwards
Department of Geography and Environment & Northern Studies Centre, University of Aberdeen, Elphinstone Road, Aberdeen AB24 3UF, Scotland

Bill Finlayson
Council for British Research in the Levant, P.O. Box 519, Jubaiha, Amman 11941, Jordan

Andrew C. Kitchener
Department of Geology and Zoology, National Museums of Scotland, Chambers Street, Edinburgh EH1 1JF, Scotland

Lars Larsson
Department of Archaeology and Ancient History, University of Lund, Sandgatan1, S-223 50 Lund, Sweden

Sinéad B. McCartan
Department of Archaeology and Ethnography, Ulster Museum, Botanic Gardens, Belfast BT9 5AB, Northern Ireland

Paul A. Mellars
Department of Archaeology, Cambridge University, Downing Street, Cambridge CB2 3DZ, England

Steven Mithen
School of Human and Environmental Sciences, University of Reading, Whiteknights, PO Box 227, Reading RG6 6AB, England

Alison J. Roberts
Department of Prehistoric Antiquities, Ashmolean Museum, Beaumont Street, Oxford OX1 2PH, England

Alan Saville
Department of Archaeology, National Museums of Scotland, Chambers Street, Edinburgh EH1 1JF, Scotland

Zofia Sulgostowska
Institute of Archaeology and Ethnology, Polish Academy of Sciences, Al. Solidarności 105, 00-140 Warsaw, Poland

Richard Tipping
Department of Environmental Science, University of Stirling, Stirling FK9 4LA, Scotland

Elizabeth A. Walker
National Museums & Galleries of Wales, Cathays Park, Cardiff CF10 3NP, Wales

Caroline R. Wickham-Jones
Cassie, Sunnybank Road, St Ola, Kirkwall, Orkney KW15 1TP, Scotland

Peter Woodman
Department of Archaeology, University College, Cork, Ireland

Section 1

INTRODUCTION

Chapter 1

Introducing Mesolithic Scotland: the Background to a Developing Field of Study

ALAN SAVILLE

The development of Mesolithic studies in Scotland is reviewed and set in context. Lacaille's Stone Age in Scotland, *published in 1954, can be seen to mark the culmination of the first phase of Mesolithic research. Subsequent changing perceptions and the recent intensification of fieldwork are discussed, with a footnote on the 'Obanian'.*

Introduction

'Mesolithic' is the term used to categorize the early Postglacial phase of the Holocene epoch in northern Europe, prior to the adoption of agriculture and associated new cultural and technological practices in the succeeding Neolithic period. Chronologically this means from the conventional start of the Holocene at *c*.10,000 BP down to a termination flexibly determined in any given part of Europe by the date at which Neolithicization can be demonstrated in the archaeological record (Price 2000). During the Mesolithic period people subsisted principally by foraging – hunting, fishing, and gathering – developing distinctive repertoires of material culture, best known generally in the archaeological record in the form of stone, bone, and antler tools. Mesolithic people seem to have been organized socially in mobile or semi-mobile extended family units, the size of group and degree of sedentism tailored to the food and other resources available in any locality and in accordance with prevailing socio-cultural strategies, most of which inevitably remain obscure. 'Mesolithic' – actually an adjective but increasingly used also as a stand-alone noun in abbreviation of 'Mesolithic period/age/times/ etc.' – thus has connotations which are chronological, economic, and cultural (Clark 1980; Mellars 1981; Mithen 1994; Price 1983; 1987).

In Scotland, the study and definition of the Mesolithic period are made potentially less complex than in many other parts of Europe, including southern Britain, by the apparent absence of any antecedent (i.e. Palaeolithic) human occupation. There is certainly no credible surviving evidence for Lower or Middle Palaeolithic presence

in Scotland – the few genuine flint handaxes recovered almost certainly represent modern losses (Saville 1997; 1998a) – nor as yet any totally firm evidence for Upper Palaeolithic/Lateglacial human activity (see Saville this volume). Therefore the terminological issues of the use of the labels Late/Final Palaeolithic or Epipalaeolithic versus Mesolithic and the nature and timing of any transition to the Mesolithic (Jacobi 1987, 163; Price 1987) have not been a specific concern in Scotland, where, for the time being at least, the first inhabitants can be regarded simply as Mesolithic.

Equally, at the opposite end of the Mesolithic timeframe there is as yet no firm indication in Scotland that foragers ever adopted pottery while retaining other aspects of their definitive material culture, in contrast to the situation in southern Scandinavia (Fischer & Kristiansen 2002). Since pottery is directly associated with the earliest indicators of Neolithic activity in Scotland, then its presence or absence can serve as a useful gauge of socio-cultural transition. The same could be said of tomb-building or monument construction in general, which – unless shell middens are considered in this latter category – does not appear to have been part of the Mesolithic way of life in Scotland or elsewhere in the UK.

It could also be claimed that part of the reason the study of the Mesolithic in Scotland is in a sense less complex than elsewhere in Britain is the relative paucity of the evidence (Fig. 1.1). Given that people were present in Scotland for some four thousand years or more before the Neolithic period, there are relatively few sites of any consequence which have been located and extensively excavated. Of course, Mesolithic sites, apart from being relatively ephemeral in the first place, are far more vulnerable than those of any subsequent period to the vicissitudes of time and chance. Such factors as changing sea levels and inundation, coastal erosion, alluviation, peat growth, and talus formation have all contributed to the destruction or concealment of the Mesolithic evidence in Scotland.

Where material culture, particularly the lithic artefact component, does survive in some quantity it has not

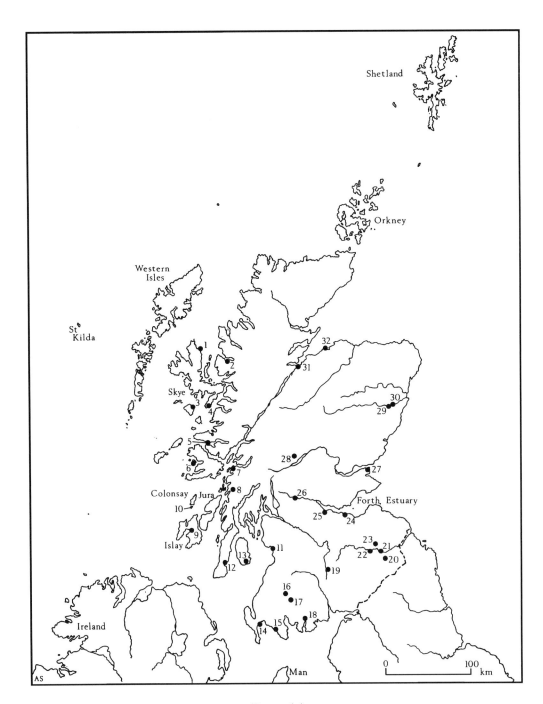

FIGURE 1.1

Map of Scotland showing places and findspots featured in the text. Key: 1 An Corran, Staffin, Skye, Highland; 2 Shieldaig, Wester Ross, Highland; 3 Kinloch, Rùm, Highland; 4 Camas Daraich, Skye, Highland; 5 Risga, Loch Sunart, Argyll & Bute; 6 Ulva Cave, Ulva, Argyll & Bute; 7 Oban (Carding Mill Bay; Druimvargie; MacArthur Cave; Raschoille Cave), Argyll & Bute; 8 Kilmelfort Cave, Argyll & Bute; 9 Newton, Islay, Argyll & Bute; 10 Oronsay, Argyll & Bute; 11 Shewalton Sands and Stevenston Sands, North Ayrshire; 12 Campbeltown, Kintyre, Argyll & Bute; 13 Auchareoch, Arran, North Ayrshire; 14 Glenluce Sands, Dumfries & Galloway; 15 Barsalloch and Low Clone, Dumfries & Galloway; 16 Starr, Loch Doon, East Ayrshire; 17 Smittons, Water of Ken, Dumfries & Galloway; 18 Cumstoun, Dumfries & Galloway; 19 Daer Reservoir, Crawford, South Lanarkshire; 20 Fairnington, Scottish Borders; 21 Dryburgh Mains, Scottish Borders; 22 Rink Farm, Scottish Borders; 23 Craigsfordmains, Scottish Borders; 24 Cramond, Edinburgh; 25 Cadger's Brae, Inveravon, Mumrills, Nether Kinneil and Polmonthill shell heaps, Falkirk; 26 Carse of Stirling (Airthrey; Blair Drummond; Meiklewood), Stirling; 27 Morton, Tentsmuir, Fife; 28 Ben Lawers, Perthshire; 29 Banchory, Aberdeenshire; 30 Nethermills, Aberdeenshire; 31 Castle Street, Inverness, Highland; 32 Culbin Sands, Highland.

4

yet been inventoried and studied in sufficient detail to permit wholly satisfactory regional or chronological subdivisions (cf. Saville 1998b). Much of the evidence for the Mesolithic in Scotland comes from coastal locations, and this is almost exclusively the case with the palaeo-environmental economic data, injecting another probable bias into the picture.

A further contrast between this and all later periods is that there is no definitive evidence, in the form of diagnostic artefacts, for Mesolithic human presence in Shetland, the Western Isles, or St Kilda. There is no conclusive *prima facie* reason why this should be so, especially as Mesolithic presence in Orkney and the Inner Hebrides attests the availability of sea-going craft, and the matter is one of continuing debate (Edwards 1996a and this volume; Edwards & Sugden 2003; Saville this volume).

The first use of the term Mesolithic is generally attributed to Westropp in 1866 (Nicholson 1983, 207; Price 1987, 227), but it did not come into common archaeological usage in Britain until after the First World War (Clark 1980, 3). The first use of the term in a specifically Scottish publication seems to be Lacaille's (1930) article on 'Mesolithic implements from Ayrshire'. It was Armand Donald Lacaille who came to be the dominant figure in Scottish Mesolithic studies in the period from 1930 until the publication of his major work *The Stone Age in Scotland* (1954) and his influence continued strongly thereafter, as reflected by the conference held in Glasgow in 1994 to mark the 40th anniversary of his *magnum opus* (Pollard & Morrison 1996). Lacaille's book (Fig. 1.2) provides a convenient marker for subdividing the account which follows.

Studying Mesolithic Scotland: from the beginnings to Lacaille

Though Lacaille's (1930) article may have been the first appearance in print in Scotland of the designation 'Mesolithic' with reference to Scottish artefacts, many of what we now recognize as key Mesolithic sites and finds in Scotland had already been discovered in the 19th century.

Thus Wilson (1851, 33) referred to the whale skeletons and antler implements from the draining operations in the Carse of Stirling, including the earliest recorded finding of what was probably an antler mattock in 1819 at Airthrey (Bald 1819) and another in 1824 at Blair Drummond (Drummond 1824). The best-known Mesolithic artefact from the carse clays of the upper Forth Valley, the Meiklewood antler-beam mattock, was

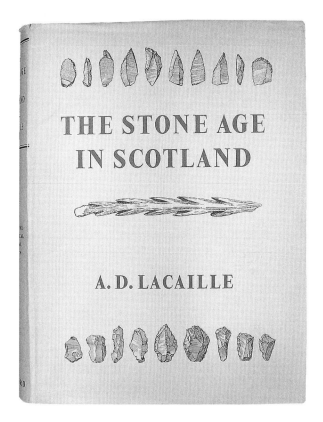

FIGURE 1.2
The Stone Age in Scotland, Lacaille's *magnum opus*, published in 1954.

found near a rorqual whale skeleton in 1877 (Turner 1889). Discoveries of highly important midden deposits in caves and rockshelters at Oban, Argyll, coincided with the expansion of that town at the end of the 19th century – MacArthur Cave (Fig. 1.3) was found in 1894 (Anderson 1895, 211) and Druimvargie rockshelter in 1897 (Anderson 1898, 298) – while exploration of the famous Oronsay shell middens started in 1881 (Fig. 1.4; Grieve 1883, 480; 1885, 48; Mellars 1987, 117). Barbed points from one of the Oronsay middens were exhibited at the International Fisheries Exhibition in London in 1883 (Anderson 1898, 307) and the biserial barbed point from the River Dee at Cumstoun, Kirkcudbrightshire, was discovered in 1895 (Munro 1908, 231). The Campbeltown flint assemblages, which were to become so important for the supposed 'Larnian' connection with Ireland, were first noted in the 1890s (Gray 1894).

For Wilson (1851) the relics from the carse clays were those of the 'Primaeval or Stone Period'; clearly of considerable antiquity, but not otherwise classifiable. Turner (1889, 791) supposed the mattocks from the carse clay to be Neolithic, but made a very good guess at

FIGURE 1.3
The exploration of MacArthur Cave, Oban, in *c.*1894.
(Photo: National Monuments Record, Royal Commission on the Ancient and Historical Monuments of Scotland)

their age being at least 5000 to 7000 years. Gray (1894, 271 & 274) considered his Campbeltown flints to be Palaeolithic, while Anderson percipiently related the Oban and Oronsay finds to:

> ... a horizon which has not heretofore been observed in Scotland, but corresponding with the intermediate layers in the cavern of Mas d'Azil ... described by M. Piette, and which he has seen reason to claim as filling up the hiatus ... supposed to exist between the palaeolithic and the neolithic (Anderson 1898, 313).

The controversy about the 'hiatus' between the Palaeolithic and Neolithic periods, which raged in the later 19th century and into the 20th, was not really a local issue in Scotland in the absence of Palaeolithic indicators. Nevertheless, as one of those most prominent in refuting the hiatus concept, Munro (1897; 1908; 1912) made full use of the Scottish evidence from Oban and elsewhere, thereby correctly identifying, as had Anderson, the pre-Neolithic position of

the cultural material, though without using the term Mesolithic. The linking by Munro and others of the barbed points from Oban with those from Mas d'Azil in Pyrenean France, while effective in making the general point of pre-Neolithic status, subsequently rather confused the issue of date and cultural affiliation (e.g. Geikie 1914, 298), once the true early status of the *Azilien* in France, now usually regarded as late Upper Palaeolithic or Epipalaeolithic, became apparent (Rozoy 1978, 320).

Hence Macalister (1921, 516), whose robust introduction of the 'Mesolithic' into his popular textbook was instrumental in establishing this as a definitive term for British prehistory, quite firmly described the Oban and Oronsay material as Azilian. The Azilian designation for this material was also followed by Breuil (1922), Burkitt (1921; 1925), Childe (1925; 1935), Clark (1932), Garrod (1926), and Sollas (1924); these references indicate how widely the Oban and Oronsay finds had permeated the general archaeological literature in Britain by this

FIGURE 1.4
Caisteal nan Gillean shell mound, Oransay, before excavation in 1881. (After Grieve 1885)

time. The distinctiveness of the Oronsay material had been noted by Bishop (1914, 102), who recommended dropping the Azilian tag in favour of the name 'Oransay [sic] culture' (cf. Mellars 1987, 129), but this did not find favour any more than Ludovic Mann's 1920 use of 'Oransay [sic] man' (Pollard *et al*. 1996, 179). McCallien (1937, 203) clearly recognized some of the chronological problems of linkage to the Azilian of France and Spain and proposed the term 'Scottish Azilian', but this was not adopted either.

It was Movius (1940; 1942) who first classified the Oronsay/Oban material as Obanian, but still without disengaging from the Azilian:

> It seems probable … that the Azilian harpoons, characteristic of this [Obanian] culture, represent a development from the Early Azilian influence at Victoria Cave [Yorkshire], reinforced by later arrivals from Southern France (Movius 1942, 198).

Movius had a rather flexible view of the Obanian, accepting the Ardantrive Cave on Kerrera with its

Neolithic/Early Bronze Age relics (Lethbridge 1950, 7–8) as a part, simply on the basis of being 'early' prehistoric and in the right location (Movius 1953, 96). Movius did subsequently recant on the Azilian connection (1953, 99), which was also more effectively dismissed by Lacaille (1954, 95; see also Thompson 1954, 206). Despite this, the Azilian connection languished in the Scottish literature for a while afterwards (e.g. Atkinson 1962, 4; Clark 1956, 98–103).

However, if in his 1954 book Lacaille attempted to remove one major confusion about the Mesolithic in Scotland, he was responsible for bolstering others. The most serious problem was the proposition, expounded in his chapter on 'Man with Mesolithic culture arrives in Scotland', that the earliest Mesolithic in Scotland was a version of the Irish Larnian. Both Lacaille and Movius (1942), whose lead Lacaille followed, seem to have envisaged actual settlement taking place from NE Ireland to SW Scotland, as indeed became the generally accepted explanation for the Mesolithic in SW Scotland (e.g. Childe 1946). This proposition hinges on the (with hindsight very curious) significance attached to lithic finds in association with raised beach deposits at Campbeltown, first reported by Gray (1894). These finds were seized upon by the Abbé Breuil when he visited Edinburgh in 1921 as one of the few potentially pre-Neolithic lithic assemblages in the National Museum which was more 'Magdalenian' than 'Tardenoisian' (Breuil 1922), though other scholars were more cautious (Garrod 1926, 176).

A new Campbeltown location was investigated in 1935 by McCallien, who rather grandly opened his publication with the sentence: 'The flint implements of the Campbeltown raised beach are well known to scientists all over the world' (McCallien & Lacaille 1941), presumably an *hommage* to Breuil. The three locations at Campbeltown – Dalaruan, Millknowe, and Albyn Distillery – have produced a variety of struck flints, including a few genuine microliths and microburins. At the Millknowe exposure, Gray observed the flints in a deposit with charcoal and bones, including fish bones, but without shells. Otherwise, there is the distinct impression of rather mixed assemblages, with rolled and fresh material in perhaps redeposited situations, all overlying the raised beach.

Nevertheless, McCallien and Lacaille (1941, 88) equated the Campbeltown material with Movius's newly defined Early Larnian. Movius (1942, 320) agreed with the Early Larnian designation, but thought this a more developed facies than in Ireland, since it had Tardenoisian and Forest Culture affinities. While Lacaille (1954, 311) persisted with the view that the Campbeltown material demonstrated that the Mesolithic was introduced into SW Scotland from Antrim by Early Larnian immigrants, rather cleverly separating the Dalaruan-Millknowe material without microburins as earlier than the Albyn Distillery finds, Movius (1953, 87–9) became more cautious on this point.

It was left to Coles, who reassessed both the Campbeltown and Antrim material, to demonstrate conclusively the fallacy of the Larnian link and to cast doubt on any Mesolithic contact between Ireland and Scotland:

> ... the overall and basic differences in tool forms are so great that it seems better ... to avoid describing the Scottish material in terms of the Irish Mesolithic (Coles 1963, 92).

Virtually no subsequent evidence for contact between Ireland and Scotland before the Neolithic has come to light, and this peculiar episode in the history of Scottish Mesolithic studies can now be seen as a temporary aberration (cf. Saville 2003a; 2003b).

With the benefit of hindsight it can now be seen that another error in Lacaille's approach was to regard much of the best lithic evidence for the Mesolithic in Scotland as being in effect post-Mesolithic in date. This was predicated upon a culture/time-lag model only credible in an era before radiocarbon dating (Saville 1996). This assumption, shared by most authorities at the time, was bound up with the perceived external relations of the Scottish lithic industries.

Mesolithic lithic tools, in particular the diagnostic microliths, had begun to be observed and recorded in Scotland early in the 20th century. The first illustrations of Scottish microliths may have been those of Scott (1895, plate 2) and Smith (1895, fig. 56), both in the final decade of the 19th century. Scott's microliths were from Craigsfordmains, Berwickshire, and he described them as 'flint implements of a peculiar type', while Smith's were from Stevenston Sands, Ayrshire, and he similarly was unable to grasp their true significance. He lumped together the Stevenston microliths, piercers, and leaf-shaped arrowheads as 'brogs', some '... so delicately pointed that one is apt to think that they have been used for tattooing and surgical purposes' (Smith 1895, 31).

Microlithic implements from the west of Scotland, akin to the 'so-called "Pygmy Flints" of other countries' (Anon. 1911, 831), were exhibited by Mann at the 1911 Scottish Exhibition of Natural History, Art and Industry in Glasgow, and Callander (1911, 177) referred to 'pigmy' flints from Culbin, Glenluce, and Shewalton Sands. Paterson (1912; 1913) noted examples from near Banchory in the Dee Valley, NE Scotland, expressing her delight that '[i]n a mole-hill ... I found my first pygmy' (1913, 104), and illustrating some indisputable microliths with the caption: 'Scottish pygmy flints of Indian type' (Paterson 1913, fig. 1). In later publications, Paterson recorded how she actually found the mole-hill 'pygmy' flint in 1906, and she recounts the anecdote that it was sent to Dr Joseph Anderson at the National Museum of Antiquities in Edinburgh – at the time Anderson was a disbeliever in microliths in Scotland – who was thereby won over (Paterson 1929; Paterson & Lacaille 1936, 420). Corrie (1916) illustrated and described a collection of 'pigmy' flints among his finds from Dryburgh, Berwickshire. He was followed by Callander (1927a), also with finds from Berwickshire, and Lacaille (1930; 1931) with finds from Ayrshire, who both reviewed occurrences elsewhere in Scotland; and by the Masons (1927; 1931) with more Tweed Valley finds.

'Pygmy (or pigmy) flint' was a widely accepted early designation for a microlith, still current in the 1920s (Callander 1927a; 1927b; Burkitt 1925, 19; Macalister 1921, 535; Paterson 1929). Lacaille referred both to 'pygmies' and microliths in 1930, but microlith is the preferred usage by the time of his 1937 overview of 'The microlithic industries of Scotland' and 'pygmies' do not feature in the 1954 book, though some non-specialists continued to use both terms (e.g. Simpson 1943, 12; 1963, 68). Interestingly, though Childe (1925, 3) favoured the term microlith early on, he still referred to 'pygmy flints' as an equivalent in a note published in 1942, presumably indicating it remained a current term for local archaeological society members.

Lacaille (1935; 1942) also took a lead in Scotland by realizing the significance of the microburin as a diagnostic Mesolithic waste product from microlith production, presumably following Clark (1932, 97–103; see also Childe 1942).

Most publications of these 'pygmy' flints referred to them as Tardenoisian, a term derived from the finds from the French locality of Fère-en-Tardenois, which was applied very loosely to designate all microlithic industries, though especially those with evidence for use of microburin technique. The term was widely used in general works (e.g. Burkitt 1921; Macalister 1921; Childe 1925), so that Callander (1927a) was able to feature Tardenoisian in the title of his article without explaining its origin or significance, though this appears to be the first specifically Scottish usage. (The term Tardenoisian was used by Geikie (1914, 314), though not with reference to Scotland, and Breuil (1922) used it tangentially in describing Scottish material.) It became the common term for microlithic industries in Scotland in the 1930s (e.g. Childe 1935, 20; Edgar 1939; Lacaille 1931) and 1940s (Childe 1946; Movius 1942; Simpson 1943) and was extensively employed by Lacaille in his 1954 book.

One of the problems with the use of these labels was that, in the French context, Azilian industries pre-dated Tardenoisian ones. Thus, if the Oban and Oronsay material was considered Azilian, but somehow late, then the microlithic industries identified as Tardenoisian elsewhere in Scotland would be even more recent. For Movius (1942, 193), the pre-existing presence of the Obanian in the north and west '... prevented ... [Tardenoisian] infiltration into the Highlands except on the east'. This kind of phasing by association is part of the explanation for Lacaille (1954) relegating his micro-lithic industries to 'post-Mesolithic developments'. Movius too saw the Scottish Tardenoisian elements as coeval with the Neolithic and Bronze Age in southern England (1953, 93).

The Tardenoisian equation in Britain was reviewed by Clark in 1955, who recommended the replacement of Tardenoisian by Sauveterrian (after the finds from the French locality of Sauveterre-la-Lémance), since it had become obvious that the most diagnostic element of

true Tardenoisian assemblages in France, the microlithic trapeze, was absent from British Mesolithic industries altogether. Affinities with the Sauveterrian microlithic industries (which were pre-Tardenoisian in France) were seen as far more appropriate for the British material, without necessarily implying non-indigenous origin. Although Clark (1955, 20) specifically reclassified the Banchory and Dryburgh finds as Sauveterrian, this appel-lation never really caught on in Scotland, other than being discussed by Mulholland (1970, 103–10) with reference to the Tweed Valley assemblages and by Mercer (1968; 1970) in the first two publications of his Jura finds.

Another problem for workers in Scotland was the apparent absence of any equivalent to the earlier Meso-lithic Maglemosian or Forest Culture of the Baltic area (Childe 1931; Clark 1932; 1936). The antler-beam mattocks were seen as the most telling evidence for Baltic links, but chronologically it was felt these related to the post-Maglemose Ertebølle horizon (Clark 1956, 105; Lacaille 1954, 175). The absence of any regular Maglemosian 'heavy flint industry', especially axeheads, meant clutching at straws to identify traces of compa-rable lithic techniques (Lacaille 1954, 149). Claims for the so-called core-tool from the Albyn Distillery site at Campbeltown being Maglemosian were, to say the least, wildly optimistic (McCallien & Lacaille 1941, fig. 6, 70; Movius 1953, 86 & 93; Saville 2003b).

It has been felt that Lacaille's *magnum opus* of 1954 was already anachronistic when it was published and yet, because of its comprehensiveness, that it may have had a numbing effect on subsequent Scottish Mesolithic studies (Morrison 1996, 14; Woodman 1989, 4). Lacaille's book, both by his own admission (1954, xix) and by any comparison, was modelled closely on that by Movius (1942), which resulted from the Harvard Archaeological Expeditions to Ireland of 1932–6 and more particularly from Movius's 1937 doctoral thesis. The survey of the Mesolithic in Scotland which Movius's book included (1942, 176–98) was itself comprehensive and rather innovative, leaving little in the way of additional data for Lacaille to cover.

Like Movius, Lacaille used 'Stone Age' in his title, even though his intention was specifically to chronicle the Mesolithic and any possible precursors, not the Neolithic. Despite its cumbersome format – not until page 140 of his book does Lacaille start to describe the Scottish archaeological material – it was undoubtedly very influential, particularly in perpetuating the notion of degenerate late Mesolithic traditions persisting till the Neolithic and Bronze Age in outlying regions (Saville 1996). Movius's subsequent updated review of the Scottish Mesolithic, written at the same time as

Lacaille's book, showed him to be even more uncritical than Lacaille, for example following Lethbridge (1950, 8) in seeing '... Mesolithic people still occupying the Oban region as late as "Beaker" times' (Movius 1953, 101), or even seeing the skeletal remains from a site at Galson, Lewis, as '... exhibiting many very striking Upper Palaeolithic features' (ibid.).

Despite all its shortcomings, however, Lacaille's book is still useful as a compendium of the Mesolithic evidence available up to about 1950, as a guide to the source literature, and generally as an indication of the contemporary state of Mesolithic studies in Scotland, to which, up until that date, Lacaille was himself unquestionably the leading contributor (Graham 1978, 301; Morrison 1996).

Studying Mesolithic Scotland: after Lacaille

Since the publication of Lacaille's major work on the Mesolithic, the Scottish database for this period has, slowly but surely, continued to expand. Although there is hardly a mention of anything Mesolithic in the *Proceedings of the Society of Antiquaries of Scotland* between Clark's Obanian article of 1956 and Mercer's first Jura paper in 1968, it would be wrong to over-exaggerate the degree to which Lacaille's book had stifled other research. In particular this was not so in the SW, where Truckell (1962) drew attention to much new material, while we have already seen that the review by Coles (1963) was significant in disengaging the local Mesolithic from the Larnian so beloved of Lacaille. Cormack's excavations at the scatter sites of Low Clone and Barsalloch were published (Cormack 1970; Cormack & Coles 1968), as were Mulholland's researches into the Tweed Valley surface scatters including important localities such as Craigsfordmains, Fairnington, and Rink Farm (Mulholland 1970). Further important finds came from rescue work at Kilmelfort Cave, Argyll, in 1956 (Coles 1983a; Saville 2003a & this volume).

Excavations of Mesolithic sites after the Second World War were small-scale, *ad hoc* affairs in general, but completely new ground was broken by the investigations at Morton Farm in Fife – begun in 1963–7

Figure 1.5
Excavations at Morton, Fife, in 1970 (site B, trenches 50/59/60 from the NW), showing the midden in section. (Photo: John Coles)

by Candow (1989), the amateur enthusiast who had discovered the site in 1957 – and then taken up by Coles in 1969–70 (Fig. 1.5). Speedy initial publication of this important site, together with its radiocarbon dates, in the *Proceedings of the Prehistoric Society* (Coles 1971) – the first and only Scottish Mesolithic site so far to appear in this journal – ensured its classic status. Paradoxically, this status has been confirmed by subsequent attempts at amplification and reinterpretation of the Morton evidence (Bonsall 1988; Clarke & Wickham-Jones 1988; Coles 1983b; Myers 1988; Woodman 1988; 1989; Saville 2003a), since the excavated evidence itself continues to be tantalizingly problematic. Because it was at the time the only well-published site exhibiting a wide range of artefactual, environmental, structural, and chronological data, Morton was unsurprisingly seized upon as a key to understanding the Scottish Mesolithic, without heeding the intricacies of its evidence. Thus the fact that there were separate sites and a probable palimpsest of intermittent occupations spread over a very long timespan (Coles 1971, 293) tended to be overlooked, and the inadequacies of the samples used for radiocarbon dating – the dates from which would not now be regarded as reliable – were ignored. Also, the publication was just in advance of a very significant shift in British Mesolithic studies in terms of nomenclature based on lithic artefact typology.

By the mid-1970s, the linkages with Continental industries had essentially been abandoned in favour of a simple 'Early' (for the former Maglemosian) and 'Later' (for the former Sauveterrian) classificatory scheme for the British Mesolithic (Jacobi 1973; 1976; 1978; Mellars 1974). The separation date between Early and Later was adopted as during the first half of the 9th millennium BP (c.8700 BP), and the defining characteristics were essentially that Early industries had mainly simple, relatively large microlith types made on 'broad' blades, while Later ones had more elaborately retouched 'narrow-blade' microliths, including small 'geometric' and rod forms.

Coles was aware of the above distinction but at the time felt forced to conclude that it was 'a little difficult to make definitive statements about the cultural affinities of the Morton assemblages' (Coles 1971, 317). Subsequently, however, the fact that the Morton evidence seemed to include predominantly Early Mesolithic microlith types in an ostensibly Later Mesolithic context, put it at the centre of debate about the existence and timing of an Early Mesolithic in Scotland (Saville this volume).

Also in the 1960s a truly remarkable campaign of excavation to study the Mesolithic began on the Isle of Jura. Starting with the excavations at Lealt Bay in 1966 (Mercer 1968), this research by the Mercers continued for 16 years until John Mercer's premature death in 1982

(Searight 1984). Mercer's (1979) ideas about the Jura Mesolithic sequence, which were not fully substantiated by radiocarbon dates, have never received wholehearted support, but it does appear that both Early and Later Mesolithic industries are represented.

Another concerted campaign began in 1970, with Mellars's project to reinvestigate the Oronsay Mesolithic shell middens, and continued until 1979 (Mellars 1987). At the same time, excavations at a mainly Bronze Age site on Islay were incidentally uncovering an underlying flint assemblage, which first indicated the potential of this island for Mesolithic research (Burgess 1976). The 1970s, in retrospect a busy decade for Mesolithic excavations in Scotland – for example Walker's work at Shieldaig, Wester Ross (Ballin & Saville 2003; Walker 1973) – finished with a major fieldwork campaign in 1978–1980 at Nethermills Farm, Crathes, on the north bank of the River Dee in Aberdeenshire (Kenworthy 1981). A major disappointment from this period was that the work of the Council for British Archaeology's Mesolithic Sub-Committee did not come to fruition in Scotland (Saville 1998b), so that the resulting gazetteer covered only England and Wales (Wymer 1977).

The end of the 1970s also saw the start of a campaign to investigate the enigmatic shell heaps (comprised predominantly of oyster shells) of the Forth Valley, focusing particularly on the most prominent example at Nether Kinneil (Sloan 1982; 1993). There are perhaps 20 or so of these 'middens', mostly along the southern shore between Falkirk and Bo'ness, but with a few on the north side in Fife and Clackmannanshire (Ashmore & Hall 1996; Sloan 1989; 1993). The size of some of the 'middens' is extraordinary. The best known are those at Inveravon (Fig. 1.6) – at least 27m and probably considerably longer (Grieve 1872; MacKie 1972; Sloan 1993); Mumrills – 43m to 50m long (Bailey 1992; Sloan 1993, 418); Polmonthill – possibly 155m long (Stevenson 1946); and Nether Kinneil – over 150m long (Sloan 1982; 1993, 70–101).

There are two major problems, apart from their sheer size, with these puzzling accumulations of shells – their origin and their date – both of which have been the cause for considerable debate. Grieve (1872) was adamant they were not natural, though perhaps not much earlier than Roman in date. Support for their artificial nature has included reports of lenses of burning at Inveravon (Sloan 1993, 103) and Polmonthill (Stevenson 1946), and the stone-built hearths, banks, and other features recorded at Nether Kinneil (Sloan 1982; 1993). Their anthropogenic origin has continued to be doubted, however, on the basis that the traces of human activity may relate to later reuse of what are in origin naturally formed shell banks (Jardine 1984, 4–5; Kinnes 1985,

FIGURE 1.6

Pipe-trench cutting through an oyster-shell accumulation at Inveravon, Falkirk, in 1983. (Photo: Tom Gray)

20). The radiocarbon dates from Nether Kinneil, a site which has anyway produced pottery and domesticated animal bones, and from another nearby site at Cadger's Brae, lie in the 5th–4th millennia BP (after marine reservoir effect correction), but there are earlier dates in the 6th millennium BP from the 'middens' at Mumrills, Inveravon, and Braehead (Ashmore this volume). Thus a Mesolithic date for some appears probable, though their status remains unclear since it is still the case that no Mesolithic artefacts have been recovered from any of the Forth Valley shell heaps.

Work on the Mesolithic in the 1980s was dominated by the important excavations at Kinloch, Isle of Rùm, from 1984 to 1986 (Wickham-Jones 1990), which did so much to rekindle wider academic and public interest in the archaeology of the period, but much was happening besides. Numerous new Mesolithic locations were reported from the SW (Edwards et al. 1983); rescue excavation at Newton, on Islay, produced a large flint assemblage (McCullagh 1989); two newly recognized rockshelter shell midden sites at Carding Mill Bay I and Raschoille Cave, Oban, were salvaged (Connock

1985; Connock et al. 1992); Tom Affleck excavated at several sites in the SW, including Starr and Smittons, and at Auchareoch on Arran (Affleck et al. 1988; Edwards 1996b); a project to record and selectively to excavate caves and rockshelters in Mid Argyll ran from 1985–1991 (Tolan-Smith 2001); excavations which still continue were started at Ulva Cave on the small island of Ulva, west of Mull, in 1987 (Bonsall et al. 1991; 1992; Russell et al. 1995); while a major campaign – The Southern Hebrides Mesolithic Project – of survey and excavation on Colonsay and Islay, was launched in 1988 (Mithen 2000a & this volume). Nor was work entirely focused on sites and artefacts, as shown by the review of early Postglacial vegetational history by Edwards and Ralston (1984), by the excavations at Castle Street, Inverness, which led to the identification of a Mesolithic tsunami horizon on the east coast (Dawson et al. 1990; Wordsworth 1985), and by many other palaeoenvironment-oriented contributions by Edwards (e.g. 1989) and others, raising issues which are still subject to lively debate (Edwards 1996a; Tipping 1996; and this volume).

Since Lacaille's book (1954) and Movius's final survey (1953), various overviews or summaries of the Mesolithic in Scotland as a whole have been published – Piggott and Henderson (1958), Atkinson (1962), Woodman (1978, 196–8), Mountain (1979), Ritchie and Ritchie (1981), Morrison (1980; 1986), Smith (1992), Wickham-Jones (1994), Finlayson and Edwards (1997), Finlayson (1998), and Mithen (2000a) – and some regional summaries have appeared (e.g. Bonsall 1997; Coles 1963; Kenworthy 1975; Mercer 1979; Ritchie & Ritchie 1972; Saville 2000; Scott 1966; Wickham-Jones & Firth 2000), of which those of the SW by Morrison (1981; 1982) were the most substantial. The Royal Commission on the Ancient and Historical Monuments of Scotland has also included several useful summaries of the Mesolithic evidence in some of its survey volumes, in particular the surveys of Stirlingshire (RCAHMS 1963, 18–20), the southern Inner Hebrides (RCAHMS 1984, 2–5), and eastern Dumfriesshire (RCAHMS 1997, 94–6). But probably of most significance has been the review by Woodman (1989), written at the invitation of the Society of Antiquaries of Scotland. In subtitling his article 'a

plea for normality', Woodman was referring to the past tendency to regard the Mesolithic in Scotland as marginal, late, obscure, and somehow irregular in comparison with the rest of mainland Britain. This criticism was justified to a degree, especially following the influence of Lacaille's work, but perhaps overstated the case by concentrating too much on the 'Obanian' question.

Nevertheless, and partly in direct response to Woodman's comments on the priority which should attach to the Oban area, detailed survey work has been undertaken (Macklin *et al.* 1992; 2000), another newly located rockshelter (Carding Mill Bay II) has been salvaged (Bonsall pers. comm.), and open-air Mesolithic locations have been located and sampled (Bonsall & Robinson 1992; Bonsall *et al.* 1993). The new excavations at Risga in Loch Sunart (Pollard 2000; Pollard *et al.* 1996) and salvage recovery of material from a rockshelter at An Corran, Skye (Fig. 1.7; Saville & Miket 1994), have contributed to new perspectives on the Obanian (Bonsall 1996; 1997), while a major new survey project to examine the 'northern Obanian' on eastern Skye, the adjacent mainland, and the islands

FIGURE 1.7
An Corran rockshelter, Staffin, Skye, from the south during excavation in December 1993. (Photo: Roger Miket)

FIGURE 1.8
Daer Reservoir site 1, South Lanarkshire, during excavation in August 2000. (Photo: Alan Saville)

between, has already made important advances (Hardy & Wickham-Jones 2001; 2002; 2003), as have research projects focused on the east of Scotland (Finlayson & Warren 2000; Warren 1998; 2001) and Caithness (Pannett 2001; 2002; Pannett & Baines 2002; Wickham-Jones & Firth 2000). The fascinating implications of the apparent discovery by the Ben Lawers Historic Landscape Project of a Mesolithic hunting camp – radiocarbon dated to c.8045 BP – at 780m above sea level in the mountains above Loch Tay, Perthshire, have yet to be assimilated (Dennison 2001a).

With the switch to mainly developer-funded rescue excavation in the 1990s, the prospect of serendipitous discovery of Mesolithic sites, including inland examples, has increased. Significant new finds have already been made in this way in the SW (MacGregor & Donnelly 2001; Pollard 1993; RCAHMS 1997, 96) and in Fife (Wickham-Jones & Dalland 1998), while systematic fieldwalking in areas such as the Scottish Borders and South Lanarkshire is also affording new insights (Barrowman 2000; Stuart 2003; Ward 2000b), especially in the case of the important new sites around Daer Reservoir in the Lowther Hills (Fig. 1.8; Ward 1995; 1997; 2000a). Amateur and local investigation continues to be the origin of significant advances, as at Cramond, where the Edinburgh Archaeological Field Society un-

covered a small feature which has yielded the earliest radiocarbon dates so far for the Scottish Mesolithic (Ashmore this volume; Denison 2001b), and at Camas Daraich, Skye, another early site from the first half of the 8th millennium BP (Birch *et al.* 2000).

Apart from fieldwork, there has been a developing interest in various Mesolithic topics involving Scotland, particularly the questions of the earliest colonization and the transition to the Neolithic. On the former, attention has focused on the one hand on the possible implications of mainly chance finds of so-called 'tanged points', which might provide a link to Lateglacial traditions elsewhere in NW Europe (Morrison & Bonsall 1989; see Ballin & Saville 2003 for a recent review), and on the other on the significance of early, potentially anthro-pogenic, disturbance indicators in the pollen record (e.g. Edwards & Mithen 1995; Edwards & Tipping this volume). The transition to Neolithic economy and culture has been seen as of particular fascination in Scotland, particularly on the west coast, because of the apparent evidence for Obanian persistence and the rela-tive absence of early Neolithic activity. One view has seen the west coast evidence as reflecting the emergence of complexity among Mesolithic people, who undergo gradual indigenous economic and social transformation (Neolithicization) while retaining many aspects of their

FIGURE 1.9
'Bender'-type temporary tent structure, Seaton Den, near Arbroath, Angus, date unknown. (Photo: Angus Council Cultural Services)

FIGURE 1.10
Open-air fish curing on Foula, Shetland, *c*.1902: see Kidd (1992, 54). (Photo: Scottish Ethnological Archive, NMS)

Mesolithic economy and settlement mobility (Armit & Finlayson 1992; 1996; Finlayson 1995; Mithen 2000b). The evidence for any emerging complexity has, however, also been disputed (Murray 2000).

Renewed recognition of possibilities for relevant ethnographic parallels for aspects of life in the Mesolithic from Scotland's recent past has followed new academic and popular interest in the travelling people or 'tinker folk' of the 19th and earlier 20th centuries (e.g. Neat 1996; Williamson 1994). These people are well known for having made use of caves and rockshelters, both for living and for work (Leitch 1987; Leitch & Smith 1993; Leitch & Tolan-Smith 1997; Martin 1984, 122–7; Tolan-Smith 2001, 168–9), and for having temporary, moveable shelters and tents (Fig. 1.9; Leitch 1989; Ritchie 1997). The latter seem to have coped with the Scottish weather and yet would leave virtually no archaeologically detectable traces once removed, offering a perspective on the interpretation of Mesolithic sites otherwise recognized solely by concentrations of stone tools. Similarly, some

elements of pre-modern foraging and fishing practices can offer insights into traditional 'ways of doing' appropriate to Scottish conditions and circumstances which may well have relevance to Mesolithic economy and technology (Fig. 1.10).

New work, exploiting the initial results from analyses of stable isotope data from the small number of Mesolithic (Richards & Mellars 1998) and early Neolithic human bones available from western Scotland has indicated a sharp contrast in dietary habits between the largely marine diet of the Mesolithic 'fish-eaters' and the almost wholly terrestrial diet of the Neolithic 'meat-eaters'. This has been taken along with other strands of evidence to suggest the possibility of a complete cultural break at the end of the Mesolithic, with Neolithic culture introduced by new colonists (Schulting & Richards 2002). Another perspective on this has been taken by those suggesting that a widespread change to drier climatic conditions at *c*.5000 BP was the catalyst for the adoption of agriculture by indigenes (Bonsall *et al.* 2002).

16

Thus, in conclusion, the current state of Mesolithic studies in Scotland, with research being undertaken both on new finds and the re-examination of old ones at an unprecedented rate, is extremely healthy. The number of new Mesolithic sites recorded by just two recent campaigns alone, the Southern Hebrides Project (26 sites on Colonsay and Islay; Mithen 2000a, 597) and the First Settlers Project (up to 30 in the Inner Sound; Hardy & Wickham-Jones 2002), is both exciting and daunting. The view it was possible to express not too long ago, that the Mesolithic population of Scotland was little more than two people for each modern county area (Atkinson 1962, 7), now seems preposterous. While it is very unlikely that the Mesolithic period in NW Europe witnessed a continuous growth in population – in fact the reverse could be the case (Price 1999) – it seems unlikely that the population in Later Mesolithic Scotland could ever have been fewer than several hundred people at any one time, and perhaps much greater (Ashmore & Edwards this volume; Gamble 1999, table 1).

Already by the time of Woodman's (1989) review the situation as regards the chronology of the Scottish Mesolithic had changed remarkably, particularly with the sequence of radiocarbon dates from Kinloch, Rùm, and the accelerator mass spectrometry (AMS) determinations on bone and antler artefacts (Ashmore this volume; Bonsall & Smith 1990; Bonsall et al. 1995; Saville this volume). A significant effect of these radiocarbon dates, and all the others coming on stream, has been to demonstrate more clearly that there is a considerable time-depth to the Mesolithic in Scotland. With the substantiation that for some four millennia Scotland was inhabited by Mesolithic foragers – and inhabited more extensively than previously appreciated – has come a new interest in the period and a determination to treat Mesolithic evidence more seriously. Workers from many disciplines have begun to focus on the Early Holocene to achieve an understanding of the processes behind the formation of the environments and habitats in Scotland today (Smout 1993). Mesolithic studies, by elucidating the anthropogenic factors involved, have a major role to play in this aspect of Quaternary investigation and their future looks sound.

A note on the Obanian

As already explained, the term Obanian was coined by Movius (1940; 1942) – and elaborated upon by him (1953) and by Lacaille (1954) – as a cultural designation for the coastal, bone- and antler-tool using, apparently non-microlithic, facies of the Scottish Mesolithic, represented at sites in and around Oban, at Risga (on

Loch Sunart), and on Oronsay. Until recently it was still possible to regard the Obanian as a localized, atypical, and rather late manifestation of coastal, niche-adapted foraging groups – 'strandloopers' – who did not manufacture microliths or other 'refined' tools but 'made do' with a scalar-core flake industry. Nobody, however, was really comfortable with this concept (cf. Woodman 1989) and with hindsight, had the finds from the early 1920s investigations on Risga been published (Pollard et al. 1996), the problems could have been resolved much earlier.

Several separate developments have allowed a more satisfactory reappraisal. Firstly, the direct radiocarbon determinations which have been made on Obanian bone and antler tools have revolutionized understanding of the duration of the Obanian, which now extends from at least c.8340 BP to ostensibly well beyond 5000 BP. Not only is this echoing almost the full known extent of the Mesolithic in Scotland, it is the Obanian dates themselves which contribute substantially to infill this timespan. Secondly, the excavation of open-air sites both at Oban and on Colonsay has demonstrated the existence of conventional microlith-using Mesolithic groups in close geographical proximity to the classic Obanian sites (an association which had always seemed a possibility from the evidence at Risga). Thirdly, a rockshelter site with a midden deposit with Obanian-type bone points and bevelled tools (one dated to c.7590 BP) was found at An Corran on the NE coast of Skye (Saville & Miket 1994). Together with the evidence from Ulva Cave, off Mull (Bonsall et al. 1992), and now that from the First Settlers Project in the Inner Sound region (Hardy & Wickham-Jones 2002), this considerably extends the geographical range of the Obanian up the west coast from Oronsay to the north of Skye. In addition, the An Corran Obanian bonework was apparently associated with a rich lithic blade industry with microliths.

In combination, these factors now make it highly plausible to see the Obanian as distinctive from the rest of the Scottish Mesolithic only in that: a) conditions for preservation of bonework are enhanced at the shell middens; b) the middens result from specific processing tasks only appropriate in certain coastal locations; and c) those processing tasks require a specialized toolkit, not the full artefactual repertoire. This position, which has recently been thoroughly examined by Bonsall (1996; 1997), effectively reunites the Obanian with the rest of the Scottish Mesolithic; it is a time-transgressive functional variant, not a cultural offshoot. This being the case, it may be acceptable, if required, to continue using the term Obanian in a limited sense with reference to the classic west-coast midden sites and their material culture, but certainly not in the former sense of an archaeological 'culture' (cf. Mithen 2000a, 622). However, even such limited usage is made more problematic by recognition of the continuation of an element of the classic Obanian tool-kit – the bevel-ended implement – into much more recent periods (Saville this volume), with the implication that, contrary to Movius's view of Mesolithic continuity as such (see above), there is a situation whereby an aspect of the basic technology suited to life on the west coast shows a persistent longevity through the Neolithic and Bronze Age and into the Iron Age and perhaps beyond. The conclusion must be that, except in retrospective survey, the days of archaeologists referring to an 'Obanian' without inverted commas are over (cf. Mellars this volume).

Acknowledgements

I am most grateful to Professor John Coles and Dr Graham Ritchie for reading this chapter in draft and offering helpful comments. They do not necessarily agree with all the opinions expressed, which remain my responsibility. For the provision of, or assistance with, the illustrations in this chapter I am indebted to Duncan Anderson, Norman Atkinson, Jim Boon, Stuart Campbell, John Coles, Lesley Fergusson, Tom Gray, Dorothy Kidd, Roger Miket, Tam Ward, and the National Monuments Record for Scotland (RCAHMS).

References

Affleck, T.L., Edwards, K. and Clarke, A. 1988. Archaeological and palynological studies of the Mesolithic pitchstone and flint site of Auchareoch, Isle of Arran. *Proceedings of the Society of Antiquaries of Scotland* **118**, 37–59.

Anderson, J. 1895. Notice of a cave recently discovered at Oban, containing human remains, and a refuse-heap of shells and bones of animals, and stone and bone implements. *Proceedings of the Society of Antiquaries of Scotland* **29** (1984–85), 211–30.

Anderson, J. 1898. Notes on the contents of a small cave or rock-shelter at Druimvargie, Oban; and of three shell-mounds in Oronsay. *Proceedings of the Society of Antiquaries of Scotland* **32** (1897–98), 298–313.

Anon. 1911. *Scottish Exhibition of National History, Art & Industry, Glasgow (1911). Palace of History: Catalogue of Exhibits*. Glasgow: Dalross Ltd.

Armit, I. and Finlayson, B. 1992. Hunter-gatherers transformed: the transition to agriculture in northern and western Europe. *Antiquity* **66**, 664–76.

Armit, I. and Finlayson, B. 1996. The transition to agriculture. *In* T. Pollard and A. Morrison (eds), *The Early Prehistory of Scotland*, 269–90. Edinburgh: Edinburgh University Press.

Ashmore, P.J. and Hall, D. 1996. Shell midden at Braehead, Alloa. *Forth Naturalist and Historian* **20**, 123–9.

Atkinson, R.J.C. 1962. Fishermen and farmers. *In* S. Piggott (ed.), *The Prehistoric Peoples of Scotland*, 1–38. London: Routledge & Kegan Paul.

Bailey, G.B. 1992. Mumrills (Polmont parish): shell midden. *Discovery and Excavation in Scotland 1992*, 11.

Bald, R. 1819. Notice respecting the discovery of the skeleton of a whale, on the estate of Airthrey, near Stirling, the property of Sir Robert Abercromby, Baronet. *Edinburgh New Philosophical Journal* **1**, 393–6.

Ballin, T.B. and Saville, A. 2003. An Ahrensburgian-type tanged point from Shieldaig, Wester Ross, Scotland, and its implications. *Oxford Journal of Archaeology* **22**(2), 115–31.

Barrowman, C. 2000. Garvald Burn (Linton parish): late Mesolithic chert scatter and knapping floor. *Discovery and Excavation in Scotland* (new series) **1**, 77–8.

Birch, S., Hardy, K., Kozikowski, G., Wickham-Jones, C.R. and Wildgoose, M. 2000. Camas Daraich (Sleat parish): Mesolithic open site. *Discovery and Excavation in Scotland* (new series) **1**, 56–7.

Bishop, A.H. 1914. An Oransay shell-mound – a Scottish pre-Neolithic site. *Proceedings of the Society of Antiquaries of Scotland* **48** (1913–14), 52–108.

Bonsall, C. 1988. Morton and Lussa Wood, the case for early Flandrian settlement of Scotland: comment on Myers. *Scottish Archaeological Review* **5**, 30–3.

Bonsall, C. 1996. The 'Obanian problem': coastal adaptation in the Mesolithic of western Scotland. *In* T. Pollard and A. Morrison (eds), *The Early Prehistory of Scotland*, 183–97. Edinburgh: Edinburgh University Press.

Bonsall, C. 1997. Coastal adaptation in the Mesolithic of Argyll. Rethinking the 'Obanian problem'. *In* G. Ritchie (ed.), *The Archaeology of Argyll*, 25–37. Edinburgh: Edinburgh University Press.

Bonsall, C. and Robinson, M. 1992. *Archaeological Survey of the Glenshellach Development Area, Oban: Report to Historic Scotland*. Edinburgh: Edinburgh University Department of Archaeology.

Bonsall, C. and Smith, C. 1990. Bone and antler technology in the British Late Upper Palaeolithic and Mesolithic: the impact of accelerator dating. *In* P.M. Vermeersch and P. van Peer (eds), *Contributions to the Mesolithic in Europe*, 359–68. Leuven: Leuven University Press.

Bonsall, C., Sutherland, D. and Lawson, T. 1991. Excavations in Ulva Cave, western Scotland 1987: a preliminary report. *Mesolithic Miscellany* **12**(2), 18–23.

Bonsall, C., Sutherland, D., Lawson, T. and Russell, N. 1992. Excavations in Ulva Cave, western Scotland 1989: a preliminary report. *Mesolithic Miscellany* **13**(1), 7–13.

Bonsall, C., Robinson, M., Payton, R. and Macklin, M. 1993. Lón Mór (Kilmore and Kilbride parish): Mesolithic site; post-ring structure. *Discovery and Excavation in Scotland 1993*, 76.

Bonsall, C., Tolan-Smith, C. and Saville, A. 1995. Direct dating of Mesolithic antler and bone artifacts from Great Britain: new results for bevelled tools and red deer antler mattocks. *Mesolithic Miscellany* **16**(1), 2–10.

Bonsall, C., Macklin, M.G., Anderson, D.E. and Payton, R.W. 2002. Climate change and the adoption of agriculture in north-west Europe. *European Journal of Archaeology* **5**(1), 9–23.

Breuil, H. 1922. Observations on the pre-Neolithic industries of Scotland. *Proceedings of the Society of Antiquaries of Scotland* **56** (1921–22), 261–81.

Burgess, C. 1976. An early Bronze Age settlement at Kilellan Farm, Islay, Argyll. *In* C. Burgess and R. Miket (eds), *Settlement and Economy in the Third and Second Millennia B.C.*, 181–207. Oxford: British Archaeological Reports (British Series **33**).

Burkitt, M.C. 1921. *Prehistory*. Cambridge: Cambridge University Press.

Burkitt, M.C. 1925. The transition between Palaeolithic and Neolithic times, i.e. the Mesolithic period. *Proceedings of the Prehistoric Society of East Anglia* **5**(1), 16–33.

Callander, J.G. 1911. Notice of the discovery of two vessels of clay on the Culbin Sands, the first containing wheat and the second from a kitchen-midden, with a comparison of the Culbin Sands and the Glenluce Sands and of the relics found on them. *Proceedings of the Society of Antiquaries of Scotland* **45** (1910–11), 158–81.

Callander, J.G. 1927a. A collection of Tardenoisian implements from Berwickshire. *Proceedings of the Society of Antiquaries of Scotland* **61** (1926–27), 318–27.

Callander, J.G. 1927b. Recent archaeological research in Scotland. *Archaeologia* **77**, 87–110.

Candow, R. 1989. *Prehistoric Morton*. Dundee: privately printed.

Childe, V.G. 1925. *The Dawn of European Civilisation*. London: Kegan Paul, Trench, Trubner & Co.

Childe, V.G. 1931. The forest cultures of northern Europe: a study in evolution and diffusion. *Journal of the Royal Anthropological Institute* **61**, 325–48.

Childe, V.G. 1935. *The Prehistory of Scotland*. London: Kegan Paul, Trench, Trubner & Co.

Childe, V.G. 1942. Rare flint in Hawick Museum. *Transactions of the Hawick Archaeological Society* (1942), 31.

Childe, V.G. 1946. *Scotland Before the Scots*. London: Methuen.

Clark, J.G.D. 1932. *The Mesolithic Age in Britain*. Cambridge: Cambridge University Press.

Clark, J.G.D. 1936. *The Mesolithic Settlement of Northern Europe*. Cambridge: Cambridge University Press.

Clark, J.G.D. 1955. A microlithic industry from the Cambridgeshire Fenland and other industries of Sauveterrian affinities from Britain. *Proceedings of the Prehistoric Society* **21**, 3–20.

Clark, J.G.D. 1956. Notes on the Obanian with special reference to antler- and bone-work. *Proceedings of the Society of Antiquaries of Scotland* **89** (1955–56), 91–106.

Clark, J.G.D. 1980. *Mesolithic Prelude*. Edinburgh: Edinburgh University Press.

Clarke, A. and Wickham-Jones, C.R. 1988. The ghost of Morton revisited: comment on Myers. *Scottish Archaeological Review* **5**, 35–7.

Coles, J.M. 1963. New aspects of the Mesolithic settlement of south-west Scotland. *Transactions of the Dumfriesshire and Galloway Natural History and Antiquarian Society* **41**, 67–98.

Coles, J.M. 1971. The early settlement of Scotland: excavations at Morton, Fife. *Proceedings of the Prehistoric Society* **37**(2), 284–366.

Coles, J.M. 1983a. Excavations at Kilmelfort Cave, Argyll. *Proceedings of the Society of Antiquaries of Scotland* **113**, 11–21.

Coles, J.M. 1983b. Morton revisited. *In* A. O'Connor and D.V. Clarke (eds), *From the Stone Age to the 'Forty-Five*, 9–18. Edinburgh: John Donald.

Connock, K.D. 1985. *Rescue Excavation of the Ossuary Remains at Raschoille Cave, Oban: an Interim Report*. Oban: Lorn Archaeological and Historical Society.

Connock, K.D., Finlayson, B. and Mills, C.M. 1992. Excavation of a shell midden site at Carding Mill Bay near Oban, Scotland. *Glasgow Archaeological Journal* **17**, 25–38.

Cormack, W.F. 1970. A Mesolithic site at Barsalloch, Wigtownshire. *Transactions of the Dumfriesshire and Galloway Natural History and Antiquarian Society* **47**, 63–80.

Cormack, W.F. and Coles, J.M. 1968. A Mesolithic site at Low Clone, Wigtownshire. *Transactions of the Dumfriesshire and Galloway Natural History and Antiquarian Society* **45**, 44–72.

Corrie, J.M. 1916. Notes on some stone and flint implements found near Dryburgh, in the parish of Mertoun, Berwickshire. *Proceedings of the Society of Antiquaries of Scotland* **50** (1915–16), 307–13.

Dawson, A.G., Smith, D.E. and Long, D. 1990. Evidence for a tsunami from a Mesolithic site in Inverness, Scotland. *Journal of Archaeological Science* **17**, 509–12.

Denison, S. 2001a. Mesolithic hunting camp found on Scottish mountain. *British Archaeology* (February 2001), 7.

Denison, S. 2001b. Earliest evidence found of settlers in Scotland. *British Archaeology* (August 2001), 4.

Drummond, H.H. 1824. Notice regarding fossil bones of a whale discovered in the District of Monteith. *Memoirs of the Wernerian Natural History Society* **5**(2), 440–1.

Edgar, W. 1939. A Tardenoisian site at Ballantrae, Ayrshire. *Transactions of the Glasgow Archaeological Society* **9**(3), 184–8.

Edwards, K.J. 1989. Meso-Neolithic vegetational impacts in Scotland and beyond: palynological considerations. *In* C. Bonsall (ed.), *The Mesolithic in Europe*, 143–55. Edinburgh: John Donald.

Edwards, K.J. 1996a. A Mesolithic of the Western and Northern Isles of Scotland? Evidence from pollen and charcoal. *In* T. Pollard and A. Morrison (eds), *The Early Prehistory of Scotland*, 23–38. Edinburgh: Edinburgh University Press.

Edwards, K.J. 1996b. The contribution of Tom Affleck to the study of the Mesolithic of southwest Scotland. *In* T. Pollard and A. Morrison (eds), *The Early Prehistory of Scotland*, 108–22. Edinburgh: Edinburgh University Press.

Edwards, K.J. and Mithen, S. 1995. The colonization of the Hebridean islands of western Scotland: evidence from the palynological records. *World Archaeology* **26**(3), 348–65.

Edwards, K.J. and Ralston, I. 1984. Postglacial hunter-gatherers and vegetational history in Scotland. *Proceedings of the Society of Antiquaries of Scotland* **114**, 15–34.

Edwards, K.J. and Sugden, H. 2003. Palynological visibility and the Mesolithic colonisation of the Hebrides, Scotland. *In* L. Larsson *et al.* (eds), *Mesolithic on the Move: Papers Presented at the Sixth International Conference on the Mesolithic in Europe, Stockholm 2000*, 11–19. Oxford: Oxbow Books.

Edwards, K.J., Ansell, M., and Carter, B.A. 1983. New Mesolithic sites in south-west Scotland and their importance as indicators of inland penetration. *Transactions of the Dumfriesshire and Galloway Natural History and Antiquarian Society* 58, 9–15.

Finlayson, B. 1995. Complexity in the Mesolithic of the western Scottish seaboard. *In* A. Fischer (ed.), *Man and Sea in the Mesolithic*, 262–4. Oxford: Oxbow Books (Oxbow Monograph **53**).

Finlayson, B. 1998. *Wild Harvesters: the First People in Scotland*. Edinburgh: Canongate/Historic Scotland.

Finlayson, B. and Edwards, K.J. 1997. The Mesolithic. *In* K.J. Edwards and I.B.M. Ralston (eds), *Scotland: Environment and Archaeology, 8000 BC–AD 1000*, 109–25. Chichester: Wiley.

Finlayson, B. and Warren, G. 2000. The Mesolithic of eastern Scotland. *In* R. Young (ed.), *Mesolithic Lifeways: Current Research from Britain and Ireland*, 133–41. Leicester: University of Leicester (Leicester Archaeology Monographs No. **7**).

Fischer, A. and Kristiansen, K. (eds). 2002. *The Neolithisation of Denmark: 150 Years of Debate*. Sheffield: J.R. Collis Publications.

Gamble, C. (ed.). 1999. *Research Frameworks for the Palaeolithic and Mesolithic of Britain and Ireland. A Report by the Working Party for the Palaeolithic and Mesolithic Annual Day Meeting and the Council of the Prehistoric Scociety*. Salisbury: The Prehistoric Society.

Garrod, D.A.E. 1926. *The Upper Palaeolithic Age in Britain*. Oxford: The Clarendon Press.

Geikie, J. 1914. *The Antiquity of Man in Europe*. Edinburgh: Oliver & Boyd.

Graham, A. 1978. Further records and opinions. *Proceedings of the Society of Antiquaries of Scotland* **109** (1977–78), 301–51.

Gray, A. 1894. Notice of the discovery of a cinerary urn of the Bronze Age, and of worked flints underneath it, at Dalaruan; also of an old flint working-place in the 30-foot raised beach at Millknowe, Campbeltown. *Proceedings of the Society of Antiquaries of Scotland* **28** (1893–94), 263–74.

Grieve, D. 1872. Notes on the shell heaps near Inveravon, Linlithgowshire. *Proceedings of the Society of Antiquaries of Scotland* **9** (1870–72), 45–52.

Grieve, S. 1883. Notice of the discovery of remains of the great auk or garefowl (*Alca impennis*, L.) on the island of Oronsay, Argyllshire. *Journal of the Linnean Society (Zoology)* **16**, 479–87.

Grieve, S. 1885. *The Great Auk, or Garefowl: its History, Archaeology and Remains*. London: Thomas C. Jack.

Hardy, K. and Wickham-Jones, C.R. 2001. Scotland's First Settlers: a project to investigate the earliest settlement of west-coast Scotland. *History Scotland* (launch issue, Winter 2001), 22–7.

Hardy, K. and Wickham-Jones, C.R. 2002. Scotland's First Settlers: the Mesolithic seascape of the Inner Sound, Skye, and its contribution to the early prehistory of Scotland. *Antiquity* **76**, 825–33.

Hardy, K. and Wickham-Jones, C.R. 2003. Scotland's First Settlers: an investigation into settlement, territoriality and mobility during the Mesolithic in the Inner Sound, Scotland, first results. *In* L. Larsson *et al.* (eds), *Mesolithic on the Move: Papers Presented at the Sixth International Conference on the Mesolithic in Europe, Stockholm 2000*, 369–81. Oxford: Oxbow Books.

Jacobi, R.M. 1973. Aspects of the 'Mesolithic Age' in Great Britain. *In* S.K. Kozlowski (ed.), *The Mesolithic in Europe*, 237–65. Warsaw: Warsaw University Press.

Jacobi, R.M. 1976. Britain inside and outside Mesolithic Europe. *Proceedings of the Prehistoric Society* **42**, 67–84.

Jacobi, R.M. 1978. The Mesolithic of Sussex. *In* P.L. Drewett (ed.), *Archaeology in Sussex to AD 1500*, 15–22. London: Council for British Archaeology (Research Report **29**).

Jacobi, R.M. 1987. Misanthropic miscellany: musings on British early Flandrian archaeology and other flights of fancy. *In* P. Rowley-Conwy, M. Zvelebil and H.P. Blankholm (eds), *Mesolithic Northwest Europe: Recent Trends*, 163–8. Sheffield: Department of Archaeology and Prehistory, University of Sheffield.

Jardine, W.G. 1984. The role of geomorphology and geology in archaeological studies: a synopsis. *Glasgow Archaeological Journal* **11**, 1–11.

Kenworthy, J.B. 1975. The prehistory of north east Scotland. *In* A.M.D. Gemmell (ed.), *Quaternary Studies in North East Scotland*, 74–81. Aberdeen: Department of Geography, University of Aberdeen.

Kenworthy, J.B. 1981. *Excavation of a Mesolithic Settlement Site at Nethermills Farm, Crathes, near Banchory, Grampian, 1978–80: Interim Statement*. Duplicated report; unpublished.

Kidd, D.I. 1992. *To See Oursels: Rural Scotland in Old Photographs*. Glasgow/Edinburgh: HarperCollins/National Museums of Scotland.

Kinnes, I. 1985. Circumstance not context: the Neolithic of Scotland as seen from outside. *Proceedings of the Society of Antiquaries of Scotland* **115**, 15–57.

Lacaille, A.D. 1930. Mesolithic implements from Ayrshire. *Proceedings of the Society of Antiquaries of Scotland* **64** (1929–30), 34–48.

Lacaille, A.D. 1931. Silex tardenoisiens de Shewalton (Comté d'Ayr), Ecosse. *Bulletin de la Société Préhistorique Française* **28**, 301–12.

Lacaille, A.D. 1935. The Tardenoisian micro-burin in Scotland. *Proceedings of the Society of Antiquaries of Scotland* **69** (1934–35), 443–5.

Lacaille, A.D. 1937. The microlithic industries of Scotland. *Transactions of the Glasgow Archaeological Society* **9**, 56–74.

Lacaille, A.D. 1942. Scottish micro-burins. *Proceedings of the Society of Antiquaries of Scotland* **76** (1941–42), 103–19.

Lacaille, A.D. 1954. *The Stone Age in Scotland*. London: Oxford University Press (for the Wellcome Historical Medical Museum).

Leitch, R. 1987. Green bottle howffs: a pilot study of inhabited caves. *Vernacular Building* **11**, 15–20.

Leitch, R. 1989. Travellers' tents. *Vernacular Building* **13**, 15–22.

Leitch, R. and Smith, C. 1993. Archaeology and ethnohistory of cave dwelling in Scotland. *Scottish Studies* **31** (1992–93), 101–8.

Leitch, R. and Tolan-Smith, C. 1997. Archaeology and the ethnohistory of cave dwelling in Scotland. *In* C. Bonsall and C. Tolan-Smith (eds), *The Human Use of Caves*, 122–6. Oxford: British Archaeological Reports (International Series **667**).

Lethbridge, T.C. 1950. *Herdsmen and Hermits: Celtic Seafarers in the Northern Seas*. Cambridge: Bowes & Bowes.

Macalister, R.A.S. 1921. *A Text-Book of European Archaeology. Vol. 1: The Palaeolithic Period*. Cambridge: Cambridge University Press.

McCallien, W.J. 1937. Late-glacial and early Post-glacial Scotland. *Proceedings of the Society of Antiquaries of Scotland* **71** (1936–37), 174–206.

McCallien, W.J. and Lacaille, A.D. 1941. The Campbeltown raised beach and its contained stone industry. *Proceedings of the Society of Antiquaries of Scotland* **75** (1940–41), 55–92.

MacGregor, G. and Donnelly, M. 2001. A Mesolithic scatter from Littlehill Bridge, Girvan, Ayrshire. *Scottish Archaeological Journal* **23**(1), 1–14.

McCullagh, R. 1989. Excavation at Newton, Islay. *Glasgow Archaeological Journal* **15**, 23–51.

MacKie, E.W. 1972. Radiocarbon dates for two Mesolithic shell heaps and a Neolithic axe factory in Scotland. *Proceedings of the Prehistoric Society* **38**, 412–16.

Macklin, M.G., Rumsby, B.T., Bonsall, C., Rhodes, A.N., and Robinson, M. 1992. Archaeological conservation in Oban, western Scotland. *In* C. Stevens, J.E. Gordon, C.P. Green, and M.G. Macklin (eds), *Conserving our Landscape*, 168–75. Crewe.

Macklin, M.G., Bonsall, C., Davies, F.M. and Robinson, M.R. 2000. Human–environment interactions during the Holocene: new data and interpretations from the Oban area, Argyll, Scotland. *The Holocene* **10**(1), 109–21.

Martin. A. 1984. *Kintyre: The Hidden Past*. Edinburgh: John Donald.

Mason, J.B. 1927. Notes on flint and other implements found near Selkirk. *Proceedings of the Society of Antiquaries of Scotland* **61** (1926–27), 111–15.

Mason, W.D. 1931. Prehistoric man at Tweed Bridge, Selkirk. *Proceedings of the Society of Antiquaries of Scotland* **65** (1930–31), 414–17.

Mellars, P.A. 1974. The Palaeolithic and Mesolithic. *In* C. Renfrew (ed.), *British prehistory: a New Outline*, 41–99. London: Duckworth.

Mellars, P.A. 1981. Towards a definition of the Mesolithic. *Mesolithic Miscellany* **2**(2), 13–16.

Mellars, P.A. 1987. *Excavations on Oronsay: Prehistoric Human Ecology on a Small Island*. Edinburgh: Edinburgh University Press.

Mercer, J. 1968. Stone tools from a washing-limit deposit of the highest post-glacial transgression, Lealt Bay, Isle of Jura. *Proceedings of the Society of Antiquaries of Scotland* **100** (1967–68), 1–46.

Mercer, J. 1970. Flint tools from the present tidal zone, Lussa Bay, Isle of Jura, Argyll. *Proceedings of the Society of Antiquaries of Scotland* **102** (1969–70), 1–30.

Mercer, J. 1979. The Palaeolithic and Mesolithic occupation of the Isle of Jura. *Almogaren (Jahrbuch des Institutum Canarium und der Gisaf)* **9–10** (1978–79), 347–67.

Mithen, S. 1994. The Mesolithic age. *In* B. Cunliffe (ed.), *The Oxford Illustrated Prehistory of Europe*, 79–135. Oxford: Oxford University Press.

Mithen, S. (ed.). 2000a. *Hunter-Gatherer Landscape Archaeology: the Southern Hebrides Mesolithic Project 1988–98. Vols.1-2*. Cambridge: McDonald Institute Monograph.

Mithen, S. 2000b. Mesolithic sedentism on Oronsay: chronological evidence from adjacent islands in the southern Hebrides. *Antiquity* **74**, 298–304.

Morrison, A. 1980. *Early Man in Britain and Ireland*. London: Croom Helm.

Morrison, A. 1981. The coastal Mesolithic in south-west Scotland. *In* B. Gramsch (ed.), *Mesolithikum in Europa*, 441–50. Berlin: VEB Deutscher Verlag der Wissenschaften.

Morrison, A. 1982. The Mesolithic period in south-west Scotland: a review of the evidence. *Glasgow Archaeological Journal* **9**, 1–14.

Morrison, A. 1986. The Mesolithic period in Scotland: a review. *In* The World Archaeological Congress Preprints, *The Pleistocene Perspective, Vol.2: Section D, Early Holocene Adaptations*, (17 A5 pages, actual volume unpaged). London: Allen & Unwin.

Morrison, A. 1996. 'The northward march of Palaeolithic man in Britain': an appreciation of Armand Donald Lacaille. *In* T. Pollard and A. Morrison (eds), *The Early Prehistory of Scotland*, 1–19. Edinburgh: Edinburgh University Press.

Morrison, A. and Bonsall, C. 1989. The early post-glacial settlement of Scotland: a review. *In* C. Bonsall (ed.), *The Mesolithic in Europe*, 134–42. Edinburgh: John Donald.

Mountain, M.-J. 1979. The later Mesolithic of Britain: Scotland and Ireland. *In* J.V.S. Megaw and D.D.A. Simpson (eds), *Introduction to British Prehistory*, 60–71. Leicester: Leicester University Press.

Movius, H.L., Jr. 1940. An early post-glacial archaeological site at Cushendun, Co. Antrim. *Proceedings of the Royal Irish Academy* **46C**, 1–84.

Movius, H.L., Jr. 1942. *The Irish Stone Age*. Cambridge: Cambridge University Press.

Movius, H.L., Jr. 1953. Curran Point, Larne, County Antrim: the type site of the Irish Mesolithic. *Proceedings of the Royal Irish Academy* **56C**, 1–195.

Mulholland, H. 1970. The microlithic industries of the Tweed Valley. *Transactions of the Dumfriesshire and Galloway Natural History and Antiquarian Society* **47**, 81–110.

Munro, R. 1897. *Prehistoric Problems*. Edinburgh: William Blackwood & Sons.

Munro, R. 1908. On the transition between the Palaeolithic and Neolithic civilizations in Europe. *Archaeological Journal* **65**, 205–44.

Munro, R. 1912. *Palaeolithic Man and the Terramara Settlements in Europe*. Edinburgh: Oliver & Boyd.

Murray, J. 2000. *Peau noire, masques blancs*: self-image in the Mesolithic–Neolithic transition in Scotland. *Antiquity* **74**, 779–85.

Myers, A.M. 1988. Scotland inside and outside of the British mainland Mesolithic. *Scottish Archaeological Review* **5**, 23–9.

Neat, T. 1996. *The Summer Walkers: Travelling People and Pearl-Fishers in the Highlands of Scotland*. Edinburgh: Canongate.

Nicholson, P.T. 1983. Hodder Westropp: nineteenth-century archaeologist. *Antiquity* **57**, 205–10.

Pannett, A. 2001. Oliclett (Wick parish): Mesolithic lithic scatter. *Discovery and Excavation in Scotland* (new series) **2**, 66.

Pannett, A. 2002. Caithness fieldwalking project. *Discovery and Excavation in Scotland* (new series) **3**, 60.

Pannett, A. and Baines, A. 2002. Oliclett (Wick parish): Mesolithic lithic scatter. *Discovery and Excavation in Scotland* (new series) **3**, 79.

Paterson, H.M.L. 1912. Pigmy flints in the Dee Valley. *Report of the British Association* (1912), 605–6.

Paterson, H.M.L. 1913. Pygmy flints in the Dee Valley. *Man* (1913), 103–5.

Paterson, H.M.L. 1929. Pygmy flints. *The Deeside Field* **4**, 64–6.

Paterson, H.M.L. and Lacaille, A.D. 1936. Banchory microliths. *Proceedings of the Society of Antiquaries of Scotland* **70** (1935–36), 419–34.

Piggott, S. and Henderson, K. 1958. *Scotland Before History*. London: Nelson.

Pollard, T. 1993. Kirkhill Farm (Johnstone parish): Mesolithic flint scatter with associated structures and burnt mound. *Discovery and Excavation in Scotland 1993*, 15.

Pollard, T. 2000. Risga and the Mesolithic occupation of Scottish islands. *In* R. Young (ed.), *Mesolithic Lifeways: Current Research from Britain and Ireland*, 143–52. Leicester: University of Leicester (Leicester Archaeology Monographs No. **7**).

Pollard, T. and Morrison, A. (eds). 1996. *The Early Prehistory of Scotland*. Edinburgh: Edinburgh University Press.

Pollard, T., Atkinson, J. and Banks, I. 1996. 'It is the technical side of the work which is my stumbling block': a shell midden site on Risga reconsidered. *In* T. Pollard and A. Morrison (eds), *The Early Prehistory of Scotland*, 165–82. Edinburgh: Edinburgh University Press.

Price, T.D. 1983. The European Mesolithic. *American Antiquity* **48**(4), 761–78.

Price, T.D. 1987. The Mesolithic of Western Europe. *Journal of World Prehistory* **1**, 225–305.

Price, T.D. 1999. Human population in Europe during the Mesolithic. *In* E. Cziesla, T. Kersting and S. Pratsch (eds), *Den Bogen spannen … Festschrift für B. Gramsch*, 185–95. Weissbach: Beier & Beran.

Price, T.D. (ed.). 2000. *Europe's First Farmers*. Cambridge: Cambridge University Press.

RCAHMS. 1963. *Stirlingshire. An Inventory of the Ancient Monuments. Vol.1*. Edinburgh: Royal Commission on the Ancient and Historical Monuments of Scotland.

RCAHMS. 1984. *Argyll. An Inventory of the Monuments. Vol. 5. Islay, Jura, Colonsay and Oronsay*. Edinburgh: Royal Commission on the Ancient and Historical Monuments of Scotland.

Richards, M.P. and Mellars, P.A. 1998. Stable isotopes and the seasonality of the Oronsay middens. *Antiquity* **72**, 178–84.

RCAHMS. 1997. *Eastern Dumfriesshire: an Archaeological Landscape*. Edinburgh: Royal Commission on the Ancient and Historical Monuments of Scotland.

Ritchie, G. 1997. Early settlement in Argyll. *In* G. Ritchie (ed.), *The Archaeology of Argyll*, 38–66. Edinburgh: Edinburgh University Press.

Ritchie, J.N.G. and Ritchie, A. 1972. *Regional Archaeologies: Edinburgh and South-East Scotland*. London: Heinemann Educational Books.

Ritchie, J.N.G. and Ritchie, A. 1981. *Scotland: Archaeology and Early History*. London: Thames & Hudson.

Rozoy, J.-G. 1978. *Les Derniers Chasseurs: L'Epipaléolithique en France et en Belgique, Essai de Synthèse*. Charleville: privately printed (Bulletin de la Société Archéologique Champenoise, numéro spécial).

Russell, N.J., Bonsall, C. and Sutherland, D.G. 1995. The exploitation of marine molluscs in the Mesolithic of western Scotland: evidence from Ulva Cave, Inner Hebrides. *In* A. Fischer (ed.), *Man and Sea in the Mesolithic*, 273–88. Oxford: Oxbow Books (Monograph **53**).

Saville, A. 1996. Lacaille, microliths, and the Mesolithic of Orkney. In T. Pollard and A. Morrison (eds), *The Early Prehistory of Scotland*, 213–24. Edinburgh: Edinburgh University Press.

Saville, A. 1997. Palaeolithic handaxes in Scotland. *Proceedings of the Society of Antiquaries of Scotland* **127**, 1–16.

Saville, A. 1998a. Musselburgh (Inveresk parish): Palaeolithic flint handaxe. *Discovery and Excavation in Scotland 1998*, 33.

Saville, A. 1998b. Studying the Mesolithic period in Scotland: a bibliographic gazetteer. *In* N. Ashton, F. Healy and P. Pettitt (eds), *Stone Age Archaeology: Essays in Honour of John Wymer,* 211–24. Oxford: Oxbow Books (Oxbow Monograph **102**/Lithic Studies Society Occasional Paper **6**).

Saville, A. 2000. Orkney and Scotland before the Neolithic period. *In* A. Ritchie (ed.), *Neolithic Europe in its European Context*, 91–100. Cambridge: Macdonald Institute Monograph.

Saville, A. 2003a. Indications of regionalisation in Mesolithic Scotland. *In* L. Larsson *et al.* (eds), *Mesolithic on the Move: Papers Presented at the Sixth International Conference on the Mesolithic in Europe, Stockholm 2000*, 340–50. Oxford: Oxbow Books.

Saville, A. 2003b. A flint core-tool from Wig Sands, Kirkholm, near Stranraer, and a consideration of the absence of core-tools in the Scottish Mesolithic. *Transactions of the Dumfriesshire and Galloway Natural History and Antiquarian Society* **77**, 13–22.

Saville, A. and Miket, R. 1994. An Corran rock-shelter, Skye: a major new Mesolithic site. *Past* 18, 9–10.

Scott, J.G. 1966. *Regional Archaeologies: South-West Scotland*. London: Heinemann Educational Books.

Scott, T. 1895. Collection of flint arrow-heads, spear-heads, knives, scrapers, borers, flakes – about 600 in all – from Craigsfordmains mostly. *History of the Berwickshire Naturalists' Club* **15**, 166–9.

Schulting, R.J. and Richards, M.P. 2002. The wet, the wild and the domesticated: the Mesolithic-Neolithic transition on the west coast of Scotland. *European Journal of Archaeology* **5**(2), 147–89.

Searight, S. 1984. The Mesolithic on Jura. *Current Archaeology* **90**, 209–14.

Simpson, W.D. 1943. *The Province of Mar*. Aberdeen: Aberdeen University Press.

Simpson, W.D. 1963. The region before 1700. *In* A.C. O'Dell and J. Mackintosh (eds), *The North-East of Scotland*, 67–86. Aberdeen: Central Press.

Sloan, D. 1982. Nether Kinneil. *Current Archaeology* **84**, 13–15.

Sloan, D. 1989. Shells and settlement: European implications of oyster exploitation. *In* J. Clutton-Brock (ed.), *The Walking Larder: Patterns of Domestication, Pastoralism, and Predation*, 316–25. London: Unwin Hyman.

Sloan, D. 1993. *Sample, Site, and System: Shell Midden Economies in Scotland, 6000–4000 BP*. Unpublished DPhil thesis, University of Cambridge.

Smith, C. 1992. *Late Stone Age Hunters of the British Isles*. London: Routledge.

Smith, J. 1895. *Prehistoric Man in Ayrshire*. London: Elliot Stock.

Smout, C. 1993. Introduction. *In* T.C. Smout (ed.), *Scotland Since Prehistory: Natural Change and Human Impact*, xii–xx. Aberdeen: Scottish Cultural Press.

Sollas, W.J. 1924. *Ancient Hunters and their Modern Representatives* (3rd edn). London: Macmillan & Co.

Stevenson, R.B.K. 1946. A shell-heap at Polmonthill, Falkirk. *Proceedings of the Society of Antiquaries of Scotland* **80** (1945–46), 135–9.

Stuart, E. 2003. Knowledge and practice: the *Scottish Lithic Scatters Project* and stoneworking in prehistory. *In* N. Moloney and M.J. Shott (eds), *Lithic Analysis at the Millennium*, 103–9. London: University College London, Institute of Archaeology.

Thompson, M.W. 1954. Azilian harpoons. *Proceedings of the Prehistoric Society* **20**(2), 193–211.

Tipping, R. 1996. Microscopic charcoal records, inferred human activity, and climate change in the Mesolithic of northernmost Scotland. *In* T. Pollard and A. Morrison (eds), *The Early Prehistory of Scotland*, 39–61. Edinburgh: Edinburgh University Press.

Tolan-Smith, C. 2001. *The Caves of Mid Argyll*. Edinburgh: Society of Antiquaries of Scotland (Monograph **20**).

Truckell, A.E. 1962. The Mesolithic in Dumfries and Galloway: recent developments. *Transactions of the Dumfriesshire and Galloway Natural History and Antiquarian Society* **40**, 43–7.

Turner, W. 1889. On implements of stag's horn associated with whales' skeletons found in the Carse of Stirling. *Report of the British Association 1889*, 789–91.

Walker, M. 1973. *Archaeological excavation of a microlithic assemblage at Shieldaig, Wester Ross, Scotland, 24/iii/73–6/iv/73: preliminary report*. Unpublished typescript (copy held at the National Monuments Record of Scotland, Edinburgh).

Ward, T. 1995. Daer reservoir (Crawford parish): bastle house, cairns, find-spots, Mesolithic knapping site. *Discovery and Excavation in Scotland 1995*, 87.

Ward, T. 1997. Daer Reservoir (Crawford parish): Mesolithic sites; burnt mounds; cairns. *Discovery and Excavation in Scotland 1997*, 75.

Ward, T. 2000a. Daer Reservoir (Crawford parish): Mesolithic flint-knapping site and other lithic scatters. *Discovery and Excavation in Scotland* (new series) **1**, 86.

Ward, T. 2000b. Weston Farm (Carnwath; Dunsyre parishes): Mesolithic and later prehistoric lithic scatters; medieval brooch. *Discovery and Excavation in Scotland* (new series) **1**, 85.

Warren, G. 1998. Upper Tweed Valley Survey. *Discovery and Excavation in Scotland 1998*, 82–3.

Warren, G. 2001. *Towards a Social Archaeology of the Mesolithic in Eastern Scotland: Landscapes, Contexts and Experience*. Unpublished PhD thesis, University of Edinburgh.

Wickham-Jones, C.R. 1990. *Rhum, Mesolithic and later sites at Kinloch: excavations 1984–86*. Edinburgh: Society of Antiquaries of Scotland (Monograph **7**).

Wickham-Jones, C.R. 1994. *Scotland's First Settlers*. London: Batsford/Historic Scotland.

Wickham-Jones, C.R. and Dalland, M. 1998. A small Mesolithic site at Craighead Golf Course, Fife Ness, Fife. *Tayside and Fife Archaeological Journal* **4**, 1–19.

Wickham-Jones, C.R. and Firth, C.R. 2000. Mesolithic settlement of northern Scotland: first results of fieldwork in Caithness and Orkney. *In* R. Young (ed.), *Mesolithic Lifeways: Current Research from Britain and Ireland*, 119–32. Leicester: University of Leicester (Leicester Archaeology Monographs No. **7**).

Williamson, D. 1994. *The Horsieman: Memories of a Traveller 1928–1958*. Edinburgh: Canongate.

Wilson, D. 1851. *The Archaeology and Prehistoric Annals of Scotland*. Edinburgh: Sutherland & Knox.

Woodman, P.C. 1978. *The Mesolithic in Ireland*. Oxford: British Archaeological Reports (British Series **58**).

Woodman, P.C. 1988. Comment on Myres. *Scottish Archaeological Review* **5**, 34–5.

Woodman, P.C. 1989. A review of the Scottish Mesolithic: a plea for normality! *Proceedings of the Society of Antiquaries of Scotland* **119**, 1–32.

Wordsworth, J. 1985. The excavation of a Mesolithic horizon at 13–24 Castle Street, Inverness. *Proceedings of the Society of Antiquaries of Scotland* **115**, 89–103.

Wymer, J.J. (ed.). 1977. *Gazetteer of Mesolithic sites in England and Wales*. London: Council for British Archaeology (Research Report **20**).

Section 2

SCOTLAND, THE SETTING

Chapter 2

After the Ice: Paraglacial and Postglacial Evolution of the Physical Environment of Scotland, 20,000 to 5000 BP

COLIN K. BALLANTYNE

This paper places the Mesolithic occupation of Scotland in the context of Lateglacial and Early Holocene environmental change. The last ice sheet covered virtually all of the present land area of Scotland. By c.9800 BP, however, climate was similar to that of the present, and during the period 7500–6000 BP average conditions were probably warmer than now. Both climate and vegetation cover were nevertheless subject to continuous change throughout the Early Holocene, forcing changes on ecosystems and probably the economic basis of Mesolithic societies. Coastal areas experienced marked and complex changes, particularly in relation to the Main Postglacial marine transgression, which culminated between 7200 and 6000 BP. Relative sea-level rise and Holocene floodplain aggradation are inferred to have destroyed many littoral and riparian Mesolithic sites. Evidence for more catastrophic change (landslides, earthquakes, coastal floods, and a tsunami) is outlined. There is no convincing evidence in the geomorphic or sedimentological record for any significant impact of Mesolithic communities on the non-biotic physical environment.

Introduction

All environments pose both opportunities and constraints for their inhabitants, and the links between environment and economy are likely to be particularly direct for hunter-gatherer societies whose livelihood was dependent on harvesting natural resources (Mithen 1999). The physical environment, moreover, exhibits continuous gradual (and occasionally catastrophic) change: climatic change over decadal to millennial timescales may dictate biotic responses that force adaptations in economy; seas may advance or recede, forcing the abandonment or relocation of littoral settlement sites; and rivers may migrate or incise their floodplains, removing all evidence of previous human occupancy. Moreover, human activity may initiate or accelerate changes in the physical environment, particularly through woodland clearance and other land-management practices that accelerate soil

erosion and alter the hydrological balance of a drainage basin.

This paper sets the period of Mesolithic occupation of Scotland in the context of the changing physical environment of the Early Holocene, conventionally regarded as lasting from c.10,000 to 5000 BP. The paper focuses in turn on four aspects of environmental change: (1) glaciation, deglaciation, and climate change in Late Pleistocene and Early Holocene times; (2) the effects on landscape of the glacial-postglacial transition; (3) landscape change and development during the Early Holocene; and (4) the possible effects of Mesolithic communities on the Early Holocene landscape.

Glaciation, deglaciation and climate change

Glaciation and deglaciation

At its maximum extent, the last (Late Devensian) ice sheet covered approximately two-thirds of the present land area of the British Isles. Although its land-based southern limits are reasonably well established (Ehlers *et al.* 1991), the limits of the ice sheet offshore from Scotland remain uncertain. Despite a long-standing view that Orkney and parts of Caithness and Buchan may have remained ice-free during the last glacial maximum (e.g. Bowen *et al.* 1986) it now seems likely that the eastern limit of the last ice sheet lay at offshore moraine complexes (Hall & Bent 1990), and there is evidence that the Scandinavian and Scottish ice sheets may have met in the North Sea basin at some time between c.29,000 and 22,000 BP (Sejrup *et al.* 1994). To the west of Scotland, the last ice sheet merged with an independent Outer Hebridean ice cap and confluent ice streams extended well out on to the continental shelf (Peacock *et al.* 1992; Stoker *et al.* 1993). To the north, Shetland appears to have supported an independent ice cap at the last glacial maximum and Orkney is known to have been overwhelmed by mainland ice, though a Late Devensian age for the last glaciation of Orkney has yet to be conclusively demonstrated (Sutherland 1991a). On

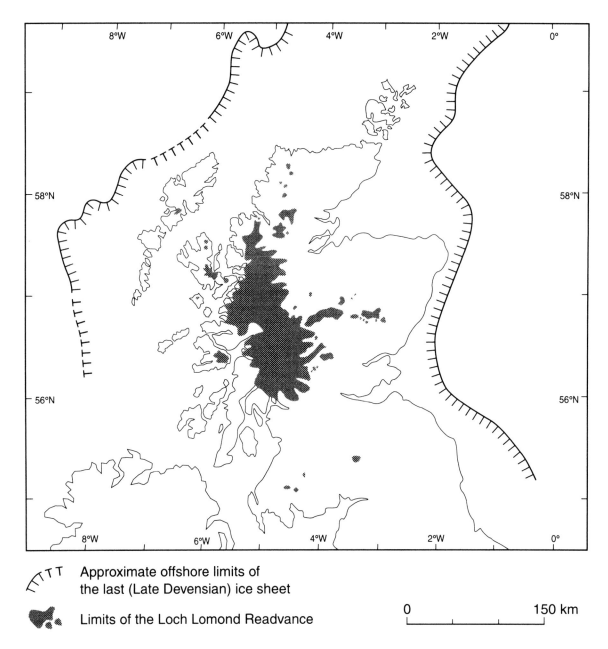

8°W   6°W   4°W   2°W   0°

58°N   58°N

56°N   56°N

8°W   6°W   4°W   2°W   0°

Approximate offshore limits of
the last (Late Devensian) ice sheet

Limits of the Loch Lomond Readvance

0   150 km

FIGURE 2.1

The approximate limits of the last (Late Devensian) ice sheet in Scotland, and the limits of the Loch Lomond Readvance. The western limit of the ice sheet is based on Stoker *et al.* (1993); the eastern limit is based on Hall and Bent (1990). Earlier accounts (e.g. Bowen *et al.* 1986; Sutherland 1984) favoured more restricted ice cover during the Late Devensian glacial maximum, with Orkney and parts of Caithness and Buchan remaining free of glacier ice.

the Scottish mainland, the ice reached a maximum thickness of over 1300m in the western Grampians (Thorp 1987), though the higher summits of the NW Highlands and Hebrides remained above the ice sheet as nunataks (Ballantyne *et al.* 1998a). In sum, current information suggests that virtually all of the present land area of Scotland and neighbouring islands lay under glacier

ice at the last glacial maximum (Fig. 2.1), creating an archaeological *tabula rasa* with extremely limited potential for the survival of Palaeolithic artefacts (Finlayson & Edwards 1997; Saville 1997).

There is limited dating evidence regarding the expansion and contraction of the last Scottish ice sheet. Uranium-series dating of calcite speleothems in Assynt suggest that ice-sheet build-up occurred after *c*.26,000 BP (Atkinson *et al.* 1986). In England, the maximum southwards extension of the ice sheet has been dated at *c*.18,000 BP, but there is strong stratigraphic evidence that the culmination of ice-sheet expansion in southern Scotland and England occurred after (possibly long after) ice nourished in the Scottish Highlands reached its maximum extent (Sutherland 1984; 1991b). Radiocarbon-dated glaciomarine sediments in Aberdeenshire (Hall & Jarvis 1989) and cosmogenic [36]Cl dates from northern Skye (Stone *et al.* 1998) indicate that retreat and downwastage of the ice sheet was well advanced by 15,000 BP, and radiocarbon dates obtained on basal lake sediments indicate that most low ground was deglaciated by *c*.13,000 BP (Fig. 2.2).

It is uncertain whether glacier ice survived the ensuing temperate interval, the Lateglacial Interstadial of *c*.13,000–11,000 BP, but if so it must have been confined to particularly favourable sites in the high corries and plateaux of the Highlands. The subsequent Loch Lomond Stadial of *c*.11,000–10,000 BP witnessed renewed expansion of glacier ice in upland areas, an event referred to as the Loch Lomond Readvance. At the readvance maximum the Western Highlands were occupied by an extensive icefield, the West Highland Icefield, which extended southwards from Glen Torridon to the southern end of Loch Lomond, and eastwards from the fjords of western Highlands to the east end of Loch Tay (Fig. 2.1). On mountains peripheral to the West Highland Icefield a number of smaller icefields and icecaps developed, for example on the islands of Skye and Mull, together with over 200 much smaller corrie and valley glaciers. This readvance probably achieved its maximum extent shortly after *c*.10,500 BP (Peacock *et al.* 1989; Rose *et al.* 1988), but radiocarbon age determinations on basal sediments within the area of the readvance suggest widespread glacier retreat by *c*.10,200 BP (Gray & Coxon 1991). By the beginning of the Holocene at *c*.10,000 BP, glacier ice was restricted to a few dwindling remnants on high ground.

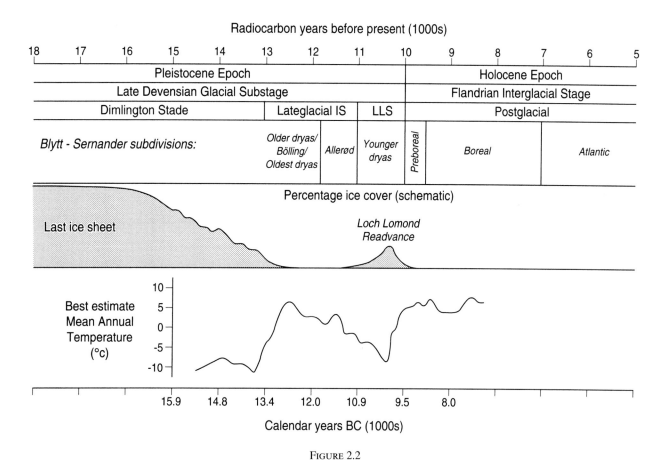

Figure 2.2

Chronology of environmental change in Scotland 18,000–5000 BP. The mean annual temperature curve is derived from temporally-smoothed data based on coleopteran assemblages (Briffa & Atkinson 1997) reduced by 1.5°C to provide an estimate for mean annual temperature in central Scotland.

Lateglacial and Early Holocene climate change

The changes in climate that controlled the expansion and contraction of glaciers in Scotland during the final 10,000 years of the Pleistocene Epoch appear to have been controlled primarily by movements of the North Atlantic oceanic polar front, which in turn reflected the vigour of thermohaline circulation (density-driven northwards movements of warm surface waters) in the Atlantic Ocean (e.g. Broeker 1990; Broeker *et al.* 1990), and by periodic meltwater pulses from the wasting northern hemisphere ice sheets (e.g. Berger & Jansen 1995). At present, the North Atlantic oceanic polar front lies between Iceland and Greenland. At the last glacial maximum, however, it lay at the latitude of northern Spain, while during the Loch Lomond Stadial it was located at the latitude of SW Ireland (Ruddiman & McIntyre 1981). At these times, therefore, Scotland was surrounded by oceanic waters much colder than those of the present (Peacock & Harkness 1990), resulting in drastic reduction of air temperatures and the expansion of glacier ice. However, climatic conditions were by no means constant during these glacial episodes. Glacier expansion occurred under cold conditions accompanied by heavy winter snowfall, and the early stages of glacier contraction appear to have been initiated by reduction in snowfall rather than climatic warming. The final stages of deglaciation, however, reflected very rapid warming at the beginning of the Lateglacial Interstadial and at the Lateglacial/Holocene transition (Fig. 2.2).

Employment of various proxy indicators of palaeo-climate, such as climatically-diagnostic periglacial phenomena (Ballantyne & Harris 1994), the equilibrium line altitudes of former glaciers (Ballantyne 2002a; Hubbard 1999), and above all the climatic implications of coleoptera and chironomid assemblages (Atkinson *et al.* 1987; Brooks & Birks 2001) have enabled a reasonably high resolution reconstruction of changes in the British climate between *c.*15,000 and 8000 BP. Extremely cold conditions appear to have persisted until *c.*13,000 BP. Within the period 13,000–12,700 BP, however, there was an astonishingly rapid warming as the North Atlantic oceanic front migrated northwards, and by *c.*12,500 BP conditions were similar to those of the present (Fig. 2.2), though perhaps more continental in character. Thereafter temperatures oscillated around a generally declining trend, with a more abrupt fall after *c.*11,300 BP heralding the onset of the Loch Lomond Stadial. At the thermal nadir of the latter, mean July sea-level temperatures in Scotland were probably of the order of 5.5–7.0°C, mean annual temperatures were as low as –6°C to –8°C, and mean January temperatures were probably no higher than –20°C. Precipitation in the west of Scotland was probably similar to, or slightly higher than, that of the present

(Ballantyne 2002a). The eastern Highlands, however, experienced marked aridity, with the Cairngorms receiving only 25–30 per cent of present precipitation (Ballantyne & Harris 1994). Thus even though climatic conditions during the earlier part of the Lateglacial Inter-stadial may have been favourable for human resettlement of the Scottish landscape, those of the Loch Lomond Stadial were certainly not, except possibly to groups adapted to survival under arctic conditions.

The transition to warmer conditions at the end of the Loch Lomond Stadial was rapid, with mean annual temperatures rising by as much as 1°C per decade (Atkinson *et al.* 1987), and by *c.*9800 BP the climate may have been as warm as at the peak of the Lateglacial Interstadial. Our understanding of climatic changes in Scotland during the ensuing five millennia, however, is remarkably limited. Much of the proxy evidence on which reconstruction of Lateglacial climatic change is based, such as periglacial phenomena and the dimen-sions of former glaciers, cannot be extended into the Holocene, and only a few well-dated records of beetle assemblages are available for the last 10,000 years. The coleopteran data that do exist for the Early Holocene in Britain indicate temperatures similar to, or very slightly higher than, those of the present (Briffa & Atkinson 1997). Moreover, evidence provided by foraminifera in North Atlantic Ocean cores demonstrates that, throughout the Holocene, polar waters remained well to the north of the British Isles (Ruddiman & Mix 1993). However, studies of Greenland ice-core data (Alley *et al.* 1997) have detected a particularly pronounced cooling at *c.*7500 BP that lasted about a century. This cooling event was probably due to disturbance of North Atlantic thermohaline circulation by catastrophic drainage of huge ice-dammed lakes as the Laurentide (North American) ice sheet retreated (Barber *et al.* 1999). Evidence from marine cores from off the west coast of Norway and from contemporaneous tree-ring records from Germany imply respectively a temperature drop of >2°C and stressing of vegetation (Klitgaard-Kristensen *et al.* 1998). The location of Scotland on the NE Atlantic margin suggests that this event was probably reflected in markedly cooler temperatures, though there is no evidence for regenera-tion of glaciers on Scottish mountains at this time.

For the remainder of the Early Holocene, however, the climate of Scotland appears to have remained generally temperate, with no drastic fluctuations in long-term average temperatures and certainly no return to cold stadial conditions. The relatively low amplitude of Holocene climatic fluctuations itself makes identi-fication of climatic changes difficult, for whereas the marked thermal fluctuations that characterized the Late-glacial period forced marked changes in fauna and flora, the comparatively small changes that appear to have occurred in the Holocene are not so readily identified in terms of biotic response.

Reconstruction of Holocene climatic change has traditionally been based on vegetation changes recorded by macrofossils and pollen assemblages preserved in peat bogs. For much of the past century a model of Holocene climate change proposed by the Scandinavian palaeobotanists A. Blytt and R. Sernander on the basis of peat stratigraphy and pollen evidence was widely accepted. They subdivided the Early Holocene into the Preboreal, Boreal, and Atlantic Periods (Fig. 2.2). The Boreal period (c.9500–7000 BP) was considered to be rather warmer and drier than at present, with a higher incidence of anticyclonic weather, while the Atlantic period (c.7000–5000 BP) was believed to be characterized by a Postglacial climatic (i.e. thermal) optimum accompanied by rather wetter conditions. As further well-dated palynological and palaeoecological evidence accumulated, however, the Blytt/Sernander scheme was recognized to be at best over-generalized, though their terminology has been retained by some authors, and especially by archaeologists, as a useful though essentially informal means of subdividing the Holocene.

Although palynological studies have furnished a rich abundance of information concerning the changing vegetation cover of Scotland during the Holocene (e.g. Birks 1996; Edwards & Whittington 1997), the usefulness of pollen-stratigraphic evidence as a climatic proxy during this period has engendered considerable debate. Some researchers, such as Huntley and Prentice (1993) have assumed that past vegetation assemblages were essentially in equilibrium with contemporaneous climate, and have employed large pollen-stratigraphic datasets to reconstruct Holocene palaeoclimates for particular time intervals. Other palaeoecologists have been more cautious in their approach, noting that because of the slow migration rates of some taxa, vegetation assemblages are likely to be out of equilibrium with climate, and stressing the importance of local ecological, edaphic, or hydrological controls on former vegetation assemblages (e.g. Birks 1990; Whittington & Edwards 1997). A further problem is that many taxa have a climatic tolerance much greater than the relatively small climatic fluctuations that are believed to have characterized the Early Holocene, limiting their use as palaeoclimatic proxies. In this respect, variations in the distribution of taxa at the extremes of their latitudinal or altitudinal range are likely to offer the greatest potential for providing useful palaeoclimatic information.

Because of the caveats identified above, palaeoclimatic reconstructions based solely on vegetation (usually arboreal) assemblages offer at best general qualitative information regarding early Holocene climate change in Scotland. Rapid warming at the onset of the Holocene is reflected in the early establishment of hazel and birch in the Scottish landscape. Other arboreal taxa such as pine, oak, and elm tended to arrive later, not necessarily because of climatic constraints but because they had farther to migrate or because of slow colonization rates. Current evidence suggests that many major arboreal species did not approach the limits of their range until c.7000 BP, at which time the climate was, in general, slightly drier and warmer than at present (Birks 1990). Huntley (1999) has suggested that the general 'first-order' climate trend in Britain during the Holocene was characterized by a tendency towards reduced seasonality and moister conditions. A quantitative reconstruction by Huntley and Prentice (1993) indicates that at c.6000 BP conditions were similar to those of the present with slightly (up to 2°C) warmer July temperatures. Huntley (1999) has emphasized, however, both the temporal and spatial variability of such conclusions; his data, for example, suggest that although winters may have been cooler around 6000 BP in southern Scotland, they were slightly warmer than now in northern Scotland (Fig. 2.3).

Because of the uncertainties inherent in the use of pollen profiles for retrodicting climate change in the Early Holocene, it is useful to review other sources of evidence. One such source of evidence relates to the climatic implications of Early Holocene glacier behaviour in SW Norway (Nesje et al. 1991). In the Jostedalen area, glacier recession at the beginning of the Holocene was briefly interrupted by a return to cooler conditions at c.9500 BP, but a climate similar to that of the present was apparently achieved by c.9000 BP. The disappearance or near-disappearance of glacier ice from the region between 7500 and 6000 BP implies summer temperatures roughly 2°C warmer than at present. After 6000 BP, however, there is evidence of thermal decline, possibly accompanied by an increase in snowfall: glaciers expanded, treelines descended, and peat growth became widespread.

The extent to which this rather distant record is relevant to Scotland is debatable, but the general pattern is broadly consistent with other lines of evidence. Radiocarbon-dated pine (Pinus sylvestris) remains in the Cairngorms demonstrate that prior to c.6500 BP the treeline was about 200m higher than at present, suggesting a warmer and perhaps less stormy climate (Dubois & Ferguson 1985). There is some evidence for a decline in treeline altitude between c.6500 and 5300 BP that may indicate climatic deterioration, but this may equally reflect sample availability and should be regarded with caution. Deuterium isotope analysis of cellulose

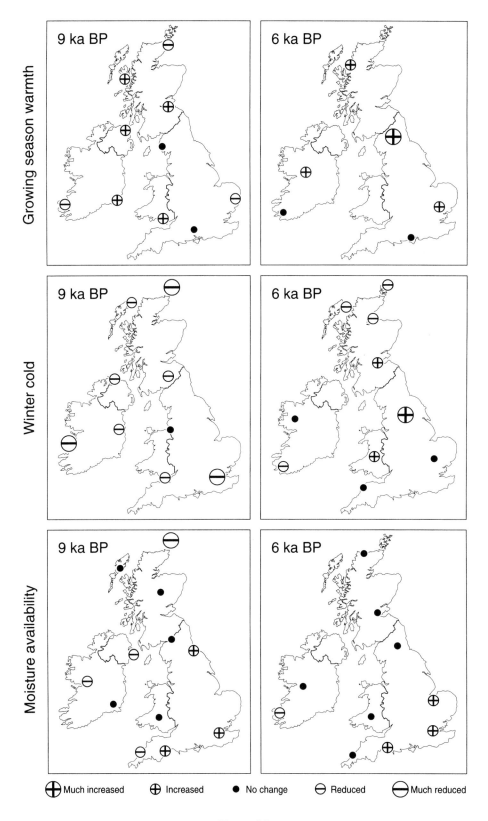

FIGURE 2.3

Holocene palaeoclimatic reconstructions based on palynological data. Differences from present-day climatic conditions are indicated for 9000 BP and 6000 BP. Based on Huntley (1999).

in wood remains in the same area indicates that there were particularly wet conditions around 7300 BP and between 6200 and 5800 BP, lending support to the notion of wetter conditions during the Atlantic chronozone and climatic deterioration around or after c.6000 BP. This is suggested also by evidence from several sites in the Loch Tulla area of Rannoch Moor, which shows that a major expansion of pine at c.6800–6600 BP was succeeded by a significant reduction in pine cover between c.6600 and 5000 BP, interpreted by Bridge *et al.* (1990) as reflecting the onset of wetter conditions.

A shift to wetter conditions in the closing centuries of the Atlantic chronozone, immediately preceding a local episode of pine decline, is also suggested by reconstruction of changes in bog hydrology in NW Scotland based on degree of peat humification (Anderson 1998). However, composite peat humification curves compiled by Anderson *et al.* (1998) for sites in the NW Highlands suggest a rather more complex pattern. Particularly wet conditions are evident at some sites prior to c.8300 BP and between c.6200 and 5800 BP, but equally there is evidence for a general drying trend between c.5400 and 5000 BP. What emerges strongly from their data is that although some major climatic trends are replicated between sites spaced a few tens of kilometres apart, the amplitude of the climatic signals varies between sites and short-term (decadal) fluctuations are not always replicated between sites. This suggests that the spatial impact of climatic changes was highly variable and that the record obtained from one area is not necessarily applicable even to areas a few tens of kilometres distant.

In sum, the limited evidence available suggests that, following rapid warming at the Lateglacial/Holocene transition, temperate conditions had been established in Scotland by c.9800 BP, and that average temperatures reached a peak between c.7500 and 6000 BP, when mean July temperatures may have been up to 2°C warmer than now. There is evidence for at least local increases in wetness prior to 9000 BP, and around 7300 BP and 6500–6000 BP, and rather more widespread evidence for climatic instability between 6000 and 5000 BP. However, this generalized summary certainly conceals numerous short-term climatic shifts that lie beyond the resolution of the available proxy evidence, and the notion of a 'stable' Early Holocene climate is certainly misguided, as is the idea that a climatic shift evident for one part of the country was necessarily replicated elsewhere (Huntley 1999). The higher resolution proxy evidence available for the Late Holocene suggests that the temperatures of the past 5000 years have oscillated around 'average' values by as much as ±2°C on a timescale of decades or longer (Briffa & Atkinson 1997), and there is no reason

to suppose that this was not equally true of the Early Holocene. Thus the notion that the Mesolithic occupants of Scotland enjoyed a climate consistently milder than that of the present is probably misguided.

Moreover, it is important to appreciate that climate was not necessarily the prime determinant of the contemporaneous biotic environment. Major tree species such as oak were still migrating towards their northern range as late as 6000 BP, four millennia after the rapid climatic amelioration that enabled such migration (Birks 1990). Both the climatic environment and the biotic environment were in a state of constant change throughout the first 5000 years of the Holocene, forcing changes on local ecosystems and thus, presumably, on the economic basis of Mesolithic society. A particularly interesting question is how sensitive the Mesolithic economy was to environmental change and whether, when adverse changes occurred, populations responded by adaption or migration. Until the resolution of palaeoclimatic reconstructions for the Early Holocene is radically improved, however, this question is likely to remain unanswered.

Effects on landscape of the glacial-postglacial transition

It has been suggested above that both the climatic and biotic environments of the Mesolithic inhabitants of Early Holocene Scotland were subject to continuous change. Change also affected the physical landscape during this period, but, outside of the littoral zone, data on the timing, rate, and magnitude of Early Holocene landscape change are remarkably limited. In terms of both climatic change and landform change the Early Holocene represents the 'Dark Age' of research on the Late Quaternary of Scotland, about which much less is known than during the preceding Lateglacial period.

It seems likely, however, that initial landscape response to deglaciation was, especially in upland areas, locally dramatic. Studies of recently deglaciated terrain have demonstrated that retreat of valley glaciers is often succeeded by rapid reworking of glacigenic sediments by slope failure, slopewash, debris flow, and rivers (Ballantyne 2002b). In upland areas that were reoccupied by glacier ice during the Loch Lomond Stadial, such *paraglacial* processes were probably responsible for extensive gullying of valley-side drift deposits and the consequent accumulation of cones and fans of debris along the flanks of glacial troughs (Ballantyne & Benn 1996). It seems likely that many (though by no means all) of the relict debris cones and alluvial fans that occupy upland valleys formed within a few centuries of deglaciation (Ballantyne 1991a).

Another effect of deglaciation on the Early Holocene landscape was destabilization of rock slopes. Over 600 major rock-slope failures (mainly rockslides) have been identified in the Scottish Highlands and Hebrides, some involving the collapse of entire mountainsides (Ballantyne 1986; Jarman & Ballantyne 2002). The majority appear to have occurred in the Early Holocene in response to debuttressing of rock slopes as the last glaciers downwasted. Failure in such cases was rarely instantaneous, but followed slow expansion of the rock mass and consequent propagation of an internal network of joints. The famous landslip on The Storr on Skye, for example, occurred at *c*.6500 BP, several millennia after deglaciation (Ballantyne *et al.* 1998b). The factors responsible for initiating rockslides in the Early Holocene remain uncertain, but a fascinating possibility is that some were triggered by earthquakes (Ballantyne 1997). Davenport

et al. (1989) have demonstrated that in the Western Highlands a combination of glacio-isostatic uplift and tectonic stress resulted in appreciable seismic activity throughout the Early Holocene, producing earthquakes of magnitude 6.5–7.0 at the end of the Loch Lomond Stadial, diminishing to magnitude 5.0–6.0 events by *c*.3000 BP. The landscape of Mesolithic Scotland was thus by no means as stable as that of the present.

Sea-level change

Causes of sea-level change
The growth and decay of the last ice sheet also had an important effect on sea-level change and the configuration of the Scottish coastline. The build-up of the last ice sheet depressed the level of the land surface, such depression being greatest near the centre of the ice sheet where the ice was thickest. During and after the

FIGURE 2.4
Raised delta and raised beach, Gruinard Bay, Wester Ross. The conspicuous raised delta reflects a relative sea level of *c*.20m OD at the time of ice-sheet deglaciation. The much lower raised beach fronting the delta is the Main Postglacial Shoreline. (Photograph by the author)

shrinkage of the ice sheet the land underwent differential glacio-isostatic rebound, with those areas that lay near the former centre of the ice sheet rising more rapidly than those near its former margins. Isostatic uplift was rapid at first, then slowed progressively throughout the Lateglacial and Holocene. Such vertical movements of the land were accompanied by glacio-eustatic changes in global sea-level. During the Early Holocene this took the form of a general rise in sea-level as the last great ice sheets melted, feeding the oceans with meltwater. As the ice sheets in North America and Eurasia did not melt completely until c.7500–6500 BP, it was not until then that global ocean volume reached its present capacity. The severance of Great Britain from continental Europe, perhaps at c.7000 BP, reflects a rapid rise in global sea-level at this time (Funnel 1995).

The interplay of glacio-eustatic sea-level rise and differential isostatic uplift resulted in marked and complex changes in the coastal configuration of Scotland. Because isostatic uplift was greater and more rapid in areas that lay close to the centre of the last ice sheet, the nature and rate of *relative* sea-level change varied spatially with distance from the centre of isostatic uplift, which lay in the vicinity of Rannoch Moor in the Western Grampian Highlands. Where the rising seas and rising land were temporarily in equilibrium (i.e. occurring at approximately the same rate), shorelines were formed. In areas where subsequent isostatic uplift outstripped sea-level rise, these ancient shorelines now take the form of raised beaches, raised rock platforms, raised deltas, and raised estuarine (*carse*) deposits (Figs 2.4 & 2.5). In areas farther from the centre of isostatic uplift, however, ancient shorelines lie below present sea-level, or are buried under deposits laid down during a later marine transgression.

The earliest raised shorelines in Scotland are those that formed in the east of the country as the sea flooded the coastline during ice-sheet retreat. Of greater significance to Mesolithic archaeology, however, is a pronounced rock platform and backing cliff, known as the Main Lateglacial Shoreline, that apparently developed during the Loch Lomond Stadial (Stone *et al.* 1996). This platform is typically 50–150m wide and is present along extensive stretches of the western seaboard (Dawson 1984). It has a maximum altitude of over 10m in the Oban area and

Figure 2.5
Raised estuarine (*carse*) deposits of the Forth Valley east of Stirling. This area was inundated by the sea at c.6800 BP.
(Photograph by the author)

gradually declines in altitude away from the centre of isostatic uplift, passing below present sea-level in Islay, western Mull, Ayrshire, and the western Moray Firth. The archaeological significance of this feature stems from the fact that caves and fissures in the backing cliff contain Mesolithic remains (Bonsall 1996; Bonsall & Sutherland 1992).

The pattern of Early Holocene sea-level change
Coastal sites located far from the centre of isostatic uplift, such as the Northern and Western Isles, tend to have been dominated by progressive submergence and coastline retreat throughout the Holocene. Indeed, in Lateglacial times the Outer Hebrides and the Orkney Islands may each have constituted a single island that became progressively fragmented by rising seas during the Holocene (Smith 1997). Coastal sites located closer to the centre of isostatic uplift experienced a more complex sequence of relative sea-level movements, in which four general phases can be identified (Fig. 2.6; Ballantyne & Dawson 1997).

1. Prior to *c*.8500–8000 BP the rate of isostatic uplift generally exceeded that of eustatic sea-level rise, and relative sea-level fell.

2. There followed a period of relative marine transgression, the Main Postglacial Transgression, when eustatic sea-level rise due to disintegration of the last mid-latitude ice sheets outstripped isostatic uplift.

3. The culmination of the Main Postglacial Transgression occurred as global ocean volume approached present levels. Because of different rates of isostatic uplift, maximum relative sea-level occurred in different places at different times within the period 7200–6000 BP, with maximum relative sea-level being latest at sites farthest from the centre of isostatic uplift.

4. The culmination of the Main Postglacial Transgression was succeeded by gradual relative marine regression due to residual isostatic uplift, interrupted by minor periods of stasis or transgression caused by small (<2m) fluctuations in eustatic sea-level.

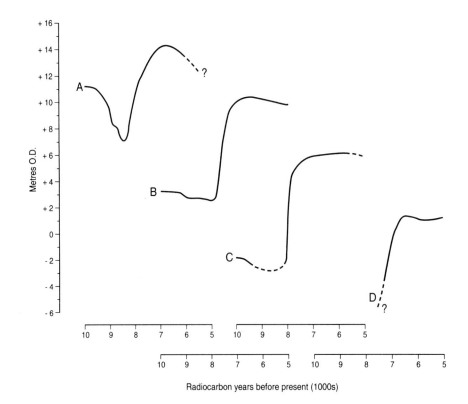

FIGURE 2.6
Graphs of Early Holocene relative sea-level change at four sites (A–D) located at increasing distance from the centre of isostatic uplift (see Fig. 2.7). A. Forth Valley (after Robinson 1993); B. The Earn-Tay confluence (after Smith *et al.* 1985); C. The Dornoch Firth (after Smith *et al.* 1992); D. Wick (after Dawson & Smith 1997).

The shoreline associated with the culmination of the Main Postglacial Transgression is known as the Main Postglacial Shoreline, and is now raised above present sea-level as a result of subsequent isostatic uplift. It forms a conspicuous raised beach or raised estuarine flats around much of the Scottish coastline, except in the northernmost mainland, Outer Hebrides, and Northern Isles. It reaches a maximum altitude of 13–14m near the centre of isostatic uplift, for example on the shores of Loch Etive and in the upper Forth Valley, and declines progressively in altitude towards more peripheral coasts (Fig. 2.7).

Implications of Early Holocene sea-level change
Given the abundance of known Mesolithic sites in coastal locations, the marked and locally rapid rise in sea-level that occurred after *c.*8500 BP has important implications for the interpretation of the pattern and chronology of Mesolithic settlement. In western Scotland the Main

Postglacial Transgression rose above the Main Late-glacial Shoreline, inundating Early Mesolithic sites and destroying shell middens and other archaeological evidence. Significantly, many of the earliest dated Meso-lithic remains in western Scotland occur at sites just above the upper limit of the transgression, for example on Rùm and in the Oban area (Bonsall & Sutherland 1992; Wickham-Jones 1990), suggesting that lower littoral sites were destroyed as sea-level rose. Similarly, Mesolithic artefacts have been found within the carse of the Forth Valley (Lacaille 1954). Collectively this evidence implies that sea-level rise associated with the Main Postglacial Transgression has effectively truncated the littoral archaeological record; coastal sites pre-dating the transgression on exposed coasts were destroyed, and those in more sheltered locations were buried under estu-arine sediments. Conversely, though the Main Postgla-cial Shoreline is a time-transgressive feature, it provides a conspicuous and locally well-dated landform for constraining the ages of *in situ* archaeological evidence recovered on or below this level. In western Scotland, for example, some Mesolithic sites, including shell middens, are located immediately adjacent to the Main Postgla-cial Shoreline, suggesting occupation at the time of the culmination of the transgression (Bonsall 1996; Jardine 1977).

Early Holocene sea-level rise resulted in striking large-scale changes in the configuration of low-lying areas of Scotland. In the west, the sea flooded low ground around the Clyde Estuary and invaded Loch Lomond. In the east the sea advanced up the Tay Estuary, flooding lower Strathearn, and inundated the Forth Valley almost as far west as Aberfoyle (Fig. 2.8). At the culmination of the transgression in the Forth Valley, *c.*6800 BP, the rising seas almost severed the Highlands from the Midland Valley, and a land bridge only 12km wide linked north and south. At a more local scale, the rapidity of relative sea-level rise after *c.*8500 BP must have had a significant impact on coastal settlements and economy. In general, rate of sea-level rise was greatest farthest from the centre of glacio-isostatic uplift. The graphs of relative sea-level in Fig. 2.6 suggest that the maximum rate of relative sea-level rise ranged from about 0.5m per century near the centre of glacio-isostatic uplift to as much as 3m per century in more distal locations. On low-lying coasts such rates imply significant marine incursion even within the span of a single human generation, and the creation of extensive inter-tidal zones that may have been very productive in terms of coastal resources (Mithen 1999). Equally, however, rapid sea-level rise increased the risk of forced abandonment of coastal settlement sites. Set within the context of rapidly-rising sea-level, extreme storm events may remodel low-lying coasts within a

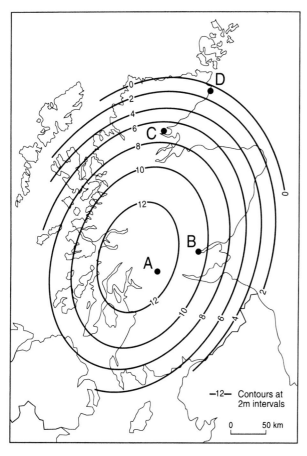

FIGURE 2.7
Isobase map for the Main Postglacial Shoreline (after Firth *et al.* 1993). Where the isobases intersect the coastline they represent the approximate present altitude of the shoreline. A–D are the locations of the reconstructed sea-level curves depicted in Fig. 2.6.

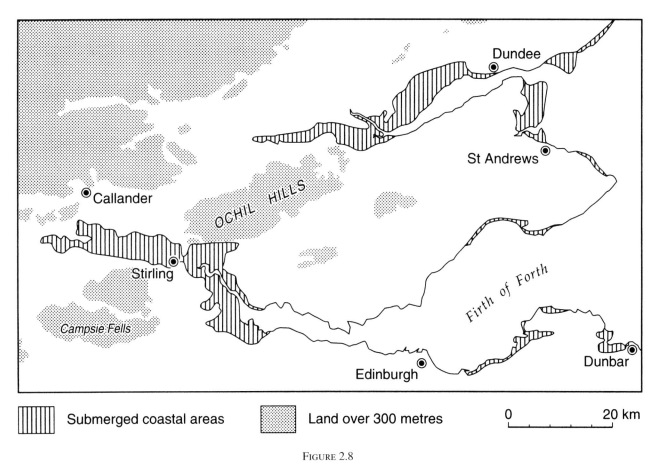

| | Submerged coastal areas | | Land over 300 metres | 0 — 20 km |

FIGURE 2.8
Extent of marine transgression of east-central Scotland at the culmination of the Main Postglacial Transgression.

matter of days or even hours, overwhelming barrier beaches and salt marshes and flooding the hinterland.

Although little is known about the influence of such exceptional storm events on littoral occupancy during the Mesolithic, evidence for another form of catastrophic flooding has been identified in the form of a conspicuous buried sand layer at numerous localities along the east coast of Scotland (Fig. 2.9) This was apparently deposited by a tsunami generated by a massive submarine landslide that occurred on the continental slope west of Norway around 7000 BP (Dawson *et al.* 1988). This tsunami is believed to have overwhelmed a Mesolithic occupation site at Inverness and may have flooded other sites at Broughty Ferry on the north side of the Tay Estuary and at Morton in NE Fife (Dawson *et al.* 1990). Although the Early Holocene coastal stratigraphic record suggests that this flooding event was unique in terms of its magnitude and widespread distribution, more localized storm events may have had equally catastrophic effects, particularly during the period of rapid sea-level rise that preceded the culmination of the Main Postglacial Transgression.

Other elements of Early Holocene landscape change

Mesolithic occupation of Scotland was not restricted to coastal sites, and a number of studies have indicated considerable inland penetration by Mesolithic communities (e.g. Affleck *et al.* 1988; Edwards 1985; Edwards *et al.* 1984). Unfortunately, current understanding of inland landscape change in the Early Holocene is slender. Research on recently deglaciated terrain (Ballantyne 2002b; Ballantyne & Benn 1996) has suggested that rapid reworking of glacigenic sediments after deglaciation typically lasts no more than a few centuries, after which a period of general hillslope and alluvial stability ensues. This pattern is supported by dates obtained on organic soil horizons and peat layers buried by debris flows, which record numerous erosional events in the Late Holocene, but very few in the Early Holocene (Curry 2000; Hinchliffe 1999). To what extent this represents a true reflection of the stability of drift-mantled hillslopes in the Early Holocene is debatable, however, as older organic layers are liable to burial

FIGURE 2.9

Conspicuous (light-coloured) sand layer within peat deposits, representing a tsunami that flooded the east coast of Scotland and the Northern Isles at *c*.7000 BP. (Photograph by A.G. Dawson)

under more recent deposits, and hence are often less accessible for sampling.

Similarly, though the last decade has witnessed a steady increase in the information available on patterns of Postglacial river incision and alluviation in Scotland (e.g. Ballantyne & Whittington 1999; Brazier *et al.* 1988; Macklin & Lewin 1993; McEwen 1997; Tipping 1994; Tipping & Halliday 1994), this has focused almost exclusively on Late Holocene events and putative causes. In the Early Holocene, changes in relative sea-level would certainly have caused floodplain aggradation (during rises in relative sea-level) and incision and associated terrace formation (during falls in relative sea-level), but such direct links apply only to river mouths and estuaries. Farther upstream, where local base level is often controlled by bedrock thresholds, the pattern of Early Holocene alluvial change is much less predictable. In the Eastern Grampian Highlands, however, a number of published (Ballantyne & Whittington 1999; Robertson-

Rintoul 1986) and unpublished (Robertson-Rintoul pers. comm.) radiocarbon dates place the culmination of Holocene floodplain aggradation, now represented by the highest Holocene terrace, after *c*.4000 BP. If this pattern is replicated elsewhere in Scotland, it implies that inland Mesolithic riparian sites are liable to have been removed by flooding or buried under floodplain sediments, and that Mesolithic sites or artefacts are liable to survive at the ground surface only above the level of the highest Holocene river terraces.

Effects of Mesolithic settlement on the physical landscape

During the Early Holocene, nearly all of Scotland except high ground was covered by a succession of woodland types (Birks 1996; Edwards & Whittington 1997). The principal impact of early human activity on the physical landscape is likely to have taken the form of deliberate or inadvertent (through burning) woodland clearance, which affects landforms in several ways. By reducing evapotranspiration and other hydrological changes, deforestation may increase stream discharge by 10–40 per cent (Moore 1985), and trigger a flashy runoff response to rainstorms, potentially causing river incision (Ferguson 1981). On hillslopes, deforestation not only reduces stability but favours rapid build-up of porewater pressures in soils, promoting shallow slope failures and associated debris flow during extreme rainstorms. Removal of vegetation, particularly by burning, causes drastic increases in rates of soil erosion by rainsplash and slopewash. In addition, clearance of woodland tends to result in increased leaching of nutrients and consequent soil acidification, degradation of soil structure, and possibly peat growth.

On the basis of pollen and charcoal evidence, a number of authors have proposed that Mesolithic communities in Scotland deliberately cleared woodland or managed heathlands, possibly to encourage grazing (e.g. Bennett *et al.* 1990; Bohncke 1988; Edwards 1996; Edwards & Mithen 1995; Edwards *et al.* 1995; Hirons & Edwards 1990), though the evidence employed in such inferences has been challenged (Macklin *et al.* 2000). It is therefore appropriate to consider whether or not there is evidence for Mesolithic woodland clearance in the geomorphological or sedimentological record. Unfortunately, as noted above, outside the coastal zone information regarding Early Holocene geomorphological changes is extremely fragmentary. There is currently no evidence for Early Holocene episodes of inland valley-floor alluviation or incision in Scotland, and though there is localized evidence for slope failure and associated debris flow activity in the NW Highlands and Hebrides between *c.*6600 and 5000 BP there is no conclusive evidence to link such activity to woodland clearance, anthropogenic or otherwise (Curry 2000; Hinchliffe 1999).

A more promising approach is to search for evidence of increased soil erosion in sediment cores retrieved from the floors of lakes. Radiocarbon dating of such cores offers the possibility of identifying periods of enhanced inwash of mineral soil, and accelerated erosion of soils within lake catchments may be reflected in an increased concentration of certain metal ions (Edwards & Rowntree 1980; Pennington *et al.* 1972), variations in magnetic susceptibility (Thompson *et al.* 1975), and the rate and grain-size of sediment influx. Where such studies have been carried out, however, they yield no conclusive evidence for significant Mesolithic land-scape disturbance, even though later deforestation or agricultural disturbance is strongly represented in lake sediment characteristics (e.g. Edwards & Rowntree 1980; Pennington *et al.* 1972; Vasari & Vasari 1968).

Absence of evidence, however, is not necessarily evidence of absence. Given the fragmentary nature of our current understanding of Early Holocene change in the physical landscape of Scotland, it is hardly surprising that no conclusive evidence has emerged concerning the impact of Mesolithic peoples on the landscape, particu-larly when the nature and extent of the landscape impact of more drastic forms of human activity (widespread deforestation and cultivation) later in the Holocene is still debatable (Ballantyne 1991b; Ballantyne & Whit-tington 1999). Probably the most promising way to establish whether or not Mesolithic woodland clearance affected the physical landscape by influencing sediment yield is through a dated association between archaeo-logical sites, palynological data, and enhanced minero-genic sedimentation within adjacent lakes. On present evidence, however, it seems reasonable to conclude that the influence of changes in the physical environment on the Mesolithic communities of Scotland was much more significant than the influence of these communities on the changing physical environment.

References

Affleck, T.L., Edwards, K.J. and Clarke, A. 1988. Archaeo-logical and palynological studies at the Mesolithic pitch-stone and flint site of Auchareoch, Isle of Arran. *Proceed-ings of the Society of Antiquaries of Scotland* **118**, 37–59.

Alley, R.B., Mayewski, P.A., Sowers, T., Stuiver, M., Taylor, K.C. and Clark, P.U. 1997. Holocene climatic instability: a prominent widespread event 8200 yr ago. *Geology* **25**(6), 483–6.

Anderson, D.E. 1998. A reconstruction of Holocene climate changes from peat bogs in north-west Scotland. *Boreas* **27**(3), 208–24.

Anderson, D.E., Binney, H.A. and Smith, M.A. 1998. Evidence for abrupt climatic change in northern Scotland between 3500 and 3900 calendar years BP. *The Holocene* **8**(1), 97–103.

Atkinson, T.C., Lawson, T.J., Smart, P.L., Harmon, R.S. and Hess, J.W. 1986. New data on speleothem deposition and palaeoclimate in Britain over the last forty thousand years. *Journal of Quaternary Science* **1**(1), 67–72.

Atkinson, T.C., Briffa, K.R. and Coope, G.R. 1987. Seasonal temperatures in Britain during the past 22,000 years, reconstructed using beetle remains. *Nature* **325**, 587–92.

Ballantyne, C.K. 1986. Landslides and slope failures in Scotland: a review. *Scottish Geographical Magazine* **102**(2), 134–50.

Ballantyne, C.K. 1991a. Holocene geomorphic activity in the Scottish Highlands. *Scottish Geographical Magazine* **107**(2), 84–98.

Ballantyne, C.K. 1991b. Late Holocene erosion in upland Britain: climatic deterioration or human influence? *The Holocene* **1**(1), 81–5.

Ballantyne, C.K. 1997. Holocene rock-slope failures in the Scottish Highlands. *Paläoklimaforschung* **19**, 197–205.

Ballantyne, C.K. 2002a. The Loch Lomond Readvance on the Isle of Mull, Scotland: glacier reconstruction and palaeo-climatic implications. *Journal of Quaternary Science* **17**(7), 759–71.

Ballantyne, C.K. 2002b. Paraglacial geomorphology. *Quater-nary Science Reviews,* **21**(12), 1935–2017.

Ballantyne, C.K. and Benn, D.I. 1996. Paraglacial slope adjustment during recent deglaciation and its implications for slope evolution in formerly glaciated environments. *In* S. Brooks and M.G. Anderson (eds), *Advances in Hillslope Processes,* 1173–95. Chichester: Wiley.

Ballantyne, C.K. and Dawson, A.G. 1997. Geomorphology and landscape change. *In* K.J. Edwards and I.B.M. Ralston (eds), *Scotland: Environment and Archaeology, 8000 BC–AD 1000,* 23–44. Chichester: Wiley.

Ballantyne, C.K. and Harris, C. 1994. *The Periglaciation of Great Britain.* Cambridge: Cambridge University Press.

Ballantyne, C.K. and Whittington, G. 1999. Late Holocene floodplain incision and alluvial fan formation in the central Grampian Highlands, Scotland: chronology, environment and implications. *Journal of Quaternary Science* **14**(7), 651–71.

Ballantyne, C.K., McCarroll, D., Nesje, A., Dahl, S.O. and Stone, J.O. 1998a. The last ice sheet in North-West Scotland: reconstruction and implications. *Quaternary Science Reviews* **17**(12), 1149–84.

Ballantyne, C.K., Stone, J.O. and Fifield, L.K. 1998b. Cosmogenic Cl-36 dating of postglacial landsliding at The Storr, Isle of Skye, Scotland. *The Holocene* **8**(3), 347–51.

Barber, D.C., Dyke, A., Hillaire-Marcel, C., Jennings, A.E., Andrews, J.T., Kerwin, M.W., Bilodeau, G., McNeely, R., Southon, J., Morehead, M.D. and Gagnon, J.-M. 1999.

Forcing of the cold event of 8,200 years ago by catastrophic drainage of Laurentide lakes. *Nature* **400**, 344–8.

Bennett, K.D., Fossit, J.A., Sharp, M.J. and Switsur, V.R. 1990. Holocene vegetational and environmental history at Loch Lang, South Uist, Western Isles, Scotland. *New Phytologist* **114**(3), 281–98.

Berger, W.H. and Jansen, E. 1995. Younger Dryas episode: ice collapse and super-fjord heat pump. *In* S.R. Troelstra, J.E. van Hinte and G.M. Ganssen (eds), *The Younger Dryas*, 61–105. Amsterdam: Koninklijke Nederlandse Akademie van Wetenschappen.

Birks, H.J.B. 1990. Changes in vegetation and climate during the Holocene of Europe. *In* M.M. Boer and R.S. De Groot (eds), *Landscape-Ecological Impact of Climate Change*, 133–58. Amsterdam: IOS Press.

Birks, H.J.B. 1996. Great Britain – Scotland. *In* B.E. Berglund, H.J.B. Birks, M. Ralska-Jasiewiczowa and H.E. Wright (eds), *Palaeoecological Events During the Last 15,000 Years: Regional Syntheses of Palaeoecological Studies of Lakes and Mires in Europe*, 95–143. Chichester: Wiley.

Bohncke, S.J.P. 1988. Vegetation and habitation history of the Callinish area, Isle of Lewis, Scotland. *In* H.H. Birks, H.J.B. Birks, P.E. Kaland and D. Moe (eds), *The Cultural Landscape – Past, Present and Future*, 445–61. Cambridge: Cambridge University Press.

Bonsall, J.C. 1996. The 'Obanian problem': coastal adaptation in the Mesolithic of western Scotland. *In* T. Pollard and A. Morrison (eds), *The Early Prehistory of Scotland*, 183–97. Edinburgh: Edinburgh University Press.

Bonsall. J.C. and Sutherland, D.G. 1992. The Oban caves. *In* M.J.C. Walker, J.M. Gray and J.J. Lowe (eds), *The South-West Scottish Highlands: Field Guide*, 115–21. Cambridge: Quaternary Research Association.

Bowen, D.Q., Rose, J., McCabe, A.M. and Sutherland, D.G. 1986. Correlation of Quaternary glaciations in England, Ireland, Scotland and Wales. *Quaternary Science Reviews* **5**, 299–340.

Brazier, V., Whittington, G. and Ballantyne, C.K. 1988. Holocene debris cone evolution in Glen Etive, Western Grampian Highlands, Scotland. *Earth Surface Processes and Landforms* **13**(6), 525–31.

Bridge, M.C., Haggart, B.A. and Lowe, J.J. 1990. The history and palaeoclimatic significance of subfossil remains of *Pinus sylvestris* in blanket peats from Scotland. *Journal of Ecology* **78**(1), 77–99.

Briffa, K.R. and Atkinson, T.C. 1997. Reconstructing Late-glacial and Holocene climates. *In* M. Hulme and E. Barrow (eds), *Climates of the British Isles: Present, Past and Future*, 84–111. London: Routledge.

Broeker, W.S. 1990. Salinity history of the North Atlantic during the last deglaciation. *Paleoceanography* **5**(6), 459–67.

Broeker, W.S., Bond, G. and Klas, M. 1990. A salt oscillator in the glacial North Atlantic? 1. The concept. *Paleoceanography* **5**(6), 469–77.

Brooks, S.J. and Birks, H.J.B. 2001. Chironomid-inferred Lateglacial air temperatures at Whitrigg Bog, southeast Scotland. *Journal of Quaternary Science* **15**(7), 759–764.

Curry, A.M. 2000. Holocene reworking of drift-mantled hill-slopes in the Scottish Highlands. *Journal of Quaternary Science* **15**(5), 529–541.

Dawson, A.G. 1984. Quaternary sea-level changes in western Scotland. *Quaternary Science Reviews* **3**(4), 345–68.

Dawson, A.G. and Smith, D.E. 1997. Holocene relative sea-level changes on the margin of a glacio-isostatically-uplifted area: an example from northern Caithness, Scotland. *The Holocene* **7**(1), 59–77.

Dawson, A.G., Long, D. and Smith, D.E. 1988. The Storegga slides: evidence from Eastern Scotland for a possible tsunami. *Marine Geology* **82**(4), 271–6.

Dawson, A.G., Smith, D.E. and Long, D. 1990. Evidence for a tsunami from a Mesolithic site in Inverness, Scotland. *Journal of Archaeological Science* **17**(6), 509–12.

Davenport, C.A., Ringrose, P.S., Becker, A., Hancock, P. and Fenton, C. 1989. Geological investigations of Late- and Postglacial earthquake activity in Scotland. *In* S. Gregersen and P. Basham (eds), *Earthquakes at North Atlantic Passive Margins: Neotectonics and Post-glacial Rebound*, 175–94. Dordrecht: Kluwer Academic Publishers.

Dubois, A.D. and Ferguson, D.K. 1985. The climatic history of pine in the Cairngorms based on radiocarbon dates and stable isotope analysis, with an account of the events leading up to its colonisation. *Review of Palaeobotany and Palynology* **46**(1), 55–80.

Edwards, K.J. 1985. Meso-Neolithic vegetational impacts in Scotland and beyond: palynological considerations. *In* C. Bonsall (ed.), *The Mesolithic in Europe*, 143–55. Edinburgh: John Donald.

Edwards, K.J. 1996. A Mesolithic of the Western and Northern Isles of Scotland? Evidence from pollen and charcoal. *In* T. Pollard and A. Morrison (eds), *The Early Prehistory of Scotland*, 23–38. Edinburgh: Edinburgh University Press.

Edwards, K.J. and Mithen, S. 1995. The colonization of the Hebridean islands of Western Scotland: evidence from the palynological and archaeological records. *World Archaeology* **26**(3), 348–65.

Edwards, K.J. and Rowntree, K.M. 1980. Radiocarbon and palaeoenvironmental evidence for changing rates of erosion at a Flandrian stage site in Scotland. *In* R.A. Cullingford, D.A. Davidson and J. Lewin (eds), *Time-scales in Geomorphology*, 207–33. Chichester: Wiley.

Edwards, K.J. and Whittington, G. 1997. Vegetation change. *In* K.J. Edwards and I.B.M. Ralston (eds), *Scotland: Environment and Archaeology, 8000 BC–AD 1000*, 63–82. Chichester: Wiley.

Edwards, K.J., Ansell, M., and Carter, B.A. 1984. New Meso-lithic sites in south-west Scotland and their importance as indicators of inland penetration. *Transactions of the Dumfries and Galloway Natural History and Antiquarian Society* **58**, 9–15.

Edwards, K.J. Whittington, G. and Hirons, K.R. 1995. The relationship between fire and long-term wet heath development in South Uist, Outer Hebrides, Scotland.

In D.B.A. Thompson, A.J. Hester and M.B. Usher (eds), *Heaths and Moorland: Cultural Landscapes,* 240–48. Edinburgh: HMSO.

Ehlers, J., Gibbard, P.L. and Rose, J. (eds). 1991. *Glacial Deposits in Great Britain and Ireland.* Rotterdam: Balkema.

Ferguson, R.I. 1981. Channel form and channel changes. *In* J. Lewin (ed.), *British Rivers,* 90–125. London: Allen & Unwin.

Finlayson, W. and Edwards, K.J. 1997. The Mesolithic. *In* K.J. Edwards and I.B.M. Ralston (eds), *Scotland: Environment and Archaeology, 8000 BC–AD 1000,* 109–25. Chichester: Wiley.

Firth, C.R., Smith, D.E. and Cullingford, R.A. 1993. Late Devensian and Holocene glacio-isostatic uplift patterns in Scotland. *Quaternary Proceedings* **3**, 1–14.

Funnel, B.M. 1995. Global sea level and the (pen-)insularity of later Cenozoic Britain. *In* R.C. Preece (ed.), *Island Britain: a Quaternary Perspective,* 3–13. London: The Geological Society, Special Publication **96**.

Gray, J.M. and Coxon, P. 1991. The Loch Lomond Stadial glaciation in Britain and Ireland. *In* J. Ehlers, P.L. Gibbard and J. Rose (eds), *Glacial Deposits of Great Britain and Ireland,* 89–105. Rotterdam: Balkema.

Hall, A.M. and Bent, A.J.A. 1990. The limits of the last British ice sheet in northern Scotland and the adjacent shelf. *Quaternary Newsletter* **61**, 2–12.

Hall, A.M. and Jarvis, J. 1989. A preliminary report on the Late Devensian glaciomarine deposits at St Fergus, Grampian Region. *Quaternary Newsletter* **59**, 5–7.

Hinchliffe, S. 1999. Timing and significance of talus slope re-working, Trotternish, Isle of Skye, Scotland. *The Holocene* **9**(4) 483–94.

Hirons, K.R. and Edwards, K.J. 1990. Pollen and related studies at Kinloch, Isle of Rhum, Scotland, with particular reference to possible early human impacts on vegetation. *New Phtyologist* **116**(6), 714–27.

Hubbard, A. 1999. High resolution modeling of the advance of the Younger Dryas ice sheet and its climate in Scotland. *Quaternary Research* **52**(1), 27–43.

Huntley, B. 1999. Climatic change and reconstruction. *In* K.J. Edwards and J.P. Sadler (eds), *Holocene Environments of Prehistoric Britain,* 513–20. Chichester: Wiley (=*Quaternary Proceedings* **7**).

Huntley, B. and Prentice, I.C. 1993. Holocene vegetation and climates in Europe. *In* H.E. Wright, J.E. Kutzbach, T. Webb, W.F. Ruddiman, F.A. Street-Perrott and P.J. Bartlein (eds), *Global Climates Since the Last Glacial Maximum,* 136–68. Minneapolis: University of Minneapolis Press.

Jardine, W.G. 1977. Location and age of Mesolithic occupation sites on Oronsay, Inner Hebrides. *Nature* **267**, 138–40.

Jarman, D. and Ballantyne, C.K. 2002. Beinn Fhada, Kintail: an example of large-scale paraglacial rock-slope deformation. *Scottish Geographical Journal* **118**(1), 59–68.

Klitgaard-Kristensen, D., Sejrup, H.P., Haflidason, H., Johnsen, S. and Spurk, M. 1998. A regional 8200 cal. yr BP cooling event in northwest Europe, induced by final stages of the Laurentide ice-sheet deglaciation? *Journal of Quaternary Science* **13**(2), 165–69.

Lacaille, A.D. 1954. *The Stone Age in Scotland.* London: Oxford University Press.

McEwen, L.J. 1997. Geomorphological change and fluvial landscape evolution during the Holocene. *In* J.E. Gordon (ed.), *Reflections on the Ice Age in Scotland,* 116–29. Glasgow: Scottish Association of Geography Teachers and Scottish Natural Heritage.

Macklin, M.G. and Lewin, J. 1993. Holocene alluviation in Britain. *Zeitschrift für Geomorphologie, Supplementband* **88,** 109–22.

Macklin, M.G., Bonsall, C., Davies, F.M. and Robinson, M.R. 2000. Human-environmental interactions during the Holocene: new data and interpretations from the Oban area, Argyll, Scotland. *The Holocene* **10**(1), 109–21.

Mithen, S.J. 1999. Mesolithic archaeology, environmental archaeology and human palaeoecology. *In* K.J. Edwards and J.P. Sadler (eds), *Holocene Environments of Prehistoric Britain,* 477–83. Chichester: Wiley (=*Quaternary Proceedings* **7**).

Moore, P.D. 1985. Forests, man and water. *International Journal of Environmental Studies* **25**(2), 159–66.

Nesje, A., Kvamme, M., Rye, N. and Løvlie, R. 1991. Holocene glacial and climate history of the Jostedalsbreen region, western Norway: evidence from lake sediments and terrestrial deposits. *Quaternary Science Reviews* **10**, 87–114.

Peacock J.D. and Harkness, D.D. 1990. Radiocarbon ages and the full glacial to Holocene transition in seas adjacent to Scotland and southern Scandinavia: a review. *Transactions of the Royal Society of Edinburgh: Earth Sciences* **81**(4), 385–96.

Peacock, J.D., Austin, W.E.N., Selby, I., Graham, D.K., Harland, R. and Wilkinson, I.P. 1992. Late Devensian and Flandrian palaeoenvironmental changes on the Scottish continental shelf west of the Outer Hebrides. *Journal of Quaternary Science* **7**(2), 145–61.

Peacock, J.D., Harkness, D.D., Housley, R.A., Little, J.A. and Paul, M.A. 1989. Radiocarbon ages for a glaciomarine bed associated with the maximum of the Loch Lomond Readvance in west Benderloch, Argyll. *Scottish Journal of Geology* **25**(1), 69–79.

Pennington, W., Haworth, E.Y., Bonny, A.P. and Lishman, J.P. 1972. Lake sediments in northern Scotland. *Philosophical Transactions of the Royal Society of London* **B264,** 191–294.

Robertson-Rintoul, M.S.E. 1986. A quantitative soil-stratigraphic approach to the correlation and dating of post-glacial river terraces in Glen Feshie, Western Cairngorms. *Earth Surface Processes and Landforms* **11**(6), 605–17.

Robinson, M. 1993. Microfossil analyses and radiocarbon dating of depositional sequences related to Holocene sea-level change in the Forth Valley, Scotland. *Transactions* of the Royal Society of Edinburgh: Earth Sciences **84**(1), 1–60.

Rose, J., Lowe, J.J. and Switsur, R. 1988. A radiocarbon date on plant detritus beneath till from the type area of the Loch Lomond Readvance. *Scottish Journal of Geology* **24**(2), 113–24.

Ruddiman, W.F. and McIntyre, A. 1981. The North Atlantic during the last deglaciation. *Palaeogeography, Palaeoclimatology, Palaeoecology* **35**(2), 145–214.

Ruddiman, W.F. and Mix, A.C. 1993. The North and Equatorial Atlantic at 9000 and 6000 yr BP. *In* H.E. Wright, J.E. Kutzbach, T. Webb, W.F. Ruddiman, F.A. Street-Perrott and P.J. Bartlein (eds), *Global Climates Since the Last Glacial Maximum,* 94–135. Minneapolis: University of Minneapolis Press.

Saville, A. 1997. Palaeolithic handaxes in Scotland. *Proceedings of the Society of Antiquaries of Scotland* **127**, 1–16.

Sejrup, H.P., Haflidason, H., Aarseth, I., King, E., Forsberg, C.F., Long, D. and Rokoengen, K. 1994. Late Weichselian glacial history of the northern North Sea. *Boreas* **23**(1), 1–13.

Smith. D.E. 1997. Sea-level change in Scotland during the Devensian and Holocene. *In* J.E. Gordon (ed.), *Reflections on the Ice Age in Scotland,* 136–51. Glasgow: Scottish Association of Geography Teachers and Scottish Natural Heritage.

Smith, D.E., Dawson, A.G., Cullingford, R.A. and Harkness, D.D. 1985. The stratigraphy of Flandrian relative sea-level changes at a site in Tayside, Scotland. *Earth Surface Processes and Landforms* **10**(1), 17–25.

Smith, D.E., Firth, C.R., Turbayne, S.C. and Brooks, C.L. 1992. Holocene relative sea-level changes and shoreline displacement in the Dornoch Firth area, Scotland. *Proceedings of the Geologists' Association* **103**(4), 237–57.

Stoker, M.S., Hitchin, K. and Graham, C.C. 1993. *The Geology of the Hebrides and West Shetland Shelves, and Adjacent Deep-Water Areas.* British Geological Survey United Kingdom Offshore Regional Geology Report. London: HMSO.

Stone, J.O., Lambeck, K, Fifield, L.K., Evans, J.M. and Cresswell, R.G. 1996. A Lateglacial age for the Main Rock Platform, western Scotland. *Geology* **24**(10), 707–10.

Stone, J.O., Ballantyne, C.K. and Fifield, L.K. 1998. Exposure dating and validation of periglacial weathering limits, northwest Scotland. *Geology* **26**(7), 587–90.

Sutherland, D.G. 1984. The Quaternary deposits and landforms of Scotland and the adjacent shelves. *Quaternary Science Reviews* **3**(2/3), 157–254.

Sutherland, D.G. 1991a. The glaciation of the Shetland and Orkney Islands. *In* J. Ehlers, P.L. Gibbard and J. Rose (eds), *Glacial Deposits of Great Britain and Ireland,* 121–8. Rotterdam: Balkema.

Sutherland, D.G. 1991b. Late Devensian glacial deposits and glaciation in Scotland and the adjacent offshore region. *In* J. Ehlers, P.L. Gibbard and J. Rose (eds), *Glacial Deposits of Great Britain and Ireland,* 53–60. Rotterdam: Balkema.

Thompson, R., Battarbee, R.W., O'Sullivan, P.E. and Oldfield, F. 1975. Magnetic susceptibility of lake sediments. *Limnology and Oceanography* **20**(10), 687–98.

Thorp, P.W. 1987. Late Devensian ice sheet in the western Grampians, Scotland. *Journal of Quaternary Science* **2**(2), 103–12.

Tipping, R. 1994. Fluvial chronology and valley-floor evolution of the upper Bowmont Valley, Borders Region, Scotland. *Earth Surface Processes and Landforms* **19**(7), 641–57.

Tipping, R. and Halliday, S.P. 1994. The age of alluvial fan deposition at a site in the Southern Uplands of Scotland. *Earth Surface Processes and Landforms* **19**(4), 333–48.

Vasari, Y. and Vasari, A. 1968. Late- and Post-glacial macrophytic vegetation in the lochs of northern Scotland. *Acta Botanica Fennica* **8**(1), 1–120.

Whittington, G and Edwards, K.J. 1997. Climate change. *In* K.J. Edwards and I.B.M. Ralston (eds), *Scotland: Environment and Archaeology, 8000 BC–AD 1000,* 11–22. Chichester: Wiley.

Wickham-Jones, C.R. 1990. *Rhum: Mesolithic and later sites at Kinloch. Excavations 1984–1986.* Edinburgh: Society of Antiquaries of Scotland (Monograph **7**).

Chapter 3

Interpretative Issues Concerning the Driving Forces of Vegetation Change in the Early Holocene of the British Isles

RICHARD TIPPING

Woodland disturbance attributed to anthropogenic activity is one of the key sources from which to understand the presence, dynamics, and behaviour of Mesolithic groups. The principles of interpretation of such woodland disturbances from upland contexts in the British Isles are critically evaluated in the light of new data which, more than previously, indicate that human activities are not the sole, or even perhaps the likeliest cause of change in plant communities. Causal hypotheses which compete with those involving human manipulation of woods have in the past been undervalued, based on assumptions that, in the absence of human groups, woodland stability would be expected. However, climate change and autogenic processes are emphasized in recent reconstructions, and natural instability characterizes ecosystems. Future interpretations of woodland disturbance may need to provide more formal, more discriminatory, and more explicit tests of competing hypotheses.

Introduction

In a period such as the Mesolithic, when archaeological traces of human presence are scarce and essentially ephemeral (Wickham-Jones 1994), identifying purposeful disturbance to plant communities by human groups has emerged as one of the most critical and significant ways by which to explore hunter-gatherer communities in many parts of the British Isles (Barton *et al.* 1995; Caseldine & Hatton 1993; Edwards 1989; 1990; Jacobi *et al.* 1976; Mellars 1976; Mellars & Dark 1998; Simmons 1969; 1975; 1996; Simmons & Innes 1987; 1988a; Smith 1970; Smith & Cloutman 1988).

The arguments assembled from which to deduce anthropogenic alterations to plants and ecosystems derive from ethnographic parallels as to why hunter-gatherers should want to manipulate their landscapes, and how they might have done it (Mellars 1976), and from detailed palaeoecological reconstructions, principally using pollen analysis (palynology), which attempt to demonstrate that this manipulation occurred. The debate has encompassed possible human effects in the partial determination of major features of Postglacial vegetation change, such as the 'early' appearance in the present interglacial of *Corylus* (hazel) (Huntley 1993; Smith 1970) and the establishment of *Alnus* (alder) (Bennett & Birks 1990; Chambers & Elliott 1989; Smith 1984; Tallantire 1992), as well as the much more subtle analysis of slight alterations to vegetation patterns over very small distances and at very short timescales (Simmons & Innes 1981; 1987; 1996a; 1996b; Smith & Cloutman 1988; Smith *et al.* 1989; Turner, Innes & Simmons 1993), in which resource manipulation (improvements in grazing quality etc.) is central to interpretation (Mellars 1976; Simmons 1975).

Classification of these diverse analyses into spatially distinct, regional *versus* local, effects is common (Edwards 1999; Smith 1981) although arbitrary. New work (e.g. Caseldine & Hatton 1993; Simmons 1996) stresses how small-scale impacts might lead to region-wide differentiation of landscapes. This paper will not exhaustively review all aspects of these analyses; such reviews are available, particularly for upland Britain (Edwards 1989; 1999; Edwards & Whittington 1997; Evans 1999; Finlayson & Edwards 1997; Simmons 1993; 1996; Tipping 1994).

The paper will instead focus on discussion of the interpretation of short-lived, ephemeral, and spatially restricted 'interference' or 'disturbance' phases in pollen diagrams. This contribution will in particular draw attention to difficulties in assigning these slight vegetation disturbances to anthropogenic activity. This attribution has, indeed, always been acknowledged to be ambiguous (Simmons 1993; 1996; Smith 1981) because of the difficulties in distinguishing the patterns to have been purposeful (and so anthropogenic) as opposed to either autogenic change in plant communities, driven by internal adjustments of complex woodland ecosystems, or climatic change in the early Holocene (Tipping 1996). No new data are presented here; rather the intention is to 'stand back' and review recently published data from a variety of sources which might place the debate in a new light.

Firstly, the long-term context of these ephemeral disturbance phases is briefly summarized, before discussion focuses on three related issues: (a) the absence of clear palynological indicators (cf. Behre 1981; 1986) of anthropogenic activity in Mesolithic disturbances; (b) the problem of equifinality in interpretations, where a range of driving forces can lead to the same vegetation response, which addresses our current lack of discrimination in dismissing particular causes; and (c) new evidence that one such driving force – climate change – has been previously undervalued or misunderstood. New data on the frequency and rapidity of Early–Mid Holocene climatic excursions may have major implications for our interpretation of vegetation changes and, possibly, for how we see the course of human change over this period.

Woodland development in the Early Holocene

The general pattern of woodland colonization and woodland restructuring following the Younger Dryas (Loch Lomond) Stadial (Lowe & Walker 1997) in the British Isles has been understood for many years (Godwin 1956). The patterns of temporal and spatial tree migration are well-known (Huntley & Birks 1983) and will not be evaluated here. They have been seen as a colonization sequence determined by gradual climatic amelioration within the Early Holocene (Godwin 1956; 1975; Lamb 1977), with different tree species being 'allowed' to migrate across Europe after specific climatic constraints and thresholds were removed. This thesis was re-examined in a highly influential paper by Birks (1989), in which the concept of gradual climatic change was replaced by one of very rapid temperature change in the first few hundred years of the Holocene, demonstrated from modelling exercises (Kutzbach & Guetter 1986) and empirical data (Atkinson et al. 1987; Dansgaard et al. 1989), data which are now widely attested (Lowe & Walker 1997).

This new paradigm implies that the colonization of tree taxa was not determined to any significant extent by any form of gradual climatic amelioration; the transition from Younger Dryas to full interglacial status was extraordinarily rapid, with data from ice-core records (Alley et al. 1993; Taylor et al. 1996) suggesting that the change took only decades. The distinct vegetation succession we observe within the Early Holocene is instead thought to be determined by: (a) the locations of Lateglacial woodland refugia; (b) contrasts in seed dispersal mechanisms and rates; and (c) 'chance' events (Birks 1989), which are required to explain the exceptional migration rates

exhibited in radiocarbon-dated pollen sequences across the British Isles. Edaphic factors (Pennington 1986) are not seen as significant in inhibiting the dispersal of early colonizing taxa such as *Betula* (birch) or *Corylus* (hazel), although pedogenesis provides increasing differentiation through time as later colonizing trees (*Quercus* (oak), *Ulmus* (elm), *Tilia* (lime), and *Pinus* (pine)) arrived. In an increasingly complex wooded landscape, autogenic adjustments like inter-species competition become important (Bennett 1986) in suppressing or displacing earlier colonizing trees.

The colonization of *Corylus* (hazel) is currently most often seen as representing migration from *refugia* close to the British Isles (Birks 1989; Edwards 1990; 1999; Rackham 1980; Tipping 1994), and a source west of the present western coastline of Scotland (Deacon 1973) has not been dismissed. Smith's (1970) suggestion of migration aided by human groups is still debated, most recently by Huntley (1993), but is not supported by the available data. Smith (1970) postulated a link between increased fire frequency and the establishment of *Corylus*, but very few pollen records can demonstrate such a relationship between burning as seen in charcoal records and the rise of *Corylus* pollen (Edwards 1989; 1990; Tipping 1994). Huntley (1993) argued that abrupt climate shifts, with increasing aridity, facilitated seedling establishment through fire, but again the data do not, except rarely (Smith 1998), support this.

The appearance of *Alnus* (alder) across the British Isles cannot be readily described as a smooth 'spread' across the country (Bennett & Birks 1990). *Alnus* is competitively inferior to the existing deciduous trees such as *Quercus* (oak) and *Ulmus* (elm) (Bennett 1986; Smith 1984), and may have required disturbance to facilitate establishment. Mesolithic human impact is one such cause (Tipping 1995a), but among many others, including autogenic, climatic, geomorphological, and biological agencies (Bennett & Birks 1990; Chambers & Elliott 1989).

By the Later Mesolithic period, woodland structure varied in many ways in space (Bennett 1989; Birks et al. 1975; Tipping 1994), at all spatial scales, and presented a variety of landscapes, extraordinarily diverse mosaics of different woodlands and open ground, within which Mesolithic communities operated. These woodland types were almost certainly not those that ecologists (Rodwell 1991) describe today (Birks 1993). We have no analogues for Later Mesolithic woodlands, because any plant community is a temporary assemblage of chance occurrences, mediated by adaptations to driving forces like soil, climate, land use, competition, and time itself. This observation, in passing, may have implications for

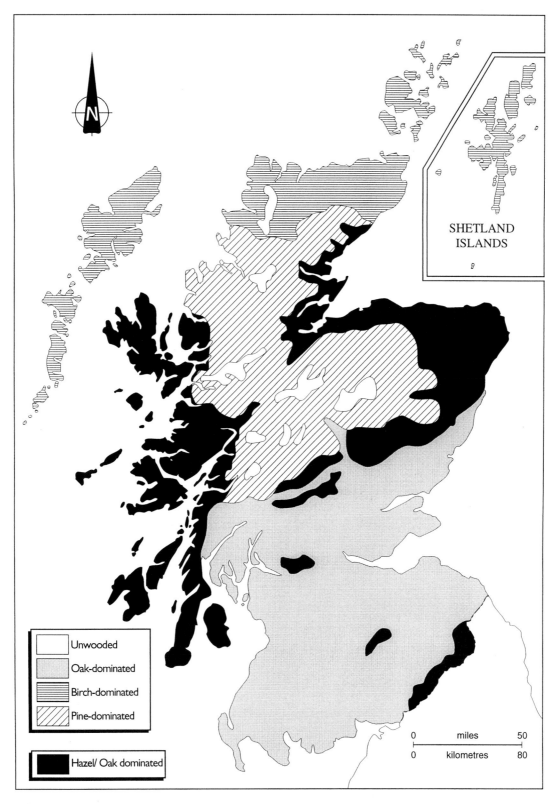

FIGURE 3.1

Reconstruction of the woodland types in Scotland at *c*.5000 ^{14}C BP (modified from Tipping 1994, illus. 3).

archaeologists in many ways. One important issue relates to the detailed modelling of factors such as terrestrial resources and biomass (e.g. Mellars 1976), which are derived from the structure, composition, and dynamics of present-day woodlands (Falinski 1986), woodlands that are different from those of the Later Mesolithic.

A number of reconstructions provide crude 'snapshots' of the regional extent and distribution of woodland types in parts of the British Isles at the transition from Mesolithic to Neolithic periods, around 5000 ^{14}C BP (Fig. 3.1; Bennett 1989; Edwards & Whittington 1997; Tipping 1994). These differ markedly between workers, and in many ways these differences indicate what we do not yet understand about local vegetation patterning, tree-lines and upland areas, ecotones, and so on (Tipping 1994). In a more specific way, these maps are problematic in imparting a false impression of stability in these landscapes. Current ecological paradigms (Botkin 1990; Shugart 1998) stress the importance in ecosystems of continuous disturbance, at all temporal and spatial scales. No plant community is stable; autogenic and external driving forces promote constant change, including the effects of single trees dying and creating short-lived canopy openings, storms causing wind-throw across hill-sides, lightning-strike fires, and anthropogenic activity (Peterken 1996).

Ephemeral disturbances in Mesolithic woodlands

It is accepted here that archaeologists and palaeoecologists have developed coherent models as to why hunter-gatherers should want to manipulate woodlands (Mellars 1976; Simmons 1969; 1975), particularly in upland settings, although many ethnographic observations are not necessarily as relevant to Mesolithic environments as often assumed. In addition, in some upland landscapes workers have generated palaeoecological data-sets which are exceptionally impressive in the detail and care with which they have been assembled, particularly the recent work of Simmons and Innes (1996a; 1996b; 1996c; Simmons *et al.* 1989; Turner *et al.* 1989; 1993) from multiple pollen profiles at North Gill on the North York Moors, summarized by Simmons (1996). These analyses have shown that woodland disturbances in this upland environment, particularly in the last 1000 or so years of the Mesolithic period, are characterized by being both very short-lived, each episode persisting only for decades, and confined to very small patches of the landscape, perhaps tens of metres around a pollen profile. Some disturbances seem to be more sustained, over hundreds of years, comparable to patterns seen at other, less highly resolved sites in the British Isles (see

Simmons 1996 for a review), but pollen recruitment characteristics at many sites make it likely that prolonged disturbances seen in single profiles are actually products of individual small-scale and ephemeral disturbances (Caseldine & Hatton 1993).

As discussed above, disturbance is now seen to be typical of ecosystems; it is a natural process. Much of the data on this derive from palaeoecological analyses which allow an appropriately long temporal perspective (Delcourt & Delcourt 1991). Work of the calibre of that at North Gill is very exciting because we can begin to understand the temporal and spatial scale of such disturbances. Each disturbance has characteristic features which are internally consistent and ecologically 'sensible', but despite the detail of the analyses, none is demonstrably anthropogenic in origin, and cause remains as inferential as ever. This is not a new criticism (Brown 1997) and it is acknowledged by Simmons (1996), but is nonetheless chastening. There seems to be a gap between the hypothetical models for hunter-gatherer woodland manipulation developed in the 1970s (e.g. Mellars 1976) and precise predictable ecological outcomes of such manipulations, from which to establish human impact. This lack of causal discrimination in pollen analyses will persist unless tests of hypotheses are developed.

There are, for example, no consistent or replicable palynological indicators within Mesolithic disturbances that can be assigned to human activity. Open ground pollen taxa are recorded in disturbances, but very few are convincing indicators of activities predicted from behaviours such as grazing (cf. Behre 1981). Pollen taxa such as *Rumex* (docks), *Melampyrum* (cow-wheat), *Pteridium* (bracken) (Simmons 1996, table 2.2) are not necessarily anthropogenic indicators; they occur in woodlands, and would respond in increased numbers, pollen production, and/or pollen dispersal to any opening of the woodland canopy. Simmons (1996, table 2.2) records *Plantago lanceolata* (ribwort plantain) as a relatively common herb in disturbance episodes within the British Isles (55 per cent of sites), and this is arguably (cf. Groenman-van Waateringe 1996) a good grazing indicator, but it is rare at profiles in North Gill, and not repeatedly recorded at other sites. Records of microscopic charcoal in pollen sequences, commonly seen as anthropogenic (Bennett *et al.* 1990; Edwards 1989; 1990; 1996; Simmons & Innes 1981; 1996b; Simmons *et al.* 1989), are in reality even more ambiguous in origin (Patterson *et al.* 1987). It can, of course, be argued that open ground herbs are no better guides to anthropogenic activity in post-Mesolithic periods, but in pollen analyses of Neolithic and later contexts there appears to be a clearer predictive use of these indicators, with, for example, woodland being substituted through clearance by a coherent suite of landuse indicators (Berglund 1969; 1985; Edwards 1993; Pilcher *et al.* 1971).

Climate change as a driving force in Early–Mid Holocene woodlands

Explanations of woodland disturbance phases in Meso-lithic contexts as anthropogenic in origin need to assume that, in the absence of human activity, stability would prevail. This is unlikely to have been the case if our new understanding of ecosystem dynamics holds true. In addition, it is probable that other external forcing factors have been underrated as explanatory variables. Chief among these is climate change. The recognition of abrupt climate change at the beginning of the Holocene period (above) has reawakened a concern that equally rapid changes may characterize the Interglacial itself. Models of a smooth and gradual amelioration in temper-ature from the Younger Dryas until a mid-Postglacial climatic 'optimum' (Lamb 1977) have been undermined in recent years, although no clear consensus has as yet been reached concerning the chronology, frequency, or magnitude of climatic changes. Synthesis is compli-cated by an emphasis on regional patterning, where neither synchroneity nor directions of climate shifts (e.g. warmer/cooler; wetter/drier) are assured between regions. Regional palaeoclimatic reconstruction requires the generation of data-sets pertinent to that spatial scale, and for much of the British Isles this is not yet possible (Berglund *et al.* 1996).

This section will not pursue the synthesis of terrestrial data-sets for NW Europe, but instead will draw attention to examples from the North Atlantic region, from new work on Greenland ice-core and ocean-sediment records. These examples may seem far removed from the British Isles, but there are sound arguments for suggesting that the major source of large-scale climatic change lies within the North Atlantic (Broecker 1994; Broecker & Denton 1990). The case-studies are new, and some need to be validated before we can fully explore their significance, but they are used here as 'markers' for a climate event stratigraphy slowly emerging (Berglund *et al.* 1996).

The major Early Holocene climate event to emerge from new analyses of the GISP2 Greenland ice core occurred at *c.*8200 cal BP/*c.*7300 ^{14}C BP (Alley *et al.* 1997). This is an abrupt change in a range of physical and geochemical indicators which together are thought to record changes in snow accumulation, temperature near the ice-sheet, storminess, and northern hemisphere atmospheric circulation. This short-lived event probably lasted 200–400 calendar years (8400–8000 cal BP/7650–

7200 ^{14}C BP). It represents the most significant climatic deterioration recorded at GISP2 in the Holocene, with an estimated temperature decline of around $6\pm2°$C in central Greenland (Alley *et al.* 1997), and 1–3°C at marine and terrestrial sites in the NE Atlantic and Scan-dinavia (Klitgaard-Kristensen *et al.* 1998). This equates to around half the amplitude of the Younger Dryas deterioration. Correlations in timing have been made between this event and reduced marine temperatures off southern Norway (Klitgaard-Kristensen *et al.* 1998), global ice advance (Beget 1983), changes in temperature and/or precipitation recorded in tree growth (Klitgaard-Kristensen *et al.* 1998) and in lake sediments (Grafen-stein *et al.* 1998) in continental Europe, with changes in tropical lake levels (Stager & Mayewski 1997) and, less clearly, with methane production, which is related to tropical plant biomass and productivity (Alley *et al.* 1997). In the British Isles this event may correlate with the first of Dubois and Ferguson's (1985) climate dislo-cations (see also Bridge *et al.* 1990; Tipping 1994), and also, more tentatively, with disturbances to woodland (Simmons 1996) and changes in climatically determined fire frequency (Tipping 1996; Tipping & Milburn 2000, and see below).

The '8200 cal BP event' currently dominates thought because the amplitude of climate change is seen to have global effects. Such impacts may well have affected human populations, particularly in NW Europe. The significance of the event might detract, however, from evidence that the Earliest Holocene (*c.*11,000–10,000 cal BP) was marked by step-wise climatic amelioration (Alley *et al.* 1997; Meese *et al.* 1994) and a succes-sion of smaller-amplitude and short-lived temperature and precipitation shifts (Björck *et al.* 1997; Digerfeldt 1988; Johnsen *et al.* 1992; Tipping 1995b; van Geel *et al.* 1981).

These Early Holocene events have been linked to the collapse of the Laurentide ice sheet and major inputs of freshwater, which may have disrupted North Atlantic ocean circulation (Barber *et al.* 1999; Björck *et al.* 1997; Klitgaard-Kristensen *et al.* 1998). Bond *et al.* (1997) seem to have registered the signal of the 8200 cal BP event, and other Holocene events, within deep-sea sedi-ments from the North Atlantic by identifying sediments derived from apparent iceberg rafting events. If supported by corroborative data, this would have major impacts on how we see Holocene climate change, because iceberg rafting, and the introduction of low-salinity freshwater to the North Atlantic, is seen as the major determinant of instabilities and shut-downs of the North Atlantic Ocean circulation (Broecker 1994; Lowe & Walker 1997). Further, Bond *et al.* (1997) suggested that these events are recorded at periodicities of around 1400–1500 calendar years throughout the Holocene; 'events' within the Mesolithic period occur at *c*.11,100, 10,300, 9400, 8100, and 5900 cal BP.

O'Brien *et al.* (1995) employed measures of snow accumulation, proxy temperature, and geochemical data on the GISP2 core to identify a number of climatic excursions within the Holocene, in addition to the '8200 cal BP event'; the major Mesolithic 'event' is a cold phase at around 5600 cal BP. These 'events' are of much lower amplitude than Lateglacial shifts, and currently 'events' understood by different measures are not necessarily synchronous (Alley *et al.* 1997; Bond *et al.* 1997; O'Brien *et al.* 1995) – a clear problem – but Holocene climate change is now best understood in terms of abrupt excursions and instability.

Fire frequency and climate change in the Early–Mid Holocene

Records of burning obtained through the analysis of macroscopic and/or microscopic charcoal preserved in sediments (Patterson *et al.* 1987) assume considerable importance in Mesolithic studies (Edwards 1989; 1990; 1996; Simmons & Innes 1981; 1988; 1996b). Increased fire frequency is assumed in many case-studies to relate to anthropogenically set fires, and burning thus becomes a convenient way of identifying human impacts on the landscape. This view seems to be predicated on two assumptions; that British woodlands are not prone to natural fire (Rackham 1980) and that climatic conditions have not been so extreme as to promote burning (e.g. Law 1998). Neither of these assumptions need be true (Bradshaw *et al.* 1996; Brown 1997; Tipping 1994; 1996).

In Boreal forests a link between fire frequency and climate change is demonstrated (Bradshaw *et al.* 1996; Clark 1988; Johnson 1992), and is suggested for the major climatic excursions recorded in the GISP2 core (Alley *et al.* 1997; Taylor *et al.* 1996). Periods of climatic aridity may have forced comparable extremes in the British Isles (Bradshaw 1993; Huntley 1993; Tipping 1996). New data from several sites in southern Scotland (Tipping & Milburn 2000) suggest that a consistent region-wide increase in fire frequency and/or intensity occurred at *c*.7300 ^{14}C BP/8200 cal BP, sustained for around 2000 years. This is the time at which a sustained 1000-year period of burning commenced around Black Ridge Brook on Dartmoor (Caseldine & Hatton 1993). Simmons (1996) saw this period as a broadly synchronous phase of woodland disturbance at upland British sites, and in Finland mires became more susceptible to fire at *c*.7300 ^{14}C BP (Pitkanen *et al.* 1999). This date coincides with the period of climatic restructuring that

would have followed the 8200 cal BP event (Alley *et al.* 1997).

Conclusions

This review has attempted to suggest that instability, through a variety of forcing mechanisms, is the natural state for ecosystems; Mesolithic-age woodlands were no different and no more stable. Disturbance regimes are now fundamental to modern approaches to ecology (Botkin 1990). Climatic instability is likely to be confirmed rather than refuted in future work. It was not the purpose of this paper to synthesize the diverse data on Early–Mid Holocene climate change for NW Europe, but simply to indicate the significance of the debate. This period is neither complacent nor stable, and the questions that need to be pursued are related to linkages of various sorts. What is the scale/magnitude of these events? How do ice-core or ocean-core events translate to terrestrial events? Is every event recognized in these sources matched in the terrestrial record? Do such events have predictable consequences (always drier or always cooler) in NW European climate? Are these impacts sufficient to perturb human resource-utilization, or to have disturbed the rhythm of hunter-gatherer life?

In this I am not concerned with an overly determinist view of the Mesolithic period, but we need to recognize that there was more than the single agent – human activity – capable of inducing change within the woodlands of the Early Holocene. Such multi-causal hypotheses have to a large extent been undervalued by a palaeoecological and archaeological community more concerned to identify the fingerprint of anthropogenic 'impacts'. In future it will be necessary to provide more formal, more discriminatory, and more explicit tests of competing hypotheses.

Acknowledgements

I would like to thank Alan Saville for inviting this contribution, and Kevin Edwards for discussion of the themes, if not the conclusions, of this paper. Bill Jamieson is thanked for the preparation of the figure.

References

Alley, R.B., Meese, D.A. Shuman, C.A., Gow, A.J., Taylor, K.C. Grootes, P.M. White, J.W.C., Ram, M., Waddington, E.D., Mayewski, P.A. and Zielinski, G.A. 1993. Abrupt increase in snow accumulation at the end of the Younger Dryas. *Nature* **362**, 527–9.

Alley, R.B., Mayewski, P.A., Sowers, T., Stuiver, M., Taylor, K.C. and Clark, P.U. 1997. Holocene climatic instability: a prominent, widespread event 8200 yr ago. *Geology* **25**, 483–6.

Atkinson, T.C., Briffa, K.R. and Coope, G.R. 1987. Seasonal temperatures in Britain during the past 22,000 years, reconstructed using beetle remains. *Nature* **325**, 587–93.

Barber, D.C., Dyke, A., Hillaire-Marcel, C., Jennings, A.E., Andrews, J.T., Kerwin, M.W., Bilodeau, G., McNeely, R., Southon, J., Morehead, M.D. and Gagnon, J-M. 1999. Forcing of the cold event of 8,200 years ago by catastrophic drainage of Laurentide lakes. *Nature* **400**, 344–8.

Barton, R.N.E., Berridge, P.J., Walker, M.J.C. and Bevins, R.E. 1995. Persistent places in the Mesolithic landscape: an example from the Black Mountain Uplands of South Wales. *Proceedings of the Prehistoric Society* **61**, 81–116.

Beget, J.E. 1983. Radiocarbon-dated evidence of worldwide early Holocene climate change. *Geology* **11**, 389–93.

Behre, K.-E. 1981. The interpretation of anthropogenic indicators in pollen diagrams. *Pollen et Spores* **23**, 225–45.

Behre, K.-E. 1986. *Anthropogenic Indicators in Pollen Diagrams*. Rotterdam: Balkema.

Bennett, K.D. 1986. Competitive interactions among forest tree populations in Norfolk, England, during the last 10,000 years. *New Phytologist* **103**, 603–20.

Bennett, K.D. 1989. A provisional map of forest types for the British Isles 5000 years ago. *Journal of Quaternary Science* **4**, 141–4.

Bennett, K.D. and Birks, H.J.B. 1990. Postglacial history of alder (*Alnus glutinosa* (L.) Gaertn.) in the British Isles. *Journal of Quaternary Science* **5**, 123–34.

Bennett, K.D., Simonson, W.D. and Peglar, S.M. 1990. Fire and man in post-glacial woodlands of eastern England. *Journal of Archaeological Science* **17**, 635–42.

Berglund, B.E. 1969. Vegetation and human influence in south Scandinavia during prehistoric time. *Oikos* Suppl. **12**, 9–28.

Berglund, B.E. 1985. Early agriculture in Scandinavia: research problems related to pollen-analytical studies. *Norwegian Archaeological Review* **18**, 77–105.

Berglund, B.E., Birks, H.J.B., Ralska-Jasiewiczowa, M. and Wright, H.E. 1996. *Palaeoecological Events During the Last 15000 Years. Regional Syntheses of Palaeoecological Studies in Lakes and Mires in Europe*. Chichester: Wiley.

Birks, H.J.B. 1989. Holocene isochrone maps and patterns of tree-spreading in the British Isles. *Journal of Biogeography* **16**, 503–40.

Birks, H.J.B. 1993. Quaternary palaeoecology and vegetation science – current contributions and possible future developments. *Review of Palaeobotany and Palynology* **79**, 153–77.

Birks, H.J.B., Deacon, J. and Peglar, S.M. 1975. Pollen maps for the British Isles 5000 years ago. *Proceedings of the Royal Society of London* **B189**, 87–105.

Björck, S., Rundgren, M., Ingólfsson, O. and Funder, S. 1997. The Preboreal oscillation around the Nordic Seas: terrestrial and lacustrine responses. *Journal of Quaternary Science* **12**, 455–65.

Bond, G., Showers, W., Cheseby, M., Lotti, R., Almasi, P., deMenocal, P., Priore, P., Cullen, H., Hajadas, I. and Bonani, G. 1997. A pervasive millennial-scale cycle in North Atlantic Holocene and glacial climates. *Science* **278**, 1257–66.

Botkin, D.B. 1990. *Discordant Harmonies: A New Ecology for the 21st Century*. Oxford: Oxford University Press.

Bradshaw, R. 1993. Forest response to Holocene climatic change: equilibrium or non-equilibrium. *In* F.M. Chambers (ed.), *Climate Change and Human Impact on the Landscape*, 57–66. London: Chapman & Hall.

Bradshaw, R.H.W., Tolonen, K. and Tolonen, M. 1996. Holocene records of fire from the boreal and temperate zones of Europe. *In* J.S. Clark, H. Cachier, J.G. Goldammer and B. Stocks (eds), *Sediment Records of Biomass Burning and Global Change*, 347–65. Berlin: Springer.

Bridge, M.C., Haggart, B.A. and Lowe, J.J. 1990. The history and palaeoclimatic significance of subfossil remains of *Pinus sylvestris* in blanket peats from Scotland. *Journal of Ecology* **78**, 77–99.

Broecker, W.S. 1994. Massive iceberg discharges as triggers for global climate change. *Nature* **372**, 421–4.

Broecker, W.S. and Denton, G.H. 1990. The role of ocean-atmosphere reorganisations in glacial cycles. *Quaternary Science Reviews* **9**, 305–41.

Brown, A. 1997. Clearances and clearings: deforestation in Mesolithic/Neolithic Britain. *Oxford Journal of Archaeology* **16**(2), 133–46.

Caseldine, C. and Hatton, J. 1993. The development of high moorland on Dartmoor: fire and the influence of Mesolithic activity on vegetation change. *In* F.M. Chambers (ed.), *Climate Change and Human Impact on the Landscape*, 119–32. London: Chapman & Hall.

Chambers, F.M. and Elliott, L. 1989. Spread and expansion of *Alnus* Mill. in the British Isles: timing, agencies and possible vectors. *Journal of Biogeography* **16**, 541–50.

Clark, J.S. 1988. Effect of climate change on fire regimes in northwestern Minnesota. *Nature* **334**, 233–5.

Dansgaard, W., White, J.W.C. and Johnsen, S.J. 1989. The abrupt termination of the Younger Dryas climatic event. *Nature* **330**, 532–4.

Deacon, J. 1973. The location of refugia of *Corylus avellana* L. during the Weichselian glaciation. *New Phytologist* **73**, 1055–63.

Delcourt, H.R. and Delcourt, P.A. 1991. *Quaternary Ecology. A Palaeoecological Perspective*. London: Chapman & Hall.

Digerfeldt, G. 1988. Reconstruction and regional correlation of Holocene lake-level fluctuations in Lake Bysjon, South Sweden. *Boreas* **17**, 165–82.

Dubois, A.D. and Ferguson, D.K. 1985. The climatic history of pine in the Cairngorms based on radiocarbon dates and tree-ring D/H ratios. *Review of Palaeobotany & Palynology* **54**, 181–5.

Edwards, K.J. 1989. Meso-Neolithic vegetation impacts in Scotland and beyond: palynological considerations. *In* C. Bonsall (ed.), *The Mesolithic in Europe*, 143–63. Edinburgh: John Donald.

Edwards, K.J. 1990. Fire and the Scottish Mesolithic: evidence from microscopic charcoal. *In* P. M. Vermeersch and P. van Peer (eds), *Contributions to the Mesolithic in Europe*, 71–9. Leuven: Leuven University Press.

Edwards, K.J. 1993. Models of mid-Holocene forest farming for north-west Europe. *In* F.M. Chambers (ed.), *Climate Change and Human Impact on the Landscape*, 133–46. London: Chapman & Hall.

Edwards, K.J. 1996. A Mesolithic of the Western and Northern Isles of Scotland? Evidence from pollen and charcoal. *In* T. Pollard and A. Morrison (eds), *The Early Prehistory of Scotland*, 23–38. Edinburgh: Edinburgh University Press.

Edwards, K.J. 1999. Palynology and people: observations on the British record. *In* K.J. Edwards and J.P. Sadler (eds), *Holocene Environments of Prehistoric Britain*, 531–44. Chichester: Wiley.

Edwards, K.J. and Whittington, G. 1997. Vegetation change. *In* K.J. Edwards and I.B.M. Ralston (eds), *Scotland: Environment and Archaeology, 8000 BC–AD 1000*, 63–82. Chichester: Wiley.

Evans, J.G. 1999. *Land and Archaeology: Histories of Human Environment in the British Isles*. Stroud: Tempus.

Falinski, J.B. 1986. *Vegetation Dynamics in Temperate Lowland Priimeval Forests. Ecological Studies in Bialowieza Forest*. Dordrecht: Dr. W. Junk Publishers.

Finlayson, B. and Edwards, K.J. 1997. The Mesolithic. *In* K.J. Edwards and I.B.M. Ralston (eds), *Scotland: Environment and Archaeology, 8000 BC–AD 1000*, 109–26. Chichester: Wiley.

Godwin, H. 1956. *History of the British Flora* (1st edn). Cambridge: Cambridge University Press.

Godwin, H. 1975. *History of the British Flora* (2nd edn). Cambridge: Cambridge University Press.

Grafenstein, U. von, Erlenkeuser, H., Müller, J., Jouzel, J., and Johnsen, S. 1998. The cold event 8200 years ago documented in oxygen isotope records of precipitation in Europe and Greenland. *Climate Dynamics* **14**, 73–81.

Groenman-van Waateringe, W. 1986. Grazing possibilities in the Neolithic of the Netherlands based on palynological data. *In* K.-E. Behre (ed.), *Anthropogenic Indicators in Pollen Diagrams*, 187–202. Rotterdam: Balkema.

Huntley, B. 1993. Rapid early-Holocene migration and high abundance of hazel (*Corylus avellana* L.): alternative hypotheses. *In* F.M. Chambers (ed.), *Climate Change and Human Impact on the Landscape*, 205–15. London: Chapman & Hall.

Huntley, B. and Birks, H.J.B. 1983. *An Atlas of Past and Present Pollen Maps for Europe: 0–13 000 Years Ago*. Cambridge: Cambridge University Press.

Jacobi, R.M., Tallis, J.H. and Mellars, P.A. 1976. The southern Pennine Mesolithic and the ecological record. *Journal of Archaeological Science* **3**, 307–20.

Johnsen, S.J., Clausen, H.B., Dansgaard, W., Fuhrer, K., Gundestrup, N., Hammer, C.U., Iversen, P., Jouzel, J., Stauffer, B. and Steffensen, J.P. 1992. Irregular glacial interstadials recorded in a new Greenland ice core. *Nature* **359**, 311–13.

Johnson, E.A. 1992. *Fire and Vegetation Dynamics: Studies from the North American Boreal Forest*. Cambridge: Cambridge University Press.

Klitgaard-Kristensen, D., Sejrup, H.-P., Haflidason, H., Johnsen, S. and Spurk, M. 1998. A regional 8200 cal. yr BP cooling event in northwest Europe, induced by final stages of the Laurentide ice-sheet deglaciation? *Journal of Quaternary Science* **13**, 165–70.

Kutzbach, J.E. and Guetter, P.J. 1986. The influence of changing orbital parameters and surface boundary conditions on climatic simulations for the past 18,000 years. *Journal of Atmospheric Science* **43**, 1726–59.

Lamb, H.H. 1977. *Climate: Present, Past and Future*. London: Methuen.

Law, C. 1998. The uses and fire-ecology of reedswamp vegetation. *In* P. Mellars and P. Dark, *Star Carr in Context*, 197–206. Cambridge: McDonald Institute Monograph.

Lowe, J.J. and Walker, M.J.C. 1997. *Reconstructing Quaternary Environments* (2nd edn). Harlow: Longman.

Meese, D.A., Gow, A.J., Grootes, P., Mayewski, P.A., Ram, M., Stuiver, M., Taylor, K.C., Waddington, E.D. and Zielinski, G.A. 1994. The accumulation record from the GISP2 core as an indicator of climate change throughout the Holocene. *Nature* **266**, 1680–82.

Mellars, P. 1976. Fire ecology, animal populations and man: a study of some ecological relationships in prehistory. *Proceedings of the Prehistoric Society* **42**, 15–45.

Mellars, P. and Dark, P. 1998. *Star Carr in Context*. Cambridge: McDonald Institute Monograph.

O'Brien, S.R., Mayewski, P.A., Meeker, L.D., Meese, D.A., Twickler, M.S. and Whitlow, S.I. 1995. Complexity of Holocene climate as reconstructed from a Greenland ice core. *Science* **270**, 1962–4.

Patterson, W.A., Edwards, K.J. and Maguire, D.A. 1987. Microscopic charcoal as an indicator of fire. *Quaternary Science Reviews* **6**, 3–23.

Pennington, W. 1986. Lags in adjustment of vegetation to climate caused by the pace of soil development: evidence from Britain. *Vegetatio* **67**, 105–18.

Peterken, G.F. 1996. *Natural Woodland. Ecology and Conservation in Northern Temperate Regions*. Cambridge: Cambridge University Press.

Pilcher, J.R., Smith, A.G., Pearson, G.W. and Crowder, A. 1971. Land clearance in the Irish Neolithic: new evidence and interpretation. *Science* **172**, 560–62.

Pitkanen, A., Turunen, J. and Tolonen, K. 1999. The role of fire in the carbon dynamics of a mire, eastern Finland. *The Holocene* **9**, 453–62.

Rackham, O. 1980. *Ancient Woodland*. Cambridge: Cambridge University Press.

Rodwell, J.S. 1991. *British Plant Communities: Volume 1 – Woodlands and Scrub*. Cambridge: Cambridge University Press.

Shugart, H.H. 1998. *Terrestrial Ecosystems in Changing Environments*. Cambridge: Cambridge University Press.

Simmons, I.G. 1969. Evidence for vegetation changes associated with mesolithic man in Britain. *In* P.J. Ucko and G.W. Dimbleby (eds), *The Domestication and Exploitation of Plants and Animals*, 111–19. London: Duckworth.

Simmons, I.G. 1975. Towards an ecology of Mesolithic man in the uplands of Great Britain. *Journal of Archaeological Science* **2**, 1–15.

Simmons, I.G. 1993. Vegetation change during the Mesolithic in the British Isles: some amplifications. *In* F.M. Chambers (ed.), *Climate Change and Human Impact on the Landscape*, 109–18. London: Chapman & Hall.

Simmons, I.G. 1996. *The Environmental Impact of Later Mesolithic Cultures. The Creation of Moorland Landscape in England and Wales*. Edinburgh: Edinburgh University Press.

Simmons, I.G. and Innes, J.B. 1981. Tree remains in a North York Moors peat profile. *Nature* **294**, 76–8.

Simmons, I.G. and Innes, J.B. 1987. Mid-Holocene adaptations and later Mesolithic forest disturbance in northern England. *Journal of Archaeological Science* **14**, 385–403.

Simmons, I.G. and Innes, J.B. 1988. The later Mesolithic period (6000–5000bp) on Glaisdale Moor, North Yorkshire. *Archaeological Journal* **145**, 1–12.

Simmons, I.G. and Innes, J.B. 1996a. Disturbance phases in the mid-Holocene vegetation at North Gill, North York Moors: form and process. *Journal of Archaeological Science* **23**, 183–91.

Simmons, I.G. and Innes, J.B. 1996b. Prehistoric charcoal in peat profiles at North Gill, Yorkshire Moors, England. *Journal of Archaeological Science* **23**, 193–7.

Simmons, I.G. and Innes, J.B. 1996c. An episode of prehistoric canopy manipulation at North Gill, North Yorkshire, England. *Journal of Archaeological Science* **23**, 337–41.

Simmons, I.G., Turner, J. and Innes, J.B. 1989. An application of fine-resolution pollen analysis to later Mesolithic peats of an English upland. *In* C. Bonsall (ed.), *The Mesolithic in Europe*, 206–17. Edinburgh: John Donald.

Smith, A.G. 1970. The influence of Mesolithic and Neolithic man on British vegetation: a discussion. *In* D. Walker and R.G. West (eds), *Studies in the Vegetational History of the British Isles*, 81–96. Cambridge: Cambridge University Press.

Smith, A.G. 1981. The Neolithic. *In* I.G. Simmons and M.J. Tooley (eds), *The Environment in British Prehistory*, 125–209. London: Duckworth.

Smith, A.G. 1984. Newferry and the Boreal-Atlantic Transition. *New Phytologist* **98**, 35–55.

Smith, A.G. and Cloutman, E.W. 1988. Reconstruction of Holocene vegetation history in three dimensions at Waun-Fignen-Felen, an upland site in South Wales. *Philosophical Transactions of the Royal Society of London* **B322**, 159–219.

Smith, A.G., Whittle, A., Cloutman, E.W. and Morgan, L.A. 1989. Mesolithic and Neolithic activity and environmental impact on the south-east fen-edge in Cambridgeshire. *Proceedings of the Prehistoric Society* **55**, 207–49.

Smith, M.A. 1998. Regional vegetation history. *In* R. McCullagh and R. Tipping (eds), *Lairg: An Archaeological Landscape*, 145–77. Edinburgh: Scottish Trust for Archaeological Research.

Stager, J.C. and Mayewski, P.A. 1997. Abrupt early to mid-Holocene climatic transition registered at the equator and the poles. *Science* **276**, 1834–6.

Tallantire, P.A. 1992. The alder [*Alnus glutinosa* (L.) Gaertn.] problem in the British Isles: a third approach to its palaeo-history. *New Phytologist* **122**, 717–31.

Taylor, K.C., Lamorey, G.W., Doyle, G.A., Alley, R.B., Grootes, P.M., Mayewski, P.A., White, J.W.C. and Barlow, L.K. 1993. The 'flickering switch' of Late Pleistocene climate change. *Nature* **361**, 432–6.

Taylor, K.C., Mayewski, P.A., Twickler, M.S. and Whitlow, S.I. 1996. Biomass burning recorded in the GISP2 core: a record from eastern Canada? *The Holocene* **6**, 1–6.

Tipping, R. 1994. The form and fate of Scotland's woodlands. *Proceedings of the Society of Antiquaries of Scotland* **124**, 1–54.

Tipping, R. 1995a. Holocene evolution of a lowland Scottish landscape: Kirkpatrick Fleming. I. Peat- and pollen-stratigraphic evidence for raised moss development and climatic change. *The Holocene* **5**, 69–82.

Tipping, R. 1995b. Holocene evolution of a lowland Scottish landscape: Kirkpatrick Fleming. II. Regional vegetation and land-use change. *The Holocene* **5**, 83–96.

Tipping, R. 1996. Microscopic charcoal records, inferred human activity and climate change in the Mesolithic of northernmost Scotland. *In* T. Pollard and A. Morrison (eds), *The Early Prehistory of Scotland*, 39–61. Edinburgh: Edinburgh University Press.

Tipping, R. and Milburn, P. 2000. The mid-Holocene charcoal fall in southern Scotland: temporal and spatial variability. *Palaeogeography, Palaeoclimatology, Palaeoecology* **164**, 177–93.

Turner, J., Innes, J.B. and Simmons, I.G. 1993. Spatial diversity in the mid-Flandrian vegetation history of North Gill, North Yorkshire. *New Phytologist* **123**, 599–647.

Turner, J. Simmons, I.G. and Innes, J.B. 1989. Two pollen diagrams from the same site. *New Phytologist* **113**, 409–16.

van Geel, B., Bohncke, S.J.P. and Dee, H. 1981. A palaeoecological study of an upper Late-Glacial and Holocene sequence from 'De Borchert', The Netherlands. *Review of Palaeobotany and Palynology* **31**, 359–448.

Wickham-Jones, C.R. 1994. *Scotland's First Settlers*. London: Batsford/Historic Scotland.

Chapter 4

Palaeoenvironments of the Late Upper Palaeolithic and Mesolithic Periods in Scotland and the North Sea Area: New Work, New Thoughts

KEVIN J. EDWARDS

Aspects of the palaeoecology and related palaeoenviron-mental elements of the Mesolithic period in Scotland are placed in the context of Lateglacial antecedents, even though a local Palaeolithic occupation is unproven. Lateglacial and Early Holocene land connections between off-shore islands, Britain, and the European mainland have implications for biotic colonization.

A consideration of Holocene palynology focuses especially upon the existence of woodland in the Outer Hebrides and phenomena in Inner Hebridean pollen diagrams which may equate with the major temperature downturn of 8200 cal BP. Studies of beetle and midge remains augment pollen records and also furnish data on Mesolithic human and animal presence, climate change, and environmental disturbance.

Tephra derived from Icelandic volcanic eruptions provides four potential isochrones for the Scottish Mesolithic period and two for the Lateglacial. Putative tsunami deposits from eastern Scotland, dating to c.7000 BP, produce a time-marker horizon and seal occupation debris which could repay forensic-style examination.

While genetic (DNA) studies have yet to prove critical for Scottish investigations, an abiding strength of Mesolithic studies is that artificial divisions between people and their environment tend to be dismissed.

Introduction

An invitation to examine aspects of the palaeoecology and related palaeoenvironmental elements of the Meso-lithic period in Scotland, to introduce new work and new thoughts, and to be speculative if necessary, produces in this writer experiences of both freedom and vulnerability. The liberty to range wherever I wish over a growing body of research, albeit with topics suggested by the editor, is an undoubted privilege. Yet, adopt a narrow focus and I could be accused of shirking my task; cast my net widely and I would lay myself open to claims of superficiality. These are as nothing, perhaps, if set against any failure to introduce fresh research and new thoughts. Nevertheless, studies of the environment of Mesolithic times (and of

the Palaeolithic period, should the term have accept-ability within a Scottish context) are yielding exciting findings, which have implications for hunter-gatherer populations.

Other papers in this volume (especially those by Ballantyne and Tipping) ably address a range of palaeo-environmental issues connected with the Mesolithic period and its antecedent conditions. Two issues in particular, climate and vegetation, are discussed later in the context of recently obtained pollen-analytical evidence. The changing disposition of land and sea, however, is critical to any consideration of human communities. Consequently, the starting point for this paper is the speculative survey of 'Doggerland' by Coles (1998).

'Doggerland' and some implications

Evidence for the former existence of a so-called 'land bridge' between Britain and the continental mainland was collated comprehensively by Reid (1913) in his book *Submerged Forests*. A realization that such connec-tions existed removes the assumption that Britain was an island to which access could only be gained by boat (Wilson 1851). The alluvial flat connecting Britain, France, the Low Countries, and Denmark had the Dogger Bank at its northern end, standing some 30m above the plain, from which animal and plant remains have been dredged. The area of alluvial plain is termed 'Doggerland' by Coles, and her thesis, anticipated by Clark (1936), who had benefited from pollen studies by Godwin and Godwin (1933), is that this was an inhabited landscape, not simply a bridge, with all that this entails for settlement and the development of biota. This landscape would have persisted from Lateglacial times, through the Lateglacial–Postglacial transition, *c.*10,000 BP (11,530 cal BP; Gulliksen *et al.* 1998) to *c.*7000 BP, when inundation of the North Sea led to the severing of connections with the continental mainland.

What the mapped reconstructions reinforce (e.g. Coles 1998; Fischer 1995; Jelgersma 1979; Lambeck 1995;

Sejrup *et al.* 1987) is the extent of land cover, not just during Mesolithic but also during Palaeolithic times (Fig. 4.1). When one sees the contiguity of southern Britain and the continent, it seems inconceivable that people did not explore, if not colonize Scotland, as soon as ice-melt in lowland areas had occurred, probably by Lateglacial Interstadial times, *c.*13,000 BP, by which time ice was confined largely to the mountains of the western Highlands (Ballantyne & Dawson 1997; Sutherland 1991). If Coles's (1998, fig. 8) depiction of 'Doggerland' in Dimlington Stadial times (16,000–13,000 BP) is too generous as to the extent of ice-free terrain, as it would be according to Ballantyne and Dawson (1997, 27), and if that of the last mentioned authors is too restrictive as to when ice-free areas appeared (ibid. fig. 3.2), then it may be the case that a middle way, geographically-speaking, is an appropriate starting point. This would see at least Orkney and, with a coastline coincident with the –100m contour (Bjerck 1995), Shetland also, as part of what is now mainland Scotland (Fig. 4.2). In any case, by Lateglacial Interstadial times, we have perhaps the maximum extent of 'Doggerland' (Coles 1998, fig. 9) – the large ice-sheets were gone and sea level had yet to rise significantly – with important implications for the migration of biota, including humans.

The subsequent Loch Lomond (Younger Dryas) Stadial only saw renewed ice sheet development and small valley and corrie glaciers *c.*10,500–10,000 BP. It may be that this was inimical to permanent settlement – indeed, why bother given the available territory over which to range? – but it would not be surprising if hunting groups decided to follow reindeer, horse, or, if still surviving, mammoth, into what is now Scotland, including Orkney. Convincing evidence for such activities eludes us, but mention may be made of the possible tanged flint points from the Inner Hebrides (cf. Edwards & Mithen 1995), which while

of a type found in Lateglacial continental Europe, may be of Early Holocene (Postglacial) age, and also of the high microscopic charcoal abundances in Loch Lomond Stadial age and earlier pollen spectra from Fife, Islay, and possibly Orkney, where greater fire incidence could be a response to increased aridity or conceivably human agency (Edwards *et al.* 2000).

Such reconstructions, if correct, place Scotland and Britain firmly in the ambit of continental Europe. The Lateglacial landscapes, during the cold stadials at least, and probably during parts of the Interstadial, would not necessarily be what *we* would call hospitable. The mean temperatures during the warmest months of the Loch Lomond Stadial may have averaged around 12°C, but temperature minima may have averaged –6 to –10°C (Lowe *et al.* 1999). There would have been much poorly vegetated terrain in which birch, willow, and juniper scrub would be the closest to a woodland cover – though sedge and perhaps grass tundra dominated in northerly areas – and soils would have been ill-developed. However, mammoth, reindeer, red deer, horse, bear, migrating wildfowl, other birds, and marine resources would have been available, if not everywhere. It may even be hypothesized (though without total conviction), that if grazing is reflected in the Mesolithic age sections of pollen diagrams from the Northern and Western Isles (see below), then the herbivores may have been relicts from a time when the islands were joined to mainland Scotland.

The coastal areas would have possessed the greatest mix of resources and may, by boat, have been the easiest areas to traverse. The find of a worked flint in a marine core from the Frigg oil field, half-way between Shetland and Norway (Long *et al.* 1986), may support the notion of a northerly early human presence.

If there was a virtual absence of people during the Loch Lomond Stadial, apart possibly from the odd

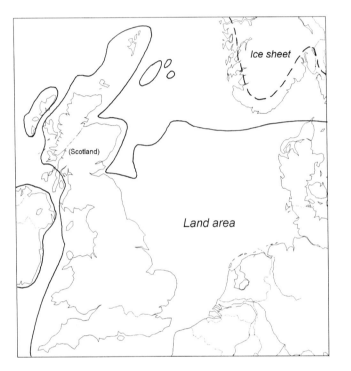

FIGURE 4.1

Predicted land/sea-level relationships for the North Sea area in Lateglacial Interstadial times, *c.*12,000 BP (after Lambeck 1995).

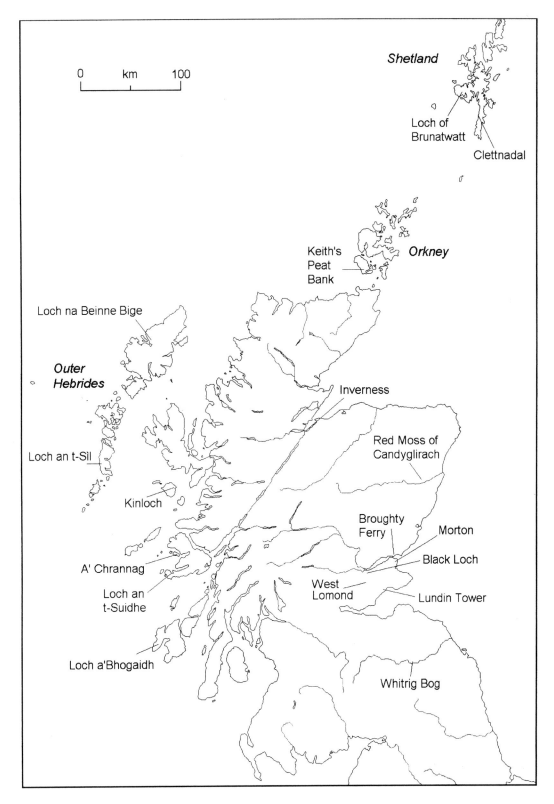

FIGURE 4.2
Location of sites mentioned in the text.

'Rambo' hunter (cf. Buckland 1984), it was more probably a reflection of the low carrying capacity of mid-latitude tundra for large vertebrate prey than the cold, to which human populations had long been adapted. It might be noted, for instance, that conditions more extreme than in Lateglacial Scotland were met by the Palaeo-Eskimo Independence I people who occupied the Greenland-Ellesmere Island High Arctic area c.4300–3800 BP (Schledermann 1996), where minimum and maximum temperatures reach around –33°C and 11°C respectively.

There may be no obvious human or technological distinction to be made between the Late Upper Palaeolithic and the Early Mesolithic periods (cf. Barton 1991). Furthermore, what comes from the preceding account is that there would be no need for a Mesolithic presence to develop suddenly at around 10,000 radiocarbon years BP in Scotland (or later if known sites are accepted as being among the earliest: e.g. Wickham-Jones (1990); Wickham-Jones & Dalland (1998); Ashmore & Saville this volume). Scotland may have already been very much part of a thriving European Upper Palaeolithic/ Mesolithic milieu by the time that rising sea-levels had inundated 'Doggerland', with a final severance of Britain from mainland Europe perhaps as early as 8000 BP or as late as sometime between 7000 and 5000 BP (Coles 1998, 66–9; Shennan et al. 2000). The relative rise in sea levels would have changed coastlines profoundly, with forced, though possibly imperceptible, alterations to the resource base. The decrease in areas of the Western and Northern Isles especially would have been fairly marked as seas developed between the island groups, their neighbours, and the mainland.

Populations

We are a long way from the estimate of Atkinson (1962, 7) that the Mesolithic population of Scotland was about 70. Cavalli-Sforza and Cavalli-Sforza (1995) suggested 5000–6000 people for Mesolithic Britain. The latest 'advance'

(Gamble 1999) suggests a figure at any one time ranging from 1560–7020 people for Scotland and 4560–20,520 for Britain (Table 4.1). Some consider these figures to be too low (Marek Zvelebil pers. comm.). Gamble (1999) emphasizes the fact that within any of these geographical areas, the distribution of population would have varied greatly, with the most productive areas being, for instance, the East Yorkshire wetlands or the Somerset Levels. In a Scottish context, the coastal zones of Aberdeenshire and the Tay, Forth, and Clyde estuaries might be nominated as candidates for higher population densities during the Mesolithic period, given the rich resource base provided by their estuarine and landward areas.

If the population density was exceedingly low then, statistically, it would probably be difficult to detect human impacts in the environmental record. Some topics associated with human-environment interactions are addressed below.

Palynology

Pollen analysis continues to provide copious data concerning the Mesolithic period. The relationships between the presence and abundance of hazel, alder, elm, and fire are still debated (Edwards 1990; 1996; Tipping 1996) and limitations of space preclude further discussion here. Similarly, advances in pollen taxonomy or macrofossil finds from cultural contexts would be necessary to advance arguments concerning the significance of pre-elm decline cereal-type pollen (Edwards & Hirons 1984; Edwards & Whittington 1997a; O'Connell 1987), although some authors (cf. Macklin et al. 2000) re-rehearse warnings.

Woodland – and a wooded Outer Hebrides?
The topic of general vegetation change, especially the colonizations, structure, and composition of primary woodlands during the Holocene, has been dealt with elsewhere (Edwards & Whittington 1997a; Tipping 1994 and this volume). The Postglacial vegetation exhibited

TABLE 4.1
Estimated hunter-gatherer population sizes for Britain (after Gamble 1999).

Density	Persons per km²	England 130,000km²	Scotland 78,000km²	Wales 20,000km²	Total population
High	0.09	11,700	7020	1800	20,520
Low	0.05	6500	3900	1000	11,400
Sparse	0.02	2600	1560	400	4560

a dynamic patterning, in which floristic mosaics varied altitudinally, latitudinally, and temporally. In spite of this variability, mapping exercises for each major tree taxon show that each has a consistent directionality of migration, although this may be an artefact of data availability.

The arrival of hazel (*Corylus avellana*), providing a ready supply of nuts as well as fast-growing wood products, must have been accepted as a wonderful resource, and the later appearance of elm and oak would have represented further opportunities for timber provision and perhaps animal browse. Although the development of deciduous hardwood forest might be thought to have been also a hindrance to easy travel and hunting, this was not necessarily so – the density of such woodland can hardly have been more impenetrable than the thicket which can characterize dense shrublands – but that may have depended on the extent to which hazel and birch had become naturally or intentionally coppiced. In any case, the patchy nature of vegetation, including nutritious herbs as well as trees, must be seen as reflecting widespread and varied potential food sources (Clarke 1976; Zvelebil 1994).

An outstanding issue remains that of a woodland presence in the Outer Hebrides and the Northern Isles. This issue has been broached in a number of publications (e.g. Bennett *et al.* 1990; 1997; Bohncke 1988; Brayshay & Edwards 1996; Edwards 1990; 1996; Tipping 1994). Wood remains in peat testify to the presence of at least pine, birch, hazel, alder, and willow in some of these localities (Fossitt 1996). The question of their density and coverage, and the non-mainland presence of such deciduous taxa as elm and oak, remain equivocal. The pollen percentages for many arboreal taxa in the islands provide strong evidence for a greatly extended woodland cover during the first half of the Holocene and this encouraged Edwards and Whittington (1997a, fig. 5.1) to be generous regarding woodland distribution.

This topic can only be touched upon here, but a potential way of approaching the issue is to look not at pollen percentages, but at absolute pollen abundance; in other words, to use pollen influx (numbers of grains accumulating in a year) as a proxy measure of vegetation density. For example, if woodland pollen influx in the islands during the Mesolithic period is similar to that found in mainland areas assumed to have been wooded, then this may provide *prima facie* evidence for the local presence of woodland in the islands. Lots of caveats need to be entered here: we do not know whether pollen productivity was lower on the islands as a result of greater exposure or salt-laden precipitation; perhaps strong westerly winds resulted in much pollen being deposited

TABLE 4.2

Mean pollen percentages (to nearest whole percent) and influx values (to nearest 10 grains cm^{-2} ^{14}C yr^{-1}) for sites in the Outer Hebrides and Fife; modern percentage pollen values are shown at the base of the table.

Site	^{14}C yr BP	Tree+shrub % (influx)	Betula % (influx)	Pinus % (influx)	Quercus % (influx)	Ulmus % (influx)	Corylus % (influx)
Loch an t-Sìl, South Uist	7650–8100	58 (3400)	21 (1320)	2 (90)	2 (100)	2 (100)	26 (1480)
Loch na Beinne Bige, Lewis	7800–8000	90 (18000)	47 (9400)	1 (200)	3 (600)	3 (600)	35 (7000)
West Lomond, Fife	6000–8300	80 (9000)	16 (1690)	3 (240)	2 (190)	3 (350)	54 (6240)
Black Loch II, Fife	5800–6500	98 (25800)	2 (460)	2 (130)	12 (3040)	12 (3050)	36 (9330)
Modern pollen % (Fossitt 1994)	–	13.8	4.6	1.0	0.8	0.2	4.4
Modern pollen % (Brayshay *et al.* 2000)	–	6.9	2.2	0.7	0.4	0.6	1.7

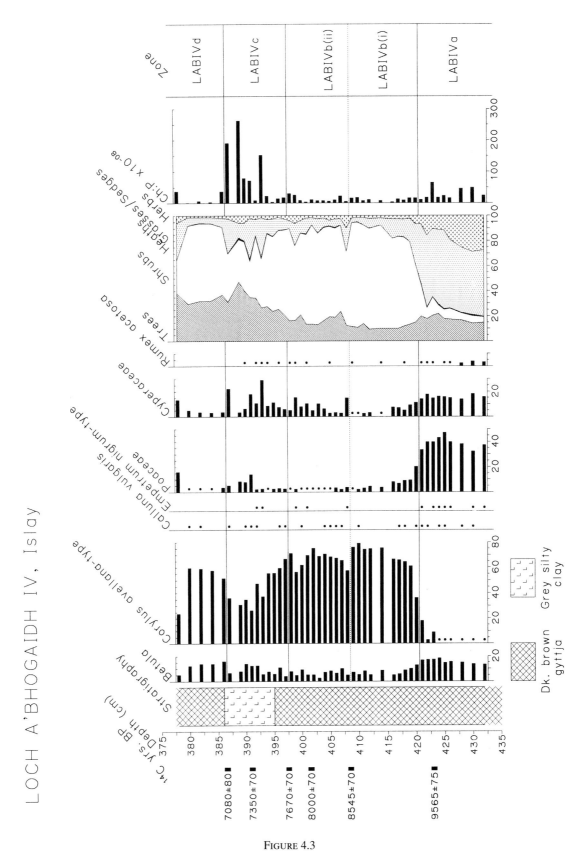

FIGURE 4.3

Selected pollen taxa and charcoal to pollen ratios from Loch a'Bhogaidh IV, Islay. Taxa are expressed as percentages of total land pollen.

off-island; mainland vegetational assemblages may not provide an acceptable analogue for island communities; we do not know what would be an acceptable mainland pollen influx figure; and, perhaps vitally important, do the taphonomic processes particular to individual lake catchments make such comparisons dubious?

In exemplification of the above, Table 4.2 compares pollen influx values for selected woodland taxa at sites in the Outer Hebrides and Fife. The time periods chosen reflect those for which consistently high influx values were found within the Mesolithic period. It is apparent that the near-coastal site of Loch an t-Sìl, South Uist (Edwards *et al.* 1995), has far lower influx values for woodland taxa (total 3400 grains cm^{-2} yr^{-1}) than the more inland site of Loch na Beinne Bige, Lewis (18,000 grains cm^{-2} yr^{-1}) (Lomax 1997). For Fife, the upland site of West Lomond, which is known to have had a local presence of *Betula* (birch) and *Corylus* (hazel) (Edwards & Whittington 1997b), seems to occupy an intermediate position (with 9000 grains cm^{-2} yr^{-1}) between the two Hebridean sites. The site of Black Loch, undoubtedly well-wooded throughout much of the Holocene (Whittington *et al.* 1991), has the highest pollen influx values (total 25,800 grains cm^{-2} yr^{-1}). Where individual taxa are concerned, the local occurrence of *Pinus* is uncertain at all sites, whereas it is assumed that *Quercus* (oak) and *Ulmus* (elm) were present at Black Loch. While this also leaves the status of oak and elm unproven for these time periods, it could be instructive to compare the data with the modern pollen percentages found in 30 surface samples for small lakes in the Western Isles (Fossitt 1994; 1996) and in 63 vegetation quadrats on a west-east transect across South Uist (Brayshay *et al.* 2000) (Table 4.2). These show that the fossil percentages for all taxa are greater than modern values, although once again, this is less impressive for pine, oak, and elm. The higher fossil values for elm and oak may derive from higher mainland abundances for these tree taxa in antiquity. From this limited exercise, it might reasonably be inferred that the Outer Hebrides sites had a strong local presence of at least birch and hazel, and that the woodland cover was probably less dense than that of lowland Fife. An imponderable for the moment is the negative effect that climatic conditions especially may have had on pollen production in the Hebrides. If this was a significant factor, the data in Table 4.2 may be leading to a down-playing of the extent of woodland in such peripheral areas.

Human or climatic impacts in the Early Holocene?
A number of Scottish pollen sites have produced evidence for Early and Mid-Holocene events that have been ascribed to possible anthropogenic impact (e.g. Bennett *et al.* 1990; Bohncke 1988; Edwards 1989;

Hirons & Edwards 1990), while others have not (Birks & Madsen 1979; Edwards 2000; Lomax 1997; Mulder 1999). The high resolution pollen diagram from Loch an t-Sìl, South Uist (Edwards 1996) reveals palynological changes which are highly suggestive of human impact and even, conjecturally, herbivore grazing, beginning at *c*.8040 BP. The difficulty is that this instance and those elsewhere (e.g. Bennett *et al.* 1992; Bohncke 1988; Edwards & Moss 1993) occur on islands for which a Mesolithic human or faunal presence is lacking. It has been suggested that artefactual evidence for such impacts would be expected beneath peat, sand, and sea (Edwards 1996). Woodman (1996, 156) has also suggested that to deny a Mesolithic presence in the Western and Northern Isles 'is to accept a proposition that some areas of Scotland were the only regions in northern Europe to remain unoccupied during the Mesolithic'. Analogues may be difficult to come by, but while we cannot physically go back in time we can move location to island sites which have produced evidence for Mesolithic people. Thus the Orkney site of Keith's Peat Bank, Hoy (Edwards 1996) is remarkably similar palynologically to those already mentioned from South Uist and Shetland, and Wickham-Jones and Firth (1990) and Saville (1996; 2000) have demonstrated the presence of Mesolithic artefacts in Mainland, Orkney.

Results arising from research in the Inner Hebrides are proving encouraging in this respect, but also open up different perspectives (Edwards & Sugden 2003; Sugden 1999). The sites of Loch a'Bhogaidh IV, Rinns of Islay (Fig. 4.3; Edwards & Berridge 1994; Sugden & Edwards 2000), Loch an t-Suidhe, Ross of Mull (Fig. 4.4), and A'Chrannag I, Ulva (Fig. 4.5) have very similar patterns of woodland reduction (birch – though not at Loch a'Bhogaidh – and hazel) with expansions in microscopic charcoal and, variously, in Poaceae (grasses), *Calluna vulgaris* (heather), and Cyperaceae (sedges). The vegetational changes occur at *c*.7670–7080, 7700–7200, and 7500–5740 BP respectively. The similarities in the start dates of these phenomena are striking and could indicate the dates at which particular bands of hunter-gatherers began sustained phases of environmental disturbance in these parts of the Inner Hebrides. (The first rise in the charcoal curve at the more northerly site of Kinloch, Rum (Hirons & Edwards 1990), does not happen until *c*.6700 BP.) An alternative explanation, or a part cause, may be sought in climatic events. When converted to calendar years (using the program *Calib 4.0*; cf. Stuiver & Reimer 1993), the beginning dates for these episodes lie at *c*.8440–8340 cal BP. These are statistically indistinguishable from the commencement of the time-band of 8400–8000 cal BP cited for the so-called '8200 cal BP event' of Alley *et al.* (1997). This was the coldest climatic

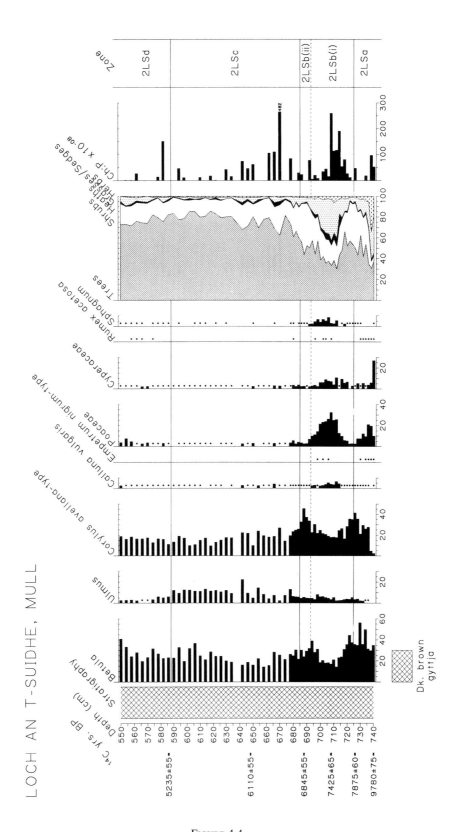

FIGURE 4.4

Selected pollen and spore taxa and charcoal to pollen ratios from Loch an t-Suidhe, Mull. Taxa are expressed as percentages of total land pollen.

62

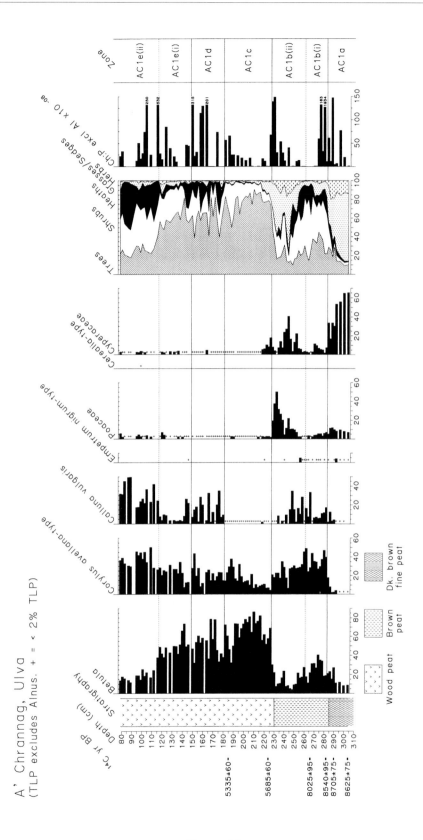

FIGURE 4.5

Selected pollen taxa and charcoal to pollen ratios from A' Chrannag I, Ulva. Taxa are expressed as percentages of total land pollen excluding Alnus glutinosa.

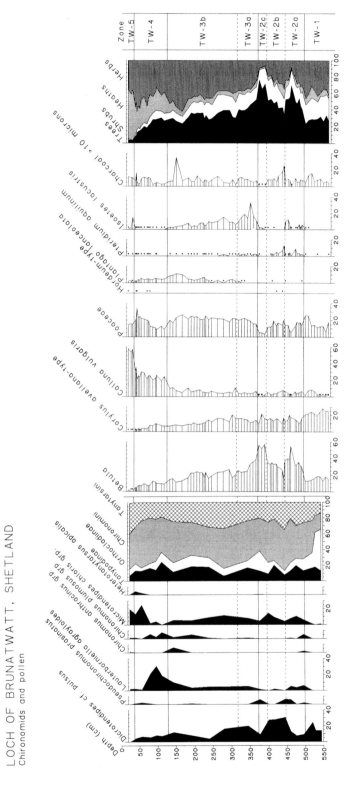

FIGURE 4.6

Selected chironomid, pollen, and spore taxa and charcoal data from Loch of Brunatwatt, Mainland, Shetland. Chironomids are expressed as percentages of total head capsules; pollen and spores are expressed as percentages of total land pollen.

event since the Younger Dryas, characterized by cold, dry conditions, and probably resulting from complex changes to thermohaline conditions consequent upon the draining of glacial lakes associated with the Laurentide ice sheet (Barber *et al.* 1999).

Are the effects of such a dramatic cold event responsible for the changes in these pollen diagrams? They could be, especially as the phenomena at Loch a'Bhogaidh and Loch an t-Suidhe come to an end *c.*7080 and 7200 BP, which is very close to the ice core end-date of *c.*7200 BP (8000 cal BP). At A'Chrannag, however, the palynological phenomena persist until *c.*5740 BP. It should be noted, however, that typically 'cold' environment indicators such as *Empetrum nigrum*-type (crowberry) and *Rumex acetosa* (common sorrel) are not especially abundant at these levels, though Cyperaceae, which often seem to respond positively to lowered temperatures, do expand. It might be reasonable to suppose at A'Chrannag that vegetational changes caused initially by a climatic revertence were sustained by human activities. There is no reason to believe that humans ceased to stay in such areas when this posited and prolonged cold phase was underway. The charcoal records during these phases are of considerable interest. People may have burnt fires to keep warm or to maintain heathland to attract browsing game. There may have been a greater aridity and incidence of lightning strikes, which finds an echo in those instances of Loch Lomond Stadial age fire already mentioned (cf. Edwards *et al.* 2000). It should be noted, however, that neither these sites, nor those from the Outer Hebrides, have the kind of *sustained* charcoal records which would fit the proposed 8000–5000 BP fire event of Tipping (1996), though they would be accommodated within it.

Earlier, more minor climatic reventences have been detected in high resolution pollen diagrams from Scotland. Two of these are from Fife: West Lomond (Edwards & Whittington 1997b) and Lundin Tower (Whittington *et al.* 1996). The latter produced stable isotope and pollen evidence for climatic oscillations, while the former has produced good pollen-statistical support for climatic oscillations (including Preboreal oscillations), which date to *c.*9745 and 9190 BP respectively. This raises the possibility that other well-known phenomena, such as interruptions to the rise of the hazel curve, *c.*9500–9000 BP, seen in a number of pollen diagrams (Edwards 1989; Edwards & Mithen 1995; Smith 1970), might also be at least partially a response to climatic perturbations.

Beetles

Sub-fossil remains of beetles (Coleoptera) are less common than those of pollen, although their ability to allow reconstructions of ecology and climate need little comment (Ashworth *et al.* 1997). Studies at Clettnadal, Shetland, reveal beetles of the genus *Aphodius* which are normally, though not exclusively, found in herbivore dung (Whittington *et al.* 2003). The site does not have the intriguing supporting palynological evidence found elsewhere in Shetland (cf. Bennett *et al.* 1992) for the possible presence of large grazing animals during the Mesolithic period. The island location, with evidence for sea level close to that of the present day, calls for more circumspection. It is possible that deep litter, accumulated in nutrient-rich grassland close to seabird or seal colonies, could have provided a suitable food or faeces surrogate (cf. Buckland *et al.* 1998), but modern comparative data are lacking. Another problem is that radiocarbon and pollen evidence are strongly indicative of inconsistent sediment accumulation; while an extrapolated date of *c.*6000 BP or even older may apply to the basal section containing dung beetles, it could be younger.

Unpublished beetle and pollen analyses from the Red Moss of Candyglirach, a lowland raised bog in Aberdeenshire, reveal pre-elm decline pollen assemblages with intermittent finds of *Scolytus scolytus*, the elm bark beetle (Clark 2002). This taxon feeds predominantly on elm and carries the fungus *Ceratocystis ulmi*, which is responsible for Dutch elm disease. The beetle is particularly attracted to trees under stress from climate or from management practices such as pollarding, coppicing, or shredding (Rackham 1986). It is possible that Mesolithic age woodland communities around Red Moss were disturbed by hunter-gatherers. Indeed, the peat has visible layers of charcoal in the stratigraphy, though this could reflect lightning strikes. More research at Red Moss is under way. One thing which will be of interest is the extent to which pyrophilic elements are evident in the insect faunas and can be shown to be a reflection of the role of fire in natural successions as opposed to anthropogenic activity.

Chironomids

The head capsules of the aquatic larvae of the Chironomidae (non-biting midges) are preserved in lake deposits and are increasingly being analysed as indicators of environmental change (Walker 1995). Chironomids are dispersed as part of the 'aerial plankton' and therefore react quickly to changes in habitat. The response of chironomids to such factors as climate change, peat growth, woodland growth, and clearance (cf. Sadler & Jones 1997) represent a potentially exciting area of palaeoecological research. At Whitrig Bog in the Borders (Brooks *et al.* 1997), chironomids purportedly show a

10°C crash in summer temperatures over a few decades at the start of the Loch Lomond Stadial. Unpublished research from Lewis and Shetland (Jon Sadler pers. comm.) demonstrates rapid Holocene warming in line with data from ice cores and beetles.

At Loch of Brunatwatt, Shetland (Fig. 4.6), the pollen data are strongly suggestive of changes to the vegetation in Mesolithic times, which could denote human interference and possible herbivore grazing: *Betula,* pteridophytes, and *Isoetes lacustris* decline; Poaceae, *Calluna,* and charcoal rise (cf. Bennett *et al.* 1992; Edwards 1996). The chironomids at this point revert back to a slightly mesotrophic fauna (e.g. *Dicrotendepes, Pseudochironomus prasinatus*) because inwashed material is resulting in slightly increased lake productivity. Strangely, deforestation in the Mid Holocene does not seem to be reflected other than in a general increase in the Tanytarsini, but acidification and blanket peat spread, shown by the rise of the *Calluna* curve, are matched by rises in the curves for *Lauterboriella agrayloides* and species of *Chironomus*. The crash in these Dipterous taxa, to be replaced by other forms common in humic waters (e.g. *Microtendipes chloris* grp and *Heterotanytarsus apicalis*), corresponds with inwashed eroded blanket peat, evident as a distinctive light brown deposit with an increased organic content.

Relative to a more established approach like palynology, chironomid-based palaeoecological research is at an early stage in its development. As improvements in taxonomy and sampling resolution occur, then contributions to the ecology of the Mesolithic period should be forthcoming.

Dating: tephra

The provision of a reliable chronology is a desirable, if not always essential part of Mesolithic studies. Artefacts may be an indication that a probable Mesolithic context is under investigation and radiocarbon dates may pinpoint events to the nearest century or two. Although rather specific with regard to its application, tephra, the vitreous, fine-grained ash ejected from volcanic eruptions, enables peat and lake sediment deposits to be dated, theoretically, with an accuracy of days, if not hours. The erupting volcano injects vast amounts of ash into the atmosphere and winds carry this over long distances, leading to ash deposition as a dusting on accumulating peat surfaces or in lake catchments (Edwards *et al.* 1994; Thorarinsson 1981). In many cases, the tephra layers are identifiable by physical and chemical means to specific dated eruptions and the material underlying the tephra is assumed to immediately pre-date the tephra. Pollen or any other palaeoenvironmental analyses of deposits adjacent to the tephra layer will be penecontemporaneous. Thus the tephra provides an isochrone, enabling temporally-controlled environmental reconstructions from different locations, whether over small or large distances (Edwards & Craigie 1998; Hall *et al.* 1994).

Since the first discovery of Hekla-4 ash in Scotland (Dugmore 1989), at least twelve Icelandic tephras are known to have formed identifiable micro-tephra marker horizons in Scotland in the last 12,000 years (cf. Dugmore *et al.* 1995; Lowe *et al.* 1999; Turney *et al.* 1997), of which four tephras fall within the Mesolithic period (Table 4.3). Clearly there is a potential for Mesolithic

TABLE 4.3
Lateglacial–Mid Holocene tephrochronology in Scotland.

Tephra	*~Date* *(^{14}C yr BP)*	
Hekla-4 tephra	3830	
		Neolithic
....		
		Mesolithic
Hoy tephra	5600	
Lairg A+B tephras	6000	
Saksunarvatn Ash	9000	
		Holocene
Vedde Ash	10,350	Loch Lomond Stadial
Borrobol Tephra	12,260	Lateglacial Interstadial

tephrochronology, but at present these particular tephras are known at only a limited number of sites in Shetland, Orkney, and Sutherland. This is primarily a reflection of the sites that have been studied to date.

Where tephra layers are not reflecting historically documented and dated eruptions, their temporal assignation is based on radiocarbon-dating. This is not as imprecise as it may seem because multiple-date (Dugmore *et al.* 1995) or 'wiggle-matching' (Pilcher *et al.* 1995) methodologies can be employed to delimit the date of tephra deposition to within a quarter-century. In any case, given appropriate stratigraphic integrity, the tephra horizon is capable of providing a precise date, correlatable over large distances, even if the numerical value of the marker horizon is uncertain.

The delimitation of tephra layers is a powerful chronological control on any accumulating deposit. Tephrochronology employed over a small area would enable tephropalynological investigations (Edwards 1996; Edwards *et al.* in press), for example, whereby 'three-dimensional' or spatial reconstructions of pollen-based vegetational or landuse variations are possible for specific time periods.

In addition to the atmospheric fallout of microtephra, during the Mesolithic period, cobble-grade, ocean-transported pumices were deposited on Scottish beaches. Recent work by Anthony Newton and Andy Dugmore (University of Edinburgh) and Guðrún Larsen (University of Iceland), has linked these pumices to a source in the silicic magma chamber of Katla, Iceland. Pumice deposits may be used to identify discrete palaeo-strandlines. When found in archaeological contexts, pumice frequently shows sign of working (e.g. Branigan *et al.* 1995).

Dating and environmental impacts: tsunamis

Along the east coast of Scotland, a layer of sand has been found in peat deposits dating to *c.*7000 BP (5840 cal BC) at a number of locations (Fig. 4.7). It has been argued by coastal geomorphologists (Dawson *et al.* 1990) that this sand was deposited by a tsunami (sea wave), which caused massive flooding during the Mesolithic period. Essentially, a submarine landslide (the Second Storegga Slide), covering an area the size of Scotland, occurred off the continental slope west of Norway at a depth of about 500m. Mesolithic people may have heard distant rumblings, or even experienced earthquakes. Water from the northern North Sea would have rushed into the space vacated by slope-failed material. People on land would have noticed that the sea receded, probably as far as the eye could see, in a matter of tens of minutes. They may have thought that the newly revealed shellfish and stranded

fish represented an amazing bonanza, that boats were now surplus to requirements, or that 'Doggerland' had re-appeared! The seawater, having piled up in the depression located in the area of slope failure, then begins to flow out again as a series of massive waves or tsunamis, travelling at 20–30m per second on shallow coasts. Four or five waves would have hit the coast over two or three hours, each separated by a strong backlash as water flowed back to sea. Any coastal settlements would have been flooded without warning, indeed the water depth would have been many metres, and people and animals would have been drowned. If the water was turbulent, with a bore of water breaking as it moved inland, then vegetation would have been stripped away and, if an appropriate sediment supply was available, a layer of sand would have been deposited. Coastal and estuarine areas, resources, and people would have been devastated.

Dawson *et al.* (1990) suggested that at least three Mesolithic sites (Inverness, Broughty Ferry, and Morton) may have produced geoarchaeological evidence for a tsunami at *c.*7000 BP. They observed that the sand layer, reaching a thickness of 0.7m in the Beauly Firth carselands, is a potentially valuable chronostratigraphic marker which would have sealed coastal sites at a single moment. In this respect, the tsunami layer would act with the precision of a tephra layer and, assuming that the sand layers derive from tsunamis and not from time-transgressive storm events, this may be its chief significance from a palaeoenvironmental perspective. Archaeologically, whatever the origins of the sand, the fortuitous burials of Mesolithic sites might be anticipated. It is instructive to cite the instance of Broughty Ferry (Hutcheson 1886), a site 'washed by an exceptional tide which disturbed the refuse of occupation and covered it with sand' (Lacaille 1954, 178). Careful, forensic-style excavation might reveal a great deal about the economies of such rapidly sealed sites.

Some final observations

We do not know if people were around in what is now the Scottish land area in the Lateglacial and the Earliest Holocene. The same uncertainty applies to any Mesolithic arrival of people in Shetland and the Outer Hebrides. As far as the Later Holocene is concerned, the human presence in mainland Scotland, the Inner Hebrides, and Orkney is proven. Whether the field of molecular genetics with its ability to trace relationships via DNA will assist in answering some of the problems is, for the moment, a moot point (Evison 1999). On the European scale, Ammerman and Cavalli-Sforza (1984) claimed that a substantial gene flow gradient from SE to

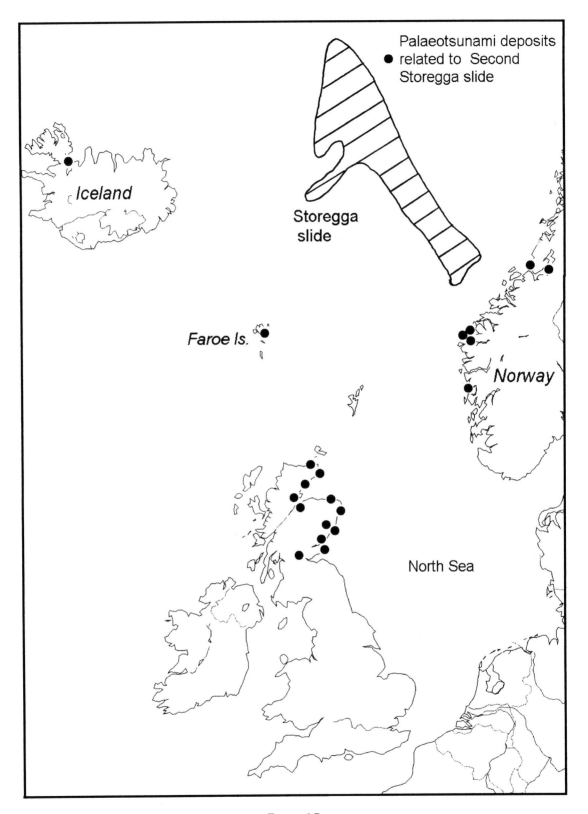

FIGURE 4.7

Tsunami deposits in the North Sea and North Atlantic areas associated with the Second Storegga Slide (after Dawson 1999).

NW Europe was probably associated with the transition to agriculture. Richards *et al.* (1996) and Sykes (2001) maintain that a large majority of maternal lineages date back well before the arrival of agriculture and are signatures of the indigenous Palaeolithic population rather than of an advancing wave of Neolithic farmers. If we had some Mesolithic, or even Palaeolithic, skeletons from Scotland, then it might be possible to plug more directly into this exciting new world. If humans are not seen as part of the biota, then genetic studies of plant DNA are showing striking agreements between the location of refugia, rates of spread, and pollen data at the European scale (Hewitt 1999). It would be exciting to see how this would work at the regional scale. Could it provide answers to such question as the origins of birch, hazel, and Scots pine in the Western and Northern Isles?

There is an understandable emphasis by environmentalists on sites bearing potential human impacts. The distribution of sites which appear to show no convincing signs of activity also tells its own story (Edwards 2000). They may be mapping areas seldom visited or which functioned as throughways for mobile populations. In island situations they may tell us that the whole island environment was not used or manipulated, or perhaps that human and/or animal populations were small. Sea-level change may have greatly reduced the land area of islands which currently have shallowly sloping, low-lying littoral zones, such as the western coastal areas of the Outer Hebrides, and it would be necessary to be aware of this before making pronouncements about resource availability and population sizes. It must be stressed that sites can only be declared mute in terms of the available data. Higher sampling resolution or higher counts of microfossils may change a site with little apparent variability into a highly sensitive indicator of hunter-gatherer activity, while multiple sites in a small area can harness the spatial dimension to reveal differential zones of activity.

An abiding strength of Mesolithic studies is that artificial divisions between people, as social organisms, and their environment, tend to be avoided (cf. Clark 1954; Mellars & Dark 1998; Mithen 2000). Indeed, so close are the relationships, that Mithen (1999, 477) regards archaeologists and environmentalists researching the Mesolithic period as being 'engaged in the study of human palaeoecology ... [a] ... rather healthy state of affairs'. Saville (1998) sees dangers in such an emphasis in that the lithic artefact record may be undervalued. If information on landscapes, plants, and animals were to be stripped from the sum total of knowledge of the Mesolithic period, however, especially for Scotland, then we might be struggling to say much beyond describing lithic typologies and distributions or analysing the dates of bone and antler artefacts, interesting though these may be. The point that barely needs making is that the fullest appreciation of the Mesolithic (and the Palaeolithic if pertinent) requires *all* factors to be researched, whether environmental, material, or social. The environmental dimension is in a good state of health and, even if more easily accomplished, though probably more time-consuming, than other aspects, must surely continue to play a key and deserved role in Mesolithic studies.

Acknowledgements

I am grateful to Heather Sugden and Sarah Clark for permission to quote from their doctoral research. Radio-carbon dating at Loch a'Bhogaidh, Loch an t-Suidhe, and Clettnadal was carried out at the NERC Radiocarbon Laboratory, East Kilbride, and the University of Arizona, with funding by NERC and guidance from Charlotte Bryant and Douglas Harkness. Valuable discussion and advice has come from Paul Buckland (Coleoptera), Alastair Dawson (sea levels), Andrew Dugmore (tephra), and Jon Sadler (chironomids). Alan Saville provided the opportunity to think about the wider issues. Paul Buckland is thanked for constructive and tempering discussions on a draft of the paper.

References

Alley, R.B., Mayewski, P.A., Sowers, T., Stuiver, M., Taylor, K.C. and Clark, P.U. 1997. Holocene climatic instability: a prominent, widespread event 8200 years ago. *Geology* **25**, 483–6.

Ammerman, A.J. and Cavalli-Sforza, L.L. 1984. *The Neolithic Transition and the Genetics of Population in Europe.* Princeton: Princeton University Press.

Ashworth, A.C., Buckland, P.C. and Sadler, J.P. (eds). 1997. *Studies in Quaternary Entomology – an Inordinate Fondness for Insects.* Chichester: Wiley (= *Quaternary Proceedings* 5).

Atkinson, R.J.C. 1962. Fishermen and farmers. *In* S. Piggott (ed.), *The Prehistoric Peoples of Scotland,* 1–38. London: Routledge & Kegan Paul.

Ballantyne, C.K. and Dawson, A.G. 1997. Geomorphology and landscape change. *In* K.J. Edwards and I.B.M. Ralston (eds), *Scotland: Environment and Archaeology, 8000 BC–AD 1000,* 23–44. Chichester: Wiley.

Barber, D.C., Dyke, A., Hillaire-Marcel, C., Jennings, A.E., Andrews, J.T., Kerwin, M.W., Bilodeau, G., McNeely, R., Southon, J., Morehead, M.D. and Gagnon, J.-M. 1999. Forcing of the cold event of 8,200 years ago by catastrophic drainage of Laurentide lakes. *Nature* **400**, 344–8.

Barton, N. 1991. Technological innovation and continuity at the end of the Pleistocene in Britain. *In* N. Barton, A.J. Roberts and D.A. Roe (eds), *The Late Glacial in*

North-West Europe, 234–45. London: Council for British Archaeology (Research Report **77**).

Bennett, K.D., Fossitt, J.A., Sharp, M.J. and Switsur, V.R. 1990. Holocene vegetational and environmental history at Loch Lang, South Uist, Scotland. *New Phytologist* **114**, 281–98.

Bennett, K.D., Boreham, S., Sharp, M.J. and Switsur, V.R. 1992. Holocene history of environment, vegetation and human settlement on Catta Ness, Lunnasting, Shetland. *Journal of Ecology* **80**, 241–73.

Bennett, K.D., Bunting, M.J. and Fossitt, J.A. 1997. Long-term vegetation change in the Western and Northern Isles, Scotland. *Botanical Journal of Scotland* **49**, 127–40.

Birks, H.J.B. and Madsen, B.J. 1979. Flandrian vegetational history of Little Loch Roag, Isle of Lewis, Scotland. *Journal of Ecology* **67**, 825–42.

Bjerck, H.B. 1995. The North Sea continent and the pioneer settlement of Norway. *In* A. Fischer (ed.), *Man and Sea in the Mesolithic,* 131–44. Oxford: Oxbow Books (Oxbow Monograph **53**).

Bohncke, S.J.P. 1988. Vegetation and habitation history of the Callanish area. *In* H.H. Birks, H.J.B. Birks, P.E. Kaland and D. Moe (eds), *The Cultural Landscape – Past, Present and Future,* 445–61. Cambridge: Cambridge University Press.

Branigan, K., Newton, A.J. and Dugmore, A.J. 1995. Pumice. *In* K. Branigan and P. Foster, *Barra: Archaeological Research on Ben Tangaval,* 144–8. Sheffield: Sheffield Academic Press.

Brayshay, B.A. and Edwards, K.J. 1996. Lateglacial and Holocene vegetational history of South Uist and Barra. *In* D.D. Gilbertson, M. Kent and J.P. Grattan (eds), *The Outer Hebrides: the Last 14,000 Years,* 13–26. Sheffield: Sheffield Academic Press.

Brayshay, B.A., Gilbertson, D.D., Kent, M., Edwards, K.J., Wathern, P. and Weaver, R.E. 2000. Surface pollen-vegetation relationships on the Atlantic seabord: South Uist, Scotland. *Journal of Biogeography* **27**, 359–78.

Brooks, S.J., Mayle, F.E. and Lowe, J.J. 1997. Chironomid-based Lateglacial reconstruction for southeast Scotland. *Journal of Quaternary Science* **12**, 161–7.

Buckland, P. C. 1984. North-west Lincolnshire 10,000 years ago. *In* F.N. Field and A.G. White (eds), *A Prospect of Lincolnshire,* 11–17. Lincoln: published privately by the editors.

Buckland, P.C., Edwards, K.J., Sadler, J.P. and Dinnin, M.H. 1998. Late Holocene insect faunas from Mykines, Faroe Islands, with observations on associated pollen and early settlement records. *Fróðskaparrit* **46**, 287–96.

Cavalli-Sforza, L.L. and Cavalli-Sforza, F. 1995. *The Great Human Diasporas: the History of Diversity and Evolution.* New York: Addison-Wesley.

Clark, J.G.D. 1936. *The Mesolithic Settlement of Northern Europe.* Cambridge: Cambridge University Press.

Clark, J.G.D. 1954. *Excavations at Star Carr.* Cambridge: Cambridge University Press.

Clark, S.H.E. 2002. *Holocene Environmental Change in Northeast Scotland: a Palaeoentomological Approach.* Unpublished PhD thesis, University of Sheffield.

Clarke, D.L. 1976. Mesolithic Europe: the economic basis. *In* G. de G. Sieveking, I.H. Longworth and K.E. Wilson (eds), *Problems in Economic and Social Archaeology,* 449–82. London: Duckworth.

Coles, B.J. 1998. Doggerland: a speculative survey. *Proceedings of the Prehistoric Society* **64**, 45–81.

Dawson, A. 1999. North Sea tsunami. The Storegga slides and the big wave. *Geography Review* **12**(3), 30–3.

Dawson, A.G., Smith, A.G. and Long, D. 1990. Evidence for a tsunami from a Mesolithic site in Inverness, Scotland. *Journal of Archaeological Science* **17**, 509–12.

Dugmore, A. 1989. Icelandic volcanic ash in Scotland. *Scottish Geographical Magazine* **105**, 168–72.

Dugmore, A.J., Larsen, G. and Newton, A.J. 1995. Seven tephra isochrones in Scotland. *The Holocene* **5**, 257–66.

Edwards, K.J. 1989. Meso-Neolithic vegetational impacts in Scotland and beyond: palynological considerations. *In* C. Bonsall (ed.), *The Mesolithic in Europe,* 143–55. Edinburgh: John Donald.

Edwards, K.J. 1990. Fire and the Scottish Mesolithic: evidence from microscopic charcoal. *In* P.M. Vermeersch and P. Van Peer (eds), *Contributions to the Mesolithic in Europe,* 71–9. Leuven: Leuven University Press.

Edwards, K.J. 1996. A Mesolithic of the Western and Northern Isles of Scotland? Evidence from pollen and charcoal. *In* T. Pollard and A. Morrison (eds), *The Early Prehistory of Scotland,* 23–38. Edinburgh: Edinburgh University Press.

Edwards, K.J. 2000. Pollen, archaeology, and burdens of proof. *In* R. Young (ed.), *Mesolithic Lifeways: Current Research from Britain and Ireland,* 67–74. Leicester: School of Archaeological Studies, University of Leicester (Leicester Archaeology Monograph **7**).

Edwards, K.J. and Berridge, J.M.A. 1994. The Late-Quaternary vegetational history of Loch a'Bhogaidh, Rinns of Islay S.S.S.I., Scotland. *New Phytologist* **128**, 749–69.

Edwards, K.J. and Craigie, R. 1998. Palynological and vegetational changes associated with the deposition of Saksunarvatn ash in the Faroe Islands. *Fróðskaparrit* **46**, 245–58.

Edwards, K.J. and Hirons, K.R. 1984. Cereal pollen grains in pre-elm decline deposits: implications for the earliest agriculture in Britain and Ireland. *Journal of Archaeological Science* **11**, 71–80.

Edwards, K.J. and Mithen, S. 1995. The colonization of the Hebridean islands of western Scotland: evidence from the palynological and archaeological records. *World Archaeology* **26**, 348–65.

Edwards, K.J. and Moss, A.G. 1993. Pollen data from the Loch of Brunatwatt, west Mainland. *In* J.F. Birnie, J.E. Gordon, K.D. Bennett and A.M. Hall, *The Quaternary of Shetland: Field Guide,* 126–9. Cambridge: Quaternary Research Association.

Edwards, K.J. and Sugden, H. 2003. Palynological visibility and the Mesolithic colonization of the Hebrides, Scotland. *In* L. Larsson, H. Kindgren, K. Knutsson, D. Loeffler and A. Åkerlund (eds), *Mesolithic on the Move: Papers Presented at the Sixth International Conference on the Mesolithic in Europe, Stockholm 2000,* 11–19. Oxford: Oxbow Books.

Edwards, K.J. and Whittington, G. 1997a. Vegetation history. *In* K.J. Edwards and I.B.M. Ralston (eds), *Scotland: Environment and Archaeology, 8000 BC–AD 1000*, 63–82. Chichester: Wiley.

Edwards, K.J. and Whittington, G. 1997b. A 12000-year record of environmental change in the Lomond Hills, Fife, Scotland: vegetational and climatic variability. *Vegetation History and Archaeobotany* **6**, 133–52.

Edwards, K.J., Buckland, P.C., Blackford, J.J., Dugmore, A.J. and Sadler, J.P. 1994. The impact of tephra: proximal and distal studies of Icelandic eruptions. *Münchener Geographische Abhandlungen* **B12**, 79–99.

Edwards, K.J., Whittington, G. and Hirons, K.R. 1995. The relationship between fire and long-term wet heath development in South Uist, Outer Hebrides, Scotland. *In* D.B.A. Thompson, A.J. Hestor and M.B. Usher (eds), *Heaths and Moorland: Cultural Landscapes*, 240–48. Edinburgh: H.M.S.O.

Edwards, K.J., Whittington, G. and Tipping, R. 2000. The incidence of microscopic charcoal in Lateglacial deposits. *Palaeogeography, Palaeoclimatology, Palaeoecology* **164**, 263–78.

Edwards, K.J., Dugmore, A.J. and Blackford, J.J. In press. Vegetational response to tephra deposition and land use change in Iceland – a modern analogue and multiple working hypothesis approach to tephropalynology. *Polar Record.*

Evison, M.P. 1999. Perspectives on the Holocene in Britain: human DNA. *In* K.J. Edwards and J.P. Sadler (eds), *Holocene Environments of Prehistoric Britain*, 615–23. Chichester: Wiley (= *Quaternary Proceedings* **7**).

Fischer, A. (ed.). 1995. *Man and Sea in the Mesolithic.* Oxford: Oxbow Books (Oxbow Monograph **53**).

Fossitt, J. 1994. Modern pollen rain in the northwest of the British Isles. *The Holocene* **4**, 365–76.

Fossitt, J.A. 1996. Late Quaternary vegetation history of the Western Isles of Scotland. *New Phytologist* **132**, 171–96.

Gamble, C. (ed.). 1999. *Research Frameworks for the Palaeolithic and Mesolithic of Britain and Ireland.* London: Working Party for the Palaeolithic and Mesolithic Day Meeting and the Council of the Prehistoric Society.

Godwin, H. and Godwin, M.E. 1933. British Maglemose harpoon sites. *Antiquity* **7**, 36–48.

Gulliksen, S., Birks, H.H., Possnert, G. and Mangerud, J. 1998. A calendar age estimate of the Younger Dryas-Holocene boundary at Kråkenes, western Norway. *The Holocene* **8**, 249–59.

Hall, V.A., McVicar, S.J. and Pilcher, J.R. 1994. Tephra-linked landscape history around 2310 BC of some sites in Counties Antrim and Down. *Biology and Environment: Proceedings of the Royal Irish Academy* **94B**, 245–53.

Hewitt, G.M. 1999. Post-glacial re-colonization of European biota. *Biological Journal of the Linnean Society* **68**, 87–112.

Hirons, K.R. and Edwards, K.J. 1990. Pollen and related studies at Kinloch, Isle of Rhum, Scotland, with particular reference to possible early human impacts on vegetation. *New Phytologist* **116**, 715–27.

Hutcheson, A. 1886. Notice of the discovery of a stratum containing worked flints at Broughty-Ferry. *Proceedings of the Society of Antiquaries of Scotland* **20** (1885–86), 166–9.

Jelgersma, S. 1979. Sea-level changes in the North Sea basin. *In* E. Oele, R.T.E. Schüttenhelm and A.J. Wiggers (eds), *The Quaternary History of the North Sea*, 233–48. Uppsala; Acta Universitatis Upsaliensis, Symposium Universitatis Upsaliensis Annum Quingentesimum Celebrantis **2**.

Lacaille, A.D. 1954. *The Stone Age in Scotland.* London: Oxford University Press.

Lambeck, K. 1995. Late Devensian and Holocene shorelines of the British Isles and North Sea from models of glacio-hydro-isostatic rebound. *Journal of the Geological Society* **152**, 437–48.

Lomax, T.M. 1997. *Holocene Vegetation History and Human Impact in Western Lewis, Scotland.* Unpublished PhD thesis, University of Birmingham.

Long, D., Wickham-Jones, C.R. and Ruckley, N.A. 1986. A flint artifact from the northern North Sea. *In* D. Roe (ed.), *Studies in the Upper Palaeolithic of Britain and Northwest Europe*, 55–62. Oxford: British Archaeological Reports (British Series **296**).

Lowe, J.J., Birks, H.H., Brooks, S.J., Coope, G.R., Harkness, D.D., Mayle, F.E., Sheldrick, C., Turney, C.S.M. and Walker, M.J.C. 1999. The chronology of palaeoenvironmental changes during the Last Glacial–Holocene transition: towards an event stratigraphy for the British Isles. *Journal of the Geological Society of London* **156**, 397–410.

Macklin, M.G., Bonsall, C., Davies, F.M. and Robinson, M.R. 2000. Human-environment interactions during the Holocene: new data and interpretations from the Oban area, Argyll, Scotland. *The Holocene* **10**, 109–121.

Mellars, P. and Dark, P. 1998. *Star Carr in Context.* Cambridge: McDonald Institute Monograph.

Mithen, S.J. 1999. Mesolithic archaeology, environmental archaeology and human palaeoecology. *In* K.J. Edwards and J.P. Sadler (eds), *Holocene Environments of Prehistoric Britain*, 477–83. Chichester: Wiley (= *Quaternary Proceedings* **7**).

Mithen, S.J. (ed.). 2000. *Hunter-Gatherer Landscape Archaeology: the Southern Hebrides Mesolithic Project, 1988–1998.* Vols. *1–2.* Cambridge: McDonald Institute Monograph.

Mulder, Y. 1999. *Aspects of Vegetation and Settlement History in the Outer Hebrides, Scotland.* Unpublished PhD thesis, University of Sheffield.

O'Connell, M. 1987. Early cereal-type pollen records from Connemara, western Ireland and their possible significance. *Pollen et Spores* **29**, 207–24.

Pilcher, J.R., Hall, V.A. and McCormac, F.G. 1995. Dates of Holocene Icelandic eruptions from tephra layers in Irish peats. *The Holocene* **5**, 103–10.

Rackham, O. 1986. *The History of the Countryside.* London: Dent.

Reid, C. 1913. *Submerged Forests.* Cambridge: Cambridge University Press.

Richards, M.R., Corte-Real, H., Forster, P., Macaula, V., Wilkinson-Herbots, H. Demaine, A., Papiha, S., Hedges, R., Bandelt, H.-J. and Sykes, B. 1996. Paleolithic and Neolithic lineages in the European mitochondrial gene pool. *American Journal of Human Genetics* **59**, 185–203.

Sadler, J.P. and Jones, J.C. 1997. Chironomids as indicators of Holocene environmental change in the British Isles. *Quaternary Proceedings* **5**, 219–32.

Saville, A. 1996. Lacaille, microliths and the Mesolithic of Orkney. *In* T. Pollard and A. Morrison (eds), *The Early Prehistory of Scotland,* 213–24. Edinburgh: Edinburgh University Press.

Saville, A. 1998. Studying the Mesolithic period in Scotland: a bibliographic gazetteer. *In* N. Ashton, F. Healy and P. Pettitt (eds), *Stone Age Archaeology: Essays in Honour of John Wymer,* 211–24. Oxford: Oxbow Books (Oxbow Monograph **102** / Lithic Studies Society Occasional Paper **6**).

Saville, A. 2000. Orkney and Scotland before the Neolithic period. *In* A. Ritchie (ed.), *Neolithic Orkney in its European Context,* 91–100. Cambridge: McDonald Institute Monograph.

Schledermann, P. 1996. *Voices in Stone: a Personal Journey into the Arctic Past.* Calgary: Komatik Series **5**, Arctic Institute of North America, University of Calgary.

Sejrup, H.P., Aarseth, I., Ellingsen, K.L., Reither, E., Jansen, E., Løvlie, R., Bent, A., Brigham-Grette, J., Larsen, E. and Stoker, M. 1987. Quaternary stratigraphy of the fladen area, central North Sea: a multidisciplinary study. *Journal of Quaternary Science* **2**, 35–58.

Shennan, I., Lambeck, K., Flather, R., Horton, B., McArthur, J., Innes, J., Lloyd, J., Rutherford, M. and Wingfield, R. 2000. Modelling western North Sea palaeogeographies and tidal changes during the Holocene. *In* I. Shennan and J. Andrews (eds), *Holocene Land-Ocean Interaction and Environmental Change around the North Sea,* 299–319. London: Geological Society of London (Special Publication **166**).

Smith, A.G. 1970. The influence of Mesolithic and Neolithic man on British vegetation. *In* D. Walker and R.G. West (eds), *Studies in the Vegetational History of the British Isles,* 81–96. London: Cambridge University Press.

Stuiver, M. and Reimer, P.J. 1993. Extended ^{14}C data base and revised CALIB 3.0 ^{14}C age calibration program. *Radiocarbon* **35**, 215–30.

Sugden, H. 1999. *High Resolution, Multiple Profile and Radiocarbon Dating Studies of Early Human Impacts and Environmental Change in the Inner Hebrides, Scotland.* Unpublished PhD thesis, University of Sheffield.

Sugden, H. and Edwards, K.J. 2000. The Early Holocene vegetational history of Loch a'Bhogaidh, southern Rinns, Islay, with special reference to hazel (*Corylus avellana* L.). *In* S. Mithen (ed.), *Hunter-Gatherer Landscape Archaeology: the Southern Hebrides Mesolithic Project 1988–1998, Vol. 1,* 129–35. Cambridge: McDonald Institute Monograph.

Sutherland, D.G. 1991. The glaciation of the Shetland and Orkney Islands. *In* J. Ehlers, P.L. Gibbard and J. Rose (eds), *Glacial Deposits in Great Britain and Ireland,* 121–7. Rotterdam: Balkema.

Sykes, B. 2001. *The Seven Daughters of Eve.* London: Bantam Press.

Thorarinsson, S. 1981. Greetings from Iceland: ashfalls and volcanic aerosols in Scandinavia. *Geografiska Annaler* **63A**, 109–18.

Tipping, R. 1994. The form and fate of Scotland's woodlands. *Proceedings of the Society of Antiquaries of Scotland* **124**, 1–54.

Tipping, R. 1996. Microscopic charcoal records, inferred human activity and climate change in the Mesolithic of northernmost Scotland. *In* T. Pollard and A. Morrison (eds), *The Early Prehistory of Scotland,* 39–61. Edinburgh: Edinburgh University Press.

Turney, C.S.M., Harkness, D.D. and Lowe, J.J. 1997. The use of microtephra horizons to correlate Late-glacial lake sediment successions in Scotland. *Journal of Quaternary Science* **12**, 525–31.

Walker, I.R. 1995. Chironomids as indicators of past environmental change. *In* P.D. Armitage, P.S. Cranston and L.C.V. Pinder (eds), *The Chironomidae: Biology and Ecology of Non-Biting Midges,* 405–22. London: Chapman & Hall.

Whittington, G., Buckland, P.C., Edwards, K.J., Greenwood, M., Hall, A.M. and Robinson, M. 2003. Multi-proxy Devensian Lateglacial and Holocene environmental records at an Atlantic coastal site in Shetland. *Journal of Quaternary Science* **18**, 151–68.

Whittington, G., Edwards, K.J. and Cundill, P.R. 1991. Late- and post-glacial vegetational change at Black Loch, Fife, eastern Scotland – a multiple core approach. *New Phytologist* **118**, 147–66.

Whittington, G., Fallick, A.F. and Edwards, K.J. 1996. Stable isotope and pollen records from eastern Scotland and a consideration of Late-glacial and early Holocene climate change for Europe. *Journal of Quaternary Science* **11**, 327–40.

Wickham-Jones, C.R. 1990. *Rhum: Mesolithic and Later Sites at Kinloch, Excavations 1984–1986.* Edinburgh: Society of Antiquaries of Scotland (Monograph **7**).

Wickham-Jones, C.R. and Dalland, M. 1998. A small Mesolithic site at Fife Ness, Fife, Scotland. *Internet Archaeology* **5**.

Wickham-Jones, C.R. and Firth, C. 1990. Mesolithic Survey. *Discovery and Excavation in Scotland 1990,* 22.

Wilson, D. 1851. *The Archaeology and Prehistoric Annals of Scotland.* Edinburgh: Sutherland and Knox.

Woodman, P.C. 1996. Archaeology on the edge: learning to fend for ourselves. *In* T. Pollard and A. Morrison (eds), *The Early Prehistory of Scotland,* 152–61. Edinburgh: Edinburgh University Press.

Zvelebil, M. 1994. Plant use in the Mesolithic and its role in the transition to farming. *Proceedings of the Prehistoric Society* **60**, 35–74.

Chapter 5

Missing Mammals from Mesolithic Middens: a Comparison of the Fossil and Archaeological Records from Scotland

ANDREW C. KITCHENER, CLIVE BONSALL and LÁSZLÓ BARTOSIEWICZ

Wild mammals were an essential source of food and materials for Mesolithic people in Scotland. However, most Mesolithic sites in Scotland contain scant evidence of the mammals that were exploited locally. In contrast, the fossil and contemporary records indicate that there was a very high and changing diversity of mammal species available to Mesolithic hunter-gatherers as the climate warmed at the end of the last Ice Age; up to 23 species of terrestrial and freshwater mammals from the fossil record compared to a maximum of 16 species from Mesolithic sites, but only four of these were found at more than two sites.

The reasons for this disparity between the fossil and archaeological records are discussed. In Scotland most Mesolithic sites with faunal remains are coastal shell middens, which may not be sites where mammals were routinely hunted and their carcasses processed. The shell midden sites are also of Later Mesolithic date and hence cannot reflect the Early Holocene fauna, which included cold climate species that had survived from the Lateglacial. Many areas have acid soils in which bones are only rarely preserved, and this may explain the absence of faunal materials from the majority of coastal and inland sites. The fact that larger mammals may have been processed at the kill site, and that some mammals were exploited for their skins, further reduces the chances of their survival in the archaeological record. Finally, optimal foraging for prey in relation to prey density may have meant that some large mammal species (e.g. moose) were not worth hunting except opportunistically. It is likely that all of these factors have contributed to the impoverished mammal fauna of the Scottish Mesolithic.

Introduction

The Early Holocene had a biodiversity unmatched in any subsequent period as Arctic faunas and floras were replaced by temperate species during the rapid climatic warming that signalled the end of the last Ice Age (Kitchener 1998; McCormick & Buckland 1997; Yalden 1999). This dynamic and wide-ranging complement of species represented a vital natural resource, which was available for exploitation by humans colonizing Scotland as hunter-gatherers in the Lateglacial or Early Holocene. Larger mammals, in particular, were among the most important of the fauna that could have been utilized by Mesolithic peoples. Not only did they provide a large and valuable source of food, but they also provided materials for making clothes, shelters, tools, and even medicines. However, the archaeological record lacks many of the larger species (Bonsall *et al.* 1999; McCormick & Buckland 1997), which are now known to have existed in Scotland from the fossil record (Kitchener 1998). Recent developments in our knowledge of the faunal history of the early Postglacial period have been possible through AMS radiocarbon dating of existing museum specimens from unreliable or poorly documented stratigraphic contexts (Kitchener & Bonsall 1997; 1999). This new information allows us to take a critical view of the faunal remains found at Mesolithic sites in comparison with the known fossil record.

Although Mesolithic peoples exploited other animal and also plant species, this review is restricted to the larger mammals, because these were most likely to be exploited by humans and the fossil record of mammals in Scotland is complete enough for a thorough comparison to be made (Kitchener 1998). Birds and molluscs were also undoubtedly important sources of foods and materials (McCormick & Buckland 1997), but poorer knowledge of their fossil records, a potentially far larger number of species, and (in the case of birds) potentially greater mobility, create greater uncertainty in comparing fossil and archaeological records than for the mammals.

In this paper we review the diversity and chronology of the large mammal species that lived in Scotland during the Early Holocene. We discuss the uses of mammals by hunter-gatherers and how this may have influenced what survived in middens. Finally, we compare the fossil and archaeological records of mammals in Mesolithic Scotland, in order to see what differences occur and discuss the possible causes of this faunal disparity.

Mesolithic mammals in Scotland

In this review we have restricted the species that were available for human exploitation to those with a body weight of more than 250 grammes. This excludes most small rodents and insectivores, but recognizes that some smaller species may have been exploited for fur (e.g. stoat/ermine, *Mustela erminea*; red squirrel, *Sciurus vulgaris*) or food (e.g. hedgehog, *Erinaceus europaeus*; water vole, *Arvicola terrestris*). Smaller mammals may occur in middens purely incidentally as, for example, temporary commensals (e.g. wood mouse, *Apodemus sylvaticus*), or they may have entered and died there long after human occupation (e.g. shrews, *Sorex* spp.). We have further divided the mammal species into terrestrial and freshwater mammals that would have been hunted routinely mainly away from the coasts, and marine mammals that may have been exploited at the coasts either seasonally (e.g. grey seals, *Halichoerus grypus*) or opportunistically (stranded cetaceans).

Although we now have a greater insight into the chronology of Scottish mammals during the Holocene from AMS radiocarbon dating (Kitchener & Bonsall 1997; 1999), there are very few sites which allow an analysis of faunal change over time. Recently, Harwood, Kitchener, and Murray (unpublished research) carried out a cluster analysis on more than 4000 bone fragments from different strata in the Creag nan Uamh caves, Sutherland. This analysis suggested that there were three distinct faunal assemblages. One cluster was dominated by reindeer (*Rangifer tarandus*) and was associated with stony deposits of Late Pleistocene age, while another cluster associated with a 'cave earth' deposit was dominated by red deer (*Cervus elaphus*) and is probably of Holocene origin. The third cluster consisted of a mixed group of species dominated by both reindeer and red deer, which may have arisen through bioturbation by badgers (*Meles meles*), rabbits (*Oryctolagus cuniculus*), and humans (*Homo sapiens*); alternatively, it may represent a very early Holocene assemblage reflecting the transition from Arctic to temperate species. A series of AMS radiocarbon dates on key species within these clusters would greatly enhance our knowledge of the faunal history of this important fossil locality.

Terrestrial mammals

During the Lateglacial and very early Holocene (c.13,000–9200 BP), when humans are likely to have recolonized Scotland (Morrison & Bonsall 1989), the landscape was dominated by treeless tundras and open grasslands (Huntley 1993), which were populated by mainly Arctic species, including reindeer, mountain hare (*Lepus timidus*), and possibly Arctic fox (*Alopex lagopus*), or open-ground species such as the wild horse (*Equus ferus*) (Kitchener 1998). As the woodland cover of Scotland developed over the next few thousand years (Tipping 1994), the fauna changed to reflect this. The wild horse probably became extinct in Britain during the Mesolithic (Clutton-Brock 1991; Yalden 1999, 78) and the latest radiocarbon date for reindeer is c.8300 BP from the Creag nan Uamh caves, Sutherland (Murray *et al.* 1993). Of these early mammals, only the mountain hare has survived until today as a relict species on high ground.

The Early Holocene forests of Scotland were inhabited by a wide range of larger species of mammals. Red deer probably colonized Scotland at the beginning of the Holocene; a set of red deer antlers from the Meadows of Edinburgh has recently been radiocarbon dated to c.8690 BP (Kitchener & Bonsall 1999; Ritchie 1920; Smith 1881). This species survives on open hillsides in Scotland today and could have adapted readily to the open ground conditions of the Early Holocene. The aurochs (*Bos primigenius*) was also an early colonizer, recorded from c.9170 BP in Fife (Harting 1880; Kitchener & Bonsall 1999; Smith 1872), which would have depended on grazing in open woodlands and could have adapted to more open habitats where grazing was possible. It survived in Scotland until at least the Bronze Age; the most recent date is from a skull from Galloway at c.3315 BP (Kitchener & Bonsall 1999; Smith 1872). We can infer from their later survival into historic times that wolf (*Canis lupus*) and wild pig (*Sus scrofa*) were also present throughout the Mesolithic. There are also Mesolithic and later dates for the brown bear (*Ursus arctos*) and beaver (*Castor fiber*) (Table 5.1).

Some Mesolithic mammals were once believed to have survived only just into the Holocene, including the moose or elk (*Alces alces*) and the lynx (*Lynx lynx*), suggesting that habitat change due to climatic amelioration or over-hunting by Mesolithic people led to their extinction (Clutton-Brock 1991; Jenkinson 1983; Simmons *et al.* 1981). Although a forest species, the moose is dependent on willow (*Salix* spp.), aspen (*Populus* spp.), birch (*Betula* spp.), and aquatic vegetation for its survival (Bryant & Kuropat 1980; Renecker & Schwartz 1998). However, recent radiocarbon dates for both species show that they survived well beyond the Neolithic period (Table 5.1). Therefore, humans probably caused the extinction of these species at much more recent dates. However, two other pieces of evidence for the later survival of the moose are highly dubious. A supposed moose antler fragment from the Roman fort at Newstead (Ewart 1911, 376; described incorrectly as an antler base in McCormick & Buckland 1997) is in fact

74

TABLE 5.1

The terrestrial mammals recorded in, or which probably survived in, Scotland during the Mesolithic period.

	Present Today	Mesolithic fossils	Post-Mesolithic occurrence	^{14}C dates BP	Date of extinction	Refs.
Hedgehog, *Erinaceus europaeus*	+		+			1
Wolf, *Canis lupus*		?	+		?*c*.17–18thC	2
?Arctic fox, *Alopex lagopus*		?			?early Holocene	2
Fox, *Vulpes vulpes*	+	?	+		1	
Brown bear, *Ursus arctos*		+	+	7590–2673	<AD500 or 10thC AD	2
Polecat, *Mustela putorius*	R		+		*c*.AD1900	1,3
Stoat, *Mustela erminea*	+	+				1
Pine marten, *Martes martes*	+	?	+			1
Badger, *Meles meles*	+	?	+			1
Otter, *Lutra lutra*	+	?	+			1
Lynx, *Lynx lynx*		+	+		<*c*.AD200	4,5
Wildcat, *Felis silvestris*	+	?	+			1
Wild horse, *Equus ferus*		?		10,165	Mesolithic	1,4
Wild pig, *Sus scrofa*		?	+		*c*.16–17thC AD	2
Red deer, *Cervus elaphus*	+	+	+	8690		1,4
Roe deer, *Capreolus capreolus*	+	?	+			1
Reindeer, *Rangifer tarandus*	R	+		9170–8300	Mesolithic	2,4
Moose, *Alces alces*		+	+	7790–3925	<*c*.1900BC	2,4
Aurochs, *Bos primigenius*		+	+	9170–3315	<*c*.1300BC	2,6
Beaver, *Castor fiber*		+	+	7690–*c*.1680	*c*.1550AD	7
Red squirrel, *Sciurus vulgaris*	?R		+			1,2
Water vole, *Arvicola terrestris*	+		+			1
Mountain hare, *Lepus timidus*	+	?	+			1

Key: + = present; ? = possibly present; R = reintroduced

References: 1 – Corbet & Harris 1991; 2 – Kitchener 1998; Yalden 1999; 3 – Birks & Kitchener 1999; 4 – Kitchener & Bonsall 1997; 5 – Bonsall *et al.* in prep.; 6 – Kitchener & Bonsall 1999; 7 – Kitchener & Conroy 1997.

the crown of a massive aberrant red deer antler (Fig. 5.1). Also, a carving on the wall of the now destroyed Michael Cave at Wemyss, Fife (Fig. 5.2) was originally thought to depict a moose (Childe 1935, 116; Edwards 1933), but could be interpreted in several ways (e.g. as an aurochs: McCormick & Buckland 1997) and we believe it to be a representation of a seal, which seems much more likely given the coastal location of the cave.

Many smaller species of mammals that survive today were also available for exploitation by Mesolithic peoples. Although fossil remains may be rare, we can infer their survival from their present occurrence and their ability to survive in habitats that were present in the Early Holocene. These mammals are also listed in Table 5.1. Therefore, in summary, Mesolithic hunter-gatherers could choose from up to 23 larger mammal species as

defined here. Given that habitat changes would have made some species unlikely to be contemporaneous, the number of species available would have varied between 10 (Earlier Mesolithic: 10,000–8300 BP) and 21 (Later Mesolithic: 8299–5000 BP), taking the most recent radiocarbon date for the reindeer as a convenient dividing point in time (Table 5.1).

Marine mammals

The fossil record of marine mammals, especially the smaller cetaceans, is very poor. In part this is because of rising sea levels since the end of the last Ice Age, which mean that stranding sites may well now be inundated. Also cetacean bone is mostly cancellous and its structure would not normally be suited to long-term preservation.

FIGURE 5.1

The putative moose antler from Newstead (NMS reg. no. X.FRA 1168). This is the crown of a very large aberrant red deer antler.
(Photo: Trustees of the National Museums of Scotland)

FIGURE 5.2

Carving in Michael Cave at Wemyss, Fife (Edwards 1933, figs 6–7). The animal has been interpreted as a large ungulate, but we suggest that it represents a seal. (Reproduced with permission from Volume 67 of the *Proceedings of the Society of Antiquaries of Scotland*)

However, based on recent observations of stranded cetaceans and records of vagrant seals, a great variety of marine mammals could have been available to Mesolithic peoples (Table 5.2), although the larger species were probably only scavenged when they became stranded sporadically on the coast. Some smaller cetacean species may have been driven ashore, as is still done in the Faroe Islands and was formerly practised in Shetland, but there is no evidence for this during the Mesolithic. Some seal species (e.g. grey seal) are terrestrial during the breeding season and so would have been vulnerable to regular seasonal hunting. There are some interesting regional differences; grey seals come ashore to give birth and mate for up to eight weeks in October/November in the Western and Northern Isles, and in November/December in the east of Scotland (Anderson 1991). It is likely that, apart from grey seals, most usage of marine mammals would have been opportunistic from strandings.

We would expect that, as with terrestrial mammals, Arctic species (e.g. narwhal, *Monodon monoceros*; beluga, *Delphinapterus leucas*; ringed seal, *Phoca hispida*) would have been replaced by temperate species (e.g. grey seal; bottle-nosed dolphin, *Tursiops truncatus*;

porpoise, *Phocoena phocoena*) as the climate warmed during the Early Holocene.

Recent investigations into strandings in Scotland have shown that many more subtropical or warm temperate species have been recorded in recent years (e.g. striped dolphin, *Stenella coeruleoalba* (Reid *et al.* 1993); Fraser's dolphin, *Lagenodelphis hosei* (Bones *et al.* 1998)). In part this is due to better recording, but also it may reflect rising global temperatures. Temperatures similar to, or higher than today may have characterized much of the Mesolithic period (Smith 1992; Walker & Lowe 1997). It is, therefore, not inconceivable that Mesolithic peoples were able to exploit a similar range of species as occurs today (Table 5.2). One notable exception is the grey whale (*Eschrichtius robustus*), which is now confined entirely to the Pacific Ocean, but which survived in the Atlantic until the 17th century AD (Yalden 1999). Lack of suitable reference material in Scottish museums means that this species may be overlooked at archaeological sites. It is essential for future research that a grey whale skeleton be acquired by the National Museums of Scotland for comparison with archaeological bone in Scotland.

TABLE 5.2

The marine mammals either recorded from the Mesolithic period in Scotland or which could have occurred there (? = probable occurrence based on the presence of vagrants in historical times or lower sea temperatures at the beginning of the Holocene).

Pinnipeds	Cetaceans
Grey seal, *Halichoerus grypus*	Porpoise, *Phocoena phocoena*
Common seal, *Phoca vitulina*	Dolphins (10 species)
?Ringed seal, *Phoca hispida*	Beaked whales (4 species)
?Harp seal, *Phoca groenlandica*	?Beluga, *Delphinapterus leucas*
?Hooded seal, *Cystophora cristata*	?Narwhal, *Monodon monoceros*
?Bearded seal, *Erignathus barbatus*	?Pygmy sperm whale, *Kogia breviceps*
?Walrus, *Odobenus rosmarus*	Sperm whale, *Physeter catodon*
	Right whale, *Eubalaena glacialis*
	?Bowhead whale, *Balaena mysticetus*
	Rorquals, *Balaenoptera* spp. (4 species)
	Humpback whale, *Megaptera novaeangliae*
	Grey whale, *Eschrichtius robustus*

The uses of mammals

Mammals were (and still are) exploited for different reasons. Many ungulate species were undoubtedly hunted for food, but could also be exploited for raw materials, including hides, bone, antler, and sinews. However, large species might be poorly represented at archaeological sites, because the carcasses would have to be butchered and defleshed at the site of the kill to reduce them to manageable pieces. This is the so-called 'schlepp effect' (Daly 1969).

Most carnivores (and possibly the red squirrel, *Sciurus vulgaris*) were probably exploited for fur, which would have greatly limited their potential for preservation in the archaeological record. It is likely that fur-bearing mammals would have been skinned at the kill site especially if the rest of the carcass had no use. Therefore, at most, the only skeletal elements that might survive in skins would be foot bones, since these may be retained in the skin. However, it is interesting to note that the skeletal remains of fur-bearing mammals have been found at some hunting/butchering stations, such as Star Carr (Clark 1954) and Ringkloster (Andersen 1995), which may indicate that similar sites have not yet been located in Scotland. As well as meat and fur, the beaver was probably exploited for the medicinal properties of the secretion (castoreum) from its castor glands. Castoreum contains a chemical similar to salycylic acid, which is derived from the bark of willows and is the active ingredient of aspirin (Marcuzzi 1986). It is believed that hunting for castoreum may have led to the beaver's extinction in Scotland in the mid-16th century AD (Kitchener & Conroy 1997).

Cetaceans and seals may have been killed for their blubber and oils, as well as for some skeletal elements used in manufacturing. Childe (1935, 240 & 248) suggested that whale bone was used opportunistically as a substitute for wood during the Iron Age. However, cetacean bone was probably not widely used because of the uncertainty of supply owing to reliance on strandings and the high degree of porosity of cetacean bone would have made it mechanically unsuitable for many purposes.

It is important to bear in mind the different ways in which various mammal species would have been used by hunter-gatherers, since this would affect which parts, if any, of the animals were preserved at archaeological sites compared with the fossil record.

The archaeological record of mammals in the Mesolithic

Mesolithic sites containing animal bone in Scotland are rare and distributed along the coast. Although these coastal sites are mostly shell middens and, hence, are dominated by a wide variety of mollusc species, they often contain some mammal bones. Table 5.3 shows the mammal species for which bones have been found at the key Mesolithic sites in Scotland. The species most often represented are red deer, wild pig, and roe deer. Some species were well represented at particular sites. For example, seal bones were particularly abundant at Cnoc Coig, Oronsay, where the presence of juvenile bones indicated that seals were exploited seasonally when they came ashore to pup in October and November

(Anderson 1991). The presence of carnivores at An Corran and in the Oban caves may indicate that these species were exploited for fur. In particular the heavily eroded, left proximal phalanx (posterior) from an adult brown bear at An Corran (Bartosiewicz forthcoming) is highly suggestive that this was all that remained from a bear skin. Although the decorative use of a bear claw (corresponding to the distal phalanx) cannot be ruled out, it is unlikely that an entire toe (including the proximal phalanx) would have been used in this way (no signs of manufacturing or wear are evident on this specimen).

Lynx remains were found at Mesolithic sites in Oban and on Ulva. In the former case, we know that the lynx dates to the period of Mesolithic occupation, though its presence was probably unrelated to human activity, but in the latter case we have no idea yet of the age of the lynx remains.

There are many mammals that are simply missing from Mesolithic sites, including moose, reindeer, wild horse, beaver, polecat, wolf, arctic fox, and stoat. We know from other sites in Britain that moose was exploited by Mesolithic peoples (e.g. Star Carr), so its

TABLE 5.3
Mammals found at Mesolithic sites in Scotland.

Species		An Corran, Staffin, Skye	Carding Mill Bay	Castle Street, Inverness	Cnoc Coig, Oronsay	Duntroon, Argyll	Forth Valley	Muirtown, Inverness	Morton, Fife	Oban, Argyll	Risga, Loch Sunart, Highland
Hedgehog	Erinaceus europaeus								+		
Domestic dog	Canis familiaris	+								+	
Red fox	Vulpes vulpes	+								+	
Brown bear	Ursus arctos	+									
Weasel	Mustela nivalis									+	
Pine marten	Martes martes				?						
Badger	Meles meles									+	
Otter	Lutra lutra	+			+					+	
Wildcat	Felis silvestris	+								+	
Lynx	Lynx lynx									+	
Grey seal	Halichoerus grypus				+						
Common seal	Phoca vitulina				+					+	
Fin whale	Balaenoptera physalus				+						
Delphinid/ phocoenid cetacean					+						
Wild pig	Sus scrofa	+	+		+				+	+	+
Red deer	Cervus elaphus	+	+	?	+	+	+	+	+	+	+
Roe deer	Capreolus capreolus	+	+		+				+	+	
Aurochs	Bos primigenius								+		+
Red squirrel	Sciurus vulgaris		+								
Water vole	Arvicola terrestris									+	
Hare	Lepus timidus	+								+	
References		1	2	3	4	5	6	7	8	6	9

References: 1 – Bartosiewicz forthcoming; 2 – McCormick & Buckland 1997; 3 – Wordsworth 1985; 4 – Grigson & Mellars 1987; 5 – Mapleton 1873; 6 – Lacaille 1954; 7 – Myers & Gourlay 1991; 8 – Coles 1971; 9 – Foxon 1991.

Note. Bioturbation and other factors make it possible that not all of these faunal remains are of Mesolithic age. Where there is uncertain contextual association, only direct radiocarbon dating of the bones would resolve any uncertainties.

absence from Scottish sites is surprising. The beaver was an important species in later periods, but it too is absent from Mesolithic sites.

Discussion

From the evidence presented in this paper, it is clear that there are major differences between the known mammal fauna of the Mesolithic and the species represented at archaeological sites. The most abundant species at the archaeological sites were red deer, wild pig, and roe deer, and they clearly represent sources of bone for tool-making as well as important sources of food, exploited even today. Other species appear only sporadically at different sites and some may well occur there incidentally rather than resulting from human hunting. What then has caused these differences between the palaeontological and archaeological records?

A major reason is that the sites in which faunal materials survive are probably not representative of human hunting activities during the Mesolithic. Shell middens were not necessarily attached to settlement sites. Many may represent special-purpose camps where molluscs were gathered and processed along with some line fishing and opportunistic hunting of otters, seals, and seabirds (Bonsall 1996). The occurrence of large mammal bones in the middens may occasionally be due to opportunistic hunting, but often can be explained in terms of particular skeletal elements brought into the sites as raw materials for tool-making.

Shell middens also benefit from favourable preservation conditions. The alkaline conditions found in the middens (pH = c.8–8.5) mean that bone is more likely to be preserved than in the vast majority of coastal and inland sites in Scotland where soil conditions are generally too acidic (pH <7.0) for survival of animal bone (Bonsall $et\ al.$ 1999). In the few English examples of inland open-air Mesolithic sites with well-preserved faunal assemblages, such as Star Carr and Thatcham (Clark 1954; Wymer 1962), it is notable that the animal remains include many of the mammals (e.g. beaver, moose, pine marten) missing from the coastal middens.

Moreover, all Scottish Mesolithic sites that have animal remains are dated to the Later Mesolithic, so that exploitation of Arctic species from the Earlier Mesolithic is unrecorded despite possible human colonization towards the end of the last Ice Age (Finlayson 1999; Morrison & Bonsall 1989).

A further possibility is that larger mammals would have been processed at the kill site and all usable materials extracted and preserved before being taken away.

For example, meat could have been dried or smoked and cut into manageable pieces for easier transport (Daly 1969). Thus much of the skeleton would not be taken from the kill site. Also, species that are exploited for their fur would be skinned at the kill site and the carcass left behind if it had no use as food or other materials. Again, there is little chance of any skeletal elements being preserved as a record of human exploitation beyond the kill site. Even where skeletal elements occur, the highly worked nature of the bone fragments may make their identification impossible using current methods and so mask the true species composition of a midden. For example, at Morton less than seven per cent of the mammal bone could be identified to species level (Coles 1971). It is easy to see how slivers of long bone from red deer, moose, and aurochs would be impossible to identify. Perhaps extracting DNA from some of these samples would allow a better appreciation of the species exploited by Mesolithic peoples.

Foraging efficiency may also provide an explanation for the limited range of species recorded at Mesolithic sites. Smith (1992, 12–16) calculated that a population density of eight reindeer per km^2 was needed to support a typical hunter-gatherer human population density of 0.006–0.02 individuals per km^2, assuming that their diet comprised 80 per cent ungulate meat and that the people lived at 20–60 per cent of their carrying capacity. In practice reindeer live at much lower densities (Table 5.4), but on migration they occur at very high population densities that could easily support high levels of seasonal exploitation. Using recent data on population densities of deer and wild pig species, and their typical body masses, it is possible to calculate the standing biomass per square kilometre that hunter-gatherers could exploit today (Table 5.4). Assuming that these were similar to those in the Mesolithic, given similarities in ecology and habitats, it is clear that red deer, wild pig, and roe deer are the most worthwhile species to hunt. These occur at high population densities and could provide a great deal of food for Mesolithic hunters. However, moose occur at very low population densities. Even though the highest biomass per square kilometre for moose could support human hunters, the opportunities for locating and exploiting a low-density population would be limited.

Therefore, it is possible that Mesolithic hunters did not develop hunting strategies for moose, because other species were more abundant and more easily encountered. However, this may not be the whole story; moose antlers and bones have been found at other Mesolithic sites in England (but only very early in the Mesolithic) and Europe (Smith 1992; Yalden 1999). In some parts of its Holarctic distribution today local population densities of moose may reach 200km^{-2} (Nowak 1999), so that strategic

TABLE 5.4

Population densities, average body masses, and standing biomasses of ungulates in Europe.

Species	Population density (per km²)	Body mass* (kg)	Biomass (kg per km²)	Refs.
Wild pig	1–30	90	90–2700	1, 2
Red deer	5–100	150	750–1500	1, 3
Roe deer	15–70	25	375–1750	1
Moose	0.1–1.1	550	55–605	1, 2, 4
Reindeer	0.4–1.9	95	38–180	1, 2
Reindeer (migration)	19,000 max.	95	1,805,000	1, 2
European bison	3–12	700	2100–8400	1, 2

* midpoint of minimum and maximum literature values

References: 1 – Macdonald & Barrett 1993; 2 – Nowak 1999; 3 – Clutton-Brock *et al.* 1982; 4 – Heptner *et al.* 1989

hunting may have been possible in some areas of Britain during the Mesolithic. In addition, unless evidence for hunting is available in the form of frontal bones attached to antlers, the possibility should be considered that cast antlers may have been collected passively rather than through active hunting (Choyke 1987, 116, tab.1).

It is conceivable that all the possible explanations mentioned above have contributed to the faunal disparity between archaeological sites and the palaeontological record in Scotland. Unfortunately, there is no prospect of elucidating further the causes or main cause of this disparity without the discovery of new Mesolithic sites with animal remains, particularly in inland locations, which may provide additional evidence of mammal species that were exploited by people during the Early Holocene.

References

Andersen, S.H. 1995. Ringkloster: Ertebølle trappers and wild boar hunters in eastern Jutland, a survey. *Journal of Danish Archaeology* **12** (1994–95), 13–59.

Anderson, S.S. 1991. Grey seal *Halichoerus grypus*. *In* G.B. Corbet and S. Harris (eds). *The Handbook of British Mammals* (3rd edn), 471–80. Oxford: Blackwell Scientific.

Bartosiewicz, L. (forthcoming). Vertebrate remains from a shell midden at An Corran, Staffin (Isle of Skye).

Birks, J.D.S. and Kitchener, A.C. 1999. *The Distribution and Status of the Polecat* Mustela putorius *in Britain in the 1990s.* London: Vincent Wildlife Trust.

Bones, M., Neill, B. and Reid, B. 1998. Fraser's dolphin (*Lagenodelphis hosei*) stranded in South Uist: first record in UK waters. *Journal of Zoology* **246**(4), 460–61.

Bonsall, C. 1996. The 'Obanian problem': coastal adaptation in the Mesolithic of western Scotland. *In* T. Pollard and A. Morrison (eds), *The Early Prehistory of Scotland*, 183–97. Edinburgh: Edinburgh University Press.

Bonsall, C., Kitchener, A.C. and Bartosiewicz, L. 1999. AMS ¹⁴C dating and the Mesolithic faunal record. *In* E. Cziesla, T. Kersting and S. Pratsch (eds), *Den Bogen spannen ... Festschrift für B. Gramsch*, 99–106. Weissbach: Beier & Beran.

Bryant, J.P. and Kuropat, P.J. 1980. Selection of winter forage by subarctic browsing vertebrates: the role of plant chemistry. *Annual Review of Ecology and Systematics* **11**, 261–85.

Childe, V.G. 1935. *The Prehistory of Scotland.* London: Kegan Paul, Trench & Trubner.

Choyke, A.M. 1987. The exploitation of red deer in the Hungarian Bronze Age. *Archaeozoologia* **1**(1), 109–116.

Clark, J.G.D. 1954. *Excavations at Star Carr.* Cambridge: Cambridge University Press.

Clutton-Brock, J. 1991. Extinct species. *In* G.B. Corbet and S. Harris (eds). *The Handbook of British Mammals* (3rd edn), 571–5. Oxford: Blackwell Scientific.

Clutton-Brock, T.H., Guinness, F.E. and Albon, S.D. 1982. *Red Deer. Behaviour and Ecology of Two Sexes.* Edinburgh: Edinburgh University Press.

Coles, J.M. 1971. The early settlement of Scotland: excavations at Morton, Fife. *Proceedings of the Prehistoric Society* **37**, 284–366.

Corbet, G.B. & Harris, S. (eds). 1991. *The Handbook of British Mammals* (3rd edn). Oxford: Blackwell Scientific.

Daly, P. 1969. Approaches to faunal analysis in archaeology. *American Antiquity* **34**, 146–53.

Edwards, A.J.H. 1933. Short cists in Roxburgh and Sutherland, and rock sculpturings in a cave at Wemyss, Fife. *Proceedings of the Society of Antiquaries of Scotland* **67** (1932–33), 164–76.

Ewart, J.C. 1911. Animal remains. *In* J. Curle, *A Roman Frontier Post and its People: the Fort of Newstead in the Parish of Melrose*, 362–77. Glasgow: James Maclehose & Sons.

Finlayson, B. 1999. Understanding the initial colonization of Scotland. *Antiquity* **73**, 879–84.

Foxon, A.D. 1991. *Bone, Antler, Tooth and Horn Technology and Utilisation.* Unpublished PhD thesis, University of Glasgow.

Grigson, C. and Mellars, P. 1987. The mammalian remains from the middens. *In* P. Mellars, *Excavations on Oronsay: Prehistoric Human Ecology on a Small Island,* 243–89. Edinburgh: Edinburgh University Press.

Harting, J.E. 1880. *British Mammals Extinct within Historic Times.* London: Trubner.

Heptner, V.G., Nasimovich, A.A. and Bannikov, A.G. 1989. *Mammals of the Soviet Union. Volume 1.* Leiden: Brill.

Huntley, B. 1993. European vegetation history: palaeovegetation maps from pollen data – 13000 yr BP to present. *Journal of Quaternary Science* **5**(2), 103–22.

Jenkinson, R.D.S. 1983. The recent history of the lynx (*Lynx lynx* Linné) in the British Isles. *Quaternary Newsletter* **41**, 1–7.

Kitchener, A.C. 1998. Extinctions, introductions and colonisations of Scottish mammals and birds since the last Ice Age. *In* R. Lambert (ed.), *Species History in Scotland,* 63–92. Edinburgh: Scottish Cultural Press.

Kitchener, A.C. and Bonsall, C. 1997. AMS radiocarbon dates for some extinct Scottish mammals. *Quaternary Newsletter* **83**, 1–11.

Kitchener, A.C. and Bonsall, C. 1999. Further AMS radiocarbon dates for extinct Scottish mammals. *Quaternary Newsletter* **88**, 1–10.

Kitchener, A.C. and Conroy, J.W.H. 1997. The history of the Eurasian beaver *Castor fiber* in Scotland. *Mammal Review* **27**(2), 95–108.

Lacaille, A.D. 1954. *The Stone Age in Scotland.* London: Oxford University Press.

McCormick, F. and Buckland, P.C. 1997. Faunal change: the vertebrate fauna. *In* K.J. Edwards and I.B.M. Ralston (eds), *Scotland: Environment and Archaeology, 8000BC–AD1000,* 83–108. Chichester: Wiley.

Macdonald, D. and Barrett, P. 1993. *Collins Field Guide to the Mammals of Britain and Europe.* London: Collins.

Mapleton, R.J. 1873. Note of a bone cave at Duntroon. *Proceedings of the Society of Antiquaries of Scotland* **10**(1) (1872–73), 306–08.

Marcuzzi, G. 1986. Man–beaver relations. *Investigations on Beavers* **5**, 15–154.

Morrison, A. and Bonsall, C. 1989. The early post-glacial settlement of Scotland: a review. *In* C. Bonsall (ed.), *The Mesolithic in Europe,* 134–42. Edinburgh: John Donald.

Murray, N., Bonsall, C., Sutherland, D.G., Lawson, T.J. and Kitchener, A. 1993. Further radiocarbon determinations on reindeer remains of Middle and Late Devensian age from the Creag nan Uamh caves, Assynt, north-west Scotland. *Quaternary Newsletter* **70**, 1–10.

Myers, A.M. and Gourlay, R.B. 1991. Muirtown, Inverness: preliminary investigation of a shell midden. *Proceedings of the Society of Antiquaries of Scotland* **121**, 17–25.

Nowak, R.M. 1999. *Walker's Mammals of the World* (6th edn). Baltimore & London: Johns Hopkins University Press.

Reid, R.J., Kitchener, A., Ross, H.M. and Herman, J. 1993. First records of the striped dolphin *Stenella coeruleoalba*, in Scottish waters. *Glasgow Naturalist* **22**, 243–5.

Renecker, L.A. and Schwartz, C.C. 1998. Food habits and feeding behaviour. *In* A.W. Franzmann and C.C. Schwartz (eds), *Ecology and Management of North American Moose,* 403–39. Washington & London: Smithsonian Institution Press.

Ritchie, J. 1920. *The Influence of Man on Animal Life in Scotland: a Study of Faunal Evolution.* Cambridge: Cambridge University Press.

Simmons, I.G., Dimbleby, G.W. and Grigson, C. 1981. The Mesolithic. *In* I.G. Simmons and M.J. Tooley (eds), *The Environment in British Prehistory,* 82–124. London: Duckworth.

Smith, C. 1992. *Late Stone Age Hunters of the British Isles.* London: Routledge.

Smith, J.A. 1872. Notes on the ancient cattle of Scotland. *Proceedings of the Society of Antiquaries of Scotland* **9**(2) (1871–72), 587–674.

Smith, J.A. 1881. Notice of the remains of the red deer (*Cervus elaphus,* Linn.) found in the bed of an old loch near Dundas Castle, Linlithgowshire; with notes on the remains of red deer found in different localities in the south of Scotland. *Proceedings of the Society of Antiquaries of Scotland* **15** (1880–81), 37–63.

Tipping, R. 1994. The form and fate of Scotland's woodlands. *Proceedings of the Society of Antiquaries of Scotland* **124**, 1–54.

Walker, M.J.C. and Lowe, J.J. 1997. Vegetation and climate in Scotland, 13,000–7,000 radiocarbon years ago. *In* J.E. Gordon (ed.). *Reflections on the Ice Age in Scotland,* 105–15. Glasgow: Scottish Association of Geography Teachers and Scottish Natural Heritage.

Wordsworth, J. 1985. The excavation of a Mesolithic horizon at 13–24 Castle Street, Inverness. *Proceedings of the Society of Antiquaries of Scotland* **115**, 89–103; fiche 1: A3–B14.

Wymer, J.J. 1962. Excavations at the Maglemosian sites at Thatcham, Berkshire, England. *Proceedings of the Prehistoric Society* **28**, 329–61.

Yalden, D.W. 1999. *The History of British Mammals.* London: Poyser.

Chapter 6

Dating Forager Communities in Scotland

PATRICK ASHMORE

Some of the consequences of variations in the proportion of radiocarbon to ordinary carbon in the atmosphere are discussed. The possibility of a sporadic human presence in Scotland before the Holocene is explored. Population estimates and coastality are assessed for various millennia, and the chronologies of environmental change and human activities are summarized.

Precision: plateaux and other problems

It is essential to remember that a calibrated radiocarbon age is arrived at by a comparison between the radio-activity of the carbon in the sample with that in tree-rings or other absolutely dated reference sets, and that the proportion of radiocarbon to ordinary carbon in the atmosphere, which determines how much there is in individual tree rings, has varied in the short, medium, and long terms. During some periods the proportion of radiocarbon to ordinary carbon in the atmosphere temporarily decreased, creating a plateau in calibration curves so that radiocarbon ages at the end of the period are indistinguishable from those at the beginning. Fig. 6.1 shows that the 1998 calibration curve (Stuiver *et al.* 1998), like its predecessors, has plateaux at several periods between 10,000 and 4000 BC.

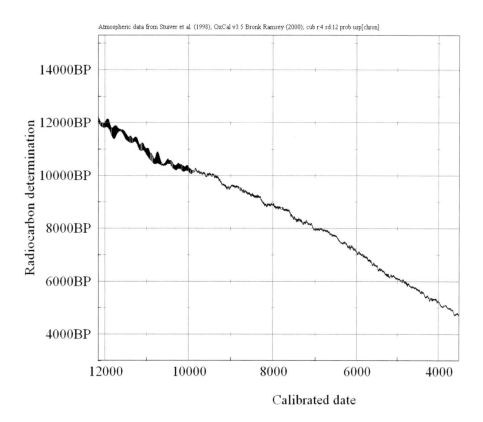

Atmospheric data from Stuiver et al. (1998), OxCal v3.5 Bronk Ramsey (2000), cub r:4 sd:12 prob usp[chron]

FIGURE 6.1

The 1998 calibration curve has plateaux at several periods between 10,000 and 4000 BC.

83

Fig. 6.2 illustrates one consequence. Radiocarbon ages with a precision of c. ±50 ^{14}C years generally leave great uncertainties about the period to which an event truly belongs. After c.9500 BC they would in general be ascribable only to a roughly 200-year period with a 95 per cent confidence or worse. Doubling the precision of ages would often not greatly improve matters. For instance, around 8500 BC, the period of the earliest published Scottish age for human activity (Lawson 2001, 124), the current calibration curve only allows dating of single events (with a 95 per cent chance of being right) to within about 350 years even with half the usual size of error. However, there are a few short periods before 4000 cal BC when much greater precision is possible. Around 9250 BC (9750 BP), 7500 BC (8500 BP), and 5750 BC (6750 BP) radiocarbon ages of ±25 years may allow the calibrated dates of events to be assigned to individual centuries.

Only a small proportion of the available ages for Scottish forager sites have an error as low as ±50 years, let alone ±25. Many ages were obtained when the radiocarbon method was far less well developed than it is today. In the 1970s and early 1980s errors were underestimated. Ages obtained before the mid-1980s should probably be corrected by multiplying the errors by between 4 and 1.4 (Ashmore et al. 2000; Baillie 1990; Stenhouse pers. comm.). A reasonable set of adjustments (Ashmore et al. 2000) leads to an average one sigma error of existing uncalibrated Scottish ages for human activity of slightly over 112 ^{14}C years. Once the dates are calibrated, the range within which available dates fall (with a probability of 19 chances out of 20) averages about 600 calibrated years.

It is worth noting that, because of the variations in atmospheric ^{14}C, uncalibrated ages can be even more misleading than calibrated dates. Their apparent

Variation in the two sigma date range of calibrated dates for C14 dates with errors of ±50 and of ±25 years

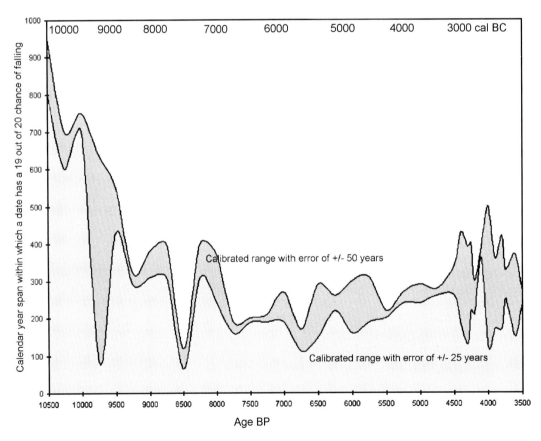

FIGURE 6.2

Radiocarbon ages with the normal precision of about ±50 ^{14}C years and those with a high precision of ±20 ^{14}C years both generally leave great uncertainties about the period to which an event truly belongs.

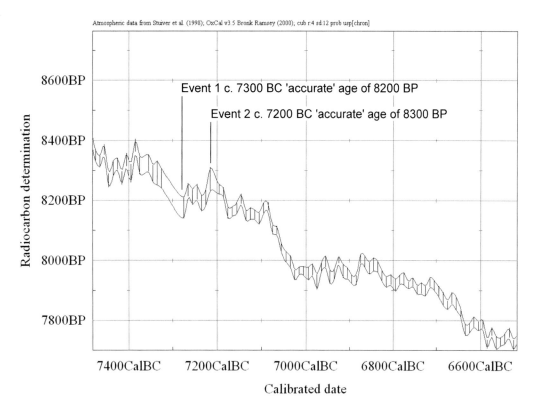

Atmospheric data from Stuiver et al. (1998); OxCal v3.5 Bronk Ramsey (2000); cub r4 sd:12 prob usp[chron]

FIGURE 6.3
An 'accurate' uncalibrated age of *c.*8200 BP may represent an event earlier than one 'accurately' aged to *c.*8300 BP.

simplicity masks some unavoidable problems. Fig. 6.3 shows that an 'accurate' uncalibrated age of about 8200 BP may represent an event earlier than one 'accurately' aged to about 8300 BP. Examination of Fig. 6.1 shows that similar reversals are possible at several periods. Although in lists of dates it is essential to quote the date BP as a conventional surrogate for the laboratory carbon isotope measurements, in the body of a discussion about archaeology, or the palaeoenvironment, it is little more meaningful to use it than to use the isotope measurements themselves. For example, the original laboratory quotation for GU-1004, a sample from Pitcairn in Fife, was '$\delta^{14}C = -776.3 \pm 5.5‰$; $^{13}C = -23.8 \pm 0.05‰$; $D = \Delta776.8 \pm 5.5‰$; ^{14}C age (Libby half life 5568 yrs): 12,050±200 yrs BP (10,100 BC); 5730-year half-life: 12,400±205 yrs BP'. The age quoted, 12,050±200 yrs BP, is no more a date than '$D = \Delta776.8 \pm 5.5‰$'; but perhaps the BP age is more tendentious. In this example, incidentally, the age was for a sample which probably comprised both coal and charcoal. Another strong argument against use of uncalibrated dates BP in discussions about past events is the proliferation of data about climate variations from ice cores and varves, which are tied to absolute time-scales.

For these reasons, ^{14}C dates quoted in the discussion of forager sites in Scotland below are presented as calibrated two sigma date ranges and labelled cal BC. The uncalibrated age measurements are presented together with their calibrated two sigma ranges in the lists in the following chapter. Absolute dates from varves and ice cores are quoted as dates BC (though in fact there are some uncertainties even in the best cores). In my text 'age' is used to refer to a laboratory measurement, and 'date' is used to refer to a calibrated date. I have not used the Bayesian methods advocated by Blackwell and Buck (2003, 233), despite their applicability in many circumstances, because their use would add considerably to the complexity of this paper without a significant improvement in understanding.

Another problem in devising a chronology for archaeological sites in Scotland (and elsewhere) has been an underestimation of the likelihood of contamination of bulk samples with residual material (Ashmore 1999). Although dating programmes for early artefacts (e.g. Bonsall *et al.* 1995) have not fallen into this error, no Scottish artefact from before 4000 BC has more than one radiocarbon age, which means that there is no check against any but the most obviously aberrant ages. Also, the ages obtained from artefacts cannot blithely be applied to the context from which the finds came, for the artefacts may have been old when lost, or have come from mixtures of older and younger deposits.

Lastly, uncertainties about the size of the marine effect during the period from *c.*8500 to 4000 BC (and indeed later) mean that calibrations of ages for shells, and for the bones of those who had a highly marine diet, perhaps underestimate the amount by which the raw ages should be corrected.

These problems mean that there is much uncertainty in the chronology of forager communities. Another major problem is that generalizations intended to average out the uncertainties in individual dates cannot be based on a statistically valid number of samples. This means that all but the most general of conjectures here are very sensitive to the dating of a few more sites. Also, there are few or no dates for many areas of Scotland, so comprehensive inter-regional studies are impossible. For all the reasons adduced above, the discussion which follows should be treated as a succession of conjectures.

Precursors to the Holocene people in Scotland

People were possibly present in Scotland, from time to time, before the Holocene. For a while it seemed that there was evidence that Ayrshire was inhabited before the peak of the last glaciation. A single piece of supposedly oak charcoal thought to be from a post in a posthole at Loudoun Hill was aged to 40,285±1435 BP (AA-20407), while indeterminate 'charcoal' under compacted gravel produced an age of 36,685±845 BP (AA-20408). Subsequent examination of material with a similar conchoidal fracture from nearby deposits, however, showed that the samples dated were probably compacted fossil soils; AA-20407 thus does not provide a useful date for the post or the posthole.

Reindeer antlers from Sourlie aged to *c.*30,000 BP (SRR-3023; Clutton-Brock & MacGregor 1988, 32) and from Woodhill Quarry, Kilmaurs, aged to before 40,000 BP (Birm-93; ibid.), nevertheless suggest that Ayrshire is one place to seek open-air Middle Palaeolithic camps because reindeer would have been a prime food source for early foragers. Further north, ages from single pieces of antler from Inchnadamph suggest that reindeer were present in NW Scotland at various ages between 45,000±2000 BP, the weighted mean of the two oldest ages, OxA-3788 and OxA-3793, and 22,300±240 BP, an age provided by OxA-3792 (Murray *et al.* 1993, table 1).

However, there are no published ages directly suggesting human activity before those of 8500 BC discussed below. The lack of proof for human activity in

the British Isles during the last glaciation before about 14000 to 12300 cal BC (Housley *et al.* 1997, 43) makes it seem unlikely that any part of Scotland was inhabited or often visited by hunting parties during the glacial period, despite the possibility, raised by Lambeck's (1995, fig. 3) isostatic rebound model for the North Sea area, that the Northern Isles and a large area of land around them may have been ice-free for long periods.

Nearly all continuous climate data are tied to absolute chronologies, so it is worth exploring the relationship between radiocarbon dates and calendar dates earlier than 9907 BC, the limit of the tree-ring dated part of the 1998 calibration curve. Uranium-thorium dating of corals provides a low-accuracy extension of the calibration curve to about 22,000 BC (Stuiver *et al.* 1998, 1041–2). Synchronization of variations in temperature-sensitive foraminifera from marine sediment cores with variations in temperature indicated by ice-core annual layers allows a conjectural extension back to about 40,000 BP (Jöris & Weninger 1998, fig. 1), although the correlation between the foraminifera and GISP2 curves depicted by Jöris and Weninger is not visually convincing and suggests that the age of the former may have been underestimated by amounts varying up to 2000 years at 40,000 BC. The Lake Suigetsu, Japan, varve chronology extends to before 40,000 BP (Kitegawa & van der Plicht 1998, fig. 1) with some gaps. The general impression from this calibration curve is that severe temporary reductions of atmospheric radiocarbon occurred in the glacial period, with particularly significant periods of diminishing radiocarbon concentrations between *c.*34,000 and 32,000 BC and between *c.*29,000 and 25,000 BC. There may be another plateau somewhere between 22,000 and 18,000 BC, where Suigetsu data are not available. A period from *c.*14,200 to 12,500 BC, around the end of the main glacial period, contains a lesser plateau.

The very low concentrations of radioactive carbon surviving in the samples from the earlier part of this period means that normal interpretations of the raw measurements bias them to younger ages (Bronk Ramsey 1998, 469–74); but the following discussion will involve only low precision interpretation of the radiocarbon ages. The Scottish dates, calibrated using the Lake Suigetsu curve, allow the following conjectures. The GISP2 ice core suggests relatively warm periods each lasting about two millennia around 42,000 cal BC and around 35,000 cal BC (Jöris & Weninger 1998, fig. 1). The mean of the two earliest Inchnadamph reindeer dates lies beyond the end of the Lake Suigetsu calibration curve between about (speculatively) 50,000 cal BC and 40,000 cal BC, and may relate either to the relatively warm period from before 50,000 to about 47,000 cal BC or to the two relatively warm millennia between 43,000 and 41,000 cal BC.

The Sourlie reindeer date seems to fall in a regular period of the calibration curve and belongs around 30,000 cal BC when there were several rapidly alternating warm and cold periods. One group of Inchnadamph reindeer dates, at about 23,000–22,000 cal BC, lies in a cold period. The period around 14,000 to 12,300 cal BC, before which there is no unambiguous evidence for Late Pleistocene human activity in Britain, is roughly the end of the main glacial period. The latest Scottish reindeer date (SRR-2105) falls in the period 7540 to 7080 cal BC, during a warm period well after the end of the Younger Dryas.

Even if it does turn out that there was human activity around 40,000 cal BC in Ayrshire (and considerably more evidence will be needed than is at present available) it seems likely that the community involved was subsequently forced out of Scotland by increased cold; and the occurrence of large mammals at various subsequent periods does not force acceptance that there was a human presence. The possibility of coastal communities hunting marine mammals in both warm and cold periods and exploiting terrestrial mammals during relatively warm periods must remain open. It is very possible that the evidence for coastal foragers has been lost or submerged through rapid sea level rise since 10,000 BC (Fig. 6.8). That said, there is no unambiguous evidence for people in Scotland until about 8500 BC.

People in Scotland from 8500 BC

The history of people in Scotland, as presently demonstrated by ^{14}C dating, starts around 8500 BC. Fig. 6.4 shows the probability distribution of dates selected from the October 2002 set (see following chapter), and thus provides a first, crude approximation to relative population sizes over time. It shows two distributions so as to ameliorate some of the difficulties presented by the methods employed by previous authors (Blockley *et al.* 2000, 114–16; Housley *et al.* 1997, 43; Smith 1992,

37). Each site is counted as having two or more periods when it has dates which are significantly different from each other, and the black distribution represents each site period with one date. The grey distribution includes all dates. Fig. 6.4 must be used with considerable caution, for it need not represent the activities of more than one or two groups of people per century. Most of the qualifications listed below in considering coastality also apply.

Also, this approach assumes that it is valid to treat much of Scotland as a single (arbitrarily bounded, of course) unit, which is superficially a doubtful proposition. But perhaps it is fair to assume that people practised exogamy, given the recent estimates of between 1560 and 7020 for forager populations in Scotland, corresponding to densities of between two and nine persons per 100km^2 (Gamble 1999, table 1); and even more so if Smith (1992, 37) is right to suggest populations of around one or two people per 100km^2 through most of this period. It is difficult otherwise to understand how adequately large genetic pools could be maintained. That is not to preclude the possibility that early forager communities were unsuccessful in passing on their genes, but the assumption here is that several parts of Scotland were continuously inhabited from about 8500 BC to the onset of farming shortly after 4000 BC. If that assumption is correct, and if population densities were as low as supposed, there must have been contacts between distant communities. However, models of spatially based, and of distance-independent, connections between clusters of people provide different answers to questions about the overall degree of connectivity. If the amount of two-way movement between communities was dependent on distance, as seems on the face of it likely, optimum connectivity would have been possible to achieve only if there were very many middle- and long-range connections between distant groups. If, on the other hand, distance was not a strong factor, a small number of almost random two-way connections between groups should have led to strong connections between all groups (Watts 1999, 136–7). Among

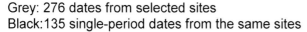

Grey: 276 dates from selected sites
Black: 135 single-period dates from the same sites

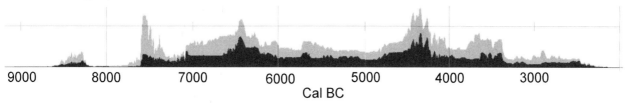

FIGURE 6.4

The probability distribution of dates from archaeological sites during the millennia succeeding 8500 BC. In both the black and grey distributions ^{14}C ages have been calibrated and summed using OxCal 3.5 and the 1998 calibration curve.

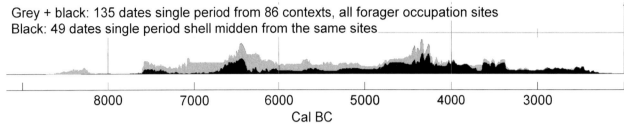

Grey + black: 135 dates single period from 86 contexts, all forager occupation sites
Black: 49 dates single period shell midden from the same sites

FIGURE 6.5

The date distribution of dates for shell midden and other occupation sites without Neolithic or later artefacts. Uncertainties in calibration of marine shells may mean that the date distributions here are skewed to slightly too early dates.

communities with perhaps a lesser attention to time than found in modern societies, distance may have not have been a dominating factor in connections between groups. If this argument is valid, even fairly infrequent two-way long distance contact could have led to a well-connected Scotland-wide network in which the foraging groups will have shared some practices and beliefs over large areas.

It is instructive to take the population estimate of between 1560 and 7020 people (while noting again that the dating evidence does not of itself provide a basis for assessing absolute figures) and equate it to the peak population a few centuries before 4000 BC. Although to do so piles conjecture on conjecture, the black area in Fig. 6.4, corresponding to one date per period, suggests low populations around 8300 BC and a peak of between 1500 and 6000 people after 6500 BC, dropping to about a third around 5000 cal BC. There was then perhaps a further rise to a peak around 4300 cal BC (the period to which the estimate of between c.1500 and c.7000 people in Scotland has here been applied). Well before the time pottery, communal burials, and other practices often associated with farmers become obvious in the dating record, around 3800 BC (Ashmore forthcoming), the population of those following forager lifestyles had halved. This does not strongly support models suggesting adoption of a sedentary lifestyle, leading to proactive adoption of farming. However, the evidence is regionally unbalanced, and the sample is small. Whether farming was introduced by incomers by at latest 3800 BC or brought in by foragers to add to their procurement strategies, the number of people following coastal foraging practices seems to have remained level until after 3400 BC.

The chronology of the use of marine resources

From c.8500 BC onward there are 49 periods of use dated from about 22 shell-midden contexts, and 86 periods of use dated from 36 other contexts without obvious Neolithic or later artefacts in occupation sites. Fig. 6.5 must be used with considerable caution, for it need not represent the activities of more than one or two groups of people per century. Also, at some sites shell may originally have been present but have failed to survive in acid soil conditions. Most of the earlier dates for shell are from the west and most of the later ones are from the east (Ashmore forthcoming). As noted above, uncertainties about the calibration of ages for shell may mean that all of these calibrated date ranges are somewhat earlier than they should be.

Nevertheless, interpreted at face value, it suggests that earlier foragers favoured non-marine resources over marine ones, and that later ones reversed that preference. Whether that is valid depends on at least six conjectures.

1. That the numbers of dated sites of particular kinds is roughly proportional to the number of originally created sites of those kinds, a doubtful proposition if early coastal sites have been destroyed or inundated by variations in sea level; see Fig. 6.8 for the possible loss of land from 10,000 BC.
2. That shell middens represent a reliance (at least a seasonal one) on coastal resources.
3. That shell middens and other occupation sites reflect population sizes in the same way as each other, a doubtful proposition if base camps tended to be preponderantly either coastal or inland.
4. That the relative degree to which shell middens and other sites reflect base camps or more transient activities did not change much over time, a conjecture which can be tested only by regional studies even more exhaustive than that recently completed in the Southern Hebrides (Mithen 2000) and the ongoing Scotland's First Settlers project (Wickham-Jones pers. comm.).
5. That either there are no sites of unrecognized types or that they have a similar chronological distribution to those of recognized types.

88

6. That the absolute number of different sites created by each group was roughly the same at all times before c.4000 BC.

Until many more areas around flint scatters and middens have been excavated the third and fourth conjectures, in particular, cannot be tested. The most rational interpretation is that changes in the proportion of coastal and inland sites may not be so marked as Fig. 6.5 suggests, because early coastal sites have disappeared through sea-level rise (see Fig. 6.8 for areas of land which may have been lost since c.10,000 to 9500 BC). There are too few data from the east to detect whether the Storegga tsunami of c.6250 to 6000 cal BC (7300 to 7200 BP) had any effect on coastal activities.

Charred hazelnut shells

Dates from hazelnut shells have a different probability distribution from those for other hazel charcoal (Fig. 6.6). The differences undoubtedly include the effects of different sample choices for producing dates. It is quite common to choose hazelnut shells to provide single entity dates for 5th millennium and earlier sites, but barley for dates in the 4th and later millennia. Nevertheless, taking the dating sample evidence in isolation from broader macro-plant studies, it seems that from about 4000 BC hazelnuts continued to be heat-treated but hazel was also used for firewood and, after 2900 BC, although hazel was much used, hazelnut shells were relatively rarely charred. The contrast suggests factors including different human choices at different periods, and the lesser reliance on hazelnuts with the availability of cereals.

None of these hazelnut shell dates comes from Shetland, Orkney, or Caithness. This is unexpected if there were people there from a fairly early date, because scrub with a hazel component is envisaged there from well before 8500 BC (Tipping 1994, 11–13; Edwards & Whittington 1997, 65–7).

An almost complete absence of charred hazelnut shell dates between 6000 and 4000 BC may well be an artefact of site and sample selection. There is a lack of evidence from pollen for a general reduction in hazel, which seems to preclude the possibility that it suffered from the hot dry summer conditions of the period from 6000 to 5000 cal BC (Edwards & Whittington 1997, 67, fig. 5.4). There remains the intriguing possibility that some more subtle explanation could be supported, such as a subordination of hazel by other species in areas favoured for occupation around 6000 cal BC, reversed for a millennium after 4000 BC by the creation of new habitats favourable to it with the introduction of farming.

Artefacts and chronology

The 21 ages for bevel-ended tools used to construct Figure 6.7 suggest a date range from between the second half of the 8th millennium cal BC (Bonsall *et al.* 1995, table 1) to about the middle of the 3rd millennium. The later dates show that bevel-ended tools are not diagnostic of pre-farming foragers even if the date from An Corran of 2230 to 1870 cal BC (AA-29313; Saville 1998, 127) is excluded from Figure 6.7 by the selection criteria used here. The sample is so small that the variations in the distribution are not significant. The most sensible conjecture is that bevel-ended tools were used in Scotland from around 8500 BC to the late 3rd millennium BC, even though they have not been dated to before 7500 BC. There are too few published dates for Scottish barbed points (5) and antler mattocks (2) to define chronological distributions, though for what it is worth the five barbed point dates are spread throughout the period and the two mattock dates are both late (Saville this volume).

A summary chronological background to human occupation

Lambeck (1995, fig. 3f) and Coles (1998, 62–4, fig. 10) speculate that Scotland was an ice-free peninsula of mainland Europe during the beginning of the present

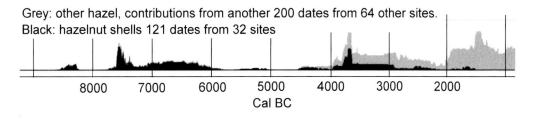

FIGURE 6.6
The probability distribution of dates for hazelnut shell and other hazel charcoal.

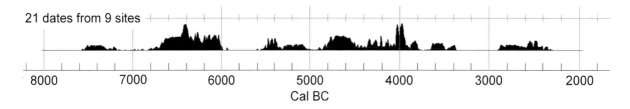

21 dates from 9 sites

8000   7000   6000   5000   4000   3000   2000

Cal BC

FIGURE 6.7
The probability distribution of dates for bevel-ended tools.

warm period, *c*.9500 BC, with Orkney forming its north-ernmost part, and Shetland and the Western Isles larger than they are at present. A North Sea inlet stretched down the east side of the peninsula from Orkney to East Anglia (Fig. 6.8). Orkney was separated from the mainland some time between 9500 and 6800 BC (Lambeck 1995, fig. 3f, 3g), perhaps not as early as suggested by McCormick and Buckland (1997, 87). Subsequent variations in Scottish coastlines differed locally.

Whittington and Edwards (1997, 14) suggest that temperature and rainfall increased rapidly from about 9500 cal BC. By a century or so after 6000 cal BC it was warmer and drier than today. Winters would have continued to be colder and summers markedly warmer than today until roughly 5000 cal BC. Figure 6.4 implies relatively lower populations during this millennium. Thereafter there seems to have been a wetter period, at least in northern Scotland (Whittington & Edwards 1997, 21).

A recent, properly cautious, review of the evidence for Early Holocene woodland by Edwards and Whit-tington (1997, 64–74) takes the pollen and microscopic charcoal evidence as far as it can be used. Birch was established throughout most of Scotland at some time between 10,000 and 9300 cal BC, and hazel spread from the extreme west of Scotland to the east during the same period. Elm spread from the south by 8300 cal BC – after people were present in southern Scotland – to the northern mainland about 5400 cal BC, and oak spread from about 7500 cal BC in the south to Aberdeenshire and Skye at some time between 4900 and 4800 cal BC. Pine was certainly present in the NW and SW before 7500 cal BC (Edwards & Whittington 1997, 65–6). The evidence for purposeful woodland clearance is usually very ambiguous (ibid., 70).

Few hard dates are available for any but a narrow range of animals. Faunal resources included elk, aurochs, red and roe deer, wild pig, and probably birds and fresh-water fish, but probably not horse, nor reindeer, although there is one date of 7540 to 7080 cal BC from a juvenile reindeer leg bone from the inner cave at Creag nan Uamh, Inchnadamph, with no known working marks or

other evidence of a human presence (SRR-2105, Murray *et al.* 1993, table 1). Marine food sources included small and large whale (including rorquals dated through their inclusion in high carse clays of the Forth to between about 6500 and 5500 cal BC), seal, shellfish, and fish (McCormick & Buckland 1997, 87, 90). However, recent work on sea-level changes in the Forth Estuary suggests maximum sea level (and thus the periods at which whales were beached further inland) may date to a significantly later period (S. Dawson pers. comm.)

A summary chronology of human occupation

Various authors have argued that Scottish tanged points imply an early occupation of Scotland (cf. Finlayson 1999, 881). However, there are no radiocarbon ages for contexts including tanged blades (Mithen 2000; Morrison & Bonsall 1989, 137) and most of these blades are part of a 'ragbag of undiagnostic forms' (Saville 2003, 343). Only those from Tiree and Shieldaig can be accepted as genuine (Ballin & Saville 2003, 124). They could be taken to support an argument that Scotland was settled at the same time as Arctic Norway (e.g. Finlayson 1999, 881; Morrison & Bonsall 1989, 135), which has produced dates that demonstrate settlement before 9500 cal BC, and perhaps before 10,000 cal BC (Thommessen 1996, fig. 1). The reindeer (associated elsewhere in Europe with foragers using tanged points) survived at least until 7540 to 7080 cal BC near Inchnadamph, not far from Shieldaig (Murray *et al.* 1993, table 1). It is therefore credible that early foragers were present soon after the end of the Younger Dryas.

However, the earliest Scottish ^{14}C ages (OxA-10143-5 & OxA-10178-80) for human activity come from single hazelnut shells at Cramond, Edinburgh, and imply settle-ment somewhere in the period between 8500 and 8300 cal BC (Lawson 2001, 124). Although now near the coast the site would have been an appreciable distance away 10,500 years ago. The next earliest date (AA-30354) comes from a single piece of *pomoideae* charcoal found in a pit at a site with abundant flake debitage, cores, and

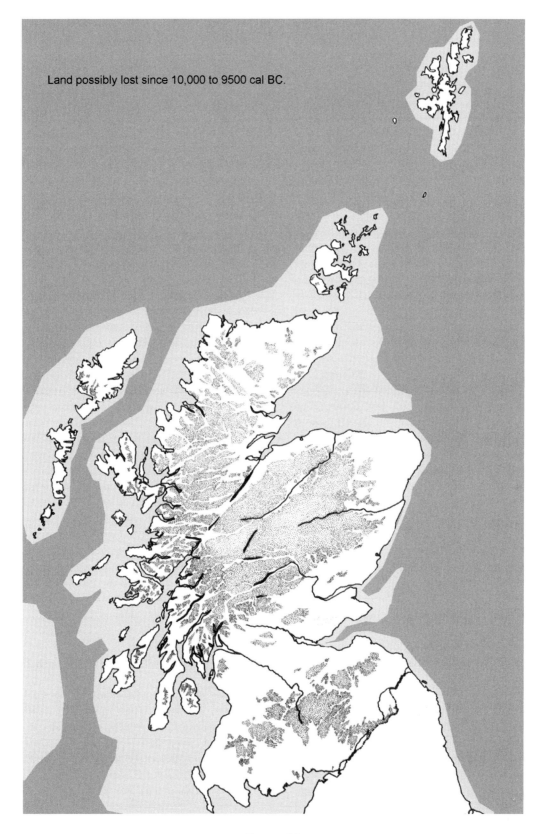

Land possibly lost since 10,000 to 9500 cal BC.

FIGURE 6.8
Scotland: land possibly lost since *c*.10,000–9500 cal BC (after Coles 1998 and Lambeck 1995).

microliths at Daer Reservoir 1 near Crawford, South Lanarkshire (Ward 1995, 87; 1997, 75; 1998, 128). It suggests occupation at some time between 8550 and 7950 cal BC.

The earliest ages (GU-1873; GU-2040) for human activity from Kinloch, the long-occupied site on the little island of Rùm, off the west coast of the Highlands (Wickham-Jones 1990, 133), and all of the 14 ages from the wind-break or shelter and hazel processing site with its microlithic assemblage at Fife Ness in eastern Scotland (Wickham-Jones & Dalland 1998a, 6; 1998b), suggest occupation near the west and east coasts within a century either way of 7500 cal BC. A recently discovered round house at East Barns, East Lothian, dates broadly around 8000 cal BC, a similar or slightly earlier date to that of another at Howick, Northumberland (Waddington *et al.* 2003; J. Gooder pers. comm.). None of these sites, however, need have been very close to the coast when they were occupied.

The next earliest site, and the earliest one showing strong evidence for a reliance on coastal resources, is a midden in the rockshelter at Druimvargie, Oban, whence a bevelled tool has been dated to between 7580 and 7180 cal BC (OxA-4608; Bonsall *et al.* 1995, table 1).

As has already been emphasized, Fig. 6.4 must be used with considerable caution, but it suggests at least a doubling of population between *c.*7500 cal BC and *c.*6500 cal BC. Even if it is not an artefact of modern site and sample selection there is no way as yet of telling whether this resulted from a steady trickle of people moving into Scotland, population growth among local groups, or a mixture of the two.

From *c.*6400 to 5000 cal BC there was a period of roughly stable forager population. A century or so after 5000 cal BC populations began to rise again, albeit slowly. The number of people engaged in this way of life peaked *c.*4400 cal BC, and fell sharply again *c.*4200 cal BC, well before the widespread adoption of farming perhaps around 3800 cal BC (Ashmore forthcoming). There is not enough information for regional comparisons within Scotland, although differences can be seen between it, Ireland, and England (Saville 2003); and it does not address some of the most challenging questions about late forager populations. It cannot contradict the possibility that Scotland became, in places, 'substantially occupied' before farming was adopted (Finlayson 1999, 883); but it does not support it. Some aspects of the forager way of life seem to have been present throughout the next two millennia, perhaps followed by people who also farmed. Shell middens and hazelnut processing sites free of distinctively non-forager artefacts diminish in numbers from *c.*3500 cal BC (*c.*5000 BP) – if current calibration of ages from marine shell are not seriously

amiss – disappearing from the dated record (except in a trivial sense) some time after *c.*2200 cal BC (*c.*3800 BP).

Conclusions

The dating evidence from Scotland summarized above does not distinguish clearly between various chronological models of settlement during Early Holocene times. It suggests the presence of foragers from *c.*8500 cal BC and a rise in population in at least the Midland Valley of Scotland and the inner western islands from *c.*7500 to 6500 cal BC, followed by a period of fairly stable population at a lower level than the peak, until a further rise starting *c.*5000 cal BC and peaking well before 4000 cal BC.

One general impression – a blend of conjectures rather than a fully-fledged model – is that practices changed gradually over the period between 8500 and 4000 cal BC, with hazelnut procurement being important in the earlier part of the period, but playing a lesser role between *c.*6000 and 4000 cal BC. Strategies including farming seem to have been widely adopted from *c.*3800 cal BC. But, while the resolution of the dates is far from optimal, it does seem that foraging practices common in the period before 4000 cal BC continued to form part of life in Scotland; indeed they continued well beyond 3500 cal BC.

Conjectures indeed; it must be remembered that known sites and artefacts represent what must be a tiny proportion of those which originally existed, and only a small proportion of the known sites and artefacts has been dated. Moreover many of the dated examples have very imprecise radiocarbon ages. If current levels of field research continue, rapid improvement can be expected, but the number of dated sites must be increased drastically, particularly north and south of the Midland Valley, if reliable patterns are to be established.

Acknowledgements

Historic Scotland funded many of the dates used here; others were kindly made available for publication in *Discovery and Excavation in Scotland* by archaeological companies and others. I am grateful to Clive Bonsall and Alan Saville for pointing me towards sources of information, to John Gooder of AOC Archaeology for information about the dates from East Barns, and to John Atkinson of GUARD for allowing me to quote the dates from Loudoun Hill. The excellent free programme Oxcal 3.5 (Bronk Ramsey 1995; 2000) was used to analyse the dates and produce some of the diagrams.

References

Ashmore, P.J. 1999. Radiocarbon dating: avoiding errors in dating by avoiding mixed samples. *Antiquity* **73**, 124–30.

Ashmore, P.J. Forthcoming. Absolute chronology. *In* G.J. Barclay and I.A. Shepherd (eds), *Scotland in Ancient Europe*. Edinburgh: Society of Antiquaries of Scotland.

Ashmore, P.J., Cook G.T. and Harkness D.D. 2000. *Radiocarbon Dates for Archaeological Sites in Scotland Issued before June 1996*. Edinburgh: Historic Scotland.

Baillie, M.G.L. 1990. Checking back on an assemblage of published radiocarbon dates. *Radiocarbon* **32**(3), 361–6.

Ballin, T. and Saville, A. 2003. An Ahrensburgian-type tanged point from Shieldaig, Wester Ross, Scotland and its implications. *Oxford Journal of Archaeology* **22**(2), 115–31.

Blackwell, P.G. and Buck, C.E. 2003. The Late Glacial human reoccupation of north-western Europe: new approaches to space-time modelling. *Antiquity* **77**, 232–40.

Blockley, S.P.E., Donahue, R.E. and Pollard A.M. 2000. Radiocarbon calibration and Late Glacial occupation in north-west Europe. *Antiquity* **74**, 112–19.

Bonsall, C., Tolan-Smith, C. and Saville, A. 1995. Direct dating of Mesolithic antler and bone artefacts from Great Britain: new results for bevelled tools and red deer antler mattocks. *Mesolithic Miscellany* **16**(1), 2–10.

Bronk Ramsey, C. 1995. Radiocarbon calibration and analysis of stratigraphy: the Oxcal program. *Radiocarbon* **37**(2), 425–30.

Bronk Ramsey, C. 1998. Probability and Dating. *Radiocarbon* **40**(1), 461–74.

Bronk Ramsey, C. 2000. OxCal 3.5 (www.rlaha.ox.ac.uk/orau.html).

Clutton-Brock, J. and MacGregor, A. 1988. An end to medieval reindeer in Scotland. *Proceedings of the Society of Antiquaries of Scotland* **118**, 23–35.

Coles, B, J. 1998. Doggerland: a speculative survey. *Proceedings of the Prehistoric Society* **64**, 45–82.

Edwards, K. J. and Whittington, G. 1997. Vegetation change. *In* K.J. Edwards and I.B.M. Ralston (eds), *Scotland: Environment and Archaeology, 8000 BC–AD 1000*, 63–82. Chichester: Wiley.

Finlayson, B. 1999. Understanding the initial colonisation of Scotland. *Antiquity* **73**, 879–84.

Gamble, C. (ed.). 1999. *Research Frameworks for the Palaeolithic and Mesolithic of Britain and Ireland*. London: Working Party for the Palaeolithic and Mesolithic Day Meeting and the Council of the Prehistoric Society.

Housley, R.A., Gamble, C.S., Street, M. and Pettitt, P. 1997. Radiocarbon evidence for the recolonisation of Northern Europe. *Proceedings of the Prehistoric Society* **63**, 35–86.

Jöris, O. and Weninger, B. 1998. Extending the 14C Calibration Curve to ca. 40,000 cal BC. *Radiocarbon* **40**(1), 495–504.

Kitegawa, H. and van der Plicht, J. 1998. A 40,000-year varve chronology from Lake Suigetsu, Japan: extension of the 14C calibration curve. *Radiocarbon* **40**(1), 505–16.

Lambeck, K. 1995. Late Devensian and Holocene shorelines of the British Isles and North Sea from models of glacio-hydro-isostatic rebound. *Journal of the Geological Society* **152**, 437–48.

Lawson, J. 2001. Cramond, Edinburgh. *Discovery and Excavation in Scotland* (new series) **2**, 124.

McCormick, F and Buckland, P.C. 1997. The Vertebrate Fauna. *In* K.J. Edwards and I.B.M. Ralston (eds), *Scotland: Environment and Archaeology, 8000 BC–AD 1000*, 83–103. Chichester: Wiley.

Mithen, S. (ed.). 2000. *Hunter-Gatherer Landscape Archaeology: The Southern Hebrides Mesolithic Project 1988-98. Vols.1–2*. Cambridge: McDonald Institute Monograph.

Morrison, A. and Bonsall, C. 1989. The early Post-Glacial settlement of Scotland: a Review. *In* C. Bonsall (ed.), *The Mesolithic in Europe*, 134–42. Edinburgh: John Donald.

Murray, N.A., Bonsall, C., Sutherland, D.G., Lawson, T.J. and Kitchener, A.C. 1993. Further radiocarbon determinations on reindeer remains of Middle and Late Devensian age from the Creag nan Uamh caves, Assynt, N W Scotland. *Quaternary Newsletter* **70**, 1–10.

Saville, A. 1998. An Corran, Staffin, Skye. *Discovery and Excavation in Scotland 1998*, 126–7.

Saville, A. 2003. Indications of regionalisation in Mesolithic Scotland. *In* L. Larsson *et al.* (eds), *Mesolithic on the Move: Papers Presented at the Sixth International Conference on the Mesolithic in Europe, Stockholm 2000*, 340–50. Oxford: Oxbow Books.

Smith, C. 1992. The population of Late Upper Palaeolithic and Mesolithic Britain. *Proceedings of the Prehistoric Society* **58**, 37–40.

Stuiver, M., Reimer, P.J., Bard, E., Beck, J.W., Burr, G.S., Hughen, K.A., Kromer, B., McCormac, G., van der Plicht, J. and Spurk, M. 1998. INTCAL98 Radiocarbon Age Calibration, 24,000–0 cal BP. *Radiocarbon* **40**(3), 1041–84.

Thommessen, T. 1996. The early settlement of northern Norway. *In* L. Larsson (ed.), *The Earliest Settlement of Scandinavia*, 235–40. Stockholm: Almquist & Wiksell International (Acta Archaeologica Lundensia, Series in 8°, No. **24**).

Tipping, R. 1994. The form and fate of Scotland's woodlands. *Proceedings of the Society of Antiquaries of Scotland* **124**, 1–54.

Waddington, C., Bailey, B., Boomer, I., Milner, N., Pederson, K., Shiel, R. and Stevenson, T. 2003. A Mesolithic coastal site at Howick, Northumberland. *Antiquity* **77** (www.antiquity.ac.uk/ProjGall/Waddington/waddington.html).

Ward, T. 1995. Daer Reservoir (Crawford Parish). *Discovery and Excavation in Scotland 1995*, 87.

Ward, T. 1997. Daer Reservoir (Crawford Parish). *Discovery and Excavation in Scotland 1997*, 75.

Ward, T. 1998. Daer Reservoir 1, Crawford. *Discovery and Excavation in Scotland 1998*, 128.

Watts, D. J. 1999. *Small Worlds*. Princeton: Princeton University Press.

Whittington, G. and Edwards, K. 1997. Climate Change. *In* K.J. Edwards and I.B.M. Ralston (eds), *Scotland: Environment and Archaeology, 8000 BC–AD 1000*, 11–22. Chichester: Wiley.

Wickham-Jones, C. R. 1990. *Rhum: Mesolithic and Later Sites at Kinloch. Excavations 1984–86.* Edinburgh: Society of Antiquaries of Scotland (Monograph **7**).

Wickham-Jones, C.R. and Dalland, M. 1998a. A small Mesolithic site at Craighead Golf Course, Fife Ness, Fife. *Tayside and Fife Archaeological Journal* **4**, 1–19.

Wickham-Jones, C.R. and Dalland, M. 1998b. Fife Ness. *Internet Archaeology* **5**.

This chapter is published with the aid of a grant from Historic Scotland.

Chapter 7

A Date List (to October 2002) for Early Foragers in Scotland

PATRICK ASHMORE

Technical comments

This list has been substantially revised since the conference and is up to date to about October 2002. It includes dates for charred remains, bone, or shell in contexts resulting from human activities, and also some wild animal bone dates. The latter are not comprehensively listed. It also includes some apparently anomalous dates for which there is usually no obvious explanation.

Ages before *c*.20,000 BP have been calibrated using the varve-based calibration curve from Lake Suigetsu, Japan (Kitegawa & van der Plicht 1998), and the rest have been calibrated using data from INTCAL98 (Stuiver *et al.* 1998) and (depending on whether they were added to this list before or after the conference) the calibration program Oxcal 2.18 or 3.5 (Bronk Ramsey 1995; 2000).

In the tables, some more realistic errors for dates obtained before the mid 1980s are indicated in the column headed 'Adjusted age BP' (although it must be emphasized that these are open to challenge, because there is no scientific basis for attaching any particular correction factor to any particular age measurement in this list, apart from those GU (Glasgow) ages covered by specific laboratory advice, and because there is no widespread agreement on how to correct early error assessment). In general, the error terms attached to more recently obtained ^{14}C age measurements are reliable (Ashmore *et al.* 2000). The calibrated dates are based on these more realistic errors because it seems most sensible to apply the precautionary principle – better to be occasionally over-cautious than to run the risk of spurious precision. The adjusted ages also attempt to take account of the marine effect on shell ages, and while it is not immediately clear that the correction of 405 years usually applied (Harkness 1983) is correct for all of the Late Pleistocene and Holocene, δ^{13}C values for shell ages do not indicate any large systematic variation.

Many of the dates are from samples which contained material from more than one entity, and may therefore contain material of different ages. They may thus correspond to no single event (Ashmore 1999). By and large the accelerator (AMS) dates – prefixed by AA- (Arizona) or OxA- (Oxford) – are from single entities.

The calibrated dates are expressed as two sigma ranges meaning that there are about 19 out of 20 chances that the true dates fall within this range. At least 15 of the dates appear to be more anomalous than can be explained by statistical variations and others, particularly some of those from Raigmore (Simpson 1996), seem to represent charcoal of mixed age. Of the remaining dates around 17 will be wrong purely because of statistical variations, in the sense that their true date will fall outside the two sigma ranges of the calibrated dates.

The date list is divided for convenience into the following major chronological groupings: before 10,000; 8000–7000; 7000–6000; 6000–5000; 5000–4000; 4000–3500 (all cal BC). Within each grouping the determinations are listed chronologically from earliest to latest, on the basis of the 'Adjusted Age BP' centrum in each case. It is appreciated that many of the samples in the final grouping probably relate to the activities of farmers, but these are of considerable relevance to questions about the transition from foraging to an economy with a strong farming element.

The columns of the date list

SITE AND COUNCIL
    The name of the site and the local authority area in which it was found.
NGR
    A four-, six-, or eight-figure British national grid reference.
REFERENCE
    The name of the submitter or a bibliographic reference.
DESCRIPTION
    A mixture of comments from the original submission and from subsequent consideration. As used here, *taphonomy* means 'how the datable material in the sample used for dating got to where it was found on the archaeological site'.

MATERIAL

A simple division of the material dated into charcoal, shell, human bone, etc.

CODE

The unique code quoted by the laboratory. Each consists of a laboratory identifier and a number. For instance, GU-1000 means age number 1000 from the GU laboratory (Glasgow University, now housed at the Scottish Universities Research Reactor Centre, East Kilbride).

CALIBRATED DATE

The Adjusted Age BP converted into a calendar date range using the programme OxCal 2.81 or 3.5 (Bronk Ramsey 1995; 2000) and the 1998 calibration curve (Stuiver *et al.* 1998). The figures quoted are for a range within which there is a 95 per cent chance that the true date lies.

LABORATORY AGE BP

The raw radiocarbon 'age' and error (one sigma) as quoted by the laboratory or primary publication. BP means before AD 1950.

ADJUSTED AGE BP

Error terms have been adjusted as explained in the introduction. Marine shell ages have been adjusted to correspond to terrestrial ages by subtracting 405 from the quoted age and increasing its error by combining it with a conversion error of ±40 radiocarbon years (Harkness 1983).

$\delta^{13}C$

Basic radiocarbon theory assumes that there is global uniformity in the natural $^{14}C/^{12}C$ ratio. This is valid for the well-mixed atmosphere, and the flora and fauna that it supports, provided an allowance is made for the extent to which isotopic fractionation occurs during the assimilation and metabolic fixation of atmospheric carbon dioxide. Although plants obtain their carbon from the atmosphere, the actual ^{14}C activity in them is lower by 3–4 per cent (equivalent to an apparent excess age of between 240 and 320 years). For each sample a $\delta^{13}C$ value is determined. This represents the difference in parts per thousand (‰) between the ratio of ^{13}C to ^{12}C in the sample to the ratio in a standard (cretaceous belemnite, *Belemnita americana*, from the Peedee formation in South Carolina, known as PDB). The fractionation between ^{14}C and ^{12}C is assumed to be twice that induced between ^{13}C and ^{12}C. A correction factor is determined which normalizes all activities to those of wood (with a ^{13}C of −25‰). Typical values for a range of sample types are as follows: −21‰ for human or animal bone; −25 to −26‰ for charcoal; −28 to −29‰ for peat; and 0‰ for marine shell. Because preparation of samples for measurement can sometimes induce a further small fractionation effect, and the quoted $\delta^{13}C$ value includes the results of this fractionation, most of the $\delta^{13}C$ measurements quoted here are not suitable for inclusion in stable isotope studies.

Acknowledgements

The technical comments are based on a collaboration with Gordon Cook and Douglas Harkness. Alan Saville helped with cross-checking and bibliographical references. I am grateful to them all, although of course any remaining errors remain my responsibility.

Dates before 10,000 cal BC

Of these 18 dates all except the purportedly charcoal dates from Loudoun Hill, which are probably from fossil soil, and four probably anomalous dates, are from reindeer antler or bone.

Site and Council	NGR	Reference	Description	Material	Code	Calibrated date	Laboratory Age BP	Adjusted Date BP	δ^{13}C
Creag nan Uamh, Highland (Sutherland)	NC 267 170	Murray et al. 1993, table 1	Single piece of reindeer calf right metacarpal from inner cave. For calibration see Kitegawa & van der Plicht (1998).	Bone, animal	OxA-3788	Out of range (c.55000 cal BC?) to 40700 ca BC	47900 ± 3600	47900 ± 3600	
Creag nan Uamh, Highland (Sutherland)	NC 267 170	Murray et al. 1993, table 1	Single piece of female reindeer shed antler from outer cave; no known working marks or other evidence of a human presence. For calibration see Kitegawa & van der Plicht (1998).	Antler	OxA-3793	Out of range (c.48100 cal BC?) to 38500 cal BC	43800 ± 2400	43800 ± 2400	
Loudoun Hill, Ayrshire	NS 6064 3734	Atkinson 2000a, 45–6	Reported as a single oak fragment (LH93/Sample 25) from a post burnt in situ and sealed beneath hard-packed gravel. The sample identification has been audited and the age has been checked for order of magnitude on a separate counter. Although the date is correct, it seems likely from subsequent analysis of samples from related deposits that the conchoidal fracture of oak has been assumed where the true identification should have been with the conchoidal fracture of fossilized soil. For calibration see Kitegawa & van der Plicht (1998).	Fossil soil	AA-20407	Out of range (c.38200 cal BC?) to c.37600 cal BC	40285 ± 1435	40285 ± 1435	−27.2
Loudoun Hill, Ayrshire	NS 6064 3734	Atkinson 2000a, 45–6	Indeterminate charcoal (LH93/Sample 30) from the primary fill of a posthole of a structure inside a palisade. Although the date is correct, it seems likely from subsequent analysis of samples from related deposits that the sample was fossil soil rather than charcoal. For calibration see Kitegawa & van der Plicht (1998).	Charcoal or fossil soil	AA-20408	c.39300 to 34700 cal BC	36685 ± 845	36685 ± 845	−25.5
Creag nan Uamh, Highland (Sutherland)	NC 267 170	Murray et al. 1993, table 1	Single piece of female reindeer shed antler from cave shaft (0–0.9m); no known working marks or other evidence of a human presence. For calibration see Kitegawa & van der Plicht (1998).	Antler	OxA-3786	c.33900 to 30600 cal BC	31580±520	31580±520	
Creag nan Uamh, Highland (Sutherland)	NC 267 170	Murray et al. 1993, table 1	Single piece of female reindeer shed antler from outer cave; no known working marks or other evidence of a human presence. For calibration see Kitegawa & van der Plicht (1998).	Antler	OxA-3985	c.34000 to 30700 cal BC	31490±570	31490±570	

Site and Council	NGR	Reference	Description	Material	Code	Calibrated date	Laboratory Age BP	Adjusted Date BP	δ¹³C
Sourlie, Irvine, Ayrshire	NS 32 38	Clutton-Brock & MacGregor 1988, 32	Fragments of reindeer antler. For calibration see Kitegawa & van der Plicht (1998).	Antler	SRR-3023	c.30800 to 30000 cal BC	29900 +430/ –410	29900 +430/ –410	
Creag nan Uamh, Highland (Sutherland)	NC 267 170	Murray et al. 1993, table 1	Single piece of female reindeer shed antler from cave shaft (1.5–2.0m); no known working marks or other evidence of a human presence. For calibration see Kitegawa & van der Plicht (1998).	Antler	OxA-3787	c.30600 to 29400 cal BC	28800 ±450	28800 ±450	
Creag nan Uamh, Highland (Sutherland)	NC 267 170	Murray et al. 1993, table 1	Single piece of female reindeer shed antler from outer cave; no known working marks or other evidence of a human presence. For calibration see Kitegawa & van der Plicht (1998).	Antler	OxA-3984	c.30200 to 29300 cal BC	28240 ±390	28240 ±390	
Creag nan Uamh, Highland (Sutherland)	NC 267 170	Murray et al. 1993, table 1	Single reindeer antler fragment from inner cave; no known working marks or other evidence of a human presence. For calibration see Kitegawa & van der Plicht (1998).	Antler	SRR-2103	c.29300 to 24400 cal BC	25360 +810/ –740	25360 +810/ –740	
Creag nan Uamh, Highland (Sutherland)	NC 267 170	Murray et al. 1993, table 1	Single reindeer antler fragment from inner cave; no known working marks or other evidence of a human presence. For calibration see Kitegawa & van der Plicht (1998).	Antler	SRR-2104	c.29300 to 23500 cal BC	24590 +790/ –720	24590 +790/ –720	
Fisher's Road East, Port Seton, East Lothian	NT 4092 7540	Haselgrove 1997	Charred barley plant remains from a grey brown sandy clay forming in the base of ditch F806, which was cut into natural; the deposit was 0.2m deep, and sealed by 1.1m ditch fills. It represents material entering the ditch after an accumulation of primary silting. This date is anomalous. For calibration see Kitegawa & van der Plicht (1998).	Charred plant remains	AA-25724	c.26000 to 23300 cal BC	23680 ±230	23680 ±230 –23.6	
Creag nan Uamh, Highland (Sutherland)	NC 267 170	Murray et al. 1993, table 1	Single piece of female reindeer shed antler from cave shaft (1.2–1.5m); no known working marks or other evidence of a human presence. For calibration see Kitegawa & van der Plicht (1998).	Antler	OxA-3792	c.23900 to 22700 cal BC	22300 ±240	22300 ±240	

Site and Council	NGR	Reference	Description	Material	Code	Calibrated date	Laboratory Age BP	Adjusted Date BP	δ¹³C
Creag nan Uamh, Highland (Sutherland)	NC 267 170	Murray et al. 1993, table 1	Mixed reindeer antler from inner cave; no known working marks or other evidence of a human presence. This sample may mix antlers of different periods (see for instance OxA-3788 at 47900±3600 BP and SRR-2105 at 8300±90 BP) and this measurement should not be used as if it dated an event.	Antler	SRR-1789	20400 to 18700 cal BC	18080±240	18080±240	
Morton A, Fife	NO 467 257	Coles 1971, 320	Charcoal pooled from lower midden T50.1/2/3. May be a mixture of older and younger charcoal.	Charcoal	NZ-1194	13600 to 11500 cal BC	12200±240	12200±340	
Pitcairn, Glenrothes, Fife	NO 273 026	Barclay 1978, 362	Probably a mixture of charcoal and coal; this measurement should not be used as if it dated an event.	Charcoal and coal	GU-1004	16000 to 8000 cal BC	12050±200	12050±2800	−23.8
Lairg, Achany Glen, Allt na Fearna, Highland (Sutherland)	NC 58 03	McCullagh & Tipping 1998, 57–8	Charcoal from context 1070, a structural posthole of House 7; most probably anomalous.	Charcoal	GU-3170	13300 to 9400 cal BC	11200±550	11200±550	
Creag nan Uamh, Highland (Sutherland)	NC 267 170	Murray et al. 1993, table 1	Mixed reindeer antler fragments from the outer cave, where there are no known working marks or other evidence of a human presence. The sample may mix antlers of different periods (see for instance OxA-3788 at 47900±3600 BP and SRR-2105 at 8300±90 BP) and this date should not be used as if it dated an event.	Antler	SRR-1788	10200 to 9300 cal BC	10080±70	10080±70	

Dates from c.10,000 cal BC to c.8000 cal BC

So far this period is only represented by the site with pits, hazelnut shells, and lithic artefacts at Cramond, Edinburgh. Although it is close to the present shoreline it may have been much further away 10,500 years ago. Any contemporaneous truly coastal sites will have been inundated during sea-level rise.

Site and Council	NGR	Reference	Description	Material	Code	Calibrated date	Laboratory Age BP	Adjusted Date BP	δ¹³C
Cramond, Edinburgh	NT 1898 7697	Lawson 2001, 124	A hazelnut shell from CR95/1066 from context 1431, the fill of a shallow scoop 1432 containing hazelnut shells and lithic artefacts, cut into the north side of Pit 1430 and sealed by context 1409.	Charred hazelnut shell	OxA-10180	8630 to 8290 cal BC	9250±60	9250±60	−26.0

Site and Council	NGR	Reference	Description	Material	Code	Calibrated date	Laboratory Age BP	Adjusted Date BP	$\delta^{13}C$
Cramond, Edinburgh	NT 1898 7697	Lawson 2001, 124	A hazelnut shell from CR95/291 context 1409, a roughly circular spread of silt with hazelnut shells and lithic artefacts sealing rubbish pits under a possible old topsoil.	Charred hazelnut shell	OxA-10145	8610 to 8290 cal BC	9230±50	9230±50	−24.9
Cramond, Edinburgh	NT 1898 7697	Lawson 2001, 124	A hazelnut shell from CR95/74/ from context 1409 a roughly circular spread of silt with hazelnut shells and lithic artefacts sealing rubbish pits under a possible old topsoil.	Charred hazelnut shell	OxA-10143	8530 to 8260 cal BC	9150±45	9150±45	−23.5
Cramond, Edinburgh	NT 1898 7697	Lawson 2001, 124	A hazelnut shell from CR95/958 from context 1426 level K from the fill of central pit 1430 with hazelnut shells and lithic artefacts.	Charred hazelnut shell	OxA-10179	8530 to 8230 cal BC	9130±65	9130±65	−23.9
Cramond, Edinburgh	NT 1898 7697	Lawson 2001, 124	A hazelnut shell from CR95/283 from context 1402, the fill of a small truncated pit 1425 sealed by context 1409.	Charred hazelnut shell	OxA-10144	8530 to 8230 cal BC	9110±60	9110±60	−23.1
Cramond, Edinburgh	NT 1898 7697	Lawson 2001, 124	A hazelnut shell from CR95/956 from context 1426 level M from the fill of central pit 1430 with hazelnut shells and lithic artefacts.	Charred hazelnut shell	OxA-10178	8530 to 8210 cal BC	9105±65	9105±65	−23.3

All of these 36 dates are from hazelnut shells apart from five charcoal dates from Daer Reservoir 1 and 2, Morton, Ben Lawers, and Lussa 1, a date from a bevel-ended tool from Druimvargie, another from Sand, a reindeer bone from Creag nan Uamh, and two probably anomalous dates from Dun Vulan and Peel of Lumphanan. Nearly all are from occupation or activity sites of forager character (the date from Druimvargie is from a rockshelter. The date from Fordhouse is from under a Neolithic burial mound. The reindeer date is an exception, as is the anomalous Lumphanan date).

Dates from c.8000 cal BC to c.7000 cal BC

Site and Council	NGR	Reference	Description	Material	Code	Calibrated date	Laboratory Age BP	Adjusted Date BP	$\delta^{13}C$
Daer Reservoir 1, Crawford, South Lanarkshire	NS 9860 0827	Ward 1998	*Pomoideae* charcoal from a pit in the flint-knapping site reported in *DES* 1995, 87 and *DES* 1997, 75.	Charcoal	AA-30354	8550 to 7950 cal BC	9075±80	9075±80	−26.7
Dun Vulan, S Uist, Western Isles	NF 7141 2982	Parker Pearson & Sharples 1999, 171, 211	Cattle toe bones in the latest soil layer (702). Anomalous.	Bone, animal	AA-10499	8300 to 7940 cal BC	8990±65	8990±65	

Site and Council	NGR	Reference	Description	Material	Code	Calibrated date	Laboratory Age BP	Adjusted Date BP	δ¹³C
Kinloch, Rùm, Highland (Lochaber)	NM 403 998	Wickham-Jones 1990, 133	Hazelnut shells from a pit fill in a settlement. Same context as GU-1874 (8515±190 BP). Recounted as 8360±70 BP (GU-1873b) in 1988.	Charred hazelnut shells	GU-1873	8000 to 7350 cal BC	8590±95	8590±95	−24.9
Kinloch, Rùm, Highland (Lochaber)	NM 403 998	Wickham-Jones 1990, 133	Hazelnut shells from a lower fill of a truncated pit in a settlement. Recounted as 8490±50 BP (GU-2040) in 1988.	Charred hazelnut shells	GU-2040	7780 to 7480 cal BC	8560±70	8560±70	−25.1
Fife Ness, Fife	NO 6365 0950	Wickham-Jones & Dalland 1998a; 1998b	A hazelnut shell from F45, the lower fill of an isolated plough truncated pit (F41) lying some 3m SW of a shelter. Though the pit could have been back-filled by old occupation deposits from the area nearby, it is most likely to be contemporary with the shelter. See also AA-25213.	Charred hazelnut shell	AA-25212	7750 to 7480 cal BC	8545±65	8545±65	−22.9
Kinloch, Rùm, Highland (Lochaber)	NM 403 998	Wickham-Jones 1990, 133	Hazelnut shells from a pit fill. Same context as GU-1873a (8590±95 BP) and 1873b (8360±70 BP). Recounted as 8060±150 BP (GU-1874b) in 1988.	Charred hazelnut shells	GU-1874	8200 to 7000 cal BC	8515±190	8515±190	−23.8
Fife Ness, Fife	NO 6365 0950	Dalland 1997; Wickham-Jones & Dalland 1998a; 1998b	A hazelnut shell from F60, the fill of pit F61, thought to be a posthole belonging to a wind-break. Part of the fill is likely to be backfill incorporating material from the surface at the time of construction of the shelter. Some of the fill may have entered the cut as the post decayed or was removed. See also AA-25209.	Charred hazelnut shell	AA-25208	7730 to 7350 cal BC	8510±70	8510±70	−23.6
Fife Ness, Fife	NO 6365 0950	Dalland, 1997; Wickham-Jones & Dalland 1998a; 1998b	A hazelnut shell from F40, the upper fill of an isolated plough truncated pit (F41), 3m SW of a shelter. The material was either dumped directly into the pit or subsided into the cut as the lower fills became more compacted. See also AA-25215.	Charred hazelnut shell	AA-25214	7680 to 7350 cal BC	8510±65	8510±65	−23.2
Fife Ness, Fife	NO 6365 0950	Dalland, 1997	A hazelnut shell from F69, the fill of a posthole (F70) situated outside and SE of a curve of postholes interpreted as part of a wind-break. It lies partly beneath a round area of dark soil (F46). Part of the fill is likely to be backfill around the post, and some of the fill may have entered the cut as the post decayed or was removed. See also AA-25205.	Charred hazelnut shell	AA-25204	7730 to 7350 cal BC	8505±75	8505±75	−23.5

Site and Council	NGR	Reference	Description	Material	Code	Calibrated date	Laboratory Age BP	Adjusted Date BP	δ¹³C
Fife Ness, Fife	NO 6365 0950	Dalland 1997; Wickham-Jones & Dalland 1998a; 1998b	Hazelnut shells from F45, the lower fill of an isolated plough truncated pit (F41), c.3m SW of a shelter. Though the pit could have been backfilled by old occupation deposits from the area nearby, it is most likely to be contemporary with the shelter. See also AA-25212.	Charred hazelnut shells	AA-25213	7610 to 7350 cal BC	8495±65	8495±65	−25.2
Kinloch, Rùm, Highland (Lochaber)	NM 403 998	Wickham-Jones 1990, 135	Hazelnut shells from a lower fill of a truncated pit in a settlement. Same sample as GU-2040a (8560±70 BP). Recounted as 8490±50 BP in 1988.	Charred hazelnut shells	GU-2040b	7650 to 7330 cal BC	8490±70	8490±70	−25.1
Fife Ness, Fife	NO 6365 0950	Dalland 1997; Wickham-Jones & Dalland 1998a; 1998b	A hazelnut shell from F40, the upper fill of an isolated plough truncated pit (F41), 3m SW of a shelter. The material was either dumped directly into the pit or subsided into the cut as the lower fills became more compacted. See also AA-25214.	Charred hazelnut shell	AA-25215	7610 to 7350 cal BC	8490±60	8490±60	−24.7
Fife Ness, Fife	NO 6365 0950	Dalland 1997; Wickham-Jones & Dalland 1998a; 1998b	A hazelnut shell from F60, the fill of pit F61, thought to be a posthole belonging to a wind-break. Part of the fill is likely to be backfill incorporating material from the surface at the time of construction of the shelter. Some of the fill may have entered the cut as the post decayed or was removed. See also AA-25208.	Charred hazelnut shell	AA-25209	7610 to 7320 cal BC	8475±75	8475±75	−26.8
Sand, Lochalsh, Highland (Skye and Lochalsh)	NG 6841 4934	Hardy 2001, 125	A bevel-ended bone artefact N62 from sample B24A NE Spit 8, from a loose unconsolidated limpet midden (013) overlying a rock-fall and covered by crushed shell and turf.	Bone, animal	OxA-10152	7750 to 7200 cal BC	8470±90	8470±90	−22.1
Fife Ness, Fife	NO 6365 0950	Dalland 1997; Wickham-Jones & Dalland 1998a; 1998b	A hazelnut shell from F46, a round area of dark soil, 2.5 × 3m, interpreted as occupation layer remains associated with the shelter. The layer was cut by plough furrows, which may indicate a high possibility of mixing with later material from the plough soil. See also AA-25210.	Charred hazelnut shell	AA-25211	7650 to 7200 cal BC	8460±85	8460±85	−25.7

Site and Council	NGR	Reference	Description	Material	Code	Calibrated date	Laboratory Age BP	Adjusted Date BP	$\delta^{13}C$
Fife Ness, Fife	NO 6365 0950	Dalland 1997; Wickham-Jones & Dalland 1998a; 1998b	A hazelnut shell from F62, the fill of pit F63, one of 7 postholes in a curve belonging to a wind-break. F62 lies partly beneath a round area of dark soil (F46). Part of the fill is likely to be backfill around the post incorporating material from the surface at the time of construction of the shelter. Some of the fill may have entered the cut as the post decayed or was removed. See also AA-25206.	Charred hazelnut shell	AA-25207	7590 to 7320 cal BC	8420±65	8420±65	−24.2
Fife Ness, Fife	NO 6365 0950	Dalland 1997; Wickham-Jones & Dalland 1998a; 1998b	A hazelnut shell from F46, a round area of dark soil, 2.5 × 3m, interpreted as occupation layer remains associated with the shelter. The layer was cut by plough furrows, which may indicate a high possibility of mixing with later material from the ploughsoil. See also AA-25211.	Charred hazelnut shell	AA-25210	7580 to 7320 cal BC	8410±60	8410±60	−21.8
Fife Ness, Fife	NO 6365 0950	Dalland 1997	A hazelnut shell from F69, the fill of a posthole (F70) situated outside and SE of a curving line of postholes interpreted as part of a wind-break structure. It lies partly beneath a round area of dark soil (F46). Part of the fill is likely to be backfill around the post, and some of the fill may have entered the cut as the post decayed or was removed. See also AA-25204.	Charred hazelnut shell	AA-25205	7580 to 7320 cal BC	8405±60	8405±60	−24.9
Kinloch, Rùm, Highland (Lochaber)	NM 403 998	Wickham-Jones 1990, 135	Hazelnut shells from a pit fill in a settlement. Same context as GU-1874 (8515±190 BP). Recounted as 8360±70 BP in 1988.	Charred hazelnut shells	GU-1873b	7580 to 7180 cal BC	8360±70	8360±70	−24.9
Fife Ness, Fife	NO 6365 0950	Dalland 1997; Wickham-Jones & Dalland 1998a; 1998b	A hazelnut shell from F62, the fill of pit F63, one of 7 postholes in a curve belonging to a wind-break. F62 lies partly beneath a round area of dark soil (F46). Part of the fill is likely to be backfill around the post incorporating material from the surface at the time of construction of the shelter. Some of the fill may have entered the cut as the post decayed or was removed. See also AA-25207.	Charred hazelnut shell	AA-25206	7580 to 7180 cal BC	8355±60	8355±60	−23.6

Site and Council	NGR	Reference	Description	Material	Code	Calibrated date	Laboratory Age BP	Adjusted Date BP	δ¹³C
Druimvargie, Oban, Argyll and Bute	NM 857 296	Bonsall et al. 1995	Bone bevelled tool from a midden in a rockshelter. (NMS X.HL 416)	Bone, animal	OxA-4608	7580 to 7180 cal BC	8340±80	8340±80	
Fife Ness, Fife	NO 6365 0950	Dalland 1997	A hazelnut shell from F83, the fill of pit F84, one of 7 postholes in a curve belonging to a wind-break. F83 lies beneath a round area of dark soil (F46). Part of the fill is likely to be backfill around the post incorporating material from the surface at the time of construction of the shelter. Some of the fill may have entered the cut as the post decayed or was removed. See also AA-25202.	Charred hazelnut shell	AA-25203	7550 to 7180 cal BC	8340±60	8340±60	−24.5
Kinloch, Rùm, Highland (Lochaber)	NM 403 998	Wickham-Jones 1990, 133	Hazelnut shells from a structural feature in settlement.	Charred hazelnut shells	GU-2150	7650 to 6800 cal BC	8310±150	8310±150	−25.7
Creag nan Uamh, Highland (Sutherland)	NC 267 170	Murray et al. 1993, table 1	Single juvenile reindeer leg bone from inner cave; no known working marks or other evidence of a human presence.	Bone, animal	SRR-2105	7540 to 7080 cal BC	8300±90	8300±90	
Fife Ness, Fife	NO 6365 0950	Dalland 1997; Wickham-Jones & Dalland 1998a; 1998b	A hazelnut shell from F83, the fill of pit F84, one of 7 postholes in a curve belonging to a wind-break. F83 lies beneath a round area of dark soil (F46). Part of the fill is likely to be backfill around the post incorporating material from the surface at the time of construction of the shelter. Some of the fill may have entered the cut as the post decayed or was removed. See also AA-25203.	Charred hazelnut shell	AA-25202	7520 to 7080 cal BC	8275±65	8275±65	−26.4
Fordhouse Barrow, Dun, Angus	NO 6658 6055	Proudfoot 2001, 122	A hazelnut shell sample 2951 from context 341, Pit 21 in a linear slot among many artefacts, mainly flint blades and flakes.	Charred hazelnut shell	OxA-10059	7450 to 7140 cal BC	8255±55	8255±55	−23.2
Lussa 1, Jura, Argyll and Bute	NR 645 874	Mercer 1980, 7	Charcoal from base of the most NE of three small rings of stones. See also SRR-159 (7963±200 BP).	Charcoal	SRR-160	8500 to 6000 cal BC	8194±350	8194±490	
Staosnaig, Colonsay, Argyll	NR 3977 9331	Mithen 2000, 373	Hazelnut shell from context 48, the fill of a small pit (cut 49), c.0.98 × 0.70m and c.0.3m deep, which is the easternmost feature located in Area A.	Charred hazelnut shell	AA-21627	7330 to 6830 cal BC	8110±60	8110±60	−25.1

Site and Council	NGR	Reference	Description	Material	Code	Calibrated date	Laboratory Age BP	Adjusted Date BP	δ¹³C
Fordhouse Barrow, Dun, Angus	NO 6658 6053	Proudfoot 1999	A single fragment of hazelnut shell from Pit 21, one of a series of Phase 1 pits sealed by the Phase 3 mound.	Hazelnut shell	OxA-8225	7310 to 6830 cal BC	8100±45	8100±45	−23.1
Kinloch, Rùm, Highland (Lochaber)	NM 403 998	Wickham-Jones 1990, 133	Hazelnut shells from a pit fill in settlement. Recounted in 1988 to 8180±50 BP.	Charred hazelnut shells	GU-2146	7310 to 6820 cal BC	8080±50	8080±50	−25.0
Peel of Lumphanan, Aberdeenshire (Kincardine and Deeside)	NJ 577 039	Newton & Talbot 1998	Waterlogged wood from a causeway, near a flint scatter (with no direct association). See also GU-1276 (50±50 BP) from the same area. Probably anomalous. Date not mentioned in Newton and Talbot 1998.	Wood	GU-1277	7450 to 6650 cal BC	8080±80	8080±110	−25.0
Auchareoch, Arran, North Ayrshire	NR 995 247	Affleck et al. 1988, 59	Hazelnut shell from pit in the south Forestry Commission quarry face.	Charred hazelnut shells	OxA-1601	7350 to 6650 cal BC	8060±90	8060±90	
Kinloch, Rùm, Highland (Lochaber)	NM 403 998	Wickham-Jones 1990, 135	Hazelnut shells from a pit fill. Same context as GU-1873 (8590±95 BP). Same sample as GU-1874a (8515±190 BP). Recounted as 8060±150 BP in 1988.	Charred hazelnut shells	GU-1874b	7500 to 6550 cal BC	8060±150	8060±150	−23.8
Daer Reservoir 2, Crawford, South Lanarkshire	NS 9842 0802	Ward 1998	Birch charcoal from a pit in the forager flint-knapping site reported in DES 1995, 87 and DES 1997, 75.	Charcoal	AA-30355	7350 to 6650 cal BC	8055±75	8055±75	−25.1
Morton A, Fife	NO 467 257	Coles 1971, 320	Charcoal pooled from occupation layers T.46.1/2. May be a mixture of older and younger charcoal.	Charcoal	NZ-1191	8000 to 6100 cal BC	8050±255	8050±355	
Ben Lawers, Perth and Kinross	NN 6139 3924	Atkinson 2000b, 125	Willow charcoal (sample 16) from the fill of a pit (16066) partly sealed by a phase 2 bank of a cellular turf structure.	Charcoal	OxA-8967	7300 to 6700 cal BC	8045±55	8045±55	−24.9

Dates from c.7000 cal BC to c.6000 cal BC

Of these 82 dates, 23 are from charcoal, 31 from hazelnut shell, and two are from mixed charcoal and hazelnut shell. Ten are from shell, 12 from animal bone, one from antler, one from wood, and two from humic soil. Most are from presumed occupation or activity sites of forager character, including several shell middens. None are self-evidently anomalous, although the soil dates probably represent material of very mixed age. The shell dates reflect a marine effect which has been allowed for in the adjusted date column by subtracting 405 years from the laboratory age. However, recent work suggests that the marine effect may have varied over time, and these adjusted ages should be used cautiously, after checking the latest work on marine reservoir corrections for this period.

Site and Council	NGR	Reference	Description	Material	Code	Calibrated date	Laboratory Age BP	Adjusted Date BP	$\delta^{13}C$
Loch Doon, South Ayrshire	NX 479 941	Edwards 1996, 118	*Rosaceae* wood charcoal from LDFS at 0.23m.	Charcoal	OxA-1598	7300 to 6600 cal BC	8000±100	8000±100	
Redkirk Point, Gretna, Dumfries and Galloway (Annandale and Eskdale)	NY 3005 6514	Masters 1981	Charcoal from an isolated hearth below transgression material. See also UB-2470 (7935±110 BP).	Charcoal	UB-2455	7350 to 6550 cal BC	8000±65	8000±110	
Camas Daraich, Skye, Highland (Skye and Lochalsh)	NG 5650 0050	Cressey *et al.* 2000a, 123	A single charred hazelnut shell (Sample 6) from fire-blackened soil rich in lithic artefacts.	Charred hazelnut shell	OxA-9783	7060 to 6690 cal BC	7985±50	7985±50	−25.1
Northton, Harris, Western Isles	NF 9753 9123	Gregory 2002, 153	A charred hazelnut shell fragment (Sample D - AMS29) from Context 7 in a possible anthropogenic horizon above natural boulder clay and sealed by layer C5. See also AA-50336 (7925±55 BP) from the same context.	Charred hazelnut shell	AA-50335	7060 to 6690 cal BC	7980±50	7980±50	−24
Lussa 1, Jura, Argyll and Bute	NR 645 874	Mercer 1980, 7	Mixed charcoal from two of three small stone rings. See also SRR-160 (8194±350 BP).	Charcoal	SRR-159	7600 to 6200 cal BC	7963±200	7963±280	
Kinloch, Rùm, Highland (Lochaber)	NM 403 998	Wickham-Jones 1990, 135	Hazelnut shells from a hollow sealed by gravel dumps on edge of burn. Same sample as GU-2147a (7880±70 BP). Recounted as 7950±50 BP in 1988.	Charred hazelnut shells	GU-2147b	7050 to 6680 cal BC	7950±50	7950±50	−25.1
Redkirk Point, Gretna, Dumfries and Galloway (Annandale and Eskdale)	NY 3005 6514	Masters 1981	Charcoal from an isolated hearth below transgression material. See also UB-2455 (8000±65 BP).	Charcoal	UB-2470	7150 to 6500 cal BC	7935±110	7935±110	

Site and Council	NGR	Reference	Description	Material	Code	Calibrated date	Laboratory Age BP	Adjusted Date BP	δ¹³C
Staosnaig, Colonsay, Argyll and Bute	NR 3977 9331	Mithen 2000, 373	Hazelnut shell from Context 17 of Pit 24, a pit used for storing hazelnuts probably capped with earlier material.	Charred hazelnut shell	AA-21624	7050 to 6650 cal BC	7935±55	7935±55	−25.1
Kinloch, Rùm, Highland (Lochaber)	NM 403 998	Wickham-Jones 1990, 133	Hazelnut shells from part of a pit complex. See also GU-2149 (7570±50 BP). Same sample recounted as 7860±50 BP (GU-2039b) in 1988.	Charred hazelnut shells	GU-2039	7050 to 6650 cal BC	7925±65	7925±65	−25.3
Northton, Harris, Western Isles	NF 9753 9123	Gregory 2002, 153	A charred hazelnut shell fragment (Sample E - AMS30) from Context 7 in a possible anthropogenic horizon above natural boulder clay and sealed by layer C5. See also AA-50335 (7980±50 BP) from the same context.	Charred hazelnut shell	AA-50336	7040 to 6650 cal BC	7925±55	7925±55	−26.3
Fordhouse Barrow, Dun, Angus	NO 6658 6054	Proudfoot 2001, 122	A hazelnut shell sample 2950 from context 330 in a layer containing numerous artefacts.	Charred hazelnut shell	OxA-10058	7040 to 6640 cal BC	7920±50	7920±50	−25.1
Kinloch, Rùm, Highland (Lochaber)	NM 403 998	Wickham-Jones 1990, 135	Hazelnut shells from a pit fill in a settlement. Same sample as GU-2145a (7850±50 BP). Recounted as 7900±50 BP in 1988.	Charred hazelnut shells	GU-2145b	7040 to 6640 cal BC	7900±50	7900±50	−25.0
Fordhouse Barrow, Dun, Angus	NO 6658 6053	Proudfoot 2001, 122	A hazelnut shell from sample 2909 from context 338, a fill of Pit 20 (context 339).	Charred hazelnut shell	OxA-10057	7040 to 6630 cal BC	7890±50	7890±50	−23.9
Druimvargie, Oban, Argyll and Bute	NM 857 296	Bonsall et al. 1995	Bone bevelled tool from a midden in a rockshelter. (NMS X.HL 424)	Bone, animal	OxA-4609	7100 to 6500 cal BC	7890±80	7890±80	
Kinloch, Rùm, Highland (Lochaber)	NM 403 998	Wickham-Jones 1990, 133	Hazelnut shells from a hollow sealed by gravel dumps on edge of burn. Recounted as 7950±50 (GU-2147b) in 1988.	Charred hazelnut shells	GU-2147	7050 to 6500 cal BC	7880±70	7880±70	−25.1
Auchareoch, Arran, North Ayrshire	NR 995 247	Affleck et al. 1988, 59	Oak wood charcoal from the west Forestry Commission quarry face.	Charcoal	OxA-1600	7050 to 6500 cal BC	7870±90	7870±90	
Kinloch, Rùm, Highland (Lochaber)	NM 403 998	Wickham-Jones 1990, 135	Hazelnut shells from part of a pit complex. See also GU-2149 (7570±50 BP). Same sample as GU-2039a (7925±65 BP), recounted in 1988.	Charred hazelnut shells	GU-2039b	7030 to 6570 cal BC	7860±50	7860±50	−25.3

Site and Council	NGR	Reference	Description	Material	Code	Calibrated date	Laboratory Age BP	Adjusted Date BP	δ¹³C
Sand, Lochalsh, Highland (Skye and Lochalsh)	NG 6841 4934	Hardy 2001, 125	A bevel-ended bone artefact N70 from sample B24A NE Spit 4, from a loose unconsolidated limpet midden (013) overlying a rock-fall and covered by crushed shell and turf.	Bone, animal	OxA-10384	7050 to 6500 cal BC	7855±60	7855±60	−21.1
Kinloch, Rùm, Highland (Lochaber)	NM 403 998	Wickham-Jones 1990, 133	Hazelnut shells from a pit fill in a settlement. Recounted as 7900±50 BP (GU-2145b) in 1988.	Charred hazelnut shells	GU-2145	7050 to 6500 cal BC	7850±50	7850±50	−25.0
Sand, Lochalsh, Highland (Skye and Lochalsh)	NG 6841 4934	Hardy 2001, 125	A bevel-ended bone artefact N60 from sample B24B NE Spit 7 from a loose unconsolidated limpet midden (013) overlying a rock-fall and covered by crushed shell and turf.	Bone, animal	OxA-10175	7050 to 6450 cal BC	7825±55	7825±55	−21.1
Cnoc Sligeach, Oronsay, Argyll and Bute	NR 3586 8801	Jardine & Jardine 1983	Inner part of shells of *Ostrea edulis*, *Patella spp.*, *Arctica islandica*, and *Littorina spp.* Within storm beach gravel deposit in CS73/11. See also Birm-463m (7210±130 BP).	Shell	Birm-463I	7500 to 6200 cal BC	8220±170	7815±240	−0.1
Druimvargie, Oban, Argyll and Bute	NM 857 296	Bonsall & Smith 1989, 38	Bone uniserial barbed point ('harpoon') NMS HL 404 from a midden in a rockshelter.	Bone, animal	OxA-1948	7050 to 6450 cal BC	7810±90	7810±90	
Newton, Islay, Argyll and Bute	NR 341 628	McCullagh 1989	Hazelnut shells from F436, the basal layer in F35, Area 2, a sub-rectangular depression full of microliths, hazelnut shells, and charcoal, interpreted as a dwelling or flint-working area.	Charred hazelnut shells	GU-1954	7050 to 6450 cal BC	7805±90	7805±90	−24.4
Ulva Cave, Argyll and Bute	NM 431 384	Bonsall *et al.* 1994	Humic fraction of a black soil from the lowermost Holocene deposit, with marine shells in hollow in Pleistocene surface. The δ¹³C value implies little contamination with carbon from marine shells.	Soil	GU-2704	7150 to 6250 cal BC	7800±160	7800±160	−26.4
Staosnaig, Colonsay, Argyll and Bute	NR 3977 9331	Mithen 2000, 373	Hazelnut shell from Context 17 of Pit 24, a pit used for storing hazelnuts, probably capped with earlier material.	Charred hazelnut shell	AA-21621	6750 to 6460 cal BC	7780±55	7780±55	−25.6
Staosnaig, Colonsay, Argyll and Bute	NR 3977 9331	Mithen 2000, 373	Hazelnut shell from Context 57, the main fill of feature 41, a stone lined boat-shaped pit, 2m SW of feature 24, the large circular pit.	Charred hazelnut shell	AA-21625	6750 to 6460 cal BC	7780±55	7780±55	−25.5

Site and Council	NGR	Reference	Description	Material	Code	Calibrated date	Laboratory Age BP	Adjusted Date BP	δ¹³C
Newton, Islay, Argyll and Bute	NR 343 627	McCullagh 1989	Hazelnut shells from F408, the uppermost layer in F35, Area 2, a sub-rectangular depression full of microliths, hazelnut shells, and charcoal, interpreted as a dwelling or flint-working area.	Charred hazelnut shells	GU-1953	7400 to 6100 cal BC	7765±225	7765±225	−25.3
Sand, Lochalsh, Highland (Skye and Lochalsh)	NG 6841 4934	Cressey et al. 2000b, 124	A single piece of birch charcoal (sample 9/8) from the same spit 8 near the edge of a midden as the bevel-ended tool N19 dated by OxA-9281 to 7715±50 BP and the antler dated by OxA-9280 to 7520±50 BP.	Charcoal	OxA-9343	6680 to 6460 cal BC	7765±50	7765±50	−24.6
Staosnaig, Colonsay, Argyll and Bute	NR 3977 9331	Mithen 2000, 373	Hazelnut shell from Context 17 of Pit 24, a pit used for storing hazelnuts, probably capped with earlier material.	Charred hazelnut shell	AA-21619	6690 to 6460 cal BC	7760±55	7760±55	−24.8
Staosnaig, Colonsay, Argyll and Bute	NR 3977 9331	Mithen 2000, 373	Hazelnut shell fragments lying immediately adjacent to each other within fill 17 of feature 24, a stone-lined pit in an area of hearths and pits.	Charred hazelnut shells	Q-3278	7050 to 6250 cal BC	7720±110	7720±110	
Sand, Lochalsh, Highland (Skye and Lochalsh)	NG 6841 4934	Cressey et al. 2000b, 124	Bevel-ended tool (N19) made from deer bone from the same spit 8 of the outer edge of a midden as the antler dated by OxA-9280 to 7520±50 BP and charcoal dated by OxA-9343 to 7765±50 BP	Bone, animal	OxA-9281	6650 to 6440 cal BC	7715±55	7715±55	−21.3
Camas Daraich, Skye, Highland (Skye and Lochalsh)	NG 5650 0050	Cressey et al. 2000a, 123	A single charred hazelnut shell (Sample 5) from a layer rich in lithic artefacts and fuel ash.	Charred hazelnut shell	OxA-9782	6640 to 6420 cal BC	7670±55	7670±55	−24.2
Staosnaig, Colonsay, Argyll and Bute	NR 3977 9331	Mithen 2000, 373	Hazelnut shell from Context 17 of Pit 24, a pit used for storing hazelnuts, probably capped with earlier material.	Charred hazelnut shell	AA-21623	6640 to 6420 cal BC	7665±55	7665±55	−27.6
Staosnaig, Colonsay, Argyll and Bute	NR 3977 9331	Mithen 2000, 373	Hazelnut shell from Context 17 of Pit 24, a pit used for storing hazelnuts, probably capped with earlier material.	Charred hazelnut shell	AA-21622	6640 to 6410 cal BC	7660±55	7660±55	−25.7

Site and Council	NGR	Reference	Description	Material	Code	Calibrated date	Laboratory Age BP	Adjusted Date BP	δ13C
Ulva Cave, Argyll and Bute	NM 431 384	Bonsall et al. 1994	Patella shell (inner) from the basal layer of a midden in area C. See also GU-2601 (8020±70 BP).	Shell	GU-2600	6660 to 6260 cal BC	8060±70	7655±80	0.5
Raschoille, Oban, Argyll and Bute	NM 8547 2888	Bonsall 1999	Humerus of a red deer from lower deposits in a cave.	Bone, animal	OxA-8396	6650 to 6260 cal BC	7640±80	7640±80	−21.8
Loch A Squir, Raasay, Highland (Skye and Lochalsh)	NG 6084 5286	Cressey et al. 2000c, 123	A single piece of birch charcoal (1/3) from spit 3 from midden layers at the rear of a rockshelter. This spit is higher than one dated by OxA-9254 to 2055±39 BP.	Charcoal	OxA-9305	6640 to 6250 cal BC	7620±75	7620±75	−26.6
Ulva Cave, Argyll and Bute	NM 431 384	Bonsall et al. 1994	Patella shell (outer) from the basal layer of a midden in area C. See also GU-2600 (8060±70 BP).	Shell	GU-2601	6640 to 6250 cal BC	8020±70	7615±80	0.5
Kinloch, Rùm, Highland (Lochaber)	NM 403 998	Wickham-Jones 1990, 135	Charcoal from a fill of pit complex in settlement; see also GU-2039 (7925±65 BP). Same sample as GU-2148a. Recounted as 7600±50 BP in 1988.	Charcoal	GU-2149b	6590 to 6260 cal BC	7600±50	7600±50	−25.3
An Corran, Skye, Highland (Skye and Lochalsh)	NG 490 685	Saville & Miket 1994	Bone (red deer) bevelled tool from a shell midden, in deposits containing microliths, on a ledge at the base of east-facing cliffs.	Bone, animal	OxA-4994	6600 to 6230 cal BC	7590±90	7590±90	
Camas Daraich, Skye, Highland (Skye and Lochalsh)	NG 5650 0050	Cressey 2001, 124	Hazelnut shell from CD 15(A), fuel deposits in a possible hearth overlain by more fuel deposits.	Charred hazelnut shell	OxA-9971	6570 to 6230 cal BC	7575±75	7575±75	−27.4
Raschoille, Oban, Argyll and Bute	NM 8547 2888	Bonsall 1999	Metatarsal of a red deer from lower deposits in a cave.	Bone, animal	OxA-8397	6590 to 6230 cal BC	7575±75	7575±75	−21.5
Kinloch, Rùm, Highland (Lochaber)	NM 403 998	Wickham-Jones 1990, 133	Charcoal from a fill of pit complex in settlement; see also GU-2039 (7925±65 BP). Recounted as 7600±50 BP (GU-2149) in 1988.	Charcoal	GU-2149	6500 to 6250 cal BC	7570±50	7570±50	−25.3
Camas Daraich, Skye, Highland (Skye and Lochalsh)	NG 5650 0050	Cressey et al. 2000a, 123	A single charred hazelnut shell (CD 15(B)) from a possible hearth under a series of layers rich in fuel ash.	Charred hazelnut shell	OxA-9784	6470 to 6240 cal BC	7545±55	7545±55	−25.4

Site and Council	NGR	Reference	Description	Material	Code	Calibrated date	Laboratory Age BP	Adjusted Date BP	δ¹³C
Sand, Lochalsh, Highland (Skye and Lochalsh)	NG 6841 4934	Cressey et al. 2000b, 124	Bevel-ended tool (N18) made from deer bone from spit 7 of a midden.	Bone, animal	OxA-9282	6470 to 6240 cal BC	7545±50	7545±50	−20.8
Coulererach, Islay, Argyll and Bute	NR 208 652	Mithen 2000, 228	Charcoal from an occupation horizon (trench 1) associated with a narrow blade artefact scatter sealed below 1.75m of peat. Abrasion on charcoal fragment suggested derivation from a hearth.	Charcoal	OxA-4924	6530 to 6210 cal BC	7530±80	7530±80	−26.4
Northton, Harris, Western Isles	NF 9753 9123	Gregory 2002, 153	A charred hazelnut fragment (Sample A – AMS26) from Context 5 in a possible occupation horizon (layer C7) sealed by layer C10. See also AA-50333 (7395±45 BP) and AA-50334 (7420±45 BP) from the same context.	Charred hazelnut shell	AA-50332	6510 to 6210 cal BC	7525±80	7525±80	−24.4
Sand, Lochalsh, Highland (Skye and Lochalsh)	NG 6841 4934	Cressey et al. 2000b, 124	A single piece of antler (sample 9/8) from the same spit 8 of the outer edge of a midden as the bevel-ended tool N19 dated by OxA-9281 to 7715±50 BP and charcoal dated by OxA-9343 to 7765±50 BP.	Antler	OxA-9280	6460 to 6240 cal BC	7520±50	7520±50	−21.8
Sketewan, Perth and Kinross	NN 9440 5210	Mercer & Midgley 1997, 303	Oak charcoal and birch stake from F206 and F274 in the pre-cairn soil layer. May mix older and younger material and probably should not be used.	Charcoal	GU-2678	6470 to 6110 cal BC	7500±80	7500±80	−26.3
Raschoille, Oban, Argyll and Bute	NM 8547 2888	Bonsall 1999, 112	Bevel-ended tool made from the metapodial of a red deer from lower deposits in a cave.	Bone, animal	OxA-8398	6460 to 6110 cal BC	7480±75	7480±75	−21.6
Northton, Harris, Western Isles	NF 9753 9123	Gregory 2002, 153	A charred hazelnut fragment (Sample C – AMS28) from Context 5 in a possible occupation horizon (layer C7) sealed by layer C10. See also AA-50333 (7395±45 BP) and AA-50332 (7525±80 BP) from the same context.	Charred hazelnut shell	AA-50334	6400 to 6100 cal BC	7420±45	7420±45	−24.1
Staosnaig, Colonsay, Argyll and Bute	NR 3977 9331	Mithen 2000, 373	Hazelnut shell from sample ST9403, spit 4, quadrat 4006. Material from exactly the same sample as AA-21620 (7040±55 BP); and see AA-21618.	Charred hazelnut shell	AA-26227	6420 to 6090 cal BC	7420±65	7420±65	

Site and Council	NGR	Reference	Description	Material	Code	Calibrated date	Laboratory Age BP	Adjusted Date BP	δ¹³C
North Carn, Jura, Argyll and Bute	NR 685 939	Mercer 1972, 4	Charcoal from the base of a small sunken L-shaped setting, perhaps a hearth and seat.	Charcoal	SRR-161	6460 to 6030 cal BC	7414±80	7414±110	
Bolsay Farm, Islay, Argyll and Bute	NR 2253 5736	Mithen 2000, 281	Hazel from context 4, quadrat (67,57), a largely undisturbed horizon of the forager occupation or activity site. See AA-21631 and AA-21633.	Charcoal	AA-21632	6400 to 6090 cal BC	7400±55	7400±55	−24.3
Northton, Harris, Western Isles	NF 9753 9123	Gregory 2002, 153	A charred hazelnut fragment (Sample B – AMS27) from Context 5 in a possible occupation horizon (layer C7) sealed by layer C10. See also AA-50332 (7525±80 BP) and AA-50334 (7420±45 BP) from the same context.	Charred hazelnut shell	AA-50333	6390 to 6090 cal BC	7395±45	7395±45	−23.7
Lón Mór, Oban, Argyll and Bute	NM 853 2835	Bonsall et al. 1993	Hazelnut shell from a midden 0.3–0.4m below the modern ground surface, in sandy loam soil, containing numerous lithic artefacts (including microliths) and charcoal fragments.	Charred hazelnut shell	AA-8793	6390 to 6080 cal BC	7385±60	7385±60	−25.0
Morton A, Fife	NO 467 257	Coles 1971, 320	Charcoal pooled from occupation layers in T.43/44/46. May be a mixture of older and younger charcoal.	Charcoal	NZ-1302	7000 to 5600 cal BC	7330±200	7330±280	
Auchareoch, Arran, North Ayrshire	NR 995 247	Affleck et al. 1988, 59	Charred hazelnut shell from a fire-spot.	Charred hazelnut shells	OxA-1599	6380 to 5990 cal BC	7300±90	7300±90	
Castle Street, Inverness, Highland (Inverness)	NH 665 452	Wordsworth 1985, 95	Elm, pine, and birch charcoal from several lenses in lower horizon of a midden.	Charcoal	GU-1376	7100 to 5500 cal BC	7275±235	7275±330	−25.5
Raschoille, Oban, Argyll and Bute	NM 8547 2888	Bonsall 1999	Bevel-ended tool made from the metatarsal of a red deer from lower deposits in a cave.	Bone, animal	OxA-8535	6340 to 5920 cal BC	7265±80	7265±80	−21.4
Bolsay Farm, Islay, Argyll and Bute	NR 2253 5736	Mithen 2000, 281	Bulked sample of charcoal fragments from fill of feature cut 26, fill 16. This feature sealed by in situ occupation deposits and colluvium.	Charcoal	Q-3219	6450 to 5800 cal BC	7250±145	7250±145	
Raschoille, Oban, Argyll	NM 8547 2888	Bonsall 1999	Single hazelnut shell from lower deposits of a cave.	Charred hazelnut shell	OxA-8439	6220 to 6010 cal BC	7250±55	7250±55	−25.1

Site and Council	NGR	Reference	Description	Material	Code	Calibrated date	Laboratory Age BP	Adjusted Date BP	δ¹³C
Loch A Squir, Raasay, Highland (Skye and Lochalsh)	NG 6084	Cressey et al. 2000c, 123	Bevel-ended deer bone tool (N25) from spit 2 from midden layers at the rear of a rockshelter. This spit is higher than one dated by OxA-9254 to 2055±39 BP.	Bone, animal	OxA-9255	6220 to 6000 cal BC	7245±55	7245±55	−21.6
Kinloch, Rum, Highland (Lochaber)	NM 403 998	Wickham-Jones 1990, 135	Charcoal and charred hazelnut shells from a buried soil at edge of burn in settlement. Same sample as GU-2211a (7140±130 BP) recounted as 7220±100 in 1988.	Charcoal and charred hazelnut shells	GU-2211b	6260 to 5840 cal BC	7220±100	7220±100	−25.8
Chapelfield, Cowie, Stirling	NS 8363 8951	Atkinson 2000c, 126	A single piece of hazel charcoal (sample 235) from charcoal stained loam (018) in the large stake-defined Pit V.	Charcoal	OxA-9298	6240 to 5910 cal BC	7220±80	7220±80	−26.4
Cnoc Coig, Oronsay, Argyll and Bute	NR 360 885	Jardine 1977	Inner part of a shell from a midden; same shell as Birm-326Y (7290±120 BP) and Birm-326Z (7240±200 BP).	Shell	Birm-326X	6500 to 5650 cal BC	7610±150	7205±215	
Newbie Cottages, Annan, Dumfries and Galloway	NY 165 652	Cressey 2000; Cressey et al. 2001	An oak stump found in an upright position on the edge of a river channel. It sat on a peat layer exposed in the channel section. The oak tree had died in situ, with root and bole as they grew.	Wood	AA-30349	6220 to 5910 cal BC	7185±65	7185±65	−31.8
Raschoille, Oban, Argyll and Bute	NM 8547 2888	Bonsall 1999	Part of a cockle shell from lower deposits of a cave.	Shell	OxA-8539	6170 to 5920 cal BC	7580±45	7175±45	3.0
Kinloch, Rum, Highland (Lochaber)	NM 403 998	Wickham-Jones 1990, 133	Charcoal and charred hazelnut shells from a buried soil at edge of burn in settlement. Recounted as 7220±100 BP (GU-2211b) in 1988.	Charcoal and charred hazelnut shells	GU-2211	6250 to 5700 cal BC	7140±130	7140±130	−25.8
Glean Mor, Islay, Argyll and Bute	NR 239 577	Mithen 2000, 203	Charcoal fragment from an occupation horizon just above and within iron pan in a heavily podsolized soil, sealed by 0.5m of peat, associated with a dense microlithic assemblage. Same context as Beta-32237 (3390±90 BP), so presumably in a secondary context.	Charcoal	Beta-32238	6220 to 5720 cal BC	7100±125	7100±125	

Site and Council	NGR	Reference	Description	Material	Code	Calibrated date	Laboratory Age BP	Adjusted Date BP	δ13C
Ulva Cave, Argyll and Bute	NM 431 384	Bonsall et al. 1994	Humin fraction of a black soil from the lowermost Holocene deposit, with marine shells in hollow in Pleistocene surface. The δ13C value implies little contamination with carbon from marine shells.	Soil	GU-2705	6220 to 5720 cal BC	7100±130	7100±130	−23.6
Castle Street, Inverness, Highland (Inverness)	NH 665 452	Wordsworth 1985, 91	Charcoal from different spots in the upper horizon of a midden, from below highest local marine transgression. (N.b. this date cited incorrectly on p.96 of the original publication.)	Charcoal	GU-1377	6210 to 5720 cal BC	7080±85	7080±120	−25.5
Staosnaig, Colonsay, Argyll and Bute	NR 3977 9331	Mithen 2000, 373	Hazelnut shell from Context 17 of Pit 24, a pit used for storing hazelnuts probably capped with earlier material. A residue of this sample was processed and produced the date AA-26227 (7420±65 BP).	Charred hazelnut shell	AA-21620	6020 to 5780 cal BC	7040±55	7040±55	−25.5
Home Farm, Castle Menzies, Perth and Kinross	NN 8305 4935	Carter 2001, 126	Oak charcoal from sample 067 from dark grey brown silty sand and charcoal 453 filling a posthole or pit 282 which did not form part of either the alignments or the arc of postholes on this site.	Charcoal	OxA-9815	6000 to 5790 cal BC	7030±45	7030±45	−24
Raschoille, Oban, Argyll and Bute	NM 8547 2888	Bonsall 1999	Part of a cockle shell from lower deposits of a cave.	Shell	OxA-8501	5990 to 5730 cal BC	7390±55	6985±55	1.4
Stoneyfield, Raigmore, Inverness, Highland (Inverness)	NH 687 456	Simpson 1996, 82–3 SC26068/2B	Charcoal from Cist III: a rough cist abutting on outer face of stone circle. This date is aberrant; archaeologically it should be after 3000 BC; it may represent mixed forager and later charcoal.	Charcoal	SRR-431	6250 to 5450 cal BC	6921±150	6920±210	−25.2
Raschoille, Oban, Argyll and Bute	NM 8547 2888	Bonsall 1999	Part of a cockle shell from lower deposits of a cave.	Shell	OxA-8540	5880 to 5660 cal BC	7300±50	6895±50	2.6
Seal Cottage, Oronsay, Argyll and Bute	NR 361 885	Jardine 1977	Shell (middle) from a midden; same shell as Birm-326X (7610±150 BP) and Birm-326Z (7240±200 BP).	Shell	Birm-326Y	6200 to 5450 cal BC	7290±120	6885±175	

Site and Council	NGR	Reference	Description	Code	Material	Calibrated date	Laboratory Age BP	Adjusted Date BP	δ¹³C
Chapelfield, Cowie, Stirling	NS 8363 8957	Atkinson 1997	Pine charcoal from the upper fill (087) of slot 066 within the entranceway to structure H (003). This deposit (087) was partially cut by post (057/058) and lay over the basal fill (085) of the slot, at the S end of the feature. The charcoal may have been burnt in situ but is probably residual.	AA-26225	Charcoal	5890 to 5560 cal BC	6840±85	6840±85	-26.1
Seal Cottage, Oronsay, Argyll and Bute	NR 361 885	Jardine 1977	Shell (outer) from a midden; same shell as Birm-326Y (7290±120 BP) and Birm-326X (7610±150 BP).	Birm-326Z	Shell	6400 to 5100 cal BC	7240±200	6835±285	
Bolsay Farm, Islay, Argyll and Bute	NR 2253 5736	Mithen 2000, 281	Alder from context 4, quadrat (67,57), a largely undisturbed horizon of the forager occupation or activity site. See AA-21631 and AA-21632.	AA-21633	Charcoal	5800 to 5620 cal BC	6810±55	6810±55	-26.2
Cnoc Sligeach, Oronsay, Argyll and Bute	NR 3586 8801	Jardine & Jardine 1983	Middle part of shells of Ostrea edulis, Patella spp., Arctica islandica and Littorina spp. Within storm beach gravel deposit in CS73/11. See also Birm-463l (8220±170 BP).	Birm-463m	Shell	6100 to 5350 cal BC	7210±130	6805±185	-1.2

Dates from c.6000 cal BC to c.5000 cal BC

Of these 38 dates 22 are from charcoal and three are from charred hazelnut shells. Five are from shell, five from animal bone, two from antler, and one from ?decayed wood. Most are from occupation or activity sites of forager character including middens, but those from Tulloch Wood, Chapelfield, Lairg, and Balnuaran of Clava are residual in later features. The antler point from Cumstoun came from a river. The shell dates reflect a marine effect which has been allowed for in the adjusted date column by subtracting 405 years from the laboratory age. However, recent work suggests that the marine effect may have varied over time, and these adjusted ages should be used cautiously, after checking the latest work on marine reservoir corrections for this period.

Site and Council	NGR	Reference	Description	Code	Material	Calibrated date	Laboratory Age BP	Adjusted Date BP	δ¹³C
Rockside, Islay, Argyll and Bute	NR 221 638	Mithen 2000, 214	Charcoal from an occupation horizon (context 2 trench 1) containing a microlithic assemblage under c.1.5m of colluvium. Context below those of Beta-37625 (3980± and Beta-37626 (3420±70BP).	Beta-37624	Charcoal	5740 to 5620 cal BC	6800±40	6800±40	
Morton A, Fife	NO 467 257	Coles 1971, 320	Charcoal pooled from occupation layers in T.47/55/56.1/2/3. May be a mixture of older and younger charcoal.	NZ-1192	Charcoal	6200 to 5300 cal BC	6790±150	6790±210	

Site and Council	NGR	Reference	Description	Material	Code	Calibrated date	Laboratory Age BP	Adjusted Date BP	$\delta^{13}C$
Tulloch Wood, Forres, Moray	NJ 089 560	Carter 1993, 228–9	Charcoal from the fill of a feature under axial bank 2; dates in-filling of feature (possibly natural).	Charcoal	GU-3096	5740 to 5480 cal BC	6740±70	6740±70	−26.2
Morton A, Fife	NO467257	Coles 1971, 320	Charcoal pooled from a pair of hearths. May be a mixture of older and younger charcoal.	Charcoal	Q-948	6200 to 5000 cal BC	6735±180	6735±250	
Chapelfield, Cowie, Stirling	NS 8363 8957	Atkinson 1997	Pine charcoal from the basal fill (694d) of pit II (776), sealed by floor layer 687, which was related to the use of structure E. Pit II dug as a single event and partially backfilled relatively rapidly with fill 694d. Largish lumps of charcoal were present throughout the fill.	Charcoal	GU-7201	5730 to 5480 cal BC	6710±70	6710±70	−25.7
Chapelfield, Cowie, Stirling	NS 8363 8957	Atkinson 1997	Pine charcoal from the upper fill (018) of pit 5 (005). This fill was a single event over the clay lining (244) of the pit and contained a high %age of carbonized material. The charcoal within 018 had not been burnt in situ.	Charcoal	AA-26226	5720 to 5480 cal BC	6705±60	6705±60	−26.1
MacArthur Cave, Oban, Argyll and Bute	NM859304	Bonsall & Smith 1989, 38	Antler from a biserial barbed point (NMS HL187) from a midden in a cave.	Antler	OxA-1949	5730 to 5480 cal BC	6700±80	6700±80	
Balnuaran Of Clava, Highland	NH 7575 4445	Bradley 2000, 115	A single piece of pine charcoal from the packing of the socket retaining one of the uprights of the stone circle enclosing the central ring cairn. The charcoal was all found in a compact group in the midst of the packing and did not occur elsewhere. It was presumably residual.	Charcoal	AA-21260	5730 to 5470 cal BC	6670±85	6670±85	−25.8
Cumstoun, Dumfries and Galloway (Stewartry)	NX 68 53	Bonsall & Smith 1992, 29	An antler biserial barbed point from the bed of the River Dee (Accession number 2755: Stewartry Museum, Kirkcudbright).	Antler	OxA-3735	5710 to 5480 cal BC	6665±70	6665±70	
Sand, Lochalsh, Highland (Skye and Lochalsh)	NG 6841 4934	Hardy 2001, 125	A bevel-ended bone artefact from sample A1B NE Spit 9 from a shell-free organic midden (022) overlying a sterile palaeosol and covered by the main shell midden.	Bone, animal	OxA-10176	5630 to 5470 AD	6605±50	6605±50	−20.9

Site and Council	NGR	Reference	Description	Material	Code	Calibrated date	Laboratory Age BP	Adjusted Date BP	δ¹³C
Tulloch Wood, Forres, Moray	NJ 089560	Carter 1993, 228–9	Charcoal from the fill of a feature, possibly natural, under a cairn.	Charcoal	GU-3092	5620 to 5360 cal BC	6530±60	6530±60	−26.8
Cnoc Sligeach, Oronsay, Argyll and Bute	NR 3586 8801	Jardine & Jardine 1983	Inner part of valve of shells of *Arctica islandica* within occupation layer in CS73/11. See also Birm-464m (6840±160 BP).	Shell	Birm-464I	5850 to 4850 cal BC	6910±160	6505±230	0.2
Sand, Lochalsh, Highland (Skye and Lochalsh)	NG 6841 4934	Hardy 2001, 125	A bevel-ended bone artefact from sample A2B SW Spit 10 from a shell-free organic midden (022) overlying a sterile palaeosol and covered by the main shell midden.	Bone, animal	OxA-10177	5540 to 5320 cal BC	6485±55	6485±55	−21.8
Raschoille, Oban, Argyll and Bute	NM 8547 2888	Bonsall 1999	Metatarsal of a red deer from lower deposits in a cave.	Bone, animal	OxA-8538	5750 to 4950 cal BC	6460±180	6460±180	−22.1
Lairg, Achany Glen, Allt na Fearna, Highland (Sutherland)	NC 58 03	McCullagh & Tipping 1998, 95	Charcoal from context 2170, compacted gravel in a pit below House 3. Artefacts in the gravel suggest association with destruction of Neolithic deposits though at 5530–5300 cal BC this seems remarkably early for Neolithic activity. The date may be anomalous or may be for derived material; it is broadly similar in date to GU-3140 from similar compacted gravel with Neolithic artefacts, and to GU-3172 and GU-3309, for charcoal which may relate to early woodland clearance. See GU-3149 (3240±100 BP) for a *TPQ* for House 3.	Charcoal	GU-3147	5530 to 5300 cal BC	6450±70	6450±70	−26.5
Morton A, Fife	NO 467 257	Coles 1971, 320	Charcoal from hearth T53.1.	Charcoal	Q-989	5630 to 5140 cal BC	6450±80	6450±110	
Seal Cottage, Oronsay, Argyll and Bute	NR 361 885	Jardine 1977	Same shell (middle) from a midden as two other Birm-326 dates: 6800±200 BP and 7180±150 BP.	Shell	Birm-326M	5750 to 4950 cal BC	6850±120	6445±175	
Cnoc Sligeach, Oronsay, Argyll and Bute	NR 3586 8801	Jardine & Jardine 1983	Middle part of valve of shells of *Arctica islandica* within occupation layer i CS73/11. See also Birm-464I (6910±160 BP).	Shell	Birm-464m	5900 to 4700 cal BC	6840±190	6435±270	0.2

Site and Council	NGR	Reference	Description	Material	Code	Calibrated date	Laboratory Age BP	Adjusted Date BP	δ¹³C
An Corran, Staffin, Skye, Highland	NG 4910 52	Saville 1998	A bone from the basal layer of red clay. The context above it contains a bone tool dated to 7590±90 BP (OxA-4994) BP. See also AA-27745.	Bone, animal	AA-27746	5530 to 5210 cal BC	6420±75	6420±75	−22.8
Balnuaran Of Clava, Highland	NH 7575 4445	Bradley 2000, 115	A single piece of hazel charcoal from the lower part of the charcoal-rich subsoil below the massive stone blocks forming the inner core of the monument. The sample was designed to provide a *TPQ*.	Charcoal	AA-21255	5530 to 5210 cal BC	6410±80	6410±80	−25.7
Lairg, Achany Glen, Allt na Fearna, Highland (Sutherland)	NC 58 03	McCullagh & Tipping 1998, 95	Alder and birch charcoal in soil in a penannular gully worn into floor of House 4. GU-3166 (3260±70 BP) and AA-10500 (3300±50 BP) are preferred as *TPQ*s for the gully. The date may be anomalous or may be from derived material; it is broadly similar in date to GU-3147 and GU-3140 from deposits with Neolithic artefacts, and to GU-3172 and GU-3309 for charcoal which may relate to early woodland clearance.	Charcoal	GU-3168	5510 to 5210 cal BC	6410±70	6410±70	−27.1
Morton A, Fife	NO 467 257	Coles 1971, 320	Charcoal from hearth T.53.1	Charcoal	NZ-1193	5700 to 4850 cal BC	6400±125	6400±175	
Seal Cottage, Oronsay, Argyll and Bute	NR 361 885	Jardine 1977	Same shell (outer) from a midden as two other Birm-326 dates: 6850±120 BP and 7180±150 BP.	Shell	Birm-326O	5900 to 4600 cal BC	6800±200	6395±285	
Morton B, Fife	NO 467 257	Coles 1971, 320	Charcoal pooled from lower midden T50.5 & T57.2. Mixture of older and younger charcoal?	Charcoal	Q-981	5650 to 4850 cal BC	6382±120	6382±170	
Morton A, Fife	NO 467 257	Coles 1971, 320, 332	'Decayed wood' in stakehole in T.42. See Spriggs and Anderson 1993 for reservations about the accuracy of many GaK dates measured in the 1970s and 80s.	?Decayed wood	GaK-2404	6100 to 4200 cal BC	6300±150	6300±450	
Biggar Common, South Lanarkshire	NT 002 388	Johnston 1997, 240–3; Sheridan 1989	Oak charcoal from one of 12 stakeholes, perhaps forming corner of sub-rectangular structure under soil below earthen long barrow. See also GU-2988 (6080±60 BP).	Charcoal	GU-2987	5550 to 4850 cal BC	6300±130	6300±130	−26.4

Site and Council	NGR	Reference	Description	Material	Code	Calibrated date	Laboratory Age BP	Adjusted Date BP	δ13C
Starr 1, Loch Doon, South Ayrshire	NX 479 941	Edwards 1996, 118	Hazel charcoal from a fire-spot ringed by a setting of rotted granite boulders.	Charcoal	OxA-1596	5370 to 4950 cal BC	6230±80	6230±80	
An Corran, Staffin, Skye, Highland	NG 4910 6852	Saville 1998	Bevel-ended bone tool found in the main shell midden (mostly of limpet shells) at the rear of the rockshelter. See also A-29315.	Bone, animal	AA-29316	5310 to 4990 cal BC	6215±60	6215±60	−20.6
Lairg, Achany Glen, Allt na Fearna, Highland (Sutherland)	NC 58 03	McCullagh & Tipping 1998, 95	Birch charcoal in a possible tree-throw between House 4 and Dyke 1; pollen analysis from nearby suggests woodland clearance at this time.	Charcoal	GU-3172	5310 to 4990 cal BC	6210±60	6210±60	−26.1
Caisteal nan Gillean, Oronsay, Argyll and Bute	NR 359 879	Mellars 1987, 140	Charcoal at base of midden layer 4, trench C.	Charcoal	Q-3008	5320 to 4850 cal BC	6190±80	6190±80	
Morton B, Fife	NO 467 257	Coles 1971, 320	Charcoal from lower midden T.50.1/3.	Charcoal	Q-988	5400 to 4700 cal BC	6147±90	6147±125	
Lairg, Achany Glen, Allt na Fearna, Highland (Sutherland)	NC 58 03	McCullagh & Tipping 1998, 95	Pine charcoal from context 3656, in a tree-throw hollow near Dyke 2; pollen analysis from nearby suggests woodland clearance at this time.	Charcoal	GU-3309	5280 to 4850 cal BC	6145±55	6145±55	
Caisteal nan Gillean, Oronsay, Argyll and Bute	NR 359 879	Mellars 1987, 140	Charcoal at base of midden layer 4, trench C.	Charcoal	Q-3007	5290 to 4800 cal BC	6120±80	6120±80	
Morton B, Fife	NO 467 257	Coles 1971, 320	Charcoal pooled from upper midden T50/59. May be a mixture of older and younger charcoal.	Charcoal	Q-928	5500 to 4600 cal BC	6115±110	6115±155	
Seal Cottage, Oronsay, Argyll and Bute	NR 361 885	Jardine 1977	Inner part of same shell from a midden as two other Birm-326 dates: 6850±120 BP and 6800±200 BP.	Shell	Birm-326I	6050 to 5350 cal BC	7180±150	6775±175	

Site and Council	NGR	Reference	Description	Material	Code	Calibrated date	Laboratory Age BP	Adjusted Date BP	δ¹³C
Cowie Road, Bannockburn, Stirling	NS 816 901	Rideout 1997, 42, 52–3	Hazelnut shells from the upper fill of 'fire-pit' P59. See also AA-20415 (4530±50 BP) and AA-20414 (4490±1100 BP) for a posthole of an enclosure 25.5–27.5m wide & >89m long cutting the fire-pit.	Charred hazelnut shells	AA-20413	5620 to 5320 cal BC	6530±75	6530±75	
Smittons, Dumfries and Galloway (Stewartry)	NX 634 918	Morrison & Bonsall 1989, 140	Hazelnut shell from a fire-spot in trench T1.	Charred hazelnut shell	OxA-1595	5470 to 4990 cal BC	6260±80	6260±80	
Lón Mór, Oban, Argyll and Bute	NM 8535 2835	Bonsall 1996	Hazelnut shell from Area F, feature 18, a lens of black soil with humified organic matter, 0.3m below the surface. Such lenses were a consistent feature of this part of the site and are interpreted as the truncated remains of decayed midden.	Charred hazelnut shell	AA-17457	5360 to 5000 cal BC	6240±65	6240±65	−27.9

Dates from c.5000 cal BC to c.4000 cal BC

Of these 78 dates 50 come from charcoal, 12 from shell, five from animal bone, six from antler, and five from charred hazelnut shells. About 50 of the dates come from artefacts or occupation or activity sites (including shell middens) of forager character. Six dates are anomalous. Seven dates come from Neolithic contexts, where they may perhaps represent inner ring-wood (as, probably, at Cleaven Dyke) residual or inner ring-wood material (as, probably, at Chapelfield), or ages some distance from the true mean age of the sample (as, possibly, at Biggar Common). None unambiguously shows Neolithic occupation or activity sites in Scotland before 4000 cal BC, though the Cleaven Dyke and Biggar dates reflect a marine effect which has been allowed for in the adjusted date column by subtracting 405 years from the laboratory age. However, recent work suggests that the marine effect may have varied over time, and these adjusted ages should be used cautiously, after checking the latest work on marine reservoir corrections for this period.

Site and Council	NGR	Reference	Description	Material	Code	Calibrated date	Laboratory Age BP	Adjusted Date BP	δ¹³C
Biggar Common, South Lanarkshire	NT 002 388	Johnston 1997, 240–3; Sheridan 1989	Oak charcoal from one of 12 stakeholes, perhaps forming corner of sub-rectangular structure under soil below earthen long barrow. See also GU-2987 (6300±130 BP).	Charcoal	GU-2988	5230 to 4800 cal BC	6080±60	6080±60	−27.1
Northton, Harris, Western Isles	NF 976 913	Simpson 1976 (BM VIII, 29)	Neolithic level in midden. Anomalous. See Spriggs & Anderson 1993 for reservations about the accuracy of many GaK dates measured in the 1970s and 80s.	Bone, animal	GaK-848	5800 to 4000 cal BC	6050±140	6050±420	

Site and Council	NGR	Reference	Description	Material	Code	Calibrated date	Laboratory Age BP	Adjusted Date BP	δ¹³C
Caisteal nan Gillean, Oronsay, Argyll and Bute	NR 359 879	Mellars 1987, 140	Charcoal in top of midden layer 4, trench C.	Charcoal	Q-3009	5210 to 4720 cal BC	6035±70	6035±70	
Carriden, Falkirk	NT 0390 8070	Saville 2001	Biserial barbed antler point from the foreshore of the Forth Estuary	Antler	OxA-7852	5060 to 4770 cal BC	6030±55	6030±55	−21.0
Boghead, Fochabers, Moray	NJ 359 592	Burl 1984, 40, 55, 71	Charcoal in or under west cairn. This sample may include residual material or may be anomalous.	Charcoal	SRR-690	5300 to 4600 cal BC	6006±60	6010±110	−28.8
Risga, Argyll and Bute	NM610600	Bonsall & Smith 1990, 360	Red deer antler mattock in a shell midden.	Antler	OxA-2023	5250 to 4600 cal BC	6000±90	6000±90	
Barsalloch, Dumfries and Galloway (Wigtownshire)	NX 343 421	Cormack 1968	Charcoal from a layer of carbonized wood beneath a stone setting in square H7. See Spriggs & Anderson 1993 for reservations about the accuracy of many GaK dates measured in the 1970s and 80s.	Charcoal	GaK-1601	5800 to 3900 cal BC	6000±110	6000±440	
Cnoc Sligeach, Oronsay, Argyll and Bute	NR 3586 8801	Jardine & Jardine 1983	Middle part of shells of *Patella* spp. within storm beach gravel deposit in CS73/11. See also Birm-462I (5850±140 BP).	Shell	Birm-462m	5500 to 4300 cal BC	6390±160	5985±230	−1.5
Inveravon, Falkirk	NS 951 798	MacKie 1972a	Lens of occupation material in a shell mound 3.55ft above the gravel.	Charcoal	GX-2334	5500 to 4300 cal BC	5955±180	5955±250	
Meiklewood, Stirling	NS 72 95	Bonsall & Smith 1989 36	Red deer antler from an antler-beam mattock (NMS HLA 3).	Antler	OxA-1159	5000 to 4550 cal BC	5920±80	5920±80	
Chapelfield, Cowie, Stirling	NS 8363 8957	Atkinson 1997	Lumps of oak charcoal from a dump of charcoal-rich material (505) at the base of Pit 1 (008). This had been immediately sealed and only one tree species was represented, suggesting a unitary deposit.	Charcoal	GU-7207	4990 to 4500 cal BC	5890±90	5890±90	−25.8
Braehead Midden, Alloa, Clackmannan	NS 8693 9370	Ashmore & Hall 1996, 112	Scallop shell from an exposure of oyster and other shells, which may have slumped from a higher position. The stratigraphy suggests that there has not been post-depositional mixing.	Shell	GU-4835	4460 to 4140 cal BC	5880±60	5475±60	0.9

Site and Council	NGR	Reference	Description	Material	Code	Calibrated date	Laboratory Age BP	Adjusted Date BP	δ¹³C
Risga, Argyll and Bute	NM 610 600	Bonsall & Smith 1992	Red deer antler bevel-ended tool from a shell midden (Hunterian Museum).	Antler	OxA-3737	4910 to 4550 cal BC	5875±65	5875±65	
Kilpatrick, Arran, North Ayrshire	NR 908 266	Barber 1997, 46	Oak charcoal from the old ground surface 16/03/318 under the primary barrow, thought to be of Neolithic date.	Charcoal	GU-1561	4920 to 4540 cal BC	5870±75	5870±75	−26.5
Priory Midden, Oronsay, Argyll and Bute	NR 346 889	Mellars 1987, 140	Charcoal from a shell midden layer (19) with a red deer antler. See also Q-3000 (5825±50 BP).	Charcoal	Q-3001	5000 to 4450 cal BC	5870±50	5870±110	
Spurryhillock, Stonehaven, Aberdeenshire (Kincardine and Deeside)	NO 852 861	Alexander 1997, 20	Oak charcoal (in Pit 619) from slow-grown oak and may be older than the context in which it was found. See also Beta-73553 (5700±70 BP). The mean of these two dates is 5780±50 BP.	Charcoal	Beta-73552	4910 to 4540 cal BC	5860±70	5860±70	−25
Shewalton, (River Irvine), North Ayrshire	NS 33 37	Bonsall & Smith 1990, 359	Antler from a biserial barbed point (NMS HLA 1).	Antler	OxA-1947	4910 to 4490 cal BC	5840±80	5840±80	
Priory Midden, Oronsay, Argyll and Bute	NR 346 889	Mellars 1987, 140	Charcoal from a shell midden layer (19) with a red deer antler mattock. See also Q-3001 (5870±50 BP).	Charcoal	Q-3000	4950 to 4400 cal BC	5825±50	5825±110	
Morton B, Fife	NO 467 257	Bonsall et al. 1995	Bevel-ended bone tool from upper midden T59. (NMS X.BNA 429)	Bone, animal	OxA-4612	4830 to 4450 cal BC	5790±80	5790±80	
Lairg, Achany Glen, Allt na Fearna, Highland (Sutherland)	NC 58 03	McCullagh & Tipping 1998, 95	Charcoal from context 2126, compacted gravel in intermediate phase of House 6, the smaller of two adjacent houses. Artefacts in the gravels suggest association with destruction of Neolithic deposits, though at 5000–4300 cal BC, this date seems to be too early for Neolithic activity. The date may be anomalous or may be derived; it is broadly similar to GU-3147 from similar compacted gravel with Neolithic artefacts, and to GU-3172 and GU-3309 for charcoal which may relate to early woodland clearance.	Charcoal	GU-3140	5000 to 4300 cal BC	5770±150	5770±150	−26.7

Site and Council	NGR	Reference	Description	Material	Code	Calibrated date	Laboratory Age BP	Adjusted Date BP	δ¹³C
Cnoc Sligeach, Oronsay, Argyll and Bute	NR 3727 8909	MacKie 1972a	Animal bones probably from various layers of the shell midden.	Bone, animal	GX-1904	5300 to 4000 cal BC	5755±180	5755±250	
Ulva Cave, Argyll and Bute	NM 431 384	Bonsall et al. 1994	Red deer antler bevel-ended tool in the upper part of a midden in area C.	Antler	OxA-3738	4780 to 4450 cal BC	5750±70	5750±70	−23.6
Priory Midden, Oronsay, Argyll and Bute	NR 346 889	Mellars 1987, 140	Charcoal from a shell midden layer (18).	Charcoal	Q-3002	4800 to 4340 cal BC	5717±50	5717±110	
Knap of Howar, Papa Westray, Orkney Islands	HY 483 578	Ritchie 1983	Animal bone from primary midden D1/9 in the wall core of House 1, period 1; from same context as SRR-452 (4080±70 BP). The two dates are very different and it is uncertain whether the midden was clearly diachronic or whether both are anomalous; the latter seems more likely.	Bone, animal	SRR-347	4840 to 4330 cal BC	5706±85	5710±120	−22.2
Spurryhillock, Stonehaven, Aberdeenshire (Kincardine and Deeside)	NO 852 861	Alexander 1997, 20	Oak charcoal (in Pit 619) from slow-grown oak and may be older than the context in which it was found. See also Beta-73552 (5860±70 BP). The mean of these two dates is 5780±50 BP.	Charcoal	Beta-73553	4710 to 4360 cal BC	5700±70	5700±70	−25
Ulva Cave, Argyll and Bute	NM 431 384	Bonsall et al. 1994	Patella shell inner fraction from the top layer of a midden in area C. See also GU-2603 (5930±70 BP).	Shell	GU-2602	4710 to 4350 cal BC	6090±70	5685±80	0.6
Cnoc Coig, Oronsay, Argyll and Bute	NR 360 885	Mellars 1987, 140	Charcoal from below shell midden.	Charcoal	Q-3006	4690 to 4360 cal BC	5675±60	5675±60	
Fordhouse Barrow, Dun, Angus	NO 6658 6053	Proudfoot 1999	Fragment of hazelnut shell from Pit 7, one of a series of Phase 1 pits, sealed by a Phase 2 surface, which also contained 7 pitchstone blades and a bifacial flint knife.	Charred hazelnut shell	OxA-8226	4600 to 4360 cal BC	5660±40	5660±40	−24.6
Cnoc Coig, Oronsay, Argyll and Bute	NR 360 885	Mellars 1987, 140	Charcoal from below shell midden.	Charcoal	Q-3005	4670 to 4350 cal BC	5650±60	5650±60	

Site and Council	NGR	Reference	Description	Material	Code	Calibrated date	Laboratory Age BP	Adjusted Date BP	δ¹³C
Cnoc Coig, Oronsay, Argyll and Bute	NR 360 885	Mellars 1987, 140	Charcoal from trench E unit 8, lower shell midden with red deer antler mattock.	Charcoal	Q-1353	4800 to 4250 cal BC	5645 ± 80	5645 ± 110	
Canal Road, Muirtown, Highland (Inverness)	NH 652 457	Myers & Gourlay 1991	Large oak charcoal lumps near the base of the midden.	Charcoal	GU-1473	4800 to 4250 cal BC	5635 ± 65	5635 ± 110	−25.6
Cnoc Sligeach, Oronsay, Argyll and Bute	NR 3586 8801	Jardine & Jardine 1983	Inner part of valve of shell of *Pectin maximus* within occupation layer in CS73/11. See also Birm-465m (5900±150 BP). Associated with a barbed point.	Shell	Birm-465I	4950 to 3950 cal BC	6010 ± 150	5605 ± 215	−1.3
Inveravon, Falkirk	NS 951 798	MacKie 1972a	Base of a shell midden, on the gravel.	Shell	GX-2331	5100 to 3800 cal BC	6010 ± 180	5605 ± 255	
Cleaven Dyke, Perth and Kinross	NO 159 404	Barclay & Maxwell 1998, 47	Rotten oak charcoal in a small pit immediately underlying a bank barrow. See also GU-3911 (5500±120 BP).	Charcoal	GU-3912	4700 to 4000 cal BC	5550 ± 130	5550 ± 130	−26.3
The Dunion, Jedburgh, The Scottish Borders (Roxburgh)	NT 621 590	Rideout 1992	Charcoal (probably an anomalous date; no explanation).	Charcoal	GU-2177	4700 to 4050 cal BC	5550 ± 100	5550 ± 100	−26.0
Cnoc Coig, Oronsay, Argyll and Bute	NR 360 885	Mellars 1987, 140	Charcoal from trench E unit 6, lower shell midden with red deer antler mattock.	Charcoal	Q-1354	4800 to 3950 cal BC	5535 ± 140	5535 ± 195	
Balnuaran Of Clava, Inverness, Highland	NH 7575 4445	Bradley 2000, 115	Birch charcoal from one of three samples (S.6–8) from a small cutting inside the kerb of the NE cairn, taken from the material of the core cairn, below the upper rubble. Micromorphological analysis suggests the material consists of redeposited turf from pre-cairn burning of the site.	Charcoal	AA-25230	4500 to 4250 cal BC	5535 ± 55	5535 ± 55	−26.6
Tulloch Wood, Forres, Moray	NJ 089 560	Carter 1993, 228–9	Charcoal from a fill of a feature, which may be natural, under a bank.	Charcoal	GU-3091	4750 to 4000 cal BC	5530 ± 150	5530 ± 150	−25.9

Site and Council	NGR	Reference	Description	Material	Code	Calibrated date	Laboratory Age BP	Adjusted Date BP	δ¹³C
Ulva Cave, Argyll and Bute	NM 431 384	Bonsall et al. 1994	*Patella* shell (outer) from the top layer of midden in area C. See also GU-2602 (6090±70 BP).	Shell	GU-2603	4550 to 4160 cal BC	5930±70	5525±80	0.4
Bharpa Carinish, N Uist, Western Isles	NF 837 604	Crone 1993, 370	Birch charcoal from spread C in hearth complex 2 overlies c.1000-year later material. The date is interpreted as anomalous rather than representing residual charcoal.	Charcoal	GU-2669	4550 to 4050 cal BC	5520±90	5520±90	−25.0
Priory Midden, Oronsay, Argyll and Bute	NR 346 889	Mellars 1987, 140	Charcoal from a shell midden layer (9/10).	Charcoal	Q-3003	4600 to 4000 cal BC	5510±50	5510±110	
Cleaven Dyke, Perth and Kinross	NO 159 404	Barclay & Maxwell 1998, 47	Rotten oak charcoal in a small pit immediately underlying a bank barrow. See also GU-3912 (5550±130 BP).	Charcoal	GU-3911	4600 to 4000 cal BC	5500±120	5500±120	−26.6
Machrie Moor, Arran, North Ayrshire	NR 912 324	Haggarty 1991	Mixed charcoal from a pit with plain Neolithic pottery, a flint knife, etc. This date is aberrant, or from old charcoal. See GU-2321 (4820±50 BP) from a nearby pit with very similar potsherds.	Charcoal	GU-2320	4500 to 4140 cal BC	5500±70	5500±70	−25.6
Cnoc Coig, Oronsay, Argyll and Bute	NR 360 885	Mellars 1987, 140	Charcoal from trench E, unit 2, upper shell midden with red deer antler mattock.	Charcoal	Q-1351	4550 to 4000 cal BC	5495±75	5495±110	
Cnoc Sligeach, Oronsay, Argyll and Bute	NR 3586 8801	Jardine & Jardine 1983	Valve of shell of *Pectin maximus* within occupation layer in CS73/11. See also Birm-465I (6010±150 BP). Associated with a barbed point.	Shell	Birm-465m	4800 to 3800 cal BC	5900±150	5495±215	−2.2
Caisteal nan Gillean, Oronsay, Argyll and Bute	NR 359 879	Mellars 1987, 140	Charcoal from midden layer 3, trench C.	Charcoal	Q-3010	4540 to 4040 cal BC	5485±50	5485±110	
Caisteal nan Gillean, Oronsay, Argyll and Bute	NR 359 879	Jardine & Jardine 1983	*Patella* shells in midden. See also SRR-1458a (4750±180 BP).	Shell	SRR-1458b	4500 to 4050 cal BC	5890±70	5485±80	0.9

Site and Council	NGR	Reference	Description	Material	Code	Calibrated date	Laboratory Age BP	Adjusted Date BP	δ¹³C
Morton B. Fife	NO 467 257	Bonsall *et al.* 1995	Bevel-ended bone tool from lower midden T59. (NMS X.BNA 440)	Bone, animal	OxA–4611	4460 to 4140 cal BC	5475±60	5475±60	
Priory Midden, Oronsay, Argyll and Bute	NR 346 889	Mellars 1987, 140	Charcoal from a shell midden layer (7).	Charcoal	Q-3004	4550 to 4000 cal BC	5470±50	5470±110	
Smittons, Dumfries and Galloway (Stewartry)	NX 634 918	Morrison & Bonsall 1989, 140	Charred hazelnut shell from fire-spot in trench T3.	Charred hazelnut shell	OxA-1594	4460 to 4040 cal BC	5470±80	5470±80	
Caisteal nan Gillean 2, Oronsay, Argyll and Bute	NR 359 879	Mellars 1987, 140	Charcoal from lower midden.	Charcoal	Q-1355	4500 to 4000 cal BC	5460±65	5460±110	
Caisteal nan Gillean 2, Oronsay, Argyll and Bute	NR 359 879	Mellars 1987, 140	Charcoal from basal midden.	Charcoal	Birm-347	4750 to 3800 cal BC	5450±140	5450±195	
Caisteal nan Gillean, Oronsay, Argyll and Bute	NR 359 879	Mellars 1987, 140	Charcoal from midden layer 3, trench C.	Charcoal	Q-3011	4500 to 3990 cal BC	5450±50	5450±110	
Cnoc Sligeach, Oronsay, Argyll and Bute	NR 3586 8801	Jardine & Jardine 1983	Shells (middle) of *Patella* spp., from storm beach gravel in CS73/11. See also Birm-462m (6390±160 BP).	Shell	Birm-462I	4800 to 3800 cal BC	5850±140	5445±200	–1.5
Caisteal nan Gillean 2, Oronsay, Argyll and Bute	NR 359 879	Mellars 1987, 141	Shells (inner) of *Patella* spp. from basal midden.	Shell	Birm-348	5400 to 3100 cal BC	5850±310	5445±435	
Cnoc Coig, Oronsay, Argyll and Bute	NR 360 885	Mellars 1987, 140	Charcoal from trench E unit 3, upper shell midden with red deer antler mattock.	Charcoal	Q-1352	4700 to 3800 cal BC	5430±130	5430±180	

Site and Council	NGR	Reference	Description	Material	Code	Calibrated date	Laboratory Age BP	Adjusted Date BP	δ¹³C
Lón Mór, Oban, Argyll and Bute	NM 8535 2835	Bonsall 1996	A large fragment of ring-porous charcoal of ash type from a thick, charcoal-rich lens at the base of a stone-lined depression, interpreted as a hearth, 0.4m below the surface, within free-draining soil 2–3m from a rectangular stone-paved area.	Charcoal	AA-17452	4370 to 4040 cal BC	5420±65	5420±65	−24.8
Cnoc Sligeach, Oronsay, Argyll and Bute	NR 369 888	Mellars 1987, 140	Charcoal from shell midden trench B layer 7.	Charcoal	BM-670	4700 to 3900 cal BC	5426±159	5416±220	
Staosnaig, Colonsay, Argyll and Bute	NR 3977 9331	Mithen 2000, 373	Hazelnut shell from context 31, the heterogeneous fill of an amorphous shaped feature in Area B of the 1994 excavations.	Charred hazelnut shell	AA-21629	4360 to 4040 cal BC	5415±60	5415±60	−23.4
Munrills, Falkirk	NS 921 798	Bonsall et al. forthcoming	Oyster shell (inner) from the bottom of a shell midden at 14m OD. See also GU-3284 (5560±70 BP) from the outer part of the same shell.	Shell	GU-3285	4360 to 3990 cal BC	5790±70	5385±80	
Summerston Landfill Site, Balmuidy, Glasgow City	NS 580 714	Baker 1998	Hazelnut shells from fill of a post-pit, 1m diam. × 0.2m deep, found at the S end of a curvilinear ditch which may be part of a settlement.	Charred hazelnut shell	AA-28390	4330 to 4000 cal BC	5345±55	5345±55	−27.3
Lairg, Achany Glen, Allt na Fearna, Highland (Sutherland)	NC 5803	McCullagh & Tipping 1998, 95	Charcoal from context 1024 in compacted gravel under primary features of House 7. Artefacts in the gravel suggest association with destruction of Neolithic deposits, though at 4550–3700 cal BC, this date seems quite early for Neolithic activity. See also, from same context, GU-3169 (2140±90 BP), which is preferred as a TPQ for House 7.	Charcoal	GU-3171	4550 to 3700 cal BC	5320±190	5320±190	−26.3
Caisteal nan Gillean 2, Oronsay, Argyll and Bute	NR 359 879	Mellars 1987, 141	Shells (middle) of Patella spp. from lower midden.	Shell	Birm-348B	4550 to 3650 cal BC	5720±140	5315±200	

Site and Council	NGR	Reference	Description	Material	Code	Calibrated date	Laboratory Age BP	Adjusted Date BP	δ13C
Lón Mór, Oban, Argyll and Bute	NM 8535 2835	Bonsall 1996	Fragment of conifer charcoal from Area F, feature 1a, a lens of black soil, rich in humified organic matter, c.0.3m below the surface. Such lenses were frequent on this part of the site and are seen as the truncated remains of decayed midden.	Charcoal	AA-17454	4320 to 3970 cal BC	5290±65	5290±65	−26.8
Stoneyfield, Raigmore, Inverness, Highland (Inverness)	NH 687 456	Simpson 1996, 82–3; (SC26068/2B)	Charcoal from Pit 4 (originally Pit 136) with potsherd, calcined bone, and flint core; see also SRR-187 (4732±90 BP), SRR-188 (4983±130 BP), SRR-424 (5000±100 BP), SRR-426 (4890±60 BP), SRR-432 (4650±120 BP). It is not archaeologically unreasonable to suppose SRR-421 reflects a true date c.3000–2500 cal BC.	Charcoal	SRR-421	6500 to 1000 cal BC	5271±650	5270±1100	−26.7
Linlithgow Priory, West Lothian	NS 99 77	Lindsay 1989	Mainly oak with 5% hazel charcoal from the fill of a pit, part of a series in which others incorporated Beaker sherds and lithic artefacts.	Charcoal	GU-1875	4230 to 3960 cal BC	5265±55	5265±55	−24.8
Biggar Common, South Lanarkshire	NT 002 388	Johnston 1997, 240–3; Sheridan 1989	Oak, hazel, birch, and willow charcoal from a bonfire beneath an earthen long barrow with early Neolithic pottery and lithic artefacts. See also GU-2986 (5150±70 BP).	Charcoal	GU-2985	4230 to 3960 cal BC	5250±50	5250±50	−25.5
Chapelfield, Cowie, Stirling	NS 8363 8957	Atkinson 2000c, 126	A single piece of hazel charcoal (sample 267) from context 008 of fill 785 of the deeply stratified Pit 1. See also OxA-9235 (214±38 BP) from a charred barley grain from the same deposit.	Charcoal	OxA-9750	4540 to 4330 cal BC	5590±55	5590±55	−24.5
Upper Largie, Argyll and Bute	NR 8330 9955	Ellis 2002, 145	Oak charcoal from sample 3117C from fill of pit 3101.	Charcoal	AA-43022	4550 to 4250 cal BC	5570±70	5570±70	−25
Fordhouse Barrow, Dun, Angus	NO 6658 6056	Proudfoot 2001, 122	A hazelnut shell sample 3049 from context 602 blocking of the passage of the chambered cairn.	Charred hazelnut shell	OxA-10060	4500 to 4330 cal BC	5565±45	5565±45	−23.5
Upper Largie, Argyll and Bute	NR 8330 9955	Ellis 2002, 145	Oak charcoal from sample 3117A from fill of pit 3101.	Charcoal	AA-43020	4540 to 4220 cal BC	5530±75	5530±75	−26

Site and Council	NGR	Reference	Description	Material	Code	Calibrated date	Laboratory Age BP	Adjusted Date BP	δ¹³C
Upper Largie, Argyll and Bute	NR 8330 9955	Ellis 2002, 45	Oak charcoal from sample 3117B from fill of pit 3101.	Charcoal	AA-43021	4500 to 4240 cal BC	5535±65	5535±65	−26
Inveresk, East Lothian	NT 3500 7130	Cook 2002, 146	Oak charcoal from a mid-brown silty soil, the basal fill of a pit (context 117 Sample 1), next to a marching camp.	Charcoal	AA-49321	4460 to 4250 cal BC	5510±40	5510±40	−27.2
Upper Largie, Argyll and Bute	NR 8330 9955	Ellis 2002, 145	Oak charcoal from sample 368A from posthole of enclosure/cursus.	Charcoal	AA-43013	4340 to 4040 cal BC	5375±55	5375±55	−25
Daer Reservoir, Crawford, South Lanarkshire	NS 975 078	Ward 2001a, 127	Single piece of hazel charcoal from Site No. 3 (sample 002) from a deposit/pit containing charcoal and lithic artefacts.	Charcoal	AA-43004	4330 to 4040 cal BC	5355±45	5355±45	−25.9
Inveresk, East Lothian	NT 3500 7130	Cook 2002, 146	Oak charcoal from a mid-brown silty soil, the basal fill of a pit (context 117 Sample 2), next to a marching camp.	Charcoal	AA-49322	4330 to 4040 cal BC	5340±45	5340±45	−27
Inveresk, East Lothian	NT 3500 7130	Cook 2002, 146	Oak charcoal from a mid-brown silty soil, the basal fill of a pit (context 117 Sample 3), next to a marching camp.	Charcoal	AA-49323	4250 to 3990 cal BC	5305±40	5305±40	−26.6
Upper Largie, Argyll and Bute	NR 8330 955	Ellis 2002, 145	Oak charcoal from sample KQ93-508 from pit of avenue leading to main timber circle or enclosure/cursus.	Charcoal	AA-48052	4230 to 3940 cal BC	5220±50	5220±50	−25.9

Dates from c.4000 cal BC to c.3500 cal BC

Of these 169 dates 103 are from charcoal and 15 from charred hazelnut shells, with one from mixed charcoal and charred nutshells. Fourteen are from human bone and 11 from animal bone, seven from shell, seven from grain or seed, four from wood, two from soil peat, and one each from antler, a plank, a crab apple, heather, and other plant remains. Around 30 of the dates come from sites generally similar to those found in earlier periods, including cave deposits and middens. Between 106 and 112 come from contexts with pottery or structures generally associated with farmers or herders such as chambered cairns or large timber settings or are associated with material such as cereals. Some of the samples dated from middens and caves have a highly ambiguous affiliation, particularly the 12 human bones dated from Raschoille Cave and Carding Mill Bay. There are a few anomalous dates, and dates such as some of those from Raigmore, which probably reflect mixed samples. The shell dates reflect a marine effect which has been allowed for in the adjusted date column by subtracting 405 years from the laboratory age. However, recent work suggests that the marine effect may have varied over time, and these adjusted ages should be used cautiously, after checking the latest work on marine reservoir corrections for this period.

Site and Council	NGR	Reference	Description	Material	Code	Calibrated date	Laboratory Age BP	Adjusted Date BP	$\delta^{13}C$
Carding Mill Bay I, Oban, Argyll and Bute	NM 8474 2935	Bonsall & Smith 1992	Antler bevel-ended tool from the lower part (XV) of a shell midden.	Antler	OxA-3740	4230 to 3790 cal BC	5190±85	5190±85	
An Corran, Staffin, Skye, Highland	NG 4910 6852	Saville 1998	A bevel-ended bone (red deer metatarsus) tool, found in the main shell midden (mostly of limpets) at the rear of the rockshelter.	Bone, animal	AA-29315	4220 to 3800 cal BC	5190±55	5190±55	−21.3
Dalladies, Aberdeenshire (Kincardine and Deeside)	NO 627 673	Piggott 1972	Charcoal (seemingly not oak) from a timber c.150mm diam. at the SW end of the Phase 2 mortuary enclosure under a long barrow. This measurement conflicts with SRR-289 (4660±50 BP) from the same piece of wood, and SRR-290 (4535±55 BP), and may be anomalous.	Charcoal	I-6113	4350 to 3700 cal BC	5190±105	5190±145	
Morton B, Fife	NO 467 257	Bonsall et al. 1995	Bevel-ended bone tool from midden T65.	Bone, animal	OxA-4610	4230 to 3790 cal BC	5180±70	5180±70	
Upper Largie, Argyll and Bute	NR 8330 9955	Ellis 2002, 145	Oak charcoal from sample 3058 from posthole of enclosure/cursus.	Charcoal	AA-43411	4220 to 3790 cal BC	5175±55	5175±55	−25.9
Balfarg Riding School, Fife	NO 285 031	Barclay & Russell-White 1993, 160–1	Hazel, oak, and willow charcoal from Context 8019B of Pit 8016 with plain pottery. See also GU-1903 (4765±55 BP) and GU-2605 (4950±70 BP) from same pit, and GU-2030 (4720±70 BP) and UtC-1302 (4830±40 BP). May represent residual material or be anomalous.	Charcoal	GU-2604	4250 to 3700 cal BC	5170±90	5170±90	−25.4
Caisteal nan Gillean 2, Oronsay, Argyll and Bute	NR 359 879	Mellars 1987, 141	Shells (outer) of Patella spp. from lower shell midden.	Shell	Birm-348C	4450 to 3500 cal BC	5570±140	5165±200	

Site and Council	NGR	Reference	Description	Material	Code	Calibrated date	Laboratory Age BP	Adjusted Date BP	δ13C
Inchtuthil, Perth and Kinross	NO 125 396	Barclay & Maxwell 1991, 35	Burnt oak fencing timbers of a long mortuary enclosure. See also GU-2761 (5070±50 BP).	Charcoal	GU-2760	4220 to 3780 cal BC	5160±70	5160±70	−25.9
Balbridie, Aberdeenshire (Kincardine and Deeside)	NO 733 959	Fairweather & Ralston 1993; Ralston 1982	Oak from the destruction level of a timber hall. See also other oak dates GU-1036–1038 and GU-1828–1832 ranging from this date to 4740±135 BP and dates from grain, flax, and linen ranging from 5010±90 to 4745±160 BP. See especially GU-1038ii at 5020±90. Oak mean is 4980±28 BP; the preferred mean is that for grain etc., which is 4910±40 BP. The calibrated mean of the oak dates is between 3900–3700 cal BC; the preferred mean of grain etc. is between 3780–3640 cal BC.	Charcoal	GU-1038I	4350 to 3650 cal BC	5160±100	5160±140	
Mumrills, Falkirk	NS 921 798	Bonsall et al. forthcoming	Oyster shell (outer) from the bottom of a shell midden at 14m OD. See also GU-3285 (5790±70 BP) from the inner part of the same shell.	Shell	GU-3284	4250 to 3700 cal BC	5560±70	5155±80	
Parks of Garden, Stirling	NS 6038 9682	Ellis 2000, 126	Alder wood (sample 1) from a well-humified peat (173), the lowest true peat under the timber platform although it overlies an initial fen carr type peat on the estuarine clay.	Peat	OxA-9289	4050 to 3800 cal BC	5153±40	5153±40	−27.5
Biggar Common, South Lanarkshire	NT 002 388	Johnston 1997, 240–3; Sheridan 1989	Oak, hazel, and birch from a bonfire below an earthen long barrow with early pottery and lithic artefacts. See also GU-2985 (5250±50 BP).	Charcoal	GU-2986	4220 to 3770 cal BC	5150±70	5150±70	−25.3
Caisteal nan Gillean 2, Oronsay, Argyll and Bute	NR 359 879	Mellars 1987, 140	Charcoal from trench B, layer 3, upper shell midden.	Charcoal	Birm-346	5300 to 2600 cal BC	5150±380	5150±530	
Cowie Road, Bannockburn, Stirling	NS 816 901	Rideout 1997, 37, 52–3	Oak charcoal from the lower charcoal fill of Pit P6 of a pit-defined enclosure (Enclosure 1), 33–36m across with a rounded end. See also AA-20409 (5130±60 BP) and AA-20411 (5135±70 BP). The mean of these three dates is 5135±40, which calibrates to between 4040 and 3800 cal BC.	Charcoal	AA-20410	4250 to 3700 cal BC	5145±80	5145±80	

Site and Council	NGR	Reference	Description	Material	Code	Calibrated date	Laboratory Age BP	Adjusted Date BP	δ13C
Cowie Road, Bannockburn, Stirling	NS 816 901	Rideout 1997, 37, 52–3	Oak charcoal from the lower charcoal fill of Pit P6 of a pit-defined enclosure (Enclosure 1), 33–36m across with a rounded end. See also AA-20409 (5130±60 BP) and AA-20410 (5145±80 BP). The mean of these three dates is 5135±40 BP, which calibrates to between 4040 and 3800 cal BC.	Charcoal	AA-20411	4250 to 3700 cal BC	5135±70	5135±70	
Cowie Road, Bannockburn, Stirling	NS 816 901	Rideout 1997, 37, 52–3	Oak charcoal from the lower charcoal fill of Pit P6 of a pit-defined enclosure (Enclosure 1), 33–36m across with a rounded end. See also AA-20410 (5145±80 BP) and AA-20411 (5135±70 BP). The mean of these three dates is 5135±40 BP, which calibrates to between 4040 and 3800 cal BC.	Charcoal	AA-20409	4050 to 3770 cal BC	5130±60	5130±60	
Home Farm, Castle Menzies, Perth and Kinross	NN 8305 4935	Carter 2001, 126	Oak charcoal from sample 024 in the centre dark grey brown silty sand fill 124 of a probable posthole, part of the most northerly of 3 alignments.	Charcoal	OxA-9813	4040 to 3790 cal BC	5130±40	5130±40	−24.5
Warden's Dykes, Dumfries and Galloway (Annandale and Eskdale)	NY 3035 6899	Banks forthcoming	Oak and unidentified charcoal from a posthole, possibly burnt in situ.	Charcoal	GU-3511	4250 to 3650 cal BC	5120±100	5120±100	−27.0
Raschoille, Oban, Argyll and Bute	NM 8547 2888	Bonsall 1999	Single hazelnut shell from lower deposits of a cave.	Charred hazelnut shell	OxA-8438	4040 to 3780 cal BC	5115±55	5115±55	−26.3
Sheep Hill, Dumbarton, East Dunbartonshire	NS 435 744	MacKie 1976	Charcoal from the base of an occupation level under a secondary rampart of a fort. See Spriggs and Anderson 1993 for reservations about the accuracy of many GaK dates measured in the 1970s and 80s.	Charcoal	GaK-2467	6000 to 1300 cal BC	5110±1020	5110±3060	
Monamore, Arran, North Ayrshire	NS 017 288	MacKie 1964	Charcoal from a hearth in the forecourt under the blocking of a chambered cairn.	Charcoal	Q-675	4350 to 3500 cal BC	5110±110	5110±155	

Site and Council	NGR	Reference	Description	Material	Code	Calibrated date	Laboratory Age BP	Adjusted Date BP	δ¹³C
Home Farm, Castle Menzies, Perth and Kinross	NN 8305 4935	Carter 2001, 126	Oak charcoal from sample 003 in the charcoal-rich black sandy silt base of the post-pipe 037 within Pit 011, part of an arc of post-pits possibly part of a circular timber structure.	Charcoal	OxA-9987	3970 to 3790 cal BC	5093±39	5093±39	−24.9
Upper Largie, Argyll and Bute	NR 8330 9955	Ellis 2002, 145	Oak charcoal from sample 3134 from posthole of enclosure/cursus.	Charcoal	AA-43024	4040 to 3700 cal BC	5090±75	5090±75	−25.1
Upper Largie, Argyll and Bute	NR 8330 9955	Ellis 2002, 145	Oak charcoal from sample 3108 from posthole of enclosure/cursus.	Charcoal	AA-43019	3990 to 3760 cal BC	5090±50	5090±50	−24.8
Maes Howe, Mainland, Orkney Islands	HY 318 128	Renfrew 1979; Renfrew *et al.* 1976	Peat (Sample 5A) from a layer (an old ground surface?) under the bank surrounding the ditch of the chambered tomb. The taphonomy of the organic material which was dated is not clear. See also SRR-792 (1045±65 BP).	Soil	SRR-791	4250 to 3600 cal BC	5090±60	5090±110	−27.8
Chapelfield, Cowie, Stirling	NS 8363 8951	Atkinson 2000c, 126	A single charred hazelnut shell (sample 432) from basal fill 694d of Pit 11. See also OxA-9233 (136±38 BP) from charred grain from the same deposit.	Charred hazelnut shell	OxA-9234	3980 to 3780 cal BC	5085±45	5085±45	−24.6
Parks of Garden, Stirling	NS 6038 9682	Ellis 2000, 126	Oak wood (W67) from a large timber lying directly on the clay in peat (F149) under the timber platform.	Wood	OxA-9613	3970 to 3780 cal BC	5080±40	5080±40	−26.1
Claish Farm, Stirling	NN 635 065	Barclay 2002, 149–50	A piece of oak charcoal (part of Sample 74) from a charcoal-rich lens (F14 1) in a linear feature (Context F14) 1.1m long. The feature is probably a constructional slot within which posts had been set, packed against SW edge. The lens (F14 1) is indicative of *in situ* burning, an interpretation which is supported by the presence of concentrations of charcoal in the upper fills.	Charcoal	AA-49638	3970 to 3780 cal BC	5080±40	5080±40	−25.2
Inchtuthil, Perth and Kinross	NO 125 396	Barclay & Maxwell 1991, 35	Burnt oak fencing timbers of a long mortuary enclosure. See also GU-2760 (5160±50 BP).	Charcoal	GU-2761	3970 to 3710 cal BC	5070±50	5070±50	−25.8

Site and Council	NGR	Reference	Description	Material	Code	Calibrated date	Laboratory Age BP	Adjusted Date BP	δ¹³C
Lochhill, Dumfries and Galloway (Nithsdale)	NX 9688 6507	Masters 1973	Charcoal? from a plank from a mortuary structure under a chambered cairn.	Planks	I-6409	4250 to 3500 cal BC	5070±105	5070±145	
Carding Mill Bay, Oban, Argyll and Bute	NM 8474 2935	Connock et al. 1992	Charcoal from upper layer of early shell midden in fissure in cliff face.	Charcoal	GU-2796	3970 to 3710 cal BC	5060±50	5060±50	−25.6
Ben Lawers, Perth and Kinross	NN 6689 3795	Atkinson 2000b, 125	Hazel charcoal (sample 4) from the upper fill (17007) of a small pit, containing an AOC beaker and fragments of calcined bone.	Charcoal	OxA-8973	3970 to 3710 cal BC	5055±45	5055±45	−27.4
Scord of Brouster, Shetland Islands	HU 255 517	Whittle et al. 1986	Birch etc. charcoal from House 2 phase 2. This date is either anomalous or represents charcoal much older than the context in which it was found.	Charcoal	CAR-253	3990 to 3650 cal BC	5050±85	5050±85	
Wardend of Durris Banchory, Aberdeenshire (Kincardine and Deeside)	NO 751 928	Russell-White 1995	Hazel, willow, and oak charcoal from remains of post burnt in situ.	Charcoal	GU-2958	3960 to 3710 cal BC	5050±50	5050±50	−26.0
Glenbatrick Waterhole, Jura, Argyll and Bute	NR 518 798	Mercer 1974	Charcoal from a trough.	Charcoal	GX-2564	4500 to 3000 cal BC	5045±215	5045±300	
Rotten Bottom, Dumfries and Galloway (Annandale and Eskdale)	NT 146 144	Sheridan 1996	Yew wood from a long bow found in a peat bog.	Wood	OxA-3540	4040 to 3640 cal BC	5040±100	5040±100	−23.6
Home Farm, Castle Menzies, Perth and Kinross	NN 8305 4935	Carter 2001, 126	Oak charcoal from sample 073 from mid-brown sandy silt 466 in the base and round the edges of a pit 239, possibly for a post of an arc of post-pits possibly part of a circular timber structure	Charcoal	OxA-9816	3970 to 3660 cal BC	5035±70	5035±70	−25.6
Carding Mill Bay I, Oban, Argyll and Bute	NM 8474 2935	Connock et al. 1992	Shell from upper layer of early shell midden in fissure in cliff face.	Shell	GU-2899	3970 to 3660 cal BC	5440±50	5035±65	.56

Site and Council	NGR	Reference	Description	Material	Code	Calibrated date	Laboratory Age BP	Adjusted Date BP	δ^{13}C
Fordhouse Barrow, Dun, Angus	NO 6658 6053	Proudfoot 1999	The 35 outer rings of a radially split oak plank used to build a structure in the phase 3B mound.	Charcoal	OxA-8222	3960 to 3710 cal BC	5035±40	5035±40	−24.4
Inveravon, Falkirk	NS 951 798	MacKie 1972a	Shell from a shell midden. See also GU-1885 (4820±90 BP) and GU 1887 (5110±60 BP).	Shell	GU-1886	3970 to 3660 cal BC	5435±60	5030±70	
Balbridie, Aberdeenshire (Kincardine and Deeside)	NO 733 959	Fairweather & Ralston 1993; Ralston 1982	Oak from the destruction level of a timber hall. See also other oak dates GU-1036–1038 and GU-1828–1832 ranging from 5160±100 to 4740±135 BP and dates from grain, flax, and linen ranging from 5010±90 to 4745±160 BP. Oak mean is 4980±28 BP; the preferred mean is that for grain etc., which is 4910±40 BP. The calibrated mean of the oak dates is between 3900–3700 cal BC; the preferred mean of grain etc. is between 3780–3640 cal BC.	Charcoal	GU-1828	3970 to 3700 cal BC	5030±60	5030±60	−24.9
Northton, Harris, Western Isles	NF 976 913	Simpson 1976; (BM VIII, 29)	Beaker 1 level midden. See Spriggs and Anderson 1993 for reservations about the accuracy of many GaK dates measured in the 1970s and 80s.	Bone, animal	GaK-847	4900 to 2600 cal BC	5030±150	5030±450	
Boghead, Fochabers, Moray	NJ 359 592	Burl 1984, 49, 71	Finely divided oak charcoal under sand filling hollow M, one of 15 hollows under the cairn.	Charcoal	SRR-685	4250 to 3500 cal BC	5031±100	5030±140	−26.4
Temple Wood, Kilmartin, Argyll and Bute	NR 826 978	Scott 1989	Oak charcoal (TW98) from Stone Hole 8 of the dismantled circle to the north of main circle, 0.5m below surface; may be heartwood from a timber of the earlier timber circle.	Charcoal	GU-1296	4350 to 3350 cal BC	5025±190	5025±190	−25
Port Charlotte, Islay, Argyll and Bute	NR 248 576	Harrington & Pierpoint 1980; RCAHMS 1984, 50–2	Hazelnut shells and charcoal from occupation layer (PC79M406), with animal bones and flints under chambered cairn. See also HAR-2836 (4660±90 BP) and HAR-3486 (4940±70 BP). There is no significant difference between the 3 dates.	Charred hazelnut shells and charcoal	HAR-3487	3980 to 3640 cal BC	5020±90	5020±90	−26.3
Upper Largie, Argyll and Bute	NR 8330 9955	Ellis 2002, 145	Oak charcoal from sample 3046 from posthole of enclosure/cursus.	Charcoal	AA-43017	3960 to 3690 cal BC	5020±55	5020±55	−26.5

Site and Council	NGR	Reference	Description	Material	Code	Calibrated date	Laboratory Age BP	Adjusted Date BP	δ¹³C
Balbridie, Aberdeenshire (Kincardine and Deeside)	NO 733 959	Fairweather & Ralston 1993; Ralston 1982	Oak from the destruction level of a timber hall. See also other oak dates GU-1036–1038 and GU-1828–1832 ranging from 5020±90 to 4740±135 BP and dates from grain, flax, and linen ranging from 5010±90 to 4745±160 BP. See especially GU-1038i (5160±100 BP). Oak mean is 4980±28 BP; the preferred mean is that for grain etc., which is 4910±40 BP. The calibrated mean of the oak dates is between 3900–3700 cal BC; the preferred mean of grain etc. is between 3780–3640 cal BC.	Charcoal	GU-1038ii	4250 to 3500 cal BC	5020±90	5020±125	−26.5
Balbridie Aberdeenshire (Kincardine and Deeside)	NO 733 959	Fairweather & Ralston 1993; Ralston 1982	Oak from the destruction level of a timber hall. See also other oak dates GU-1036–1038 and GU-1828–1832 ranging from 5020±90 to 4740±135 BP and dates from grain, flax and linen ranging from 5010±90 to 4745±160 BP. The oak mean is 4980±28 BP; the preferred mean is that for grain etc., which is 4910±40 BP. The calibrated mean of the oak dates is between 3900–3700 cal BC; the preferred calibrated mean of grain etc. is between 3780–3640 cal BC.	Charcoal	GU-1831	4250 to 3500 cal BC	5015±125	5015±125	−26.4
Balbridie Aberdeenshire (Kincardin and Deeside)	NO 733 959	Ralston 1982; Fairweather & Ralston 1993	Crab apple from the destruction level of a timber hall. See also oak dates GU-1036–1038 and GU-1828–1832 ranging from 5160±100 to 4740±135 BP and dates from grain, flax, and linen ranging from 5010±90 to 4745±160 BP. Oak mean is 4980±28 BP; the preferred mean is that for grain etc., which is 4910±40 BP. The calibrated mean of the oak dates is between 3900–3700 cal BC; the preferred mean of grain etc. is between 3780–3640 cal BC.	Charred crab apple	OxA-1769	3970 to 3640 cal BC	5010±90	5010±90	
Carzield, Dumfriesshire, Dumfries and Galloway	NX 970 821	Sheridan 1995	Charcoal from a pit with carinated bowls.	Charcoal	Beta-68480	3960 to 3660 cal BC	5010±70	5010±70	

Site and Council	NGR	Reference	Description	Material	Code	Calibrated date	Laboratory Age BP	Adjusted Date BP	$\delta^{13}C$
Home Farm, Castle Menzies, Perth and Kinross	NN 8305 4935	Carter 2001, 126	Oak charcoal from sample 047 in the dark grey-brown sandy silt fill 433 of a post-pipe overlain by silt (442) in pit 233, part of an arc of post-pits possibly part of a circular timber structure.	Charcoal	OxA-9814	3950 to 3700 cal BC	5010±40	5010±40	−24.5
Carding Mill Bay I, Oban, Argyll and Bute	NM 8474 2935	Connock et al. 1992	Shell from lower layer of early shell midden in cliff face.	Shell	GU-2898	3960 to 3660 cal BC	5410±60	5005±70	.95
Claish Farm, Stirling	NN 635 065	Barclay 2002, 149–50	A piece of hazel charcoal (part of Sample 86) from the post-pipe of a steep-sided sub-rectangular feature (Context F30) with eight fills.	Charcoal	AA-49645	3950 to 3660 cal BC	5000±50	5000±50	−26.7
Stoneyfield, Raigmore, Inverness, Highland (Inverness)	NH 687 456	Simpson 1996, 82–3; (SC26068/2B)	Charcoal from Pit 18 (originally coded as Pit 151) with fragments of bone. See also, for similar pits, SRR-187 (4732±90 BP), SRR-188 (4983±130 BP), SRR-421 (5270±650 BP), SRR-426 (4890±60 BP), SRR-432 (4650±120 BP). According to Ministry of Works file this was 3045±95 BP.	Charcoal	SRR-424	4250 to 3350 cal BC	5004±95	5000±135	−26.8
Raschoille, Oban, Argyll and Bute	NM 8547 2888	Bonsall 1999	Single hazelnut shell from lower deposits of a cave.	Charred hazelnut shell	OxA-8440	3940 to 3660 cal BC	4995±45	4995±45	−21.8
Parks of Garden, Stirling	NS 6038 9682	Ellis 1999	Ten outer rings of an oak log, which may have fallen naturally, from peat underlying the platform.	Wood	OxA-8125	3940 to 3660 cal BC	4995±40	4995±40	−25.5
Ulva Cave, Argyll and Bute	NM 431 384	Bonsall et al. 1994	Charcoal from the lower infill of a pit containing charcoal, charred cereal grains, and marine shells.	Charcoal	GU-2707	3950 to 3650 cal BC	4990±60	4990±60	−25.4
Biggar Common East, South Lanarkshire	NT 030 395	Ward 1996, 140	Hazel charcoal from a spread of charcoal (103) in Area 2, near to shallow pits and containing large quantities of hazel kernels and early Neolithic potsherds. Presence of carbonized material with kernels indicates an area of food processing, possibly associated with a fire and cooking.	Charcoal	GU-4279	4050 to 3500 cal BC	4990±110	4990±110	−24.6

Site and Council	NGR	Reference	Description	Material	Code	Calibrated date	Laboratory Age BP	Adjusted Date BP	δ¹³C
Stoneyfield, Raigmore, Inverness, Highland (Inverness)	NH 687 456	Simpson 1996, 82–3; (SC26068/2B)	Charcoal from Pit 9 (originally coded as Pit 14 with cremation) with large stone slab with single cupmark on lower side.	Charcoal	SRR-188	4250 to 3350 cal BC	4983±130	4983±180	
Carding Mill Bay, Oban, Argyll and Bute	NM 8474 2935	Connock et al. 1992	Charcoal from lower layer of shell midden in fissure in cliff face.	Charcoal	GU-2797	3940 to 3650 cal BC	4980±50	4980±50	−25.8
Raschoille, Oban, Argyll and Bute	NM 8547 2888	Bonsall 1999	Humerus of a human child or juvenile from upper deposits of a cave.	Bone, human	OxA-8432	3940 to 3650 cal BC	4980±50	4980±50	−20.4
Upper Largie, Argyll and Bute	NR 8330 9955	Ellis 2002, 145	Oak charcoal from sample 2074 from posthole of enclosure/cursus.	Charcoal	AA-43015	3940 to 3650 cal BC	4975±50	4975±50	−24.1
Balbridie, Aberdeenshire (Kincardine and Deeside)	NO 733 959	Fairweather & Ralston 1993; Ralston 1982	Oak from the destruction level of a timber hall. See also other oak dates GU-1036–1038 and GU-1828–1832 ranging from 5020±90 to 4740±135 BP and dates from grain, flax, and linen ranging from 5010±90 to 4745±160 BP. The oak mean is 4980±28 BP: the preferred mean is that for grain etc., which is 4910±40 BP. The calibrated mean of the oak dates is between 3900–3700 cal BC; the preferred mean of grain etc. is between 3780–3640 cal BC.	Charcoal	GU-1830	3950 to 3640 cal BC	4970±75	4970±75	−25.9
Balbridie, Aberdeenshire (Kincardine and Deeside)	NO 733 959	Fairweather & Ralston 1993; Ralston 1982	Oak from the destruction level of a timber hall. See also other oak dates GU-1036–1038 and GU-1828–1832 ranging from 5020±90 to 4740±135 BP and dates from grain, flax, and linen ranging from 5010±90 to 4745±160 BP. The oak mean is 4980±28 BP: the preferred mean is that for grain etc., which is 4910±40 BP. The calibrated mean of the oak dates is between 3900–3700 cal BC; the preferred mean of grain etc. is between 3780–3640 cal BC.	Charcoal	GU-1832	3940 to 3640 cal BC	4970±60	4970±60	−25.8
Newton, Islay, Argyll and Bute	NR 341 628	McCullagh 1989	Alder, hazel, and oak charcoal from Pit F3, a small pit with pottery, incl. carinated bowls, cut by possible fence lines, which were in turn earlier than Pit F4 dated by GU-1951 (4880±60 BP).	Charcoal	GU-1952	3940 to 3640 cal BC	4965±60	4965±60	−27.4

Site and Council	NGR	Reference	Description	Material	Code	Calibrated date	Laboratory Age BP	Adjusted Date BP	δ¹³C
Fordhouse Barrow, Dun, Angus	NO 6658 6053	Proudfoot 1999	Large fragments from an oak timber used to build a structure in the phase 3B mound.	Charcoal	OxA-8224	3910 to 3650 cal BC	4965±40	4965±40	−26.4
Tulloch of Assery B, Highland (Caithness)	ND 067 618	Sharples 1986	Animal bone on the floor of the chambered tomb.	Bone, animal	GU-1332	3990 to 3520 cal BC	4965±60	4965±110	−20.4
Tulloch Wood, Forres, Moray	NJ 089 560	Carter 1993, 228–9	Charcoal from a buried A horizon of soil under Bank 2.	Charcoal	GU-3083	3960 to 3630 cal BC	4960±80	4960±80	−25.9
Brownsbank Farm, Biggar, South Lanarkshire	NT 0765 4280	Ward 2001, 126	Single piece of hazel charcoal from Trench No. 1 from a pit (Feature 1.) Containing carinated pottery and pitchstone.	Charcoal	AA-42172	3940 to 3640 cal BC	4960±45	4960±45	−25.9
Boghead, Fochabers, Moray	NJ 359 592	Burl 1984, 40, 55, 71	Charcoal from black layer beneath the mound with pottery. See also SRR-686 (4900±60 BP).	Charcoal	SRR-689	4250 to 3350 cal BC	4959±110	4960±155	−28.5
Balfarg Riding School, Fife	NO 28 5031	Barclay & Russell-White 1993, 160–1	Oak charcoal from Context 8019B of Pit 8016 with plain pottery bowls. See also GU-1903 (4765±55 BP) and GU-2604 (5170±90 BP) from the same pit, and GU-2030 (4720±70 BP) and UtC-1302 (4830±40 BP).	Charcoal	GU-2605	3960 to 3530 cal BC	4950±90	4950±90	−25.2
Camster, Highland (Caithness)	ND 260 443	Masters 1980; Masters 1997, 133, 157	Charcoal flecks from the B horizon under the tail of the chambered long cairn. See also GU-1708 (4915±60 BP) and GU-1709 (4920±125 BP). The old ground surface contained pottery, incl. carinated bowls in Grimston style, flaked stones, postholes, and stakeholes.	Charcoal	GU-1707	3960 to 3630 cal BC	4950±80	4950±80	−26.0
Upper Largie, Argyll and Bute	NR 8330 9955	Ellis 2002, 145	Oak charcoal from sample 3131.	Charcoal	AA-43023	3940 to 3640 cal BC	4950±55	4950±55	−26.2
Claish Farm, Stirling	NN 635 065	Barclay 2002, 149–50	A charred hazelnut shell (part of Sample 107) from a pit (Context F19) with 13 fills. The pit is striking for the substantial quantities of pottery used, apparently deliberately, to line its sides. The sample came from a heavily burnt layer, probable representing in situ burning. See also AA-49642 (4845±40) from the same context.	Charred hazelnut shell	AA-49643	3940 to 3640 cal BC	4950±50	4950±50	−24.9

Site and Council	NGR	Reference	Description	Material	Code	Calibrated date	Laboratory Age BP	Adjusted Date BP	δ¹³C
Boghead, Fochabers, Moray	NJ 359 592	Burl 1984, 50, 55, 71	Finely divided oak charcoal in sand infill of Pit 1, in the old ground surface under the North Cairn.	Charcoal	SRR-683	4400 to 3000 cal BC	4950±180	4950±250	−26.0
Deer's Den, Kintore Bypass. Aberdeenshire	NJ 784 160	Alexander 1999	Single hazelnut shell from one of a concentration of pits containing burnt bone, lithic artefacts, and pottery.	Charred hazelnut shell	OxA-8132	3800 to 3640 cal BC	4945±40	4945±40	−25.2
Port Charlotte, Islay, Argyll and Bute	NR 248 576	Harrington & Pierpoint 1980; RCAHMS 1984, 50–2	Hazelnut shells and charcoal from occupation layer (PC79M405), with animal bones and flints under chambered cairn. See also HAR-2836 (4660±90 BP) and HAR-3487 (5020±90 BP). There is no significant difference between the 3 dates.	Charred hazelnut shells and charcoal	HAR-3486	3950 to 3630 cal BC	4940±70	4940±70	−26.4
Balbridie, Aberdeenshire (Kincardine and Deeside)	NO 733 959	Ralston 1982; Fairweather & Ralston 1993	Flax from destruction level of a timber hall. See also oak dates GU-1036–1038 and GU-1828–1832 ranging from 5160±100 to 4740±135 BP and dates from grain, flax, and linen ranging from 5010±90 to 4745±160 BP. Oak mean is 4980±28 BP; the preferred mean is that for grain etc., which is 4910±40 BP. The calibrated mean of the oak dates is between 3900–3700 cal BC; the preferred mean of grain etc. is between 3780–3640 cal BC.	Charred seed	OxA-1768	3950 to 3630 cal BC	4940±70	4940±70	
Deer's Den, Kintore Bypass. Aberdeenshire	NJ 784 160	Alexander 1999	Single piece of oak roundwood charcoal from one of a concentration of pits, containing flint, pitchstone, and pottery.	Charcoal	OxA-8131	3800 to 3640 cal BC	4940±40	4940±40	−25.5
Upper Largie, Argyll and Bute	NR 8330 9955	Ellis 2002, 145	Oak charcoal from sample 2073 from posthole of enclosure/cursus.	Charcoal	AA-43014	3910 to 3630 cal BC	4935±50	4935±50	−25.1
Claish Farm, Stirling	NN 635 065	Barclay 2002, 149–50	A hazelnut shell (part of Sample 6) from an oval re-cut posthole (Context F13) related to slot F14 that runs across the N half of the structure. There were 12 fills.	Charred hazelnut shell	AA-49637	3790 to 3640 cal BC	4935±40	4935±40	−23.2
Midtown of Pitglassie, Aberdeenshire (Banff and Buchan)	NJ 686 434	Shepherd 1996, 22	Charred material forming a deposit on a carinated bowl of early type in the main pit in the area surrounded by the ring-mound.	Charcoal	GU-2014	4000 to 3500 cal BC	4935 ±105	4935±105	−26.0

Site and Council	NGR	Reference	Description	Material	Code	Calibrated date	Laboratory Age BP	Adjusted Date BP	δ¹³C
Raschoille, Oban, Argyll and Bute	NM 8547 2888	Bonsall 1999	Femur of a human child from upper deposits of a cave.	Bone, human	OxA-8431	3910 to 3630 cal BC	4930±50	4930±50	−20.6
Claish Farm, Stirling	NN 635 065	Barclay 2002, 149–50	Birch charcoal (part of Sample 19) from a charcoal-rich dark brown-black sandy loam and orange red silt sand (Context f15c), representing burning *in situ*, in a regular five-sided pit with seven fills. The pit was also used for the insertion of deposits that contained artefactual remains. See also AA-49639 (4895±40 BP) and AA-49641 (4885±50 BP) from the same context.	Charcoal	AA-49640	3790 to 3640 cal BC	4930±40	4930±40	−26
Balbridie, Aberdeenshire (Kincardine and Deeside)	NO 733 959	Ralston 1982; Fairweather & Ralston 1993	Oak charcoal from destruction level of a timber hall. See also other oak dates GU-1036–1038 and GU-1828–1832 ranging from 5020±90 to 4740±135 BP and dates from grain, flax, and linen ranging from 5010±90 to 4745±160 BP. The oak mean is 4980±28 BP; the preferred mean is that for grain etc., which is 4910±40 BP. The calibrated mean of the oak dates is between 3900–3700 cal BC; the preferred mean of grain etc. is between 3780–3640 cal BC.	Charcoal	GU-1037	4000 to 3350 cal BC	4930±80	4930±110	−25.7
Raschoille, Oban, Argyll and Bute	NM 8547 2888	Bonsall 1999	Humerus of an adult human from upper deposits of a cave.	Bone, human	OxA-8433	3800 to 3630 cal BC	4920±50	4920±50	−20.2
Fordhouse Barrow, Dun, Angus	NO 6658 6053	Proudfoot 1999	The outer rings of a radially split oak plank used to build a structure in the phase 3B mound.	Charcoal	OxA-8223	3790 to 3640 cal BC	4920±45	4920±45	−24.9
Camster, Highland (Caithness)	ND 260 443	Masters 1980; Masters 1997, 133, 157	Charcoal flecks from the B horizon under the tail of the chambered long cairn. See also GU-1708 (4915±60 BP) and GU-1707 (4950±80 BP). The old ground surface contained pottery, including carinated bowls in Grimston style, flaked stones, postholes, and stakeholes.	Charcoal	GU-1709	4000 to 3350 cal BC	4920±125	4920±125	−25.9
Carzield, Dumfriesshire, Dumfries and Galloway	NX 970821	Sheridan 1995	Charcoal from a pit with carinated bowls.	Charcoal	Beta-68481	4000 to 3350 cal BC	4920±110	4920±110	

Site and Council	NGR	Reference	Description	Material	Code	Calibrated date	Laboratory Age BP	Adjusted Date BP	δ¹³C
Camster, Highland (Caithness)	ND 260 443	Masters 1980; Masters 1997, 133, 157	Charcoal flecks from the B horizon under the tail of the chambered long cairn. See also GU-1707 (4950±80 BP) and GU-1709 (4920±125 BP). The old ground surface contained pottery, including carinated bowls in Grimston style, flaked stones, postholes, and stakeholes.	Charcoal	GU-1708	3940 to 3530 cal BC	4915±60	4915±60	−26.0
Claish Farm, Stirling	NN 635 065	Barclay 2002, 149–50	A hazelnut shell (part of Sample 24) from a sub-circular posthole (Context F9) on the E wall of the structure. No evidence of recut. 8 white quartz pebbles at bottom. The charcoal is probably remains of surface material fallen into post-pipe during rotting.	Charred hazelnut shell	AA-49635	3715 to 3645 cal BC	4915±40	4915±40	−28.3
Claish Farm, Stirling	NN 635 065	Barclay 2002, 149–50	A charred hazelnut shell (part of Sample 83) from a sub-circular large posthole (Context F21) with ten fills forming part of the curving NE wall of the building. The nutshell came from a heavily charcoal-flecked layer about half way down the fill which probably represents material from surface burning that has fallen into the posthole. The feature may well have been re-cut and there is evidence for burning of at least one post *in situ* and perhaps the deposition of burnt material and broken pottery.	Charred hazelnut shell	AA-49644	3800 to 3540 cal BC	4910±50	4910±50	−25
Claish Farm, Stirling	NN 635 065	Barclay 2002, 149–50	A hazelnut shell (part of Sample 39) from a sub-circular probable posthole (Context F8), with ten fills with clear evidence for replacement, on the E wall of the structure.	Charred hazelnut shell	AA-49636	3790 to 3630 cal BC	4910±45	4910±45	−22.5
Raschoille, Oban, Argyll and Bute	NM 8547 2888	Bonsall 1999	Humerus of an adult human from upper deposits of a cave.	Bone, human	OxA-8441	3780 to 3630 cal BC	4900±45	4900±45	−21.2
Boghead, Fochabers, Moray	NJ 359 592	Burl 1984, 40, 55, 71	Charcoal from black layer under the mound with pottery. See also SRR-689 (4960±110 BP).	Charcoal	SRR-686	4000 to 3350 cal BC	4898±60	4900±110	−25.9
Douglasmuir, Friockheim, Angus	NO 617 481	Kendrick 1995, 33	Oak charcoal from posthole (DM80 BAV) of an enclosure, from a depth of 0.75m in a post-pipe. See also GU-1210 (4855±55 BP) and GU-1469 (4895±70 BP).	Charcoal	GU-1470	4000 to 3350 cal BC	4900±65	4900±110	−25.2

Site and Council	NGR	Reference	Description	Material	Code	Calibrated date	Laboratory Age BP	Adjusted Date BP	δ¹³C
Eilean Domhnuill, N Uist, Western Isles	NB 747 753	Armit 2000, 127	A single piece of heather (ED 1003-2) from underwater deposits representing the earliest settlement traces located. Oxa-9084 (4735±45 BP), OxA-9086 (4775±50 BP), and OxA-9160 (4690±65 BP) from the same deposit.	Heather	OxA-9085	3790 to 3530 cal BC	4895±50	4895±50	
Deer's Den, Kintore Bypass, Aberdeenshire	NJ 784 160	Alexander 1999	Single hazelnut shell from one of a concentration of pits, containing burnt bone, lithic artefacts, and pottery.	Charred hazelnut shell	OxA-8133	3770 to 3630 cal BC	4895±40	4895±40	−24.7
Claish Farm, Stirling	NN 635 065	Barclay 2002, 149–50	A charred hazelnut shell (part of Sample 19) from a charcoal-rich dark brown-black sandy loam and orange red silt sand (Context f15c), representing burning in situ, in a regular five sided pit with seven fills. The pit was also used for the insertion of deposits that contained artefactual remains. See also AA-49640 (4930±40 BP) and AA-49641 (4885±50 BP) from the same context.	Charred hazelnut shell	AA-49639	3770 to 3630 cal BC	4895±40	4895±40	−24
Douglasmuir, Friockheim, Angus	NO 617 481	Kendrick 1995, 33	Oak charcoal from posthole (DM80 BDD) of an enclosure. Depth of posthole c.0.5–0.7m. See also GU-1470 (4900±65 BP) and GU-1210 (4855±55 BP).	Charcoal	GU-1469	4000 to 3350 cal BC	4895±70	4895±110	−24.6
Raschoille, Oban, Argyll and Bute	NM 8547 2888	Bonsall 1999	Humerus of an adult human from upper deposits of a cave.	Bone, human	OxA-8442	3780 to 3540 cal BC	4890±45	4890±45	−21.0
Stoneyfield, Raigmore, Inverness, Highland (Inverness)	NH 687 456	Simpson 1996, 82–3; (SC26068/2B)	Charcoal from Pit 41 (originally coded as Pit 174) with Grooved Ware sherds, lithic debitage, fragments of calcined bone and a carbonized hazelnut shell. See similar pits SRR-187 (4732±90 BP), SRR-188 (4983±130 BP), SRR-421 (5270±650 BP), SRR-424 (5000±100 BP), SRR-432 (4650±120 BP). This date is curiously early; another set of similar pits has dates well after 3000 cal BC. N.b. the Ministry of Works file gives this as 4588±60 BP or c.3600–3050 cal BC.	Charcoal	SRR-426	3950 to 3350 cal BC	4888±60	4890±110	−26.1

Site and Council	NGR	Reference	Description	Material	Code	Calibrated date	Laboratory Age BP	Adjusted Date BP	δ¹³C
Claish Farm, Stirling	NN 635 065	Barclay 2002, 149–50	A charred wheat grain (part of Sample 19) from a charcoal-rich dark brown-black sandy loam and orange red silt sand (Context f15c), representing burning *in situ*, in a regular five-sided pit with seven fills. The pit was also used for the insertion of deposits that contained artefactual remains. See also AA-49640 (4930±40) and AA-49639 (4895±40) from the same context.	Charred grain	AA-49641	3790 to 3530 cal BC	4885±50	4885±50	–25
Newton, Islay, Argyll and Bute	NR 341 628	McCullagh 1989	Oak charcoal from context 4 in Pit F4, a large pit, possibly the socket for a single massive post, cutting possible fence lines, which were in turn later than pit F3 dated by GU-1952 (4965±60 BP).	Charcoal	GU-1951	3800 to 3520 cal BC	4880±60	4880±60	–26.3
Raschoille, Oban, Argyll and Bute	NM 8847 2888	Bonsall 1999	A charred twig of hazel or similar species from lower deposits in a cave.	Charcoal	OxA-8536	3800 to 3520 cal BC	4880±60	4880±60	–27.2
Biggar Common West, South Lanarkshire	NT 000 390	Ward 1996, 140	Crab-apple charcoal from a charcoal spread (105) in an isolated spot with a concentration of early Neolithic potsherds mixed with charcoal; possible food preparation area.	Charcoal	GU-4276	3780 to 3530 cal BC	4880±50	4880±50	–26.2
Cleigh, Argyll and Bute	NM 878 257	Gilmour & Henderson 2002, 144; NM82NE 21	Hazel charcoal fragment (from Soil Sample 26) recovered from a compact silt deposit with charcoal inclusions (Context 33). Abutted stonework forming a possible cairn on top of original foundation material.	Charcoal	Beta-107675	3760 to 3530 cal BC	4870±40	4870±40	–27.8
Brownsbank Farm, Biggar, South Lanarkshire	NT 0765 4280	Ward 2001b, 126	Single piece of hazel charcoal from Trench No. 1 from a pit (Feature 2) containing carinated pottery and pitchstone.	Charcoal	AA-42173	3770 to 3520 cal BC	4865±45	4865±45	–26.2
Garvald Burn, Scottish Borders	NT 1015 4865	Barrowman 2001, 126	A piece of charred birch (sample CS4) from context 402 a sand layer; the charcoal almost certainly comes from a hearth c.1m to the east.	Charcoal	OxA-10449	3760 to 3530 cal BC	4865±40	4865±40	–24.4
Glenvoidean, Bute, Argyll and Bute	NR 997 705	Marshall & Taylor 1977, 14	Charcoal under the west slab of the main chamber.	Charcoal	I-5974	4050 to 3100 cal BC	4860±115	4860±160	

Site and Council	NGR	Reference	Description	Material	Code	Calibrated date	Laboratory Age BP	Adjusted Date BP	δ¹³C
Chapelfield, Cowie, Stirling	NS 8363 8957	Atkinson 1997	Hazel charcoal from the final fill (350) of Pit 7 (441) containing up to five early pottery vessels undisturbed in the period after deposition; no evidence to suggest burning *in situ*. See GU-7208 from the overlying layer.	Charcoal	GU-7203	3950 to 3350 cal BC	4860±100	4860±100	−25.9
Claish Farm, Stirling	NN 635 065	Barclay 2002, 149–50	A charred hazelnut shell (part of Sample 80A) from the post-pipe of a light sub-circular posthole (Context F37), with two fills, in the N wall. The sample probably reflects burnt material on the surface during demolition or rotting of the post.	Charred hazelnut shell	AA-49646	3790 to 3380 cal BC	4855±70	4855±70	−27.1
Douglasmuir, Friockheim, Angus	NO 617 481	Kendrick 1995, 33	Oak charcoal from a post-pipe (DM79/T11/F514/LO1) in a truncated posthole forming part of enclosure. See also GU-1470 (4900±65 BP) and GU-1469 (4895±70 BP).	Charcoal	GU-1210	3950 to 3350 cal BC	4855±55	4855±110	−24.8
Raschoille, Oban, Argyll and Bute	NM 8547 2888	Bonsall 1999	Humerus of an adult human from upper deposits of a cave.	Bone, human	OxA-8404	3790 to 3380 cal BC	4850±70	4850±70	−21.6
Claish Farm, Stirling	N N635 065	Barclay 2002, 149–50	A charred hazelnut shell (part of Sample 100) from a pit (Context F19) with 13 fills. The pit is striking for the substantial quantities of pottery used, apparently deliberately, to line its sides. The sample came from a heavily burnt layer, probable representing *in situ* burning. See also AA-49643 (4950±50 BP) from the same context.	Charred hazelnut shell	AA-49642	3710 to 3520 cal BC	4845±40	4845±40	−25.2
Upper Largie, Argyll and Bute	NR 8330 9955	Ellis 2002, 145	Oak charcoal from sample 3045 from posthole of enclosure/cursus.	Charcoal	AA-43016	3720 to 3510 cal BC	4840±50	4840±50	−26.3

Site and Council	NGR	Reference	Description	Material	Code	Calibrated date	Laboratory Age BP	Adjusted Date BP	δ¹³C
Balbridie, Aberdeenshire (Kincardine and Deeside)	NO 733 959	Fairweather & Ralston 1993; Ralston 1982; Ralston & Reynolds 1981	Oak charcoal from destruction level of a timber hall. See also other oak dates GU-1036–1038 and GU-1828–1832 ranging from 5020±90 to 4740±135 BP and dates from grain, flax, and linen ranging from 5010±90 to 4745±160 BP. The oak mean is 4980±28 BP; the preferred mean is that for grain etc., which is 4910±40 BP. The calibrated mean of the oak dates is between 3900–3700 cal BC; the preferred calibrated mean of grain etc. is between 3780–3640 cal BC.	Charcoal	GU-1035	4300 to 2900 cal BC	4840±165	4840±230	−25.6
Tulloch of Assery B, Highland (Caithness)	ND 067 618	Sharples 1986	Charcoal from the pre-cairn surface beneath the chambered tomb.	Charcoal	GU-1339	3950 to 3350 cal BC	4840±65	4840±110	−24.7
Cowie Road, Bannockburn, Stirling	NS 816 901	Rideout 1997, 37, 52–3	Hazel charcoal from phase 2 fill of Pit P25 of an enclosure, 33–36m across, with a rounded end.	Charcoal	AA-20412	3760 to 3380 cal BC	4830±60	4830±60	
Carding Mill Bay I, Oban, Argyll and Bute	NM 848 290	Bonsall and Smith 1992; Connock et al. 1992; Schulting 2000a, 122	Human bone from lower layer of the earlier shell midden deposit (Contexts XV and XIV), which yielded all the previous ¹⁴C dates on charcoal, shell, and artefacts; the new date fits in well with this group, and suggests that the whole midden deposit can be viewed within a 'Neolithic' context – one that included burial as well as other activities.	Bone, human	OxA-7664	3710 to 3520 cal BC	4830±45	4830±45	−20.9
Eilean Domhnuill, N Uist, Western Isles	NB 747 753	Armit 2000, 127	A single grain of barley (ED 681-2) from a phase 9 hearth deposit. See also OxA-9157 (4675±60 BP) from the same deposit	Charred seed	OxA-9079	3710 to 3520 cal BC	4830±45	4830±45	−23.6
Balfarg Riding School, Fife	NO 285 031	Barclay & Russell-White 1993, 160–1	Carbonized barley from a sherd (in Pit 2212) of globular pottery. See also GU-2030 (4720±70 BP) from a pit with similar pottery, and GU-1903 (4765±55 BP), GU-2604 (5170±90 BP) and GU-2605 (4950±70 BP), all from a pit with plain pottery.	Charred grain	UtC-1302	3700 to 3520 cal BC	4830±40	4830±40	−24.2

Site and Council	NGR	Reference	Description	Material	Code	Calibrated date	Laboratory Age BP	Adjusted Date BP	δ¹³C
Crarae, Argyll and Bute	NR 986 973	Scott 1961; Schulting 2000b, 122	Cockle shell from sample NN 1161 which may refer to the construction/initial use phase of the monument. Oxa-7880 part of a large group of shells in the burial chamber, interpreted by the excavator as probably a foundation deposit.	Shell	OxA-7880	4230 to 3950 cal BC	5230±55	4825±55	
Rascholie, Oban, Argyll and Bute	NM 8547 2888	Bonsall 1999	Humerus of an adult human from upper deposits of a cave.	Bone, human	OxA-8443	3710 to 3380 cal BC	4825±55	4825±55	−20.4
Balbridie, Aberdeenshire (Kincardine and Deeside)	NO 733 959	Fairweather & Ralston 1993; Ralston 1982	Oat grain from destruction level of a timber hall. See also oak dates GU-1036–1038 and GU-1828–1832 ranging from 5160±100 to 4740±135 BP and dates from grain, flax, and linen ranging from 5010±90 to 4745±160 BP. Oak mean is 4980±28 BP; the preferred mean is that for grain etc., which is 4910±40 BP and the calibrated mean of the oak dates is between 3900–3700 cal BC; the preferred mean of grain etc. is between 3780–3640 cal BC.	Charred oat	OxA-1767	3770 to 3370 cal BC	4820±80	4820±80	
Alt Chrysal, Barra, Western Isles	NL 642 977	Branigan & Foster 1995	Birch charcoal in a layer below a pottery clamp and above a circular/apsidal timber building at the base of the sequence. See also GU-3923 (4470±60 BP) for the top of the sequence.	Charcoal	GU-3922	3710 to 3370 cal BC	4820±60	4820±60	−25.8
Machrie Moor, Arran, North Ayrshire	NR 912 324	Haggarty 1991	Mixed charcoal from pits with bits of six plain pots incl. carinated bowls. See also GU-2320 (5500±70 BP), with very similar potsherds.	Charcoal	GU-2321	3710 to 3380 cal BC	4820±50	4820±50	−25.5
Boghead, Fochabers, Moray	NJ 359 592	Burl 1984, 43, 50, 55, 71	Large fragments of oak from layer XIII, debris on the old ground surface under North Cairn.	Charcoal	SRR-684	3950 to 3350 cal BC	4823±60	4820±110	−24.7
Duntreath, Stirling	NS 5328 8072	MacKie 1972b, 38–9; RCAHMS 1979, 16	Charcoal from the top of Layer 3, in one of several white ashy spreads containing flecks of charcoal. The socket for the one remaining upright stone was cut through Layer 3, but Layer 2 appeared to have accumulated against it.	Charcoal	GX-2781	4500 to 2500 cal BC	4810±270	4810±380	

Site and Council	NGR	Reference	Description	Material	Code	Calibrated date	Laboratory Age BP	Adjusted Date BP	δ¹³C
Pitnacree, Strathtay, Perth and Kinross	NN 928 533	Coles & Simpson 1965, 40	Charcoal, thought by the excavators to represent burning of vegetation before construction of a mortuary enclosure. Under the soil were two massive postholes. These remains were all below an embanked stone and turf enclosure under or forming part of the construction of a round mound. See Spriggs and Anderson 1993 for reservations about the accuracy of many GaK dates measured in the 1970s and 80s.	Charcoal	GaK-601	4300 to 2800 cal BC	4810 ± 90	4810 ± 270	
Warden's Dykes, Dumfries and Galloway (Annandale and Eskdale)	NY 3035 6899	Banks forthcoming	Oak, alder, hazel, and unidentified charcoal from a probably later posthole in the sequence also dated by GU-3508 (4670 ± 60 BP).	Charcoal	GU-3509	3720 to 3370 cal BC	4800 ± 80	4800 ± 80	−25.9
Chapelfield, Cowie, Stirling	NS 8363 8957	Atkinson 1997	Hazel charcoal from charcoal-rich basal fill (440) of Pit 7 (441), under a redeposited fill containing up to five early vessels (See GU-7203). There was no evidence of burning in situ.	Charcoal	GU-7208	3720 to 3370 cal BC	4800 ± 80	4800 ± 80	−26.0
Carding Mill Bay I Oban, Argyll and Bute	NM 848 290	Connock et al. 1992; Schulting 2000a, 122	Human phalanx from the upper layer C XIV:1 of the earlier shell midden deposit, overlying C XV. The date is indistinguishable from OxA-7664 (and could conceivably belong to the same individual).	Bone, human	OxA-7663	3700 to 3380 cal BC	4800 ± 50	4800 ± 50	−21.5
Knap of Howar, Papa Westray, Orkney Islands	HY 4830 5180	Ritchie 2000, 124–5	A sheep foetus metatarsal from Trench III, layer 3, secondary midden c.20m south of House 1.	Bone, animal	OxA-9759	3660 to 3380 cal BC	4800 ± 45	4800 ± 45	−18.9
Tulloch of Assery A, Highland (Caithness)	ND 068 618	Sharples 1986	Disarticulated human bone on the SW bench of the N chamber of the chambered tomb.	Bone, human	GU-1338	3950 to 3300 cal BC	4800 ± 60	4800 ± 110	−20.7

Site and Council	NGR	Reference	Description	Material	Code	Calibrated date	Laboratory Age BP	Adjusted Date BP	δ¹³C
Balbridie, Aberdeenshire (Kincardine and Deeside)	NO733959	Fairweather & Ralston 1993; Ralston 1982	Oak from destruction level of a timber hall. See also other oak dates GU-1036–1038 and GU-1828–1832 ranging from 5020±90 to 4740±135 BP and dates from grain, flax, and linen ranging from 5010±90 to 4745±160 BP. The oak mean is 4980±28 BP; the preferred mean is that for grain etc., which is 4910±40 BP. The calibrated mean of the oak dates is between 3900–3700 cal BC; the preferred mean of grain etc. is between 3780–3640 cal BC.	Charcoal	GU-1829	3950 to 3100 cal BC	4785±150	4785±150	−25.2
Camster, Highland (Caithness)	ND 260 443	Masters 1980; Masters 1997, 133, 157	Charcoal from a burnt area in the SW forecourt of the chambered long cairn. The date is younger than, but statistically indistinguishable from, three other dates from the old ground surface under the cairn GU-1707 (4950±80 BP), GU-1708 (4915±60 BP), and GU-1709 (4920±125 BP).	Charcoal	GU-1706	4000 to 3050 cal BC	4780±170	4780±170	−25.1
Lairg, Achany Glen, Achaidh Mór, Highland (Sutherland)	NC 580 024	McCullagh 1996; McCullagh & Tipping 1998, 95, 156	Alder charcoal distributed throughout a shallow, well-stratified sandy loam containing a small assemblage of pottery. Interpreted as an early sediment that accumulated prior to the first phase of a multi-phase cairn. See also AA-17460±60 BP.	Charcoal	AA-17461	3660 to 3370 cal BC	4775±60	4775±60	−25.4
Eilean Domhnuill, N Uist, Western Isles	NB 747 753	Armit 2000, 127	An uncharred hazel twig (ED 1008-2) from underwater deposits representing the earliest settlement traces located. See also OxA-9084 (4735±45 BP) OxA-9085 (4895±50 BP) and OxA-9160 (4690±65 BP) from the same deposit.	Wood	OxA-9086	3660 to 3370 cal BC	4775±50	4775±50	
Machrie Moor, Arran, North Ayrshire	NR 912 324	Haggarty 1991, 58	Oak charcoal in a pit cutting an early ditch terminal; another such pit contained plain pottery.	Charcoal	GU-2315	3710 to 3350 cal BC	4770±90	4770±90	−26.4
Knap of Howar, Papa Westray, Orkney Islands	HY 483 578	Ritchie 1983	Animal bone from the primary midden of Period I in Trench V.	Bone, animal	Birm-816	4300 to 2800 cal BC	4770±180	4770±250	−19.4

Site and Council	NGR	Reference	Description	Material	Code	Calibrated date	Laboratory Age BP	Adjusted Date BP	δ13C
Knap of Howar, Papa Westray, Orkney Islands	HY 483 578	Ritchie 1983	Animal bone from E/II/3, secondary midden of Period II in Trench II outside S wall of house. See also F/II/11 SRR-344 (4450±70 BP).	Bone, animal	SRR-348	3900 to 3100 cal BC	4765±70	4770±110	−21.9
Balfarg Riding School, Fife	NO 285 031	Barclay & Russell-White 1993, 160–1	Alder, hazel, and ash charcoal from Context 8019B of Pit 8016 with plain pottery bowls. See also GU-2604 (5170±90 BP) and GU-2605 (4950±70 BP) from the same pit, and GU-2030 (4720±70 BP) and UtC-1302 (4830±40 BP).	Charcoal	GU-1903	3700 to 3360 cal BC	4765±85	4765±85	−24.8
Carding Mill Bay I, Oban, Argyll and Bute	NM 8474 2935	Bonsall & Smith 1992	Bone bevel-ended tool from the upper part (XIV) of a shell midden.	Bone, animal	OxA-3739	3660 to 3370 cal BC	4765±65	4765±65	
Knap of Howar, Papa Westray, Orkney Islands	HY 4830 5180	Ritchie 2000, 124–5	A pig humerus distal fragment from Trench III, layer 4, primary midden some 20 m south of House 1.	Bone, animal	OxA-9760	3650 to 3370 cal BC	4750±50	4750±50	−20.1
Caisteal nan Gillean. Oronsay, Argyll and Bute	NR 359 879	Jardine & Jardine 1983	Charcoal in midden. See also SRR-1458b (5890±70 BP).	Charcoal	SRR-1458a	4300 to 2800 cal BC	4750±180	4750±250	−26
Balbridie, Aberdeenshire (Kincardine and Deeside)	NO 733 959	Fairweather & Ralston 1993; Ralston 1982	A bulk sample BB79 WS14,17,36,38,85 of emmer from destruction level of a timber hall. See also oak dates GU-1036–1038 and GU-1828–1832 ranging from 5020±90 to 4740±135 BP and dates from grain, flax, and linen ranging from 5010±90 to this date. Oak mean is 4980±28 BP; the preferred mean is that for grain etc., which is 4910±40 BP. The calibrated mean of the oak dates is between 3900–3700 cal BC; the preferred mean of grain etc. is between 3780–3640 cal BC.	Charred grain	GU-1421	4000 to 2900 cal BC	4745±160	4745±225	−25.3
Ardnadam, Cowal, Argyll and Bute	NS 163 791	Rennie 1984, 17–18	Charcoal from the lowest hearth of a small sub-rectangular structure, No 5, middle to late in the sequence of a small settlement, with pottery close by.	Charcoal	GU-1549	3710 to 3340 cal BC	4740±90	4740±90	

Site and Council	NGR	Reference	Description	Material	Code	Calibrated date	Laboratory Age BP	Adjusted Date BP	δ¹³C
Shurton Hill, Lerwick, Shetland Islands	HU 441 403	Whittington 1978	Charcoal beneath a sub-peat dyke; also quoted as 4750, and as 4800 by Ralston 1986.	Charcoal	UB-2122	3640 to 3370 cal BC	4740±50	4740±50	
Bolsay Farm, Port Charlotte, Islay, Argyll and Bute	NR 2253 5736	Mithen 2000, 281	Willow from context 4, quadrat (67,57), a largely undisturbed horizon of the Mesolithic occupation or activity site. See AA-21632 and AA-21633.	Charcoal	AA-21631	3640 to 3370 cal BC	4740±50	4740±50	−27.9
Balbridie, Aberdeenshire (Kincardine and Deeside)	NO 733 959	Fairweather & Ralston 1993; Ralston 1982; Ralston & Reynolds 1981	Oak charcoal from destruction level of a timber hall. See also other oak dates GU-1036-1038 and GU-1828-1832 ranging from 5020±90 to this date and dates from grain, flax, and linen ranging from 5010±90 to 4745±160 BP. The oak mean is 4980±28 BP; the preferred mean is that for grain etc., which is 4910±40 BP. The calibrated mean of the oak dates is between 3900–3700 cal BC; the preferred calibrated mean of grain etc. is between 3780–3640 cal BC.	Charcoal	GU-1036	4000 to 2900 cal BC	4740±135	4740±190	−25.2
Eilean Domhnuill, N Uist, Western Isles	NB 747 753	Armit 2000, 127	A single hazelnut (ED 1003-1) from underwater deposits representing the earliest settlement traces located. See also OxA-9085 (4895±50 BP), OxA-9086 (4775±50 BP) and OxA-9160 (4690±65 BP) from the same deposit.	Charred hazelnut shell	OxA-9084	3640 to 3370 cal BC		4735±45	
Crarae, Argyll and Bute	NR 986 973	Scott 1961; Schulting 2000b, 122	Human phalanx from NN 1186.2, part of a small group of human bones and teeth at the east end of the middle segment of the burial chamber. The date confirms the 4th millennium attribution of the human bones.	Bone, human	OxA-7662	3640 to 3370 cal BC	4735±40	4735±40	−21.5
Stoneyfield, Raigmore, Inverness, Inverness, Highland (Inverness)	NH 687 456	Simpson 1996, 82–3	Charcoal in Pit 6 (originally Pit 11 with cremation) with potsherd. See also SRR-188 (4983±130 BP), SRR-421 (5270±650 BP), SRR-424 (5000±150 BP) SRR-426 (4890±60 BP), SRR-432 (4650±120 BP). This date is curiously early. Another set of similar pits has dates after 3000 cal BC.	Charcoal	SRR-187	3800 to 3100 cal BC	4732±90	4732±125	
Cadgers Brae, Grangemouth, Falkirk	NS 9297 7944	Sloan 1985	Shell from a shell midden.	Shell	GU-1884	3640 to 3360 cal BC	5130±60	4725±70	

Site and Council	NGR	Reference	Description	Material	Code	Calibrated date	Laboratory Age BP	Adjusted Date BP	δ13C
Dunloskin Wood, Cowal, Argyll and Bute	NS 166 785	Rennie 1986	Charcoal from the hearth on period 1 floor of either a 9.5m round house, or possibly an oval turf house, on a platform (Platform 9). See also GU-2064 (4570±150 BP) from same context.	Charcoal	GU-2063	3950 to 3000 cal BC	4725±150	4725±150	−27.1
Kinloch, Rum, Highland (Lochaber)	NM 403 998	Wickham-Jones 1990, 134	Charcoal from a fill of a hollow in an earlier settlement. See also GU-2148 (4080±60).	Charcoal	GU-2043	3800 to 3000 cal BC	4725±140	4725±140	−27.3
Meldon Bridge, Peebles, Scottish Borders (Tweeddale)	NT 205 404	Speak & Burgess 1999, 103	Charcoal from small pit (LY77 N45 87) in large timber enclosure.	Charcoal	GU-1057	3800 to 3050 cal BC	4725±90	4725±125	−25.5
Kinloch Farm, Collessie, Fife	NO 279 115	Barber 1982, 532	Flecks of charcoal from the inner ditch of a double-ditched enclosure; the features inside contained pottery.	Charcoal	GU-1375	3800 to 3100 cal BC	4725±70	4725±110	−25.4
Balfarg Riding School, Fife	NO 285 031	Barclay & Russell-White 1993, 160–1	Hazel charcoal from Pit 2050 with globular pottery bowls; see also UtC-1302 with similar pottery and GU-1903 (4765±55 BP), GU-2604 (5170±90 BP), and GU-2605 (4950±70 BP), all from a pit with plain pottery bowls.	Charcoal	GU-2606	3640 to 3360 cal BC	4720±70	4720±70	−27.4
Raschoille, Oban, Argyll and Bute	NM 8547 2888	Bonsall 1999	Femur of a human child from upper deposits of a cave.	Bone, human	OxA-8434	3640 to 3370 cal BC	4720±50	4720±50	−21.1
Knap of Howar, Papa Westray, Orkney Islands	HY 48305 180	Ritchie 2000, 124–5	A sheep bone from layer 9/14, primary midden redeposited within the wall-core of House 1.	Bone, animal	OxA-9754	3640 to 3370 cal BC	4720±50	4720±50	−20.5
Raschoille, Oban, Argyll and Bute	NM 8547 2888	Bonsall 1999	Humerus of an adult human from upper deposits of a cave.	Bone, human	OxA-8444	3640 to 3370 cal BC	4715±45	4715±45	−21.1
Port Charlotte, Islay, Argyll and Bute	NR 248 576	Harrington & Pierpoint 1980; pers. comm. 13 Oct. 1980; RCAHMS 1984, 50–2	Charcoal from the chamber of chambered cairn. See also HAR-2084 (4540±70 BP). There is no significant difference between the two dates.	Charcoal	HAR-2406	3640 to 3360 cal BC	4710±70	4710±70	

Site and Council	NGR	Reference	Description	Material	Code	Calibrated date	Laboratory Age BP	Adjusted Date BP	δ¹³C
Home Farm, Castle Menzies, Perth and Kinross	NN 8305 4935	Carter 2001, 126	Hazel charcoal from sample 001 in the charcoal-rich black silty loam basal fill 027 of posthole 004, which did not form part of either the alignments or the arc of postholes on this site.	Charcoal	OxA-9811	3640 to 3360 cal BC	4701 ± 38	4700 ± 40	−24.7
Eilean Domhnuill, N Uist, Western Isles	NF 7500 7529	Armit 2002, 152	Plant remains (Rhytidiadephus) from contexts interpreted as more or less contemporary floor levels submerged by subsequent lake level rise, representing the earliest settlement traces located. See also OxA-9084 (4735 ± 45 BP), OxA-9085 (4895 ± 50 BP) and OxA-9086 (4775 ± 50 BP) from the same deposit.	Plant remains	OxA-9160	3640 to 3350 cal BC	4690 ± 65	4690 ± 65	−25.8
Carding Mill Bay I, Oban, Argyll and Bute	NM 848 290	Connock et al. 1992; Schulting 2000a, 122	Human, parietal bone from a remnant deposit C VII:130 against the SE rock face, attributed to the earlier shell midden but seen by the excavators as possibly disturbed.	Bone, human	OxA-7665	3630 to 3360 cal BC	4690 ± 40	4690 ± 40	−21.4
Knap of Howar, Papa Westray, Orkney Islands	HY 4830 5180	Ritchie 2000, 124–5	A cattle metatarsal from layer 7, a secondary floor deposit of House 2.	Bone, animal	OxA-9757	3630 to 3360 cal BC	4680 ± 50	4680 ± 50	−20.6
Eilean Domhnuill, N Uist, Western Isles	NB 747 753	Armit 2000, 127	A single grain of barley (ED 681-1) from a phase 9 hearth deposit. See also OxA-9079 (4830 ± 45 BP) from the same deposit.	Charred grain	OxA-9157	3640 to 3350 cal BC	4675 ± 60	4675 ± 60	−22.5

References

Affleck, T.L., Edwards, K. and Clarke, A. 1988. Archaeological and palynological studies at the Mesolithic pitchstone and flint site of Auchareoch, Isle of Arran. *Proceedings of the Society of Antiquaries of Scotland* **118**, 37–59.

Alexander, D. 1997. Excavation of pits containing decorated Neolithic pottery and early lithic material of possible Mesolithic date at Spurryhillock, Stonehaven, Aberdeenshire. *Proceedings of the Society of Antiquaries of Scotland* **127**, 17–27.

Alexander, D. 1999. Deer's Den, Kintore Bypass, Aberdeenshire. *Discovery and Excavation in Scotland 1999*, 110.

Armit, I. 2000. Eilean Domhnuill, North Uist. *Discovery and Excavation in Scotland* (new series) **1**, 127.

Armit, I. 2002. Eilean Domhnuill, North Uist. *Discovery and Excavation in Scotland* (new series) **3**, 152.

Ashmore, P.J. 1999. Radiocarbon dating: avoiding errors by avoiding mixed samples. *Antiquity* **73**, 124–30.

Ashmore, P.J. and Hall, D. 1996. Shell midden at Braehead, Alloa. *Forth Naturalist and Historian* **20**, 123–9.

Ashmore, P.J., Cook G.T. and Harkness D.D. 2000. *Radiocarbon Dates for Archaeological Sites in Scotland issued before June 1996*. Edinburgh: Historic Scotland.

Atkinson, J.A. 1997. Chapelfield, Cowie. *Discovery and Excavation in Scotland 1997*, 116.

Atkinson, J.A. 2000a. Excavations on the Leven, Loudoun Hill, Ayrshire, 1993. *Scottish Archaeological Journal* **22**(1), 31–68.

Atkinson, J.A. 2000b. Ben Lawers, Perth and Kinross. *Discovery and Excavation in Scotland* (new series) **1**, 125.

Atkinson, J.A. 2000c. Chapelfield, Cowie, Stirling. *Discovery and Excavation in Scotland* (new series) **1**, 126.

Baker, F.M. 1998. Summerston Landfill Site, Balmuidy. *Discovery and Excavation in Scotland 1998*, 126.

Banks, I. Forthcoming. The excavation of multi-period remains adjacent to the banked enclosure of Warden's Dykes, Gretna: Neolithic, Bronze Age and Early Historic Evidence from the M74.

Barber, J.W. 1982. The investigation of some plough truncated features at Kinloch Farm, Collessie in Fife. *Proceedings of the Society of Antiquaries of Scotland* **112**, 524–33.

Barber, J.W. (ed.). 1997. *The Archaeological Investigation of a Prehistoric Landscape: Excavations on Arran 1978–1981*. Edinburgh: Scottish Trust for Archaeological Research (Monograph **2**).

Barclay, G.J. 1978. The excavation of a cairn at Pitcairn, Glenrothes, Fife. *Proceedings of the Society of Antiquaries of Scotland* **109** (1977–78), 361–6.

Barclay, G.J. 2002. Claish Farm, Stirling. *Discovery and Excavation in Scotland* (new series) **3**, 149–50.

Barclay, G.J. and Maxwell, G.S. 1991. Excavation of a Neolithic long mortuary enclosure within the Roman legionary fortress at Inchtuthil, Perthshire. *Proceedings of the Society of Antiquaries of Scotland* **121**, 27–44.

Barclay, G.J. and Maxwell, G.S. 1998. *The Cleaven Dyke and Littleour: Monuments in the Neolithic of Tayside*. Edinburgh: Society of Antiquaries of Scotland (Monograph **13**).

Barclay, G.J. and Russell-White, C.J. 1993. Excavations in the ceremonial complex of the fourth to second millennium BC at Balfarg/Balbirnie, Glenrothes, Fife. *Proceedings of the Society of Antiquaries of Scotland* **123**, 43–210.

Barrowman, C. 2001. Garvald Burn, Scottish Borders. *Discovery and Excavation in Scotland* (new series) **2**, 126.

Bonsall, C. 1996. Lón Mór, Oban. *Discovery and Excavation in Scotland 1996*, 136.

Bonsall, C. 1999. Raschoille, Oban. *Discovery and Excavation in Scotland 1999*, 112.

Bonsall, C. and Smith, C. 1989. Late Palaeolithic and Mesolithic bone and antler artifacts from Britain: first reactions to accelerator dates. *Mesolithic Miscellany* **10**(1), 33–8.

Bonsall, C. and Smith, C. 1990. Bone and antler technology in the British Late Upper Palaeolithic and Mesolithic: the impact of accelerator dating. *In* P.M. Vermeesch and P. Van Peer (eds), *Contributions to the Mesolithic in Europe*, 359–68. Leuven: Leuven University Press.

Bonsall, C. and Smith, C. 1992. New AMS ¹⁴C dates for antler and bone artifacts from Great Britain. *Mesolithic Miscellany* **13**(2), 28–34.

Bonsall, C., Robinson, M., Payton, R, and Macklin, M. 1993. Lón Mór. *Discovery and Excavation in Scotland 1993*, 76.

Bonsall, C., Sutherland, D.G., Russell, N.J., Coles, G., Paul, C.R.C., Huntley, J.P. and Lawson, T.J. 1994. Excavations in Ulva Cave, western Scotland 1990–91: a preliminary report. *Mesolithic Miscellany* **15**(1), 8–21.

Bonsall, C., Tolan-Smith, C. and Saville, A. 1995. Direct dating of Mesolithic antler and bone artifacts from Great Britain: new results for bevelled tools and red deer antler mattocks. *Mesolithic Miscellany* **16**(1), 2–10.

Bonsall, C., Bailey, G. and Sloan, D. Forthcoming. Mumrills shell midden.

Bradley, R. 2000. *The Good Stones: a New Investigation of the Clava Cairns*. Edinburgh: Society of Antiquaries of Scotland (Monograph **17**).

Branigan, K. and Foster, P. 1995. *Barra: Archaeological Research on Ben Tangaval*. Sheffield: Sheffield Academic Press.

Bronk Ramsey, C. 1995. Radiocarbon calibration and analysis of stratigraphy: the program OxCal. *Radiocarbon* **37**(2), 425–30.

Bronk Ramsey, C. 2000. OxCal 3.5 (www.rlaha.ox.ac.uk/orau.html).

Burl, H.A.W. 1984. Report on the excavation of a Neolithic mound at Boghead, Speymouth Forest, Fochabers, Moray, 1972 and 1974. *Proceedings of the Society of Antiquaries of Scotland* **114**, 35–73.

Carter, S. 1993. Tulloch Wood, Forres, Moray: the survey and dating of a fragment of prehistoric landscape. *Proceedings of the Society of Antiquaries of Scotland* **123**, 215–33.

Carter, S. 2001. Home Farm, Castle Menzies, Perth and Kinross. *Discovery and Excavation in Scotland* (new series) **2**, 126.

Clutton-Brock, J. and MacGregor, A. 1988. An end to medieval reindeer in Scotland. *Proceedings of the Society of Antiquaries of Scotland* **118**, 23–35.

Coles, J.M. 1971. The early settlement of Scotland: excavations at Morton, Fife. *Proceedings of the Prehistoric Society* **37**(2), 284–366.

Coles, J.M. and Simpson, D.D.A. 1965. The excavation of a Neolithic round barrow at Pitnacree, Perthshire, Scotland. *Proceedings of the Prehistoric Society* **31**, 34–57.

Connock, K.D., Finlayson, B. and Mills, C.M. 1992. Excavation of a shell midden site at Carding Mill Bay near Oban, Scotland. *Glasgow Archaeological Journal* **17**, 25–38.

Cook, M. 2002. Inveresk, East Lothian. *Discovery and Excavation in Scotland* (new series) **3**, 146.

Cormack, W.F. 1968. Barsalloch, Wigtownshire. *Discovery and Excavation in Scotland 1968*, 46.

Cressey, M. 2000. Solway Phase 3, Dumfries and Galloway. *Discovery and Excavation in Scotland* (new series) **1**, 122.

Cressey, M. 2001. Camas Daraich, Skye, Highland. *Discovery and Excavation in Scotland* (new series) **2**, 124.

Cressey, M., Hardy, K. and Wickham-Jones, C.R. 2000a. Camas Daraich, Skye, Highland. *Discovery and Excavation in Scotland* (new series) **1**, 123.

Cressey, M., Hardy, K. & Wickham Jones, C.R. 2000b. Sand, Highland. *Discovery and Excavation in Scotland* (new series) **1**, 124.

Cressey, M., Hardy, K. and Wickham-Jones, C.R. 2000c. Loch A Squir, Raasay, Highland. *Discovery and Excavation in Scotland* (new series) **1**, 123.

Cressey M, Milburn, P and Crone, A. 2001. *Solway Firth Environmental Assessment and Coastal Management Survey (Newbie Cottages to Broom Knowes, near Powfoot)*. Edinburgh: Scottish Natural Heritage (SNH Research, Survey and Monitoring report **172**).

Crone, A. 1993. Excavation and survey of sub-peat features of Neolithic, Bronze and Iron Age date at Bharpa Carinish, North Uist, Scotland. *Proceedings of the Prehistoric Society* **59**, 361–82.

Dalland, M. 1997. Fife Ness. *Discovery and Excavation in Scotland 1997*, 113–14.

Edwards, K.J. 1996. The contribution of Tom Affleck to the study of the Mesolithic of Southwest Scotland. *In* T. Pollard and A. Morrison (eds), *The Early Prehistory of Scotland*,108–22. Edinburgh: Edinburgh University Press.

Ellis, C. 1999. Parks of Garden, Stirling. *Discovery and Excavation in Scotland 1999*, 114.

Ellis, C. 2000. Parks of Garden, Stirling. *Discovery and Excavation in Scotland* (new series) **1**, 126.

Ellis, C. 2002. Upper Largie, Argyll and Bute. *Discovery and Excavation in Scotland* (new series) **3**, 145.

Fairweather, A.D. and Ralston, I.B.M. 1993. The Neolithic timber hall at Balbridie, Grampian Region, Scotland: the building, the date, the plant macrofossils. *Antiquity* **67**, 313–23.

Gilmour, S. and Henderson J. 2002. Cleigh, Argyll and Bute. *Discovery and Excavation in Scotland* (new series) **3**, 144.

Gregory, R. 2002. Northton, Harris, Western Isles. *Discovery and Excavation in Scotland* (new series) **3**, 153.

Haggarty, A. 1991. Machrie Moor, Arran: recent excavations at two stone circles. *Proceedings of the Society of Antiquaries of Scotland* **121**, 51–94.

Hardy, K. 2001. Sand, Highland. *Discovery and Excavation in Scotland* (new series) **2**, 125.

Harkness, D.D. 1983. The extent of the natural ^{14}C deficiency in the coastal environment of the United Kingdom. *PACT* **8**, 351–64.

Harrington, P. and Pierpoint, S. 1980. Port Charlotte chambered cairn, Islay: an interim note. *Glasgow Archaeological Journal* **7**, 113–15.

Haselgrove, C. 1997. Fisher's Road East, Port Seton. *Discovery and Excavation in Scotland 1997*, 113.

Jardine, W.G. 1977. Location and age of Mesolithic coastal occupation sites on Oronsay, Inner Hebrides. *Nature* **267**, 138–40.

Jardine, W.G. and Jardine, D.C. 1983. Minor excavations and small finds at three Mesolithic sites, Isle of Oronsay, Argyll. *Proceedings of the Society of Antiquaries of Scotland* **113**, 22–34.

Johnston, D.A. 1997. Biggar Common, 1987–93: an early prehistoric funerary and domestic landscape in Clydesdale, South Lanarkshire. *Proceedings of the Society of Antiquaries of Scotland* **127**, 185–253.

Kendrick, J. 1995. Excavation of a Neolithic enclosure and an Iron Age settlement at Douglasmuir, Angus. *Proceedings of the Society of Antiquaries of Scotland* **125**, 29–67.

Kitegawa, H. and van der Plicht, J. 1998. A 40,000-year varve chronology from Lake Suigetsu, Japan: extension of the ^{14}C calibration curve. *Radiocarbon* **40**(1), 505–16.

Lawson, J. 2001. Cramond, Edinburgh. *Discovery and Excavation in Scotland* (new series) **2**, 124.

Lindsay, W.J. 1989. Linlithgow: the excavations. *In* J.A. Stones (ed.), *Three Scottish Carmelite Friaries*, 57–94. Edinburgh: Society of Antiquaries of Scotland (Monograph **6**).

McCullagh, R.P.J. 1989. Excavation at Newton, Islay. *Glasgow Archaeological Journal* **15**, 23–51.

McCullagh, R.P.J. 1996. Lairg scheduled area, Highland. *Discovery and Excavation in Scotland 1996*, 139.

McCullagh, R.P.J. and Tipping, R. (eds). 1998. *The Lairg Project 1988–1996: the Evolution of an Archaeological Landscape in Northern Scotland*. Edinburgh: Scottish Trust for Archaeological Research (Monograph **3**).

MacKie, E.W. 1964. New excavations on the Monamore Neolithic chambered cairn, Lamlash, Isle of Arran, in 1961. *Proceedings of the Society of Antiquaries of Scotland* **97** (1963–64), 1–34.

MacKie, E.W. 1972a. Radiocarbon dates for two Mesolithic shell heaps and a Neolithic axe factory in Scotland. *Proceedings of the Prehistoric Society* **38**, 412–6.

MacKie, E.W. 1972b. Duntreath, standing stones, Stirlingshire. *Discovery and Excavation in Scotland 1972*, 38–9. Edinburgh: Council for Scottish Archaeology.

MacKie, E.W. 1976 The vitrified forts of Scotland. *In* D.W. Harding (ed.), *Hillforts: Later Prehistoric Earthworks in Britain and Ireland*, 205–35. London: Academic Press.

Marshall, D.N. and Taylor, I.D. 1977. The excavation of the chambered cairn at Glenvoidean, Isle of Bute. *Proceedings of the Society of Antiquaries of Scotland* **108** (1976–77), 1–39.

Masters, L. 1973. The Lochhill long cairn. *Antiquity* **47**, 96–100.

Masters, L. 1980. Camster Long chambered cairn, Caithness. *Discovery and Excavation in Scotland 1980*, 17.

Masters, L. 1981. A Mesolithic hearth at Redkirk Point, Gretna, Annandale and Eskdale District. *Transactions of the Dumfriesshire and Galloway Natural History and Antiquarian Society* **56**, 111–14.

Masters, L. 1997. The excavation and restoration of the Camster Long chambered cairn, Caithness, Highland, 1967–80. *Proceedings of the Society of Antiquaries of Scotland* **127**, 123–83.

Mellars, P.A. 1987. *Excavations on Oronsay: Prehistoric Human Ecology on a Small Island*. Edinburgh: Edinburgh University Press.

Mercer, J. 1972. Microlithic and Bronze Age camps, 75–26ft OD, N Carn, Isle of Jura. *Proceedings of the Society of Antiquaries of Scotland* **104** (1971–72), 1–22.

Mercer, J. 1974. Glenbatrick Waterhole: a microlithic site on the Isle of Jura. *Proceedings of the Society of Antiquaries of Scotland* **105** (1972–74), 9–32.

Mercer, J. 1980. Lussa Wood 1: the Late-Glacial and early Post-Glacial occupation of Jura. *Proceedings of the Society of Antiquaries of Scotland* **110** (1978–80), 1–31.

Mercer, R.J. and Midgley, M.S. 1997. The Early Bronze Age cairn at Sketewan, Balnaguard, Perth & Kinross. *Proceedings of the Society of Antiquaries of Scotland* **127**, 281–338.

Mithen, S. (ed.). 2000. *Hunter-Gatherer Landscape Archaeology: the Southern Hebrides Mesolithic Project 1988–98. Vols.1–2*. Cambridge: Macdonald Institute Monograph.

Morrison, A. and Bonsall, C. 1989. The early post-glacial settlement of Scotland: a review. *In* C. Bonsall (ed.), *The Mesolithic in Europe*, 134–42. Edinburgh: John Donald.

Murray, N.A., Bonsall, C., Sutherland, D.G., Lawson, T.J. and Kitchener, A.C. 1993. Further radiocarbon determinations on reindeer remains of Middle and Late Devensian Age from the Creag nan Uamh caves, Assynt, NW Scotland. *Quaternary Newsletter* **70**, 1–10.

Myers, A.M. and Gourlay, R.B. 1991. Muirtown, Inverness: preliminary investigation of a shell midden. *Proceedings of the Society of Antiquaries of Scotland* **121**, 17–25.

Newton, N.S. and Talbot, E.J. 1998. Excavations at the Peel of Lumphanan, Aberdeenshire, 1975–9. *Proceedings of the Society of Antiquaries of Scotland* **128**, 653–70.

Parker Pearson, M. and Sharples, N. 1999. *Between Land and Sea: Excavations at Dun Vulan, South Uist*. Sheffield: Sheffield Academic Press.

Piggott, S. 1972. Excavation of the Dalladies long barrow, Fettercairn, Kincardineshire. *Proceedings of the Society of Antiquaries of Scotland* **104** (1971–72), 23–47.

Proudfoot, E. 1999. Fordhouse barrow, Dun. *Discovery and Excavation in Scotland 1999*, 111.

Proudfoot, E. 2001. Fordhouse Barrow, Angus. *Discovery and Excavation in Scotland* (new series) **2**, 122.

Ralston, I.B.M. 1982. A timber hall at Balbridie Farm and the Neolithic in north-east Scotland. *Aberdeen University Review* **168** (Autumn 1982), 238–49.

Ralston, I.B.M. 1986. n.p. A Scottish Radiocarbon Date List.

Ralston, I.B.M. and Reynolds, N. 1981. *Balbridie: Excavations 1977–80*. Unpublished Interim Report, Scottish Development Department (Ancient Monuments).

RCAHMS. 1979. *The Archaeological Sites and Monuments of Stirling District, Central Region*. Edinburgh: Royal Commission on the Ancient and Historical Monuments of Scotland.

RCAHMS. 1984. *Argyll, an Inventory of the Monuments. Vol. 5. Islay, Jura, Colonsay and Oronsay*. Edinburgh: Royal Commission on the Ancient and Historical Monuments of Scotland.

Renfrew, C. 1979. *Investigations in Orkney*. London: Society of Antiquaries of London (Research Report **38**).

Renfrew, C., Harkness, D. and Switzer, R. 1976. Quanterness, radiocarbon and the Orkney cairns. *Antiquity* **50**, 194–204.

Rennie, E.B. 1984. Excavations at Ardnadam, Cowal, Argyll, 1964–1982. *Glasgow Archaeological Journal* **11**, 13–39.

Rennie, E.B. 1986. Dunloskin (Dunoon and Kilmun parish), recessed platform. *Discovery and Excavation Scotland 1986*, 26–7.

Rideout, J.S. 1992. The Dunion, Roxburgh, Borders. *In* J.S. Rideout, O.A. Owen and E. Halpin, *Hillforts of Southern Scotland*, 73–119. Edinburgh: AOC Scotland Ltd (Monograph **1**).

Rideout, J.S. 1997. Excavation of Neolithic enclosures at Cowie Road, Bannockburn, Stirling, 1984–5. *Proceedings of The Society of Antiquaries of Scotland* **127**, 29–68.

Ritchie, A. 1983. Excavation of a Neolithic farmstead at Knap of Howar, Papa Westray, Orkney. *Proceedings of the Society of Antiquaries of Scotland* **113**, 40–121.

Ritchie, A. 2000. Knap of Howar, Papa Westray *Discovery and Excavation in Scotland* (new series) **1**, 124–5.

Russell-White, C.J. 1995. The excavation of a Neolithic and Iron Age settlement at Wardend of Durris, Aberdeenshire. *Proceedings of the Society of Antiquaries of Scotland* **125**, 9–27.

Saville, A. 1998. An Corran, Staffin, Skye. *Discovery and Excavation in Scotland 1998*, 126–7.

Saville, A. 2001. A Mesolithic barbed antler point from the foreshore of the Forth Estuary, near Carriden, Falkirk. *Calatria (= Journal of the Falkirk Local History Society)* **15** (Autumn 2001), 70–80.

Saville, A. and Miket, R. 1994. An Corran, Staffin, Skye. *Discovery and Excavation in Scotland 1994*, 40–1.

Schulting, R.J. 2000a. Carding Mill Bay, Argyll and Bute. *Discovery and Excavation in Scotland* (new series) **1**, 122.

Schulting, R.J. 2000b. Crarae, Argyll and Bute. *Discovery and Excavation in Scotland* (new series) **1**, 122.

Scott, J.G. 1961. The excavation of the chambered cairn at Crarae, Loch Fyneside, Mid Argyll. *Proceedings of the Society of Antiquaries of Scotland* **94** (1960–61), 1–27.

Scott, J.G. 1989. The stone circles at Temple Wood, Kilmartin, Argyll. *Glasgow Archaeological Journal* **15**, 53–124.

Sharples, N.M. 1986. Radiocarbon dates from three chambered tombs at Loch Calder, Caithness. *Scottish Archaeological Review* **4**(1), 2–10.

Shepherd, A. 1996. A Neolithic ring-mound at Midtown of Pitglassie, Auchterless, Aberdeenshire. *Proceedings of the Society of Antiquaries of Scotland* **126**, 17–51.

Sheridan, J.A. 1989. Biggar Common (Biggar Liberton parish), round cairn, long mound, surface scatter. *Discovery and Excavation in Scotland 1989*, 60.

Sheridan, J.A. 1995. Irish Neolithic pottery: the story in 1995. *In* I. Kinnes and G. Varndell (eds.), *'Unbaked Urns of Rudely Shape': Essays on British and Irish Pottery*, 3-21. Oxford: Oxbow (Oxbow Monograph **55**).

Sheridan, J.A. 1996. The oldest bow ... and other objects. *Current Archaeology* **149**, 188–90.

Sheridan, J.A. 1997. Pottery. *In* D.A. Johnston, Biggar Common, 1987–93: an early prehistoric funerary and domestic landscape in Clydesdale, South Lanarkshire. *Proceedings of the Society of Antiquaries of Scotland* **127**, 202–23.

Simpson, D.D.A. 1976. The later Neolithic and Beaker settlement site at Northton, Isle of Harris. *In* C. Burgess and R. Miket (eds), *Settlement and Economy in the Third and Second Millennia B.C.*, 221–31. Oxford: British Archaeological Reports (British Series **33**).

Simpson, D.D.A. 1996. Excavation of a kerbed funerary monument at Stoneyfield, Raigmore, Inverness, Highland, 1972–3. *Proceedings of the Society of Antiquaries of Scotland* **126**, 53–86.

Sloan, D. 1985. Cadger's Brae (Grangemouth parish), shell midden. *Discovery and Excavation in Scotland 1985*, 6.

Speak, S. and Burgess, C. 1999. Meldon Bridge: a centre of the third millennium BC in Peeblesshire. *Proceedings of the Society of Antiquaries of Scotland* **129**, 1–118.

Spriggs, M, and Anderson, A. 1993. Late colonisation of East Polynesia. *Antiquity* **67**, 200–17.

Stuiver, M., Reimer, P.J., Bard, E., Beck, J.W., Burr, G.S., Hughen, K.A., Kromer, B., McCormac, G., van der Plicht, J. and Spurk, M. 1998. INTCAL98 radiocarbon age calibration, 24,000–0 cal BP. *Radiocarbon* **40**(3), 1041–84.

Ward, T. 1993. Biggar Common (Biggar parish): Neolithic/Bronze Age artefact scatters. *Discovery and Excavation in Scotland 1993*, 87.

Ward, T. 1996. Biggar Common East. *Discovery and Excavation in Scotland 1996*, 140.

Ward, T. 1998. Daer Reservoir 1 and 2, Crawford. *Discovery and Excavation in Scotland 1998*, 128.

Ward, T. 2001a. Daer Reservoir, Crawford, South Lanarkshire. *Discovery and Excavation in Scotland* (new series) **2**, 127.

Ward, T. 2001b. Brownsbank Farm, Biggar, South Lanarkshire. *Discovery and Excavation in Scotland* (new series) **2**, 126.

Whittington, G. 1978. A sub-peat dyke on Shurton Hill, Mainland, Shetland. *Proceedings of the Society of Antiquaries of Scotland* **109** (1977–78), 30–5.

Whittle, A, Keith-Lucas, M., Milles, A., Noddle. B., Rees, S and Romans, J.C.C. 1986. *Scord of Brouster, an Early Agricultural Settlement on Shetland: Excavations 1977–1979*. Oxford: Oxford University Committee for Archaeology (Monograph **9**).

Wickham-Jones, C.R. 1990. *Rhum: Mesolithic and Later Sites at Kinloch. Excavations 1984–86*. Edinburgh: Society of Antiquaries of Scotland (Monograph **7**).

Wickham-Jones, C.R. and Dalland, M. 1998a. A small Mesolithic site at Craighead Golf Course, Fife Ness, Fife. *Tayside and Fife Archaeological Journal* **4**, 1–19.

Wickham-Jones, C.R. and Dalland, M. 1998b. Fife Ness. *Internet Archaeology* **5**.

Wordsworth, J. 1985. The excavation of a Mesolithic horizon at 13–24 Castle Street, Inverness. *Proceedings of the Society of Antiquaries of Scotland* **115**, 89–103.

This chapter is published with the aid of a grant from Historic Scotland.

Chapter 8

Conference Discussion Session: Sunday Morning, 7 September 1999
Scotland in the Early Holocene

CHAIR: KEVIN EDWARDS

[The speakers in this session were Colin Ballantyne, Richard Tipping, Kevin Edwards, and Patrick Ashmore]

ROB YOUNG	It's a question all the speakers might want to comment on. If Richard's [Tipping] work suggests there's a lot more to the climatic side of vegetation change than the human side; and you've [Kevin Edwards] shown with your work that obviously there are cases where you've got evidence that suggests quite intensive human activity, how do you tease the two things out in terms of the way forward? What's the method of progression given the kind of thing Patrick [Ashmore] said about the problems of radiocarbon dates? Because I'd have thought that one way round it might be if you've got some really, really fine-resolution pollen work, then it's fine-resolution chronology that you need to go with it, and what I've just heard kind of undermines that as a way forward as well.
PATRICK ASHMORE	Well, I suppose you can in some circumstances wiggle-match. In other words, if you have got very even peat deposition – which personally I don't believe in, but I know a lot of people do – then you can date successive layers and try and match them up with the calibration curve. So in some circumstances you may be able to get that very much higher precision chronology. Increasingly also we're finding trees in Mesolithic and Neolithic contexts. For instance, there's a recent Mesolithic date from an oak in the north coast of the Solway, which Mike Cressey's obtained. So I think there are various avenues which will help, but your basic point is right and radiocarbon is a very blunt tool.
KEVIN EDWARDS	I would hope that when we get more tephra layers identified that that will help us a great deal, even if we can only date them with radiocarbon. That in a sense doesn't matter, as long as we know that that horizon represents what is a few hours' deposition then we could be getting somewhere. But the big problem with a tephra is that it's likely to be spatially incredibly specific because of the way that the tephra plume came from Iceland and blanketed or, blanketed is the wrong word, dusted parts of Scotland – so it's rather hit and miss. And I think all we can do to tease those things apart is to just continually operate a multiple working hypothesis approach but hopefully we'll get sites where we have got multiple proxies, not just pollen.
RICHARD TIPPING	Yes, I had written down as my answer that what probably should be done now is to identify those sites where we can get multi proxy. We know that pollen and charcoal are effectively responding to something and we don't actually know what it is. If you're going to take away the climatic part of that signal, then you need sites from which you can get climate data, proxy climate data, at the same time and at the same resolutions as you're getting your pollen and charcoal signatures. You're basically just trying to take one away from the other, and that has to be the approach, I think.
COLIN BALLANTYNE	I've very little to add to that except perhaps to emphasize what we actually mean by climate in terms of vegetation, ecological landscape change, and possibly the impact of changing ecosystems on human communities. And that is that we tend to look at

climate in terms of average climate, and there is a great deal of literature for later in the Holocene about the influence of, for example, the Sub-Atlantic thermal decline and how this might have influenced vegetation or how this might have influenced human communities. What's really important about climate are not the means but the extremes. An extreme climatic event is the one that does the damage, it's the one that fells the forests, it's the one that upsets the ecosystem, and unfortunately these are much more difficult to predict in terms of a lot of the climatic proxies that we presently have. And I think that also, if I may comment, and this is something I think that our pollen analysts perhaps might like to take on board a little bit more, is the fact that ecologists have been showing with regard to more recent times that ecosystems themselves are self-regulating with particular fluctuations going on. I think there is a certain caveat to be introduced here and that is that vegetation itself is likely to change, or vegetation assemblages are likely to change, irrespective of any external perturbation. And I wonder to what extent some of the fluctuations we have seen in pollen diagrams and so on today actually reflect such internal regulation, particularly where we've got very fine resolution sampling?

KEVIN EDWARDS   Richard, you are the biodiversity expert, what do you think?

RICHARD TIPPING   Am I? Thank you. The idea of internal regulation I think was in part alluded to in what I said. I'm not entirely sure that these systems are regulated entirely internally. Disturbance factors are through things like trees falling over or hillsides being knocked over by trees. So they do have an external factor. The regulatory effect from some of the newest ecology is producing paradigms which suggest that the inherent instability can in fact take you in a whole series of different pathways, in that it's not necessarily the case that things will actually come back to position one, if you like. You move from position one to position two, and from that point you can actually move to position three, position four, [or even] further away from your starting point, so the regulatory factors I think are less significant now than they were perhaps ten years ago.

KEVIN EDWARDS   And I think although you get – for example in birch populations – you get senescence and they decline, they come back, and in some cases that may be what we're seeing with fine-resolution pollen analysis. But in many cases the pollen rain is going to average what you have got and you are going to miss these things. It comes down to the whole patch dynamics of the vegetational cover and the danger is that if we think we can try and pick some of these things up by finer and finer resolution. Although I greatly admire the Simmons and Innes work, I do have doubts about millimetre-level pollen analysis because of the whole smoothing nature of peat deposits, and when you come to lakes that's another matter altogether, so, well …

PAUL MELLARS   Well, obviously these arguments about the incidence of fire and clearance and how they are explained are going to run and run. It's now been running for what, the best part of 30 years and a lot of the arguments are much the same now as they were when Dimbleby and others started [to raise] these problems. I fully accept all the problems. My own perspective on this has been very much coloured by the fact that if you look at the ethnographic evidence, fire control of vegetation was used by nearly all hunter-gatherers in a very, very wide range of environments. So the ethnographic evidence cross-culturally suggesting that hunter-gatherers do tend to use fire control is very impressive. And it really follows from that that you would almost have to be suggesting that the European Mesolithic populations were verging on the mentally retarded not to use it, granted that in certain contexts the advantages of using it are so obvious. But what it all leads to is that we desperately need a strategy for how we differentiate between humanly controlled burning and natural burning, and I think that's the '$64,000 question' and it's what we are having a lot of difficulty getting to grips with. And I wonder if one of the things is not so much what started the fire but how the fire was controlled, because most hunter-gatherers when they light fires do try to control them spatially. So if we could get more of a handle on the spatial extent of burning and if we find that this was very localized, that might be an argument for thinking that it's humanly controlled as compared to natural fires, which presumably would not be spatially controlled. Or otherwise I can see us having these arguments in another 30 years' time.

CLIVE BONSALL

Can I ask Colin Ballantyne a question? You showed two slides which gave completely different limits for the last ice sheet, the last glaciation. What is your opinion on the prospects of ice-free areas in Scotland?

COLIN BALLANTYNE

In the present land area of Scotland, virtually nil. Let me go through the evidence stage by stage. As far as the west of Scotland goes, to take the shelf areas to the west, I think there's general consensus now that the seismo-stratigraphic evidence from the shelf shows that the last ice sheet went quite a distance to the west of the Outer Isles, perhaps to roughly about the longitude of St Kilda, although St Kilda itself appears to have escaped glaciation by the last ice sheet. That would have left, of course, an unglaciated enclave but it's one that is now under the sea. In the north it does appear that Shetland supported its own ice cap and on balance the evidence favours that the last ice sheet from the mainland encroached on Orkney. This is not conclusive. The Orkney question still remains up for grabs, but I think the balance of evidence favours it being overrun by mainland ice. As for the supposed areas of Caithness and Buchan being left unglaciated by the last ice sheet I think that's now extremely unlikely. Partly because of the evidence from radiocarbon dates, partly because of the morphological evidence of offshore moraine sequences in the North Sea basin. They tend to suggest that the last ice sheet was perhaps about 50–80km at least out from the present east shore of Scotland. If you wanted to go to an ice free part of Scotland you would probably have had to go up onto some of the higher mountains, perhaps in the Hebrides and the north-west Highlands or perhaps out to St Kilda. So as regards major enclaves of unglaciated terrain, at balance the evidence says no.

KEVIN EDWARDS

Could you tell us what date that was? When did ice cease to be a major factor in Shetland would you say?

COLIN BALLANTYNE

I was rather hoping that nobody would ask that question! One big problem is this. There's a convention grown up that the last British ice sheet, I'll call it that, reached its maximum round about 18,000 radiocarbon years ago. This is actually first of all rather poorly dated and secondly it assumes that the ice sheet everywhere expanded to its limits at the same time which is absolute nonsense. It was a very large ice sheet and it was almost certainly still advancing to the south when it was retreating up in the north. So this makes it very, very difficult for us to establish an age for the ice maximum, and besides the ice maximum was different in different places. The best bet is that in Scotland, and particularly in northern Scotland, the ice expanded more rapidly and earlier in the north than it did in England. And that effectively, if we are looking at a ball-park estimate for when we had maximal glaciation, in say the Scottish Highlands and further north in the Northern Isles, [it] would be something like about 22–20,000 radiocarbon years ago – perhaps add about 3000 to get that into calendar years.

PETER WOODMAN

It's really two related observations about island colonization. The first one is that I must admit I always feel a little bit uneasy when people are looking at pollen diagrams and inferring that there is either human interference or else animal interference or else human interference to benefit the animals, and yet we are not even absolutely sure if the animals, the large browsing mammals, were actually there in the first place. Which means that we really have gone out on a limb and that one of the major problems is trying to find the mammalian fauna. And as I said, as appears to be coming out of [the evidence from Ireland], you can't necessarily guarantee that these large mammals would be on these islands. The issue about colonizing the Northern Isles, Orkney and Shetland, if I could agree and fundamentally disagree at the same time with what Patrick [Ashmore] was saying, [in terms of] the quality of radiocarbon dating in north Norway, there are certain individual dates I would have very, very serious doubts about. But we are faced with the fact – and if any of you have seen Bernard Gramsch's recent Festschrift I've a paper just about this very topic in that – faced with the fact that there is a robust pattern of dates earlier than 9000 BP uncalibrated and that, unfortunately, because [in] that volume [I] was talking about the earliest colonization or settlement of Scandinavia it was also perhaps not emphasized enough that those are the earliest of a whole series of dates that are running over the next millennium and a half and that they by-and-large can be mirrored by inferred datings from sea-level change at places like Mortensnes where there are hut sites, and actually with a typological and technological sequence that we are beginning now to be able now to tie back in with the Fosna in southern Norway, so the idea of phase one being early, before 9000 BP, I think is tenable. The individual dates are open to question; [that from] Slettnes is probably a bit better, but the point is – and I know that that was a throwaway remark to justify talking about something else – I think the important thing is that Hein Bjerck and his work has emphasized that one of the fundamental issues is when was an effective marine technology available? There may be a subtle difference between very rapidly moving up along the Norwegian coastline … They did not come from the east. I've actually looked at that evidence, I've worked on the Kola [Peninsula] material, they certainly came up along the coast, they didn't come the other way. But the issue really for Shetland I think is when was that marine technology there that would allow them to exploit both Shetland and Orkney as a marine resource? And Hein [Bjerck] is saying that that was probably in Norway happening round about 9000 BP, therefore there is no reason why in Scotland we couldn't have the same situation.

RICHARD TIPPING

Can I respond to the first point which was your argument, your point, about going out on a limb in inferring mammalian faunas on islands like the Shetlands, which Kevin [Edwards] talked about [with reference to] Keith Bennett's work up on Shetland. Kevin has explained the chain of reasoning [about] the suppression of tall herbs, which necessitates, seemingly, for Keith, the introduction of red deer, probably by human beings, to an island which did not have red deer, in order to suppress the tall herb vegetation. I would agree absolutely with what Kevin said and with what you are indicating as well, that this is a chain of reasoning which is very tortuous and very extended and somewhere along the line we have to introduce Occam's razor or the law of parsimony and simply say: what is required to suppress the production of tall herbs, or the pollen productivity, or the recognition of tall herb vegetation? And the simplest way of doing that is simply to put trees over them. So what I think Keith is looking at, and [is the case at] other sites where this happens, is simply increasing density of woodland cover, which is suppressing tall herb vegetation – it is simple!

PETER WOODMAN

This business about red deer being brought in, in fact this may sound really way out on a limb, but I actually find it easier to believe in Mesolithic communities bringing in domesticated cattle to these islands than I do bringing in red deer. Because we're back – Paul [Mellars] was talking about things that have run for decades – one of the issues is this old issue: is it possible to domesticate red deer? What are you doing? Are you bringing these animals over, landing them off a boat, and then say well run off and we'll come back in two or three generations' time and there will be a viable resource there? I think it's very different from what's happening in Oronsay, where it may well be for very particular reasons that red deer are either being brought in or else there is a dwarf

162

population or something like that, but on these other islands the idea of bringing red deer in is raising all sorts of other questions.

KEVIN EDWARDS

Could I just show one overhead? I appreciate what you [Richard Tipping] are saying and I think it may be a question of taphonomy, where if you have got trees ... I remember arguing this one with Keith [Bennett] at the time just before he wrote it about trying to look at alternative ways of looking at it. But I think the important thing to note in all these instances from Orkney – and here's one from Orkney, Keith's Peat Bank [on Hoy] – from three Shetland sites now, and from a site in the Outer Isles, is that in all the cases where the ferns go down, trees go down. So I understand what you are saying but I think the evidence actually doesn't show it. The evidence shows a woodland reduction, not an increase. Now when we look at the influx it may say something different, but I don't think so.

TAM WARD

It's not a question, just a point, referring to the early date that Patrick [Ashmore] alluded to from Daer Reservoir [South Lanarkshire], which was calibrated [to] 8,080 BC. That date came from a series of contexts which gave us mixed woodland charcoal up there and we do actually intend to carry out further dating on that site. Just as a matter of interest, I know other speakers today will allude to that site, there was a very, very unusual lithic assemblage from the site, which may also have repercussions for early people in Scotland.

CHRIS TOLAN-SMITH

Just taking up a point of Patrick's [Ashmore] – actually he rather kindly referred to some of my earlier efforts in this demographic business. What I was doing then was not mapping or recording numbers of sites, the point I'm making – I think this makes an important difference – is that I was recording radiocarbon records of a human presence within 10km squares. That gets away from quite a lot of the problems I think that he may refer to in his printed text, to do with logging numbers of sites and that kind of thing. The way I was trying to approach the problem was to look more at a human presence in particular areas. Now we could argue about whether it should be 10km^2 or 100km^2 or 5km^2 or whatever, but it's very different to mapping individual site occurrences. I just wanted to make the point because I was specifically in that paper trying to get away from using sites, it was intended to be a non-site approach to this problem.

PATRICK ASHMORE

I was just taking a 1000km^2 site! Yes, I quite take your point. The method I'm using is not identical to yours, not only in that way, but in other ways too, in the way I've averaged the dates. I'm totally lost in terms of understanding how people interacted with each other in [Mesolithic] Scotland, I don't know whether they had big territories or whether they had lots of long distance connections or whether they had smallish territories, [or] how much it varied over time, so I've taken a very crude, consciously crude and simplistic, approach and I'm just basically counting the number of sites which seem to occur in each century. In effect in an area from Inverness to SW Scotland, because we don't have good dates from north of there and until we have a lot more and a lot better evidence we certainly can't start to try to do it on a smaller scale, that's my belief anyway, so it's a very crude first approximation to something slightly different from what you were doing.

PAUL PETTITT

Can I stick on that topic and ask Patrick just to clarify a point? I couldn't quite make out the figures on your graphs, or the captions on the graphs anyway, so I wonder if you can clarify how you worked it out? I was reading it, I hope incorrectly, that your first rise in numbers of sites was a rise from one site per century to two, and your second peak was a rise from two to three. Have you standardized that or anything, or is that real?

PATRICK ASHMORE

Yes, about half a site a century to about two. When you say you want me to clarify the methodology, do you want me …

PAUL PETTITT

I just wondered if I was reading it correctly.

PATRICK ASHMORE

You were reading it roughly correctly, except it's on average about half a site. Well, it depends on where you start, of course, it starts with zero if you go far enough off to the left!

PUBLICATIONS REFERRED TO, OR WHICH CONTAIN AMPLIFICATION OF POINTS RAISED, IN THIS DISCUSSION SESSION:

Bennett, K.D. and Sharp, M.J. 1993. Holocene vegetation and environment. *In* J. Birnie, J. Gordon, K. Bennett and A. Hall (eds), *The Quaternary of Shetland: Field Guide*, 18–22. London: Quaternary Research Association.

Bjerck, H.B. 1995. The North Sea Continent and the pioneer settlement of Norway. *In* A. Fischer (ed.), *Man and Sea in the Mesolithic*, 131–44. Oxford: Oxbow Books (Monograph **53**).

Blackford, J.J., Edwards, K.J., Buckland, P.C. and Dobney, K. 1996. Keith's Peat Bank, Hoy: Mesolithic human impact? *In* A.M. Hall (ed.), *The Quaternary of Orkney: Field Guide*, 62–8. London: Quaternary Research Association.

Simmons, I.G., Turner, J. and Innes, J.B. 1989. An application of fine-resolution pollen analysis to later Mesolithic peats of an English upland. *In* C. Bonsall (ed.), *The Mesolithic in Europe*, 206–17. Edinburgh: John Donald.

Smith, C. 1992. The population of late Upper Palaeolithic and Mesolithic Britain. *Proceedings of the Prehistoric Society* **58**, 37–40.

Woodman, P.C. 1999. The early Postglacial settlement of Arctic Europe. *In* E. Cziesla, T. Kersting and S. Pratsch (eds), *Den Bogen Spannen … Festschrift für Bernhard Gramsch, Teil 1*, 297–312. Weissbach: Beier & Beran.

Section 3

SCOTLAND, THE ARCHAEOLOGY

Chapter 9

Mesolithic Scotland, Coastal Occupation, and the Role of the Oronsay Middens

PAUL MELLARS

The paper presents a broad review of some of the key issues in current studies of the Scottish Mesolithic: the evidence for the initial Postglacial colonization of Scotland; the significance of the coastal factor in Mesolithic economies; the particular role of shellfish in these coastal economies; and the special problems posed by the interpretation of the Oronsay shell middens. A review of new evidence from Oronsay and elsewhere points to the conclusion that the Oronsay middens were probably the product of semi-permanent occupation of the island by a single social group, rather than a result of many intermittent visits to the sites by a range of different social groups. On Oronsay and elsewhere, the concentration of shell middens during the later stages of the Mesolithic may indicate increasing economic stress, resulting from either increasing population density, or heavy over-use of resources by the human groups themselves.

Introduction

The Mesolithic period in Scotland presents a fascinating challenge to those studying the early Postglacial settlement of northern Europe on several different fronts. To attempt a review of these issues within the space of a single paper poses a significant challenge in itself, so to provide a focus for the present discussion I intend to examine four separate, and it seems to me particularly interesting, aspects of the topic, all of which have generated some lively debate in the recent literature:

1. the initial Postglacial colonization of Scotland;

2. the general significance of the coastal element in the Scottish Mesolithic;

3. the particular role of molluscs and shell middens in these coastal economies; and,

4. the special problems posed by the interpretation of the Oronsay middens.

Climatic change and the earliest Postglacial colonization of Scoland

One of the most striking features to emerge from recent research is the scale and speed of the climatic changes which marked the end of the last Ice Age in northern Europe. The most detailed evidence at present comes from studies of the oxygen isotope and deuterium records in the Greenland ice cores combined, for the British Isles, with detailed studies of the highly temperature-dependent records of beetle faunas recovered from well-preserved organic deposits over the Lateglacial and Early Holocene periods (Atkinson *et al*. 1987; Dansgaard *et al*. 1993; Lowe *et al*. 1994; 1995). As shown in Fig. 9.1, these converge on a closely similar pattern, in which an initial temperature rise of perhaps 15°C marked the start of the major 'Lateglacial Interstadial' at *c*.13,000 BP (in raw radiocarbon terms – closer to *c*.14,500 BP in 'absolute terms': Becker 1993; Lowe *et al*. 1994), followed by a progressive climatic decline into the period of the so-called 'Younger Dryas' episode, which reached its bitterly cold peak at *c*.10,500 BP. It is generally agreed that the retreating Scottish glaciers experienced a sudden re-expansion during the cold conditions of the Younger Dryas, marking the phase of the so-called 'Loch Lomond Stadial', in which ice apparently covered much of the northern and western mountains of Scotland (Jones & Keen 1993; see Ballantyne this volume).

Equally dramatic was the sudden sharp increase in temperatures which defined the start of the full Postglacial or 'Holocene' period at *c*.10,000 ^{14}C BP. Both the ice cores and beetle records suggest that at this point average summer and winter temperatures rose by as much as 10–12°C in northern Europe, probably within the space of a century or less. Even if the speed of colonization of northern Europe by forests lagged a few centuries behind the climatic changes themselves, there is good evidence that predominantly birch and pine forests had replaced the pre-existing open vegetation over most of the British isles by *c*.9300 BP, with the possible exception of some of the more exposed, windswept areas of northern and western Scotland (Edwards 1996).

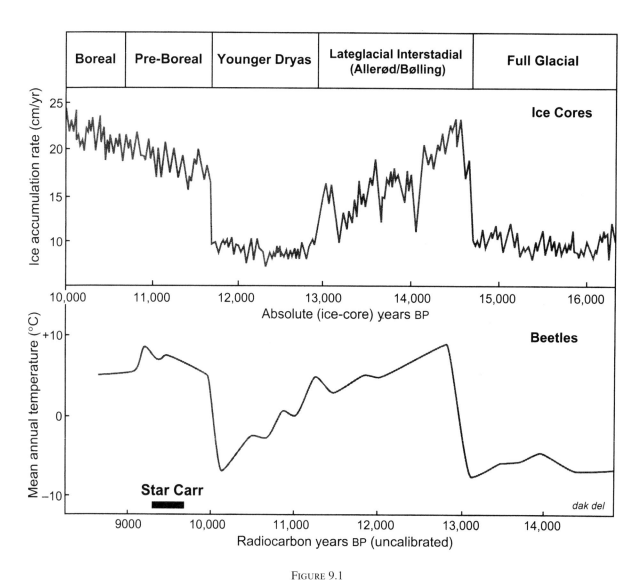

FIGURE 9.1
Climatic changes over the Lateglacial and early Postglacial periods as reconstructed from (upper) Greenland ice cores and (lower) beetle faunas from British sites (after Atkinson *et al.* 1987; Lowe *et al.* 1994).

The pattern of human recolonization of northern Europe in the wake of these dramatic climatic and ecological changes is now reasonably well documented. Typical 'Creswellian' communities, hunting mainly horse and (more sporadically) reindeer, were clearly established over most parts of southern and central England by *c.*12,500 BP, and may have extended northwards at least to the Lake District before the onset of the ensuing Younger Dryas cold phase (Barton 1997; Housley *et al.* 1997; Jacobi 1991).

The critical issue in respect of Scotland, of course, is whether this episode of colonization during the Lateglacial interstadial extended beyond the bounds of northern England. On ecological grounds there seems no reason

to doubt that both climatic conditions and the availability of essential food supplies would have been adequate to permit the human colonization of many areas of Scotland, especially perhaps along the Atlantic coastline, where a combination of relatively mild winters (due to the adjacent Gulf Stream) and the rich coastal resources would arguably have provided optimal conditions for colonization by Lateglacial hunter/fisher/gatherer groups.

At present, direct archaeological evidence for this hypothetical phase of Lateglacial occupation in Scotland remains at best sparse and at worst highly ambiguous (Ballin & Saville 2003; Mithen 2000a; Morrison & Bonsall 1989). Potentially the most significant finds are a series of discoveries of what appear to be distinctively tanged point forms, distributed at various points from Stronsay and Mainland Orkney to Tiree and Jura in the Inner Hebrides. Typologically the most convincing of these finds are the pieces from Balevullin on Tiree (Fig. 9.2), and Shieldaig in Wester Ross (Saville this volume), which bear a strong resemblance to the classic Ahrensburgian tanged points from northern Germany, Holland, and southern Scandinavia (Ballin & Saville 2003; Bang-Andersen 1996; Larsson 1999), and to some of the equally dispersed discoveries of similar tanged points from a number of southern British sites, such as Hengistbury Head, Avington VI, and Cranwich (Barton 1992; 1997). But even if the typology of these west Scottish tanged points seems convincing, their chronology remains enigmatic.

In other parts of northern Europe tanged points of essentially the same form seem to span the period from the later part of the Lateglacial Interstadial (in the Danish Bromme sites) to the first few centuries of the Holocene (in some of the Ahrensburgian sites) and we must presumably accept a similar latitude in the dating of the Scottish specimens. Only at Lussa Wood on Jura is there a possible association of these forms with a high-level raised beach formation of apparently Lateglacial age (Mercer 1980), but this association again remains uncertain (Morrison & Bonsall 1989).

Nevertheless, even if the exact age of these finds remains ambiguous, one could make out a reasonable argument on purely technological grounds for regarding them as evidence for the earliest phase of human colonization of Scotland in the wake of the retreating ice sheets. Evidence recently documented from along the western, Atlantic coastline of Norway should make us especially open to this suggestion (Fig. 9.3). At sites extending to at least 70°N there are now records of typically Ahrensburgian-like tanged points, dated in some cases back to at least 9600 BP, and apparently reflecting an extremely rapid and strongly coastally oriented colonization of the northern Atlantic coastline – almost certainly with the use of boats – at a surprisingly early stage in the Postglacial (Bang-Andersen 1996; Larsson 1999; Rowley-Conwy 1999). A similar pattern of colonization of the Atlantic coastline of England and Scotland should hardly come as any surprise.

Following this initial, enigmatic tanged-point phase, the second apparently well-documented phase of Scottish Postglacial settlement is marked by a scatter of very different industries which have generally been compared to the classic, Early Mesolithic 'broad blade' microlithic assemblages of the kind best documented at Star Carr and a range of related sites in northern England (Jacobi 1978; Mellars & Dark 1998; Reynier 1998). The highly distinctive type fossils of these industries consist of simple obliquely blunted microlithic points, combined with a range of larger, isosceles triangular forms and others of distinctively trapezoidal shape (Fig. 9.2). Industries combining this range of forms have now been recorded from a wide spread of Scotland, ranging from Morton, Elginhaugh, and Craigsfordmains in the east, to Shewalton Moor and Auchrocher Moss in the west, and to the Inner Hebrides coastal sites of Lussa Bay and Glenbatrick on Jura and An Corran on Skye (Coles 1971; Mercer 1970; 1974; 1979; 1980; Morrison & Bonsall 1989; Saville this volume; Wickham-Jones 1994). None of these sites is at present securely dated by radiocarbon, since in all of the reported cases (such as Morton in Fife and Lussa Wood on Jura, with dates in the seventh and ninth millennia BP respectively) the association of the dated samples with the archaeological material is at best controversial (Morrison & Bonsall 1989).

There are also uncertainties as to whether some of these predominantly 'broad blade' microlithic industries are associated with some smaller 'narrow blade' or 'geometric' forms (as for example at Morton and Lussa Wood) or whether these apparent associations are simply a result of reoccupation and accidental mixtures of material on the same locations at different periods during the Mesolithic. At least at the site of Glenbatrick (area G1) on Jura the assemblage of typically broad-blade forms seems to be largely detached from any component of apparently later, narrow-blade forms (Mercer 1974).

Setting all these caveats aside, it would hardly be surprising to find a major episode of colonization of large areas of Scotland at a period broadly equivalent to the time of the Star Carr occupation in northern England – that is during the initial Postglacial period of rapidly expanding birch woodland, and probably dating to substantially prior to 9000 BP in radiocarbon terms (Mellars & Dark 1998; Reynier 1998). Again, one can point to the rapid spread of early Postglacial human colonization along the whole length of the Norwegian coast (Fig. 9.3) under conditions probably not very different from those in western Scotland (Bang-Andersen 1996; Larsson 1999). And of course large areas of the present North Sea would have been dry land at this time owing to the low sea levels at the start of the Holocene (the so-called 'Doggerland' province: Coles 1998), allowing easy penetration of Britain from a large part of northern Europe.

Any speculation as to the actual patterns of subsistence at this time is unfortunately undermined by the total absence of organic remains from the Scottish sites. One can only presume that at inland locations the prime food resources are likely to have come from hunting species such as aurochs, elk, wild boar, and (above all) red

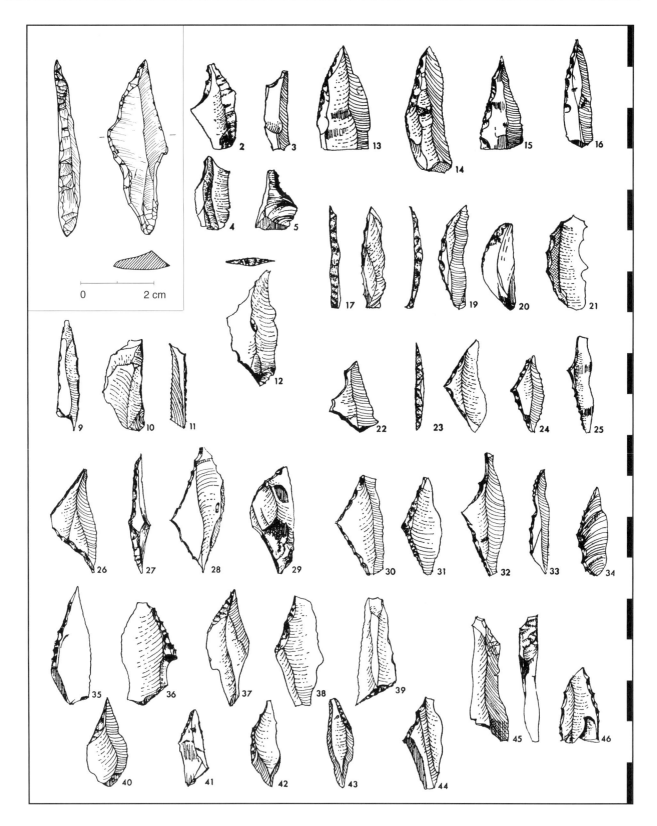

FIGURE 9.2

'Broad blade' microlithic assemblage from Morton (Fife) showing a range of forms closely similar to those from Star Carr and other Early Mesolithic sites in England (after Coles 1971). Inset: tanged point from Balevullin, Tiree (after Morrison & Bonsall 1989).

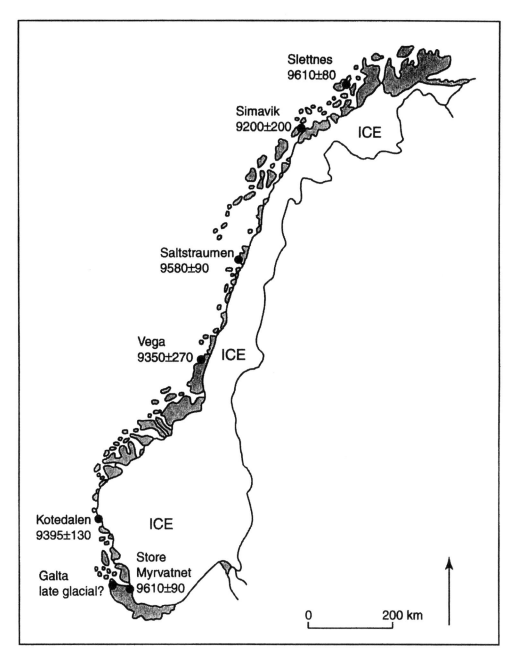

FIGURE 9.3

Radiocarbon dates (in uncalibrated years BP) for sites showing rapid human colonization along the Norwegian
coast in the early Postglacial period (after Bang-Andersen 1996; Rowley-Conwy 1999).

deer – as at Star Carr – while along the coastlines it is reasonable to assume that the economies were dependent equally (and perhaps alternating between the seasons) on the exploitation of both terrestrial and a wide range of marine resources. Certainly the rich lithic assemblages recovered from sites such as Lussa Wood on Jura (many times richer than the assemblage from Star Carr itself) would suggest that some of these coastal locations were repeatedly and intensively occupied over periods amounting perhaps to several centuries.

The coastal factor

It is hard to look at any distribution map of Mesolithic sites in Scotland without being impressed by the number

171

of sites which are located either on, or in relatively close proximity to, the coast. To anyone familiar with the general literature on hunter-gatherer societies this should come as no surprise. The conventional explanation for this concentration of coastal occupation is an essentially ecological one. The coastal habitats in many areas provide a range of economic resources which are not only highly productive and concentrated in spatial terms (such as shellfish beds, red deer over-wintering 'yards', seal-breeding colonies, migrating fish, etc.) but which are also exceptionally diverse in both ecological and economic terms (e.g. Renouf 1984; Rowley-Conwy 1999; Yesner 1980). Essentially, coastal locations can provide the best of three different economic worlds: the resources of the sea itself; the varied resources of the adjacent land; and the special 'ecotone' resources of the intertidal and immediate coastal zone – such as molluscs, crustaceans, seaweed, and certain specifically maritime plants, such as samphire.

The sheer wealth and concentration of many coastal resources could be expected to provide exceptionally rich and concentrated food supplies to coastal-living groups, supporting commensurately high human population densities. But if one adds to this the broad *diversity* of these combined sea and land resources, then the additional, critically important element of more long-term economic security is added to the equation. The point here is essentially the ecological 'law of the minimum', which dictates that the maximum level of any population which can be supported in any habitat depends not on the overall abundance and productivity of food resources in the environment as a whole, but on the quantity and security of these resources available during periodic episodes of resource decline or failure (e.g. Boughey 1973, 26–8).

In terms of hunter-gatherer subsistence, these episodes of resource scarcity can occur either on a more or less regular annual cycle (such as the general scarcity of plant foods during the winter and spring months, or seasonal migration patterns of deer or fish) or at more irregular periods caused, for example, by especially severe winters or drought, or even by heavy over-exploitation of the resources by the human groups themselves. In this situation the point quite simply is that in locations which have access to the widest possible range of different food resources, the probability of all these resources failing simultaneously is drastically reduced. The wide range and diversity of food resources available in many coastal locations therefore provides the best long-term insurance strategy against recurrent episodes of food failure for hunter-gatherer groups. Other significant advantages of coastal locations lie in the relative ease and speed of communications (by boat), and the consequent ability to maintain both economic and social contacts with other human groups over large areas of the coastal zone (Hardy & Wickham-Jones 2002).

A second set of generalizations which has often been made for coastal-living hunter-gatherer groups is that the relatively high densities of human populations which can often be supported in these habitats, and the occurrence of many of the essential resources in spatially concentrated forms (such as shellfish beds, winter deer yards, seal-breeding colonies, etc.) can often lead to significant social consequences among coastal hunter-gatherers (Renouf 1984; Rowley-Conwy 1999; Yesner 1980; and papers in Price & Brown 1985). Using ethnographic analogies drawn from areas such as the NW coast of North America (the Tlingit, Salish, etc.), northern Japan (the Ainu), SE Australia (the coastal aborigines), and with some South American groups, it is often clear that hunter-gatherers in these locations can form relatively large social units (almost amounting to villages in some locations), which can frequently remain largely sedentary in the same location over a large part of the year. It is often argued in turn that these large, semi-sedentary communities are likely to develop not only more 'complex' forms of social organization (including, for example, certain kinds of economic or social role specialization, assigned leadership, or even explicit social ranking within the individual groups) but also more elaborate forms of technology, and perhaps domestic architecture. Other embellishments, such as increased ceremonial, ritual, or artistic expression, may be tagged on to the cultural repertoire of these coastal groups (Keeley 1988; Rowley-Conwy 1999).

How does this rather impressive hypothetical scenario measure up to the available archaeological evidence for the character of coastal occupation in Mesolithic Scotland? As noted earlier, Mesolithic sites appear to be densely distributed around most parts of the coastline of Scotland which have been systematically explored, and over periods ranging from the Early Mesolithic (as represented for example by the broad-blade sites on Jura) to the latest stages, as exemplified by the 'Obanian' shell middens of Argyll and the narrow-blade microlithic industries from around the islands of Jura, Islay, and Colonsay, and along many parts of the coastline of SW Scotland (Mithen 2000a; Wickham-Jones 1994). These concentrations of sites could be taken to support the hypothesis of an unusually high density of human population in these coastal habitats throughout much if not all of the Mesolithic.

It is also clear that many of these coastal sites are exceptionally rich in archaeological terms, with quantities of microliths (for example on several of the Jura sites or at Bolsay Farm on Islay), which are hard to parallel at most inland locations, either in Scotland or in Britain as a whole (Mithen 2000a). This could certainly be taken to indicate a highly intensive pattern of occupation on the sites, almost certainly extending in many cases over several centuries, and possibly hinting at relatively prolonged individual episodes of occupation on the same sites. One might add that the artefact inventories recorded from many of these locations seem to include a wide range of functionally different forms (microliths, scrapers, burins, awls, saws, 'limpet scoops', pitted pebbles, etc.) together with large quantities of cores and other flaking debris, which could be taken to suggest functionally generalized 'base-camp' type locations, rather than more ephemerally occupied and more functionally (or socially) focused 'special activity' sites. All of these patterns could no doubt be seen as consistent with the idea that certain coastal locations served as relatively sedentary (or at least relatively long-term) settlements over at least a substantial part of the annual cycle. The presence of well-defined structural features at several of the sites (as discussed below) could be seen as a further indication of the relatively intensive patterns of occupation and associated economic activities at many of the sites.

How far the available evidence can support some of the other proposed generalizations about the nature of coastal societies remains much less clear. Any speculations as to the overall size of the social groups who occupied the sites are inevitably undermined by the effects of frequently repeated occupation on the sites and the resultant occupational palimpsests. In the virtual absence of organic remains from all except a small handful of (mostly) shell midden sites, it is hard to speculate on either the precise range and nature of the economic activities practised on the sites, or the character or duration of any seasonal patterns of occupation.

Arguably the most significant features reported from Scottish Mesolithic sites are the well-defined traces of various structural features (Wickham-Jones this volume). Substantial pits which most probably represent storage facilities have been reported from sites on Rùm, Jura, Islay, Colonsay, and elsewhere, while traces of either stakeholes or the scooped foundations of living structures have been documented from at least a dozen coastal sites. The most impressive structural feature so far published from Scotland is the large circular depression, almost five metres in diameter, recently excavated at Staosnaig on Colonsay (Mithen 2000a). At least in terms of size and shape this feature seems to be strongly reminiscent of the substantial hut structure excavated at Mount Sandel in Northern Ireland (Woodman 1985). As noted above, these features at least could be taken as an indication of relatively prolonged and stable periods of perhaps semi-sedentary residence on these sites, most

probably (to judge by the abundance of hazelnut shells in the Staosnaig feature) spanning the autumn and perhaps winter months.

As to the possibility of increased ceremonial or artistic activity associated with coastal settlements, there is effectively nothing to report from the Scottish sites (again bearing in mind the general absence of organic remains) apart from the concentrations of perforated cowrie-shell beads recovered from the five Late Mesolithic shell middens on Oronsay (Mellars 1987; Simpson 1996). It is of course tempting to think that further explorations will bring to light large-scale Mesolithic cemeteries of the kind documented from Vedbaek in Denmark and Skateholm in south Sweden (Larsson 1999), but for the present (and in view of the poor conditions for the preservation of bone on most Scottish sites) this may remain a forlorn hope. In short, even if one can make out a case for at least some of the speculative features of social and cultural 'complexity' for the Mesolithic coastal exploitation of Scotland, it is hard to claim that this case is overwhelming, from the evidence at present to hand.

Shell middens and molluscs in Mesolithic Scotland

The significance of the large-scale exploitation of marine molluscs has stimulated some lively debate in the archaeological literature. Most of the debate has centred on the fact that on both economic cost/benefit grounds and recent ethnographic and historical parallels, the harvesting of molluscs generally appears to be a relatively inefficient economic strategy, which in recent contexts seems to have been resorted to mainly as a 'stress' or 'crisis' activity, when other food resources either fail or are in seriously short supply (e.g. Bailey 1982; Cohen 1977; Mannio & Thomas 2000; Waselkov 1987). Clearly, the strength of these arguments varies with different species of molluscs and their general abundance in specific locations, but for most species the generalizations seem to apply.

Essentially, molluscs tend to be labour-intensive and time-consuming to collect, to provide relatively low calorific returns for the time and labour invested, to require large amounts of processing time to extract the small quantities of food involved, are generally heavy to transport (unless the shells are removed at the point of collection), and in some cases (most notoriously limpets) are relatively tough and tasteless to eat. The argument generally runs that under these conditions, shellfish would normally be collected in large quantities only under circumstances of economic stress or scarcity, either at particular times of the year when other food resources in general were in short supply, or during more occasional periods of economic hardship when other, more 'staple' food supplies were either dwindling, or perhaps exhausted by intensive local over-exploitation of the resources by the human populations themselves (Bailey 1982; Cohen 1977; Mannio & Thomas 2000; Waselkov 1987). One might add that the harvesting of molluscs generally involves irregular patterns of labour investment (i.e. heavily concentrated at periods of low tide) and ethnographically has usually been the main preserve of women and children in the local groups (Meehan 1982).

Clearly, these generalizations should not be over-played. In most coastal situations molluscs represent an obvious and immediately available source of food, and it would be surprising if any coastal living group did not incorporate some component of shellfish into its regular diet, if only to add an element of variety to the staple diet, much in the way that we enjoy most species of shellfish at the present day. In these terms we would expect to find some component of shellfish in almost all coastal sites, and it comes as no surprise that the archaeological record of at least sporadic mollusc exploitation can be traced well back into the Middle and even Lower Palaeolithic periods (Klein 1999; Parkington 1999). The real interest in cultural and economic terms centres on the contexts in which shellfish seem to have become a major and central element in dietary systems leading, archaeologically, to the appearance of major shell midden accumulations.

Any study of the archaeological records of shellfish exploitation must of course take account of the various sources of potential distortion in the surviving archaeological evidence. Since most of the archaeologically documented shell middens seem to be located very close to the contemporaneous beaches (as for example those on Oronsay, or in the Firth of Forth) we can only realistically expect to find traces of these middens where the related shorelines themselves are preserved. In the Scottish context this generally means that only sites dating from the later stages of the Mesolithic – and in particular those associated with the period of the maximum Postglacial marine transgression, from *c.*7000 BP onwards – are likely to retain any substantial traces of midden deposits. But there are other, potentially equally serious, sources of bias in the archaeological record. Evidence from Oronsay and elsewhere leaves no doubt that in recent historical times shell middens were often exploited as a convenient source of lime-rich fertilizer in areas of naturally acidic soils (Mellars 1987, 202). It is virtually impossible to estimate the potential impact of this factor on the survival of shell middens in areas subjected to systematic farming over the past 5000 years, but in many areas the impact could have been dramatic.

Seen in these terms it should hardly come as a surprise that the main contexts in which Mesolithic shell middens have survived more or less intact down to the present day derive mainly from either cave and rockshelter sites (where systematic mining of the deposits for fertilizer would presumably have been difficult) or from areas of naturally highly alkaline soils, such as the extensive 'machair' deposits of the islands and west Scottish coasts, where the superficial wind-blown deposits themselves are composed largely of shell sand (as for example over large areas of Oronsay and most of the other Hebridean islands). In areas of naturally highly acidic soils, the effects of natural leaching over the past 5000 years may have been sufficient to eliminate all traces of at least the thinner and more short-term shell middens. Any attempt to calculate the potential impact of these combined factors on the extent of survival of shell middens can hardly amount to more than a wild guess, but it might not be unrealistic to suggest that the surviving sample of Mesolithic shell middens may represent no more than one or two per cent of those originally present on the associated coasts.

So, with all these caveats, what can we say about the documented chronological distribution of shell middens in Mesolithic Scotland? The archaeological record effectively starts with the apparently typical, limpet-dominated midden discovered in the 1890s in the Druimvargie rockshelter at Oban (Lacaille 1954), which has been dated on the basis of the associated artefacts (including two uniserially barbed bone points and typical 'limpet-scoops') to between 8300 and 7800 BP (Bonsall 1996). Broadly similar dates have now been reported for an apparently similar midden, with associated microlithic technology, at Sand on the Applecross peninsula (Hardy & Wickham-Jones 2002). There are slightly later dates for the midden deposits excavated in the Ulva cave adjacent to Mull (Bonsall 1996) and (rather less well documented in stratigraphic terms) for those in the An Corran rockshelter on Skye (Saville & Miket 1994). The bulk of the classic 'Obanian' shell middens of the west coast are generally associated with the period of the maximum of the Postglacial marine transgression, and have dates ranging from *c.*6700 BP (MacArthur Cave, Oban) down to *c.*5400 BP (Cnoc Coig, Caisteal nan Gillean I & II, Cnoc Sligeach, and Priory Midden on Oronsay) (Bonsall 1996; Mellars 1987). Broadly the same period seems to be represented by the cockle-dominated midden at Morton in Fife (Coles 1971), and by at least the earlier stages of formation of some of the massive oyster middens around the shores of the Firth of Forth, as at Inveravon and Nether Kinneil, near Falkirk (Sloan 1984). The concentration of these sites during the later Mesolithic phases – especially from *c.*6500 BP – is therefore striking, but arguably hardly surprising in view of the history of relative land/sea-level changes during the course of the Postglacial period.

If the conspicuous clustering of shell middens during the later stages of the Mesolithic is a real feature of the archaeological record, and not simply a product of the various distorting factors discussed above, then of course it could have significant implications for the whole pattern of socio-economic change over the period of the Mesolithic/Neolithic transition, and perhaps even provide a major explanatory factor for at least some of these changes. In other areas of Europe it has often been noted that there seems to be a curious outbreak of shell midden formation shortly before the first appearance of fully Neolithic communities in the different areas, and this has been seen by some workers as a potential reflection of a general pattern of economic crisis which would at least have accelerated, if not initiated, the adoption of new agricultural practices (Bailey 1982; Cohen 1977). The large-scale use of labour-intensive shellfish collection strategies could, in other words, be seen as part of a general pattern of economic 'intensification' during the final Mesolithic stages, which could have provided a major stimulus for the adoption of the new Neolithic regime (Harris 1996; Zvelebil *et al.* 1998), as discussed further below.

The 'Obanian' phenomenon and the interpretation of the Oronsay middens

The whole topic of the 'Obanian' phenomenon in Mesolithic Scotland has generated a long and (recently) fairly lively debate in the literature (e.g. Bonsall 1996; Mithen 2000a; Mithen & Finlayson 1991; Richards & Mellars 1998), which at least in part reduces to some issues of terminology. If by 'Obanian' we imply almost any midden deposits heavily dominated by limpets, then one could no doubt identify Obanian sites at almost any period from the ninth millennium BP onwards down to the end of the Mesolithic period, and no doubt far beyond (Bonsall 1996). To have any meaning in a cultural or even technological sense, we must clearly identify the Obanian by at least some distinctive artefact forms. The usual candidates cited in this context are the much-discussed 'limpet-scoop' forms (i.e. artificially bevelled, more or less finger-shaped pieces of bone, antler, or elongated stone pebbles) together with other forms such as pitted beach-pebbles (probably used as anvilstones for working flint), larger and more heavily worn 'limpet hammers', bone awls, perforated cowrie-shell beads, and the more sporadic occurrence of single- or double-barbed 'harpoons' of bone or antler and

occasional perforated red-deer antler mattocks (Bonsall 1996; Lacaille 1954; Mellars 1987). It could be argued that none of these forms is especially distinctive in either typological or technological terms, at least when taken in isolation. Indeed, in certain cases, most notably the bevel-ended bone and stone forms, and the engaging cowrie-shell beads, they are now known to be distributed around large parts of the western and northern coastline of Britain during the later stages of the Mesolithic, extending as far south as Wales and Devon (Barton 1997). From the east coast we have apparently typical bone 'limpet-scoop' forms from the midden at Morton in Fife (Coles 1971), and a typical, double-barbed harpoon head washed up on the beach at Whitburn, Tyne and Wear (Mellars 1970).

As noted above, at least some of these 'typical' features of the Obanian can now be identified in west-Scottish shell midden deposits back to the ninth millennium BP (notably in the Druimvargie rockshelter at Oban) and could be seen as a normal component of the technology employed in these explicitly coastal, shellfish harvesting sites throughout at least the second half of the Mesolithic period as a whole. Leaving aside all the issues of the potentially highly specialized economic function of these sites, as discussed very clearly by Bonsall (1996), it is clear that any notion of the 'Obanian' as a distinctive, sharply defined cultural or social entity, specific to the final stages of the Mesolithic in western Scotland, must be set to one side.

Over the past decade, most of the focus of the debate over the general 'Obanian' problem seems to have shifted to the specific interpretations of the remarkable concentration of shell middens on the small island of Oronsay (immediately to the south of Colonsay) in the Inner Hebrides (Bonsall 1996; Mellars 1987; Mithen 2000a; 2000b; Mithen & Finlayson 1991; Richards & Mellars 1998). As the person responsible for the main campaign of fieldwork on these sites, I can hardly conclude the present paper without some discussion of these recent, highly stimulating debates.

The basic pattern of the evidence from Oronsay is perhaps too well known to need detailed description here (Mellars 1978; 1987; Mellars & Wilkinson 1980). The island itself has a present land area of only six km^2 and at the time of the Mesolithic occupation this would have been reduced to around four km^2 by the effects of the main Postglacial marine transgression, which seems to have reached its maximum in this particular region around 6500 BP. Five major shell middens have now been documented and excavated on the island, with a range of radiocarbon dates spanning the period *c.*6200–5400 BP (Fig. 9.4). The middens are all of a broadly similar size (mostly *c.*25–30m in diameter) and at all the sites

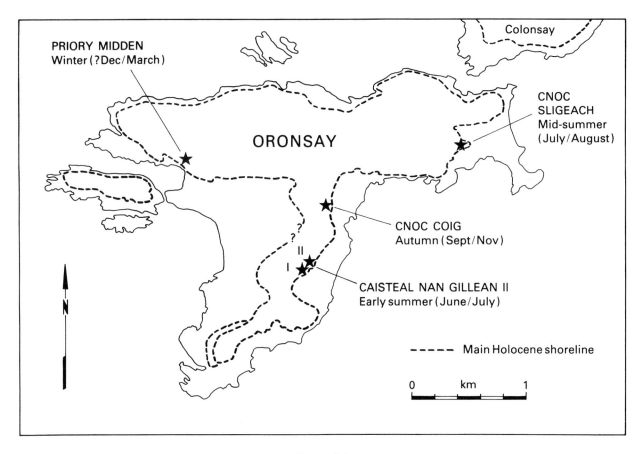

FIGURE 9.4
Location of shell middens on Oronsay, with main seasons of occupation as indicated by fishing for saithe
(after Mellars 1987).

there is clear stratigraphic evidence for a relatively long and complex succession of closely repeated occupation and shellfish collection (with many associated hearths), spanning periods of at least 200–300 years.

All the midden deposits are heavily dominated by limpets, with much smaller proportions of periwinkles (*Littorina littorea*) and dogwhelks (*Nucella lapillus*), and very sporadic traces of a wide range of other species (oysters, cockles, topshells, razor-shells, mussels, dog cockle, etc.). Fine-sieving and analysis of the deposits has shown that fishing – especially for young saithe (*Pollachius virens*) – must have contributed almost as much to the diet of the midden occupants as the shellfish. The collection of at least two species of crabs was clearly a significant component of the diet at all the sites, with more sporadic traces of grey seal, otter, a range of sea birds (especially the Great Auk), and relatively abundant traces of burnt and broken hazelnut shells. Remains of land mammals are extremely rare on all the sites, and consist mainly of segments of red deer antler, which were

probably imported into the sites largely if not entirely for the manufacture of artefacts such as 'limpet scoops' and, much more rarely, barbed antler points and perforated mattock heads (Grigson & Mellars 1987). Other artefacts include the normal repertoire of 'Obanian' forms, including abundant bevel-ended stone 'limpet scoops', bone or antler awls, pitted pebble-hammers or anvil-stones, and abundant examples of small, double perforated cowrie-shell beads or pendants. Significantly, the relatively abundant flintwork recovered from all the middens seems to have been produced almost entirely on small, local beach pebbles, and is conspicuously lacking in either typical microlithic or micro-blade technology, or virtually any clearly recognizable retouched tool forms.

One of the most significant and intriguing patterns revealed by the recent work on Oronsay is the evidence for a sharply seasonal pattern of fishing for saithe at the different sites, based on detailed comparative studies of the size distribution of the distinctive otoliths (Mellars 1978; 1987; Mellars & Wilkinson 1980). This revealed

176

clearly that at least the main season of fishing for this species had varied sharply and systematically between the different sites, spanning the period from early to mid-summer (at Cnoc Sligeach and Caisteal nan Gillean II), through autumn (Cnoc Coig) to at least the early or mid-winter months (Priory Midden) (Fig. 9.4). The only periods of fishing not clearly represented in the middens are late winter and spring, when it is known that the saithe retreat into deeper, offshore waters, and are effectively impossible to catch (Note 1).

Stated briefly, there are two basic and sharply conflicting hypotheses which have been debated in the recent literature on the Oronsay middens, which in many ways encapsulate the more general issues of the interpretation of the 'Obanian' phenomenon as a whole (Bonsall 1996; Mithen 2000a; 2000b; Mithen & Finlayson 1991; Richards & Mellars 1998). Reduced to the essentials, these can be summarized as follows:

1. That the occupation and use of the different shell middens on Oronsay was essentially the product of a single social group, which remained on the island throughout most if not all of each year, but moving seasonally between the different sites (Richards & Mellars 1998).

2. That the occupations documented in the different middens represent much more sporadic and intermittent visits to the sites by a range of different social groups, who spent the remainder of each year on some of the larger adjacent islands, such as Jura, Islay, or Colonsay, or possibly the Scottish mainland, most probably practising economies in these other locations dependent largely on the hunting of red deer or other land mammals (Mithen 2000a, 623; Mithen & Finlayson 1991) (see Fig. 9.5).

A full analysis of these two hypotheses would occupy much more space than is available here, and in earlier publications I have tried to take a fairly open-ended view of the different alternatives (Mellars 1978; 1987; Mellars & Wilkinson 1980). There is now no doubt, however, that the gradual accumulation of evidence from different sources poses a much more serious obstacle to the second of the above hypotheses than it does to the first. Very briefly, the main considerations can be summarized as follows..

Clearly, the seasonal evidence referred to above demonstrates the use of the different Oronsay middens spanning virtually all seasons of the year, with the occupation of each individual site being apparently specific to one season (mid-summer at Cnoc Sligeach, autumn at Cnoc Coig, winter at Priory midden, etc.) (Mellars & Wilkinson 1980) (Note 1). To explain this pattern

in terms of the 'sporadic visits' hypothesis one would presumably need to assume two things: first that there was some form of convention among the different groups who visited the island as to exactly which sites should be occupied at which seasons of the year; and second (assuming relatively brief visits) that some groups were deliberately making the crossing to Oronsay to exploit the rich coastal resources there at times of the year when other groups were leaving the island to exploit resources elsewhere. On the face of it neither of these seems a very plausible scenario. Clearly, Oronsay provided rich and probably economically reliable food resources at all seasons of the year. In this situation it is difficult to visualize why a range of hypothetically different social groups should have found it necessary to come and go between the islands in such a highly patterned way, but one which varied in seasonal terms between the different groups involved.

There is no reason to doubt that the rich, concentrated, and highly varied food resources available on Oronsay would have been adequate to support a single human group throughout most if not all seasons of the year. In addition to the wealth of coastal resources (fish, shell-fish, crabs, seals, sea-birds, etc.) clearly documented in the middens, it is possible that certain land-based resources (such as hazelnuts or other plant foods) would have provided a much larger component of the diet than the archaeological evidence suggests (Mithen 2000a). Moreover, the resources of the adjacent parts of southern Colonsay would have been potentially available within at most two or three kilometres of movement (by boat) from the Oronsay sites. In purely subsistence terms there seems no reason to doubt the viability of essentially year-round occupation on the Oronsay sites, by a relatively small social unit. For groups adept at the harvesting of coastal resources, it would have been difficult to go short of food on Oronsay at any season of the year.

As already noted, the character of the flaked stone industries recovered from the Oronsay middens provides no hint whatever that the sites were occupied by groups who at other times of the year, or in other locations, manufactured typical microlithic industries of the kind represented at many sites on the adjacent islands of Jura, Islay, and indeed Colonsay (Fig. 9.5; Mercer 1979; Mithen 2000a; Mithen & Lake 1996). The flint assemblages from all of the Oronsay sites have proved to be conspicuously lacking not only in any trace of micro-lithic or typical micro-blade technology, but of almost any clearly retouched tool forms. Even if one were to postulate a highly specialized economic function for the Oronsay sites, it would seem odd that no trace whatever of these microlithic or micro-blade technologies should ever have been imported, or produced, in the Oronsay

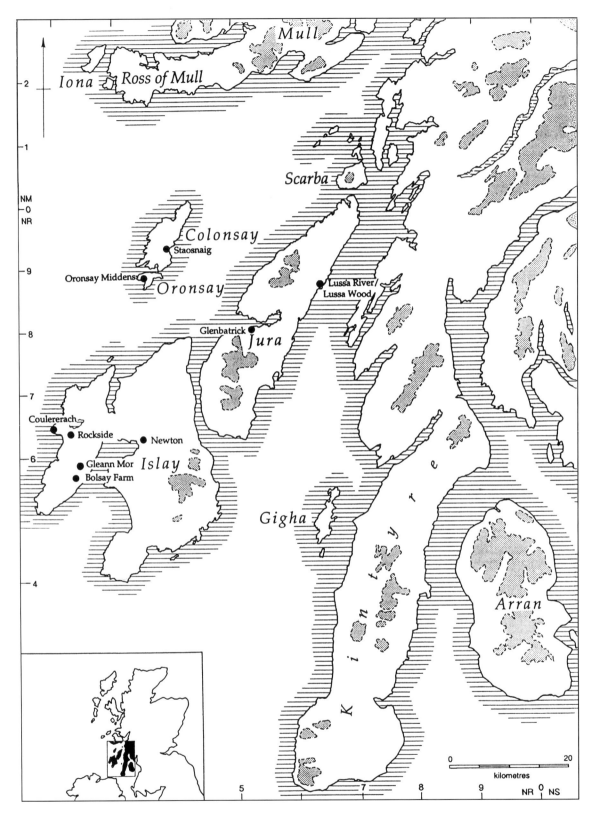

FIGURE 9.5

Location of the Oronsay middens in relation to Later Mesolithic microlith-yielding sites on the adjacent islands of Colonsay, Islay, and Jura (after Mithen 2000b).

sites, by groups coming from the hypothetically complementary sites elsewhere. Nor, so far as we can tell, do the lithic assemblages include any component of clearly imported flint.

Similar observations can be applied to the general scarcity of red deer bones and antler at the Oronsay sites. At 'Obanian' sites on the Scottish mainland (such as Risga, on Loch Sunart, or the MacArthur Cave at Oban) either red deer bone or antler seems to have been the strongly preferred material for the manufacture of 'limpet scoops', with tools made on these materials heavily outnumbering those made on stone (Lacaille 1954). On the Oronsay sites, by contrast, all traces of red deer bones are conspicuously scarce (Grigson & Mellars 1987) and the 'limpet scoops' are manufactured far more commonly from beach pebbles than from fragments of either bone or antler. Once again it is hard to imagine how or why this situation should arise, among groups who were hypothetically spending the greater part of each year on some other adjacent islands, largely dependent on the hunting of red deer, and therefore presumably with almost unlimited access to bone and antler as raw materials.

How far the Oronsay sites can in fact be interpreted as highly specialized functional or activity locations is itself equally open to question (cf. Bonsall 1996). Quite apart from the wide range of food resources now reported from all of the sites there is clear evidence for an equal diversity in the range of technologies and functional tool forms employed on the different sites ('limpet scoops', 'limpet hammers', hammer/anvilstones, worked flints, bone chisels, bone awls, antler harpoons, mattock heads, cowrie-shell beads, etc.), together with evidence for the on-site manufacture of many of these forms. There is also explicit evidence from at least one of the sites (Cnoc Coig), not only for large and repeatedly reused hearths, but also for at least two clearly defined hut structures (Fig. 9.6; Mellars 1987). In short, at least the Cnoc Coig midden could be seen as reflecting much more substantial occupation than a mere 'shellfish processing site' (Bonsall 1996; Meehan 1982). Perhaps more to the point, one should keep in mind that other major 'residential' or 'base-camp' locations could well exist in some of the interior parts of Oronsay, in areas at present covered by deep deposits of wind-blown sand (Note 2).

Lastly, and most significantly, we now have recent carbon and nitrogen isotope analyses carried out on a number of human bones from two of the Oronsay middens (Cnoc Coig and Caisteal nan Gillean II), which in five out of the six analysed cases point to a diet consisting almost entirely of marine resources, and with no apparent evidence of a significant terrestrial element in the diet (Richards & Mellars 1998). Clearly, whichever way this evidence is viewed it is not consistent with the view that the individuals in question spent a large part of each year in some other locations, subsisting primarily on land-based resources, such as red deer or terrestrial plant foods. The evidence is more consistent with the hypothesis of essentially residential occupation on Oronsay – or in some other purely coastally oriented location – at all seasons of the year.

Recently, Mithen (2000a; 2000b) has reviewed the new aspects of the evidence from Oronsay and elsewhere and has adopted a rather different stance from that adopted in his earlier article on 'Red deer hunters on Colonsay' (Mithen & Finlayson 1991). In particular, he has presented a detailed analysis of the available radiocarbon dates for both the Oronsay sites and the various microlithic/micro-blade dominated sites on the adjacent islands of Colonsay, Islay, and Jura (Fig. 9.5). In brief, Mithen concludes that there appears to be a curious gap in the overall distribution of radiocarbon dates for these microlithic sites between c.6500 and 5400 BP, which coincides almost exactly with the main date distribution of the Oronsay sites. As he points out, unless this reflects some kind of strange, accidental bias in the available radiocarbon measurements, or a simple accident in the sites chosen for excavation and dating, this would pose an obvious problem for viewing both the microlithic sites and the Oronsay shell middens as directly inter-dependent parts of the same economic and social systems, leaving aside all the other technological, economic, and seasonal objections to this particular hypothesis outlined above.

So we appear to be left with the model of a permanent, or at least semi-permanent, human population on Oronsay as the most likely hypothesis for the archaeological evidence as a whole. But this still leaves scope for a number of other, related options. There can be no doubt whatever that the Oronsay communities must have maintained some kind of regular contact with human groups on other adjacent islands, or just possibly the Scottish mainland. This would have been essential on purely demographic grounds to maintain the mating patterns and genetic viability of the Oronsay groups. And we already have strong evidence that the Oronsay communities must have been importing at least some of the red deer antler supplies employed for tool manufacture from one or more of the adjacent islands, or the Scottish mainland (Grigson & Mellars 1987). The mixed marine and terrestrial diet implied by the isotopic analysis of one of the human bones from the Caisteal nan Gillean II midden (Richards & Mellars 1998) would point in the same direction, possibly reflecting an individual who was co-opted by marriage into the Oronsay community from elsewhere.

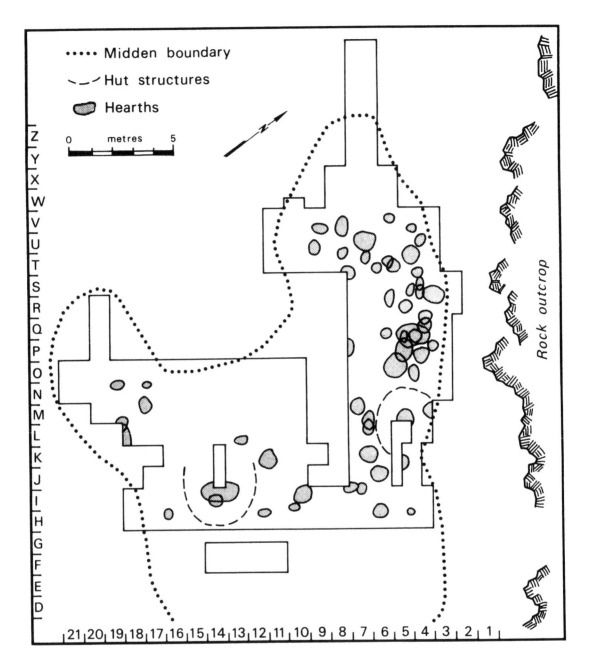

FIGURE 9.6

Plan of the Cnoc Coig midden (Oronsay) showing location of hearths and associated hut structures (after Mellars 1987).

A further and in some ways particularly intriguing possibility is that the overall 700–800 year span of the occupation now clearly documented by radiocarbon dating of the different Oronsay sites was not in fact strictly continuous in chronological terms, but reflects a more 'punctuated' pattern, consisting of a series of separate, shorter interludes of intensive occupation, separated by other periods of non-occupation. One possibility, for example, is that the separate episodes of intensive occupation on the Oronsay sites could have been precipitated by certain kinds of resource crisis or failure in other adjacent locations, such as the immediately adjacent island of Colonsay. If one were to pursue this hypothetical scenario, one might envisage, for example, that the Late Mesolithic groups who practised a predominantly hunting economy (for red deer) on the adjacent island of Colonsay (cf. Mithen & Finlayson 1991) would on occasions have over-exploited the local red deer populations either to the point of extinction, or to near extinction, especially in view of the small size of Colonsay, and especially if the hunting practices involved systematic vegetation-burning strategies designed to attract and control the movements of the animal herds (Mellars 1976). Arguably, if this were to happen, then an obvious and perhaps inevitable response would have been to shift the economy onto an intensive exploitation of predominantly coastal resources, until the local land-based resources had time to recover (Note 3).

It is precisely in situations of this kind that the rich, concentrated, and seasonally dependable coastal resources available on Oronsay might have provided the essential safety-net to maintain the local human groups over these periods of local resource crisis. If cycles of this kind were to happen at, say, 50- or 100-year intervals, then one could potentially have several separate episodes of occupation on the Oronsay sites, distributed at various points over the combined 800-year span of occupation on the sites. Unfortunately, the available radiocarbon dates for the Oronsay sites are hardly adequate to test this particular hypothesis with any rigour or precision. But this is certainly one potential model for the Oronsay sites which can hardly be dismissed from the evidence at present to hand.

One final aspect of the model discussed above is that it would reinforce the potential interest of the apparent epidemic of Late Mesolithic shell middens in Europe, as a symptom of a progressive and repeated process of resource over-exploitation which eventually precipitated – and perhaps necessitated – the widespread adoption of new agricultural economies (Bailey 1982; Cohen 1977; Harris 1996). The process could be seen as one of either progressive depletion and over-use of the available resources, or more simply (in Cohen's terms) as a shifting balance between human population numbers and the available 'natural' resources needed to support these populations. In either case one could see the curious concentration of Late Mesolithic shell middens on Oronsay – as well as those in other parts of Scotland, and perhaps Europe more broadly – as a specific argument in favour of a general 'economic stress' model for the diffusion and widespread adoption of fully agricultural economies throughout Europe (Harris 1996; Zvelebil et al. 1998).

There is, of course, another dimension to the Oronsay middens. The dense scatters of limpets and other shells spread over the surface of the middens, bleached by the sun, would inevitably have formed a conspicuous feature in the local landscape, which would almost certainly have been visible from the adjacent parts of both Islay and Jura, as well as from boats passing between the islands. Viewed from this perspective, the shell midden sites could well have served as significant social or terri-

torial markers in the Later Mesolithic environment of the Inner Hebrides, potentially analogous to the chambered tombs and round barrows of the ensuing Neolithic and Bronze Ages. This might also help to explain why the middens tend to be located on some of the higher parts of the eastern Oronsay coastline, and why the successive episodes of occupation on the different sites were so closely tied to the same locations. To push the speculative boat out further, one might even go on to recall that the overall form of middens such as Caisteal nan Gillean I and Cnoc Sligeach are in many ways strikingly similar to the shapes of limpet shells (see Mellars 1987, figs.11.19 & 13.2), and that the same shapes are equally reminiscent of the outlines of the Jura Mountains (the so-called Paps of Jura), which form the dominating feature of the skyline immediately to the east of Oronsay (ibid., fig. 2.4)! But again, these interpretations should not be stretched too far. There are, of course, other reasons why naturally elevated locations could have been deliberately selected as major activity locations, either to improve visibility from the sites over the adjacent coastline, or to reduce the impact of attacks from midges and other insects, which form a perennial feature of the Hebridean environment – as anyone who has conducted fieldwork in these areas will be acutely aware. As in most other areas of prehistory, a full understanding of the behaviour of the Mesolithic communities on Oronsay will only be achieved by taking a balanced view of the prosaically functional, as well as more exciting social and ideological, dimensions of the human societies involved.

Notes

1. As discussed elsewhere (Mellars 1987), a major question which remains to be resolved is whether the collection of molluscs on Oronsay was carried out at precisely the same seasons as the fishing activities at the different sites, or whether the harvesting of shellfish was concentrated primarily during the late winter and spring months, when fishing for saithe was effectively impossible. Drying and storage of fish for use over the winter is of course another possibility – a practice in use until recently on Colonsay.

2. A further (more extreme) possibility is that the principal base-camp locations of the Oronsay groups could have been located on the adjacent parts of southern Colonsay, from which smaller groups (perhaps mainly women and children) would have made daily visits to the Oronsay sites by boat along the eastern coast – though this model would of course encounter many of the interpretative problems

discussed in the preceding paragraphs. If the groups were dependent almost entirely on coastal resources for their annual food supplies, as the isotope evidence suggests (Richards & Mellars 1998), it is hard to see why base-camps on Colonsay would have any advantages over those on Oronsay itself – and they would certainly have involved a greater investment in commuting time! The east coast of Oronsay still has the reputation as the most productive and reliable fishing grounds for saithe of the two islands, and has a much greater length of coastline accessible within a short radius of movement than any location on Colonsay. It also supports a large seal colony.

3. This would of course assume that Colonsay once supported a red deer population – either as a result of natural migration to the island early in the Postglacial or (perhaps more likely) by the deliberate introduction of red deer by the Mesolithic groups themselves (see Grigson & Mellars 1987).

References

Atkinson, T.C., Briffa, K.R. and Coope, G.R. 1987. Seasonal temperatures in Britain during the past 22,000 years, reconstructed using beetle remains. *Nature* **325**, 587–92.

Bailey, G.N. 1982. Coasts, lakes and littorals. *In* M.R. Jarman, G.N. Bailey and H.N. Jarman (eds), *Early European Agriculture*, 72–106. Cambridge: Cambridge University Press.

Ballin, T.B. and Saville, A. 2003. An Ahrensburgian-type tanged point from Shieldaig, Wester Ross, Scotland, and its implications. *Oxford Journal of Archaeology* **22**(2), 115–31.

Bang-Andersen, S. 1996. The colonization of southwest Norway: an ecological approach. *In* L. Larsson (ed.), *The Earliest Settlement of Scandinavia*, 219–314. Stockholm: Almquist & Wiksell International (*Acta Archaeologica Lundensia*, Series in 8°, No. **24**).

Barton, N. 1992. *Hengistbury Head, Dorset. Vol. 2. The Late Upper Palaeolithic and Early Mesolithic Sites*. Oxford: Oxford University Committee for Archaeology (Monograph **34**).

Barton, N. 1997. *Stone Age Britain*. London: Batsford/English Heritage.

Becker, B. 1993. An 11,000-year German oak and pine dendrochronology for radiocarbon calibration. *Radiocarbon* **35**, 201–13.

Bonsall, C. 1996. The 'Obanian problem': coastal adaptations in the Mesolithic of western Scotland. *In* T. Pollard and A. Morrison (eds), *The Early Prehistory of Scotland*, 183–97. Edinburgh: Edinburgh University Press.

Boughey, A.S. 1973. *The Ecology of Populations*. New York: Macmillan.

Cohen, M.N. 1977. *The Food Crisis in Prehistory*. Yale: Yale University Press.

Coles, B.J. 1998. Doggerland: a speculative survey. *Proceedings of the Prehistoric Society* **64**, 45–81.

Coles, J.M. 1971. The early settlement of Scotland: excavations at Morton, Fife. *Proceedings of the Prehistoric Society* **37**, 284–365.

Dansgaard, W., Johnsen, S.J., Clausen, H.B., Dahl-Jensen, D., Gundestrup, N.S., Hammer, C.U., Hvidberg, C.S., Steffensen, J.P., Sveinbjörnsdottir, A.E., Jouzel, J. and Bond, G. 1993. Evidence for general instability of past climate from a 250-kyr ice record. *Nature* **364**, 218–20.

Edwards, K. 1996. A Mesolithic of the Western and Northern Isles of Scotland? Evidence from pollen and charcoal. *In* T. Pollard and A. Morrison (eds), *The Early Prehistory of Scotland*, 23–38. Edinburgh: Edinburgh University Press.

Grigson, C. and Mellars, P. 1987. The mammalian remains from the middens. *In* P. Mellars (ed.), *Excavations on Oronsay: Prehistoric Human Ecology on a Small Island*, 243–89. Edinburgh: Edinburgh University Press.

Hardy, K. and Wickham-Jones, C.R. 2002. Scotland's First Settlers: the Mesolithic seascape of the Inner Sound, Skye and its contribution to the early prehistory of Scotland. *Antiquity* **76**, 825–33.

Harris, D.R. (ed.). 1996. *The Origins and Spread of Agriculture and Pastoralism in Eurasia*. London: UCL Press.

Housley, R.A., Gamble, C.S., Street, M. and Pettitt, P. 1997. Radiocarbon evidence for the Lateglacial human recolonisation of Europe. *Proceedings of the Prehistoric Society* **63**, 25–54.

Jacobi, R. 1978. Northern England in the eighth millennium bc: an essay. *In* P. Mellars (ed.), *The Early Postglacial Settlement of Northern Europe*, 295–332. London: Duckworth.

Jacobi, R. 1991. The Creswellian, Creswell and Cheddar. *In* N. Barton, A.J. Roberts and D.A. Roe (eds), *The Late Glacial in North-West Europe: Human Adaptation and Environmental Change at the End of the Pleistocene*, 128–40. London: Council for British Archaeology (Research Report **77**).

Jones, R.L. and Keen, D.H. 1993. *Pleistocene Environments in the British Isles*. London: Chapman & Hall.

Keeley, L.H. 1988. Hunter-gatherer economic complexity and 'population pressure': a cross-cultural analysis. *Journal of Anthropological Archaeology* **7**, 373–411.

Klein, R.G. 1999. *The Human Career: Human Biological and Cultural Origins*. Chicago: University of Chicago Press.

Lacaille, A.D. 1954. *The Stone Age in Scotland*. London: Oxford University Press.

Larsson, L. 1999. Settlement and palaeoecology in the Scandinavian Mesolithic. *In* J. Coles, R. Bewley and P. Mellars (eds), *World Prehistory: Studies in Memory of Grahame Clark*, 87–106. Oxford: Oxford University Press (=*Proceedings of the British Academy* **99**).

Lowe, J.J., Ammann, B., Birks, H.H., Bjork, S., Coope, G.R., Cwynar, L., de Beaulieu, J.-L., Mott, R.J., Peteet, D.M. and Walker, M.J.C. 1994. Climatic changes in areas adjacent to the North Atlantic during the last glacial-interglacial transition (14–9 ka BP): a contribution to IGCP-253. *Journal of Quaternary Science* **9**, 185–98.

Lowe, J.J., Coope, G.R., Harkness, D.D. and Walker, M.J.C. 1995. Direct comparison of UK temperatures and Greenland snow accumulation rates, 15000–12000 yr ago. *Journal of Quaternary Science* **10**, 175–80.

Mannio, M.A. and Thomas, K.D. 2000. Depletion of a resource? The impact of prehistoric human foraging on intertidal mollusc communities and its significance for human settlement, mobility and dispersal. *World Archaeology* **33**, 452–74.

Meehan, B. 1982. *Shell Bed to Shell Midden*. Canberra: Australian Institute for Aboriginal Studies.

Mellars, P. 1970. An antler harpoon-head of Obanian affinities from Whitburn, County Durham. *Archaeologia Aeliana* **48**, 337–46.

Mellars, P. 1976. Fire ecology, animal populations and man: a study of some ecological relationships in prehistory. *Proceedings of the Prehistoric Society* **42**, 15–46.

Mellars, P. 1978. Excavation and economic analysis of Mesolithic shell middens on the island of Oronsay (Inner Hebrides). *In* P. Mellars (ed.), *The Early Postglacial Settlement of Northern Europe*, 371–96. London: Duckworth.

Mellars, P. 1987. *Excavations on Oronsay: Prehistoric Human Ecology on a Small Island*. Edinburgh: Edinburgh University Press.

Mellars, P. and Dark, P. 1998. *Star Carr in Context: New Archaeological and Palaeoecological Investigations at the Early Mesolithic Site of Star Carr, North Yorkshire*. Cambridge: McDonald Institute Monograph.

Mellars, P. and Wilkinson, M.R. 1980. Fish otoliths as indicators of seasonality in prehistoric shell middens; the evidence from Oronsay, (Inner Hebrides). *Proceedings of the Prehistoric Society* **46**, 19–44.

Mercer, J. 1970. Flint tools from the present tidal zone, Lussa Bay, Isle of Jura, Argyll. *Proceedings of the Society of Antiquaries of Scotland* **102** (1969–70), 1–30.

Mercer, J. 1974. Glenbatrick Waterhole: a microlithic site on the Isle of Jura. *Proceedings of the Society of Antiquaries of Scotland* **105** (1972–74), 9–32.

Mercer, J. 1979. The Palaeolithic and Mesolithic occupation of the Isle of Jura, Argyll, Scotland. *Almogaren: Jahrbuch des Institutum Canarium und der Gisaf* **9–10** (1978–79), 347–67.

Mercer, J. 1980. Lussa Wood I: the Late-glacial and early Postglacial occupation of Jura. *Proceedings of the Society of Antiquaries of Scotland* **110** (1978–80), 1–32.

Mithen, S. (ed.). 2000a. *Hunter-Gatherer Landscape Archaeology: The Southern Hebrides Mesolithic Project 1988–98. Vols. 1–2*. Cambridge: McDonald Institute Monograph.

Mithen, S.J. 2000b. Mesolithic sedentism on Oronsay: chronological evidence from adjacent islands in the southern Hebrides. *Antiquity* **74**, 298–304.

Mithen, S.J. and Finlayson, B. 1991. Red deer hunters on Colonsay? The implications of Staosnaig for the interpretation of the Oronsay middens. *Proceedings of the Prehistoric Society* **57**, 1–8.

Mithen, S.J. and Lake, M. 1996. The Southern Hebrides Mesolithic Project: reconstructing Mesolithic settlement in western Scotland. *In* T. Pollard and A. Morrison (eds), *The Early Prehistory of Scotland*, 123–51. Edinburgh: Edinburgh University Press.

Morrison, A. and Bonsall, C. 1989. The early post-glacial settlement of Scotland: a review. *In* C. Bonsall (ed.), *The Mesolithic in Europe*, 134–42. Edinburgh: John Donald.

Parkington, J. 1999. Western Cape landscapes. *In* J. Coles, R. Bewley and P. Mellars (eds), *World Prehistory: Studies in Memory of Grahame Clark*, 25–36. Oxford: Oxford University Press (= *Proceedings of the British Academy* **99**).

Price, T.D. and Brown, J.A. (eds). 1985. *Prehistoric Hunter-Gatherers: the Emergence of Cultural Complexity*. New York: Academic Press.

Renouf, M.A.P. 1984. Northern coastal hunter-fishers: an archaeological model. *World Archaeology* **16**, 18–27.

Reynier, M.J. 1998. Early Mesolithic settlement in England and Wales: some preliminary observations. *In* N. Ashton, F. Healy and P. Pettitt (eds), *Stone Age Archaeology: Essays in Honour of John Wymer*, 174–84. Oxford: Oxbow Books (Oxbow Monograph **102**/Lithic Studies Society Occasional Paper **6**).

Richards, M.P. and Mellars, P.A. 1998. Stable isotopes and the seasonality of the Oronsay middens. *Antiquity* **72**, 178–84.

Rowley-Conwy, P. 1999. Economic prehistory in southern Scandinavia. *In* J. Coles, R. Bewley and P. Mellars (eds), *World Prehistory: Studies in Memory of Grahame Clark*, 126–60. Oxford: Oxford University Press (=*Proceedings of the British Academy* **99**).

Saville, A. and Miket, R. 1994. An Corran rock-shelter, Skye: a major new Mesolithic site. *Past* **18**, 9–10.

Simpson, B. 1996. Self and social identity: an analysis of Mesolithic body adornment from the Scottish Western Isles. *In* T. Pollard and A. Morrison (eds), *The Early Prehistory of Scotland*, 237–51. Edinburgh: Edinburgh University Press.

Sloan, D. 1984. Shell middens and chronology in Scotland. *Scottish Archaeological Review* **3**, 73–9.

Waselkov, G.A. 1987. Shellfish gathering and shell midden archaeology. *Advances in Archaeological Method and Theory* **10**, 93–210.

Wickham-Jones, C.R. 1994. *Scotland's First Settlers*. London: Batsford/Historic Scotland.

Woodman, P.C. 1985. *Excavations at Mount Sandel 1973–1977, County Londonderry*. Belfast: HMSO.

Yesner, D.R. 1980. Maritime hunter-gatherers: ecology and prehistory. *Current Anthropology* **21**, 727–50.

Zvelebil, M., Domańska, L. and Dennell, R. (eds) 1998. *Harvesting the Sea, Farming the Forest*. Sheffield: Sheffield Academic Press.

Chapter 10

The Material Culture of Mesolithic Scotland

ALAN SAVILLE

The fundamental elements of material culture – essentially stone, bone and antler tools – surviving from the Mesolithic period in Scotland are described and discussed in terms of significance and chronology.

Introduction

My object in this chapter is to give an overview of the type and nature of material culture *surviving* from the Mesolithic period in Scotland, before turning to some of the continuing problems of its interpretation in terms of chronology.

There has to be an emphasis on the word *surviving*, since the archaeological record for the Scottish Mesolithic period is an impoverished one. There are no wooden bows and arrows, no basketry holdalls or fishtraps, no birchbark containers, no bone fishhooks with attached twine, and so on, as survive from Mesolithic times in other parts of Europe. More surprisingly perhaps, in view of the number of coastal, riverine, and island sites, there are no logboats or skinboats; and, rather more depressingly, there are no art objects. All these things must once have been present, but what remains, as in most of the UK, is largely the real 'hardcore' of prehistory – the stone tools – plus some objects made of bone, antler, and shell. It is from this foundation that much of our understanding of the character and extent of human settlement in the Scottish Mesolithic must perforce be built, and it is incumbent upon prehistorians to make the most of the evidence available.

Stone tools

Mesolithic flaked stone tools are found throughout most of the more obviously habitable, lower-lying parts of Scotland, except, at least to date, in Shetland, the Western Isles, or St Kilda. The raw material exploited was predominantly flint where available, chert in those areas where it was a common resource, and a whole plethora of other silicious rocks in areas where neither

flint nor chert were so readily to hand (Finlayson 1990a; Saville 1994a). Given the relative scarcity of flint in Scotland, it is remarkable how few Mesolithic flaked stone assemblages from anywhere in the country seem without any flint at all (Note 1), and it is the resourcefulness with which flint and other appropriate rocks were sought out and exploited, which is one of the triumphs of human endeavour at this period (Saville 2003a).

One aspect of this exploitation, which contrasts with the subsequent Neolithic period, is that it was, irrespective of the raw material involved, on a local or at best regional scale, there being no obvious inter-regional dispersal of raw materials (Saville 2003b). Pitchstone, despite previous claims for quite far-flung Mesolithic occurrences (Williams Thorpe & Thorpe 1984), must be included here until it can be convincingly demonstrated that Mesolithic items made from pitchstone regularly occur in assemblages of this period well away from their origin in Arran and the immediate hinterland of dispersal in the SW.

Raw material diversity in the Scottish Mesolithic was made especially apparent by the study of the finds from excavations at Morton, Fife, where it was concluded that 'the variety of materials used ... seems among the greatest from anywhere in Britain' (Coles 1971, 298). Suffice it to say that quartz, quartzite, rock crystal, chalcedony, bloodstone, jasper, pitchstone, baked mudstone, agate, silicified limestone, and opal were among the rocks utilized by Mesolithic toolmakers in those parts of the country where they could be found locally.

As far as stone tool typology is concerned, pride of place must be given to that most distinctive yet recurrent of Mesolithic implements, the microlith (Figs 10.2; 10.16–20), in its many geometric and non-geometric manifestations, and its equally diagnostic co-respondent, the microburin (Lacaille 1935; 1942). Microliths, normally fashioned on a bladelet or segment thereof, are defined by their small size (in Scotland less, usually much less, than 50mm long and less, usually much less, than 5mm thick) and their tendency to distinctive shapes in plan (oblique points, triangles, crescents, rods, etc.), but also – and most crucially – by the definitive

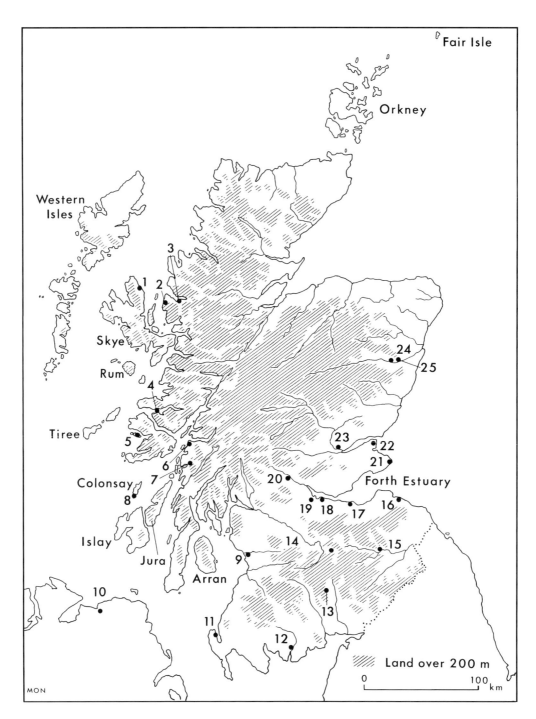

FIGURE 10.1

Map of Scotland showing some of the places and findspots featured in the text. (Drawn by Marion O'Neil)

Key: 1 An Corran, Staffin, Skye, Highland; 2 Sand, Lochalsh, Highland; 3 Shieldaig, Wester Ross, Highland; 4 Risga, Loch Sunart, Argyll & Bute; 5 Ulva Cave, Ulva, Argyll & Bute; 6 Oban (Carding Mill Bay; Druimvargie Rockshelter; Lón Mór; MacArthur Cave; Raschoille Cave), Argyll & Bute; 7 Kilmelfort Cave, Argyll & Bute; 8 Oronsay, Argyll & Bute; 9 Shewalton (River Irvine), North Ayrshire; 10 Mount Sandel, County Londonderry, Northern Ireland; 11 Wig Sands, Kirkcolm, Dumfries & Galloway; 12 Cumstoun (River Dee), Dumfries & Galloway; 13 Daer Reservoir, South Lanarkshire; 14 Cambwell, Scottish Borders; 15 Dryburgh Mains (River Tweed), Scottish Borders; 16 East Barns, Dunbar, East Lothian; 17 Cramond, Edinburgh; 18 Carriden, Falkirk; 19 Inveravon, Falkirk; 20 Meiklewood, Stirling; 21 Fife Ness, Fife; 22 Morton, Fife; 23 Friarton (River Tay), Perth, Perth & Kinross; 24 Banchory (River Dee), Aberdeenshire; 25 Nethermills (River Dee), Aberdeenshire.

blunting retouch on one or more edges, without which no microlith can be classified as such. The microburin is a waste product resulting from the most normal method of microlith manufacture, by which the bulbar, or less frequently the distal, end of the bladelet blank is detached by notching and snapping (Fig. 10.2, nos. 28–29).

There is room for disagreement about the precise method of hafting and function of microliths in general (Clarke 1976; Finlay 2000), and of the various shape-types in particular, since it is still the case that no hafted examples have been found in Britain or Ireland and since some microwear analyses of microliths are

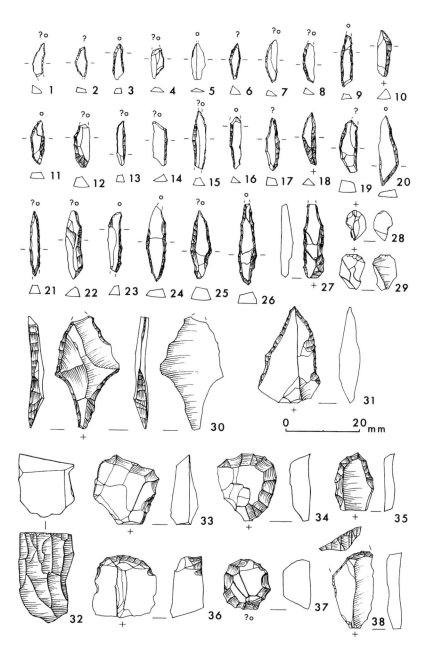

FIGURE 10.2

Artefacts from Shieldaig, Wester Ross. 1–26 microliths; 27 *mèche de foret*; 28–9 microburins; 30 tanged point; 31 piercer; 32 platform core; 33–8 scrapers (quartz: 1–3, 6, 12–15, 17, 19–20, 22, 25, 36–7; flint/chalcedony: 5, 7–11, 16, 18, 21, 23–4, 26–8, 30–1, 32, 34–5; bloodstone: 29, 33; flint/bloodstone: 4). (Drawn by Marion O'Neil)

entirely negative or suggest a variety of modes of utilization (Dumont 1988; Finlayson 1990b; Finlayson & Mithen 1997; 2000; Grace 1992). Nevertheless, what evidence there is for the use of microliths elsewhere in Mesolithic Europe – or indeed world-wide since they are a remarkably widespread tool-form – is that a major function was as the armatures of arrowheads. They were hafted with the blunted edge inserted into a lateral slot or slots in the shaft (though, with the use of resin or other adhesive, slots are not essential: David (1998)), leaving the naturally sharp edge protruding, as is made clear by finds of the actual arrowheads (Clark 1975; Nuzhnyj 1989). Use in this fashion seems confirmed by the wear and fracture patterns on some microliths (Fischer *et al.* 1984), by the injuries to game animals indicated by bone damage (Noe-Nygaard 1974), and by microliths in association with human remains (Nuzhnyj 1989) and animal carcasses (Fischer 1989, 36).

Scottish microliths have been studied in depth mainly on a site by site or island basis, rather than regionally or nationally, and there is often difficulty in making any wider cross-comparisons because of idiosyncratic classification and nomenclature (cf. Woodman 1989, 12–14). Recently some detailed attribute analyses have been applied to microlith assemblages excavated on Colonsay

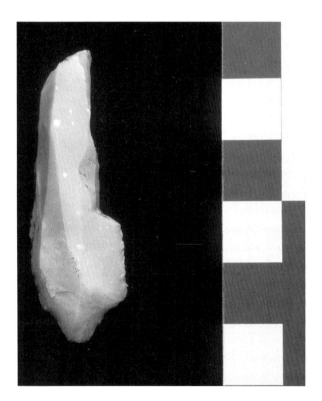

FIGURE 10.3
Flint burin, Banchory, Deeside. Scale in cms.
(Photo: Trustees of the National Museums of Scotland)

and Islay (Finlay *et al.* 2000; Finlayson *et al.* 2000), but even these have raised questions of terminology which might hinder further inter-assemblage comparisons (Saville 2002). One point which has emerged clearly from these detailed analyses, however, is the very small average size of microliths in these scalene triangle dominated assemblages. The means of the lengths of large samples of Later Mesolithic microliths from Gleann Mor and Bolsay Farm, Islay, and Staosnaig, Colonsay, are 12.8mm, 14.1mm, and 14.3mm respectively (Mithen 2000). Analysis of a sample of 141 complete microliths from Kinloch, Rùm, also dominated by scalene triangles, gives an entirely similar figure for mean length of 14.1mm, despite the differences in raw materials (unpublished analysis of sample in the NMS collections by A. Saville; cf. Wickham-Jones & McCartan 1990, ill. 61). Only slightly larger mean values were obtained from samples of Later Mesolithic microliths from the Pennines and North Yorkshire Moors (Eerkens 1997, table 2) and it will be interesting to see, when comparable Later Mesolithic assemblages are analysed from elsewhere in Scotland, if any significant metrical differences emerge.

It is, of course, microliths which provide the most obvious typological difference between Early and Later Mesolithic industries (see below and Saville this volume) and size is a significant attribute in this context, though difficult to demonstrate statistically because of the small total size of available assemblages. Just to hint at the contrast, however, the 14 complete microliths (9 isosceles triangles and 5 obliquely blunted points) from the SW corner of Site A at Morton, Fife (NMS collection), have a mean length of 22.1mm (Fig. 10.16). Any microlith found in Scotland which is longer than *c*.30mm (e.g. Fig. 10.18, no. 1) immediately raises the possibility of an Early Mesolithic presence, but such examples are often surface finds from potentially chronologically mixed scatters.

The most common of the more extensively modified, struck lithic tools is the scraper (Fig. 10.2, nos. 33–38). This tool-type continues on through the Neolithic and Bronze Age periods and only sometimes is it possible to distinguish Mesolithic scrapers typologically, usually by a combination of traits such as: small size; asymmetry or amorphousness of outline; extensive, non-invasive scraper retouch; and snapped or retouched bases. Much less frequent are forms such as piercers of various forms (Fig. 10.2), rarely sufficiently diagnostic to be categorized as Mesolithic as single finds or within an otherwise undated assemblage, the exception being the rare *mèche de foret*-type of bilaterally blunted awl (Fig. 10.2, no. 27), which is a Mesolithic type-fossil (Clark 1975, 108; Jacobi 1980, 154). Burins seem far less common in Scotland than some of the older literature would suggest,

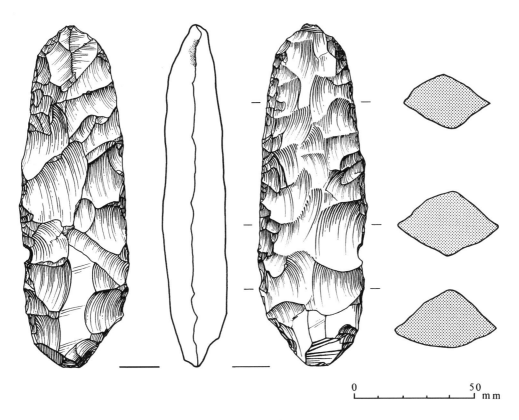

FIGURE 10.4
Flint core-tool, Wig Sands, Dumfries and Galloway. (Drawn by Marion O'Neil)

indeed it is a moot point how much of a real burin tradition existed in Mesolithic Scotland. Other than the exceptional burin spalls from Kilmelfort Cave (Coles 1983a; Saville & Ballin forthcoming), one of the rare entirely convincing burins is from Banchory on Deeside (Fig. 10.3; Paterson & Lacaille 1936, fig. 4.1). Various kinds of edge-trimmed flakes and blades, including serrated (or microdenticulate) types occur, as do truncated blades, of which those with obliquely blunted truncations are the most distinctively Mesolithic (Paterson & Lacaille 1936, fig. 2, 16–17).

Extremely rare, almost non-existent, are heavy-duty flaked core-tools of axehead, adze, or pick type. Only three possibilities are known from Scotland, all of flint and all isolated surface finds from widely separate localities: Fair Isle, between Orkney and Shetland (Cumming 1946; Saville 1994b; 2000); Morton, Fife (Coles 1971, 314; Saville 1994b; 2003c); and Wig Sands, Wigtownshire (Saville 2003b; 2003c). The Fair Isle find, which typologically seems undoubtedly Mesolithic, is very hard to explain as a genuinely local find and must remain problematic. The Morton artefact is a subsequent chance find from the vicinity of the well-known

excavated Mesolithic site, and though it could be Mesolithic, it is insufficiently distinctive typologically to regard it as definitely Mesolithic, rather than Neolithic, in type and date. The Wig Sands core-tool (Fig. 10.4), arguably much more likely to be a Mesolithic artefact, is probably best regarded as an import from Ireland.

The debitage or waste material from the knapping of flint and similar raw materials, at least when present at a location in any quantity (Fig. 10.5), can also be distinctively Mesolithic in character by virtue of the dominance within an assemblage of blades and bladelets produced from platform cores (Fig. 10.2, no. 32). Many of the cores themselves are often distinctively Mesolithic, particularly the pyramidal single-platform microblade cores or opposed-platform bladelet cores with parallel flake scars, though it is unwise to over-emphasize these distinctive types, much favoured by antiquarian collectors. The reality in most large assemblages is that less distinctive types of core predominate. There has been some past uncertainty over the degree to which bipolar, anvil-struck knapping was a regular part of Mesolithic technology. This reduction method is present in association with shell middens on Oronsay and in the caves and rockshelters at

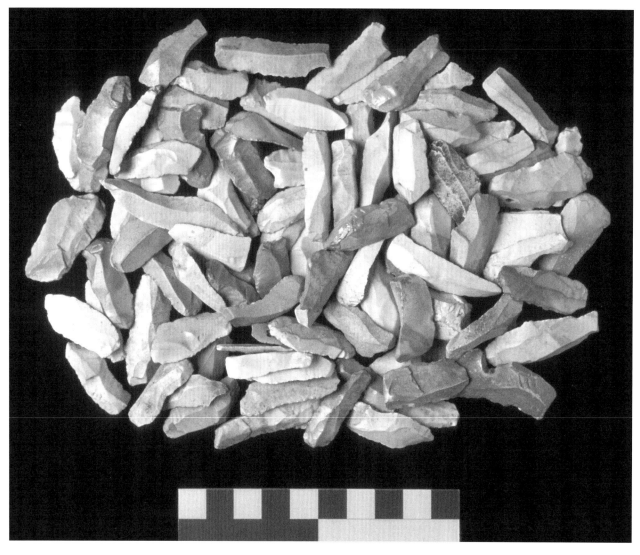

FIGURE 10.5
Unretouched flint blades and flakes, Lussa Bay, Jura. Scale in cms. (Photo: Trustees of the National Museums of Scotland)

Oban, and also in the Mesolithic assemblage at Kinloch, on Rùm (Zetterlund 1990), but how universal it may have been and its relationship to specific raw material types is difficult to determine. This is because, as it is important to remember whenever discussing such issues, there are very few stratified or otherwise closed assemblages of any size from Mesolithic Scotland. Most Mesolithic flaked stone tools derive from surface occurrences in locations where it is the norm to find some degree of undoubted or potential contamination by admixture from later prehistoric activity. However, it is interesting that re-examination of the Mesolithic assemblage from Kilellan, Islay, indicates that both platform and anvil reduction strategies coexisted in a situation where the raw material

used – beach pebble flint – is entirely uniform for both strategies (Saville in Ritchie forthcoming).

Apart from the flaked lithic tools, there are various types of artefact, generally grouped in Scottish archaeological studies under the rubric of 'coarse stone tools' (Clarke 1990), which exploit natural pebbles and cobbles for a variety of purposes, such as hammers, pounders, grinders, anvils, and weights. Mercer (1979, 353) regarded the double-notched quartzite hammer-anvil as a type fossil of his Late Mesolithic (phase 3) sites on Jura, and probably correctly connected them with bipolar-core technology. Unique so far is the small hollowed stone from Fife Ness, to which no specific function has been assigned (Wickham-Jones & Dalland 1998, illus. 9). Few

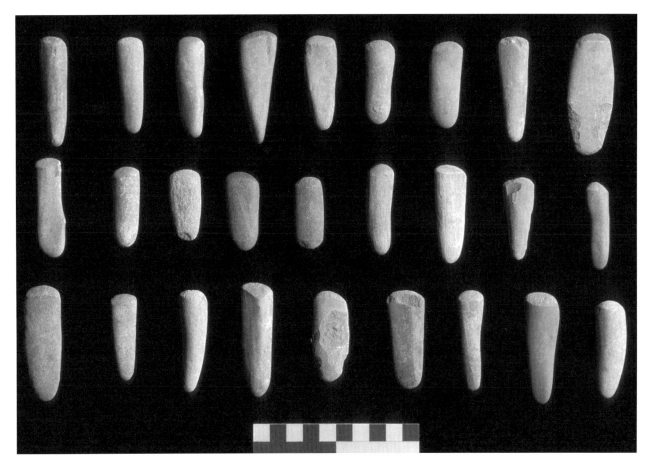

FIGURE 10.6

Bevel-ended stone tools, Cnoc Sligeach, Oronsay. Scale in cms. (Photo: Trustees of the National Museums of Scotland)

coarse stone tools are reliably diagnostic, however, since they are a continuing facet of tool-use in Scotland well into the first millennium AD (Saville 2003a), thus unless there is a close association with other, more culturally specific or dated material, it is often difficult to be sure if such implements are of Mesolithic age.

Until recently, the exception to this rule would have been the bevel-ended stone tools (Fig. 10.6), which are present in very large numbers at the Oronsay middens and to a lesser extent at the Oban caves and other sites (Anderson 1898, figs 24–8; Bishop 1914, fig. 36; Clarke 1990, illus. 81; Finlayson 1995, fig. 1; Mellars 1987, fig. 8.7). They are natural elongated pebbles of schistose (or similar) rock, collected from the beach, modified at one end or occasionally at both ends by abrasion, and sometimes perfunctorily shaped. This is the artefact known in the earlier literature as a limpet hammer (Grieve 1885, 57) or limpet scoop/gouge (Bishop 1914, 95), though Anderson (1898, 312) thought only the larger tools could have served as limpet hammers and that the

more common small variety was more likely to be for dressing and working skins (Anderson 1895, 222). Breuil (1922, 267–71) took the view that these implements were flaking tools for flint-working; Jacobi (1980, 189) associated them with the cleaning of seal-skins; and Finlayson (1995, 263) has supported the hide-working hypothesis. Despite the considerable interest shown in this tool category (Mellars 1987, 129; Reynolds 1983), their precise function has proved elusive. Recent experimental work has shown that such tools could indeed be used for flintknapping, hide-softening, hazelnut-cracking, and limpet harvesting, with the latter considered the activity producing abrasion, breakage, and fracture-patterns most similar to the archaeological specimens (Barlow & Mithen 2000). It is certainly the case that bevelled pebbles are most numerous at the 'Obanian' middens (there are hundreds of examples from the Oronsay sites), but they do occur in smaller numbers at non-midden sites somewhat away from the coast in Mesolithic times, such as Kinloch, Rùm (Clarke 1990, 122) and East Barns,

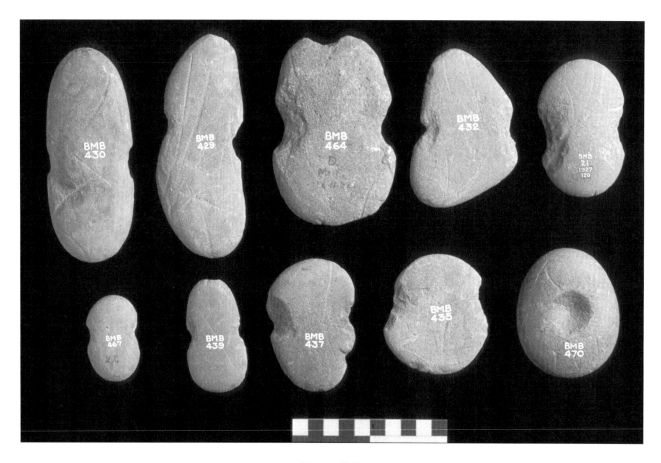

FIGURE 10.7

Waisted pebbles (and countersunk pebble, bottom right), Dryburgh Mains, Scottish Borders. Scale in cms.
(Photo: Trustees of the National Museums of Scotland)

Dunbar (J. Gooder pers. comm.). The size range is quite wide, and it is unclear whether this reflects deliberate choice or the dominant size of available pebbles, and in turn whether the variation in size has any meaning in terms of variation in function, need for hafting, and so on. The reason for expressing some doubt as to whether all bevel-ended stone tools are Mesolithic relates to their presumed equivalence to bevel-ended tools of bone and antler, which have been shown by direct radiocarbon dating to continue into Bronze Age times (see below).

Countersunk (Fig. 10.7) and hourglass-perforated quartzitic pebbles from various locations have often been considered as definitely or potentially Mesolithic (Candow 1989, fig. 16; Lacaille 1954, fig. 61; Mulholland 1970, 93), but these are not finds with any other close association to assist in dating. Elsewhere in Britain, though well-contexted cases are virtually non-existent, there is a presumption that some hourglass-perforated pebbles are Mesolithic (Mellars & Reinhardt 1976, 274–80; Jacobi in discussion, this volume). These

perforated implements do not usually exhibit any external wear, so the suggested functions as weights for digging-sticks, hand-drills, nets, and roof-ties seem more plausible than as percussion tools. Similar artefacts occur elsewhere in Europe in ostensibly early (Gramsch & Kloss 1989, fig. 6.2; Matiskainen 1989, fig. 12) and late Mesolithic contexts (Price 1987, 254), and may in some instances be decorated, encouraging a description in such cases as 'mace-heads' (Matiskainen 1989).

Also considered as weights are the so-called 'waisted pebbles' (Fig. 10.7). These are flat, ovoid, water-worn pebbles, usually modified (notched) by simple removals from opposite medial sections of the two longer sides to create bilateral indentations or a 'waist', presumably for the attachment of a string or rope (Note 2). These are known principally from surface finds along the north banks of the River Tweed, most particularly from the location of Dryburgh Mains, Berwickshire, and immediate surroundings, which have produced a whole series of these arte- facts of various sizes (Corrie 1914; 1916; Lacaille 1954,

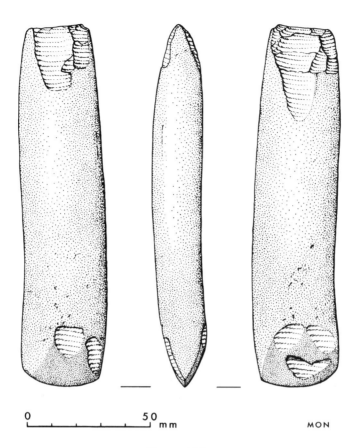

0   50 mm   MON

FIGURE 10.8
Sandstone pebble axehead, Cambwell, Scottish Borders.
(Drawn by Marion O'Neil)

166; Warren 2001, 154–61). The conventional interpretation, recognizing their river-side location (the Tweed is still an important salmon river), is as net-weights or line-sinkers, that is as fishing gear, though other uses, for example as weights for bird-nets (Mann, quoted in Warren 2001, 152), have also been mooted. The functional association with fishing seems reasonable, given the world-wide occurrence of very similar simple pebble-tools with this role (cf. Moore 2000, 174–6), but again there must be caution as to whether they are in this instance necessarily Mesolithic in date.

Naturally formed pumice fragments or pebbles, presumably collected as drift pumice from beaches (Binns 1972), were used as abraders, perhaps especially for shaping, smoothing, and resharpening bone needles and piercers (Bishop 1914, fig. 40; Clarke & Dugmore 1990).

Stone axeheads have yet to be recorded from any Scottish Mesolithic sites. Only one possible candidate has been suggested, a pebble axehead from Cambwell, near Biggar (Fig. 10.8; Saville 1994b). This is a completely unassociated find, suggested as Mesolithic purely on the basis of its typological contrast with Scottish Neolithic axeheads, particularly its parsimonious use of a suitably shaped pebble. Mesolithic stone axeheads are common in Ireland (Woodman 1978) and occur in coastal Wales (David 1989; 1991; David & Walker this volume), but not in England where flint axeheads and picks may be the equivalent. Given the absence of sufficiently large flints for axehead manufacture in Scotland, yet the availability of abundant supplies of suitable stone, it is hard to understand why stone axeheads were not part of the Mesolithic tool-kit here, since there must have been a requirement for implements to undertake heavy-duty tasks, unless antler tools were used instead (see below and Saville 2003c).

Bone and antler tools

The most common bone implement (also, but less commonly, made from antler) from Mesolithic Scotland is the bevel-ended tool (Fig. 10.9), known almost exclusively from coastal midden sites (Anderson 1895, figs

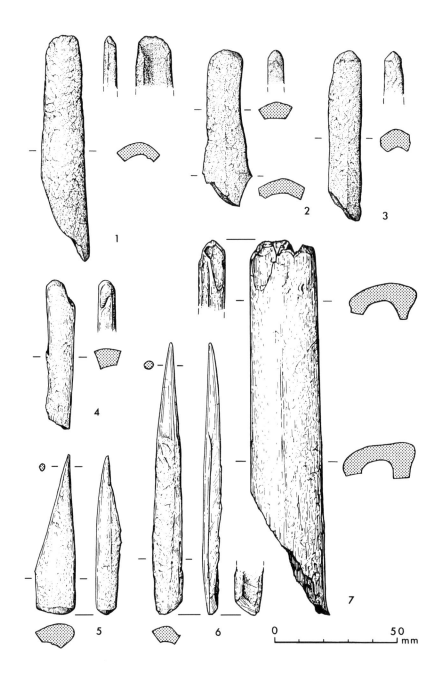

FIGURE 10.9

Bone tools from Morton site B, Fife (1–2); Druimvargie rockshelter, Oban, Argyll (3–4);
and An Corran, Skye, Highland (5–7). 1–4, & 7: bevel-ended tools; 5: combined point and
bevel-ended tool; 6: point. Some of these tools have been directly AMS dated: 1 – 5790±80
BP (OxA-4612); 2 – 5475±60 BP (OxA-4611); 3 – 8340±80 BP (OxA-4608); 4 – 7890±80
BP (OxA-4609); 7 – 7590±90 BP (OxA-4994). (Drawn by Marion O'Neil)

5–8; Anderson 1898, figs 10–15, 19–23; Bishop 1914, fig. 37; Coles 1971, fig. 15). This tool can so closely resemble its stone counterpart (above) that there must at least be a functional overlap if not a complete inter-changeability in the purpose these tools served, though the bone and antler varieties are equally stubborn about

revealing their precise function. Like the stone versions, they occur in large numbers, for example over 150 were recovered from MacArthur Cave.

The bone versions are most often fabricated on split fragments from deliberate shattering of longbones, principally the metapodials of red deer in those cases

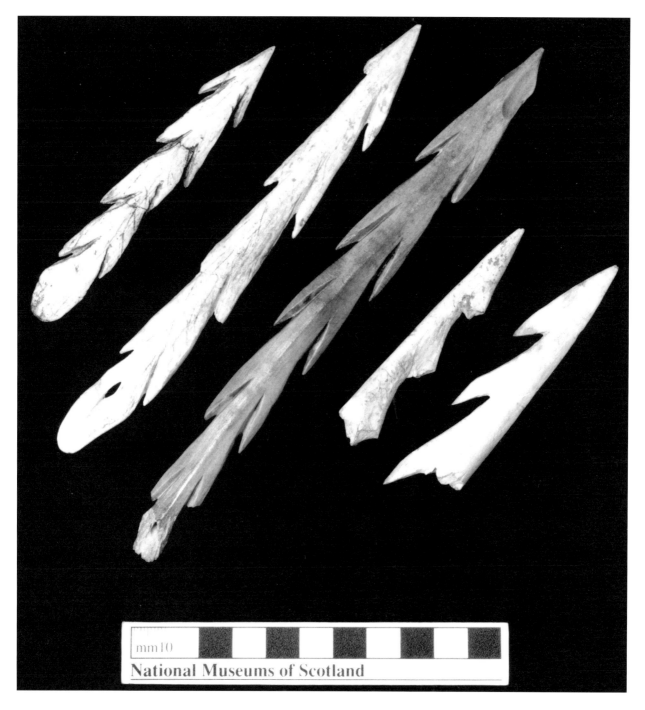

FIGURE 10.10

Barbed points from MacArthur Cave, Oban, Argyll (two on the left, both antler); Shewalton, North Ayrshire (centre, antler); Druimvargie rockshelter, Oban, Argyll (two on the right, both bone). Of these, only the Shewalton point (OxA-1947) and the Druimvargie point on the far right (OxA-1948) have been directly AMS dated (see Table 10.2). (Photo: Trustees of the National Museums of Scotland)

where it is possible to identify the species (Foxon 1991, 108; Y. Hallén pers. comm.). The antler versions are formed on split fragments of beam, presumably detached by groove-and-splinter technique (Griffitts & Bonsall

2001; Bonsall in discussion, this volume). Double-ended forms do occur, but much less frequently than the single-ended, which will normally have an unmodified butt formed by the original split end. Combinations of the bevel-ended tool and piercers sometimes occur (Fig. 10.9, no. 5). Both bone and antler versions of the bevelled tools are normally small, less than 70–80 mm in length, but a small number of larger bone examples are known from two of the Oban sites (Anderson 1895, figs 9–10; Anderson 1898, figs 7–8) and from An Corran, Skye (Fig. 10.9, no. 7), sometimes retaining an articular end of the bone as the butt.

Examination of these tools in large numbers shows that some bear clear signs of being the reused pieces of broken larger tools of completely different type, such as barbed points (Anderson 1895, fig. 13; at least three bevelled tools at MacArthur Cave are made on fragments of barbed points), piercers, mattocks, or other unidentified tools (Breuil 1922, fig. 5.2). This factor helps to reinforce the impression, gained from the frequency of their discard in apparently still usable form, that these implements are at the bottom end of the bone tool hierarchy.

They are easy to make, obviously highly serviceable, but of no particular value and thus highly expendable. It seems very likely that the small examples were hafted for use, even though such a haft has never been found; unlike the expendable bevelled tools, the hafts would have been reuseable and were presumably curated.

Despite the detailed studies by Reynolds (1983) and Foxon (1991), many aspects of the bevel-ended tools remain unresolved (cf. Finlayson 1998, 25). Even the fundamental issue of the bevelling itself is confused, with Reynolds (1983, 53) and Foxon (1991, 110) maintaining that the blanks are deliberately ground to produce the bevel before use, whereas other authorities see the bevelling as purely a product of use (Clark 1956, 92). Reynolds (1983, 58) retains the label 'limpet scoop', but suggests the function is rubbing, smoothing, and possibly scraping. Foxon (1991, 115) felt that most were used for hide-working and this interpretation is

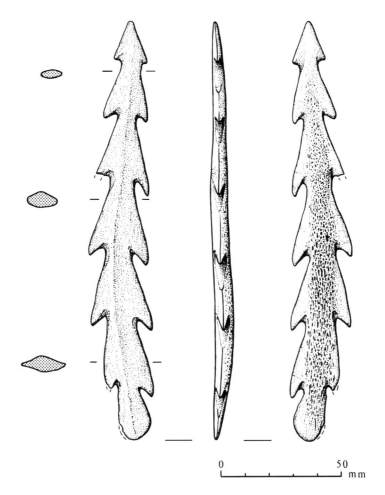

FIGURE 10.11
Barbed antler point from Carriden, Falkirk, directly AMS dated to 6030±55 BP
(OxA-7852). (Drawn by Marion O'Neil)

followed by Finlayson (1995), whereas Bonsall (1996, 194) reverts to the collection and processing of limpets as the explanation, with further support for this adduced from recent experimental and use-wear analysis (Griffitts & Bonsall 2001).

Some 26 bevelled tools have now been directly ^{14}C-dated, producing an astonishing age-range from c.8470 to 3010 BP (Table 10.2), which makes this an extraordinarily long-lived tool-type. It continued in use virtually unchanged for five millennia, and can no longer be regarded as a purely Mesolithic type-fossil (Saville 1998b).

Simple bone piercers (Anderson 1898, figs 2–3; Mellars 1987, fig. 8.4), of various shapes and sizes, although often similarly made on split longbone fragments, seem to have been less expendable than the bevelled tools, since they sometimes exhibit a high degree of use polish, which suggests curation (Fig. 10.9, no. 6). These tools could obviously have been used in fish- and shell-fish processing (Bonsall 1996, 194), though when discussing the Risga material Foxon (1991, 101) draws a distinction between points and points/pins, with the former being piercing tools and the latter suggested to be for fastening clothing or bags.

Boars' tusks were used for small, sharply chisel-edged tools, though only single examples have been found at MacArthur Cave and Druimvargie rockshelter, Oban. These have been described as scraping-tools (Clark 1956, 93) but were perhaps blades to be sleeved and hafted, in the manner of examples from Zealand (Clark 1975, plate II). As yet unexplained are the finely worked fragments of antler with 'chisel'-like terminations which occur in 'Obanian' assemblages (e.g. Breuil 1922, fig. 5:1–2, the latter reused as a bevelled tool after breakage) (Note 3).

General evidence for antler-working has been found at many of the midden sites (Clark 1956, figs 4–6; Grigson & Mellars 1987, figs 15.2 & 15.4), and Clark's study (1956, 93) showed how the technique involved 'nibbling', cutting, splitting, and perforating using flint tools. Antler and wooden wedges were probably also used for splitting antler, though none has been noted from the 'Obanian' sites. Clark (1956) thought there was no evidence for the use of groove-and-splinter technique in Scotland, but this is now disputed (Griffitts & Bonsall 2001; Bonsall in discussion, this volume).

Cetacean bone, which has especially attractive properties of size, density, and resilience, was undoubtedly exploited when available, though the block from Priory Midden, Oronsay, used as an anvil or for chopping, is one of the few specific Mesolithic instances recorded (Grigson & Mellars 1987, fig. 15.15). A fragment of whale rib with traces of human use was found in the carse clay at Causewayhead in the Forth Valley (Morris 1898,

60) and Piggott and Henderson (1958, 27) mentioned a whale-bone vertebra used as a chopping-block from the Carse of Stirling.

Much more elaborate as tools are the mattocks (Clark 1956, figs 1–3; Mellars 1987, fig. 8.8) and the barbed points (Anderson 1895, figs 11–12; Anderson 1898, figs 1–2 & 16–18; Bishop 1914, fig. 38), which have from an early stage been recognized as important and distinctive elements of the Scottish Mesolithic. Both categories have recently been the subject of renewed study, largely as part of the spin-off from direct AMS ^{14}C dating (Bonsall & Smith 1990; Smith & Bonsall 1991).

Barbed points

The barbed points (Figs 10.10–11) are of two basic varieties, the uniserial and the biserial (Bonsall & Smith 1990; Smith & Bonsall 1991). Most of the Scottish examples are biserial, the exceptions being the two broken bone points from Druimvargie rockshelter (Anderson 1898, figs 1–2) and a single bone example from 'Glenavon' (Morrison & Bonsall 1989, fig. 4). The latter has generally been regarded, since Lacaille's (1954, 184) original publication, as of 'Maglemosian' type, identified with Clark's (1936, 116) type 9, with large recurved barbs and therefore 'early' (Note 4). The Druimvargie examples are both much flatter with pronounced oblique cut-marks forming the sharp-angled barbs. It is interesting that the two Druimvargie points are very similar in dimensions and style, and that, placed flat surface downwards, one has the barbs on its right side, the other on the left (Fig. 10.10). Thus they complement each other and could conceivably, and perhaps probably, have been a leister pair (cf. Saville 2001, 78).

There are some differences in the detailed morphology of the biserial points (Lacaille 1939, 49; Saville 2001), many of which are made on antler rather than bone, but the range of variation in terms of blank, butt, and barb shape is relatively limited in Scotland (Morrison 1980, fig. 7.10), in contrast to the variety of types found on the European mainland (Kozlowski & Kozlowski 1977; Verhart 1990, fig. 1). Barbs are normally alternate or slightly staggered rather than arranged in exactly opposite positions (Jardine & Jardine 1978, 354).

Only two of the Scottish barbed points, one from MacArthur Cave, Oban (Anderson 1895, fig. 11), the other from Risga, Loch Sunart (Foxon 1991, fig. 5.4:29), have a basal perforation entitling them technically to be classified as harpoon heads, though Foxon (1991, 103) doubts the rather odd Risga implement could have functioned as a harpoon point. It is also true, however, that all the examples except two from MacArthur Cave and that from Carriden, Falkirk (Saville 2001), are broken at the base, making exact classification impossible. It is also true that the many fragmentary examples of barbed points from the 'Obanian' sites, including the three lost examples from Caisteal nan Gillean, Oronsay (Anderson 1898, figs 16–18; Lacaille 1954, fig. 86; Mellars 1987, fig. 8.3), lack their bases.

There are no further details, other than of its former existence, about the bone barbed point from the north end of Loch Asgog, Cowal (RCAHMS 1988, 3; G. Ritchie pers. comm.), but it should be noted that the findspots of all the other barbed points are from 'Obanian' middens or from riverine or estuarine contexts (Carriden, Forth estuary; Cumstoun, River Dee; Shewalton, River Irvine).

Foxon (1991, 102) has suggested biserial barbed points were the armatures for thrusting spears rather than javelins, but in reality the function of both uniserial and biserial types is, strictly speaking, unknown (Smith & Bonsall 1991, 209). The coastal or riverine provenance of most of them could be a bias of the occurrence of suitable contexts for preservation rather than indicating a function to do with fishing or other boat-borne or shore-side hunting. The only clear-cut functional association of barbed points from Britain, however, is with the terrestrial hunting of elk in the Lateglacial (Hallam *et al.* 1973).

The Shewalton, Ayrshire, antler point (Fig. 10.10), with five barbs per side, is the largest of the barbed points from Scotland. It is damaged at the base so the precise basal form is unknown, which is also the case with the shorter example (155mm), again with five pairs of barbs, from Cumstoun, Kirkcudbrightshire (Lacaille 1954, 157; Munro 1908). Next largest is the Carriden antler point, with six barbs per side and an intact, unperforated, spatulate base (Fig. 10.11). Both the MacArthur Cave barbed points have four barbs per side, the larger having a perforated spatulate base, the smaller an unperforated one (Fig. 10.10). All four have a plano-convex section, the flatter face corresponding to the interior of the antler. The barbs are sharp, angular, and steeply down-turned.

Apart from the fact that one has a basal perforation, the size and weight difference of these four examples is so marked that a different function may have been the case (Table 10.1).

The direct dating of one of the flat, uniserial, barbed points from Druimvargie Rockshelter to *c.*7810 BP, in contrast to the earliest and latest dates for biserial points of *c.*6700 BP at MacArthur Cave and *c.*5840 BP at Shewalton, raises the possibility of a typological shift from uniserial to biserial during the Mesolithic (Bonsall & Smith 1990, 364), but this may not be comparing like with like if the Druimvargie points are from a leister (see above). The assemblage from Risga includes one uniserial point as well as several biserial fragments, but none of these is yet directly dated and the uniserial point is atypical, not only in having a perforation but in being made on a jawbone (Foxon 1991, 103). One of the points from Cnoc Sligeach, Oronsay, is possibly made from a seal rib-bone (Jardine & Jardine 1978).

Antler mattocks

British red-deer antler mattocks have been studied by Smith (1989), who defined four types (A–D) according to the part of the antler used and the positioning of the perforation. The only Mesolithic type recognized in Scotland is type C, the T-shaped antler-beam mattock, made from a segment of beam around the stump of the removed trez-tine (Note 5). The perforation is through the trez-tine stump in the same plane as the blade, which has a cutting edge formed by an oblique truncation, presumably fashioned with a flint or similar tool.

The best known of the Scottish mattocks is that from Meiklewood, Stirlingshire (Fig. 10.12; Bonsall & Smith 1990, fig. 2), a fairly hefty example (weighing 508g), which gives a reminder of the sheer size of deer antler available for use during the Mesolithic. Other type C mattocks are the fragmentary examples from Risga

TABLE 10.1

Dimensions and weights of the four most complete barbed points from Scotland,

Location	Length in mm	Width in mm	Thickness in mm	Weight in grams	Reference
Shewalton	192	19	11	29	Lacaille 1939
Carriden	168	25	8	18	Saville 2001
MacArthur Cave	165	18	9	15	Anderson 1895
MacArthur Cave	107	16	5	6	Anderson 1895

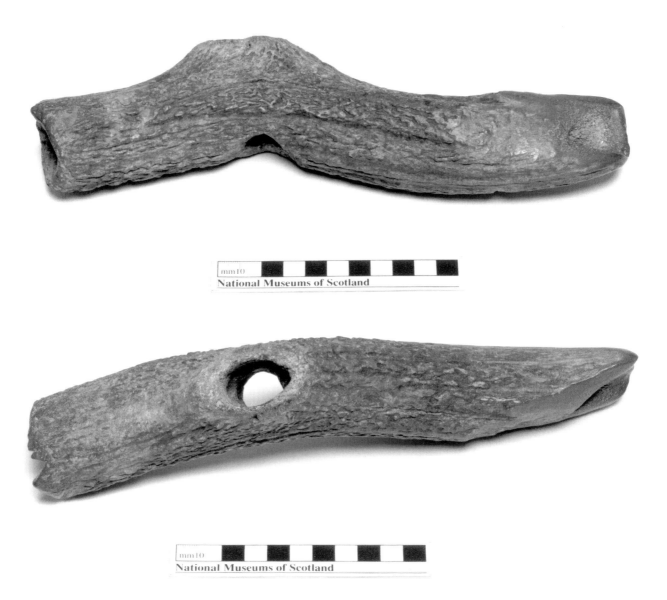

FIGURE 10.12
Antler beam mattock from Meiklewood, Stirling, directly AMS dated to 5920 ± 80 BP (OxA-1159).
(Photo: Trustees of the National Museums of Scotland)

(Clark 1956, fig. 1) and Priory Midden, Oronsay (Mellars 1987, fig. 8.8). The latter is of particular interest in that it originally had a cutting edge at both ends. Fragments of perforated antler tools, almost certainly parts of mattocks, occur at most of the 'Obanian' middens and suggest they were quite common tools.

When first discovered, both the Meiklewood mattock and another probable example from the carse clay, which is now lost, had the remains of wooden hafts in their perforations (Turner 1889). The use of wooden handles for such tools is confirmed by discoveries elsewhere where parts of the haft do survive, as with one of the elk antler mattocks at Star Carr (Clark 1954, 158), which retained a carbonized stub in the perforation. More revealingly, in Denmark complete handles survive with some antler mattocks, as at Dyrholmen (Childe 1950, fig. 17) and Ringkloster (Andersen 1974, fig. 59), in the latter case identified as unworked three-year-old hazel branches.

Opinion on the function of antler mattocks has oscillated between wood-working, digging, and flenching (Smith 1989, 282), or even hunting (Childe 1950, 33). The suggested use as flenching axes or blubber mattocks in dismembering whale carcasses derives inspiration and support from the discovery of one definite, another probable, and possibly one or two other examples from the carse clays of the Forth Valley, adjacent to the remains of stranded whales (Clark 1947, 91). It seems possible that mattocks could be used as flenching tools, though as Smith (1989, 282) suggested, the chance nature of such strandings is perhaps unlikely to have warranted such a specific tool type, and we cannot be sure that the coastal provenance of the extant examples is not simply an artefact of the available contexts for preservation. On the other hand, Woodman (1989, 19) proposed that the normal function for the mattocks was the butchery of seals, which were presumably regularly hunted, with occasional use on whales when opportunity arose.

Smith (1989) himself favoured an identification as digging tools (cf. Zvelebil 1994, 55), mainly because of preliminary observations of use-wear on a type A antler-base mattock from England, now known to be of Bronze Age date (Bonsall & Smith 1990, 361). The T-shaped mattocks would seem to be unnecessarily hefty and elaborate for general digging purposes, for which a

FIGURE 10.13
Patrick Cave-Browne chopping a birch log with a modern replica antler mattock. (Photo: Alan Saville)

simple digging stick would suffice, and ill-suited because of the angled blade. The blade edge is clearly crucial to the function; Childe (1942, 263) suggested some could be used as wedges in woodworking, the handle serving as a lever. Recent experiments (Jensen 1991; 1996; P. Cave-Browne pers. comm.) have shown that such an edge is extremely robust and can be used quite satisfactorily to chop wood (Fig. 10.13). Once blunt, the edge can easily be resharpened by grinding against an abrasive stone, such as sandstone. In view of the absence of any other obvious woodworking tools of stone or flint in the Scottish Mesolithic (see above), the possibility that antler mattocks were in fact the otherwise missing axeheads seems very attractive (Saville 2003c). It would perhaps not explain the occurrence of identical mattocks in large numbers at both coastal and inland Ertebølle sites in Denmark (e.g. 23 T-shaped mattocks at Ringkloster; Andersen 1974, 100) alongside numerous flint axeheads, which were themselves presumably woodworking tools, except that Mesolithic people in Denmark had equal access to flint and antler. In Scotland, where suitable flint was non-existent, but the red deer plentiful, antler was the obvious choice (Saville 2003c).

Both the Meiklewood mattock and a supposed mattock fragment from Risga have been directly dated, to c.5920 BP and c.6000 BP respectively (Table 10.2). Associated dates for the example from Priory Midden, and for fragments from other Oronsay middens and from Risga, are all in the range c.6200 to 5400 BP, but the dating could be extended much earlier if the supposed fragment from Druimvargie is accepted as from a mattock (Bonsall & Smith 1990, 365).

Implements and ornaments of other materials

The use of shell for artefacts in the Scottish Mesolithic was apparently restricted to the cowrie (*Trivia monacha*) and scallop (*Pecten maximus*) (Note 6). Cowrie shells were single- or double-perforated to form beads (Fig. 10.14), which were presumably used as ornaments, though whether in necklace or bracelet form, or on clothing, or in the hair, remains unknown (Simpson 1996). Perforated cowries have now been found on the mainland at Carding Mill Bay I, Oban (Connock *et al.* 1992, fig. 4) and Sand, Wester Ross (Hardy & Wickham-Jones 2003, fig. 49.11), complementing those previously known from the islands of Oronsay (Bishop 1914, fig. 42; Mellars 1987, fig. 8.9) and Ulva (Bonsall *et al.* 1992). Cowrie-shell beads are a widespread British type and not always coastal in occurrence, as the cache of eleven beads from Madawg rockshelter in the Wye Valley demonstrates (Barton 1994,

TABLE 10.2

Direct AMS radiocarbon determinations on bone and antler artefacts, listed chronologically by uncalibrated ^{14}C age BP

^{14}C BP	Lab. no.	Artefact type	Find location	Reference
8470±90	OxA-10152	bevelled tool, bone	Sand, Highland	Hardy 2001
8340±80	OxA-4608	bevelled tool, bone	Druimvargie rockshelter, Oban, Argyll	Ashmore 1997; Bonsall et al. 1995
7890±80	OxA-4609	bevelled tool, bone	Druimvargie rockshelter, Oban, Argyll	Ashmore 1997; Bonsall et al. 1995
7855±60	OxA-10384	bevelled tool, bone	Sand, Highland	Hardy 2001
7825±55	OxA-10175	bevelled tool, bone	Sand, Highland	Hardy 2001
7810±90	OxA-1948	uniserial barbed point, bone	Druimvargie rockshelter, Oban, Argyll	Ashmore 1997; Bonsall & Smith 1990
7715±55	OxA-9281	bevelled tool, bone	Sand, Highland	Cressey et al. 2000a
7590±90	OxA-4994	bevelled tool, bone	An Corran rockshelter, Skye, Highland	Saville 1998a
7545±50	OxA-9282	bevelled tool, bone	Sand, Highland	Cressey et al. 2000a
7480±75	OxA-8398	bevelled tool, bone	Raschoille Cave, Oban, Argyll	Bonsall 1999
7265±80	OxA-8535	bevelled tool, bone	Raschoille Cave, Oban, Argyll	Bonsall 1999
7245±55	OxA-9255	bevelled tool, bone	Loch A Squir, Raasay, Highland	Cressey et al. 2000b
6700±80	OxA-1949	biserial barbed point, antler	MacArthur Cave, Oban, Argyll	Ashmore 1997; Bonsall & Smith 1990
6665±70	OxA-3735	biserial barbed point, antler	Cumstoun, Dumfries & Galloway	Bonsall & Smith 1992
6605±50	OxA-10176	bevelled tool, bone	Sand, Highland	Hardy 2001
6485±55	OxA-10177	bevelled tool, bone	Sand, Highland	Hardy 2001
6215±60	AA-29316	bevelled tool, bone	An Corran rockshelter, Skye, Highland	Saville 1998a
6030±55	OxA-7852	biserial barbed point, antler	Carriden, Forth Valley, Falkirk	Saville 2001
6000±90	OxA-2023	?mattock, antler	Risga, Loch Sunart, Argyll	Ashmore 1997; Bonsall & Smith 1990
5920±80	OxA-1159	mattock, antler	Meiklewood, Forth Valley, Stirling	Bonsall & Smith 1990
5875±65	OxA-3737	bevelled tool, antler	Risga, Loch Sunart, Argyll	Ashmore 1997; Bonsall & Smith 1992

¹⁴C BP	Lab. no.	Artefact type	Find location	Reference
5840±80	OxA-1947	biserial barbed point, antler	Shewalton, North Ayrshire	Bonsall & Smith 1990
5790 ± 80	OxA-4612	bevelled tool, bone	Morton B, Tentsmuir, Fife	Bonsall *et al.* 1995
5750±70	OxA-3738	bevelled tool, antler	Ulva Cave, Ulva, Argyll	Ashmore 1997; Bonsall & Smith 1992
5475±60	OxA-4611	bevelled tool, bone	Morton B, Tentsmuir, Fife	Bonsall *et al.* 1995
5190±55	AA-29315	bevelled tool, bone	An Corran rockshelter, Skye, Highland	Saville 1998a
5190±85	OxA-3740	bevelled tool, antler	Carding Mill Bay I, Oban, Argyll	Ashmore 1997; Bonsall & Smith 1992
5180±70	OxA-4610	bevelled tool, bone	Morton B, Tentsmuir, Fife	Bonsall *et al.* 1995
4765±65	OxA-3739	bevelled tool, bone	Carding Mill Bay I, Oban, Argyll	Ashmore 1997; Bonsall & Smith 1992
4175±60	AA-29311	bevelled tool, bone	An Corran rockshelter, Skye, Highland	Saville 1998a
3975±50	AA-29314	bevelled tool, bone	An Corran rockshelter, Skye, Highland	Saville 1998a
3660±65	AA-29313	bevelled tool, bone	An Corran rockshelter, Skye, Highland	Saville 1998a
3010±50	OxA-7887	bevelled tool, bone	Balephuil Bay, Tiree, Argyll	Saville 1998b

fig. 7). Cowrie-shell beads are also very widespread in Mesolithic NW Europe (Newell *et al.* 1990), so their presence in Scotland is entirely unsurprising. By contrast, small stone beads, of the kind known at Star Carr, Yorkshire (Clark 1954, 165), and The Nab Head, Pembrokeshire (Jacobi 1980, 158; David & Walker this volume), have not yet been noted from any Mesolithic sites in Scotland.

Large, fan-like scallop shells (Bishop 1914: fig. 41; Hardy & Wickham-Jones 2003, fig. 49.11; Mellars 1987: fig. 8.10) were occasionally trimmed around the edges, edge-worn though use, perhaps as scoops or containers, or worked for other unknown purposes.

Otherwise, the Mesolithic material culture repertoire from Scotland, as it comes down to us through the archaeological record, is patently a pale shadow of its real extent. Outstandingly, we lack items of wood altogether, though any relevant ethnographic parallel, or any archaeological parallel from cultural contexts blessed with waterlogged preservation (Andersen 1987),

serve to emphasize the key role that woodworking is likely to have played (Coles 1983b, 11). This must also be true of the related area of bark-working, and similarly of basketry, netting, rope-making, hide- and skin-working; in fact whole categories of material culture activity involving organics susceptible to rapid decomposition are lost. There are clearly so many everyday activities and aspects of life for which we have no artefactual or precious little other surviving evidence – for example, fire-making, food-preparation, cooking and eating, clothing, burial, carrying, and transport – that study of the Mesolithic in Scotland can become in this respect frustrating.

The temptation to draw over-simplistic parallels and to make unwarranted extrapolations must be resisted, but it is equally useful to keep an open mind about those possibilities which other forager cultures provide (Orme 1979). To take a single ethnographic example, Grigson and Mellars (1987, 272) speculated that one very appropriate potential use for seal-skin during the Mesolithic on Oronsay would be for making boots in 'Eskimo' fashion, and one might also reflect on the 'Eskimo' use of seal-skin for boat-building (see below).

Missing elements in the material culture record must be kept firmly in mind, otherwise there is a danger of falling into the trap of thinking of the Mesolithic as culturally impoverished. It is fortunately increasingly unnecessary to have to refer to the ethnographic record for comparative data, since the spectacular organic finds of Mesolithic date being made in many parts of Europe help visualize the type of equipment which would have been available in Scotland, including ropes and textiles, wooden bows and leister prongs, basketry fish-traps, birch-bark containers, and even bone fishhooks with twine attached by a clove-hitch (Andersen 1985; Burov 1989; 1998; Gramsch 1992; Gramsch & Kloss 1989; Gron & Skaarup 1991; Mordant & Mordant 1992; Oshibkina 1989; Skaarup 1993; Zhilin & Matiskainen 2003).

Decorated bone and antler objects (Andersen 1980), figurines and pendants of amber, and other artwork are common in the Mesolithic, particularly the later Mesolithic, of Scandinavia (Larsson 1990, 286). In Britain Mesolithic art is rare (Jacobi 1980, 160), the best known instance being the pebbles with incised decoration from Rhuddlan, North Wales (Berridge & Roberts 1994; David & Walker this volume), and as yet there are no examples of artwork from Scotland.

Water transport

One of the most perplexing of all the missing elements of material culture, since it is inevitable from the distribution of Mesolithic sites and materials in the Inner Hebrides that sea travel was practised, is the absence of any evidence for boats. The distribution of Mesolithic sites inland suggests that river and loch navigation would also have been undertaken. Smith (1992, 139–43) has recently reviewed the evidence from the British Mesolithic, concluding that skinboats were much more likely to have been used in coastal waters and the open sea (cf. Clark 1952, 283) especially off the Scottish coast (Johnstone 1980, 27), while logboats could have served for loch and river transport. No instances of actual skinboats are known from this early in Europe, but the survival of evidence for such flimsy vessels, if coracle-type or similar construction is envisaged, would of course be exceptional. On the other hand, no logboats of Mesolithic date are known from Britain, where the only extant Mesolithic artefact possibly related to water transport is the birch-wood 'paddle' from Star Carr, Yorkshire (Clark 1954, fig. 77).

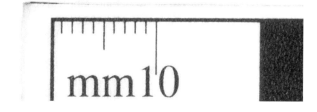

FIGURE 10.14
Perforated cowrie-shell beads, Oronsay.
(Photo: Trustees of the National Museums of Scotland)

In Denmark, however, there is now a substantial body of information on Mesolithic logboats, with ^{14}C dates going back to the end of the 7th millennium BP (Andersen 1986; Christensen 1990; Skaarup 1995). The Danish evidence clearly indicates that logboats were being used in coastal waters, and experimental work suggests that sea passage in logboats is feasible (Christensen 1990). Burial in or under logboats is also a significant feature of Mesolithic culture in Denmark (Grøn & Skaarup 1991; Skaarup 1995). Older still is the logboat from Noyen-sur-Seine, France, which has a ^{14}C date of c.7960 BP (Mordant & Mordant 1992, 61). This logboat, and another early example from Pesse, Holland, are made of pine, while all those identified from Denmark are from lime (Christensen 1990).

Numerous instances of the finding of logboats or possible logboats have been reported in Scotland. The (?)pine-wood 'logboat' found c.1879 in the River Tay alluvium at the Friarton Brickworks, Perth (Geikie 1880), has until recently been accepted as Mesolithic because of its apparent stratigraphic position below carse clay in the Firth of Tay (e.g. Coles 1971, 361; Jacobi 1982, 14; Mountain 1979, 69), which Mowat (1996, 35) has estimated would make it approximately of later Boreal age. However, not only are the stratigraphy and dating very open to question, it is not altogether certain that this object, now lost, was a logboat at all (Smith 1992, 142).

Tantalizing though all the old accounts of logboat finds are – especially the example of the Oban logboat with its sheets of birch bark and copious hazelnut shells (Mapleton 1879) – without proper records and ^{14}C dating their ages are impossible to guess (Note 7). This applies particularly to the many supposed dugouts found in the 18th and 19th centuries (Munro 1899, 66–72), but also to more recent finds. Thus the speculation that the Lochar Water, Dumfries, logboat found in 1973 might be Mesolithic was halted when the Early Bronze Age ^{14}C date of c.3754 BP was obtained (Jardine & Masters 1977; Jardine & Morrison 1976, 190). Similarly, ^{14}C dating of what was previously thought to be an early prehistoric dugout from Loch Doon showed it to belong to the mid-1st millennium AD (MacKie 1984). The recent reporting of a Mesolithic logboat from the Shannon estuary in Ireland, which was subsequently reassessed as a natural 'plank' of poplar wood, is a further salutatory case in point (O'Sullivan 2001, 71–2).

Mowat (1996) has now collated all the available information on logboats in Scotland and has shown how, with the possible exception of Friarton, much more recent contexts than the Mesolithic are likely to be the norm. Perhaps the most convincing argument against the possibility of logboats being manufactured in Scotland during the Mesolithic has been the absence of heavy-duty wood-working tools for their construction. Detailed examination of the Mesolithic logboats from Tybrind Vig and elsewhere in Denmark has shown that all identifiable instances are made from substantial lime-tree trunks, worked using the flint-bladed adzes commonly found on Ertebølle sites (Andersen 1986, 97; Christensen 1990). It is simply impracticable to believe that logboats could have been manufactured in Scotland during the Mesolithic without comparable tools, despite suggestions deriving from Geikie's (1880, 2) comments on the Friarton find that some logboats may have been worked by charring and scraping rather than chopping (Andersen & Hay in discussion, this volume; Jacobi 1982, 14; Morrison 1980, 168). Indeed, the Danish evidence indicates that fire was never used in the manufacture of dugouts, only axeheads/adzes and probably wooden wedges and mallets, with charring where it occurs relating to secondary use or abandonment (Christensen 1990; Grøn & Skaarup 1991,

50). On the other hand, preliminary reports of the logboat from Noyen-sur-Seine suggest that this pine trunk had been hollowed out using fire (Mordant & Mordant 1992, 61), and anyway, as we have seen, in Scotland there were heavy-duty antler tools potentially capable of use for working wood.

Material culture and chronology

In terms of chronology, the very big advantage of organic artefacts is that they can be directly ^{14}C dated, and their disadvantage is that over most of Scotland such artefacts have a low survival rate and when they do survive they are often completely isolated finds. While these direct dates do, in a very tangible way, demonstrate Mesolithic presence in Scotland from c.8470 to c.5840 BP (Table 10.2), they have little capacity for correlation with the lithic artefact evidence outwith the 'Obanian' context and are from too small a sample to contribute towards phasing within this period. They also, as in the case of the bevel-ended tools, have the potential to be misleading chronologically if one prejudges the 'Mesolithic-ness' of the implement type being dated. While there are 15 bevelled tools dated between c.8470 and c.5875 BP (i.e. prior to the latest date for a truly Mesolithic type-fossil, the Shewalton barbed point, at c.5840 BP), there are a further 11 which postdate this. There is debate as to when the conventional end of the Mesolithic/beginning of the Neolithic should be placed in northern Britain, with suggestions ranging from c.5500 to c.5000 BP. Even if the latest end of this range is taken, however, only six of the later 11 bevelled tools are from the 6th millennium BP, leaving two from the 5th millennium and three from the 4th millennium. The An Corran dates seem unequivocally to indicate the continuation of this type well into the Bronze Age (the Late Bronze Age example from Balephuil Bay, Tiree, could be argued to be slightly outwith the typological norm: Fig. 10.15). Apart from the fact that this means the bevelled tools can no longer be seen as Mesolithic indicators, it also removes the possibility of extrapolating from their dates any indication of the actual duration of the Mesolithic in Scotland (Note 8).

By contrast, the ubiquitous stone tools cannot be directly dated, but comparative typological analysis should enable the injection of some chronological structure into the picture of the Scottish Mesolithic. In this regard it is the microliths – and we can be certain that the microlith is an implement type which has no post-Mesolithic currency – which are potentially the most useful, since the long history of research on these in the UK should permit some chronological and perhaps regional subdivision to take place. At the very least, it should be possible to have some insight into the comparative presence and distribution of so-called 'Earlier'/'Early' and 'Later' Mesolithic activity (Jacobi 1973; Mellars 1974), with regard to the 'broad' and 'narrow' blade subdivision and associated contrasts in size and shape of microliths, and the blanks on which they are made, as established in England (Pitts & Jacobi 1979). As outlined previously (Saville this volume), these subdivisions equate at base to the former Maglemosian and Sauveterrian designations on the basis of Continental comparanda. The conventional boundary between Early and Later Mesolithic lies at c.8700/8650 BP, though recent research is beginning to show a rather more complex picture (cf. Barton & Roberts this volume; David & Walker this volume), and Reynier (2002) has suggested the Early/Later nomenclature may now have outlived its usefulness.

Until very recently the situation in Scotland could be summarized as indicating an early (but not unacceptably early on the English model) introduction/adoption of Later Mesolithic microlith forms from c.8500 BP, as at Kinloch, Rùm (Wickham-Jones 1990), and Fife Ness (Wickham-Jones & Dalland 1998). Other Later Mesolithic types of microliths and their associated assemblages found anywhere in Scotland were either seen to postdate c.8500 BP on the basis of associated ^{14}C dates, or assumed to do so by analogy. In fact, the majority of reliable dates for these Later Mesolithic lithic assemblages fall within the bracket c.8000–6000 BP (Ashmore this volume) and, as Mithen (2000, 601) has discussed, there are currently no strong grounds for typological subdivision of this apparently homogeneous Later Mesolithic cultural phase. Woodman's (1989) suggestion of an early, pre-8000 BP phase of the Later Mesolithic, characterized by dominant scalene triangle microliths, followed after c.8000 BP by assemblages with increased proportions of crescent and double-backed needle microliths, has been undermined by the evidence for the early crescent-dominated collection from Fife Ness (Wickham-Jones & Dalland 1998), confirming the sense of Later Mesolithic homogeneity from the beginning. As in some other parts of the UK, it is difficult to find microlithic assemblages attributable to the 6th millennium BP, leaving in lithic terms only the non-microlithic anvil-struck flake industries of the classic 'Obanian' sites (Lacaille 1954, 199–245). There is no indication thus far of any specifically 'Late' or 'Terminal' Mesolithic element, in the form of rod-dominated microlithic assemblages – which would be datable by analogy to the later 6th millennium BP (Spikins 2002, 29) – among the Scottish finds.

Equally the recent consensus was that, though undated by ^{14}C, there were indicators of Early Mesolithic presence

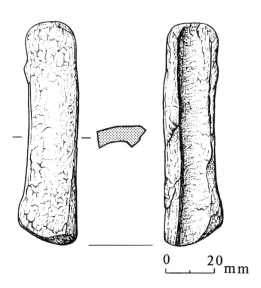

FIGURE 10.15
Bevel-ended bone tool, Balephuil Bay, Tiree, directly AMS dated to 3010±50 BP (OxA-7887). (Drawn by Marion O'Neil)

in Scotland, most clearly reflected by the 'broad blade' microliths in assemblages at Morton site A, Fife (Coles 1971), and Lussa Bay and Glenbatrick Waterhole site G1, Jura (Mercer 1970; 1974). Some of the debate these assemblages have engendered (cf. Woodman 1989; Saville this volume) seems with hindsight unnecessary, specially in the case of Morton A, where the microlith assemblage can now be seen to be entirely Early Mesolithic in character and to come from spatially specific locations (Note 9). The combination of relatively large isosceles triangles and obliquely blunted points (Fig. 10.16), all made from flint, concentrated in the SW corner of Site A at Morton, is of classic Star Carr-type, and is therefore best dated by analogy with the most specific dates from Star Carr and elsewhere to c.9350–9200 BP (Roberts et al. 1998), or perhaps more broadly to somewhere in the range c.9700–9000 BP (Dark 2000; Reynier 1997; 2000).

The microliths at Lussa Bay (Fig. 10.17) and Glenbatrick Waterhole G1 also fit this picture, though at the former in particular there appears to be contamination by Later Mesolithic material, as indeed is the case with those surface finds, which include arguably Early Mesolithic types, from Shewalton Moor, Ayrshire (Lacaille 1930; 1954, 286), with which Mercer (1970, 21) correctly made comparison. The microlithic element of the assemblage from An Corran, Skye, with its obliquely blunted points and large triangles (Fig. 10.18), also appears distinctly Early Mesolithic. The earliest date for this site of c.7590 BP from a bevelled bone tool (Table 10.2) suggests a possible separation between an Early Mesolithic lithic

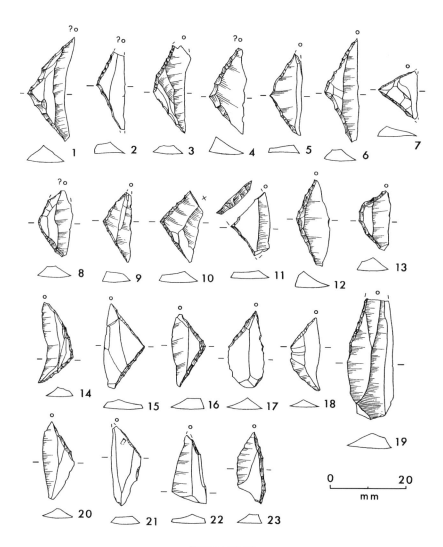

FIGURE 10.16

Flint microliths from Morton site A, Fife. 1–16 broad triangles; 17–22 obliquely blunted points; 23 edge blunted point (trench 44: 9, 10, 12, 18, 20–22; trench 47: 3, 5, 6–8, 11, 17; trench 53: 2, 14, 16, 23; trench 55/56: 1, 4, 15, 19; test-pits, trenches 48/49/52: 13). (Drawn by Marion O'Neil)

assemblage and a Later Mesolithic midden and bone and antler assemblage, with the earlier phase and its microliths undated except by *terminus ante quem*. From elsewhere in Scotland there are individual microliths, either found completely separately or in mixed surface or excavated assemblages, which would, on the basis of their size and/or shape, also fit more appropriately in an Early rather than Later context (e.g. Mulholland 1970, fig. 12), though it would in these cases be unwise to place too much weight on subjective typological chrono-indicators.

Otherwise there has been no recognized indication that other strands of the Early Mesolithic or transitional Early/Later Mesolithic found in England – the Deepcar-type, Horsham-type, and Honey Hill-type assemblages (Reynier 1997; 1998; 2000) – were present in Scotland.

A possible hint of conflict with the picture painted by the above summary came with the single (and perhaps misleading – there is a later date from the same site), ^{14}C date of *c*.9075 BP from Daer Reservoir site 1, South Lanarkshire (Ward 1998), in apparent association with a typologically Later Mesolithic assemblage (Fig. 10.19) at what is an inland upland site at *c*.340m above current sea-level in the Lowther Hills. This possible conflict has now become a reality with the series of six ^{14}C dates obtained on carbonized hazelnut shells from Cramond, Edinburgh. These dates, between *c*.9250 and *c*.9105 BP (Lawson 2001; Ashmore this volume), are the earliest so far available for Mesolithic activity in Scotland, and are associated with what would also, conventionally, be regarded as a Later Mesolithic microlithic assemblage

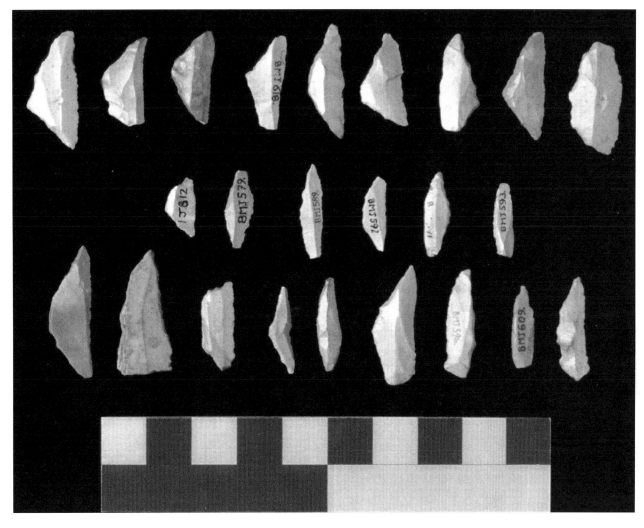

Figure 10.17

Flint microliths from Lussa Bay, Jura. Scale in cms. (Photo: Trustees of the National Museums of Scotland)

with crescents and scalene triangles (Fig. 10.20). It would be wrong to attempt to draw too many conclusions about either the Cramond or Daer Reservoir assemblages in advance of their full publication, but the implication is that a fully 'Later Mesolithic' microlithic repertoire with crescents and scalene triangles was established in southern Scotland before, perhaps well before, c.9000 BP. If it is assumed that typologically Early Mesolithic microlith assemblages must be earlier than typologically Later Mesolithic ones, then the indications from Morton and some of the Jura sites must, as already mentioned, indicate Early Mesolithic habitation in Scotland at some point rather earlier in the 10th millennium BP, on both the east and west coasts.

That, strictly speaking, is as far as the evidence for chronology and chrono-typological subdivision currently

allows for Scotland. The Scottish position does, of course, have interesting implications for the rest of the UK, since at the moment the Later Mesolithic appears earlier here than in England. This may be seen as further support for Reynier's (2002) proposition of a time-transgressive initial Later Mesolithic occurring first in the north, or it might be simply a matter of current chance availability of dates, and that earlier Later Mesolithic dates will emerge from England and Wales in due course.

Scotland before the Early Mesolithic?

The question inevitably arises as to whether there is any surviving material culture of pre-Neolithic type which might point to occupation of Scotland even earlier than the Early Mesolithic, in particular in the Lateglacial or in very earliest Postglacial times?

Various claims for Upper Palaeolithic human presence made on the basis of excavations which took place at Bone Cave and Reindeer Cave, Inchnadamph, Sutherland, in 1889 and 1926–27 respectively, can be discounted following re-evaluation of the accumulated reindeer antlers as natural (Murray *et al.* 1993), the human skeletal remains as Neolithic (Bonsall & Kitchener 1998), and the surviving bone and ivory artefacts as Early Historic (Saville 1993 & in preparation).

No stone tools were ever found at Inchnadamph, but what lithic or other artefactual evidence might be expected to result from any pre-Early Mesolithic inhabitation? In England, the immediate predecessors in the terminal Pleistocene/earliest Holocene are the long-blade technology (LBT) industries with their *lames mâchurées* (bruised blades), dated very approximately to the period *c.*10,300–9700 BP (Barton 1989; 1997; 1998; 1999; and this volume; Dumont 1997). These in turn have wider, North European Plain connections with the Ahrensburgian techno-complex (Ballin & Saville 2003). Chronologically linked bone and antler artefacts would be the so-called 'Lyngby axes' or reindeer antler clubs (Cook & Jacobi 1994) and various types of uniserial barbed antler and bone points (Smith & Bonsall 1991).

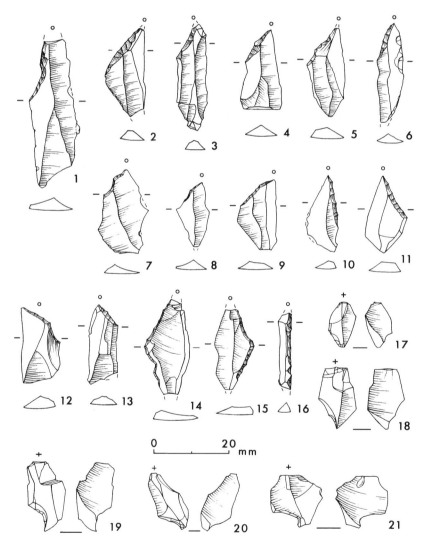

FIGURE 10.18

Microliths and microburins from An Corran, Staffin, Skye. 1–13 obliquely blunted points; 14–15 broad triangles; 16 ?rod; 17–21 microburins (baked mudstone: 1–2, 6, 12, 14, 16, 18, 20; chalcedonic silica: 3–5, 7–11, 13, 15, 17, 19, 21). (Drawn by Marion O'Neil)

FIGURE 10.19
Flint/chalcedony microliths from Daer Reservoir site 1, South Lanarkshire. Scale in cms.
(Photo: Trustees of the National Museums of Scotland)

There are no 'Lyngby axes' from Scotland, and the only example of an 'early' ('Maglemose') form of uniserial barbed point is the 'Glenavon' one (see above), which, apart from its uncertain provenance (Note 4), cannot be directly dated because of conservation contaminants (Morrison & Bonsall 1989).

LBT-type industries have always been thought unlikely in Scotland, if for no other reason than the absence of suitably sized flint for the cores from which long blades could be struck. Discoveries at An Corran, Skye, have somewhat undermined this reasoning, since one of the raw materials exploited at that site, baked mudstone, was clearly capable of producing substantial blades up to at least 90mm in length (Fig. 10.21) and potentially much longer. There is no suggestion, however, that the An Corran blades (which together with most of the microlith forms at that site (Fig. 10.18) suggest activity by Early Mesolithic people with a Star Carr-type lithic industry) represent a LBT presence in date or typology, and indeed the only possible indicators

of human activity in Scotland in the period following the Loch Lomond Stadial cold phase and before the Early Mesolithic (i.e. c.10,200–9,800 BP) would be the few finds of Ahrensburgian-type flint points. These finds have recently been reviewed, with the conclusion that only two, those from Shieldaig, Wester Ross (Fig. 10.2, no. 30), and from Balevullin, Tiree, are acceptable candidates (Ballin & Saville 2003; Morrison & Bonsall 1989). Isolated finds of this kind are probably too flimsy a basis on which to satisfactorily populate Scotland at this period, but a human presence can at least be seen as feasible (Ballin & Saville 2003), and such finds do reinforce the need to keep an open mind about pre-Early Mesolithic occupation.

Perhaps an equally open mind should be kept about the possibility of Late and Final Upper Palaeolithic human presence in Scotland prior to the height of the Loch Lomond Stadial, especially given the favourable climate and habitats of Windermere Interstadial times. In terms of material culture this would require the finding of

209

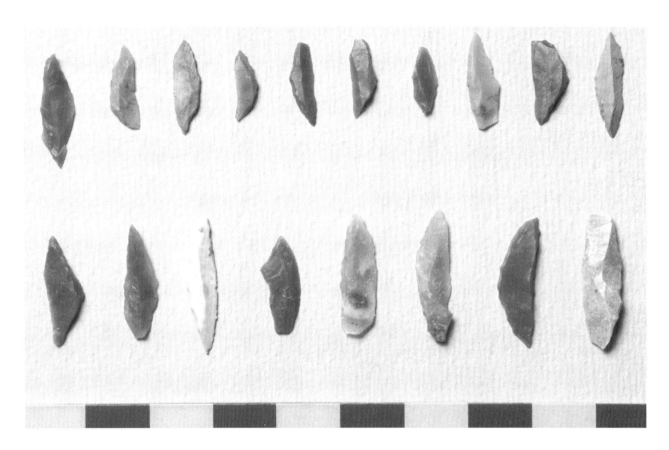

FIGURE 10.20
Chert and flint/chalcedony microliths from Cramond, Edinburgh. Scale in cms.
(Photo: Trustees of the National Museums of Scotland)

stone tools of Creswellian and related technocomplexes from the 13th millennium BP (Barton 1999; Jacobi 1991; 1997) and of Federmesser and related traditions from the 12th millennium into the 11th millennium BP (Barton 1997; 1999). The most northerly findspots for any accepted Lateglacial artefacts in Britain are from caves in the Morecombe Bay area of south Cumbria (Campbell 1977; Salisbury 1988; 1992) and there have hitherto been no significant claims for any Scottish evidence, though there have been optimistic predictions (Jacobi 1991, 129).

While there are no known diagnostic parallels from Scotland for the distinctive sharply angle-backed blades of the Creswellian (Barton *et al.* 2003), there are distinct hints of curved- and angle-backed points of Federmesser-related type in the intriguing, rather odd assemblage from Kilmelfort Cave, Argyll (Fig. 10.22; Coles 1983a; Saville 2003b). With its mixture of large (in Scottish terms) microlithic and non-microlithic backed-blade forms, but no independent dating, the position of this assemblage remains problematic, though there are grounds for

suggesting better parallels (in terms of the form, size, thickness, and number of bulbar backed pieces; the absence of microburins; and the presence of burins) with Final Upper Palaeolithic rather than Early Mesolithic industries (Saville & Ballin forthcoming) (Note 10). This would by analogy situate the Kilmelfort Cave assemblage somewhere within the time bracket *c.*11,750–10,700 BP (Barton 1999), prior to the more extreme downturn of temperature at the height of the Loch Lomond Stadial.

There are also occasional isolated finds of very distinctive individual implements, such as the surface find of a flint angle-backed point (length 52mm) from Fairnington, near Kelso in the Tweed Valley (Fig. 10.23; NMS collection X.ABA164), which offer the hope of eventually finding Lateglacial open-air sites in Scotland.

Conclusion

As this chapter has shown, the range of surviving material culture is limited, and in the case of bone and

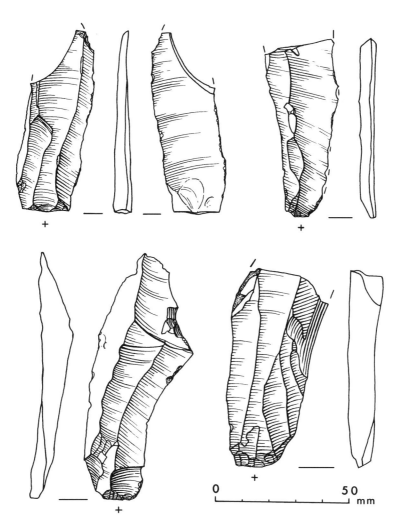

FIGURE 10.21
Unretouched or slightly edge-trimmed blades of baked mudstone from An
Corran, Staffin, Skye. (Drawn by Marion O'Neil)

antler tools, of very restricted distribution, related to the limited availability in Scotland of conditions conducive to their preservation. Nevertheless, the increasingly widely recognized distribution and density of Mesolithic stone tools throughout most parts of Scotland is pointing to a more determined and sustained settlement during this period than previously envisaged. Thus the massive increase in various kinds of Mesolithic sites known in two small areas of western Scotland as a result of the Southern Hebrides and Inner Sound Projects (Saville this volume), must indicate significant levels of population, at least during the Later Mesolithic.

Tolan-Smith (2003) recently proposed that Early Mesolithic colonization of Scotland may in fact have been delayed because a phase of 'landscape learning' was necessary for foragers to accommodate to the terrain and habitats of northern Britain. The combination of new ^{14}C dates and renewed typological inquisition of the available material culture has, however, substantiated a scenario of Mesolithic activity in the 10th millennium BP, if not earlier activity in the Lateglacial. It seems more priority should rather be given to the ecological and sociobiological arguments – given the inextricable link in terms of habitat, food, and materials dependency between humans and their prey and other resources – in favour of rapid colonization of any readily accessible areas where the preconditions for settlement existed. The explanation for why settlement of the Western Isles and Shetland may not have happened during the Mesolithic could lie in the more restricted food and material resources those habitats offered, together with the difficult open sea crossings needed to access them. There is no reason

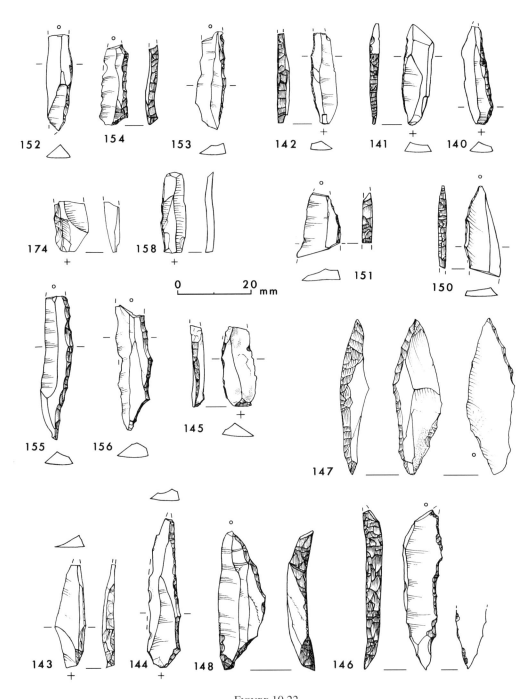

FIGURE 10.22

Flint microliths and backed bladelets from Kilmelfort Cave, Argyll. (Drawn by Marion O'Neil)

to suppose Mesolithic people had eremitic or similar tendencies to propel them beyond locations where their resource requirements could not easily be fulfilled and, unlike their Neolithic successors, they had no tradition of taking their resources with them.

To conclude, Scotland does have a Mesolithic material culture which, though impoverished in terms of what survives, is distinctive in several respects, such as its use of a very wide range of lithic raw materials and its relatively prolific, in UK terms, bone and antler tools. There is now a reasonably large dataset of material culture from many parts of Scotland, but there is still uncertainty as to how to subdivide or phase this chronologically, and this is one of the last regions in Europe where this is the case.

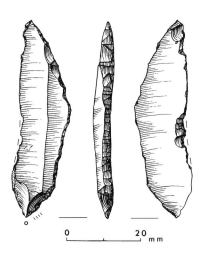

FIGURE 10.23
Large microlith or backed point from Fairnington, near Kelso, Scottish Borders. (Drawn by Marion O'Neil)

The 'Holy Grail' of Mesolithic research in Scotland is to find sites with the stratification and organic preservation to resolve this question and finally link the archaeology and economy, but progress in our understanding of the period will nevertheless continue to be made by the detailed analysis of both new and existing collections of material culture, even where only stone tools are involved. In this regard, it can be predicted that a more targeted investigation of the nature and source of the lithic raw materials exploited will contribute significantly towards unravelling the story of Mesolithic Scotland.

Acknowledgements

I am grateful to Dr Andrew Foxon and Dr Graeme Warren for providing copies of their unpublished theses and allowing me to refer to them. For assistance with illustrations I am grateful to Marion O'Neil, Duncan Anderson, Patrick Cave-Browne, Tam Ward, John Lawson, and Roger Miket.

Notes

1. There has to be some caution here, since it is not always easy to discriminate in hand specimen between flint and volcanic silicas, such as chalcedony, especially when dealing only with small size artefacts (e.g. microliths) and there is therefore always some potential for misidentification.

2. The author noted similar waisted stones (using angular slabs rather than rounded cobbles, but modified in exactly the same way) in use as weights tied to the bases of lobster pots at Seahouses harbour, Northumberland, in 2003.

3. The antler spatula from the Distillery Cave, Oban (Lacaille 1954, fig. 83), is another instance of a tool previously accepted as 'Obanian' because of the location of its findspot, whereas radiocarbon dating has shown it to be, as its typology would otherwise suggest, an example of a Beaker/Early Bronze Age implement (Sheridan 1995).

4. A record in the National Museums of Scotland indicates that this barbed point arrived at the Hunterian Museum labelled only as 'from a peat-moss at Glenavon', and that it was registered as from the Glenavon (or Glenaven) in Banffshire simply as a guess. With hindsight it seems just as probable that the findspot could have been one of the several Glenavons in the Central Belt but, in fact, unless any new evidence in substantiation of its provenance comes to light, it is impossible to attach much significance to this regrettably pedigree-less object.

5. The type D mattock previously recorded as from Cnoc Sligeach, Oronsay (Clark 1956, fig. 3; Morrison 1980, plate 11; Smith 1989, 274) has now been re-identified as being the implement found in a Bronze Age cist at Crantit Farm, Kirkwall, Orkney, in 1909, and a Bronze Age ^{14}C date has been obtained (MacKie 1995). It has also been shown to have been made on an antler tine rather than a beam. It seems very unlikely that the mooted fragmentary type C mattock from St Columba's Cave, Argyll, was actually a Mesolithic artefact of this type (Tolan-Smith 2001, 66).

6. The putatively perforated Pelican's Foot shell from the Morton B site, Fife (Coles 1971, 347; Saville 2003b, 341) has recently been acquired by the National Museums of Scotland. Re-examination suggests the hole is fortuitous and that this shell has not obviously been used, either as a bead or in any other way.

7. In fact the 'logboat' from Dalrigh, Oban, which was made from an oak trunk, was convincingly re-assessed by Abercromby (1905, 182) as being a log-coffin rather than a boat of any kind (cf. Mowat 1996, 102). One of the associated pieces of birch bark has recently been ^{14}C dated to 3555 ± 60 BP (OxA-6813), which suggests an Early Bronze Age date for the log-coffin (Sheridan et al. 2002, 55).

8. It is instructive to reflect that the new late dating of bevelled tools potentially reopens aspects of the old debate about the chronological position and socio-economic character of the 'Obanian' (see Saville

this volume). There is little doubt that Lacaille and Movius would have regarded the late dates from An Corran simply as a confirmation of the anticipated continuation of 'Obanian culture' on the west coast of Scotland into what would elsewhere be fully Bronze Age culture.

9. In fact the surface finds, including large obliquely blunted and isosceles triangle microliths, from the Tentsmuir Sands (the area around the site at Morton), had already given a clear indication that there was an Early Mesolithic presence here. Lacaille (1954, 278–81) recognized this, and drew attention to the 'broad-blade' aspect of the Tentsmuir material, but the logic of the model by which he was constrained dictated he regard this nevertheless as an Early Bronze Age 'Mesolithic survival' industry.

10. Well before the Kilmelfort Cave excavation report was published (Coles 1983a), in which the excavator only cautiously expressed the view that the flint industry was 'early' in the settlement of Scotland, Atkinson (1962, 5) had already suggested the affinities for the assemblage were with 'the later stages of the Creswellian'. The very fact that the Kilmelfort finds come from a cave does provide additional circumstantial support for the possibility of a Lateglacial context for them in view of the prominence of this site type in the known database for the period (Jacobi 1991).

References

Abercromby, J. 1905. Report on excavations at Fethaland and Trowie Knowe, Shetland; and of the exploration of a cairn on Dumglow, one of the Cleish Hills, Kinross-shire. *Proceedings of the Society of Antiquaries of Scotland* **39** (1904–05), 171–84.

Andersen, S.H. 1974. Ringkloster, en jysk indlandsboplads med Ertebøllekultur. *Kuml 1973–74*, 10–108.

Andersen, S.H. 1980. Ertebøllekunst: nye østjyske fund af mønstrede Ertebølleoldsager. *Kuml 1980*, 7–62.

Andersen, S.H. 1985. Tybrind Vig: a preliminary report on a submerged Ertebølle settlement on the west coast of Fyn. *Journal of Danish Archaeology* **4**, 52–69.

Andersen, S.H. 1986. Mesolithic dug-outs and paddles from Tybrind Vig, Denmark. *Acta Archaeologica* **57**, 87–106.

Andersen, S.H. 1987. Tybrind Vig: a submerged Ertebølle settlement in Denmark. *In* J.M. Coles and A.J. Lawson (eds), *European Wetlands in Prehistory*, 253–80. Oxford: Clarendon Press.

Anderson, J. 1895. Notice of a cave recently discovered at Oban, containing human remains, and a refuse-heap of shells and bones of animals, and stone and bone implements. *Proceedings of the Society of Antiquaries of Scotland* **29** (1894–85), 211–30.

Anderson, J. 1898. Notes on the contents of a small cave or rock-shelter at Druimvargie, Oban; and of three shell-mounds in Oronsay. *Proceedings of the Society of Antiquaries of Scotland* **32** (1897–98), 298–313.

Ashmore, P. 1997. Radiocarbon dates from archaeological sites in Argyll and Arran. *In* G. Ritchie (ed.), *The Archaeology of Argyll*, 236–83. Edinburgh: Edinburgh University Press.

Atkinson, R.J.C. 1962. Fishermen and farmers. *In* S. Piggott (ed.), *The Prehistoric Peoples of Scotland*, 1–38. London: Routledge and Kegan Paul.

Ballin, T.B. and Saville, A. 2003. An Ahrensburgian-type tanged point from Shieldaig, Wester Ross, Scotland, and its implications. *Oxford Journal of Archaeology* **22**(2), 115–31.

Barlow, C. and Mithen, S. 2000. The experimental use of elongated pebble tools. *In* S. Mithen (ed.), *Hunter-Gatherer Landscape Archaeology: the Southern Hebrides Mesolithic Project 1988–98. Vol. 2*, 513–21. Cambridge: McDonald Institute Monograph.

Barton, R.N.E. 1989. Long blade technology in southern Britain. *In* C. Bonsall (ed.), *The Mesolithic in Europe*, 264–71. Edinburgh: John Donald.

Barton, R.N.E. 1994. Second interim report on the survey and excavations in the Wye Valley, 1994. *Proceedings of the University of Bristol Spelaeological Society* **20**(1), 63–73.

Barton, R.N.E. 1997. *Stone Age Britain*. London: Batsford/ English Heritage.

Barton, R.N.E. 1998. Long blade technology and the question of British Late Pleistocene/Early Holocene lithic assemblages. *In* N. Ashton, F. Healy and P. Pettitt (eds), *Stone Age Archaeology: Essays in Honour of John Wymer*, 158–64. Oxford: Oxbow Books (Oxbow Monograph **102**/Lithic Studies Society Occasional Paper **6**).

Barton, R.N.E. 1999. The Lateglacial or Late and Final Upper Palaeolithic colonization of Britain. *In* J. Hunter and I. Ralston (eds), *The Archaeology of Britain*, 13–34. London: Routledge.

Barton, R.N.E., Jacobi, R.M., Stapert, D. and Street, M.J. 2003. The Late-glacial reoccupation of the British Isles and the Creswellian. *Journal of Quaternary Science* **18**(7), 631–43.

Berridge, P. and Roberts, A. 1994. The Mesolithic decorated and other pebble artefacts: synthesis. *In* H. Quinnell and M.R. Blockley (eds), *Excavations at Rhuddlan, Clwyd 1969–73: Mesolithic to Medieval*, 115–31. York: Council for British Archaeology (Research Report **95**).

Binns, R.E. 1972. Pumice on postglacial strandlines and in prehistoric sites in the British Isles. *Scottish Journal of Geology* **8**(2), 105–14.

Bishop, A.H. 1914. An Oransay shell-mound – a Scottish pre-Neolithic site. *Proceedings of the Society of Antiquaries of Scotland* **48** (1913–14), 52–108.

Bonsall, C. 1996. The 'Obanian problem': coastal adaptation in the Mesolithic of western Scotland. *In* T. Pollard and A. Morrison (eds), *The Early Prehistory of Scotland*, 183–97. Edinburgh: Edinburgh University Press.

Bonsall, C. 1999. Oban – Raschoille [radiocarbon dates]. *Discovery and Excavation in Scotland 1999*, 112.

Bonsall, C. and Kitchener, A. 1998. Comment [on Neolithic human remains from the Creag nan Uamh caves]. *In* R.E.M. Hedges, P.B. Pettitt, C. Bronk Ramsey and G.J. van Klinken, Radiocarbon dates from the Oxford AMS system: *Archaeometry* datelist 26. *Archaeometry* **40**(2), 438.

Bonsall, C. and Smith, C. 1990. Bone and antler technology in the British Late Upper Palaeolithic and Mesolithic: the impact of accelerator dating. *In* P.M. Vermeersch and P. van Peer (eds), *Contributions to the Mesolithic in Europe*, 359–68. Leuven: Leuven University Press.

Bonsall, C. and Smith, C. 1992. New AMS ¹⁴C dates for antler and bone artifacts from Great Britain. *Mesolithic Miscellany* **13**(2), 28–34.

Bonsall, C., Sutherland, D., Lawson, T. and Russell, N. 1992. Excavations in Ulva Cave, western Scotland 1989: a preliminary report. *Mesolithic Miscellany* **13**(1), 7–13.

Bonsall, C., Tolan-Smith, C, and Saville, A. 1995. Direct dating of Mesolithic antler and bone artifacts from Great Britain: new results for bevelled tools and red deer antler mattocks. *Mesolithic Miscellany* **16**(1), 2-10.

Breuil, H. 1922. Observations on the pre-Neolithic industries of Scotland. *Proceedings of the Society of Antiquaries of Scotland* **56** (1921–22), 261–81.

Burov, G.M. 1989. Some Mesolithic wooden artifacts from the site of Vis I in the European north east of the U.S.S.R. *In* C. Bonsall, *The Mesolithic in Europe*, 391–401. Edinburgh: John Donald.

Burov, G.M. 1998. The use of vegetable materials in the Mesolithic of northeast Europe. *In* M. Zvelebil, L. Domańska and R. Dennell (eds), *Harvesting the Sea, Farming the Forest*, 53–63. Sheffield: Sheffield Academic Press.

Campbell, J.B. 1977. *The Upper Palaeolithic of Britain. Vols. 1–2*. Oxford: Clarendon Press.

Candow, R. 1989. *Prehistoric Morton*. Dundee: privately printed.

Childe, V.G. 1942. The antiquity and function of antler axes and adzes. *Antiquity* **16**, 258–64.

Childe, V.G. 1950. *Prehistoric Migrations in Europe*. Oslo: H. Aschehaug & Co (Instituttet for Sammenlignende Kulturforskning; Serie A: Forelesninger, XX).

Christensen, C. 1990. Stone Age dug-out boats in Denmark: occurence, age, form and reconstruction. *In* D.E. Robinson (ed.), *Experimentation and Reconstruction in Environmental Archaeology*, 119–41. Oxford: Oxbow books.

Clark, J.G.D. 1936. *The Mesolithic Settlement of Northern Europe*. Cambridge: Cambridge University Press.

Clark, J.G.D. 1947. Whales as an economic factor in prehistoric Europe. *Antiquity* **21**, 84–104.

Clark, J.G.D. 1952. *Prehistoric Europe: the Economic Basis*. London: Methuen & Co.

Clark, J.G.D. 1954. *Excavations at Star Carr*. Cambridge: Cambridge University Press.

Clark, J.G.D. 1956. Notes on the Obanian with special reference to antler- and bone-work. *Proceedings of the Society of Antiquaries of Scotland* **89** (1955–56), 91–106.

Clark, J.G.D. 1975. *The Earlier Stone Age Settlement of Scandinavia*. Cambridge: Cambridge University Press.

Clarke, A. 1990. Coarse stone tools. *In* C.R. Wickham-Jones, *Rhum: Mesolithic and Later Sites at Kinloch, Excavations 1984–86*, 117–26. Edinburgh: Society of Antiquaries of Scotland (Monograph **7**).

Clarke, A. and Dugmore, A. 1990. Pumice. *In* C.R. Wickham-Jones, *Rhum: Mesolithic and Later Sites at Kinloch, Excavations 1984–86*, 130–1. Edinburgh: Society of Antiquaries of Scotland (Monograph **7**).

Clarke, D.L. 1976. Mesolithic Europe: the economic basis. *In* G. de G. Sieveking, I.H. Longworth and K.E Wilson (eds), *Problems in Economic and Social Archaeology*, 449–81. London: Duckworth.

Coles, J.M. 1971. The early settlement of Scotland: excavations at Morton, Fife. *Proceedings of the Prehistoric Society* **37**(2), 284–366.

Coles, J.M. 1983a. Excavations at Kilmelfort Cave, Argyll. *Proceedings of the Society of Antiquaries of Scotland* **113**, 11–21.

Coles, J.M. 1983b. Morton revisited. *In* A. O'Connor and D.V. Clarke (eds), *From the Stone Age to the 'Forty-Five*, 9–18. Edinburgh: John Donald.

Cook, J. and Jacobi, R. 1994. A reindeer antler or 'Lyngby' axe from Northamptonshire and its context in the British Late Glacial. *Proceedings of the Prehistoric Society* **60**, 75–84.

Connock, K.D., Finlayson, B. and Mills, C.M. 1992. Excavation of a shell midden site at Carding Mill Bay near Oban, Scotland. *Glasgow Archaeological Journal* **17**, 25–38.

Corrie, J.M. 1914. Notes on a collection of polishers and other objects found on the site of the Roman fort at Newstead, Melrose. *Proceedings of the Society of Antiquaries of Scotland* **48** (1913–14), 338–43.

Corrie, J.M. 1916. Notes on some stone and flint implements found near Dryburgh, in the parish of Mertoun, Berwickshire. *Proceedings of the Society of Antiquaries of Scotland* **50** (1915–16), 307–13.

Cressey, M., Hardy, K. and Wickham-Jones, C.R. 2000a. Sand, Highland [radiocarbon dates]. *Discovery and Excavation in Scotland* (new series) **1**, 124.

Cressey, M., Hardy, K. and Wickham-Jones, C.R. 2000b. Loch A Squir, Raasay, Highland [radiocarbon dates]. *Discovery and Excavation in Scotland* (new series) **1**, 123.

Cumming, G.A. 1946. Flint core axe found on Fair Isle, Shetland. *Proceedings of the Society of Antiquaries of Scotland* **80** (1945–46), 146–8.

Dark, P. 2000. Revised 'absolute' dating of the early Mesolithic site of Star Carr, North Yorkshire, in the light of changes in the early Holocene tree-ring chronology. *Antiquity* **74**, 304–7.

David, A. 1989. Some aspects of the human presence in West Wales during the Mesolithic. *In* C. Bonsall (ed.), *The Mesolithic in Europe*, 241–53. Edinburgh: John Donald.

David, A. 1991. Late Glacial archaeological residues from Wales: a selection. *In* N. Barton, A.J. Roberts and D.A. Roe (eds), *The Late Glacial in North-West Europe: Human Adaptation and Environmental Change at the End of the Pleistocene*, 141–59. London: Council for British Archaeology (Research Report **77**).

David, A. 1998. Two assemblages of Later Mesolithic microliths from Seamer Carr, North Yorkshire: fact and fancy. *In* N. Ashton, F. Healy and P. Pettitt (eds), *Stone Age Archaeology: Essays in Honour of John Wymer*, 196–204. Oxford: Oxbow Books (Oxbow Monograph **102**/Lithic Studies Society Occasional Paper **6**).

Dumont, J.V. 1988. *A Microwear Analysis of Selected Artefact Types from the Mesolithic Sites of Star Carr and Mount Sandel*. Oxford: British Archaeological Reports (British Series **187**).

Dumont, S. 1997. Nouvelles recherches sur la transition Tardiglaciaire-Préboréal dans le sud et l'est de l'Angleterre. *In* J.-P. Fagnart and A. Thévenin (eds), *Le Tardiglaciaire en Europe du Nord-Ouest*, 517–27. Paris: CTHS.

Eerkens, J. 1997. Variability in Later Mesolithic microliths of northern England. *Lithics* **17/18**, 51–65.

Finlay, N. 2000. Microliths in the making. *In* R. Young (ed.), *Mesolithic Lifeways: Current Research from Britain and Ireland*, 23–31. Leicester: University of Leicester (Leicester Archaeology Monographs No. **7**).

Finlay, N., Finlayson, B. and Mithen, B. 2000. The secondary technology: its character and inter-site variability. *In* S. Mithen (ed.), *Hunter-Gatherer Landscape Archaeology: the Southern Hebrides Mesolithic Project 1988–98. Vol. 2*, 571–87. Cambridge: McDonald Institute Monograph.

Finlayson, B. 1990a. Lithic exploitation during the Mesolithic in Scotland. *Scottish Archaeological Review* **7**, 41–57.

Finlayson, B. 1990b. The function of microliths: evidence from Smittons and Starr, SW Scotland. *Mesolithic Miscellany* **11**(1), 2–6.

Finlayson, B. 1995. Complexity in the Mesolithic of the western Scottish seaboard. *In* A. Fischer (ed.), *Man and Sea in the Mesolithic*, 261–4. Oxford: Oxbow Books (Monograph **53**).

Finlayson, B. 1998. *Wild Harvesters: the First People in Scotland*. Canongate Books/Historic Scotland.

Finlayson, B. and Mithen, S. 1997. The microwear and morphology of microliths from Gleann Mor. *In* H. Knecht (ed.), *Projectile Technology*, 107–29. New York: Plenum Press.

Finlayson, B. and Mithen, S. 2000. The morphology and microwear of microliths from Bolsay Farm and Gleann Mor: a comparative study. *In* S. Mithen (ed.), *Hunter-Gatherer Landscape Archaeology: the Southern Hebrides Mesolithic Project 1988–98. Vol. 2*, 589–93. Cambridge: McDonald Institute Monograph.

Finlayson, B., Finlay, N. and Mithen, S. 2000. The cataloguing and analysis of the lithic assemblages. *In* S. Mithen (ed.), *Hunter-Gatherer Landscape Archaeology: the Southern Hebrides Mesolithic Project 1988–98. Vol. 1*, 61–72. Cambridge: McDonald Institute Monograph.

Fischer, A. 1989. Hunting with flint-tipped arrows: results and experiences from practical experiments. *In* C. Bonsall (ed.), *The Mesolithic in Europe*, 29–39. Edinburgh: John Donald.

Fischer, A., Hansen, P.V. and Rasmussen, P. 1984. Macro and micro wear traces on lithic projectile points. *Journal of Danish Archaeology* **3**, 19–46.

Foxon, A.D. 1991. *Bone, Antler, Tooth and Horn Technology and Utilisation in Prehistoric Scotland*. Unpublished PhD thesis: Department of Archaeology, University of Glasgow.

Geikie, J. 1880. Discovery of an ancient canoe in the old alluvium of the Tay at Perth. *The Scottish Naturalist* **5**, 1–7.

Grace, R. 1992. Use wear analysis. *In* F. Healy, M. Heaton and S.J. Lobb, Excavations of a Mesolithic site at Thatcham, Berkshire. *Proceedings of the Prehistoric Society* **58**, 53–63.

Gramsch, B. 1992. Friesack Mesolithic wetlands. *In* B. Coles (ed.), *The Wetland Revolution in Prehistory*, 65–72. Exeter: The Prehistoric Society and WARP.

Gramsch, B. and Kloss, K. 1989. Excavations near Friesack: an early Mesolithic marshland site in the northern plain of central Europe. *In* C. Bonsall (ed.), *The Mesolithic in Europe*, 313–24. Edinburgh: John Donald.

Grieve, S. 1885. *The Great Auk, or Garefowl: its History, Archaeology and Remains*. London: Thomas C. Jack.

Griffitts, J. and Bonsall, C. 2001. Experimental determination of the function of antler and bone 'bevel-ended tools' from prehistoric shell middens in western Scotland. *In* A.M. Choyke and L. Bartosiewicz (eds), *Crafting Bone: Skeletal Technologies through Time and Space*, 207–20. Oxford: British Archaeological Reports (International Series **937**).

Grigson, C. and Mellars, P. 1987. The mammalian remains from the middens. *In* P.A. Mellars, *Excavations on Oronsay*, 243–89. Edinburgh: Edinburgh University Press.

Grøn, O. and Skaarup, J. 1991. Mollegabet II – a submerged Mesolithic site and a 'boat burial' from Aero. *Journal of Danish Archaeology* **10**, 38–50.

Hallam, J.S., Edwards, B.J.N., Barnes, B. and Stuart, A.J. 1973. The remains of a Late Glacial elk associated with barbed points from High Furlong, near Blackpool, Lancashire. *Proceedings of the Prehistoric Society* **39**, 100–28.

Hardy, K. 2001. Sand, Highland [radiocarbon dates]. *Discovery and Excavation in Scotland* (new series) **2**, 125.

Hardy, K. and Wickham-Jones, C.R. 2003. Scotland's First Settlers: an investigation into settlement, territoriality and mobility during the Mesolithic in the Inner Sound, Scotland, first results. *In* L. Larsson *et al.* (eds), *Mesolithic on the Move: Papers Presented at the Sixth International Conference on the Mesolithic in Europe, Stockholm 2000*, 369–81. Oxford: Oxbow Books.

Jacobi, R.M. 1973. Aspects of the 'Mesolithic Age' in Great Britain. *In* S.K. Kozlowski (ed.), *The Mesolithic in Europe*, 237–65. Warsaw: Warsaw University Press.

Jacobi, R.M. 1980. The early Holocene settlements of Wales. *In* J.A. Taylor (ed.), *Culture and Environment in Prehistoric Wales*, 131–206. Oxford: British Archaeological Reports (British Series **76**).

Jacobi, R.M. 1982. Later hunters in Kent: Tasmania and the earliest Neolithic. *In* P.E. Leach (ed.), *Archaeology in Kent to AD 1500*, 12–24. London: Council for British Archaeology (Research Report **48**).

Jacobi, R.M. 1991. The Creswellian, Creswell and Cheddar. *In* N. Barton, A.J. Roberts and D.A. Roe (eds), *The Late Glacial in North-West Europe: Human Adaptation and Environmental Change at the End of the Pleistocene*, 128–40. London: Council for British Archaeology (Research Report **77**).

Jacobi, R.M. 1997. The «Creswellian» in Britain. *In* J.-P. Fagnart and A. Thévenin (eds), *Le Tardiglaciaire en Europe du Nord-Ouest*, 497–505. Paris: CTHS.

Jardine, W.G. and Jardine, D.C. 1978. A Mesolithic barbed point from Cnoc Sligeach, Isle of Oronsay, Argyll. *Proceedings of the Society of Antiquaries of Scotland* **109** (1977–78), 352–5.

Jardine, W.G. and Masters, L.J. 1977. A dug-out canoe from Catherinefield Farm, Locharbriggs, Dumfriesshire. *Transactions of the Dumfriesshire and Galloway Natural History and Antiquarian Society* **52**, 55–65

Jardine, W.G. and Morrison, A. 1976. The archaeological significance of Holocene coastal deposits in south-western Scotland. *In* D.A. Davidson and M.L. Shackley (eds), *Geoarchaeology: Earth Science and the Past*, 175–95. London: Duckworth.

Jensen, G. 1991. Ubrugelige økser? Forsøg med Kongemose- og Ertebøllekulturens økser af hjortetak. *Eksperimentel Arkæologi* **1**, 9–21.

Jensen, G. 1996. Effektive økser af kronhjortens tak. *In* M. Meldgaard and M. Rasmussen (eds), *Arkæologiske Eksperimenter i Lejre*, 40–8. Lejre: Naturens Verden/ Historisk-Arkæologisk Forsøgscenter.

Johnstone, P. 1980. *The Sea-Craft of Prehistory*. London: Routledge & Kegan Paul.

Kozlowski, J.K. and Kozlowski, S.K. 1977. Pointes, sagaies et harpons du Paléolithique et du Mésolithique en Europe du Centre-Est. *In* H. Camps-Fabrer (ed.), *Méthodologie appliquée a l'industrie de l'os préhistorique*, 205–27. Paris: Centre National de la Recherche Scientifique.

Lacaille, A.D. 1930. Mesolithic implements from Ayrshire. *Proceedings of the Society of Antiquaries of Scotland* **64** (1929–30), 34–48.

Lacaille, A.D. 1935. The Tardenoisian micro-burin in Scotland. *Proceedings of the Society of Antiquaries of Scotland* **69** (1934–35), 443–5.

Lacaille, A.D. 1939. A barbed point of deer-antler from Shewalton, Ayrshire. *Proceedings of the Society of Antiquaries of Scotland* **73** (1938–39), 48–50.

Lacaille, A.D. 1942. Scottish micro-burins. *Proceedings of the Society of Antiquaries of Scotland* **76** (1941–42), 103–19.

Lacaille, A.D. 1954. *The Stone Age in Scotland*. London: Oxford University Press (for the Wellcome Historical Medical Museum).

Larsson, L. 1990. The Mesolithic of southern Scandinavia. *Journal of World Prehistory* **4**(3), 257–309.

Lawson, J. 2001. Cramond, Edinburgh [radiocarbon dates]. *Discovery and Excavation in Scotland* (new series) **2**, 124.

MacKie, E.W. 1984. A late single-piece dug-out canoe from Loch Doon, Ayrshire. *Glasgow Archaeological Journal* **11**, 132–3

MacKie, E.W. 1995. An 'Obanian' antler mattock re-attributed. *Mesolithic Miscellany* **16**(1), 11–15.

Mapleton, R.J. 1879. Notice of the discovery of an old canoe in a peat-bog at Oban. *Proceedings of the Society of Antiquaries of Scotland* **13** (1878–79), 336–8.

Matiskainen, H. 1989. The chronology of the Finnish Mesolithic. *In* C. Bonsall (ed.), *The Mesolithic in Europe*, 379–90. Edinburgh: John Donald.

Mellars, P.A. 1974. The Palaeolithic and Mesolithic. *In* C. Renfrew (ed.), *British Prehistory: a New Outline*, 41–99. London: Duckworth.

Mellars, P.A. 1987. *Excavations on Oronsay: Prehistoric Human Ecology on a Small Island*. Edinburgh: Edinburgh University Press.

Mellars, P.A. and Reinhardt, S.C. 1978. Patterns of Mesolithic land-use in southern England: a geological perspective. *In* P.A. Mellars (ed.), *The Early Postglacial Settlement of Northern Europe: an Ecological Perspective*, 243–93. London: Duckworth.

Mercer, J. 1970. Flint tools from the present tidal zone, Lussa Bay, Isle of Jura, Argyll. *Proceedings of the Society of Antiquaries of Scotland* **102** (1969–70), 1–30.

Mercer, J. 1974. Glenbatrick Waterhole, a microlithic site on the Isle of Jura. *Proceedings of the Society of Antiquaries of Scotland* **105** (1972–74), 9–32.

Mercer, J. 1979. The Palaeolithic and Mesolithic occupation of the Isle of Jura. *Almogaren (Jahrbuch des Institutum Canarium und der Gisaf)* **9–10** (1978–79), 347–67.

Mithen, S. (ed.). 2000. *Hunter-Gatherer Landscape Archaeology: the Southern Hebrides Mesolithic Project 1988–98. Vols. 1–2*. Cambridge: McDonald Institute Monograph.

Moore, A.M.T. 2000. Stone and other artifacts. *In* A.M.T. Moore, G.C. Hillman and A.J. Legge, *Village on the Euphrates: from Foraging to Farming at Abu Hureyra*, 165–86. New York: Oxford University Press.

Mordant, D. and Mordant, C. 1992. Noyen-sur-Seine: a Mesolithic waterside settlement. *In* B. Coles (ed.), *The Wetland Revolution in Prehistory*, 55–64. Exeter: The Prehistoric Society and WARP.

Morris, D.B. 1898. Whale remains, prehistoric implements, etc., found at Causewayhead. *Transactions of the Stirling Natural History and Archaeological Society* 1897–98, 57–61.

Morrison, A. 1980. *Early Man in Britain and Ireland*. London: Croom Helm.

Morrison, A. and Bonsall, C. 1989. The early post-glacial settlement of Scotland: a review. *In* C. Bonsall (ed.), *The Mesolithic in Europe*, 134–42. Edinburgh: John Donald.

Mountain, M.-J. 1979. The Later Mesolithic of Britain: Scotland and Ireland. *In* J.V.S. Megaw and D.D.A. Simpson (eds), *Introduction to British Prehistory*, 60–71. Leicester: Leicester University Press.

Mowat, R.J.C. 1996. *Logboats of Scotland*. Oxford: Oxbow Books (Oxbow Monograph **68**).

Mulholland, H. 1970. The microlithic industries of the Tweed Valley. *Transactions of the Dumfriesshire and Galloway Natural History and Antiquarian Society* **47**, 81–110.

Munro, R. 1899. *Prehistoric Scotland and its Place in European Civilisation*. Edinburgh: Blackwood & Sons.

Munro, R. 1908. On the transition between the Palaeolithic and Neolithic civilizations in Europe. *Archaeological Journal* **65**, 205–44.

Murray, N.A., Bonsall, C., Sutherland, D.G., Lawson, T.J. and Kitchener, A.C. 1993. Further radiocarbon determinations on reindeer remains of Middle and Late Devensian age from the Creag nan Uamh caves, Assynt, NW Scotland. *Quaternary Newsletter* **70**, 1–10.

Newell, R.R., Kielman, D., Constandse-Westermann, T.S., Van der Sanden, W.A.B. and Van Gijn, A. 1990. *An Inquiry into the Ethnic Resolution of Mesolithic Regional Groups*. Leiden: E.J. Brill.

Noe-Nygaard, N. 1974. Mesolithic hunting in Denmark illustrated by bone injuries caused by human weapons. *Journal of Archaeological Science* **1**(3), 217–48.

Nuzhnyj, D. 1989. L'utilisation des microliths géometriques et non géometriques comme armatures de projectiles. *Bulletin de la Société Préhistorique Française* **86**(3), 88–96.

Orme, B. 1979. Boundaries of the forager's life. *Proceedings of the Devon Archaeological Society* **37**, 195–202.

Oshibkina, S.V. 1989. The material culture of the Veretye-type sites in the region to the east of Lake Onega. *In* C. Bonsall, *The Mesolithic in Europe*, 402–13. Edinburgh: John Donald.

O'Sullivan, A. 2001. *Foragers, Farmers and Fishers in a Coastal Landscape: an Intertidal Archaeological Survey of the Shannon Estuary*. Dublin: Royal Irish Academy (Discovery Programme Monograph **5**).

Paterson, H.M.L. and Lacaille, A.D. 1936. Banchory micro-liths. *Proceedings of the Society of Antiquaries of Scotland* **70** (1935–36), 419–34.

Piggott, S. and Henderson, K. 1958. *Scotland Before History*. London: Thomas Nelson & Sons.

Pitts, M.W. and Jacobi, R.M. 1979. Some aspects of change in flaked stone industries of the Mesolithic and Neolithic in southern Britain. *Journal of Archaeological Science* **6**, 163–77.

Price, T.D. 1987. The Mesolithic of western Europe. *Journal of World Prehistory* **1**, 225–305.

RCAHMS. 1988. *Argyll. Vol. 6. Mid Argyll & Cowal: Prehistoric and Early Historic Monuments*. Edinburgh: Royal Commission on the Ancient and Historical Monuments of Scotland.

Reynier, M.J. 1997. Radiocarbon dating of early Mesolithic stone technologies from Great Britain. *In* J.-P. Fagnart and A. Thévenin (eds), *Le Tardiglaciaire en Europe du Nord-Ouest*, 529–42. Paris: CTHS.

Reynier, M.J. 1998. Early Mesolithic settlement in England and Wales: some preliminary observations. *In* N. Ashton, F. Healy and P. Pettitt (eds), *Stone Age Archaeology: Essays in Honour of John Wymer*, 174–84. Oxford: Oxbow Books (Oxbow Monograph **102**/Lithic Studies Society Occasional Paper **6**).

Reynier, M.J. 2000. Thatcham revisited: spatial and strati-graphic analyses of two sub-assemblages from Site III and its implications for early Mesolithic typo-chronology in Britain. *In* R. Young (ed.), *Mesolithic Lifeways: Current Research from Britain and Ireland*, 33–46. Leicester: University of Leicester (Leicester Archaeology Monographs No. **7**).

Reynier, M.J. 2002. Kettlebury 103: a Mesolithic 'Horsham' type stone assemblage from Hankley Common, Elstead. *Surrey Archaeological Collections* **89**, 211–31.

Reynolds, T.E.G. 1983. *Form, Function and Technology: a Test Case of Limpet Scoops*. Unpublished BA dissertation: Archaeology Department, University of Cambridge.

Roberts, A., Barton, N. and Evans, J. 1998. Early Mesolithic mastic: radiocarbon dating and analysis of organic residues from Thatcham III, Star Carr and Lackford Heath. *In* N. Ashton, F. Healy and P. Pettitt (eds), *Stone Age Archaeology: Essays in Honour of John Wymer*, 185–92. Oxford: Oxbow Books (Oxbow Monograph **102**/Lithic Studies Society Occasional Paper **6**).

Ritchie, A. (ed.). forthcoming. Excavations at Kilellan, Islay.

Salisbury, C.R. 1988. Late Upper Palaeolithic artefacts from Lindale Low Cave, Cumbria. *Antiquity* **62**, 510–13.

Salisbury, C.R. 1992. The Pleistocene exploitation of Cumbria: a review of the evidence. *Transactions of the Cumberland and Westmorland Antiquarian and Archaeological Society* **92**, 1–6.

Saville, A. 1993. Comment [on 1st millennium AD ivory pin from Reindeer Cave, Inchnadamph]. *In* R.E.M. Hedges, R.A. Housley, C. Bronk Ramsey and G.J. van Klinken, Radiocarbon dates from the Oxford AMS system: *Archaeometry* datelist 16. *Archaeometry* **35**(1), 155.

Saville, A. 1994a. Exploitation of lithic resources for stone tools in earlier prehistoric Scotland. *In* N. Ashton and A. David (eds), *Stories in Stone*, 57–70. London: Lithic Studies Society (Occasional Paper **4**).

Saville, A. 1994b. A possible Mesolithic stone axehead from Scotland. *Lithics* **15**, 25–8.

Saville, A. 1998a. An Corran, Staffin, Skye [radiocarbon dates]. *Discovery and Excavation in Scotland 1998*, 126–7.

Saville, A. 1998b. Comment [on bone tool from Balephuil Bay, Tiree]. *In* C. Bronk Ramsey, P.B. Pettitt, R.E.M. Hedges, G.W.L. Hodgins and D.C. Owen, Radiocarbon dates from the Oxford AMS system: *Archaeometry* datelist 30. *Archaeometry* **42**(2), 466.

218

Saville, A. 2000. Orkney and Scotland before the Neolithic period. *In* A. Ritchie (ed.), *Neolithic Europe in its European Context*, 91–100. Cambridge: Macdonald Institute Monograph.

Saville, A. 2001. A Mesolithic barbed antler point from the foreshore of the Forth Estuary, near Carriden, Falkirk. *Calatria (Journal of the Falkirk Local History Society)* **15**, 70–80.

Saville, A. 2002. Mesolithic: a Hebridean 'trend-setter' [review article]. *Antiquity* **76**, 258–61.

Saville, A. 2003a. Lithic resource exploitation for artefacts in prehistoric and early historic Scotland. *In* T. Stöllner, G. Körlin, G. Steffens and J. Cierny (eds), *Man and Mining – Mensch und Bergbau: Studies in Honour of Gerd Weisgerber*, 404–13. Bochum: Deutschen Berbau-Museum (= *Der Anschnitt* **16**).

Saville, A. 2003b. Indications of regionalisation in Mesolithic Scotland. *In* L. Larsson *et al.* (eds), *Mesolithic on the Move: Papers Presented at the Sixth International Conference on the Mesolithic in Europe, Stockholm 2000*, 340–50. Oxford: Oxbow Books.

Saville, A. 2003c. A flint core-tool from Wig Sands, Kirkholm, near Stranraer, and a consideration of the absence of core-tools in the Scottish Mesolithic. *Transactions of the Dumfriesshire and Galloway Natural History and Antiquarian Society* **77**, 13–22.

Saville, A. and Ballin, T.B. forthcoming. Kilmelfort Cave, Argyll.

Saville, A. and Miket, R. 1994. An Corran rock-shelter, Skye: a major new Mesolithic site. *Past* 18, 9–10.

Sheridan, J.A. 1995. Comment [on antler spatula from Distillery Cave, Oban]. *In* R.E.M. Hedges, R.A. Housley, C. Bronk Ramsey and G.J. van Klinken, Radiocarbon dates from the Oxford AMS system: *Archaeometry* datelist 20. *Archaeometry* **37**(2), 424.

Sheridan, J.A., Cowie, T.G. and Hunter, F.J. 2002. NMS dating programme: 1994–98. *In* C. Bronk Ramsey, T.F.G. Higham, D.C. Owen, A.W.G. Pike and R.E.M. Hedges, Radiocarbon dates from the Oxford AMS system: *Archaeometry* datelist 31. *Archaeometry* **44**(3), 55–61.

Simpson, B. 1996. Self and social identity: an analysis of the Mesolithic body ornament from the Scottish western isles. *In* T. Pollard and A. Morrison (eds), *The Early Prehistory of Scotland*, 237–51. Edinburgh: Edinburgh University Press.

Skaarup, J. 1993. Submerged settlements. *In* S. Hvass and B. Storgaard (eds), *Digging Into the Past: 25 Years of Archaeology in Denmark*, 70–5. Copenhagen and Moesgard: The Royal Society of Northern Antiquaries and the Jutland Archaeological Society.

Skaarup, J. 1995. Stone-Age burials in boats. *In* O. Crumlin-Pedersen and B.M. Thye (eds), *The Ship as Symbol in Prehistoric and Medieval Scandinavia*, 51–8. Copenhagen: National Museum of Denmark.

Smith, C. 1989. British antler mattocks. *In* C. Bonsall (ed.), *The Mesolithic in Europe*, 272–83. Edinburgh: John Donald.

Smith, C. 1992. *Late Stone Age Hunters of the British Isles*. London: Routledge.

Smith, C. and Bonsall, C. 1991. Late Upper Palaeolithic and Mesolithic chronology: points of interest from recent research. *In* N. Barton, A.J. Roberts and D.A. Roe (eds), *The Late Glacial in North-West Europe: Human Adaptation and Environmental Change at the End of the Pleistocene*, 208–12. London: Council for British Archaeology (Research Report **77**).

Spikins, P. 2002. *Prehistoric People of the Pennines*. Leeds: West Yorkshire Archaeology Service.

Tolan-Smith, C. 2001. *The Caves of Mid Argyll: an Archaeology of Human Use*. Edinburgh: Society of Antiquaries of Scotland (Monograph **20**).

Tolan-Smith, C. 2003. The social context of landscape learning and the lateglacial–early postglacial recolonization of the British Isles. *In* M. Rockman and J. Steele (eds), *Colonization of Unfamiliar Landscapes: the Archaeology of Adaptation*, 116–29. London: Routledge.

Turner, W. 1889. On implements of stag's horn associated with whales' skeletons found in the Carse of Stirling. *Report of the British Association 1889*, 789–91.

Verhart, L.B.M. 1990. Stone Age bone and antler points as indicators for 'social territories' in the European Mesolithic. *In* P.M. Vermeersch and P. Van Peer (eds), *Contributions to the Mesolithic in Europe*, 139–51. Leuven: Leuven University Press.

Ward, T. 1998. Daer Reservoir, Crawford [radiocarbon dates]. *Discovery and Excavation in Scotland 1998*, 128.

Warren, G. 2001. *Towards a Social Archaeology of the Mesolithic in Eastern Scotland: Landscapes, Contexts and Experience*. Unpublished PhD thesis, University of Edinburgh.

Wickham-Jones, C.R. 1990. *Rhum: Mesolithic and Later Sites at Kinloch, Excavations 1984–86*. Edinburgh: Society of Antiquaries of Scotland (Monograph **7**).

Wickham-Jones, C.R. and Dalland, M. 1998. A small Mesolithic site at Craighead Golf Course, Fife Ness, Fife. *Tayside and Fife Archaeological Journal* **4**, 1–19.

Wickham-Jones, C.R. and McCartan, S. 1990. The lithic assemblage: secondary technology. *In* C.R. Wickham-Jones, *Rhum: Mesolithic and Later Sites at Kinloch, Excavations 1984–86*, 87–102. Edinburgh: Society of Antiquaries of Scotland (Monograph **7**).

Williams Thorpe, O. and Thorpe, R.S. 1984. The distribution and sources of archaeological pitchstone in Britain. *Journal of Archaeological Science* **11**, 1–34.

Woodman, P.C. 1978. *The Mesolithic in Ireland*. Oxford: British Archaeological Reports (British Series **58**).

Woodman, P.C. 1989. A review of the Scottish Mesolithic: a plea for normality! *Proceedings of the Society of Antiquaries of Scotland* **119**, 1–32.

Zetterlund, P. 1990. The lithic assemblage: primary technology. *In* C.R. Wickham-Jones, *Rhum: Mesolithic and Later Sites at Kinloch, Excavations 1984–86*, 64–86. Edinburgh: Society of Antiquaries of Scotland (Monograph **7**).

Zhilin, M.G. and Matiskainen, H. 2003. Deep in Russia, deep in the bog. Excavations at the Mesolithic sites Stanovoje 4 and Sakhtysh 14, Upper Volga region. *In* L. Larsson *et al.* (eds), *Mesolithic on the Move: Papers Presented at the Sixth International Conference on the Mesolithic* *in Europe, Stockholm 2000*, 694–702. Oxford: Oxbow Books.

Zvelebil, M. 1994. Plant use in the Mesolithic and its role in the transition to farming. *Proceedings of the Prehistoric Society* **60**, 35–74.

Chapter 11

The Use of Stone Tools in Mesolithic Scotland:
Function, Value, Decision-Making, and Landscapes

BILL FINLAYSON

The detailed analysis of stone tool assemblages remains important at the scale of landscape analysis to ensure that such an approach does not produce an over-generalized description of hunter-gatherer behaviour. Especially in Scotland, where other data are often lacking, stone tools remain the key to understanding what people were doing at specific points in the landscape. By examining how tools functioned, what raw materials were used in their manufacture, and how different materials might be selected for specific tool types, which could be curated differently at various places, we can begin to approach an understanding of Mesolithic landscapes.

Introduction

Research into the Mesolithic period has been dominated for many years by a focus on environmental and economic data. In the 1980s significant new insights were made through the work of Rowley-Conwy (1983; 1985), which concentrated on the economic use of landscapes in southern Scandinavia, largely based on organic data, and pointing out the limitations of stone-tool studies (Rowley-Conwy 1987). However, the recognition of these limitations made it very clear that because of the predominance of stone tools as a form of evidence, it was necessary to develop the approaches to their study. The truth of this becomes far more vital if we consider how partial the organic data tend to be, especially in Scotland. Here, apart from rare occasions such as at Staosnaig on Colonsay (Mithen 2000), the bulk of organic information comes from shell middens, which clearly only represent one specialist facet of Mesolithic life. How partial that is can be seen in debates about the nature of the 'Obanian' material (Bonsall 1996; Finlayson 1995; Pollard 1996; Woodman 1989), where for a long time archaeologists assumed that this represented a separate culture, as these middens preserved such a distinctive array of material. Equally, suggestions that the Mesolithic inhabitants of Oronsay spent their lives moving around this small island are the result not only of interpreting the available

seasonal data (Mellars & Wilkinson 1980), but also because of the apparent archaeological invisibility of these people away from their middens.

A second problem lies with the organic reconstruction of landscape use, largely based on site-catchment analysis. At its worst this approach produces a terribly static view of the Mesolithic period (cf. Armit & Finlayson 1992; 1996). The landscape is divided into zones in terms of what subsistence resources can be obtained. Sites are identified that may relate to these resources, and debate concerns whether people were living at a base-camp and sending out task groups to collect seasonal resources, or were moving as a community. It is the stuff of classic hunter-gatherer archaeology, and, when supported by good data regarding economic activities on specific sites, has helped to make important advances in how we understand people to have behaved, especially perhaps with the development of the idea of the complex hunter-gatherer. Unfortunately, very often the data behind such models are not so good, and interpretation is based more upon the generalized application of the model onto a universal landscape, where people hunt in the hills and catch fish in the sea. What is even more of a problem is that this is all they do. Studies of the Mesolithic period tend to be concerned with episodes of colonization and the transition to Neolithic culture, with perhaps a third area of interest regarding the change to complex hunter-gatherer societies. Unless the particular area of study is rich in burial sites, the Mesolithic period tends to be seen as essentially timeless within the boundaries of beginning and end. The maps of economic exploitation of the landscape serve to reinforce this approach.

Stone tools in context

The function of stone tools is of course how their makers used them; and this is the important link to how we as archaeologists make use of stone tools. We cannot simply study them as dead items for classification; the whole point is that as day-to-day artefacts they can serve to bring us insights into how people were behaving. It is because stone tools had functions given to them by people; because people will have given their tools value; and because the whole process of how to obtain the raw materials, work the stone, make the tool, use it, and discard it are bound up with human decision-making, that they are worthy of study. For this study we need to escape the bounds of our own archaeological heuristic devices; typological systems designed to seriate tools to allow chronological or regional divisions have little, if any, explicative powers regarding how society worked. Research on the Southern Hebrides Mesolithic Project (SHMP) suggests that there is no chronological change in typology or technology between c.9000 and 6500 BP (Mithen 2000).

Above all else, we should not want to commence from a generalized anthropological model of how modern hunter-gatherers behave and impose this onto a standardized landscape. We need to wrestle much more closely with our principal source data and look at what is happening on each site, within its own landscape context, and in relationship to other sites. Given the quality of our dating evidence, and the problems we have in determining length of occupation of sites, this last becomes very difficult. However, we should not simply retreat to the fall-back position of assuming that all Mesolithic sites are roughly contemporary, or perhaps that we can treat them as contemporary, as if nothing ever happened in the Mesolithic period. In fact, the period is one of major climate change, sea-level change, and consequently of changes in resources, of changes to the base map, of inevitable movement of people. Life did not stand still till the first peasants rolled up with their packets of seeds.

One reason why most research on the Mesolithic period in Scotland has focused on the west coast is that the existing database from eastern Scotland, apart from the well-known exceptions of Morton (Coles 1971; 1983) and Fife Ness (Wickham-Jones & Dalland 1998), both in Fife, is dominated by stone tools, often with little, or no, organic, structural, or contextual information. This makes it appear relatively impoverished. The consequent emphasis on the west coast has led to an assumption that the economy was based on marine resources, and indeed that Scotland may have been initially colonized along this coast. At the end of the Mesolithic, early Neolithic dates associated with large buildings and other sites (Barclay et al. 2002) have suggested that a truly Neolithic way of life may have commenced rather earlier in the east than the west.

Unfortunately, today's distribution of lithic artefacts bears neither a straightforward nor simple relationship to human activity in the past. Their distribution is the result of a combination of geomorphological and human processes, which have affected the east coast more than the west. It appears from both site location and the historically documented numbers of salmon in the major rivers of the east that these would have provided very significant resources. At the same time these rivers could have provided important access routes inland where dense forest may otherwise have obstructed travel. This is an important difference for the way the east of Scotland may have been occupied, compared to the west, where it is not only the coastal form that is different, but that the large river systems of the east offer very different possibilities. However, we should not continue to build universal landscape-derived settlement models. Mesolithic societies will not all have used their landscapes in the same manner, especially not over the entire time range of the period.

It is very easy to say more must be done with the stone tool evidence, but harder to bring this into effect. Ten years ago one of the key problems was that stone-tool studies had been focusing very hard on methodological issues, specialisms had become more and more narrow, and their value to understanding human behaviour had apparently become less and less (cf. Torrence 1989). Since then there has been more of an interest in addressing the theoretical issues surrounding the use of stone-tool data, and the information from stone-tool studies has begun to be made to work. Function is the key to this. Function that is, not in the prosaic sense of the microwear analyst, but in the holistic sense advocated by Edmonds (1987). Above and beyond everything else, chipped stone tools have a function, be it utilitarian, ceremonial, ritual, an expression of self and status, or a combination of all of these. To connect stone tools with people we have to appreciate their purpose. Functional analysis is a primary, direct means for inferring this.

Typology remains an important aspect of this study. It can indicate style and it can indicate functional potential. The interplay between these two aspects is crucial; high morphological sophistication combined with low functional potential, for example in the 'over-crafted' Neolithic projectile point, clearly means something entirely different from the low morphological sophistication but high functional potential of the quartz scraper. However, formal typologies may serve to do little other than pigeon-hole artefacts.

Technology is the means to achieve the morphological target within the constraints of the planned function and the base raw material. Our study of technology only makes sense when viewed in this way. The great advantage of the situation in Scotland is that the wide range of raw materials utilized provides scope to study the way in which technology is used to produce the desired end product, and how much morphological homogeneity is lost on the way.

The raw stone material provides a base line for tool manufacture and use. However, the raw material differences and potentials do not determine all that follows. The solutions found to operating with the different materials are specific to culture and involve cost-benefit considerations of using non-local material, political access to non-local material, and the importance of cultural norms including style and technology. Within these constraints, variables such as access, quantity, and required quality become more important than simple presence/absence of a material. It appears that raw material procurement patterns in Later Mesolithic Scotland are generally locally based (Wickham-Jones 1986). But our understanding of the organization of stone procurement in the Mesolithic period is still dominated by Binford's (1980) models of expedient and embedded collection. Scotland offers some promise for such analyses because the range of materials chipped and flaked in prehistory facilitates recognition of diverse attitudes to stones.

Mesolithic sites often appear to be palimpsests of repeated occupation, which present major problems for stone-tool analysis. However, if these sites represent the rule, or at least one important aspect of Mesolithic settlement patterns, it is imperative that we try to study them. The resolution of the difficulties will not be found by searching for and dating single occupation sites such as Fife Ness. What is more, the midden sites are as affected by this problem as the simple artefact scatters.

The application of detailed analyses of stone-tool data to Scottish Mesolithic sites is clearly important, and has been conducted in an incremental fashion over the last decade. The relative lack of fieldwork in Scotland has often been used for special pleading (Woodman 1989) but there is now a substantial quantity of data. This principally consists of material from Rùm (Wickham-Jones 1990), from Arran and upland SW Scotland (Afleck 1986; Afleck et al. 1988), and, in between, from the southern Hebrides (Mithen 2000). Supporting this, although not quite as accessible, are Mercer's collections from Jura (Mercer 1970; 1971; 1972; 1974). These collections between them comprise several hundred thousand artefacts, made principally of flint, bloodstone, pitchstone, chert, and quartz. The approximate sources of all these materials are known, and a generally similar, Late Mesolithic date established. In broad terms, with the exception of the quartz component, the assemblages are typologically very similar, comprising mostly narrow-blade microliths, few micro-burins, and generally low frequencies of scrapers. Technologically there are differences, with flint and pitchstone having the

highest frequencies of microliths and blades, followed by bloodstone and chert producing higher frequencies of flakes, then chunks, with finally quartz, not producing conventional blades at all. Core techniques run from high frequencies of conical blade cores, through amorphous flake cores, to bipolar cores.

These sites vary from inland upland sites to sites either on or near the coast, yet the variation in retouched tool proportions seems to be more easily explained as raw material variation and/or related to specialized site functions than by a simple economic/functional divide as once postulated by Mellars (1976).

Regardless of local material availability, supplementary materials are always used, normally in small quantities. Even on Islay, where flint appears to be relatively abundant on the beaches, low frequencies of quartz tools are found (Finlay et al. 2000a). In the centre of the Dumfries and Galloway region, where chert is plentiful, flint is found (Finlayson 1990). On Rùm, despite the ready availability of bloodstone and other volcanic chalcedonies, flint actually dominates the assemblages during the Mesolithic, despite no known flint from Rùm's beaches (Wickham-Jones 1990).

Technology is matched perfectly to raw material, and the end product is not identical. This raises questions as to how we interpret the traces left by mobile people, who might fail to leave an identical signature as they move between different raw material zones. In a quartz-only assemblage, several of which are known, how can we identify the Late Mesolithic artefacts? The midden sites are dominated by bipolar technique in both flint and quartz, and there is therefore a tendency to lump all local bipolar industries into the post-6500 BP period. Furthermore, Woodman has observed that in Ireland the bipolar technique is more representative of the Neolithic than the Mesolithic (Woodman 1978). This is certainly the case in Orkney, where the Neolithic assemblages are often dominated by bipolar technique.

How can functional analysis help here? First of all, it cannot, generally, help to sort out subsistence economics by simple one-by-one descriptions of tool functions. It can, however, begin to cast some insights into the intriguing tangle of assemblage variability present. This is a two-edged sword. Functional analysis cannot do any more than examine individual tool histories unless there is a good understanding of assemblage variability, based on typology, technology, and material.

Firstly, through the study of use-wear, actual use-rates (or the proportion of tools used) can be considered. This has to be analysed by assemblage, by blank type, by tool type, and by material type.

Secondly, types of use can be examined. Not in terms of individual function, but in degrees. Do wear traces, macro and micro, suggest intensive or light use? Are tools expedient or curated? Does this vary between different components of the assemblage?

Thirdly, homogeneity can be assessed. Are classes of tool used in uniform ways? Are the wear traces in similar locations on the tools? Do patterns of use-rate and type of use vary between or within tool types?

Fourthly, inter-site variability can be considered. For example, does use-rate and intensity of use go up away from a raw material source, or is distance not significant? This is one important way to link tools to landscape.

Microliths

One main area of concern in Mesolithic studies is the homogeneity of microliths as functional items, especially given their historical interpretation as projectile points, and the models built upon this assumption. Microlith samples from a number of sites, including Starr and Smittons in the Southern Uplands (Finlayson 1990), and a larger sample of over 200 microliths from Gleann Mor (Finlayson & Mithen 1997) and Bolsay Farm on Islay have been examined (Finlayson & Mithen 2000). It appears quite clear that microliths were used for a variety of tasks, including, but not restricted to, projectile use. What is more, the morphological variability between microliths does not appear to coincide with the functional variation. Finally, variation does not appear to relate to site location or size.

Perhaps this should not be entirely surprising. In the typological system established for the SHMP an attempt was made to avoid the pigeon-holing of microliths in recognition of the continuous variability in form (Finlayson *et al.* 1996). A detailed examination rapidly reveals that a very large proportion is not clearly classifiable into types. While it is possible to quickly describe pieces as 'points', 'triangles', and 'backed bladelets', further meaningful sub-division becomes increasingly difficult. Even on the simplest level, the distinction between 'crescents' and 'triangles' in particular is fuzzy, and all the major classes grade into each other. The purpose of the SHMP system was to get away from a classificatory mentality founded on diagnostic tool types as representative of discrete 'objects', be they territorial groups, chronological phases, or functionally defined tool-kits.

The majority of identified wear-traces do not relate to projectile use. It is possible that projectile use is under-represented, perhaps due to pieces lost off site and to pieces not showing wear. However, even if these factors are taken into account, the large number of pieces with positive evidence for non-projectile use provides irrefu-

table evidence that microliths are not a single-function tool form and they do not equate entirely with the act of hunting.

Interesting variations occur between Bolsay Farm and Gleann Mor, separated by only a few kilometres. To start with, the microliths at Gleann Mor are much smaller than at Bolsay. Significantly fewer (35 per cent) have wear traces than at Bolsay (50 per cent). At Gleann Mor scalene triangles are used more frequently than other forms; at Bolsay there is a greater variation in used tool form. Even among the scalene triangles there are differences, the most marked being that motion of tool use at Gleann Mor is mostly longitudinal, while at Bolsay it is predominantly transverse.

Not surprisingly the overall use-rates vary from site to site. Within that, they vary from material to material. A number of preferences appear, for example in the choice of flint against chert in the Southern Uplands, using flint for tools with predominantly longitudinal motions, where a finer tool is more suited to a task. What do these indicate with regard to how the lithic economy is working? The differences between Starr and Smittons (Finlayson 1990) can perhaps be explained by perceived material value. Although more flint is present at Starr than at Smittons, the flint is more intensely utilized, suggesting a greater value placed on it. This may indicate that flint was a material for which a specific procurement effort had to be made. At Smittons there is a lower proportion of flint, treated in a more casual manner. The implication is that the flint is embedded into the Smittons economy as a local material somewhere on a mobile round. A steady fall-off in a mobile round would account for the low proportion of flint. Again, the high proportion combined with the intensity of use at Starr argues for deliberate curation of flint. The results can be summarized as follows:

1. There is a general continuity of form between microlith types. There is no sharp distinction between crescents and triangles for example, just a gradual increase in angularity from crescents to triangles.

2. Microliths are not always used as projectiles; their function varies. It can even be suggested on the basis of use wear that projectile use may be a relatively minor function, however this may be exaggerated by loss of used projectiles and the lower visibility of projectile use traces.

3. This variation occurs within, not between, microlith types. It is not the case that scalene triangles are used for one function, while, say, rods are used for another. Scalene triangles are used for a

range of different functions, indeed there is little relationship between overall microlith form and specific function. The shape of the microlith does not appear to determine its use.

4. Overall, there is a preference to use microliths with sharply defined angles. The morphological criteria that are important are micro-morphological, concerning attributes rather than the overall tool form.

These results may reinforce notions that the microlith represents a standardized 'plug-in' type of replaceable component in composite tools, whether they are projectiles or non-hunting alternatives. It appears that conventional typology may be looking at the wrong attributes, although, of course, we remain a long way from understanding how Mesolithic people perceived the different forms. Work on the SHMP suggests that overall microlith form is most likely to relate to social learning, and that the variations in style are passive rather than emblematic (Finlay et al. 2000b).

The point of this is not to deny that some Mesolithic sites may have been hunting camps. However, we must be wary of functional reductionism in understanding all sites in terms of subsistence activities. Sites such as Gleann Mor, Islay, may well have been located to observe game movements, but even if this were a prime reason for site location, it does not determine what activities were carried out on site. While the site may relate to hunting, the artefacts abandoned on site may not relate to maintaining hunting tool-kits. We cannot attribute site function on the basis of a single artefact type. Indeed, one of the clearest lessons is that the analysis of stone tools has to both be in depth and to encompass many strands for it to serve any purpose.

Future Directions

A new research project has commenced on the west coast (Finlayson et al. 1999). The Scotland's First Settlers Project is a regional study of the area of the Inner Sound, from the eastern coast of Skye to the western shore of the mainland. The main chronological focus of the project is on both the Mesolithic and the earliest evidence for the Neolithic in the area. A principal reason for commencing a new west-coast project is to develop an innovative approach. Regional approaches have already been developed, most notably in the SHMP. The Scotland's First Settlers Project is trying to develop this by accepting the importance of the sea in this time and place, and by considering the seascape defined by Skye and the mainland. This provides a contained space for

the study and will allow the relationship between people and the sea to be examined. Initial results suggest that although a greater density of sites, both middens and lithic scatters, is being identified than was predicted, these consist of many small sites, similar to those previously identified.

What has come out of all of the projects conducted recently is that, although there is plenty of evidence for intensive exploitation of marine resources, there is no evidence for complexity as argued for southern Scandinavia (Rowley-Conwy 1983). This is interesting on a number of counts. First of all, it is important to make the general point that the parallels often made with the culture and economy of the native peoples of the North American NW coast and that of the Mesolithic west of Scotland could ecologically be applicable throughout Scotland. The west coast may have an abundance of middens and a very rich resource base, but the east coast has some considerable resources of its own, not least the presence of what would have been phenomenally rich salmon rivers. It can be argued that even in the heartland of the complex Mesolithic, in southern Scandinavia, there is still no evidence for anything as striking as the American NW coast societies, but the evidence throughout Scotland does not suggest a situation that really even parallels southern Scandinavia. This is an important point in considering the value of the eastern and the western lands and seas. The middens have created a mental image of a marine-based Mesolithic lifestyle, often referring to the Scandinavian evidence for examples of what may be missing from the Scottish archaeological record.

Recent discussion of 'Doggerland' has reinforced this perspective, arguing that developed coastal Mesolithic societies would have retreated back with the coast, superseding more scattered inland communities, and providing a real alternative to farming, so that when the two economic systems met, they were both expansionist and resistant to one another (Coles 1998; 1999). Yet the point has to be made that the length of coastline would have been increasing and that therefore the lands available for such a marine-based complex Mesolithic would have been increasing. Would such an abundance of resources have meant that the complex system would not have been needed?

Much of the focus of research on the Mesolithic period in recent years has been for complexity, or for traits that would make Mesolithic cultures more or less willing to adopt Neolithic practices. Rowley-Conwy (1983) has argued that complexity is a package, and that multiple elements have to be adopted together. Working in this general framework, there has been a tendency to look for base-camps, wherever possible. Mithen

(2000) has observed that in fact all the lithic scatter sites excavated by the SHMP appear to be either small specialized sites, or are actually probably palimpsests of such sites. There does not appear to be the structural complexity, nor the generalized assemblages, that would be expected of substantial base-camps. The largest lithic scatter so far excavated, at Bolsay Farm, Islay, appears to have had an important role in microlith manufacture, but with no evidence that this was conducted as a base-camp activity, rather than a specialized repeated task.

This would suggest that we are dealing with a society of foragers, rather than collectors, to use Binford's (1980) terms. The main potential missing element is that contemporary base-camps may have been coastal and may have been lost after marine transgression. The chief obstacle to this is that for the period when coastal sites are best preserved, in the form of the midden sites, we still have no evidence for substantial base-camps. The middens never attain the sizes of the Ertebolle middens, and many are tiny. In fact, they appear very much as another set of specialized sites, typical of the foraging economy.

One of the key questions regarding the landscape is over what size of area did people move? The assumption has generally been that areas were large, from a starting point that Scotland may have been the territory of one family (Atkinson 1962), down to somewhat smaller, but still substantial, regions. The lithic evidence is beginning to point away from this. The distinctive raw materials really do not seem to move very far until the Neolithic period (cf. Finlayson 1997). There is a very, very rapid fall in the quantities of lithic artefacts present on sites even only short distances from sources, seen for example in the relative scarcity of bloodstone in the Inner Sound (and its absence in the southern Hebrides), or in the abundance of quartz usage on Jura. The flint-rich sites on the Rhinns of Islay almost appear to be confined to that peninsula where the raw material is sourced. Indeed, even within that settlement zone there is a surprising pattern of decline in material, from Coulererach, where the use of cores appears wasteful, with pieces discarded well before exhaustion; to Bolsay, where use of cores appears more parsimonious; to Gleann Mor, where pebbles appear to have been small, the microliths are small, and a much wider range of knapping techniques appears to have been used to deal with the small size of raw material (Finlay et al. 2000a; 2000b).

In the Southern Uplands there appears to have been a similar prolific use of local chert (in the Upper Tweed only 10 per cent of Mesolithic assemblages are flint), but different approaches to the imported flint, where the patterns of raw material usage, as seen in the microwear analysis of the Starr and Smittons assemblages, suggest

marked territorial behaviour either side of the local watershed (Finlayson 1990).

Furthermore, while we may talk of a single, narrow-blade microlithic tradition, increasingly there appears to be variation in microlith form from area to area. Graeme Warren (pers. comm.) is now beginning to see each of the main river systems of the East Coast as containing a distinctive suite of microlith forms. As functional data suggest that these microlith forms are not a reflection of specific tool needs, they must reflect some sort of local tradition.

What I have attempted to do in this paper is provide an indication that stone tools can provide us with important and useful information regarding society in the Mesolithic, covering aspects such as decision-making, how the landscape was occupied, and how the different sites connect to each other. This allows the economic data to be used to examine more than the patterns of subsistence. It should be clear that the apparently dramatic qualities of economic data should not be prioritized to the exclusion of the stone tool data. Equally, the stone tool data will repay detailed analyses, as long as that analysis takes place in a holistic context, considering the function of the tools, the raw material procurement strategies, the effects of raw material on technology and form, as well as the environmental location of the site, and any organic economic data present.

Acknowledgements

This paper is very much the result of working on many projects, and I would like to thank all my colleagues on the Southern Hebrides Mesolithic Project, the East of Scotland Mesolithic Project, and the Scotland's First Settlers Project.

References

Affleck, T.L. 1986. Excavation at Starr, Loch Doon 1985. *Glasgow Archaeological Society Bulletin* **22**, 10–21.

Affleck, T.L., Edwards, K.J. and Clarke, A. 1988. Archaeological and palynological studies at the Mesolithic pitchstone and flint site of Auchareoch, Isle of Arran. *Proceedings of the Society of Antiquaries of Scotland* **118**, 37–59.

Armit, I. and Finlayson, B. 1992. Hunter-gatherers transformed: the transition to agriculture in northern and western Europe. *Antiquity* **66**, 664–76.

Armit, I. and Finlayson, B. 1996. The transition to agriculture. *In* T. Pollard and A. Morrison (eds), *The Early Prehistory of Scotland*, 269–90. Edinburgh: Edinburgh University Press.

Atkinson, R.J.C. 1962. Fishermen and farmers. *In* S. Piggott (ed.), *The Prehistoric Peoples of Scotland*, 1–38. London: Routledge & Kegan Paul.

Barclay, G.J., Brophy, K. and MacGregor, G. 2002. Claish, Stirling: an early Neolithic structure in its context. *Proceedings of the Society of Antiquaries of Scotland* **132**, 65–137.

Binford, L. 1980. Willow smoke and dog's tails: hunter-gatherer settlement systems and archaeological site formation. *American Antiquity* **45**(1), 4–20.

Bonsall, C. 1996. The 'Obanian problem': coastal adaptation in the Mesolithic of western Scotland. *In* T. Pollard and A. Morrison (eds), *The Early Prehistory of Scotland*, 183–97. Edinburgh: Edinburgh University Press.

Coles, B. 1998. Doggerland: a speculative survey. *Proceedings of the Prehistoric Society* **64**, 45–81.

Coles, B. 1999. Doggerland's loss and the Neolithic. *In* B. Coles, J. Coles and M.S. Jørgensen (eds), *Bog Bodies, Sacred Sites, and Wetland Archaeology*, 51–7. Exeter: WARP Occasional Paper **12**.

Coles, J.M. 1971. The early settlement of Scotland: excavations at Morton, Fife. *Proceedings of the Prehistoric Society* **37**(2), 284–366.

Coles, J.M. 1983. Morton revisited. *In* A. O'Connor and D.V. Clarke (eds), *From the Stone Age to the 'Forty-five*, 9–18. Edinburgh: John Donald.

Edmonds, M.R. 1987. Rocks and risk: problems with lithic procurement strategies. *In* A.G. Brown and M.R. Edmonds (eds), *Lithic Analysis and Later British Pre-history: Some Problems and Approaches,* 155–79. Oxford: British Archaeological Reports (British Series **162**).

Finlay, N., Finlayson, B. and Mithen, S. 2000a. The primary technology: its character and inter-site variability. *In* S. Mithen (ed.), *Hunter-Gatherer Landscape Archae-ology: the Southern Hebrides Mesolithic Project 1988–98. Vol. 2*, 553–69. Cambridge: McDonald Institute Monograph.

Finlay, N., Finlayson, B. and Mithen, S. 2000b. The secondary technology: its character and inter-site variability. *In* S. Mithen (ed.), *Hunter-Gatherer Landscape Archae-ology: the Southern Hebrides Mesolithic Project 1988–98. Vol. 2*, 571–87. Cambridge: McDonald Institute Monograph.

Finlayson. B. 1990. Lithic exploitation during the Mesolithic in Scotland. *Scottish Archaeological Review* **7**, 41–57.

Finlayson, B. 1995. Complexity in the Mesolithic of the western Scottish seaboard. *In* A. Fischer (ed.), *Man and Sea in the Mesolithic: Coastal Settlement Above and Below Present Sea Level*, 261–4. Oxford: Oxbow Books (Oxbow Monograph **53**).

Finlayson, B. 1997. Chipped stone; hammerstone and axeheads. *In* D. Johnston, Biggar Common, 1987–93: an early prehistoric funerary and domestic landscape in Clydesdale, South Lanarkshire. *Proceedings of the Society of Antiquaries of Scotland* **127**, 223–34.

Finlayson, B. and Mithen, S. 1997. The microwear and morphology of microliths from Gleann Mor. *In* H. Knecht (ed), *Projectile Technology*, 107–29. New York: Plenum Press.

Finlayson, B. and Mithen, S. 2000. The morphology and microwear of microliths from Bolsay Farm and Gleann Mor: a comparative study. *In* S. Mithen (ed.), *Hunter-Gatherer Landscape Archaeology: the Southern Hebrides Mesolithic Project 1988–98. Vol. 2*, 589–93. Cambridge: McDonald Institute Monograph.

Finlayson, B., Finlay, N. and Mithen, S. 1996. Mesolithic chipped stone assemblages: descriptive and analytical procedures used by the Southern Hebrides Mesolithic Project. *In* T. Pollard and A. Morrison (eds), *The Early Prehistory of Scotland*, 252–66. Edinburgh: Edinburgh University Press.

Finlayson, B., Hardy, K. and Wickham-Jones, C. 1999. Inner Sound: survey and trial excavation. *Discovery and Excavation in Scotland 1999*, 49–50.

Mellars, P.A. 1976. Settlement patterns and industrial variability in the British Mesolithic. *In* G. de G. Sieveking, I.H. Longworth and K.E. Wilson (eds), *Problems in Economic and Social Archaeology*, 375–99. London: Duckworth.

Mellars, P.A. and Wilkinson, M.R. 1980. Fish otoliths as indicators of seasonality in prehistoric shell middens: the evidence from Oronsay (Inner Hebrides). *Proceedings of the Prehistoric Society* **46**, 19–44.

Mercer, J. 1970. Flint tools from the present tidal zone, Lussa Bay, Isle of Jura, Argyll. *Proceedings of the Society of Antiquaries of Scotland* **102** (1969–70), 1–30.

Mercer, J. 1971. A regression-time stone-workers' camp, 33ft OD, Lussa River, Isle of Jura. *Proceedings of the Society of Antiquaries of Scotland* **103** (1970–1), 1–32.

Mercer, J. 1972. Microlithic and Bronze-Age camps, 75–26ft OD, N Carn, Isle of Jura. *Proceedings of the Society of Antiquaries of Scotland* **104** (1971–2), 1–22.

Mercer, J. 1974. Glenbatrick Waterhole, a microlithic site on the Isle of Jura. *Proceedings of the Society of Antiquaries of Scotland* **105** (1972–4), 9–32.

Mithen, S. (ed.). 2000. *Hunter-Gatherer Landscape Archae-ology: the Southern Hebrides Mesolithic Project 1988–98. Vols 1–2*. Cambridge: McDonald Institute Monograph.

Pollard, T. 1996. Time and tide: coastal environments, cosmology and ritual practice in early prehistoric Scotland. *In* T. Pollard and A. Morrison (eds), *The Early Prehistory of Scotland*, 198–210. Edinburgh: Edinburgh University Press.

Rowley-Conwy, P. 1983. Sedentary hunters: the Ertebølle example. *In* G. Bailey (ed.), *Hunter-Gatherer Economy in Prehistory: a European Perspective*, 111–26. Cambridge: Cambridge University Press.

Rowley-Conwy, P. 1985. The origin of agriculture in Denmark: a review of some theories. *Journal of Danish Archaeology* **4**, 188–95.

Rowley-Conwy P. 1987. Animal bones in Mesolithic studies: recent progress and hopes for the future. *In* P. Rowley-Conwy, M. Zvelebil and H.P. Blankholm (eds), *Mesolithic Northwest Europe: Recent Trends*, 74–81. Sheffield: Department of Archaeology and Prehistory, University of Sheffield.

Torrence, R. (ed.). 1989. *Time, Energy and Stone Tools*. Cambridge: Cambridge University Press.

Wickham-Jones, C.R. 1986. The procurement and use of stone for flaked tools in Prehistoric Scotland. *Proceedings of the Society of Antiquaries of Scotland* **116**, 1–10.

Wickham-Jones, C.R. 1990. *Rhum: Mesolithic and Later Sites at Kinloch, Excavations 1984–86*. Edinburgh: Society of Antiquaries of Scotland (Monograph **7**).

Wickham-Jones, C.R. and Dalland, M. 1998. A small Mesolithic site at Fife Ness, Fife, Scotland. *Internet Archaeology* **5**.

Woodman, P.C. 1978. *The Mesolithic in Ireland*. Oxford: British Archaeological Reports (British Series **58**).

Woodman, P.C. 1989. A review of the Scottish Mesolithic: a plea for normality! *Proceedings of the Society of Antiquaries of Scotland* **119**, 1–32.

Chapter 12

Structural Evidence in the Scottish Mesolithic

C. R. WICKHAM-JONES

The paper considers the evidence for upstanding structures in the Scottish Mesolithic. In contrast to a generally supposed paucity, there are some 20 sites with evidence for a variety of structures varying from the large and robust to smaller, less substantial constructions (Fig. 12.1). Several sites have evidence for more than one structure and there are in all over 23 buildings or shelters, together with four paved areas, and various stone settings. Despite the richness of the evidence it is still difficult to draw generalized patterns, but this is typical of our understanding of the Mesolithic period in Scotland, where increasing research continues to reveal further variety in the cultural remains. Nevertheless, it is clear that there was a rich architectural tradition on which people drew to provide themselves with appropriate shelter for a variety of tasks and situations.

The Evidence

The Mesolithic in Scotland contrasts with more recent periods in the paucity of upstanding structures. It has long been considered that the majority of the evidence for the Scottish Mesolithic comes in the form of lithic artefact scatters. Few of these have ever been excavated so information has to be derived from the surface collection of artefacts that may be of more or less purely Mesolithic type. On excavated sites poor preservation conditions have also lead to an emphasis on lithic information. There is, however, plenty of other evidence relating to Mesolithic activity, and this paper considers that pertaining to structures. What does the evidence comprise (Note 1), and how may it be interpreted?

One of the best known sites with detailed structural evidence is Morton in Fife. In the late 1960s, excavations by Coles (1971), on the site discovered by the late Reg Candow, yielded evidence – in the form of arcs of stakeholes and discoloured occupation deposits (not necessarily coinciding) – that has been interpreted as representing a variety of structures, including windbreaks. In all, the patterns of stakeholes indicated that a minimum of five separate structures could be discerned scattered across site A at Morton.

Morton is interesting for the range of evidence that it presents, from apparently substantial stake-built structures, to large structures with no evidence for stakes, and also small, shallow shelters composed of four or five stakes (Fig. 12.2). One structure is composed of a wide stake-built windbreak up against a natural volcanic bank (Fig. 12.2.E). With the exception of the small shelters, evidence for hearths in association with the structural evidence was abundant. On site B at Morton, however, where the shell midden was preserved, the evidence was less clear. There were stakeholes, but they formed less of a pattern, though some are recorded as having had stone packing. An arc of stones, only one course high, enclosed part of a circular shape *c*.2.5m in diameter, and elsewhere localized concentrations of flat boulders and rocks were thought to represent deliberate levelling of the midden. Overall the picture in the midden area was much less clear and the excavator felt that successive activities in this zone had destroyed much of the preceding evidence. This is a problem that recurs on other midden sites.

Prior to the work at Morton the likelihood of surviving structural evidence from the Mesolithic was thought remote. So much so that Lacaille's (1954) great work on *The Stone Age in Scotland* is largely an artefact-based study. Structural indications in the form of postholes were recorded on the Oronsay shell middens, but these were felt to post-date the Mesolithic period. Work on these middens by Mellars in the 1970s, however, showed that structural remains could be preserved within and below the middens (Mellars 1987). Evidence within the middens mainly comprised hearth structures, sometimes associated with apparent depressions or levelled areas. Below the middens more complex evidence was recovered, comprising at Caisteal nan Gillean II a posthole, found in section, in association with an apparently artificial depression in the pre-midden land surface. At Cnoc Coig (originally known as Druim Arstail (or Harstell): Mellars 1987, 127; Wickham-Jones *et al.* 1982, 18), the excavator records unequivocal evidence for two roughly circular stakehole

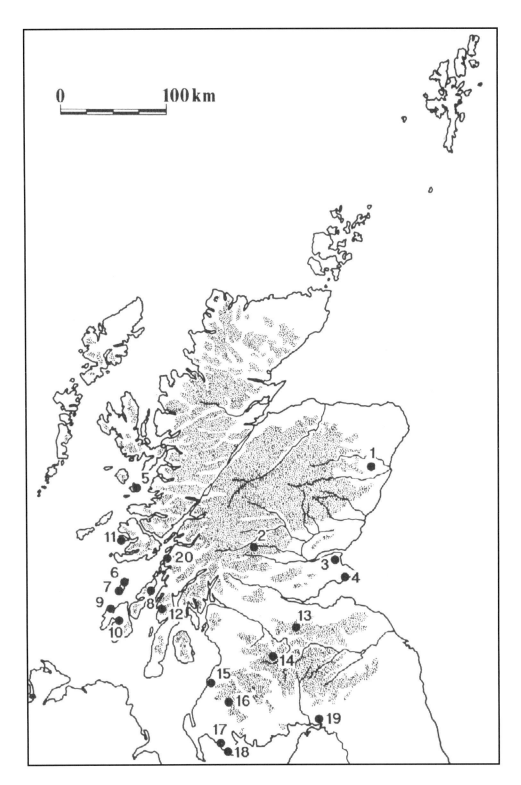

FIGURE 12.1

Location of sites mentioned in the text: 1. Nethermills, Aberdeenshire; 2. Ben Lawers, Perthshire; 3. Morton, Fife; 4. Fife Ness, Fife; 5. Kinloch, Rùm; 6. Staosnaig, Colonsay; 7. Cnoc Coig and Caisteal nan Gillean, Oronsay; 8. Lussa Wood, Jura; 9. Kilellan, Islay; 10. Newton, Islay; 11. Ulva Cave, Ulva; 12. Ellary Boulder Cave, Argyll; 13. The Popples, Peeblesshire; 14. Daer Reservoir, South Lanarkshire; 15. Littlehill Bridge, Ayrshire; 16. Starr 1, Ayrshire; 17. Low Clone, Wigtownshire; 18. Barsalloch, Wigtownshire; 19. Redkirk Point, Dumfriesshire; 20. Lón Mór, Argyll.

structures, c.3–3.5m in diameter, with hearths at the centre (Fig. 12.3.A). Both had small pit-like features around the hearth, interpreted as deposits of cooking stones, and both seem to have been composed of inclined stakes c.40–60mm thick. Elsewhere at Cnoc Coig a pre-midden hearth was associated with occupation debris and a stone 'arrangement'.

In the mid-1980s excavations took place at Kinloch on the island of Rùm, and these, though not associated with shell midden deposits, also revealed structural evidence (Wickham-Jones 1990). This evidence is derived from a palimpsest of stakeholes and is hard to interpret. There was no clear evidence for hearths at Kinloch, but five separate alignments could be discerned comprising both stakeholes and slots (Fig. 12.3.E). Four are curved, one is rectangular. None represents a complete circle, or square, and so it is impossible to derive much information on size or form, but it is interesting to note that each surviving stretch of stakes runs for just over 2m. As for form, as the excavation report tried to show, the stakehole 'dots' may be joined together in several different ways in order to provide flimsy shelters or structures that are more substantial.

At Newton, on Islay, excavations in the 1980s revealed a sub-rectangular depression, c.0.35m deep and just over 4m wide, cut into gravels (Fig. 12.3.C; McCullagh 1989). There was a central pit, and at one edge a gully linked three angled pits. It was not possible to excavate the whole site, but the remains found have been interpreted as those of a square or rectangular structure, with a pitched roof. There was clear evidence for numerous hearths inside, together with a substantial lithic assemblage. Intriguingly, this site had originally shown up as an 'ambiguous' cropmark, and there were others on the same terrace (now destroyed). This may be a rare recorded instance of a Mesolithic cropmark and it should surely act as a timely reminder for those studying this period to be aware of such traces.

Most of the sites covered so far have yielded evidence for several structures, and this raises the problem of their contemporaneity, or otherwise, of use. At Fife Ness this is not a problem because only one possible structure was revealed (Wickham-Jones & Dalland 1998a; 1998b). The evidence at Fife Ness comprises an arc of pits with a central hearth and a single outlying pit (Fig. 12.2.D). These features more-or-less coincide with a clear discolouration or 'occupation' layer in the soil and the overall diameter is just over 1m. The problems at Fife Ness arise in interpreting the remains. Do they represent a built structure, in which case the excavators argue that it is best interpreted as a flimsy windbreak? Alternatively, other explanations such as an open activity area can be put forward. Whatever the interpretation of the site at

Fife Ness, prospection during the course of excavation suggested that it stood alone.

At Lussa Wood, on the Isle of Jura, excavation in the 1970s yielded evidence for a stone structure that remains unparalleled in Scottish archaeology (Mercer 1980). This structure comprises a line of three interconnecting stone rings each with an internal diameter of just over 1m and an external diameter of 2m (Fig. 12.5.A). The rings are very similar and each shares the central stones with its neighbour; the excavator was convinced that they were all contemporary. They appear to have been filled with gravels which contained lithic artefacts, charcoal, burnt hazelnut shells, and tiny fragments of bone. Above them and slightly to one side lay a patch of angular slabs (Fig. 12.5.B). The excavations at Lussa Wood did not extend far beyond the edges of the structure, so it is difficult to interpret, but the excavator saw it as some sort of hearth or cooking arrangement and drew parallels with stone rings at Téviec in the Morbihan (Péquart et al. 1937).

Low Clone, on the Solway Firth, lies on a low cliff just above the raised beach and excavation there in the 1960s by Cormack and Coles (1968) yielded evidence interpreted as at least one light shelter or windbreak. A series of stakeholes and linear stone settings was associated with a long, scooped hollow, outside of which lay a substantial hearth (Fig. 12.4.A). The hollow measured c.20m in length and it was c.0.5m deep with a flat bottom. It may have been occupied repeatedly for there were various arrangements of features within it, including a stone setting fairly high up, and the excavators noted the possibility that two inter-cutting hollows had blurred into one another. A second scooped hollow lay c.25m to the west, but was not examined in detail.

Two miles to the SE of Low Clone lies the site of Barsalloch, which was excavated in the late 1960s (Cormack 1970; Cormack & Coles 1968). The evidence here was less clear than that from Low Clone. A natural sandy hollow on the raised beach had been made use of, and was associated with various indistinct stone settings and hearths, some in pits, as well as a widespread lithic scatter (Fig. 12.4.B). The evidence perhaps shares more similarities with the stone settings from Kilellan on Islay (see below) and it is difficult to interpret, though the excavator felt that the stone settings indicated the erection of temporary shelters.

In the southern Hebrides an extensive programme of fieldwork has lead to the discovery of many new Mesolithic sites on the islands of Colonsay and Islay, and much detail about the Mesolithic landscape and its population (Mithen 2000). Excavations were carried out at a number of sites, but, interestingly, few yielded structural information. One of the most positive signs came from Staosnaig, on Colonsay, where a large circular

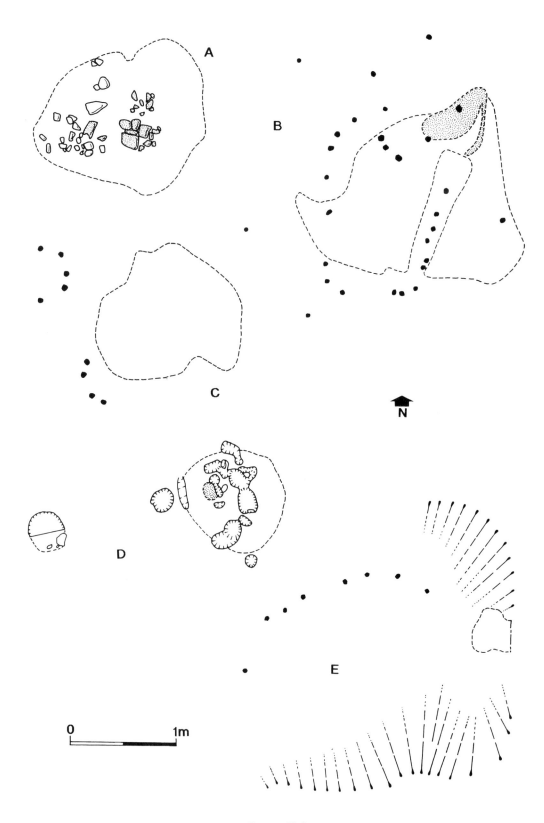

FIGURE 12.2

A: Morton Site A, occupation T46; B: Morton Site A, occupation II, T47; C: Morton Site A, occupation I, T47; D: Fife Ness; E: Morton Site A, occupation T43. See Fig. 12.5 for key to conventions. (A–C & E: redrawn from Coles 1971; D: redrawn from Wickham-Jones & Dalland 1998b)

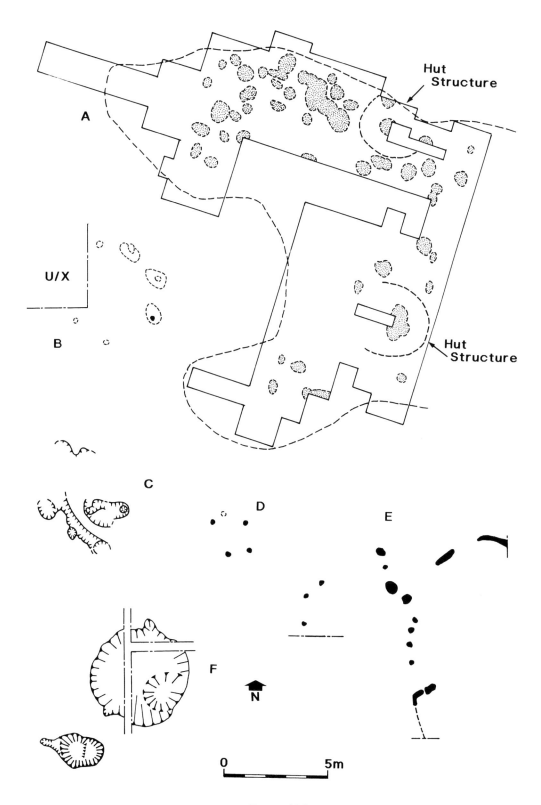

FIGURE 12.3

A: Cnoc Coig, composite plan of hearths at various levels within the shell midden and the structures at the base of the midden; B: Nethermills; C: Newton; D: Daer Reservoir; E: Kinloch, composite plan of structural features in main trench; F: Staosnaig. See Fig. 12.5 for key to conventions. (Redrawn from the following sources: A: Mellars 1987; B: Kenworthy 1981; C: McCullagh 1989; D: T. Ward pers. comm.; E: Wickham-Jones 1990; F: Mithen 2000)

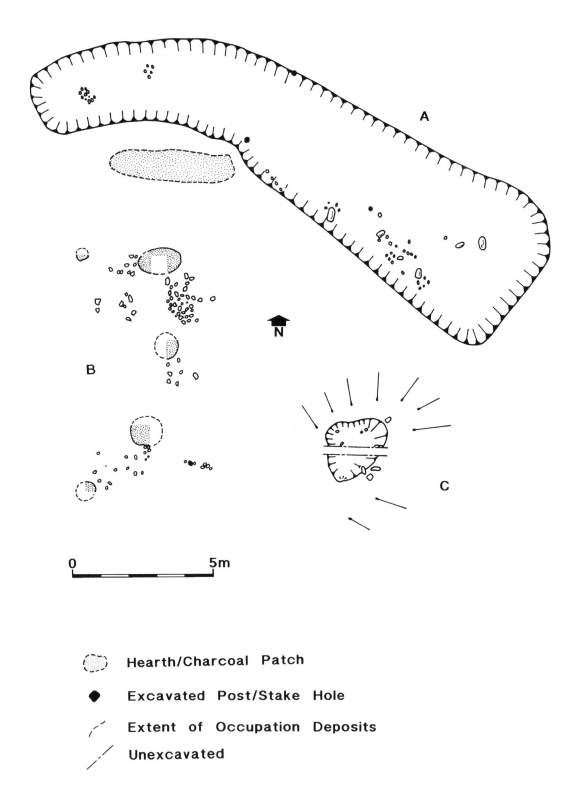

N

0   5m

Hearth/Charcoal Patch

Excavated Post/Stake Hole

Extent of Occupation Deposits

Unexcavated

FIGURE 12.4

A: Low Clone; B: Barsalloch; C: Ben Lawers. (Redrawn from the following sources: A: Cormack & Coles 1968; B: Cormack 1970; C: Atkinson *et al.* 1999)

feature (4.5m diameter) was clearly artificially cut and has been interpreted as the base of a hut (Fig. 12.3.F). It has been compared with the structure at Newton on Islay (McCullagh 1989), and with the site at Cass ny Hawin on the Isle of Man (Woodman 1987). There was no clear evidence for hearths within the hut, which seems to have been filled with later midden material, but there was a series of small hearth features away from the main structure, and other features may have served as ovens. The only other site with numerous features was Bolsay Farm, on Islay (Mithen 2000), but the excavators felt that the stakeholes here could not be convincingly interpreted as a single structure.

In Dumfriesshire, a site at Redkirk Point, on the Solway Firth, was observed to be eroding on the foreshore in 1976 and much had already washed away; the rest was excavated by Masters (1981) before the next tide came in. He found a 'pear-shaped' hollow measuring 1.03m×0.65m and 0.25m deep (Fig. 12.6.A). The sand within the hollow was clearly burnt, and it included numerous fragments of charcoal, but no artefacts. Towards the bottom of the hollow lay a semicircular setting of burnt sandstone pebbles that measured 0.5m×0.7m and was interpreted as a hearth. Two radiocarbon dates of 8000±65 BP (UB-2445) and 7935±110 BP (UB-2470) were obtained on charcoal from the hearth. The lack of artefacts from Redkirk Point makes interpretation difficult, but the excavators were in no doubt that the features were artificial. Could this be the remains of a structure? It certainly bears a strong resemblance to features on many of the other sites discussed here, such as Low Clone, Starr 1, and Morton. Palaeo-environmental work in the area suggests that the site pre-dates the maximum Postglacial marine transgression which, due to extensive coastal marsh conditions at the head of the Solway Firth, may have consisted only of infrequent inundation during flood tides (Jardine 1975; 1980). Sadly, within a week of its discovery the site was buried under boulders as part of a coastal protection scheme, so that wider examination for Mesolithic features is not currently possible.

SW Scotland seems to be associated with Mesolithic coastal structures in sandy hollows and further evidence for this comes from the site at Littlehill Bridge, near Girvan, Ayrshire, where excavations by Glasgow University Archaeological Research Division (GUARD) uncovered an occupation horizon within a scooped hollow (G. MacGregor pers. comm.). There seemed to be three phases of activity here, the first involving the creation of a scoop *c*.4m × 2.5m and up to 0.25m deep. The excavations here were very limited and no evidence for post- or stakeholes was recovered, but phase three of the activity involved the digging of a pit, together with a series of dumps of material. Phase two comprised the formation of deposits inside the scoop, and this included much flint-working debris. The material associated with this site includes charcoal deposits as well as lithic artefacts. One radiocarbon determination has been obtained, 7350±60 BP (Beta-108701), and the artefacts include narrow-blade microliths as well as cores and waste material. Littlehill Bridge lies well within the local traditions for the early settlement of Scotland.

Dictated by the distribution of Mesolithic sites in Scotland (and by most of the Mesolithic research projects), much of the above detail comes from coastal sites. A rare inland structure comes from the site at Starr 1, Loch Doon, Ayrshire, excavated by Tom Affleck (Edwards 1996). Here a series of stakeholes associated with other evidence suggested some type of shelter, but unfortunately the trench was inundated by a rise in the level of the loch after bad weather, so that a detailed record could not be made. Less clear structural evidence from the site was revealed in 1984 and comprised discoloured 'occupation' deposits together with small artificial depressions and a stone setting 0.4m in diameter (Fig. 12.6.C; Affleck 1985).

Other inland structures have recently been revealed by a team from GUARD, together with the National Trust for Scotland, on Ben Lawers, Perthshire, where various turf and stone structures have been excavated along a natural, moraine bank (Atkinson *et al.* 1997; 1999). There is evidence for both medieval and prehistoric activity here, and it is very difficult to separate the two, but it is suggested that there were Mesolithic structures, and that activity may have continued into the Neolithic period. Only one structure (structure B) seems clearly associated with Mesolithic material and thus may be dated to that period; the other structures are of indeterminate age. Structure B comprised a roughly circular hollow *c*.3m in diameter. It seems to have

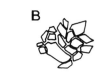

FIGURE 12.5

A: Lussa Wood, stone circles; B: Lussa Wood, stone setting. See Fig. 12.5 for key to conventions. (Redrawn from Mercer 1980)

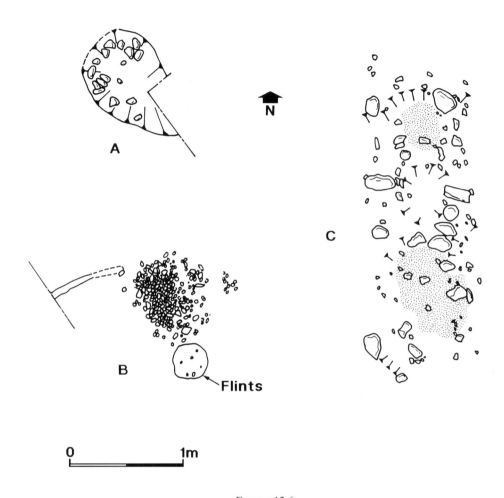

Flints

0   1m

FIGURE 12.6

A: Redkirk Point; B: Kilellan; C: Starr 1. See Fig. 12.5 for key to conventions. (Redrawn from the following sources: A: Masters 1981; B: Ritchie forthcoming; C: Affleck 1985)

included external banks, but there was no evidence for post- or stakeholes (Fig. 12.4.C).

In general the Ben Lawers site was associated with knapped flint and quartz including microliths and snapped blades, and the structures comprised depressions, of various shapes, with stakeholes, postholes, and hearths as well as external banks. The site has been interpreted as a possible hunting camp and the excavators note that it would be unlikely to have been occupied except for brief periods in the summer. The presence of several structures here raises the possibility that activity was extensive, though the site may well have been used repeatedly over a number of years. It would seem that the Mesolithic structures were subsequently reused as the basis for shieling huts in the medieval period, though, of course, the reverse possibility can not be discounted – that the shieling huts incorporated turves from the area of a pre-existing Mesolithic site. The location of

this site is particularly interesting because of its considerable height above sea level. Like Fife Ness it rounds out our picture of the different types of site that occur in the Mesolithic, whether or not the structures themselves are early. A date of 7300–6700 cal BC has recently been obtained from charcoal within a pit below one of the Ben Lawers structures (see Ashmore this volume). Full publication of this site is awaited with interest.

Another possible inland, upland structure has been excavated at Daer Reservoir, South Lanarkshire, by a team from Biggar Museums (Ward 1995; T. Ward pers. comm.). A number of sites have been investigated here, including Daer 1, which lies on the NE side of the reservoir, on the north bank of a former minor stream channel. Considerable numbers of lithic artefacts have been recovered together with charcoal fragments and a few features, interpreted as the base of postholes. The full interpretation of the site awaits post-excavation analysis, but the evidence seems to suggest a small post-built hut c.1.5m × 2m (Fig. 12.3.D). This site has produced the very early date of 9075±80 BP (AA-30354) from a single sample of *pomoidea* charcoal from one of the structural pits.

In Aberdeenshire, excavations by Kenworthy (1981) at Nethermills, beside the River Dee, in the late 1970s yielded considerable evidence for stakeholes, together with discoloured occupation deposits containing both lithic artefacts and charcoal fragments. The stakeholes are recorded as randomly scattered across the site so that it was difficult to reconstruct any coherent pattern, but they were accompanied by more substantial postholes which the excavator has interpreted as the remains of a circular structure c.4.5m in diameter (Fig. 12.3.B). Detailed information about this site has yet to be published, but preliminary inspection of the microliths suggests an associated narrow-blade assemblage.

Of relevance to this paper, if not comprising precisely structural deposits, are those sites in caves, where use of a natural structure could be said to diminish the need for an artificial construction. Scotland is rich in cave sites, many of which are well known, especially those at Oban, Argyll (Lacaille 1954). Many of the discoveries at Oban were made before modern techniques of archaeological recovery, so there is little detail of the deposits either within or outside the caves. There are tantalizing hints, such as the recovery of hearth deposits at Druimvargie rockshelter, but interpretation in terms of human activity is difficult. Pollard (1990), among others, has discussed the inadequacies of the archaeological record from Oban. Even where cave sites have been discovered recently the circumstances of their finding all too often mean that much of the archaeological material has been removed prior to investigation, as at Raschoille Cave (Connock 1985) and Carding Mill Bay (Connock 1990; Connock *et al.* 1992).

In this light the recent projects at Ulva Cave and the Mid Argyll Cave and Rockshelter Survey are particularly important. At Ulva, the recent excavations have uncovered considerable evidence for Mesolithic activity in the form of midden deposits within the cave. There were no obvious signs of internal structures of Mesolithic age, but research at this site is on-going (Bonsall *et al.* 1994). In Mid Argyll there were remains of early occupation from several of the sites, but only Ellary Boulder Cave had associated structural evidence (Tolan-Smith 2001, 86). This took the form of an arc of three substantial postholes arranged across the west entrance to the cave. The excavator has interpreted this as a screen to protect the interior, though he notes that it is impossible to reconstruct its height. Knapping debris at the foot of the screen suggests that natural light could still penetrate.

Further information relating to cave and rockshelter occupation to the north in Scotland is now coming from a new project, started in 1998, around the Inner Sound between Skye and the Scottish mainland. This has already resulted in the discovery of numerous new rockshelter sites with shell middens, of which one, at Sand, has been confirmed as Mesolithic, while two others are apparently early (Hardy & Wickham-Jones 2002). Hopefully, excavation of both rockshelters and lithic scatter sites in the area will lead to the recovery of new detail over the next few years.

Finally, before turning to the discussion, there is one further type of evidence to be considered, and that is the evidence for cobbled areas and other stone settings. The small stone settings from Lussa Wood and Low Clone have already been mentioned, but they are not alone. Perhaps the best examples of cobbled settings come from Kilellan Farm, Islay, excavated in the 1970s (Burgess 1976; Ritchie forthcoming). The variety of stone features here included an irregular setting of small flat stones c.1.4m across, a small arc of stones, and two patches of cobbles, one just over 2m long and the other 1m in diameter (Fig. 12.6.B). These were associated with the basal sand horizon, rich in Mesolithic flint artefacts, and the smaller patch of cobbles lay between two artefact scatters and to the SW of a small, shallow scoop c.0.75m long (A. Ritchie pers. comm.). To the west of these cobbles lay an enigmatic feature (recorded by the excavators as a 'ginger strip'), which was not excavated. There was not enough organic material to allow ^{14}C determinations, but the associated lithic artefacts did include narrow-blade microliths.

A rather enigmatic example of a stone setting was recorded by Warren (1998) at the Popples, Peebles. This comprises three large sub-angular boulders observed in a small trial pit (1m × 0.5m). They formed a rough surface and there were associated lithic artefacts and charcoal fragments. The site is located on a low rocky outcrop immediately above a well-known salmon river, the Tweed. These excavations comprised only trial trenches, and the evidence recovered is hard to interpret.

Evidence of more substantial stone paving came from a site at Lón Mór, Oban, which was excavated in the 1990s as part of the Oban Archaeological Project (Bonsall 1996; Bonsall *et al.* 1993 & in press; Macklin *et al.* 2000). Here, an area of stone paving c.2m across was uncovered to the NW of a lithic artefact scatter with Mesolithic age dates ranging between 7385±60 BP (AA-8793) and 5290± 65 BP (AA-17454). The paving was associated with a stone-lined hearth dated to 5420±65 BP (AA-17452).

Discussion

Having reviewed the evidence it is necessary to ask what does it all mean? Can any insights be gained into the behaviour of Mesolithic people with regard to shelter from the information available? Three avenues of enquiry present themselves: the first relates to types of architecture; the second to function; and the third to site organization.

With regard to Mesolithic architecture we run into the problems of deducing structure from relatively scanty and disparate evidence (Table 12.1). The reconstructionist's bible in this field must be Faegre's (1979) work on nomadic tents. Faegre's information is drawn from around the world and he illustrates structures that are devised to cope with a wide variety of climatic conditions and terrain. All have one thing in common, however, in that all relate to nomadic settlement. It is clear from the Scottish evidence that, albeit relating to one general geographical and climatic zone, there is little continuity of form, or even size. Certain principles are clear, however: many structures are based on inclined stakes; a circular plan seems to predominate (though there are a few rectangular structures); some structures have a complete circumferences of timber, while others have only an arc or isolated posts, and many incorporate settings of stones; a few sites have evidence of other work with stones, for example areas of paving or cobbling are not uncommon; and scooped hollows, both natural and artificial, are a common feature of many structures, especially in the SW of Scotland.

Some general architectural principles emerge. With regard to size, there is clearly a tradition of large structures and these may be round or rectangular. Structures at Staosnaig, Nethermills, and Newton, all measure c.4.5m in diameter and can be regarded as robust. The two structures at Cnoc Coig are in a similar league at 3.5m diameter, as apparently is that at Ben Lawers (though interestingly this structure was considered small by its excavators). Structures of medium size, 2–2.5m diameter, predominated at Morton, and the Daer Reservoir site falls into this group, as may the shelters at Kinloch, though it is difficult to estimate their overall size. Each of these could also be regarded as fairly well built. Then there are the small, less substantial shelters of 1m diameter or less: there were two at Morton; Starr 1 seems to fall into this group; and Fife Ness would also be included.

The eagle-eyed will no doubt note that this division into large, medium, and small masks an apparently continuous spectrum of architectural detail from dimensions of 4.5m and over to c.0.5m. It should come as no surprise that some buildings were big and others small; different buildings no doubt served different needs and perhaps the most important feature for us is the variety. Should we be looking for patterns at all? We have, after all, only a handful of structures in comparison to the great length of time over which the Mesolithic occupation of Scotland took place. From the well-built round and rectangular structures at Kinloch and the fragile shelter of Fife Ness some 8500 ^{14}C years ago, to the large, robust structures at Cnoc Coig some 5600 ^{14}C years ago, there is remarkably little change in the overall picture, but we are dealing with very few sites (if more than were previously thought). Morton is particularly important here because it has such a variety of structures that we are reminded of the normality of variety, even on a single site.

House plans are all very well, but what about the real three-dimensional article? What did these structures look like? There have been several attempts at reconstruction, both as drawings and for real at interpretation centres. The path is fraught with problems. As Faegre (1979) shows, even apparently flimsy remains can be reconstructed into something quite robust, and this is something particularly reported by those who have set out to build Mesolithic-style shelters. You do not need deep foundations to support a stable 'bender', nor do you need many posts. This is especially true where settlement takes place in a woodland environment. Complex foundations are not needed when the wind whistles over the top of the trees. It is interesting to note that many Plains Indians in North America only regarded it as necessary to set poles into the ground in areas troubled by high winds, or for permanent settlement, and even then some dug holes only for the poles of the main supporting tripod (Laubin & Laubin 1977). Stones and smaller pegs may all give added support. Furthermore, there are many ways in which any one stake setting may have been built up and Scotland offered a variety of potential coverings from hides, to bark, or brushwood. A quick glance at the reconstruction drawings for structures at Rùm (Wickham-Jones 1990; Wickham-Jones & Pollock 1995; 1996) shows how our ideas changed over time, and all are quite possible. In this way we can see that three-dimensional reconstructions may also vary.

Here I should perhaps say that 'chance would be a fine thing', as Scotland lacks the 'reconstruction museums' of other countries, but it is possible to see some variation even in the views represented by reconstructions in the open air at Archaeolink Prehistory Park, Oyne, Aberdeenshire, and inside a museum gallery at Dundee, made some five and 15 years ago respectively. It is interesting, however, that there is a tendency for reconstructing buildings of 'bender'-type. Recent cultural heritage clearly has great influence over us, though here we can note another problem with reconstruction. Our picture is too clouded with images of Plains Indians, New Age folk, or local tinkers of the very recent past. We need to try to avoid that and think more adventurously.

Mesolithic architecture did not have modern rules to follow, and it would be nice to see some reconstruction of the small fragile, wobbly, shelters as well. Of course they would have to be firmed up enough to last an interpreta-

TABLE 12.1
Summary of structural evidence from Mesolithic sites in Scotland (as at April 2003).

Site Name	Full circle	Part circle	Rectangular	Turf	Stone setting	Hearth	'Occupation' Deposit	Depression
Morton	•	•			•	•	•	
Cnoc Coig	•					•	•	•
Nethermills	•						•	
East Barns	•					•	•	•
Howick	•					•	•	•
Fife Ness		•				•	•	•
Low Clone		•			•	•	•	•
Daer Reservoir		•				•	•	
Ellary Boulder Cave		•					•	
Starr 1		•			•		•	•
Kinloch		•	•		•			
Ben Lawers				•		•	•	•
Staosnaig						•		•
Sands of Forvie							•	•
Newton			•			•	•	•
Lussa Wood					•		•	
Redkirk Point					•	•		•
Littlehill Bridge							•	•
Barsalloch					•	•	•	•
Kilellan					• cobbles			
Lón Mór					• paving	•		
The Popples					• paving?			
Casteal nan Gillean II								•

tional lifetime and not the two or three nights for which they may have originally been designed, but anything that gives an impression of the richness and variety of Mesolithic life would be useful.

Turning to function, the page remains disappointingly blank. Many of the structures had related hearths and all (bar one: Redkirk Point) are associated with lithic, and sometimes other, material. Elsewhere, detailed studies have been made of internal organization and function, based on microlith distribution patterns, the location of hearths, and so forth (e.g. Grøn 1990), but it was not possible to carry out analysis at this level within the confines of the present study. Nevertheless, there is a clear suggestion in the various excavation reports of functional difference and perhaps others will now take up the challenge of looking at the relevant artefactual evidence.

It is important to remember that structures may not always have served as dwelling, or sleeping, places. On occasion, this has been highlighted by the excavators themselves, as at Fife Ness where the structure was ascribed a working, rather than a dwelling, function (Wickham-Jones & Dalland 1998a; 1998b). Generally, however, shelter for sleeping is regarded as being of particular importance to Mesolithic people, as at Morton (Coles 1971) and at Staosnaig, where sleeping, or possibly storage, are suggested (Mithen 2000). Given the Scottish climate, a host of other possible purposes presents itself, from shelters within which to work skins or to work on stone tools, to shelters for cooking and drying shelters. Storage is unlikely to need an associated hearth, unless some more complex process is involved, but a fire would obviously be important for many reasons including heat and light as well as a practical part of many tasks. One feature which arises out of the reconstruction at Archaeo-link is the great amount of light there can be inside a medium-sized structure of this type, and, also from other reconstructions there, just how quickly one does adjust to working within reduced light conditions. Thus at the Ulster History Park, while there is not much light inside the Mount Sandel Mesolithic house reconstruction, this might not have been a problem.

Turning back to the associated artefacts, there is the standard problem of ascertaining whether these relate to activities that went on inside an extant structure, or whether they relate to the dumping of waste into a derelict building. This problem has been addressed at some sites, for example Staosnaig (Mithen 2000) and Fife Ness (Wickham-Jones & Dalland 1998a; 1998b), but elsewhere the picture is often disappointingly simplistic. Issues such as the relationship of settlement to midden need to be further explored, and just what does all the lithic waste mean? Mesolithic site

reports often refer frequently to 'knapping floors', but is that really the case? Even the briefest episode of flint knapping leads to a huge amount of waste, and we rarely find deposits of that size. Waste may have been disposed of in many different ways, so that the actual knapping floors remain elusive. Furthermore, many other activities in which stone tools were implicated would also leave lithic debris.

Included within function I would add the factor of time; thus function relates to two separate issues – the purpose of an activity and its duration. In this way sites may be divided into three gross categories of occupation: long, medium, and short (cynics may discern the continuous spectrum once again) – and within each of these a variety of purposes may be postulated.

At Kinloch I interpreted the site as the remains of a long-term base-camp type of occupation. Fife Ness, however, was interpreted as a short-lived specialist processing site. Ben Lawers is interpreted as a short-lived hunting camp, while Morton and the Oronsay middens stand out as very different examples of medium-term marine exploitation sites. Most sites have the added complication that repeated activity on the same site has added to the evidence while blurring the individual picture. Despite the evidence for several structures on a few sites, no individual site can yet show clear evidence for the contemporaneous use of more than one structure. At Kinloch this was not resolved, but at Morton discontinuous use was postulated (Coles 1971).

The issue of repeated return also clouds the interpretation of site organization. The relationship of different structures, one to another, and to other features on site, is clearly important in our attempt to assess their overall function. But it is a hard nut to crack. For various reasons many excavations have concentrated on relatively small areas around obvious structures, so that the picture is incomplete. The structure at Fife Ness seemed to stand alone, but what of the hut at Nethermills, or that at Newton? Even where area excavation has been undertaken, interpretation is difficult. At Staosnaig there were few cut features, and little evidence for other structures. At Kinloch, however, a palimpsest of features was revealed, probably extending over a much larger area than that explored. Direct dating did not elucidate the relationships of the structures one to another and detailed interpretation of the ways in which the site had operated were impossible. The trenches at Morton revealed very different pictures for different parts of the site, while on Oronsay there was the added complication of elucidating the relationships between the different shell middens on the same small island. Gross pictures may be drawn, but the minutiae of intra-site life continue, for the moment, to elude us.

Conclusions

I have to admit that when I set out to write this paper I had no idea of the wealth of structural evidence that existed from Scottish Mesolithic sites, nor of the richness and variety that would be revealed. You will notice, however, that I still tend to be a pessimist in the matter of overall interpretation. I am not a great believer in grand-scale patterns, they still smack too much of pigeon-holing for me. We have to refine our individual site interpretations before we can start looking at the big picture. Nevertheless, that picture is increasingly interesting. We have long postulated that the Mesolithic approach to the landscape was particularly sophisticated and involved a range of specific types of site. We can now begin to cite the evidence to support that theory.

Note

1. Since this paper was written work on the Mesolithic of Scotland has continued apace. In 1999 fieldwork at the Sands of Forvie focused on a scooped feature some 6m in diameter in the surface of a glacial deposit. Though there were no clear structural elements it was associated with a microlithic flint industry and the excavator has suggested that it may have parallels with the site at Staosnaig (G. Warren pers. comm.). In the months preceding publication of this volume two new sites of great relevance have come to light. At East Barns in East Lothian work by AOC (Scotland) has uncovered a large oval (c.5m internal diameter) structure with postholes set around a natural hollow, with an associated narrow-blade microlithic industry (J. Gooder pers. comm.). Just over the border in Northumberland a similar structure has been found at Howick where a setting of postholes lay round the edge of a roughly circular hollow to define an occupation area that had internal hearths (Waddington *et al.* in press). The Howick lithic artefacts also included narrow-blade microliths. Both Howick and East Barns lie near the coast, though neither site had preserved midden deposits.

Acknowledgements

First of all my greatest thanks go to Alan Saville for inviting me to write the paper, and to himself and Fionna Ashmore for organizing such a wonderful conference. Inevitably, I have merely put together the work of others and the contributions of all the individual excavators cited here must be acknowledged. There are, however, several people who have freely made available information from unpublished material and to them a special debt is owed: Clive Bonsall; John Gooder; Gavin MacGregor; Steven Mithen; Anna Ritchie; Chris Tolan-Smith; Clive Waddington; Tam Ward; and Graeme Warren. As ever, faults in the interpretation lie with the author. The illustrations were prepared by Alan Braby and great thanks are owed to the Society of Antiquaries of Scotland, which generously grant-aided the illustration work.

References

Affleck, T.L. 1985. *Starr 1 – An Inland Mesolithic Site in S.W. Scotland. Trial Excavation, 1984.* Privately Circulated Interim Report.

Atkinson, J.A., Donnelly, M. and MacGregor, G. 1997. Ben Lawers Historic Landscape Project. *Discovery and Excavation in Scotland 1997*, 63.

Atkinson, J.A., Donnelly, M., Lelong, O. and MacGregor, G. 1999. *Ben Lawers Historic Landscape Project, the Final Pilot Season.* Glasgow: Glasgow University Archaeological Research Division, Report **290.4**.

Bonsall, C. 1996. Lón Mór, Oban: radiocarbon dates. *Discovery and Excavation in Scotland 1996*, 136.

Bonsall, C., Robinson, M., Payton, R. and Macklin, M. 1993. Lón Mór. *Discovery and Excavation in Scotland 1993*, 76.

Bonsall, C., Sutherland, D.G., Russell, N.J., Coles, G., Paul, C.R.C., Huntley, J.P. and Lawson, T.J. 1994. Excavations in Ulva Cave, western Scotland 1990–1: a preliminary report. *Mesolithic Miscellany* **15**(1), 8–21.

Bonsall, C., Payton, R., Macklin, M., Bartosiewicz, L. and Gooder, J.G. In press. Microlithic sites in the Oban area, central-west Scotland. *Mesolithic Miscellany.*

Burgess, C. 1976. An early Bronze Age settlement at Kilellan Farm, Islay, Argyll. *In* C. Burgess and R. Miket (eds), *Settlement and Economy in the Third and Second Millennia B.C.*, 181–207. Oxford: British Archaeological Reports (British Series **33**).

Coles, J.M. 1971. The early settlement of Scotland: excavations at Morton, Fife. *Proceedings of the Prehistoric Society* **37**(2), 284–366.

Connock, K. D. 1985. *Raschoille Cave, Oban, Interim Report.* Lorn Archaeological and Historical Society. Privately Circulated Interim Report.

Connock, K. D. 1990. A shell midden at Carding Mill Bay, Oban. *Scottish Archaeological Review* **7**, 74–6.

Connock, K.D., Finlayson, B. and Mills, C.M. 1992. Excavation of a shell midden site at Carding Mill Bay near Oban, Scotland. *Glasgow Archaeological Journal* **17**, 25–38.

Cormack, W.F. 1970. A Mesolithic site at Barsalloch, Wigtownshire. *Transactions of the Dumfriesshire and Galloway Natural History and Antiquarian Society* **47**, 63–80.

Cormack, W.F. and Coles, J.M. 1968. A Mesolithic site at Low Clone, Wigtownshire. *Transactions of the Dumfriesshire and Galloway Natural History and Antiquarian Society* **45**, 44–72.

Edwards, K.J. 1996. The contribution of Tom Affleck to the study of the Mesolithic of southwest Scotland. *In* T. Pollard and A. Morrison (eds), *The Early Prehistory of Scotland*, 108–22. Edinburgh: Edinburgh University Press.

Faegre, T. 1979. *Tents: Architecture of the Nomads.* London: John Murray.

Grøn, O. 1990. A large Maglemosian winter house? *Mesolithic Miscellany* **11**(1), 7–13.

Hardy, K. and Wickham-Jones, C.R. 2002. Scotland's First Settlers: the Mesolithic seascape of the Inner Sound, Skye, and its contribution to the early prehistory of Scotland. *Antiquity* **76**, 825–33.

Jardine, W.G. 1975. Chronology of the Holocene marine transgression and regression in south-western Scotland. *Boreas* **4**, 173–96.

Jardine, W.G. 1980. Holocene raised coastal sediments and former shorelines of Dumfriesshire and eastern Galloway. *Transactions of the Dumfriesshire and Galloway Natural History and Antiquarian Society* **55**, 1–59.

Kenworthy, J.B. 1981. *Excavation of a Mesolithic Settlement Site at Nethermills Farm, Crathes, near Banchory, Grampian, 1978–80. Interim Statement.* Privately Circulated Interim Report.

Lacaille, A.D. 1954. *The Stone Age in Scotland.* London: Oxford University Press.

Laubin, R. and Laubin, G. 1977. *The Indian Tipi: its History, Construction, and Use.* Norman: University of Oklahoma Press.

McCullagh, R. 1989. Excavation at Newton, Islay. *Glasgow Archaeological Journal* **15**, 23–51.

Macklin, M.G., Bonsall, C., Davies, F.M. and Robinson, M.R. 2000. Human-environment interactions during the Holocene: new data and interpretations form the Oban area, Argyll, Scotland. *The Holocene* **10**(1), 109–21.

Masters, L. 1981. A Mesolithic hearth at Redkirk Point, Gretna, Annandale and Eskdale District. *Transactions of the Dumfriesshire and Galloway Natural History and Antiquarian Society* **56**, 111–14.

Mellars, P.A. 1987. *Excavations on Oronsay: Prehistoric Human Economy on a Small Island.* Edinburgh: Edinburgh University Press.

Mercer, J. 1980. Lussa Wood 1: the Late Glacial and early Post-Glacial occupation of Jura. *Proceedings of the Society of Antiquaries of Scotland* **110** (1978–80), 1–32.

Mithen, S. (ed). 2000. *Hunter-Gatherer Landscape Archaeology: the Southern Hebrides Mesolithic Project 1988–1998.* Cambridge: MacDonald Institute Monograph.

Péquart. M., Péquart, St-J., Boule, M. and Vallois, H. 1937. *Téviec. Station-Nécropole Mésolithique du Morbihan.* Paris: Masson (Archives de l'Institut de Paléontologie Humaine, mémoire **18**).

Pollard, A. 1990. Down through the ages: a review of the Oban Cave deposits. *Scottish Archaeological Review* **7**, 58–74.

Ritchie, A. (ed.). Forthcoming. *Excavations at Kilellan Farm, Islay.* Edinburgh: Society of Antiquaries of Scotland.

Tolan-Smith, C. 2001. *The Caves of Mid Argyll: an Archaeology of Human Use.* Edinburgh: Society of Antiquaries of Scotland (Monograph Series **20**).

Waddington, C., Bailey, G., Bayliss, A., Boomer, I., Milner, N., Pedersen, K. and Shiel, R. In press. A Mesolithic settlement site at Howick, Northumberland: a preliminary report. *Archaeologia Aeliana* (5th series) **31**.

Ward, T. 1995. Daer Reservoir. *Discovery and Excavation in Scotland 1995*, 87.

Warren, G. 1998. Manor Bridge – 'The Popples', Mesolithic Settlement. *Discovery and Excavation in Scotland 1998*, 82.

Wickham-Jones, C.R. 1990. *Rhum: Mesolithic and Later Sites at Kinloch, Excavations 1984–86.* Edinburgh: Society of Antiquaries of Scotland (Monograph Series **7**).

Wickham-Jones, C.R. and Dalland M. 1998a. A small Mesolithic site at Fife Ness, Crail, Scotland. *Internet Archaeology* **5**.

Wickham-Jones, C.R. and Dalland, M. 1998b. A small Mesolithic site at Craighead golf course, Fife Ness, Fife. *Tayside and Fife Archaeological Journal* **4**, 1–19.

Wickham-Jones, C.R. and Pollock, D. 1995. *Rhum, the excavations.* Edinburgh: privately published.

Wickham-Jones, C.R. and Pollock, D. 1996. *Rhum, the excavations 2.* Edinburgh: privately published.

Wickham-Jones, C.R., Brown, M.M., Cowie, T.G., Gallagher, D.B. and Ritchie, J.N.G. 1982. Excavations at Druim Arstail, Oronsay, 1911–12. *Glasgow Archaeological Journal* **9**, 18–30.

Woodman, P.C. 1987. Excavations at Cass ny Hawin, a Manx Mesolithic site and the position of the Manx microlithic industries. *Proceedings of the Prehistoric Society* **53**, 1–22.

Chapter 13

The 'Mesolithic Experience' in Scotland

STEVEN MITHEN

The author seeks to engage more closely with the life actually lived by Mesolithic people in Scotland. Aspects of the experience of weather, landscape, wildlife, and archaeological experiment gained during ten years' work with the Southern Hebrides Project offer scope for useful insights into the world of the Mesolithic hunter-gatherer.

Archaeologists who study the prehistoric hunter-gatherers of the Mesolithic period in Scotland take upon themselves an immense challenge. Our goal is to reconstruct the prehistoric way of life of these hunter-gatherers in as much detail as possible, ideally exposing every facet of technology, economy, society, and ideology. Often we have to work with poorly preserved data which are open to numerous competing interpretations. But just as serious as this, is that our interpretations of the data are inevitably constrained by our own experience of the world. For the vast majority of prehistorians that experience will be one of living in permanent homes in an industrialized state society, a life with limited engagement with the natural world. As such it could hardly be more distant and detached from that of the Mesolithic experience.

This vast gulf between our own experience and that of the Mesolithic inhibits our abilities as archaeologists to reconstruct the past. But it could be seen as a blessing in disguise. For if even for a moment we thought that there was an iota of contact between our own experience and that of Mesolithic people, we would be tempted to believe that there was another iota, and then another, and then another. Eventually we would be doing no more than writing our own experience of the world into the past and so be fooling ourselves about our understanding of prehistory.

So perhaps it is not only honest but of maximum utility to accept and be grateful for the disjunction between the Mesolithic and the modern experience. Once we have accepted that, we can get on with our archaeology without the risk of slipping into the dangerous grasp of subjectivity. And hence we can collect and catalogue the microliths and other stone artefacts, plan the features,

undertake the soil chemistry, and – if lucky – study the plant remains and animal bones. By so doing we can reconstruct some aspects of Mesolithic life: the technology, the subsistence, the mobility patterns, the manner in which people manipulated their environments, the time of their demise, and the rise of Neolithic communities.

This is indeed what we should be doing – questing towards an objective understanding of the past – and the last decade has seen substantial developments to that end. Indeed, our understanding of the Scottish Mesolithic has been transformed beyond all recognition by new fieldwork, new analyses, and the application of new techniques from archaeological science. Peter Woodman's (1989) 'plea for normality' in Scottish Mesolithic studies was well-heeded. In that review of Scottish Mesolithic studies he asked whether there was the will within present-day Scottish archaeology to tackle the challenges posed by the Mesolithic record. Challenges not only in terms of that record's less than perfect preservation and the often difficult working conditions posed by the Scottish environment, but the challenge of escaping from a parochialism that had divorced Scottish Mesolithic studies from those of Europe, and indeed from hunter-gatherer studies in general.

The last decade or so of research on the Mesolithic period in Scotland, represented by papers in this volume and elsewhere, demonstrated that the will was there. Scottish Mesolithic studies are certainly now part of the mainstream, and 'normality' has been attained. Hence we now have models for settlement systems and foraging patterns, where once we just had lists of artefacts and cultures (cf. Bonsall 1996). We now view stone artefacts as products of a series of knapping decisions; part functional instruments for engaging with the natural world, part tools for social discourse (e.g. Finlay 1997; Finlayson 1990). We are sensitive to gender-biased interpretations of the record and seek to talk as much about the role of women as that of men in our interpretations of the evidence, and also about the young and the old (Finlay 1997; Wickham-Jones 1994). And we

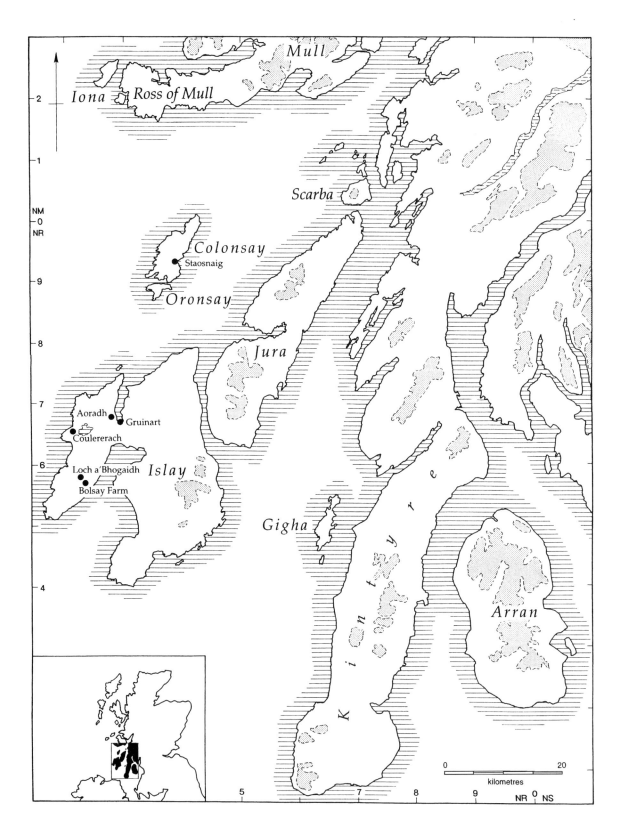

FIGURE 13.1
The Southern Hebrides, Scotland, showing places referred to in the text.

seek to apply the latest scientific techniques to our studies, ranging from programmes of AMS ^{14}C dating, to soil micromorphology and computer simulation (e.g. Ashmore 1997; Bonsall *et al.* 1995; Lake *et al.* 1998; Mithen 2000, 426–31). But perhaps the most significant achievement has been the willingness to collect new data, to engage in new field projects, such as those by Clive Bonsall around Oban and at Ulva Cave (e.g. Bonsall *et al.* 1994), and what may be the most productive of all, the new work on and around Skye being undertaken by Caroline Wickham-Jones, Bill Finlayson, and Karen Hardy in the First Settlers' Project (Hardy & Wickham-Jones 2002).

With this new work a more extensive and profound understanding of Mesolithic lifestyles has developed than seemed possible a decade ago. Of course our understanding is still appallingly limited; the Scottish Mesolithic continues to be the poor relation to that of much of Europe due to the scarcity of sites, their limited range, and the immense rarity of organic preservation.

The impoverished record of Mesolithic Scotland may one day be transformed by the discovery of waterlogged sites; even one of these would undoubtedly further our understanding of Mesolithic lifestyles very substantially. But even with such sites, our understanding will remain deficient as we will still lack knowledge of the Mesolithic experience. By finding more artefacts, we will not necessarily move towards understanding the experience of making or using those artefacts; by finding well preserved faunal assemblages, we will not necessarily move further towards the Mesolithic hunter-gatherer's experience of watching, hunting, and eating animals. Hence one might argue that the Mesolithic lifestyle will always remain alien, and our understanding will always be quite superficial.

I hope that this will not be the case. Indeed I think it will not be the case for we can connect with the Mesolithic experience. Although our daily lives may be quite different from those of Mesolithic people, our bodies and our brains are made of quite the same stuff. We are members of the same species, we share the same perceptional and cognitive apparatus, and the same physiological needs. Indeed I think that there is not just an iota but a vast wealth of common experience that we can share with that of Mesolithic people.

FIGURE 13.2
Excavating in the rain at Gleann Mor, Islay, August 1989.

The crux of my argument concerns the nature of the human mind and how it has evolved. Strong arguments can be made that our mentality has been substantially conditioned by a hunter-gatherer way of life, since it was when our ancestors were living that lifestyle that the human body and brain evolved from those of an ape-like predecessor five million years ago to that of modern humans, who first appeared *c*.130,000 years ago (Barkow *et al*. 1992). Some psychologists argue that many aspects of modern human behaviour, such as our patterns of food consumption and the structure of our social relations, remain fundamentally structured by a hunter-gatherer mentality that we still possess (e.g. Cosmides 1989; Pinker 1997). They argue that the switch to a farming lifestyle, the adoption of sedentism, the developments of towns and cities, and of a diverse and complex material culture, have just been too recent to have had any profound impact on the way we think. Moreover, some psychologists argue that many of the ills of our society – literally in terms of the patterns of, say, heart disease, and metaphorically in terms of social disintegration within urban ghettos – derive from the conflict between the hunter-gatherer way of life to which our bodies and minds are adapted and the cultural environments within which we find ourselves today.

I have contributed to such arguments myself due to my strong belief that an understanding of the past, and especially of past minds, is central to understanding the human condition today (Mithen 1996). But I do not want to dwell on these theoretical arguments but focus myself back onto Mesolithic Scotland. For I feel that the Scottish landscapes provide us with one of the best opportunities for finding those connections between our own and that of the Mesolithic experience. The reason is quite simple; when working in Scotland, and especially in the Highland region, one is forced into a direct and intensive engagement with the natural world, an engagement that may remain a pale shadow of that experienced by Mesolithic hunter-gatherers but is nevertheless in some sense in continuity with that experience. This is why Mesolithic archaeology in wild landscapes, such as the Highlands and Islands of Scotland, is always more rewarding, for me at least, than that in the tamed landscapes of, say, southern England, where conurbations and intensive farming have removed any chance of a significant engagement with the natural world. In Scotland, with its wilder landscapes, there is a chance of our modern experience engaging with and informing us about that of Mesolithic people. For all we need to do is to give our evolved, and perhaps repressed, hunter-gatherer mind a chance, give it the right environment and the right stimuli, and we can indeed catch a glimpse, however

FIGURE 13.3
Flooded trenches at Staosnaig, Colonsay, July 1992.

small and fleeting and superficial that may be, of the Mesolithic experience.

I appreciate that such views verge on the subjective, empathetic approaches to the past that are readily open to criticism, if not ridicule. But I do feel compelled to address such matters as they have been absent, intentionally absent, from my previous writings on the Mesolithic, and indeed they are largely absent from my publication of the Southern Hebrides Mesolithic Project (Mithen 2000). That project involved working on the islands of Islay and Colonsay (Fig. 13.1), excavating Mesolithic sites, and, along with colleagues, notably Bill Finlayson and Nyree Finlay, attempting to squeeze as much information as possible from the data we acquired. Within the final publication we tried to make an objective analysis of Mesolithic settlement patterns within the southern Hebrides. It includes a major review of Mesolithic studies in Scotland, sections on palaeo-environmental reconstruction with specific reference to vegetation history and sea levels, chapters about raw material distributions, a report on fieldwalking surveys on Islay and Colonsay, extensive and detailed

FIGURE 13.4
Heatwave at Staosnaig, Colonsay, September 1991.

FIGURE 13.5
Bolsay Farm, Islay, looking towards Beinn Tart a'Mhill.

FIGURE 13.6
Trench II, Bolsay Farm, Islay, August 1992.

FIGURE 13.7
Eastwards view from summit of Beinn Tart a'Mhill looking towards the Paps of Jura.

FIGURE 13.8
Test-pitting at Coulererach, Islay, September 1993.

site reports from excavations at ten Mesolithic sites on these islands (many of which include numerous specialist reports), chapters about using GIS to predict site location and computer simulation of colonization and island exploitation, chapters on experimental archaeology, lithic studies, inter-site comparisons, and then a synthesis of these lines of evidence to reconstruct the history of colonization, the nature of Mesolithic settlement patterns, and the transition to farming in the southern Hebrides. This is a publication replete with tables and graphs, plans and sections, and all the other elements of a scientifically based fieldwork report. But I list all of these not to stress what is present, but what is absent. For there is little within the volume about the Mesolithic experience, and that may be a serious omission (Note 1). Certainly it is one that provides an inaccurate reflection of my own experience during the project.

Throughout the course of working on Colonsay and Islay I did indeed believe I was gaining some aspects of the Mesolithic experience, such as the way the Mesolithic inhabitants had seen and felt about their landscapes and their artefacts. Perhaps this derived from no more than a false sense of empathy with those distant prehistoric people. Or perhaps it does indeed reflect the fact that all members of *Homo sapiens* share a common set of

perceptional and cognitive mechanisms that remain impervious to any cultural influences; hence Mesolithic hunter-gatherers and twenty-first-century university academics can and do share a fundamentally similar experience of the world.

Let me now provide some examples of this 'Mesolithic experience' – some possible points of contact between the experience of a Mesolithic archaeologist and that of the Mesolithic hunter-gatherer. I readily acknowledge that these may well be all in my imagination, reflecting a forlorn optimism that as archaeologists we can go beyond the reconstruction of settlement and subsistence into the minds of those who lived and died long ago in prehistory. And if there is indeed no legitimate academic basis to the following 'Mesolithic experience', at least the following may convey a little more of the Mesolithic archaeologist's experience than is normally found in site publications and works of synthesis.

The first point of contact must, of course, be with the weather. We know that the climate of the early Postglacial is likely to have been different to that of today, perhaps rather warmer and rather drier. But I am thinking here not about climate but about weather – something of constant interest to both prehistoric hunter-gatherers and Mesolithic archaeologists working in Scotland. Even the

FIGURE 13.9
Trial-trenching at Coulererach, Islay, September 1993.

most ardent lover of Scotland will admit that the Scottish weather is not always ideal. All those who have excavated in Scotland will have been frustrated by the wind, rain, and cold that either prevents fieldwork altogether or inhibits the quality of that work.

Scottish archaeologists, however, tend to be a hardy breed and often find themselves working in appalling weather conditions. This may be unavoidable when field seasons are short and funds limited – one can simply not afford to sit indoors waiting for the rain to stop. This was certainly the case during the Southern Hebrides Mesolithic Project (Figs 13.2–3). One benefit of this is that working through such weather is a remarkably good reminder of how it must have been to have always lived close to nature. For I suspect that the Mesolithic people also disliked the rain and the cold, and – just like frustrated archaeologists – that they too looked out across the landscape waiting for the storms to pass, cursing the rain that was ruining their fishing and plant

gathering. And, just like us, I imagine that they enjoyed the experience of returning to their warm huts, of drying out, of eating hot food and having a drink. And when the sun was hot, really unusually hot, I have no doubt that they enjoyed that experience as much as we do today; as much as we did when excavating at Staosnaig in the heatwave of September 1991 (Fig. 13.4).

My argument is simply that the weather of Scotland is conducive to engaging with the Mesolithic experience. And I contrast this very favourably with the constant sun and heat of Wadi Faynan, Jordan, where Bill Finlayson and I were recently working. After I have been in the Jordanian desert for a couple of weeks I am almost pleading for some rain and some mist; the very sight of a cloud is thrilling, even though one knows that it will very soon be burnt off by the sun. In such landscapes, which today have a very different climate and landscape to that of the Early Holocene, it is far more difficult to engage with the lives of the prehistoric hunter-gatherers whom we study.

I now wish to consider some specific localities in the landscapes of Islay and Colonsay where I believe we can engage with further aspects of the Mesolithic experience.

The first locality is that of Bolsay Farm, Islay, the site of a major Mesolithic settlement (Mithen 2000, 259–328). This location provides an almost insurmountable hurdle to cross from the modern to the Mesolithic experience. For today this is a patch of startling green pasture amid an open landscape with hardly a tree in sight, and those which can be found are small, scrubby affairs (Fig. 13.5). All that remains of the existence of a prehistoric settlement are chipped stone artefacts, coarse stone tools, charred plant materials, chemical traces in the sediments, and a few ephemeral features within the soil (Fig. 13.6). But we know from our studies, and from the palynological studies conducted by Kevin Edwards in the nearby Loch a'Bhogaidh, that when Bolsay Farm was occupied this was a heavily wooded landscape, a rich and vibrant landscape (Edwards & Berridge 1994). The vast quantity of chipped stone at Bolsay Farm, and the extensive time range over which the radiocarbon dates are spread, suggests that there was something special about this specific place in the landscape, causing people to keep returning here throughout both the Mesolithic and Neolithic periods.

A study of the sediments at the site has suggested that there was once a natural spring at Bolsay Farm and people came for that reason, chucking much of their waste into the wet and boggy ground. But trying to imagine what that experience may have been like, to have sat by the spring while knapping stone, cooking plants, and I guess drinking 'tea', surrounded by oak and hazel, and all sorts

FIGURE 13.10
Searching for flint pebbles on a west coast beach of Islay.

FIGURE 13.11
Flint pebbles from Islay. Scale in cms.

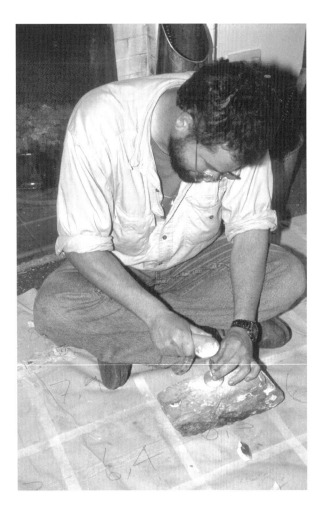

FIGURE 13.12
Gilbert Marshall flint knapping with Islay pebbles.

would have been well above the Mesolithic tree-line and, just like today, Mesolithic people could have surveyed their island world. I suspect they did, and that they too found the view spectacular, and sat to regain their breath from the climb and named the landmasses they could see. Here, on the summit of Beinn Tart a'Mhill a modern person like me, one who lives in the suburbia of southern England, can indeed share a little of the Mesolithic experience.

This is true not just on Beinn Tart a'Mhill, but at other special places on these islands. Consider that of Coulererach on the west coast of Islay. As with Bolsay Farm, this does not initially appear very promising for gaining access to the Mesolithic experience. We know little about this site as our only evidence was that gained from test-pitting and trial-trenching (Figs 13.8–9), there having been no possibility of making an open-area excavation. The fieldwork produced a chipped stone assemblage indicating that this had been a locality where considerable primary working of flint nodules had been undertaken – the initial testing and decortication of pebbles – before partially worked cores were transported away from the site (Mithen 2000, 553–69). As at Bolsay Farm, the project was able to make a detailed study of the chipped stone artefacts, pursuing detailed comparisons with those from elsewhere. It became evident that both highly skilled and novice knappers had worked stone at Coulererach (Finlay 1997; Mithen 2000, 217–29), but beyond that we have hardly any further knowledge of the site and its past activities. So what can we know about the Mesolithic experience at this locality?

Once again it is profitable to take a short walk from the site, this time to the beaches of the west coast (Fig. 13.10). The first thing to do on those beaches is to search for flint pebbles. These are found randomly scattered on the beach. The Southern Hebrides Mesolithic Project made a detailed survey of their distribution, both here and on the beaches around the whole of the southern Hebridean islands, and indeed further afield (Mithen 2000, 75–90). It was found that the beaches close to Coulererach are today the richest in terms of pebble abundance and quality, and that is most likely to have been the same during the Mesolithic (Fig. 13.11). So the searching for and collecting of pebbles replicates that during Mesolithic times, for how else did people then acquire their pebbles other than by strolling along the shoreline? And I suspect that the delight in finding a decent nodule today is much the same delight as that found in prehistory. One can then, of course, knap the pebbles and seek to replicate the artefacts and debitage products found at Coulererach and other Mesolithic sites.

Experimental flint knapping (Fig. 13.12) – and indeed experimental archaeology in general – must surely edge

of herbs, flowers, and grasses, is all but impossible in the bland green pasture of Bolsay Farm today.

So what to do to gain a little inkling of the Mesolithic experience? My suggestion – and one that I have followed through many times – is simply to climb Beinn Tart a'Mhill, the hill rising behind the site and which is almost constantly on the Islay horizon (Fig. 13.6). I suspect that this hill was wrapped up in all sorts of stories and myths of the local Mesolithic people; it may even have had specific religious significance. But we do not need to speculate about these to appreciate the hill – we can simply climb it and then be awed by the view from the summit (Fig. 13.7). When the weather is fine one can see Ireland and Kintyre to the south, Tiree and Ben Nevis to the north. The view is spectacular. Back in Mesolithic times the key elements of this view would have been identical. The summit of Beinn Tart a'Mhill

FIGURE 13.13
Sperm whale close to Coulererach, Islay, September 1993.

FIGURE 13.14
Excavation at Aoradh, Islay, August 1995.

FIGURE 13.15
View across Gruinart Estuary from location close to Aoradh.

FIGURE 13.16
Staosnaig, Colonsay, September 1994.

FIGURE 13.17
Feature F17, Staosnaig, Colonsay, September 1994.

us a little closer to the Mesolithic experience than would otherwise be possible. In my own case, the results of my knapping fit most closely with those clumsy, wasteful efforts that we found at Coulererach and which are most probably the work of young children. But again I suspect that the delight an experienced modern knapper gains from the removal of fine blades is one shared with that of the equally experienced Mesolithic knapper who once sat at Coulererach.

In 1993 a whale was washed ashore close to this site (Fig. 13.13). It was an 11m-long sperm whale that had died at sea and then gradually rotted on the beach over the following years. One of the Project team watched the carcass wash ashore. We all marvelled at the size of the beast in 1993, and then in succeeding years we were all revolted at the smell of the decaying flesh. Such whales are not infrequently washed ashore on Islay and indeed throughout Scotland. Though there are no direct traces, I think it cannot be doubted that such animals were also washed up on the beaches of Islay during the Mesolithic period. Such events may have been occasions for feasting or possibly no more than wonderment – just as we had felt in the summer of 1993. For although we frequently assume that Mesolithic people had much greater knowledge of animals and plants than we have

today, as with us they would have had very few occasions to see whales in the full splendour of their whole body. Not for them wildlife documentaries, museums to visit, films to watch; sea mammals would, I think, have been animals of very considerable interest and amazement to Mesolithic people. And hence when we marvelled at the Coulererach whale in 1993, I suspect that that was not only a modern but also a Mesolithic experience – as indeed was the stink of the rotting flesh in the years that followed.

With this whale we are engaging with the Mesolithic experience of seeing animals, and if those Mesolithic foragers were anything like the hunter-gatherers documented in the ethnographic record, they would have spent a great deal of time watching the animals of their world. Not simply the animals that they wished to hunt, but all types of animals, for hunter-gatherers are naturalists *par excellence*, having interests in wildlife that seem to far exceed utilitarian need.

With this in mind it is useful to consider another of the excavated Islay sites, that of Aoradh (Mithen 2000, 231–9), located on the eastern edge of Loch Gruinart, this being another location where there is a chance to engage with the Mesolithic experience (Fig. 13.14). Aoradh is simply known as a scatter of artefacts, one

255

similar in certain respects to Coulererach, and where extensive area excavation could have been undertaken had it been worthwhile. But this site is substantially damaged by farming and erosion, and it is difficult to say anything about it beyond the fact that Mesolithic people had once sat at this spot. Perhaps this is, however, all we need to know. The view from Aoradh looks across Loch Gruinart (Fig. 13.15), which is one of the prime locations in the Hebrides, indeed in Scotland – perhaps the whole of Britain – for bird-watching. A vast array of wildfowl exploit the rich estuarine sediments and it is at Gruinart that the annual October arrival and March departure of the vast flocks of geese that winter on Islay are seen at their most dramatic.

It is not only wildfowl that are seen at Gruinart. One memorable evening in the summer of 1996 I went with my family to watch the peregrine falcons that swoop across the estuary and sit on the sands. And after having seen those we were able to watch seals, then spotted an otter, and when heading back across the island red deer were silhouetted against the setting sun. I recount this because it was an intense and for me unique experience of seeing such wildlife within one evening, though one perhaps rather more familiar to our Mesolithic forebears. But I think that it is not mere coincidence that within 100m of our Mesolithic site at Aoradh is a large nature reserve of the Royal Society for the Protection of Birds, which is a magnet for ornithologists today. For I have no doubt that the Mesolithic people who camped at Aoradh were also keen bird-watchers and they had sat there just as we sit today, waiting and watching for the birds. Watching wildlife is indeed one way to engage with the Mesolithic experience, and there are few better places to do this than on the island of Islay.

Bolsay Farm, Coulererach, and Aoradh are on Islay, but possibly the most interesting and important Mesolithic site excavated by the Southern Hebrides Mesolithic Project was that of Staosnaig on Colonsay (Fig. 13.16; Mithen 2000, 359–441). The key feature at this site is the large, circular, shallow pit, most likely to have once been the base of a hut and then used as a rubbish pit for lithic debris and charred plant remains (Fig. 13.17). Once again the initial possibility of engaging with the Mesolithic experience at a site such as Staosnaig appears quite remote. The principal reconstructed activity at this site is an intense exploitation of hazelnuts, together with a substantial use of apples and lesser celandine (*Ranunculus ficaria* L.). Hazelnuts seem to have been roasted in small ovens and much of the debris, of shells and the accidentally charred nuts, was discarded across the site, filling the hollow left from an abandoned hut. I think that the site is most likely to have been a scene

of rather short-term but quite frenzied activity as very large quantities of plants were processed before people departed, returning to the larger islands of Jura and Islay.

But today frenzied is the last word that comes to mind when one visits Staosnaig, or indeed Colonsay in general. On a warm sunny day it is the essence of tranquillity as one explores the rock pools and picnics upon the beach. There are no surface traces of the archaeology and it requires an enormous leap of the imagination to conceive of this as a hive of Mesolithic activity. So there is little chance of engaging with the Mesolithic experience.

Again to help one with this task, one might resort to experimental archaeology, such as attempting to replicate the roasting of hazelnuts (Fig. 13.18; Mithen 2000, 507–12). However accurate our hazelnut roasting ovens may or may not have been, the experience of trying to replicate Mesolithic plant processing was immensely rewarding and provided substantial help when interpreting the archaeological remains. The

FIGURE 13.18
David Score roasting hazelnuts, July 1995.

FIGURE 13.19
The author hammering limpets, Colonsay, September 1994.

smell of woodsmoke, the taste of a roasted kernel, the sticky ooze seeping from those nuts which became charred; these were some of our modern experiences which we surely shared with those of our Mesolithic forebears at Staosnaig. Other types of experimental archaeology were also inspired by finds from Staosnaig. For instance we tried using elongated pebble tools similar to those from the site to remove limpets from rocks (Fig. 13.19; Mithen 2000, 513–21), to see if the tools we found really could have been limpet hammers. And by so doing we learnt more in a few hours about limpet gathering than had been acquired from no end of books and articles. We cuffed our knuckles against the rocks, broke hammers by mis-hits, and discovered bountiful patches of limpets. I have little doubt that our sensations when doing so were not too far divorced from those who used limpet hammers on the coast of Colonsay 8000 years ago.

The most profound Mesolithic experience that can be gained from the site of Staosnaig, however, is by leaving this site, in the sense of departing from it on foot to explore the island of Colonsay. For Staosnaig was surely a key landing place for the island, and once Mesolithic foragers had arrived and dragged their boats ashore, they too would have left to search the island. They would

have partly searched for resources – were there flints on the beaches, deer to hunt, plants to gather? – and partly searched for no reason other than that of searching itself: walking, looking, and learning about their world. For that is the essence of being a hunter-gatherer. That too was frequently my experience at Staosnaig, leaving my field-team digging at the site and departing for walks around the remarkable island of Colonsay (Fig. 13.20). I too was searching, searching for Mesolithic artefacts eroding out of peat bogs and sand dunes, but also searching for searching's sake: walking, looking, and learning about the island. It is in doing this, doing no more than just walking, I believe, that one can engage most closely with the Mesolithic experience. Even now on Colonsay one may well gain sensations which had been shared by those of the Mesolithic people. The woods of the east coast provide a glimpse, perhaps, of the woodland within which they had walked, and the awesome sight of Kiloran Bay must surely have been just as awesome to Mesolithic eyes, seeing it for the first time more than 8000 years ago (Fig. 13.21). The sunsets, the starry skies, the sunrises of Colonsay are not new events, unique to the modern world; Mesolithic eyes also watched those events. While Mesolithic people may have imbued the sun, the moon, and stars with symbolic meanings forever unknown to

FIGURE 13.20
Looking towards Kiloran Bay from Beinn nan Gudairean, Colonsay.

FIGURE 13.21
Kiloran Bay, Colonsay.

us, I suspect that many basic sensations would have been quite similar to our own.

I am not suggesting that one should sit still and attempt to commune with the Mesolithic mindset. Quite the reverse, since if we are to gain insight into the Mesolithic experience the key is not to be still but to be mobile. The key is to leave the sites, to get walking, to feel the sun, the rain, and the sea spray upon one's face, to watch the birds and the animals, to climb the crags and cross the rivers, to walk within the hills, on the beaches, and across the moors. Do that and one can begin to engage with the Mesolithic experience, engage with it in a more profound manner than one can by studying any number of lithic artefact reports, pollen diagrams, and site plans.

I spent much time during the Project doing just that: being out in the rain, the wind, and the sun; climbing to the tops of hills; scouring the beaches for flint pebbles; watching animals and birds; and walking across the landscape – very often from site to site along the pathways I imagined that Mesolithic feet may have trodden. I like to think that the intense experience of the Scottish landscape gained in this manner was similar to the experience gained by Mesolithic hunter-gatherers. I have strong theoretical reasons why that should be the case, as our minds, emotions, perceptions, indeed our bodies themselves have been moulded to the way they are by millions of years of evolution while our human ancestors lived a hunter-gatherer lifestyle. We are no longer hunter-gatherers, but all we need to do is to give our bodies and our minds a chance and they will respond accordingly to provide us with a glimpse, perhaps no more than a tiny, ephemeral, transient glimpse, but a glimpse nevertheless of a hunter-gatherer experience, one of the Mesolithic era.

Or perhaps not; was that really a Mesolithic experience I gained when I abandoned my field-team and went walking and bird-watching in the Hebrides? Or was it simply the experience of a Mesolithic archaeologist who enjoys to walk and to embed himself into the natural world, an experience of one who deludes himself that we can enter the minds of people long dead? I'm not sure.

But what I do know is that the Mesolithic experience in Scotland is a remarkable experience. The last decade has seen a transformation in Scottish Mesolithic studies so that they are now part of the European mainstream. It is a period in which much remains to be discovered – large areas of Scotland need to be surveyed for Mesolithic sites – and the time is ripe for further field projects, innovative analyses of both new and old artefact collections, and for the application of further techniques from archaeological science. A momentum

has developed in Scottish Mesolithic studies during the last decade and it is essential that that is maintained into the new millennium. And we will then be able to make far more detailed, objective reconstructions of life in the Scottish Mesolithic. So the future experience of the Mesolithic archaeologist in Scotland is, I am sure, going to be highly rewarding. And by virtue of the landscapes within which we work in Scotland, and with the evolved mind that we all possess, and with a willingness to take time out from digging itself, there is a chance, perhaps just a slim, marginal chance, that what we experience might also include a tiny glimpse of the Mesolithic experience itself.

Acknowledgements

I am very grateful to Alan Saville and Fionna Ashmore for having invited me to participate in the Mesolithic Scotland conference and contribute to its publication. I would also like to thank those who provided comments on an earlier version of this manuscript. This article is based on experiences during the Southern Hebrides Mesolithic Project, none of which would have been possible without the support from my colleagues on that project, most notably Bill Finlayson, Nyree Finlay, and Mark Lake, to whom I am eternally grateful. Of course none of those colleagues necessarily share the views expressed in this article which are mine alone.

Note

1. As a result of giving the presentation which forms the basis for this paper at the Edinburgh conference at the end of 1999, I decided at a late stage to add a version of it as a tailpiece to my publication of the work of the Southern Hebrides Mesolithic Project (Mithen 2000, 627–33).

References

Ashmore, P. 1997. Radiocarbon dates from archaeological sites in Argyll and Arran. *In* G. Ritchie (ed.), *The Archaeology of Argyll*, 236–83. Edinburgh: Edinburgh University Press.

Barkow, J.H., Cosmides. L. and Tooby. J. 1992. *The Adapted Mind: Evolutionary Psychology and the Generation of Culture.* Oxford: Oxford University Press.

Bonsall, C. 1996. The 'Obanian Problem': coastal adaptation in the Mesolithic of western Scotland. *In* T. Pollard and A. Morrison (eds), *The Early Prehistory of Scotland*, 183–97. Edinburgh: Edinburgh University Press.

Bonsall, C., Sutherland, D.G., Russell, N.J., Coles, G., Paul, C.R.C., Huntley, J.P. and Lawson, T.J. 1994. Excavations in Ulva Cave, western Scotland 1990–1: a preliminary report. *Mesolithic Miscellany* **15**(1), 8–21.

Bonsall, C., Tolan-Smith, C. and Saville, A. 1995. Direct dating of Mesolithic antler and bone artifacts from Great Britain: new results for bevelled tools and red deer antler mattocks. *Mesolithic Miscellany* **16**(1), 2–10.

Cosmides, L. 1989. The logic of social exchange: has natural selection shaped how humans reason? Studies with the Wason selection test. *Cognition* **31**, 187–276.

Edwards, K.J. and Berridge, J.M.A. 1994. The Late-Quaternary vegetational history of Loch a'Bhogaidh, Rinns of Islay S.S.S.I., Scotland. *New Phytologist* **128**, 749–69.

Finlay, J.N. 1997. *Exploring the Social Dimensions of Microlithic Technology: Experimental and Analytic Approaches with a Case Study from Western Scotland.* Unpublished PhD thesis, University of Reading.

Finlayson, B., 1990. Lithic exploitation during the Mesolithic in Scotland. *Scottish Archaeological Review* **7**, 41–57.

Hardy, K. and Wickham-Jones, C. 2002. Scotland's First Settlers: the Mesolithic seascape of the Inner Sound, Skye, and its contribution to the early prehistory of Scotland. *Antiquity* **76**, 825–33.

Lake, M.W., Woodman, P.E. and Mithen, S.J. 1998. Tailoring GIS software for archaeological applications: an example concerning viewshed analysis. *Journal of Archaeological Science* **25**, 27–38.

Mithen, S. 1996. *The Prehistory of the Mind.* London: Thames & Hudson.

Mithen, S. (ed.). 2000. *Hunter-Gatherer Landscape Archaeology: The Southern Hebrides Mesolithic Project 1988–98. Vols. 1–2.* Cambridge: McDonald Institute Monograph.

Pinker, S. 1997. *How the Mind Works.* New York & London: Norton.

Woodman, P.C. 1989. A review of the Scottish Mesolithic: a plea for normality! *Proceedings of the Society of Antiquaries of Scotland* **119**, 1–32.

Wickham-Jones. C.R. 1994. *Scotland's First Settlers.* London: Batsford/Historic Scotland.

Chapter 14

Conference Discussion Session: Sunday Afternoon, 7 September 1999
Mesolithic Scotland, the Evidence: Part 1

CHAIR: NICK BARTON

[The speakers in this session were: Alan Saville, Caroline Wickham-Jones, and Tony Pollard]

CLIVE BONSALL	Two points, one of which is a joint point between Alan's [Saville] and Tony's [Pollard] papers. Regarding implements for woodworking – experiments conducted in Denmark with replicas of T-shaped antler axes, together with the very limited experiments that were done [in Edinburgh] with Patrick Cave-Browne using replica T-shaped antler axes, show that these things are actually very effective for woodworking, particularly on fresh wood. And in fact some archaeological specimens from Denmark actually have wood embedded in the blade. So I think there is very little doubt that T-shaped antler axes were used in the Late Mesolithic for working wood. And coming to your point, Alan, about the lack of the groove-and-splinter technique in the Scottish Mesolithic, there is absolutely no doubt that the groove-and-splinter technique was used. Careful study of bevel-ended tools shows the traces and the grooving on the edges of these things and, in fact, experiments show that you simply cannot obtain splinters from red deer antler if you don't groove it, you just cannot get the splinters out. You can do it with bone, on a deer cannon-bone you have a natural groove running down the length of it, you can drive a wedge in there, but you'll find that when you actually start working bone it's a lot easier if you groove it first.
PAUL MELLARS	Clive, were you suggesting they were using groove-and-splinter on Oronsay?
CLIVE BONSALL	You have to, to work the antler.
PAUL MELLARS	How did we miss it? I saw absolutely no trace of any kind of groove-and-splinter [working]. Grahame Clark wrote an article on this in, I think, 1956 – 'Notes on the Obanian with special reference to bone- and antler-working' – and the main point of that, having just dug and published Star Carr, was to argue that in the Obanian there's no groove-and-splinter work, so unless he got that very wrong … certainly we never saw any evidence for it. But I always assumed – we haven't done experimental work on this and perhaps Clive [Bonsall] has – but I wondered whether they were using these little *pièces écaillées*, these scaled pieces, as a kind of chisel that could be driven in to split the antler down the side. Now I haven't tried to do it and if Clive says he has tried to do it and it doesn't work I'd be interested.
CLIVE BONSALL	I can assure you if you take a careful look at the margins, the lateral margins, of the better preserved bevel-ended tools from the middens, you will see the traces of the longitudinal striations of grooving. And it is actually very difficult to work antler without grooving it.
SØREN ANDERSEN	I'm completely in agreement with Clive Bonsall about the absence or presence of groove-and-splinter technique. I also think it's impossible to make harpoons of your type without an advanced groove-and-splinter technique. That [can be] stated, I would just say, [whether] you find them or you don't – you are arguing on negative evidence here – so I

think it's a question of [do] you have the right sites? If you look at the whole record we have lots of sites with very few single stray finds, single harpoons, without any trace of groove-and-splinter technique. Then [at] another site, you [may] have many, many pieces reflecting the presence of groove-and-splinter technique. That depends on the type of site. That's one point. Another point that's more a comment – I want here and now to stress a point to erase a widespread misunderstanding [about] the production of dugout canoes. They are never, never, never made by fire! Never! They are always made by chopping and splitting the wood, by use of adzes and axes and by wedges, and by using wedges [that] are just as usefully made of hardwood as they are made of stone and antler or bone. We have never, never so far seen any trace of fire used for Danish Mesolithic, Neolithic, Bronze Age, Iron Age, and Viking boats in Denmark, or southern Scandinavia for that matter. Just forget that!

TONY POLLARD

I will bow to your knowledge there. This was an idea that just came to me without following it through, but how would evidence of fire manifest itself on a vessel that the fire has simply been used to remove the heart [-wood of the trunk] and it has then been totally finished with an axe? That would remove any traces of any burning whatsoever.

SØREN ANDERSEN

That has something to do with … when you are making a boat, you are using a very, very fresh tree. You can't get it to burn, that's one thing, if you really are so lucky to get it to burn you can't control the burning – it will burn very, very irregularly into the trunk. And you know, if you have found a nice tree, let us say the best tree within the territory, why the devil should you destroy it by letting some fire burn completely out of control into it? No, that's impossible!

IAN SHEPHERD

Just to say, I quite take what the Professor is saying, but we have in the audience someone who has actually burnt out a logboat this summer at Archaeolink [Prehistory Park at Oyne, Aberdeenshire] using only fire and an antler pick. Perhaps Linda Hay would like to say something more, but it's perfectly possible and you control the fire by quenching. You don't just sit back and let it rip, it's a perfectly possible technique.

LINDA HAY

I have to say you can burn a boat, I mean we used quite old wood, but it's a long job I have to say and if I had the option of using a couple of 'Stone Age men' with some stone axes or some antler axes that would be a much better way. They have done experiments in Denmark using … a couple of guys who know what they are doing, using the proper sort of tools and they have made excellent boats in a matter of days, whereas I've been labouring over my 'Stone Age' boat. It's taken me weeks, about six weeks I'd say altogether at least. It can be done but it won't be as good as using the stone tools or antler tools. Don't do it! [Editor's note: see Wheeler et al. (2003) for the use of fire-hollowed logs for prehistoric dugout canoes in Florida.]

REG CANDOW

This is a question directed I think to Alan [Saville]. It's actually about an artefact which wasn't flint, but half of a perforated macehead-type tool. Is it accepted that it could be Mesolithic? It was a surface find, after the excavation [at Morton, Fife], but I was always led to believe that the perforated maceheads with the hour-glass perforation were a Mesolithic type of tool and of course they could be going [on] into the Neolithic, a prototype for Neolithic types of club-heads, etc. But is that particular type of tool accepted as being Mesolithic and would you find them perhaps in a Palaeolithic industry or is it just starting off in the Mesolithic? It was just actually a question out of curiosity. Do these types of implements appear in an earlier period?

ALAN SAVILLE

Well, certainly the hour-glass perforated pebbles are a very general type, which can occur in a variety of chronological contexts, although, to be honest, the majority of them occur out of any archaeological context whatsoever. But there are examples of hour-glass perforated pebbles of this kind which have been found elsewhere in Europe from good Mesolithic contexts, and indeed there are decorated examples from eastern Europe. The problem comes when you try and find really concrete examples of these in Mesolithic contexts from the UK ... and I know that Roger Jacobi has done some work on this, I don't know whether he wants to comment on that?

ROGER JACOBI

These perforated pebbles are a real problem chronologically. Certainly over the last few weeks I've encountered three from Mesolithic contexts in England; one is Oakhanger, the site just near Oakhanger site 7 in Hampshire, which is probably Early Mesolithic, one from a site in Kent called Addington, which is both Early and Late Mesolithic probably, and the third excavated from the site at Lower Halstow [Kent] in the 1920s by J.P.T. Burchell. I believe, and I don't know whether Paul [Mellars] has ever traced this one, I've seen a reference by Jeffrey Radley to a perforated pebble as a surface find from one of the Flixton [Yorkshire] sites ... a paper in the 1950s.

PAUL MELLARS

No.

STEVEN MITHEN

Caroline [Wickham-Jones], you are a bit equivocal about the quality of the structural evidence, because you began by saying that you were surprised as to how much you had found in the literature and then you finished by saying that there is just not enough to do any generalizations and we have got to look at it on a site-to-site basis. So I was wondering whether you thought it was sensible at all to bring together structural evidence from not just Scotland but also England, Wales, and Ireland, and whether once you put that all together there might be sufficient to start generalizing about the nature of Mesolithic structures we have in the record?

CAROLINE WICKHAM-JONES

I have to say that I tend to see Scotland as having quite a diversity of Mesolithic population and I tend to shy away from saying, so they are building a round structure in SW Scotland and they are building a round structure in East Anglia – that's not really earth-shattering because they must have been living in some sort of shelter! I would go for looking for more structural evidence and looking at the structural evidence that we have in more detail, perhaps trying to extend away from it as you did at Staosnaig [on Colonsay]. So I would try to – although I think we have got more than I thought we had – I would still try to improve the quality of our record and I think there is quite a lot to be done there. But other people can look at the rest of it; that would be good fun!

NICK BARTON

Is it possible to infer structure using the ring-and-sector method or something like this or is that just too fanciful for you?

CAROLINE WICKHAM-JONES

What's the ring-and-sector method? Is this something that the English know about and we don't?

NICK BARTON

I think we can talk about it over tea!

Conference Discussion Session: Sunday Afternoon, 7 September 1999
Mesolithic Scotland, the Evidence: Part 2

CHAIR: PAUL MELLARS

[The speakers in this session were: Bill Finlayson, Clive Bonsall, and Steven Mithen]

PAUL MELLARS

Thank you very much indeed Steve for that wonderfully evocative and poetic account. As someone who worked for about ten years on Colonsay and Oronsay myself, so much of what Steve said really rang true with me, and in fact it occurred to me that the people who were collecting shellfish – a large part of their experience is waiting for the tide to go out!

UNIDENTIFIED MEMBER OF THE AUDIENCE

A comment for Clive Bonsall. He addressed a lot of questions about the Mesolithic/ Neolithic transition, but he seemed to miss the most important one, which is what the transition was. There's a lot of assumptions about it being the adoption of farming, and you went on at the end to talk about the importance of cereal and the environment. But it seems in the Neolithic in Scotland, which I'm studying, that cereal doesn't really become important until the middle Neolithic and that's being picked up in the sort of $\delta^{13}C$ evidence where it's more about the meat and the animals, and picks up on what Peter Woodman was saying yesterday about cattle. So I was wondering if you could comment?

CLIVE BONSALL

Well, cereal cultivation was certainly going on shortly after 5000 BP, if not before. I would be a little bit more – I'm not naturally cautious as you realize! – but I would be a little bit circumspect about the stable isotope evidence. I think we need more of it and I think if you're going to talk about whether you can tell from stable isotopes whether people are ingesting plant foods or meat, or the proportions in which they were ingesting these things [then] I'd like to see that backed up by other things. I'd like to see some trace element work and so forth before I commit myself on that. So far as I can see, I just look at the broad picture and what I see in the evidence so far is that before 5000 BP, admittedly on a very poor data set, a very limited data set, people have a predominantly marine diet – and that's Mesolithic to me. Then you get this shift when people have a predominantly terrestrial diet, and I don't know what proportion of plant versus animal produce went into that diet, but I'm pretty certain that it was mainly agricultural produce.

KEVIN EDWARDS

A question for Clive [Bonsall] or a series of comments perhaps and questions. I was somewhat disturbed by your paper, but I don't in a sense blame you, I blame us as palynologists, I think. Are we not actually getting across what we have been saying for several decades? Let's look at the elm decline and its predecessors. You seem to be very surprised about finding these declines at an earlier stage, but we wouldn't be surprised in the slightest. You can find them in Britain, you don't need to go to France or to Holland, and if the declines or some of the declines are due to, primarily down to *Scolytus* and Dutch elm-type disease, then that's to be expected. I mean the *Scolytus* didn't suddenly evolve at the elm decline – it's been around for presumably hundreds of thousands of years – but those early reductions in elm may be due to an elm-type disease; or they may not be; they may be climatic or whatever. I didn't actually say that the elm decline was disease, what I said was that there was a decline and that Dutch elm disease is spread by *Scolytus*. That's not the same as saying that the elm decline was caused by *Scolytus*, but in the palynological literature you'll find that most palynologists, if you like, hedge their bets, and they will talk about the fact that you've got a combination of features here, and that indeed that it is at times when you have climate stress, times when you have

264

management stress on trees, that's particularly when *Scolytus* gets into trees; they're under stress, so that's when it can happen. But of course it's not necessarily a sharp divide either; it's not a sudden happening, it's got a standard deviation on that if you like, and of course it is right across that part of NW Europe, it's not just Britain as you have suggested. That's one thing. Another thing I would say is about your cereal-type pollen. As I indicated we've got them in the Lateglacial – *Plantago lanceolata*, of course – we have known that's been around since forever, it's just a question of when it really starts to expand. A problem with the sites that you showed is that you're in a rising sea-level situation, it could be *Glyceria* in particular but you don't show any stratigraphies. We don't know the taphonomy of your sites in terms of what you have presented or in the written paper [Macklin *et al.* 2000; a pre-publication copy was given to all conference speakers, courtesy of Clive Bonsall], so we can't actually judge the veracity of what you are saying. The inferences may be flawed, certainly in terms of what you presented, not necessarily in terms of the data, but it's the data that's not presented so we can't judge it. I think I better stop there.

CLIVE BONSALL

I could say that I have the same problem with your publications actually! So I think we'll call it quits on this one!

PAUL MELLARS

Shall we move on?

ROB YOUNG

Just a point to Clive [Bonsall]. I was kind of disturbed, because I thought there was a real sort of lapse back into serious environmental determinism in what you said and there's a contradiction I think, if I heard it right. You said at the start that the transition was to do with animals and the control of animals – you thought that was fairly central – and then at the end you said it was to do with a climatic change. You don't need to invoke the mechanisms you invoke really if animals become important for that transition. And one thing you have undermined, I think, and you haven't really addressed, is the kind of issues that Bill's [Finlayson] interested in, which is decision-making within the landscape and why people actually choose to make these decisions. It's something you didn't really touch on, so …

CLIVE BONSALL

No, I don't think I can be accused of environmental determinism …

ROB YOUNG

I just did it!

CLIVE BONSALL

You did, yes! But I don't think you're justified to do that! What I said was that climate was a permissive factor and climate is a very critical factor that affects most if not all agricultural systems. And what I also said with regard to the animals is that you've got to keep them and what do you feed them on?

UNIDENTIFIED MEMBER OF THE AUDIENCE

Grass!

CLIVE BONSALL

Exactly! Well, you have got to grow it. It's got to be grown and you have to feed [the animals] over the winter. So, I think you've got to take into account the technology of the time. If it's hunter-gatherers adopting new materials and agricultural practices … they're not seasoned farmers, they've got to get this system going, it's an alien system which they've got to get going, in a very difficult environment. I mean you can't compare this with modern agriculture or even medieval agriculture. Sure, cereals were grown in Scotland in medieval times, it was an extensive lazy-bed system, [but] I'm quite sure that wasn't going on initially. So all I'm saying is …

ROB YOUNG

What makes them do it though, it's the issue of choice, you're not addressing that issue of what makes them do it, the why of it?

CLIVE BONSALL

Well, I did address that. Something comes along that they want – the animals. Something comes along that's extremely desirable, extremely attractive to hunter-gatherers and that's the animals. Something they can own and control ...

PAUL MELLARS

A new opportunity?

CLIVE BONSALL

A new opportunity, which they seize, but there are limits. They want, as I see it, they want the animals, they want the wealth and the power that goes with this, but climate is one of the controlling factors that they have to take account of. They may try to get the system going in northern Europe, something comes along – the area's marginal – something comes along to make that area available for a major expansion of agriculture and that possibly is climate change. I said it was very tentative because I think we don't understand enough about climate change in the Holocene, there's a lot going on in the Holocene in terms of climatic change but it's not going on in the same scale as at the Lateglacial/Holocene transition. It's going on on a smaller scale but there's a lot going on there and I think a lot more research needs to be done into what exactly is going on, how it varied geographically across northern Europe.

PAUL MELLARS

I'd like to move on to any questions for the other speakers. Clearly Clive has raised one of the great critical issues in the whole of prehistory – the origins of agriculture – so it is enormously important. Is there anything else urgently on that or do people have points for the other speakers?

NICK BARTON

A question really for Steve [Mithen], and I guess Bill [Finlayson] as well, but in relation to that rather fantastic feature at Staosnaig [on Colonsay]. I'm not quite sure that I understood how you interpreted [it], but are you saying that it most probably was a hut structure or house structure of some form? Are you saying that they were living on a midden or that it was actually material dumped back in afterwards as a result of the roasting of the hazelnuts and the seeds and so forth?

STEVEN MITHEN

Yes. We think it was originally the base of a house, a hut, but the current fill within it that we excavated was a secondary use of the feature. So after it had been abandoned as a hut and the site had been abandoned, midden debris spread across the site and filled surviving hollows there. Then later truncation of the surface leaves it within those hollows, so I don't think it's an occupation fill of that hut but, as I say, I was surprised when I was at Ohalo II [Israel] in September to see the huts there with an almost identical density of plant debris and chipped stone, looking extremely similar to the Staosnaig feature. And there they can actually demonstrate that that was an occupation fill because around the edge of those they have surviving charcoal, carbonized wood – I suppose small branches – still sticking vertically, showing that this was a brushwood wall around it. So our feelings are that the fill is a secondary fill of this feature that had once been used as a hut.

NICK BARTON

A subsidiary question. Did you find any postholes underneath all of this at the base?

STEVEN MITHEN

No. We don't have any very clear postholes around it, there's a gully that might be related structurally. One doesn't know whether they would survive because it's been built on top of a sand deposit and pebble beach deposit so one doesn't know whether postholes would survive, but we certainly don't have strong features to support some sort of superstructure.

266

PAUL MELLARS	Did you ever make any estimate of the number of hazelnuts possibly represented in the feature? Are we talking about thousands or hundreds of thousands?
STEVEN MITHEN	We made loads of estimates and nobody could possibly agree with each other. I think the final estimate that is going to appear in an article in the *Journal of Archaeological Science* next year some time is something like half a million hazelnuts. It's a vast quantity.
CAROLINE WICKHAM-JONES	This is really just to say first of all how much I enjoyed Steven's [Mithen] paper, I really thought it was great hearing that aspect of interpretation brought out. It's brilliant to hear someone giving it that sort of due influence at the end of the conference. This is a slightly facetious comment, perhaps for Steven or Bill [Finlayson], that you missed out one very important aspect of the Mesolithic experience that I know Bill has experienced, [and have all] those of us who work in the west of Scotland … which is the role of the midge! And I just wondered if this is an environmental factor or what you think about it?
BILL FINLAYSON	Not really one I'd like to talk about or dwell on! We don't really know what the role of the midge would be at that time, I think that's one of the big questions. Johnson and Boswell don't really mention the midge either, so there is always the question as to whether the midges, to the extent that they are there now, are a recent thing. We didn't really have the same problems when we were on Islay – you saw [from the slides] that the weather that we had was usually pretty blustery – so we didn't have the same problems that we had this year on Skye, when it was pretty ghastly … and I'm now leaving the country!
PAUL MELLARS	I'd just make two observations about that from years on Oronsay when we did have terrible problems with midges and if you get a really bad attack of midges it absolutely drives people mad – people who break out in red spots and are almost screaming. There are only two things you could do about it, one was to light a fire of damp bracken somewhere near the site and let the smoke drift across and that would clear it – and one might well ask whether that had anything to do with some of the burning that we see in the Scottish Mesolithic! But of course the other thing is the higher you are the more air movement there is. The worst place you could possibly be is in a trench where the air is still and damp. And I wonder whether one of the reasons why shell middens are where they are and why they were allowed to build up so high, like Caisteal nan Gillean, is precisely because sitting, this is a serious comment, precisely because sitting …
BILL FINLAYSON	Unfortunately all the cave sites are the exact opposite, they're fairly nasty to be in. But it is a cultural thing, it's one of the things [where] we perhaps don't share the experience because certainly most of the people I know on Lewis will try and assure you that midges are a state of mind and that they're not really a problem.
PAUL HUMPHREYS	I'd like to address a question to Dr Mithen. It seems to me that one of the problems we have in perceiving how past peoples might have viewed their world is that we can't escape from what we know. And I wondered how you might imagine, just as an example, how the Mesolithic people might have viewed the aurora borealis for example, where for us because we understand it from our perspective, we can no longer escape that …
STEVEN MITHEN	Well, yes, an interesting question. I think in one sense of course you are right, we can't escape from our own experience, we can't look at the world with past eyes, but I do think there is a profound sense that we can't take relativism too far and that we do share similar perceptual apparatus. When we look at such things as the aurora borealis or any natural phenomenon that we understand through mechanisms of science these days, what is noticeable is that science doesn't take away the mystery of it. We may well know how

267

these things work and why it's like that and aspects about the universe, but we can still look at it and feel awed by it and inspired by it. So I feel that our minds are not dominated by our scientific world, but we do still have those sensations.

PAUL HUMPHREYS

You were using words like awe, but I was thinking of responses perhaps like fear, and that's really what I was getting at.

STEVEN MITHEN

Well we're back to the midges really aren't we! Yes indeed, all these sorts of sensations – I'm sure we share them in a very fundamental way.

PUBLICATIONS REFERRED TO, OR WHICH CONTAIN AMPLIFICATION OF POINTS RAISED, IN THIS DISCUSSION SESSION:

Bonsall, C., Anderson, D.E. and Macklin, M.G. 2002. The Mesolithic–Neolithic transition in western Scotland and its European context. *Documenta Prehistorica* 29, 1–19.

Bonsall, C., Macklin, M.G., Anderson, D.E. and Payton, R.W. 2002. Climate change and the adoption of agriculture in north-west Europe. *European Journal of Archaeology* **5**(1), 9–23.

Boswell, J. 1785. *The Journal of a Tour to the Hebrides with Samuel Johnson LL.D.* London: Charles Dilly.

Candow, R. 1989. *Prehistoric Morton: the Story of the Mesolithic Discoveries at Morton Farm on Tentsmuir in North East Fife.* Dundee: privately published.

Clark, J.G.D. 1956. Notes on the Obanian with special reference to antler- and bone-work. *Proceedings of the Society of Antiquaries of Scotland* **89** (1955–56), 91–106.

Jensen, G. 1996. Effektive økser af kronhjortens tak. *In* M. Meldgaard and M. Rasmussen (eds), *Arkaeologiske Eksperimenter i Lejre*, 40–48. Lejre: Naturens Verden/ Historisk-Arkaeologisk Forsøgscenter.

Macklin, M.G., Bonsall, C., Davies, F.M. and Robinson, M.R. 2000. Human-environment interactions during the Holocene: new data and interpretations from the Oban area. *The Holocene* **10**(1), 109–21.

Mithen, S. (ed.). 2000. *Hunter-Gatherer Landscape Archaeology: the Southern Hebrides Mesolithic Project 1988–98. Vols 1–2.* Cambridge: McDonald Institute Monograph.

Mithen, S. 2003. *After the Ice: a Global Human History, 20,000–5000 BC.* London: Weidenfeld & Nicolson.

Mithen, S., Finlay, N., Carruthers, W., Carter, S. and Ashmore, P. 2001. Plant use in the Mesolithic: evidence from Staosnaig, Isle of Colonsay, Scotland. *Journal of Archaeological Science* **28**, 223–34.

Parker, A.G., Goudie, A.S., Anderson, D.E., Robinson, M.A. and Bonsall, C. 2002. A review of the mid-Holocene elm decline in the British Isles. *Progress in Physical Geography* **26**(1), 1–45.

Stapert, D. 1989. The ring and sector method: intrasite spatial analysis of Stone Age sites, with special reference to Pincevent. *Palaeohistoria* **31**, 1–57.

Wheeler, R.J., Miller, J.J., McGee, R.M., Ruhl, D., Swann, B. and Memory, M. 2003. Archaic period canoes from Newnans Lake, Florida. *American Antiquity* **68**(3), 533–51.

Section 4

BRITAIN AND IRELAND

Chapter 15

The Mesolithic in the Isle of Man: an Island Perspective

SINÉAD B. McCARTAN

The Isle of Man lies in the middle of the Irish Sea and the archaeological evidence from the island indicates influences from both Ireland and Britain alongside insular developments. The island was settled extensively during the Mesolithic period and this evidence is examined and discussed in relation to the island context.

Introduction

The interaction of British and Irish influences and the occasional insular development are the chief features of the prehistory of the island (Clark 1935, 70). The Isle of Man lies in the middle of the Irish Sea and is just over 53km long and 21km wide, with a total area of 588km². It is approximately 60km from the coasts of both Ireland and NW England, some 70km from Anglesey in Wales, and just 20km from the Mull of Galloway in SW Scotland (Fig. 15.1). The island's position in the middle of the Irish Sea, far from being isolating, was pivotal in permitting contact between the island communities and those from neighbouring Ireland and Britain. Evidence of this contact exists from earliest times alongside that for more insular developments and it is the study of the interplay between these two elements that provides an understanding of the role of the Isle of Man in prehistoric times.

The purpose of this paper is to outline, within an environmental context, the history and current state of Mesolithic research on the island. Following a discussion of the characteristics of islands and of the issues raised by island archaeology, the influences of the island environment upon the Mesolithic settlement of the island will be addressed.

Environmental background

The central valley running between Douglas and Peel separates the northern and southern uplands which dominate the Isle of Man (Dackombe & McCarroll 1990, 10; Dackombe & Thomas 1985, 1) (Fig. 15.2). The coastal plateaux lie to the east and, to a lesser extent, to the west of the uplands. The east coast plateau merges into the plain of Malew and, in the extreme south of the island, the Mull Hill and the Calf of Man overlook this low-lying plain. At the opposite end of the island the northern uplands end abruptly to give way to the northern plain which is composed entirely of glacial drift, and is broken at the extreme northern end by the Bride Hills.

A radiocarbon date of 15,150 ± 350 BP (Birm-754) from a kettle hole on the Jurby Ridge on the west of the island indicates that the island, or at least that area, was free of ice by c.15,000 years ago (McCarroll *et al.* 1990, 55). The Lateglacial sea-level is a point of some controversy and opinion radically differs over the existence of landbridges (Boulton 1990; Eyles & McCabe 1989; Lambeck 1991; Wingfield 1995). Wingfield's proposed models for landbridges indicate that one probably existed between the Isle of Man and NW England/north Wales c.10,000 years ago and another from the island to Ireland by c.9700 BP. By 9500 years ago the land-link with Ireland was broken and it is not until c.9000 BP that the link with Britain was finally severed (Wingfield 1995, 233). This severance date confirms previous speculations by Allen (1978, 13; 1984, 10).

Very little information is available on the range and dating of the Holocene vertebrate fauna on the island. Both the Isle of Man and Ireland have a very restricted range of Postglacial fauna owing primarily to early isolation and island status. Recent research (Woodman *et al.* 1997) in Ireland, however, has provided a broad chronology for its Pleistocene and Holocene faunal record and this information can perhaps provide some insight into the Manx record. The largest land mammals available for exploitation by British Mesolithic hunter-gatherers include aurochs (*Bos primigenius*), brown bear (*Ursus arctos*), red deer (*Cervus elaphus*), wild pig (*Sus scrofa*), elk (*Alces alces*), and roe deer (*Capreolus capreolus*). At present none of these animals have been found to be contemporary with Manx Mesolithic assemblages. Aurochs, elk, and roe deer are unknown in Ireland and it is uncertain as to whether they ever

FIGURE 15.1
Location map of the Isle of Man in the British Isles.

reached the Isle of Man. The discovery of a possible elk antler from near Ballaugh in the north-west of the island has been dismissed and the only archaeological record for roe deer is from Chapel Hill, Balladoole (McCarroll *et al.* 1990, 76). Brown bear was present in Ireland during the Mesolithic, but has not been found in association with cultural material (McCormick 1999, 359; Woodman *et al.* 1997, 138), and it may also have colonized the Isle of Man.

It has long been assumed that red deer was the main large mammal exploited during the Mesolithic period in Britain and Ireland. This proposition, however, has now been seriously questioned in the Irish context (Woodman *et al.* 1997, 152) where red deer is not known to occur between *c.*12,000 and 4000 BP. McCormick (1999, 360)

argues that red deer was deliberately reintroduced into Ireland during the Neolithic, and van Wijngaarden-Bakker (1989, 132) suggests that the Irish Mesolithic hunter-gatherers may have exploited seals in place of red deer, as their skins are similar in size and texture. This might also have been the situation in the Isle of Man, although if a landbridge to NW England and north Wales existed until *c.*9000 BP it is possible that red deer were able to colonize the island. Jawbones have been dredged from the Lhen Trench at the Guilcaugh, Isle of Man (McCarroll *et al.* 1990, 76), but their context is uncertain and the material has not been dated.

In contrast to the situation in Britain, wild pig appears to have been the primary mammal exploited in Ireland during the Mesolithic and it accounts for 98 per cent

272

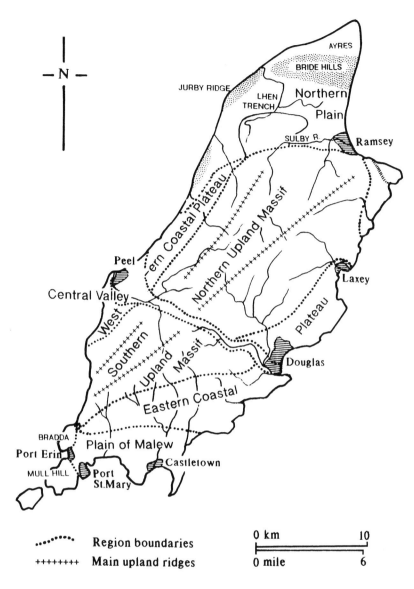

FIGURE 15.2
The Manx landscape divided into eight physiographic regions
(after Dackombe & McCarroll 1990).

of faunal remains from the sites of Mount Sandel, Co. Londonderry, and Lough Boora, Co. Offaly (van Wijngaarden-Bakker 1989, 127). By analogy it might be assumed that wild boar was an important element in the Manx hunter-gatherer's subsistence strategies and indeed the tusk of a wild boar is known from the shell midden at Port St Mary, Isle of Man (Woodman 1987, 20). Wild cat (*Felis silvestris*) has been found at Lough Boora, Co. Offaly (van Wijngaarden-Bakker 1989, 127) and its bones have also been found at Port St Mary. Garrad (1978, 68) claims that the latter were from the Mesolithic midden, although this is not entirely apparent from the original

excavation report (Swinnerton 1889), and the midden appears to have been more disturbed than previously realized. Finally, migratory fish undoubtedly colonized the Isle of Man's river systems during the Postglacial period. In the absence, therefore, of dated evidence the range of Holocene fauna in the Isle of Man is uncertain, but it may be assumed that it was no less than that of Ireland, and indeed possibly more extensive.

The study of the vegetational history for the early Postglacial period depends on a limited number of pollen cores, the most detailed and dated information coming from those taken at Lough Cranstal in the north

273

of the island. A date of 7825±120 BP (Hv-5226) from Lough Cranstal marks the approximate beginning of the marine transgression which ended at *c*.7370±110 BP (Hv-5225) when it is clear from the pollen evidence that a well-developed mixed oak woodland comprising alder (*Alnus*), elm (*Ulmus*), oak (*Quercus*), and hazel (*Corylus*) was present (McCarroll *et al.* 1990, 67; Tooley 1978, 22). Lime (*Tilia*) is absent from the record, with the exception of a couple of grains before and after the elm decline, and this sparse evidence can be paralleled in Ireland.

Past and present research

Swinnerton's (1889; 1892) papers on the investigations at the sites of Port St. Mary and Glen Wyllin marked the initial work on the Manx Mesolithic period, although at the time the chronological position of the sites was not fully appreciated. Clark's (1935) seminal paper – 'The Prehistory of the Isle of Man' – represented the first collation and interpretation of the evidence for the

Mesolithic settlement of the island. Clark (1935, 71–5) identified two Mesolithic stone tool traditions. The first he called 'Tardenoisian', which he believed marked the earliest human activity on the island, with eleven microlith findspots distributed in the extreme south, the west, and north-west (Figs 15.3 & 15.4).

Clark's (1935, 74) second Mesolithic stone tool tradition he called the 'Bann River Culture', which featured butt-trimmed and tanged forms, and was widespread across the island with some 21 findspots occurring in the east and further north in Ayre, sometimes overlapping in the areas where the 'Tardenoisian' was also found (Figs 15.5 & 15.6). Clark was the first to draw attention to the similarity of this group of material to that found in Northern Ireland, particularly along the River Bann. This Manx material was sometimes also associated with artefacts of the Neolithic period, such as leaf-shaped arrowheads, and this prompted Clark (1935, 75) to claim that '... the Bann culture, though Mesolithic in origin, seems to have flourished at a later date'.

Woodman reappraised the evidence for the Manx Mesolithic period in 1978 and suggested that two distinct microlith industries could be identified. The first, and probably the earliest, was best represented at Port St Mary and was characterized by 'a large number of elongated scalene triangles and rather broad hollow-based points' (Woodman 1978a, 126); the second, and somewhat later, industry was most clearly defined by the assemblages from Glen Wyllin/Ballacregga, which have 'numerous different types of geometric microliths including small scalene triangles, isosceles triangles and crescents and small needle points' (Woodman 1978a, 126). Woodman (1978a, 127) viewed the hollow-based point as an insular development, perhaps indicative of population continuity on the island during the Mesolithic period and he concluded that its resemblance to the British Horsham point was simply fortuitous, particularly since other elements of the so-called Horsham culture were absent.

Woodman (1978a, 127–34) renamed Clark's 'Bann River Culture' the 'Heavy-Bladed Industry', noting a superficial similarity between the Manx and Irish butt-trimmed and tanged forms, and he suggested that the similarity with the Irish material was primarily in the knapping technique, in particular the use of the so-called 'Larnian core'. However, major differences between the Irish and Manx assemblages were also noted (Woodman 1978a, 133–4). For example, tanged forms are more common on the Isle of Man than Ireland and two types occur: a very narrow form and a rather more splayed form (probably an insular development). Another difference noted by Woodman is that among the Irish assemblages there is a range of other artefacts including bar-forms,

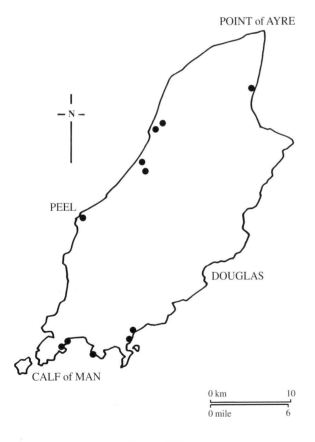

POINT of AYRE

– N –

PEEL

DOUGLAS

0 km   10

0 mile   6

CALF of MAN

FIGURE 15.3
Distribution of Clark's 'Tardenoisian' sites (after Clark 1935).

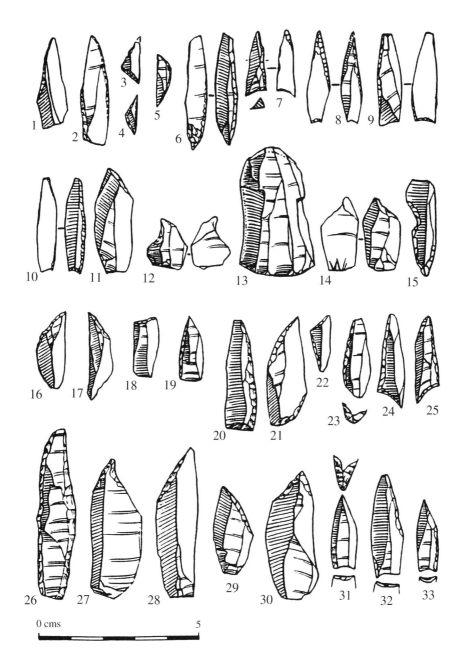

FIGURE 15.4
'Tardenoisian' flints: 1–15 Glen Wyllin; 16–33 Port St. Mary (after Clark 1935).

points, and polished axeheads, which do not seem to occur in the Manx assemblages. Woodman (1978a, 133) concluded that, despite these differences, the origins for the Manx Mesolithic culture must lie within the later phases of the Mesolithic occupation of Ireland.

Excavations by Woodman (1987) in 1982–3 at Cass ny Hawin, Malew, provided the first dates for a Manx Mesolithic presence, with a series ranging between 7695±95 BP (UB-2660) and 7350±95 BP (UB-2593)

for a microlithic industry. Woodman (1987, 20) viewed Cass ny Hawin as bridging the gap between the earlier and later microlithic industries. In 1982 an Early Mesolithic pit was discovered during excavations at the Half Moon Battery, Peel Castle, although unfortunately no radiocarbon date was obtained. This material was ascribed by Smart (1986, 6) to the 'Glen Wyllin/ Ballacregga complex' since it comprised primarily geometric forms. An excavation at the site of Rhendhoo

275

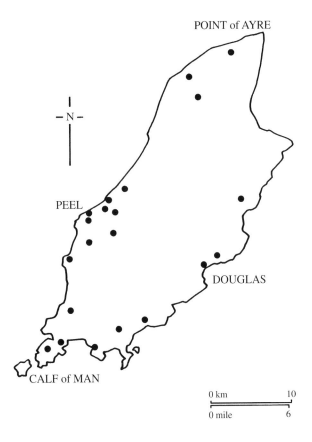

POINT of AYRE

– N –

PEEL

DOUGLAS

CALF of MAN

```
0 km          10
0 mile         6
```

FIGURE 15.5
Distribution of Clark's 'Bann River Culture'
(after Clark 1935).

in the Lhen Trench in 1989 produced three dates in association with 'Heavy-Bladed' material including two butt-trimmed flakes (McCartan 1994). These dates indicate sporadic activity at the site between 6100 ± 50 BP (BM-2694) and 5170 ± 50 BP (BM-2695). Similar butt-trimmed flakes from Zone 3 at Newferry, Co. Antrim, are associated with dates of 5705 ± 90 BP (UB-630) and 5415 ± 90 BP (UB-489) (Woodman 1977, 177–8).

The Rhendhoo site indicates the contemporaneous use of such tools in both Ireland and the Isle of Man, but also that they were used at a later date on the island. The radiocarbon dates from Cass ny Hawin confirm that the microlithic industries date to the Early Mesolithic and those from Rhendhoo confirm the later chronological position of the 'Heavy-Bladed' or 'macrolithic' industry. This change from an Early Mesolithic microlithic to Late Mesolithic macrolithic industry is paralleled in Ireland (Woodman 1978b). In the late 1980s two AMS dates on shells from the Port St Mary site were obtained. The first on shells from within one of the cists produced a date of 2870 ± 80 BP (OxA-2480) and a second on shells from the red earth below the cists produced a date of

4970 ± 80 BP (OxA-2481) (Chiverrell *et al.* 1999). This latter date was disappointing since it had been hoped to date the microlithic industry from the site, but as mentioned previously the midden appears to have been more contaminated than formerly thought and the date seems to confirm this view.

By the late 1980s a vast collection of unidentified archaeological material was accumulating in the Manx Museum stores through the work of a number of active field-walkers on the Island. The three excavated assemblages together with the field collections provided a new database of material for analysis and since no detailed survey had been undertaken since 1978, it seemed opportune to embark on a reassessment of the evidence for the Manx Mesolithic period (McCartan 1990; 1994; 1999; 2003).

Prior to the reassessment, Manx lithic industries were known only in a very broad and general manner. While 'type fossils' such as microliths and 'Bann flakes' were easily identifiable, the associated lithic material was poorly understood, particularly for the Neolithic and Bronze Age industries. The lack of independently dated lithic material from excavations compounded the problem and inadvertently made the surface-collected material the primary quantitative source of information. A high percentage of material can be located to an individual field. Each field, sometimes referred to as a 'plot', within a Manx parish has a number and the vast majority of the recent surface collections can be securely linked to a field/plot number. As a matter of convenience the field is taken as a defined unit or site. It is recognized, of course, that where material is recovered from two or more adjoining fields, this may in fact be a single site. The following paragraphs present some of the conclusions of this reassessment.

The reassessment has revealed a total of 81 findspots for Early Mesolithic material – roughly one site per 6km². Of these 81 sites, 61 (75 per cent) can be provenanced to a field or plot. In general, the distribution map has not changed dramatically from that noted by Clark (1935), with the most obvious exceptions being the new sites around the Lhen Trench, the Sulby River, and those on the east coast at Ballavarkish, *c.*4km north of Ramsey, Cronk y Chule near Laxey, and Finch Hill in Douglas. The concentration of findspots along the Lhen valley undoubtedly reflects the home base of one of the field-walkers and the intensity with which he has examined the ploughed fields. In the broadest sense the Early Mesolithic material can be divided into two groups: findspots where microliths are present and those where they are absent. Some 50 findspots, of which 37 are provenanced, have microliths (sometimes a single microlith). Another 31, 24 of which

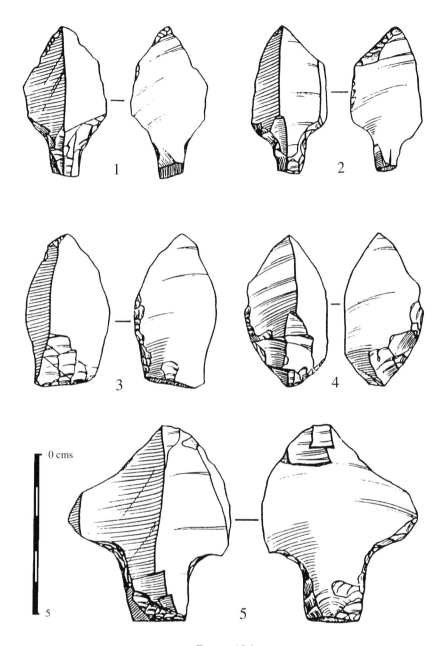

FIGURE 15.6
'Bann River Culture' flints: 1, 3 and 4 Kirkill, Rushen; 2 Cronk y Chule, Lonan; 5 Glencrutchery, Douglas (after Clark 1935).

can be provenanced, are represented solely by knapping debris (Fig. 15.7). This difference could be interpreted as reflecting distinct functions, as knapping debris by itself is often viewed simply as evidence of stone-tool manufacture, while the presence of finished tools can be interpreted in a number of ways including evidence of domestic activity or task-specific sites. The two groups of sites overlap in their distribution and it is possible that in some instances both types may represent an extension to the one site.

In terms of the economic basis and the subsistence strategies, and particularly given the size of the Isle of Man, the distributional evidence would seem to suggest that there may have been no need for groups to move around the Island. The coastal lowlands may have supported base camps for most of the year with small groups moving to other areas, on a temporary basis, to exploit specific resources. This might have maximized the utilization of available food resources and, with the use of storage, there would have been a reduced risk of

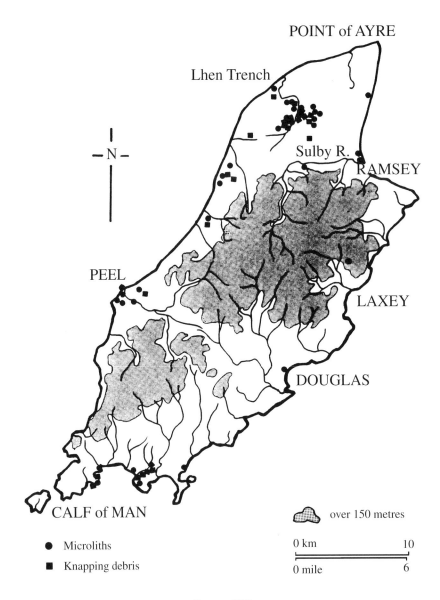

POINT of AYRE

Lhen Trench

Sulby R.

RAMSEY

– N –

PEEL

LAXEY

DOUGLAS

CALF of MAN

over 150 metres

● Microliths

■ Knapping debris

0 km   10

0 mile   6

FIGURE 15.7
The current distribution of Early Mesolithic sites.

food shortages over the winter months. There is meagre evidence for the use of the uplands and although the opportunities for making discoveries in such areas are much more limited compared to lowland areas, this is not to say that such areas were not exploited or settled.

Variation in microlith types does occur between localities. It is beyond the scope of this paper, however, to discuss in detail the extent of variation and its interpretation, but it has been dealt with provisionally in another paper (McCartan 1999).

There are now approximately 325 findspots show-ing evidence of the Late Mesolithic 'Heavy-Bladed' material.

Of these, 168 are represented solely by knapping debris and these assemblages contain enough diagnostic Late Mesolithic elements to distinguish them from the Neolithic and Bronze Age traditions. Some 157 of the 325 sites are represented by either tanged points, butt-trimmed flakes, or both types of artefacts. Again this difference between findspots with and without the finished tool forms may reflect function, but similar to the earlier material, the distribution of both types of sites overlaps.

Of the 157 sites, 86 (55 per cent) are provenanced. Seventy-five sites have tanged points only, 49 sites have butt-trimmed forms only, and 33 sites have both

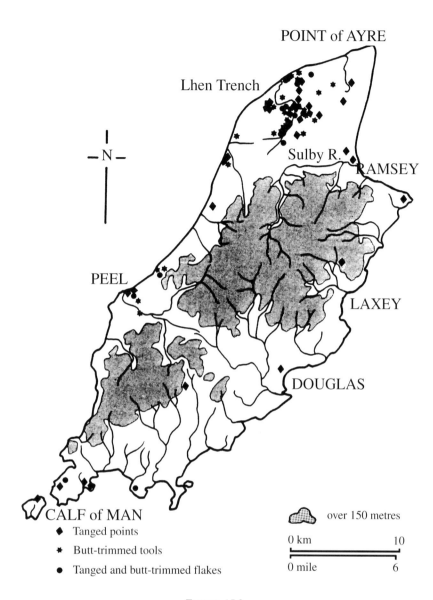

POINT of AYRE

Lhen Trench

Sulby R.

RAMSEY

PEEL

LAXEY

DOUGLAS

CALF of MAN

◆ Tanged points

✳ Butt-trimmed tools

● Tanged and butt-trimmed flakes

over 150 metres

0 km   10

0 mile   6

FIGURE 15.8
The current distribution of Late Mesolithic sites with tanged and butt-trimmed tools.

types (Fig. 15.8). This variation may reflect either function or chronology. The distribution differs from Clark's 'Bann River Culture' with a greater density of finds now along the NW coast and in particular the Lhen Trench.

Activity still seems to be restricted to the coastal lowlands. The east coast, particularly the Malew Plain, is generally lacking sites and this seems unusual, but it may simply reflect a lack of fieldwork in the area. The uplands also still show sparse activity, but a date from a pollen core from Bienn-y-Phott in the northern uplands possibly indicates forest clearance at 6240±60 BP (Beta-81358) (Tomlinson 1997).

The island context

Within the last forty years, research using islands as the unit of study has steadily increased. MacArthur and Wilson (1967, 3) observed that '... the island is the first unit that the mind can pick out and begin to comprehend'. An island has clearly defined boundaries, unlike a regional mainland landscape, and can have unique properties and characteristics. Fosberg (1963a, 5) suggested that:

> Some of the more significant characteristics of the island ecosystem are relative isolation; limitation in size (space resource); limitation in, or even absence of certain other

279

resources; limitation in organic diversity; reduced inter-species competition; protection from outside competition and consequent preservation of archaic, bizarre, or possibly ill-adapted forms; tendency towards climatic equability; extreme vulnerability, or tendency toward great instability when isolation is broken down; and tendency toward rapid increase in entropy when change has set in.

While MacArthur and Wilson (1967), as bio-geographers, were principally concerned with plants and animals, others have focused on 'man's place in the island ecosystem' (Fosberg 1963b). Evans (1973; 1977) suggested that islands could be viewed as 'laboratories for the study of culture process' and his work assessed the levels of interaction between some of the Mediterranean islands, and between the islands and the mainland, rather than studying their development in isolation. Research has probably been most prolific in the Pacific region (Kirch 1986; Terrell 1986), while within the European context it has been pursued in particular by Cherry (1981) and by Renfrew and Wagstaff (1986) in the Mediterranean, and by Patton (1995) in the Channel Islands.

The Isle of Man offers an opportunity to consider some of the issues pertinent to island archaeology and to assess the influence that the island environment may have had on the archaeology and, in this case, the impact on the Mesolithic settlement of the Isle of Man. Before considering some of the general island characteristics suggested by Fosberg (1963a, 5), in a Manx context there are certain fundamental issues that must be addressed such as when, how, and from where the first settlers arrived. The earliest dates for the Manx Mesolithic period centre on 7600 BP, and these dates are associated with an assemblage which includes unique 'insular' forms. It may be inferred, therefore, that initial colonization took place earlier, perhaps around 8000 BP. This date is still 1000 years later than the severance date suggested by Wingfield (1995), which implies that colonization took place by boat. Evidence for Mesolithic watercraft technology from Ireland and Britain is limited. The wooden paddle from Star Carr (Clark 1954, 23) is often quoted, but in 1995 a fragmentary boat of oak exhibiting axe marks was found on the western shore of Lough Neagh in Brookend townland, Co. Tyrone (Fry 2000, 116), and has been dated to $6449 \pm 51/6465 \pm 50$ BP (UB-4066). It has been suggested that logboats or dugout canoes were used along the river systems and for navigating the coastline, and that skin boats performed more effectively and safely in open sea conditions (Fry 1995, 14), although the sea-worthiness of some logboats has now been proposed (Robinson et al. 1999).

The question of the origins of the Manx Mesolithic is still unclear. Clark (1935, 75) was confident that it was possible to 'distinguish influences from the east and from the west'. There is little doubt that the origins of Manx Late Mesolithic culture are to be found in Ireland, but the earliest settlers might have arrived from north Wales, NW England, SW Scotland, or from even further field. Whether by accident or design, curiosity may have been a major motivating factor in the colonization of the island as availability of limited island-based food resources alone was unlikely to have been the main purpose. Woodman (1981, 96) has suggested that absolute distance may have been less important than perceived distance, and this is particularly relevant since the Isle of Man can be clearly seen from parts of Ireland and Wales, and especially from NW England and SW Scotland.

Only when the settlers had been ensconced for some time would the full impact of living on a small island have been fully realized. One of the basic distinctive characteristics of islands suggested by Fosberg (1963a, 5) is 'relative isolation'. Given that watercraft technology was available to the initial colonizers it may be assumed that it remained an important element in the Mesolithic lifestyle. The degree of isolation was therefore dependent on the needs and requirements of the island population, and possibly also of that of the groups in neighbouring mainland areas. The term 'insular developments' has been used in relation to the Manx hollow-based microliths and some of the later tanged points. Insularity can be a factor of isolation, and therefore if isolation was not complete these 'insular developments' might instead be viewed as either a local adaptation of the tool-kit to island resources, evidence of contact with groups elsewhere, or even as a signature of social identity in a region which may have been more susceptible than most to outside influences. Of particular interest is the difference between the Manx and Irish Late Mesolithic assemblages. Vayda and Rappaport (1963, 134–5) studying the evidence from some of the Pacific islands suggest that if a small group of people migrate to an isolated place they may be unable 'to reproduce in full the culture of the population from which they derived, then the culture in the new place will be immediately different from the culture in the homeland'. This might possibly explain why the Manx Later Mesolithic is only partly similar to the Irish Later Mesolithic.

Two characteristics of islands – scarcity of resources and limitation in organic diversity – are probably a factor of both size limitation and isolation (Murdock 1963, 146). As mentioned previously, the Isle of Man probably had a more restricted range of Holocene fauna compared to Britain and it also has fewer ecological habitats (Allen 1978, 9; Garrad 1972, 24). On the other hand the island, by its very nature, offers both the resources of terrestrial and marine environments for exploitation. A maritime economy might have provided the main food resources for the hunter-gatherers, which were supplemented by terrestrial products, particularly during leaner, colder periods of the year. The greatest danger in such an island economy was the over-exploitation of resources, as a hunter-gatherer economy can have just as devastating an impact on limited resources as an agricultural one. The over-hunting of land and sea mammals, over-fishing of the river systems, and even the intensive collection of birds' eggs could have had devastating consequences. The permanence of hunter-gatherers on the island would have been dependent not only on the availability of food resources, but also on their ability to manage, rather than over-exploit, these resources. Another factor which may also have required management was population level and there is evidence among more recent island populations that levels can be controlled when required (Hayden 1972; Vayda & Rappaport 1963, 137–9).

Long-term sustainability and viability of the population may also have been dependent on access to mating networks (Woodman 1981, 100–1). If colonization of the island was the result of successive waves of small groups, then a feasible breeding population may have been in place. Without such renewals, links on a social level with hunter-gatherer groups elsewhere would have been necessary to sustain a healthy on-island population. The maintenance of a permanent population on the island may have been dictated by social and economic issues. Patton (1995, 6) suggests that unlike Neolithic communities on the continental mainland, those living on the Channel Islands had direct access to the sea which may have been an important mechanism in maintaining an island population.

Two other characteristics of islands are the preservation of traits and the tendency towards vulnerability and instability when isolation is broken down. If the Isle of Man was isolated from outside influences it may have been possible for a Mesolithic way of life to continue unhindered after its abandonment elsewhere. Indeed, the latest dates from Rhendhoo (McCartan 1994, 115) overlap with some of the earliest known for Neolithic food production in Ireland and Britain (Williams 1989). However, the Isle of Man may never have functioned within a totally closed system. There may well have been periods when there was less contact, which was only re-established when dictated by necessity. Although, once isolation was broken down the impact of changes was probably quite profound and new ideas and equipment may have been adopted and spread quite quickly (Fosberg 1963a, 5). It is possible therefore that once the Late Mesolithic 'macrolithic' technology was introduced (either by new settlers or through the diffusion of ideas) that it spread and became established fairly rapidly and

certainly the evidence indicates a greater number of Late Mesolithic sites, which are distributed extensively across the island.

The absence of a definitive early Neolithic might also be explained by a period of less contact. Once contact was re-established, however, and for whatever reasons, then changes occurred quite rapidly with the replacement of a hunting-gathering lifestyle with an agricultural one. Burrow (1997, 11) has stated that the middle Neolithic period amply compensates for the paucity of early Neolithic evidence and that 'from the start of the 4th millennium BC onwards … it appears that the Isle of Man was well integrated into a network of Neolithic cultural interaction within the Irish Sea province'.

Conclusions

There is evidence for the extensive settlement of the Isle of Man during the Mesolithic period, with initial colonization sometime before 7600 BP and the continuation of a Mesolithic way of life to c.5000 BP. The island probably sustained a permanent hunter-gatherer population, which was primarily dependent on a maritime economy, supplemented by terrestrial resources. In order to avoid the over-exploitation of food supplies some form of regulation, and possibly management, would have been required. Assuming accessibility to watercraft technology, isolation from Ireland and Britain may not have been complete, and economic and social needs may have dictated contact with these adjacent lands. Patton (1995) used a socio-geographic approach rather than a bio-geographic one in order to understand the development of Neolithic communities in the Channel Islands. The evidence led him to suggest that control of access to boats and the knowledge of how to sail them, as well as control of access by other Channel Island communities to regional interaction networks, may have contributed to the development of greater social differentiation in island communities when compared to mainland societies. The evidence also suggests that the Isle of Man did not function within a closed system and understanding the nature of the contacts and influences between island and mainland hunter-gatherer groups may help elucidate the role of the island within the Irish Sea province.

Note

Further aspects of the Manx Mesolithic, especially its environmental background, are discussed in McCartan (2003).

Acknowledgements

I would like to thank the Trustees of the National Museums and Galleries of Northern Ireland. Richard Warner, Ulster Museum, commented on drafts of this paper and Deirdre Crone produced the illustrations. Thanks are also due to Peter Woodman.

References

Allen, D.E. 1978. The present-day fauna and flora of Man as indicators of the date of the Flandrian severance. *In* P. Davey (ed.), *Man and Environment in the Isle of Man*, 9–13. Oxford: British Archaeological Reports (British Series **54**(i)).

Allen, D.E. 1984. *Flora of the Isle of Man*. Douglas: Manx Museum and National Trust.

Boulton, G.S. 1990. Sedimentation and sea level changes during glacial cycles and their control on glacimarine facies architecture. *In* J.A. Dowdeswell and J.D. Scourse (eds), *Glacimarine Environments: Processes and Sediments*, 15–52. London: Geological Society (Special Publications **53**).

Burrow, S. 1997. *The Neolithic Culture of the Isle of Man*. Oxford: British Archaeological Reports (British Series **263**).

Cherry, J.F. 1981. Pattern and process in the earliest colonisation of the Mediterranean islands. *Proceedings of the Prehistoric Society* **47**, 41–68.

Chiverrell, R.C., Davey, P.J., Gowlett, J.A.J. and Woodcock, J.J. 1999. Radiocarbon dates for the Isle of Man. *In* P.J. Davey (ed.), *Recent Archaeological Research on the Isle of Man*, 321–36. Oxford: British Archaeological Reports (British Series **278**).

Clark, G. 1935. The Prehistory of the Isle of Man. *Proceedings of the Prehistoric Society* **1**, 70–92.

Clark, J.G.D. 1954. *Excavations at Star Carr*. Cambridge: Cambridge University Press.

Dackombe, R. and McCarroll, D. 1990. The Manx landscape. *In* V. Robinson and D. McCarroll (eds), *The Isle of Man: Celebrating a Sense of Place*, 10–17. Liverpool: Liverpool University Press.

Dackombe, R.V. and Thomas, G.S.P. 1985 *Field Guide to the Quaternary of the Isle of Man*. Cambridge: Quaternary Research Association.

Evans, J.D. 1973. Islands as laboratories for the study of culture process. *In* C. Renfrew (ed.), *The Explanation of Culture Change*, 517–20. London: Duckworth.

Evans, J.D. 1977. Island archaeology in the Mediterranean: problems and opportunities. *World Archaeology* **9**, 12–26.

Eyles, N. and McCabe, A.M. 1989. The Late Devensian (<22,000 BP) Irish Sea Basin: the stratigraphic record of a collapsed ice-sheet margin. *Quaternary Science Reviews* **8**, 307–51.

Fosberg, F.R. 1963a. The island ecosystem. *In* F.R. Fosberg (ed.), *Man's Place in the Island Ecosystem*, 1–6. Hawaii: Bishop Museum Press.

Fosberg, F.R. (ed.). 1963b. *Man's Place in the Island Ecosystem*. Hawaii: Bishop Museum Press.

Fry, M.F. 1995. Communicating by logboat: past necessity and present opportunity in the North of Ireland. *Irish Studies Review* **12**, 11–16.

Fry, M.F. 2000. *Coití: Logboats from Northern Ireland*. Belfast: Department of Environment (Northern Ireland Archaeological Monograph **4**).

Garrad, L.S. 1972. *The Naturalist in the Isle of Man*. Newton Abbot: David & Charles.

Garrad, L.S. 1978. Evidence for the history of the vertebrate fauna of the Isle of Man. *In* P. Davey (ed.), *Man and Environment in the Isle of Man*, 61–75. Oxford: British Archaeological Reports (British Series **54**(i)).

Hayden, B. 1972. Population control among hunter/gatherers. *World Archaeology* **4**(2), 205–21.

Kirch, P.V. 1986. *Island Societies: Archaeological Approaches to Evolution and Transformation*. Cambridge: Cambridge University Press.

Lambeck, K. 1991. Glacial rebound and sea-level change in the British Isles. *Terra Nova* **3**, 379–89.

MacArthur, R.J. and Wilson, E.O. 1967. *The Theory of Island Biogeography*. Princeton: Princeton University Press.

McCarroll, D., Garrad, L. and Dackombe, R. 1990. Lateglacial and Postglacial environmental history. *In* V. Robinson and D. McCarroll (eds), *The Isle of Man: Celebrating a Sense of Place*, 55–76. Liverpool: Liverpool University Press.

McCartan, S.B. 1990. The Early Prehistoric colonisation of the Isle of Man: Mesolithic hunter-gatherers. *Proceedings of the Isle of Man Natural History and Antiquarian Society* **9**(4), 517–34.

McCartan, S. B. 1994. A Later Mesolithic site at Rhendhoo, Jurby, Isle of Man. *Proceedings of the Isle of Man Natural History and Antiquarian Society* **10**(2), 87–117.

McCartan, S.B. 1999. The Manx Early Mesolithic: a story in stone. *In* P.J. Davey (ed.), *Recent Archaeological Research on the Isle of Man*, 5–11. Oxford: British Archaeological Reports (British Series **278**).

McCartan, S.B. 2003. Mesolithic hunter-gatherers in the Isle of Man: adaptations to an island environment? *In* L. Larsson, H. Kindgen, K. Knutsson, D. Loeffler and A. Åkerlund (eds), *Mesolithic on the Move: Papers Presented at the Sixth International Conference on the Mesolithic in Europe, Stockholm 2000*, 331–9. Oxford: Oxbow Books.

McCormick, F. 1999. Early evidence for wild animals in Ireland. *In* N. Benecke (ed.), *The Holocene History of the European Vertebrate Fauna: Modern Aspects of Research*, 355–71. Archäologie in Eurasien, Band **6**. Rahden/Westf: Verlag Marie Leidorf GmbH.

Murdock, G.P. 1963. Human influences on the ecosystems of high islands of the tropical Pacific. *In* F.R. Fosberg (ed.), *Man's Place in the Island Ecosystem*, 145–52. Hawaii: Bishop Museum Press.

Patton, M. 1995. *Neolithic Communities of the Channel Islands.* Oxford: British Archaeology Reports (British Series **240**).

Renfrew, C. and Wagstaff, M. 1982. *An Island Polity: the Archaeology of Exploitation in Melos.* Cambridge: Cambridge University Press.

Robinson, M.E., Shimwell, D.W. and Cribbin, G. 1999. Reassessing the logboat from Lurgan Townland, Co. Galway, Ireland. *Antiquity* **73**, 903–8.

Smart, R. 1986. Flint Report. *In* R.H. White (ed.), *The Peel Castle Excavation: the Half Moon Battery*, 6–7. Douglas: St Patrick's Isle (IOM) Archaeological Trust.

Swinnerton, F. 1889. The early Neolithic cists and refuse heap at Port St. Mary. *Yn Liaor Manninagh* **1**(1), 241–4.

Swinnerton, F. 1892. Pre-Aryan remains at Glen Wyllin, Isle of Man. *Yn Liaor Manninagh* **1**(2), 262–4.

Terrell, J. 1986. *Prehistory in the Pacific Islands.* Cambridge: Cambridge University Press.

Tomlinson, P. 1997. The Manx hill-land: the palaeoenvironmental resource. In *Proceedings of the Man Hill-Land Seminar*, 57–64. Douglas: Manx Nature Conservation Trust.

Tooley, M.J. 1978. Flandrian sea-level changes and vegetational history of the Isle of Man: a review. *In* P. Davey (ed.), *Man and Environment in the Isle of Man*, 15–24. Oxford: British Archaeological Reports (British Series **54**(i)).

van Wijngaarden-Bakker, L.H. 1989. Faunal Remains and the Irish Mesolithic. *In* C. Bonsall (ed.), *The Mesolithic in Europe*, 125–33. Edinburgh: John Donald.

Vayda, A.P. and Rappaport, R.A. 1963. Island cultures. *In* F.R. Fosberg (ed.), *Man's Place in the Island Ecosystem*, 133–42. Hawaii: Bishop Museum Press.

Williams, E. 1989. Dating the introduction of food production into Britain and Ireland. *Antiquity* **63**, 510–21.

Wingfield, R.T.R. 1995. A model of sea-levels in the Irish and Celtic seas during the end-Pleistocene to Holocene transition. *In* R.C. Preece (ed.), *Island Britain: a Quaternary perspective*, 209–42. London: The Geological Society.

Woodman, P.C. 1977. Recent excavations at Newferry, Co. Antrim. *Proceedings of the Prehistoric Society* **43**, 155–99.

Woodman, P. 1978a. A re-appraisal of the Manx Mesolithic. *In* P. Davey (ed.), *Man and Environment in the Isle of Man*, 119–39. Oxford: British Archaeological Reports (British Series **54**(i)).

Woodman, P.C. 1978b. *The Mesolithic in Ireland: Hunter-Gatherers in an Insular Environment.* Oxford: British Archaeological Reports (British Series **58**).

Woodman, P.C. 1981. The post-glacial colonisation of Ireland: the human factors. *In* D. Ó Corráin (ed.), *Irish Antiquity*, 93–110. Cork: Tower Books.

Woodman, P.C. 1987. Excavations at Cass ny Hawin, a Manx Mesolithic site, and the position of the Manx microlithic industries. *Proceedings of the Prehistoric Society* **53**, 1–22.

Woodman, P., McCarthy, M. and Monaghan, N. 1997. The Irish Quaternary Fauna Project. *Quaternary Science Reviews* **16**, 129–59.

Chapter 16

Some Problems and Perspectives:
Reviewing Aspects of the Mesolithic Period in Ireland

PETER WOODMAN

In some ways Mesolithic research in Ireland and Scotland has developed significantly in the last few decades, but it is apparent that some of the fundamental questions remain unchanged and to a great extent the similarities of these problems are due to the similar contexts in which research takes place. In both countries we still have a lot to learn from each other in terms of research objectives.

Introduction

Mesolithic studies in Ireland and Scotland have been linked in many ways for a large part of the twentieth century. Authors such as Lawlor (1928) saw the origins of Irish Mesolithic habitation as a product of communities making the short sea crossing from SW Scotland to NE Ireland and, in return, Lacaille's *Stone Age of Scotland* (1954) was very heavily influenced by Movius's *Irish Stone Age* (1942) in suggesting Mesolithic immigration from Ireland to Scotland. While many of the ideas associated with this connection across the 'Sea of Moyle' have been set aside, there is no doubt that Mesolithic studies in Ireland and Scotland continue to share many similar problems. Therefore this paper will look at how both regions have faced the same challenges of roughly the last quarter of the twentieth century. The fact that the World Holocene session of INQUA included a joint paper on Scotland and Ireland shows that this traditional link still exists (Wickham-Jones & Woodman 1998).

The period 1970 to 1975 has been chosen as the starting point as it was during these few years that new perspectives were brought to bear on Mesolithic studies in both areas. In Ireland, excavations at Newferry (Woodman 1977a) and the commencement of excavations at Mount Sandel (Woodman 1985) had allowed Irish Mesolithic studies to escape from all the baggage associated with the 'Larnian' (Lacaille 1954; Movius 1942), while in Scotland the publication of excavations at Morton (Coles 1971), the beginning of re-excavations of the Oronsay middens (Mellars 1987), and the publication of various

sites on Jura (Mercer 1968; 1970; 1974; 1980) laid the foundation for a new view of the Mesolithic period in Scotland. In both regions a new and yet remarkably similar perspective was emerging.

In each region the earliest known Mesolithic material was a product of a technology which used a range of microliths readily identifiable elsewhere in Western Europe, and there was growing evidence that this technology had been brought to Ireland and Scotland at an earlier date than had hitherto been suspected. Perhaps equally importantly the idea of Ireland and Scotland being occupied by 'Palaeolithic refugees' (see Mitchell 1955, for an assumption that material from Toome, Co. Londonderry, had an Aurignacian affinity) had begun to vanish from an explicit position in conceptions of the Mesolithic period in the region.

It was also appreciated that more localized technologies may have emerged, especially in the case of the macrolithic Later Mesolithic in Ireland, while in Scotland the role of the so-called 'Obanian' (Lacaille 1954) and the shift from a platform- to a scalar-core technology also suggested regional differentiation.

In the publication of his doctoral thesis, the author noted several questions which needed to be tackled (Woodman 1978, 211). These included the following.

> To what extent was the island of Ireland occupied during the Mesolithic period? (Identified as the query which perhaps presented the most manageable task to answer.)
>
> What is the nature of the chronological gap in the Irish Mesolithic?
>
> How and why was there a change in the technology used during the Irish Mesolithic period?
>
> What were the roles of base camps and was there any evidence of extensive activity associated with major base camps?

Although not listed specifically as a question, the absence of any early assemblages predating Mount Sandel was also noted (Woodman 1978, 208). This absence, and the extent of occupation, are questions which could equally have been posed in a Scottish context and are

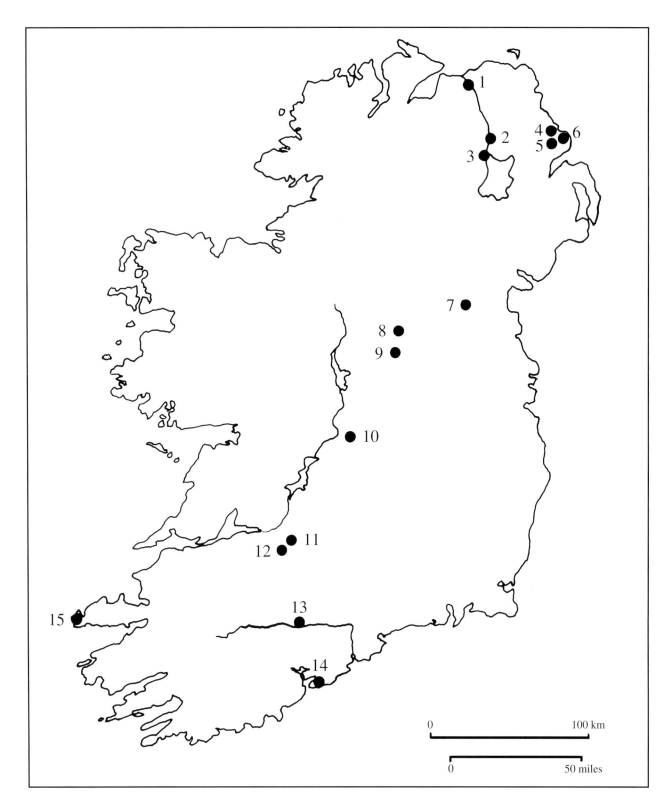

FIGURE 16.1

Outline map of Ireland showing the location of Mesolithic sites. Key: 1. Mount Sandel; 2. Newferry; 3. Toome; 4. Larne; 5. Glynn; 6. Ballydown; 7. Ballyhoe Lough; 8. Lough Kimale; 9. Lough Derravarragh; 10. Lough Boora; 11. Killuragh Cave; 12. Rathjordan; 13. Kilcummer; 14. Dunpower Head; 15. Ferriter's Cove.

still relevant in both regions today. The question of changing technology has some relevance to Scotland as many underlying attitudes towards lithic technological change tend to be coloured by a series of often unchallenged assumptions about the impact of different raw materials on stone tool manufacturing (Woodman 1987). Lack of progress on the question of base camps can be understood in that, like many regions in Europe, both Ireland and Scotland lack sufficient sites of the kind which would allow this type of discourse to take place. The location of those Irish sites mentioned in the text is shown in Fig. 16.1.

Chronology and typology

At this stage it is useful to review the current state of knowledge of the chronology and typology of the Irish Mesolithic. As in Scotland, this phase of prehistory represents the first unequivocal evidence for human settlement, but unlike the situation on the British mainland, in Ireland there are strong indicators that the Mesolithic period can be divided into two very different phases with, still today, a gap in evidence in the middle. This is illustrated in Fig. 16.2.

Irish Early Mesolithic occupation was thought to be associated with a controlled percussion blade technology and the production of a series of microlithic forms, of which elongated triangles, backed rods, and a range of needle points are the more distinctive forms. However, recent analysis of an Early Mesolithic assemblage (Costa et al. 2001) has shown that the reduction sequence includes the use of hard hammer percussion in the early stages of production while the blades themselves were usually produced with a soft hammer-stone rather than a punch. Few scrapers and no burins exist. Axeheads occur in this phase of the Mesolithic and can consist of core axeheads, chopping tools, flake axe/adzes, and, on certain sites, a range of ground stone axeheads. It is difficult to find evidence that this technology continued to any great extent after c.7000 cal BC. By at the latest c.6500 cal BC a new technology had replaced that associated with the Early Mesolithic period (see discussion below).

The later phase of the Irish Mesolithic in its classic form is clearly associated with a hard-hammer technology used to produce a series of large, comparatively robust blades and blade-like flakes, which in turn were used as the blanks for the production of a series of tools such as the butt-trimmed and bar-forms. Polished stone axeheads appear to have been more prevalent in this phase and are also associated with a series of large picks and borers. Recent excavations at Ferriter's Cove

(Woodman et al. 1999) suggest that a number of other forms of stone tool may be associated with the Later Mesolithic period.

Ireland's Early Holocene ecology may have more in common with some of the larger Scottish islands rather than with the Scottish mainland (cf. Yalden 1999), in that many of the larger mammals usually associated with this phase of the Holocene are not present in Ireland (i.e. aurochs, elk, and even perhaps – which would be more notable – red and roe deer: Woodman et al. 1997). Perhaps for this reason Irish Mesolithic artefacts have a tendency to occur in riverine, lacustrine, and coastal locations, as if fishing and the exploitation of marine resources were the key elements in the economy. The distribution of Irish Mesolithic artefacts, therefore, is very different from that found in Scotland and England. Several authors (e.g. MacLean 1993) have pointed to the possibility that the role of plant food should not be underestimated, but as yet there is little evidence in the form of site location or equipment to suggest that this was a major form of sustenance during the Irish Mesolithic period.

Dealing with the chronological gap

Both Ireland and Scotland have had their own particular Mesolithic chronological problems, but it is obvious that these are rather different. While Britain as a whole has a problem with Mesolithic specialists being unable to provide a convincing set of explanations for the typological sequence of lithic industries in the period after 7000 cal BC, Ireland still suffers, as it did in 1978, from a lack of understanding of the process of change from the Early to Later Mesolithic periods. There are still no significant assemblages from a substantial portion of the seventh millennium cal BC. The obvious alternative explanations to a continuous human presence throughout the Mesolithic period in Ireland do not appear to have any validity.

There is, as noted by Woodman (1981), enough evidence of human activity throughout the gap to show continuity of settlement and the fact that Early Mesolithic assemblages can be found throughout the island negates Mitchell's explanation that his 'Sandelians' died out (Mitchell 1976). Similarly there appears to be no functional differentiation. There are inland Early Mesolithic microlithic assemblages such as at Lough Boora (Ryan 1980) and Kilcummer (Woodman 1984), while Later Mesolithic macrolithic assemblages have been found inland at Lough Kinale and Ballyhoe Lough (Woodman 1998). On the coast in Larne, a site on Lough Glynn (Woodman 1977b) has produced a substantial Early

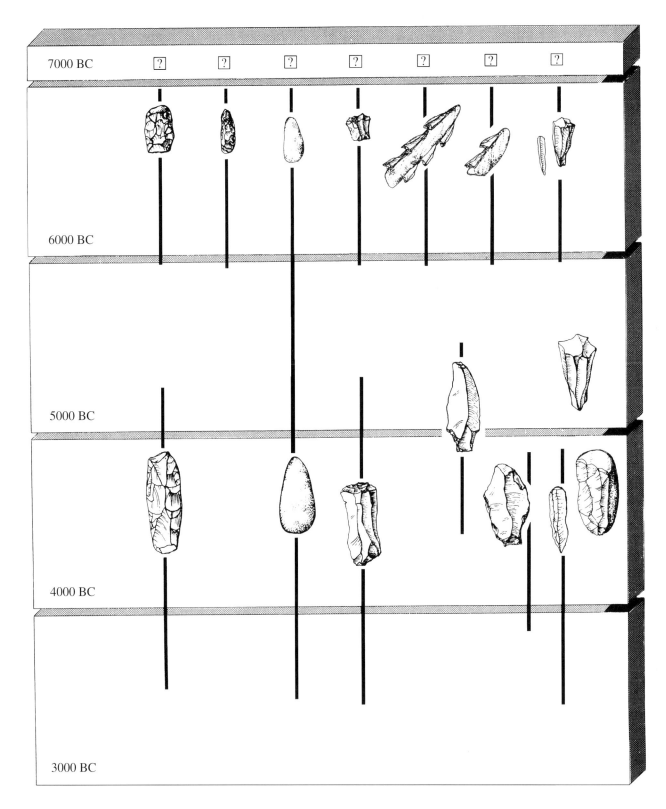

FIGURE 16.2
A chrono-typological chart of the Irish Mesolithic industries (after Woodman 1985, fig. 90).

Mesolithic assemblage, yet the 'Larnian' type site and another Later Mesolithic site at Ballydown (Moore 1998), on Island Magee, lie within a few kilometres, and Later Mesolithic sites are also present on Larne Lough.

What is apparent – other than the chronological gap – is how much Irish Mesolithic research, as in Scotland, has been dominated by a few major research excavations. In Ireland, in particular, if it were not for the work at Newferry, Mesolithic studies would lack a chronological backbone. There are approximately 100 ^{14}C dates associated with the Irish Mesolithic period, but roughly half (45) come from three sites – Mount Sandel, Ferriter's Cove, and Newferry – while it is Newferry which has produced the longest sequence. In fact, without Newferry there would only be a small group of sites before 7000 cal BC and a significant group after 5000 cal BC, with very few satisfactory assemblages or sites in between (Fig. 16.3). In reality, many of the dates from this middle period relate to poor, small, or not particularly instructive assemblages such as Toome, Cushendum, and so on (Woodman 1978).

Woodman (1981) has suggested that the context for technological change may have been social – that is the development of a socially self-sufficient island

population – but this does not really explain the actual change in lithic technology. The suggestion that the creation of the macrolithic Later Mesolithic is due to the abundance of raw materials cannot withstand scrutiny. It is the old argument based on flint availability once again (Woodman 1987). High-quality blade tools were also made in rhyolite and chert and the rare early phase assemblages of the Later Mesolithic, such as Zone 7 at Newferry, probably produced some of the finest long blades to be recovered in Ireland. Therefore it would be incorrect to view the change as some form of lithic 'island pauperization'.

Perhaps, as suggested by Woodman and Anderson (1990), the greater emphasis on the creation of fixed facilities, such as fish traps, could have led to technological change and may explain the concentration of Later Mesolithic artefacts at key locations, for example at fords on rivers or within lakes. In fact much of the Later Mesolithic material comes from specialist food procurement locations such as at Newferry and perhaps Dunpower, Co. Cork (Woodman 1989). These would appear to be located where certain specific activities took place rather than locations which Mesolithic groups used primarily as campsites. In fact, actual campsites,

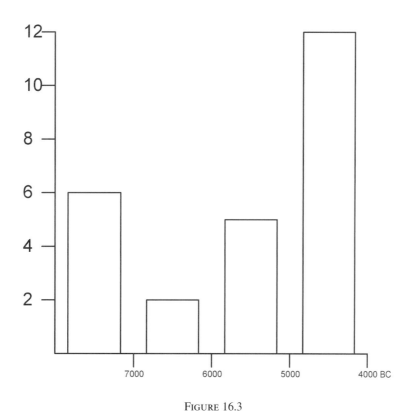

FIGURE 16.3

Chart showing the number of archaeological sites in Ireland which have produced ^{14}C dates in each millennium between 8000 and 4000 cal BC.

particularly from the Later Mesolithic, are still quite rare. Sutton, Co. Dublin (Mitchell 1956), and Ballydown, Co. Antrim (Moore 1998), are two of the few sites. This distinctive nature of many Later Mesolithic sites representing, in some cases, the accumulation of caches and/or discarded artefacts, and in many others having little more than one tool, is very different from what is found in most other parts of Europe and presents its own challenges in trying to understand the distribution of Later Mesolithic artefacts.

The commencement of human settlement

The chronological frontier for Mesolithic settlement in both Scotland and Ireland has remained remarkably stable for over two decades, and until very recently has shown little change in Scotland since the excavations on Rùm (Wickham-Jones 1990). Yet unlike in the 1970s, when mutual marginality was a sufficient explanation for lateness (the *ultima Thule* explanation), we have for some time been aware of the fact that an even earlier Mesolithic is possible but so far 'no unequivocal evidence has emerged' (Woodman 1996). To some extent there is still the tendency to explain these absences by the vicissitudes of nature, such as the 'Caledonian forest' in the case of Scotland (discussion at the 1978 Scottish Archaeological Forum conference in Glasgow), or in the case of Ireland the 'formidable' barrier of the Irish Sea. (Have things changed since Tacitus wrote about these islands in the first century AD?)

We should set to one side the nevertheless real possibility of Palaeolithic settlement, which could predate the last Glacial maximum (Woodman *et al.* 1997; cf. Ashmore this volume). We are concerned about

extending back in time the continuity of Mesolithic settlement rather than recording occasional visits at a much earlier date.

It is, of course, tempting to look for the equivalent of the English Early Mesolithic industries, that is non-geometric/obliquely blunted points and/or isosceles triangles, and to assume that their occurrence indicates occupation before *c*.8000 cal BC (Reynier 1997). However, some Irish assemblages containing these forms may be later in date. One pit at Mount Sandel (F100/5: Woodman 1985), which was cut through the main occupation, produced six simple obliquely blunted points, while at the as yet unpublished site of Killuragh Cave, Co. Limerick, two ^{14}C dates close to 7000 cal BC, on samples taken from human remains, may have been associated with another group of small obliquely blunted points. Therefore, in Ireland, as at Lussa Bay (Mercer 1970) and Glenbatrick (Mercer 1974) on Jura, where assemblages which resemble aspects of the English Early Mesolithic have been found, there is no guarantee that they indicate an earlier phase of settlement.

In the case of the Mount Sandel ^{14}C dates there may be another element which is rarely recognized – inter-laboratory variations. Most of the ^{14}C dates were obtained from the methane gas counter in Belfast, but two dates were also obtained from Groningen and, as a precaution, these samples were taken from the same features as samples which had been dated in Belfast. In F100/2 the Groningen sample was taken from a higher level than the Belfast sample. The differences between laboratories should be noted (Table 16.1).

The large standard deviation for sample UB-951 supports a possibility that the two dates from F56/1 may not be significantly different, but combined with

TABLE 16.1
Mount Sandel, Co. Londonderry (Woodman 1985): variant radiocarbon dates from features F100/2 and F56/1.

Feature	Layer	Lab Number	Date
F 100/2	4	UB-912	8725±115 BP
F 100/2	2	GRN-10470	8380±50 BP
F 56/1	3	UB-951	8790±185 BP
F 56/1	3	GRN-10471	8430±60 BP

the difference between the dates from F100/2 there is a strong suggestion of inter-laboratory or in this case inter-machine differences in dates. It is not a question of which is correct but it should be noted that until the mid 1980s, and in particular during the period in which many key Mesolithic sites were excavated, virtually all ^{14}C dates for the Irish Mesolithic were obtained from the original Belfast methane gas counter. Therefore, as these four dates come from late in the occupation at Mount Sandel, it is possible that the initial phase of settlement began at or just after 8000 cal BC rather than slightly earlier.

The weakness of other early dates is that one date of *c*.9000 BP from Lough Boora, Co. Offaly, has a large standard deviation (8980±360 BP), while the date of 9440±100 BP from Woodpark, Co. Sligo, was from a very disturbed context (a beach deposit which was likely to be 4000 years younger).

On the positive side, an assumption that the classic assemblages found in the Mount Sandel area are not to be associated with a date of *c*.9000 BP, but could be closer to *c*.8600 BP, allows a possible explanation for the local or insular character of the Mount Sandel assemblage, that is for an as yet undiscovered phase in which local forms, such as the needle points and flake axeheads, developed. The question again must be whether this developed from a geometric assemblage. In the 1980s, northern England seemed the best possible source of the origin for the Irish Early Mesolithic culture, but even then it was not a satisfactory source, as the Irish dates were so much earlier (Woodman 1981; and in particular 1985, 171). David's (1990) work in Wales, in particular at Prestatyn, where ^{14}C dates of *c*.8700 BP are associated with an assemblage containing a number of large scalene triangles, negates the impression based on the evidence from sites like Trwyn Ddu, that geometric assemblages only occurred in Wales later, after *c*.8600 BP. In fact, the Prestatyn assemblage, when combined with the older 'non-geometric' Nab Head and Caldey assemblages (David 1989), suggests a much more gradual change in technology and it is possible that this would have existed throughout England as well as Wales. This type of change is more in keeping with what has been suggested for the Maglemose of Denmark (Brinch Petersen 1966; Fischer 1978).

In summary, it could be argued that the Irish Early Mesolithic did not begin at an impossibly early date and that, based on the evidence from Wales, an origin can be suggested from within a gradually changing British Mesolithic. However, the absence of any assemblage from either Scotland or Ireland which is unequivocally much earlier than *c*.9000 BP still leaves the question as to whether the occupation of both regions was the product of a specific event (Note 1).

This of course brings up again the question of the absence of discoveries in Ireland of anything earlier than the Mount Sandel assemblages. Unlike the period of research prior to 1970, when there was an assumption that everything in Ireland and Scotland would be later than in England, there has been for fifteen, if not twenty, years a recognition that there could be an earlier phase of settlement in both regions. Surely at this point we must begin to ask whether there was a genuine delay in the Early Holocene settlement of Ireland and Scotland, or whether we are simply not looking in the right places?

Scandinavia was occupied at an early date, probably along the Norwegian coast where, in spite of the weakness of some of the data, the overall combination of the ^{14}C dates fits with the geological evidence and with a typological sequence. There is good reason to believe that human settlement was established in Arctic Norway well before 9000 BP (Woodman 1999), and many parts of Sweden and Finland were occupied shortly after the retreat of the ice of the Fenno-Scandinavian Ice Sheet (cf. articles in Larsson 1996). In the absence of archaeological sites from the first millennium of the Holocene, it is not surprising that there is difficulty in obtaining an overall impression of the land-based fauna in both regions (most dates for faunal remains come from archaeological excavations: see Bonsall *et al.* 1999; Woodman *et al.* 1997). However, even if the lack of information on early faunas genuinely reflects a restricted range of mammals before *c*.9000 BP, the Scandinavian evidence surely points to extremely rich coastal and marine resources but, unlike the Scandinavian coastline, it is probable that much of the Early Holocene coast around the British Isles has been drowned due to rising relative sea levels, or in the case of Ireland obliterated under the Mid-Holocene transgression. This lack of key parts of the Holocene coastal record is reflected in the impact of the Tapes Transgression on the Norwegian coast (Bjerck 1986)

Therefore the challenge remains. Is the absence of early settlement genuine, particularly if the earliest settlement of Ireland is roughly contemporaneous with that known in Scotland?

The extent of occupation

As suggested in 1978 (Woodman 1978, 211), extending the area of known occupation was the easiest aspect of Mesolithic study in which to make progress. In fact, though the excavation of a Late Mesolithic site at Ferriter's Cove (Woodman *et al.* 1999), in the previously 'Mesolithic-free' extreme SW of Ireland, would be like the discovery in Scotland of a Mesolithic

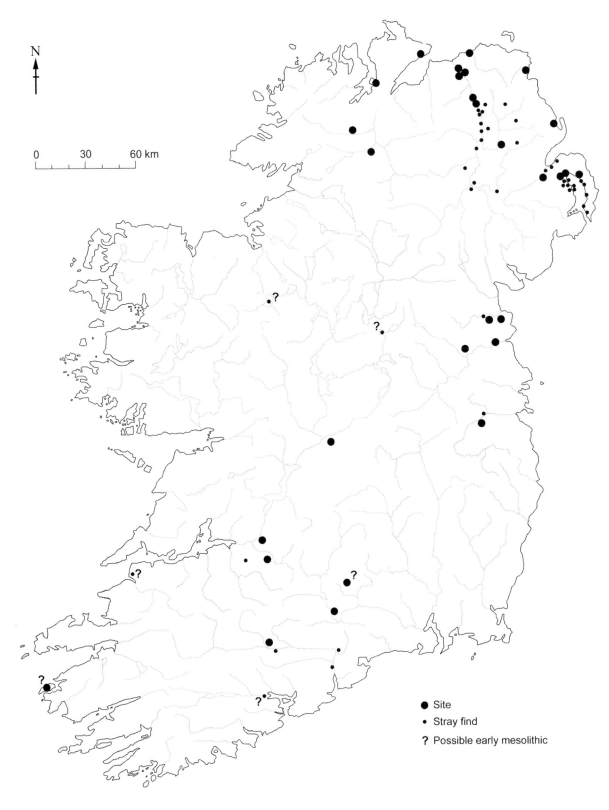

FIGURE 16.4
Locations of Early Mesolithic material in Ireland.

site on Shetland, the author would actually put greater emphasis on his discovery of the Mesolithic assemblage on a cliff overlooking Kilcummer, Co. Cork (Woodman 1984). Although subsequent excavations at this site did not reveal any *in situ* deposits which could be ^{14}C dated (Anderson 1993), the absence of any microlithic assemblages in Ireland which significantly postdate 8000 BP clearly indicates that the Kilcummer assemblage should be considered part of the Irish Early Mesolithic.

Therefore, once Mesolithic settlement had begun in Ireland, human populations spread quite rapidly through the island and now Early Mesolithic/microlithic assemblages are being found in the SW in Cork and Limerick and in the NW in Donegal (Fig. 16.4). Thus there is no evidence of a slow migration from one end of the island to the other through imagined hostile environments. There are still certain areas where there is a lack of known Mesolithic settlement, but today it would be assumed that we simply have not found traces of Mesolithic settlement rather than considering these areas as empty landscapes (see Fig. 16.5 for changes in the known distribution of Mesolithic settlement in Ireland).

In retrospect, the only limitation was our expectations. The assumption that a large part of the island was not colonized was due mostly to the mindset created by Lawlor (1928) and the belief that, outside NE Ireland there was no flint available from which early settlers could have made stone tools. Our self-limiting expectation is perhaps best illustrated by the fact that Ó Ríordáin (1948) found a fine example of a scalene triangle microlith during the excavation of a ring barrow at Rathjordan, overlooking the Camoge River, Co. Limerick. As there was an expectation that the Mesolithic occupation of Ireland was a northern phenomenon, the implications of this discovery were never followed through.

In Ireland, perhaps the most difficult problem is establishing a 'parity of esteem' between a century-old tradition of Mesolithic research based in NE Ireland and research in the rest of the island. There is, perhaps, a tendency to assume that sites found outside the historic core research area of NE Ireland are only of very local significance and marginal to the real discourse established elsewhere. Ferriter's Cove at the western end of the Dingle Peninsula can be regarded as an interesting local phenomenon with only the question of the early dates for cattle being of significance, whereas its evidence for spatial patterning, range of organic remains, and new implement forms should allow realization of the exceptional value of this site to research in the Irish Later Mesolithic. The criteria by which Irish Mesolithic research has been carried out have been inadvertently prejudiced by the mindset

created by Lawlor and others (including the author). What is being found elsewhere may be different but no less significant. In fact, it may become apparent that the paradigms of research in the flint-rich areas will be shown to be hidebound and not fully relevant to research elsewhere.

Similarly, it is of interest that both Ireland and Scotland have had difficulties divesting themselves of the assumption that availability of flint limited the extent of occupation. In fact it is only in the last decade or so that we have moved beyond a grudging acceptance that other materials might be used as a substitute to realizing that each island had a diverse range of raw materials, and that each material has advantages and disadvantages in usability and accessibility. Thus rhyolites, cherts, and other raw materials were used in Ireland (Woodman *et al.* 1999), while in Scotland Wickham-Jones (1986) and Saville (1994) have documented the diversity of raw materials exploited.

Besides our own intellectual restrictions, our contemporary demography and landscape/landuse have limited discoveries that extend known Mesolithic settlement. In SW Ireland, over the last fifteen years, there have been four major discoveries of locations of Mesolithic assemblages. (1) Ferriter's Cove, found by Dr Vernon (1976) (a geologist interested in archaeology with a summer home in the area); (2) Killuragh Cave (Woodman 1997) explored by Benny O'Neill (a landowner interested in geology and archaeology); (3) Kilcummer on the Cork Blackwater; and (4) the east Cork Later Mesolithic sites (both found by the author as part of a landscape project funded by the Royal Irish Academy and the Wenner-Gren Foundation). While the latter two might seem to indicate the role of the professional, it should be noted that each of these areas is within easy access of Cork. Woodman (1978) noted that throughout the last 150 years most lithic scatters were found by collectors within an hour's travel of their homes. While many were prepared to travel long distances to the known archaeologically rich sand dunes, most major discoveries were made by people who knew their local landscape, such as Buick and Grainger (late nineteenth-century collectors in mid-Antrim), Kirk in the Strangford Lough area (1930s); Jimmy Brennan in Tyrone (1950–60s); and, more recently, Peter Carr in the Comber area (1980s) and today Brian MacNaught and Tommy Gallagher in Derry and Donegal.

From personal experience, those of us who live in areas where artefact density in lithic scatters is quite low will always have to act as amateurs in our landscapes, taking advantage of the accumulation of chance half-days – when fields are just right and the weather has been suitable – in order to discover new sites. For these reasons

Extent of known occupation up to 1978

Extent of known occupation up to 2000

FIGURE 16.5
Changing recognition of the extent of Mesolithic occupation in Ireland, prior to 1978 and in 2000.

settlement. However, where the circumstances are right, as with the changing water levels at Loch Doon, Ayrshire, where sites were discovered by Tom Affleck (Edwards 1996), or with the Scotland's First Settlers Project on Skye and the adjacent mainland (Hardy & Wickham-Jones 2002), then surely we should concentrate our research effort in expanding our information about these specific landscapes? This will mean that, barring chance finds, there may be areas where research cannot take place, but it does not mean that we should assume that these areas lack a Mesolithic presence.

In other words, we do not have to find Mesolithic material everywhere, but targeted research projects in specific localities where there is a chance of being 'an amateur in the landscape' must follow the excitement of first discoveries; it is time spent in the landscape which is most likely to produce results.

Contacts between Ireland and Scotland during the Mesolithic period

Aside from the questions of initial colonization of Ireland and the role of Scotland in that process, there has been very little discussion on contact between the two regions. In part this is because there is so little evidence of contact during this period.

However, this lack of evidence for contact must be a matter of comment. There are numerous caches of Irish Later Mesolithic artefacts in Ireland (Woodman 1978), but none have been found across the Irish Sea in adjacent parts of Scotland. This can be contrasted with the known 'exchange' of Neolithic artefacts. In western Scotland, there are the spectacular caches of Irish Neolithic flint from Campbeltown and Stranraer, with final stage roughout flint axeheads in the cache from Campbeltown (Saville 1999). It should be remembered that while similar caches, such as the Ballynease MacPeake cache are known from Ireland, no caches of similar size to the Scottish examples have been found (Woodman 1992). Many axeheads of Irish porcellanite have been found in Scotland, while there is a growing corpus of Scottish Arran pitchstone from Irish Neolithic sites (Simpson & Meighan 1999), as well as a small group of what would appear to be Group VI axes (Cooney & Mandal 1998) imported from Langdale, Cumbria (see Fig. 16.6).

This contrast between evidence of Mesolithic and Neolithic exchange in lithic artefacts between the two regions is even more paradoxical when the degree of inter-visibility between parts of Antrim, the southern Hebrides, the Mull of Kintyre, and Galloway is considered (Fig. 16.6).

a stretch of the Blackwater River and the east Cork coast have provided easy access to substantial areas of ploughed land, which is beginning to allow us to understand how landscapes were used through time (Woodman 1989). Similarly, projects in SE Ireland, where there was no amateur tradition of fieldwalking, required very large inputs of time and resources as in the Ballylough survey (Zvelebil *et al.* 1987) or to a lesser extent along the Barrow River (Zvelebil *et al.* 1996).

One of the biggest challenges in areas such as northern Scotland or the west of Ireland is to get past that first discovery, as at Ferriter's Cove (Woodman *et al.* 1999) or Rùm (Wickham-Jones 1990), and to realize that while many regions will have been utilized during Mesolithic times, not all regions will be suitable for present-day research. We should recognize the fact that large parts of both research areas are sparsely occupied today and that these are often regions where very extensive accumulations of Quaternary deposits have covered earlier landscapes, reducing the chances of discovering

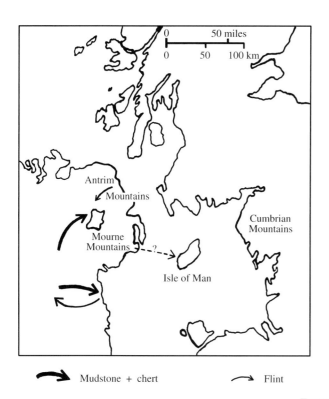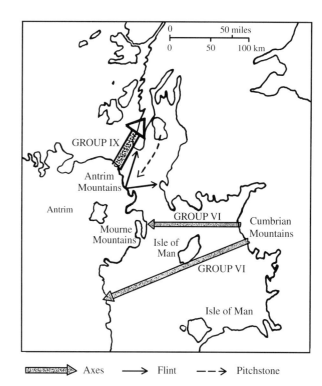

FIGURE 16.6

Movement of raw materials in the northern Irish Sea zone: left map – Mesolithic; right map – Neolithic.

While it is tempting to see Ireland as totally isolated, there is the obvious fact that similar technology to that of the Irish Later Mesolithic industries is found in the Isle of Man (McCartan this volume), which is less convenient of access from/to Ireland than are many parts of Scotland. Despite the similarity in technology, however, there is no evidence that artefacts nor flint raw material were imported from Ireland to Man. The recent discoveries of what may be domesticated cattle bones which significantly predate 4000 cal BC, if not 4500 cal BC, at Ferriter's Cove, Co. Kerry, in what would appear to be Later Mesolithic contexts, also highlight the possibility that contacts between regions may not always be reflected in the lithic artefacts as opposed to other aspects of the economy (Woodman *et al.* 1999).

In this case research on contacts within the Irish Sea basin might represent a fruitful area for analysis.

Note

1. The so-called tranverse arrowhead, published by Burenhult (1984, fig. 45), was a natural artefact and was in any case not associated with the early radiocarbon date as it was found some considerable distance from the location of the sample.

References

Anderson, E. 1993. The Mesolithic: fishing for answers. *In* E. Shee-Twohig and M. Ronayne (eds), *Past Perceptions: the Prehistoric Archaeology of South-West Ireland,* 16–24. Cork: Cork University Press.

Bjerck, H.B. 1986. The Fosna-Nøstvet problem. A consideration of archaeological units and chronozones in the south Norwegian Mesolithic period. *Norwegian Archaeological Review* **19**(2), 103–21.

Bonsall, C., Kitchener, A.C. and Bartosiewicz, L. 1999. AMS ¹⁴C dating and the Mesolithic faunal record. *In* E. Cziela, T. Kersting and S. Pratsch (eds), *Den Bogen spannen ... Festschrift für B. Gramsch,* 99–106. Weissbach: Beier and Beran.

Brinch Petersen, E. 1966. Klosterlund – Sønder Hadsund – Bøllund. Les trois sites principaux du Maglémosien ancien en Jutland. Essai de typologie et de chronologie. *Acta Archaeologica* **37,** 77–185

Burenhult, G. 1984. *The Archaeology of Carrowmore: Environmental Archaeology and the Megalithic Tradition at Carrowmore, Co. Sligo, Ireland.* Stockholm: Institute of Archaeology, University of Stockholm (Theses and Papers in North-European Archaeology **14**).

Cooney, G. and Mandal, S. 1998. *The Irish Stone Axe Project: Monograph 1.* Bray: Wordwell.

Coles, J. 1971. The early settlement of Scotland: excavations at Morton, Fife. *Proceedings of the Prehistoric Society* **37**(2), 284–366.

Costa, L., Sternke, F. and Woodman, P.C. 2001 An Analysis of the Lithic Assemblage from Eleven Ballyboes, Co Donegal: a contribution to the study of Early Mesolithic tool production in Ireland. *The Ulster Journal of Archaeology* **60**, 1–8.

David, A. 1989. Some aspects of the human presence in west Wales during the Mesolithic. *In* C. Bonsall (ed.), *The Mesolithic in Europe*, 241–53. Edinburgh: John Donald.

David, A. 1990. *The Palaeolithic and Mesolithic Settlement of Wales.* Unpublished PhD thesis, University of Lancaster.

Edwards, K.J. 1996. The contribution of Tom Affleck to the study of the Mesolithic of southwest Scotland. *In* T. Pollard and A. Morrison (eds), *The Early Prehistory of Scotland*, 108–22. Edinburgh: Edinburgh University Press.

Fischer, A. 1978. På sporet af overgangen mellem palæoliticum og mesolithicum i Sydskandinavien. *Hikuin* **4**, 27–50.

Hardy, K. and Wickham-Jones, C. 2002. Scotland's First Settlers: the Mesolithic seascape of the Inner Sound, Skye, and its contribution to the early prehistory of Scotland. *Antiquity* **76**, 825–33.

Lacaille, A.D. 1954. *The Stone Age in Scotland.* London: Oxford University Press.

Lawlor, H.C. 1928. *Ulster: its Archaeology and its Antiquities.* Belfast: Carswell & Sons.

Larsson, L. (ed.) 1996. *The Earliest Settlement of Scandinavia.* Stockholm: Almquist & Wiksell International (*Acta Archaeologica Lundensia,* Series in 8°, No. **24**).

MacClean, R. 1993. Eat your greens: an examination of the potential diet available in Ireland during the Mesolithic. *Ulster Journal of Archaeology* **56**, 1–8.

Mellars, P.A. 1987. *Excavations on Oronsay: Prehistoric Human Ecology on a Small Island.* Edinburgh: Edinburgh University Press.

Mercer, J. 1968. Stone tools from a washing-limit deposit of the highest post-glacial transgression, Lealt Bay, Isle of Jura. *Proceedings from the Society of Antiquaries of Scotland* **100** (1967–8), 1–46.

Mercer, J. 1970. Flint tools from the present tidal zone, Lussa Bay, Isle of Jura, Argyll. *Proceedings of the Society of Antiquaries of Scotland* **102** (1969–70), 1–30.

Mercer, J. 1974. Glenbatrick Waterhole, a microlithic site on the Isle of Jura. *Proceedings of the Society of Antiquaries of Scotland* **105** (1972–4), 9–32.

Mercer, J. 1980. Lussa Wood 1: the Late-Glacial and early Post-Glacial occupation of the Isle of Jura. *Proceedings of the Society of Antiquaries of Scotland* **110** (1978–80), 1–32.

Mitchell, G.F. 1955. The Mesolithic site at Toome Bay, Co. Londonderry. *Ulster Journal of Archaeology* **18**, 1–16.

Mitchell, G.F. 1956. An early kitchen-midden at Sutton, Co. Dublin. *Journal of the Royal Society of Antiquaries of Ireland* **86**, 1–26.

Mitchell, G.F. 1976. *The Irish Landscape.* London: Collins.

Moore, D. 1998. *Analysis of the Lithic Assemblages from Early Prehistoric Sites along the South Antrim Coast.* Unpublished M.Phil thesis, Queens University Belfast.

Movius, H. 1942. *The Irish Stone Age: its Chronology, Development and Relationships.* Cambridge: Cambridge University Press.

Ó Ríordáin, S.P. 1948. Further barrows at Rathjordan, Co. Limerick. *Journal of the Cork Historical and Archaeological Society* **53**, 19–31.

Reynier, M. 1997. Radiocarbon dating of early Mesolithic stone technologies from Great Britain. *In* J.-P. Fagnart and A. Thévenin (eds), *Le Tardiglaciaire en Europe du Nord-Ouest*, 529–42. Paris: CNRS.

Ryan, M. 1980. An early Mesolithic site in the Irish midlands. *Antiquity* **54**, 46–7.

Saville, A. 1994. Exploitation of lithic resources for stone tools in earlier prehistoric Scotland. *In* N. Ashton and A. David (eds), *Stories in Stone,* 57–70. London: Lithic Studies Society (Occasional Paper **4**).

Saville, A. 1999. A cache of flint axeheads and other flint artefacts from Auchenhoan, near Campbeltown, Kintyre, Scotland. *Proceedings of the Prehistoric Society* **65**, 83–123.

Simpson, D. and Meighan, I. 1999. Pitchstone – a new trading material in Neolithic Ireland. *Archaeology Ireland* **13**(2), 26–30.

Vernon, P.D. 1976. A Neolithic scraper from Ferriter's Cove, Dingle Peninsula, Co. Kerry. *Journal of the Cork Historical and Archaeological Society* **81**, 118–19.

Wickham-Jones, C.R. 1986. The procurement and use of stone for flaked tools in prehistoric Scotland. *Proceedings of the Society of Antiquaries of Scotland* **116**, 1–10.

Wickham-Jones, C.R. 1990. *Rhum, Mesolithic and Later Sites at Kinloch: Excavations 1984–86.* Edinburgh: Society of Antiquaries of Scotland (Monograph **7**).

Wickham-Jones, C.R. and Woodman, P.C. 1998. Studies on the early settlement of Scotland and Ireland. *Quaternary International* **49/50**, 13–20.

Woodman, P.C. 1977a. Recent excavations at Newferry, Co. Antrim. *Proceedings of the Prehistoric Society* **43**, 155–99.

Woodman, P.C. 1977b. A narrow-blade Mesolithic site at Glynn, County Antrim. *Ulster Journal of Archaeology* **40**, 12–20.

Woodman, P.C. 1978. *The Mesolithic in Ireland.* Oxford: British Archaeological Reports (British Series **58**).

Woodman, P.C. 1981. The post-glacial colonization of Ireland: the human factors. *In* D. Ó Corráin (ed.), *Irish Antiquity*, 93–110. Cork: Tower Books.

Woodman, P.C. 1984. The early prehistory of Munster. *Journal of the Cork Historical and Archaeological Society* **89**, 1–11.

Woodman, P.C. 1985. *Excavations at Mount Sandel 1973–77, County Londonderry.* Belfast: HMSO (Northern Ireland Archaeological Monographs No. **2**).

Woodman, P.C. 1987. The impact of resource availability on lithic industrial traditions in prehistoric Ireland. *In* P. Rowley-Conway, M. Zvelebil and H.P. Blankholm (eds), *Mesolithic Northwest Europe: Recent Trends*, 138–46. Sheffield: Department of Archaeology and Prehistory, University of Sheffield.

Woodman, P.C. 1989. The Mesolithic of Munster: a preliminary assessment. *In* C. Bonsall (ed.), *The Mesolithic in Europe*, 116–24. Edinburgh: John Donald.

Woodman, P.C. 1992 Excavations at Mad Man's Window, Glenarm, Co. Antrim: problems of flint exploitation in east Antrim. *Proceedings of the Prehistoric Society* **58**, 77–106.

Woodman, P.C. 1996. Archaeology on the edge: learning to fend for ourselves. *In* T. Pollard and A. Morrison (eds), *The Early Prehistory of Scotland,* 152–61. Edinburgh: Edinburgh University Press.

Woodman, P.C. 1997. Killuragh. *In* I. Bennett (ed.), *Excavations 1996*, 67–8. Bray: Wordwell.

Woodman, P.C. 1998. George Morant and the Mesolithic of Ballyhoe Lough. *In* M. Ryan (ed.), *Irish Antiquity: Essays in Memory of Joseph Raftery*, 1–16. Bray: Wordwell.

Woodman, P.C. 1999. The early Postglacial settlement of Arctic Europe. *In* E. Cziela, T. Kersting and S. Pratsch (eds), *Den Bogen spannen ... Festschrift für B. Gramsch,* 297–312. Weissbach: Beier and Beran.

Woodman, P.C. and Anderson, E. 1990. The Irish later Mesolithic: a partial picture. *In* P.M. Vermeersch and P. van Peer (eds), *Contributions to the Mesolithic in Europe*, 377–87. Leuven: Leuven University Press.

Woodman, P.C., McCarthy, M. and Monaghan, N. 1997. The Irish Quaternary Fauna Project. *Quaternary Science Reviews* **16**, 129–59.

Woodman, P.C., Anderson, E. and Finlay, N. 1999. *Excavations at Ferriter's Cove 1983–95: Last Foragers, First Farmers in the Dingle Peninsula*. Bray: Wordwell.

Yalden, D.W. 1999. *The History of British Mammals*. London: Poyser.

Zvelebil, M., Moore, J., Green, S. and Henson, D. 1987. Regional survey and the analysis of lithic scatters: a case study from Southeast Ireland. *In* P. Rowley-Conway, M. Zvelebil and H.B. Blankholm (eds), *Mesolithic Northwest Europe: Recent Trends*, 9–32. Sheffield: Department of Archaeology and Prehistory, University of Sheffield.

Zvelebil, M., Macklin, M.G., Passmore, D.G. and Ramsden, P. 1996. Alluvial archaeology in the Barrow Valley, southeast Ireland: the 'Riverford Culture' re-visited. *Journal of Irish Archaeology* **7**, 13–40.

Chapter 17

Wales During the Mesolithic Period

ANDREW DAVID and ELIZABETH A. WALKER

Any understanding of the Mesolithic period in Wales remains heavily dependent on description and analysis of lithic collections from a small number of excavated open sites, caves, and foreshore locations, backed up by a limited ^{14}C record. This database is reviewed here and indicates the first appearance of a techno-logically characteristic Early Mesolithic at c.8170 cal BC, rather later than the earliest of equivalent technolo-gies in England. Although intriguing items such as shale beads and carved stones are shown to be a part of this material culture, there is very little evidence presently available to allow the reconstruction of subsistence strategies or lifestyle. Change is signalled from as early as c.7900 cal BC when narrow-blade lithic assemblages are introduced in north Wales, though most dated lithic material of this type occurs between 6000–5000 cal BC. Despite recent investigations at intertidal sites, where significant remnants of contemporary landscapes are preserved, interpretation remains highly constrained. Although upland exploitation is indicated, this appears to be contrasted with a very marked preference for coastal site location, a phenomenon which persists into the early Neolithic.

Introduction

In this paper we review current evidence for human activities in Wales during the first few millennia of the Holocene (*c*.9600–3750 cal BC) (Note 1). This so-called 'Middle Stone Age', sandwiched between the Palaeolithic and the Neolithic, was recognized as a feature of Welsh prehistory even before the publication of Mortimer Wheeler's *Prehistoric and Roman Wales* (1925), in which that author was then obliged to confess that '… at present the opening phases of the New Stone Age in Wales are lost in uncertainty' (Wheeler 1925, 46). Despite the later recognition of a 'Mesolithic' to fill this gap in Wales (Clark 1932), the evidence for this was not extensively reviewed until much later (Wainwright 1963). A subsequent synthesis (Jacobi 1980) showed that

the database had changed little and, in particular, that no reliable ^{14}C chronology existed which could place the many finds of lithic material within the apparent sequence of Earlier and Later phases of the Mesolithic seen to be emerging elsewhere in Britain and parts of Europe. Within the last twenty years additional fieldwork and ^{14}C dating have improved the picture somewhat (Barton *et al.* 1995; Bell *et al.* 2000; David 1989; 1990), while more recent research is expanding the database and its interpretation further still (Aldhouse-Green 2000; Burrow 2003; Walker 2000 & forthcoming).

Background

The origins of Mesolithic inhabitation are as obscure in Wales as they seem to be elsewhere in Britain. The presence or absence of humans here during the Younger Dryas stadial, when climate deteriorated at *c*.13,700 cal BC and remained severe for 1200–1300 years (Alley 2000), remains equivocal. The prevailing tundra con-ditions, encouraging the re-growth of cirque glaciers in the Cambrian Mountains, seem not to have been so extreme as to deter reindeer, wild horse, and man, among other animals, from entering parts of the British Isles. The worst of the cold may have been moderated along the western maritime fringe but this zone, and any evidence it contained, is now submerged. However, a clue that man may indeed have been present in Wales during this cold hiatus is provided by cutmarks recently observed on a carnivore bone (A. Currant & R. Jacobi pers. comm.), with an age of 11,010–10,380 cal BC (OxA-6500), found among Neolithic ritual deposits at Parc le Breos Cwm on Gower (Whittle & Wysocki 1998). The only other certain evidence for an approximately contemporary human presence is provided by the well-known decorated horse jaw from Kendrick's Upper Cave, Llandudno (Sieveking 1971), upon which there is an AMS determination of 10,620–8860 cal BC (OxA-111; Gillespie *et al.* 1985). A decorated bovid molar from the cave has since produced a determination of 11,000–10,160 cal BC (OxA-4573; Aldhouse-Green 2000). There are no certain examples of the Ahrensburgian or long-blade flint technologies that have been linked with a Final Palaeolithic exploitation of eastern and southern Britain at about this time (Barton 1991; Jacobi 1982).

According to ^{14}C determinations obtained from pollen profiles (e.g. Walker & Harkness 1990) the onset of Holocene climatic conditions occurs in Wales, as elsewhere, at c.9600 cal BC. Other evidence, from ice core data (Dansgaard et al. 1993), suggests the likelihood that this transition was very abrupt, perhaps occurring over as little as 50 years at c.11,500 cal BC (Alley 2000; Alley et al. 1993). Such swift climatic amelioration, outpacing the spread of tree migration, may well account for the persistence of horse and reindeer in places. Thereafter, forest animals moved from refugia further south.

The sequence of Holocene vegetation change in Wales follows the same pattern as elsewhere in Britain. Following an initial florescence of herb and heathland species the appearance of juniper is usually short-lived, succumbing quickly to the invasion of extensive birch woodlands, with hazel and local pine, willow, and alder stands (Hibbert & Switsur 1976; Moore 1972; Taylor 1973). Indeed, in some areas of Wales the juniper phase is barely detectable at all in the pollen record. Birch arrived relatively late, at or after c.8700 cal BC (Donald 1987). The following hazel expansion appears early in the Tregaron Bog pollen profile at c.9200 cal BC (Hibbert & Switsur 1976), while at Mynydd Bach, west of Tregaron, hazel starts to rise before the juniper peak. Hazel becomes more widespread at c.8900 cal BC (Birks 1989) and the boundary between the decline of birch and the expansion of hazel has been dated to 9120–8280 cal BC (CAR-690) at the inland site of Waun Fignen Felen in the Brecon Beacons (Barton et al. 1995) confirming Caseldine's (1990, 33) observation that hazel expanded away from the coastal lowlands later.

As hazel reached its maximum throughout Wales, birch declined in favour of oak, elm, and pine in the lowlands, with pine and birch predominating on higher ground. This gradually gave way to the arrival of alder and lime, particularly near the coast (Taylor 1980, fig. 3.4). In SW Wales, mixed alder-oak-elm forest became established in sheltered valley locations although elm may not have been able to compete in the more exposed areas (Donald 1987). Throughout this period the vegetation over the Welsh landscape is likely to have been very variable at local and regional scales owing also to changes in elevation, soil type, and aspect. Such abrupt changes in environment remain a distinctive feature of Wales today.

Postglacial sea levels were rising at a rate approximately in step with climatic improvement (Fairbanks 1989; Fairbridge 1961) – rapidly throughout the early part of the Holocene – only decelerating at about the climatic optimum of c.4850 cal BC (West 1977). Several curves for eustatic sea-level rise have been plotted, although they are not all in exact agreement. A general curve developed for Britain suggests a level of about –37m at c.9600 cal BC (Godwin et al. 1958), which is in rough agreement with a depth of –34m at c.8900 cal BC (Ters 1973). Suggestions that by 8250 cal BC the sea level was about 25–30m below the present level, based on evidence from sites along Cardigan Bay, also fit into this pattern (Lambeck 1996). Despite this rapid rise, substantial areas of the Bristol Channel lowlands and Cardigan Bay would have remained dry at the time of the first Mesolithic human activity there (Fig. 17.1).

The effect of an advancing sea would be to raise the local water-table, creating a margin of swamp and carr in areas of formerly well-drained woodland. In many circumstances peat might then develop until overtaken by increasing salinity and finally inundation. Marine transgression is likely to have been somewhat uneven and marked by sudden incursions as natural barriers were breached during storms and tidal surges (Kidson & Heyworth 1973). Today, submerged clays and peats in the intertidal zone include deposits dating from the Later Mesolithic and have for long been an important resource for research (e.g. Balaam et al. 1987; Bell et al. 2000).

Occasional finds from such intertidal sediments and from within caves provide what very few faunal data are available for Wales. By comparison with the rather more abundant finds from other British sites it seems likely that the influx of woodland brought with it a distinct mammalian fauna which included red and roe deer, wild cattle, wild pig, and elk.

An Early Mesolithic occupation

Within the changing environmental scenario outlined above, Wales inherits a fully recognizable technical and economic Early Mesolithic tradition already familiar on sites elsewhere in Britain (although not necessarily in Scotland) and from the European mainland.

Wales is no more fortunate than many other areas of Britain which, with few exceptions, lack sites with good dating evidence for the Early Mesolithic period. Necessarily therefore, most efforts to understand the human presence in Wales at this time depend upon the location and study of lithic assemblages, which can be linked in only a few cases with reliable ^{14}C determinations. From the very limited dating evidence available

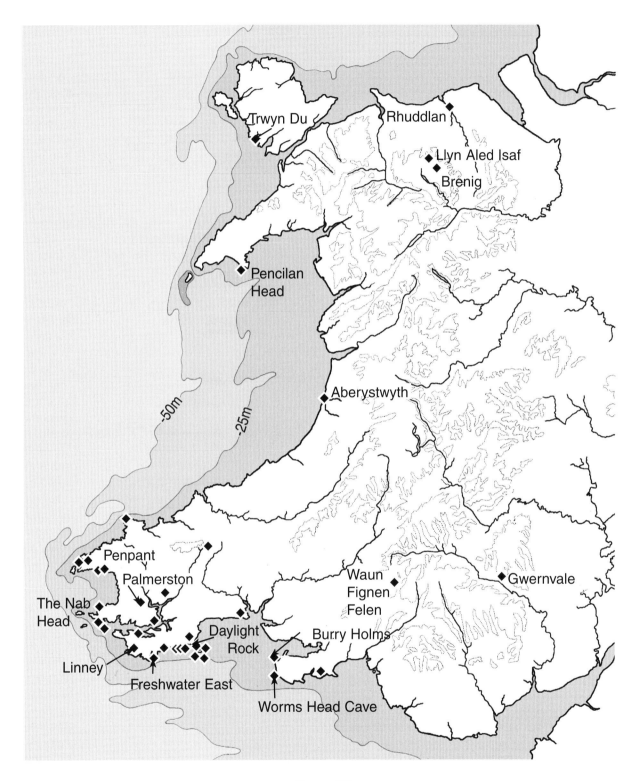

FIGURE 17.1
Distribution map of Early Mesolithic findspots in Wales.

301

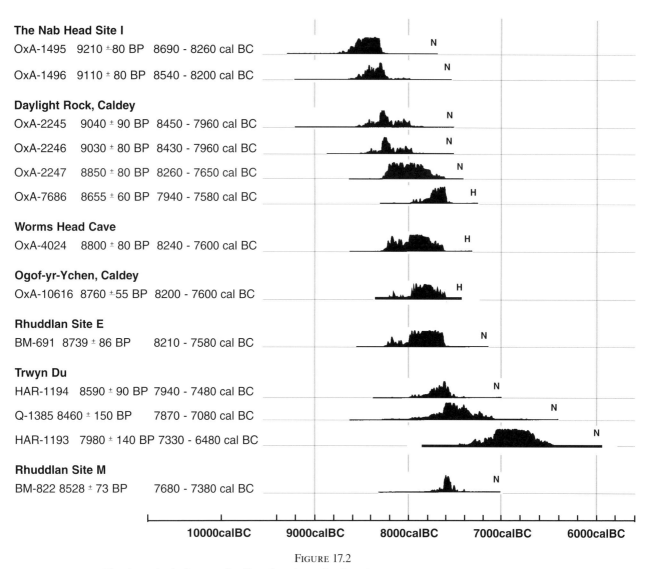

The Nab Head Site I

OxA-1495 9210 ±80 BP 8690 - 8260 cal BC

OxA-1496 9110 ± 80 BP 8540 - 8200 cal BC

Daylight Rock, Caldey

OxA-2245 9040 ± 90 BP 8450 - 7960 cal BC

OxA-2246 9030 ± 80 BP 8430 - 7960 cal BC

OxA-2247 8850 ± 80 BP 8260 - 7650 cal BC

OxA-7686 8655 ± 60 BP 7940 - 7580 cal BC

Worms Head Cave

OxA-4024 8800 ± 80 BP 8240 - 7600 cal BC

Ogof-yr-Ychen, Caldey

OxA-10616 8760 ±55 BP 8200 - 7600 cal BC

Rhuddlan Site E

BM-691 8739 ± 86 BP 8210 - 7580 cal BC

Trwyn Du

HAR-1194 8590 ± 90 BP 7940 - 7480 cal BC

Q-1385 8460 ± 150 BP 7870 - 7080 cal BC

HAR-1193 7980 ± 140 BP 7330 - 6480 cal BC

Rhuddlan Site M

BM-822 8528 ± 73 BP 7680 - 7380 cal BC

10000calBC   9000calBC   8000calBC   7000calBC   6000calBC

FIGURE 17.2

The chronological range of radiocarbon determinations for the Welsh Early Mesolithic period.
Key: H = human bone; N = nutshell.

(Fig. 17.2), it would appear that an Early Mesolithic presence is detectable in Wales only after it has become established further to the north and east.

Prior to the 1990s, the chronology for the Welsh Early Mesolithic was dependant on a small series of ^{14}C determinations from three sites in the north of the country: Trwyn Du on Anglesey (White 1978); and Rhuddlan sites E and M, in Denbighshire (Berridge 1994). These dates are all significantly later than might be predicted from dating evidence obtained elsewhere in Britain and Europe (Jacobi 1980, 146). In each case, too, there are grounds for believing them to be in error or, at least, to be unrepresentative of the earliest Mesolithic settlement of Wales.

The determinations from Trwyn Du, a site which lies below a Bronze Age cairn, were all on bulked hazelnut shell samples. The date of 7330–6480 cal BC (HAR-1193) relates to the contents of a pit but the ^{14}C determination was considered unreliable by the dating laboratory on account of the sample's low carbon content (White 1978). The other determinations (Q-1385 & HAR-1194) were obtained from the fill of a hollow that overlies the pit from which sample HAR-1193 was obtained. The stratigraphic relationship of this pit and the Bronze Age cuts is unclear owing to earthworm sorting of the two main layers into one (White 1978); consequently some doubt must exist about the integrity of the context from which the samples came. In addition, determinations on aggregates of carbonized nutshells from locations with significant evidence for post-Mesolithic usage should clearly be treated with caution (Jacobi 1987).

The ¹⁴C determinations from samples taken from Rhuddlan come from two different sites, E and M, in separate parts of the medieval town. Both sites have produced large lithic assemblages, mostly from derived contexts. Two ¹⁴C determinations came from large pit features containing Mesolithic material. The result of 7680–7380 cal BC (BM-822) from Site M has been discounted as it arises from a sample gathered from the fill of a large pit or hollow that was truncated by a later prehistoric gully (Berridge 1994). However, the result from a pit at Site E of 8210–7580 cal BC (BM-691) is believed to be reliable, possibly 'one of the most secure Mesolithic dates obtained for Wales' (Berridge 1994, 127). The pit concerned has a stratified sequence of mixed yellow and grey sand in which there was a black sand lens containing hazelnut shells. However, the pit was cut by a later soil and also by a medieval ditch and possible contamination cannot therefore be ruled out, given that comparable sites in England are significantly earlier (David 1989). A single determination of 9150–8600 cal BC (Beta-098452; Mein 1996) taken on the fill of a stakehole at Trostrey Castle, Monmouthshire, is also considered to be unreliable in the light of other dating evidence at the site and an absence of any associated Early Mesolithic artefacts (Walker forthcoming).

Excavation at two sites in Pembrokeshire, The Nab Head and Daylight Rock, was intended in part to obtain further evidence for dating Early Mesolithic settlement in Wales (David 1990, 104). AMS determinations on charred hazelnut shell fragments associated with a distinctive Early Mesolithic flint and stone industry at The Nab Head Site I provided an age range of 8690–8200 cal BC (David 1990, 115). At Daylight Rock, on Caldey Island, AMS determinations on charred hazelnut shells associated with a discrete lithic assemblage closely similar to that at The Nab Head Site I, provided a slightly later age range of 8450–7650 cal BC.

Together, the Pembrokeshire determinations draw the earliest evidence so far obtained for a Welsh Mesolithic technology slightly nearer to its inception in England. The central dating of c.8170 cal BC, when compared with those for equivalent lithic collections in England, falls towards the later end of an Early Mesolithic continuum. On the basis of tool typology we might have expected an earlier dating by up to 500 years, in line with that for Star Carr (Yorks) or Thatcham (Berks). It would seem, for instance, that the earliest occupation at Star Carr preceded that at The Nab Head by at least 300 years or so (Day & Mellars 1994; Mellars & Dark

1998, 120). Instead, the Pembrokeshire dates fall in line with those from other sites in England, such as the series from Oakhanger VII (Hants), centred at c.8250 cal BC (but this latter dating depends on bulked samples and is associated with lithic material typologically distinct from that in Wales: Jacobi 1978).

Although these few ¹⁴C determinations provide an initial conception of timescale it is clear that many more are required before a chronological pattern is established that can be relied upon. Until then we continue to depend upon characterization of lithic assemblages for further information on the Early Mesolithic in Wales.

The artefacts

Perhaps most distinctive among lithic assemblages attributed to this period are large and 'broad' (>8mm) microliths (for a definition of the term 'broad blade' see Radley & Mellars 1964). The dominant form is the obliquely backed point, found with varying proportions of large isosceles and scalene triangles, and bi-truncated trapezoidal pieces. These microliths are usually accompanied by end scrapers and burins and sometimes by axeheads or adzes. Serrated or microdenticulated blades and narrow, steeply trimmed drill-bits (*mèches de foret*: Clark 1975, 108), as well as utilized flakes and blades can also occur. So far absent from Wales are any of the distinctive organic artefacts such as uniserially barbed points of bone and antler which have also been noted to be a part of this 'techno-complex' (Verhart 1988).

Groups of microliths from Welsh sites display some significant variation. Those from The Nab Head Site I and Daylight Rock have a higher proportion of large triangular forms to obliquely backed points (Figs 17.3–4); while at Trwyn Du, Rhuddlan, and Burry Holms (Figs 17.5–6), obliquely backed points predominate over far fewer large triangles. One could speculate that this variation in Wales is shared with that observed more widely (Jacobi 1984, 46) and which has been vested with possible chronological significance (Reynier 1998) – the assemblages with proportionally more triangular microliths ('Star Carr' type) occurring earlier than those in which obliquely backed points predominate. However, the dating evidence, as summarized above, is still too meagre to develop this proposal for Wales.

Despite the surface find of a hollow-based point at Merthyr Mawr Warren, Bridgend (Jacobi pers. comm.), there is no other evidence from Wales for this microlith type. In SE England, broad-blade isosceles triangles and obliquely backed points are combined with hollow-based, or 'Horsham', points. On the limited evidence so far available, the chronological position of these 'Horsham' assemblages seems to lie between the local

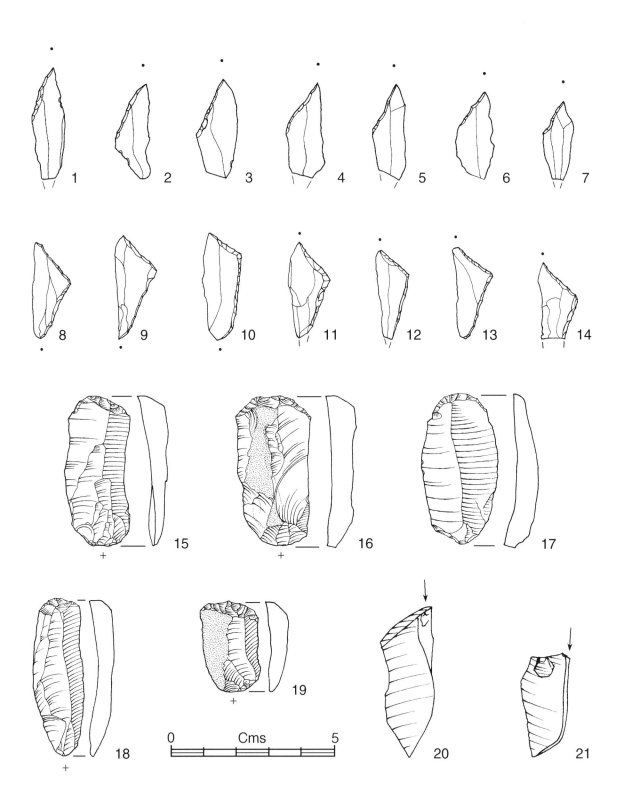

FIGURE 17.3
The Nab Head Site I Early Mesolithic finds: 1–14 microliths; 15–19 end scrapers; 20–21 burins.

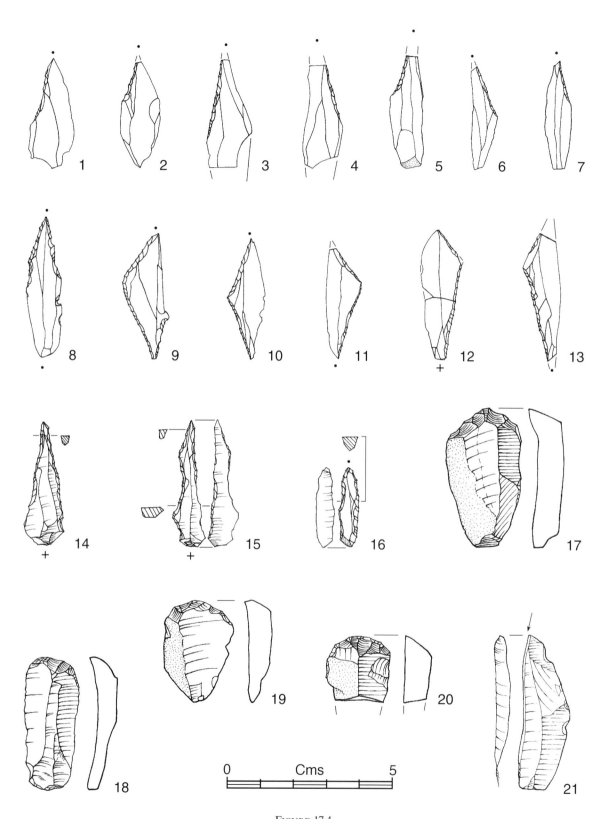

FIGURE 17.4
Daylight Rock Early Mesolithic finds: 1–13 microliths; 14–16 *mèches de foret*; 17–20 end scrapers; 21 burin.

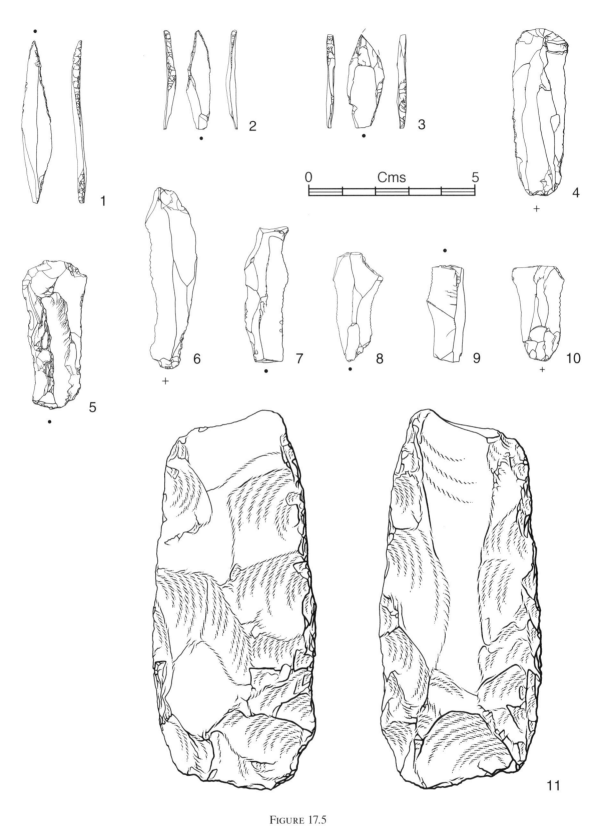

FIGURE 17.5
Trwyn Du Early Mesolithic finds: 1–3 microliths; 4–5 end scrapers; 6–10 microdenticulates; 11 core axehead/adze.

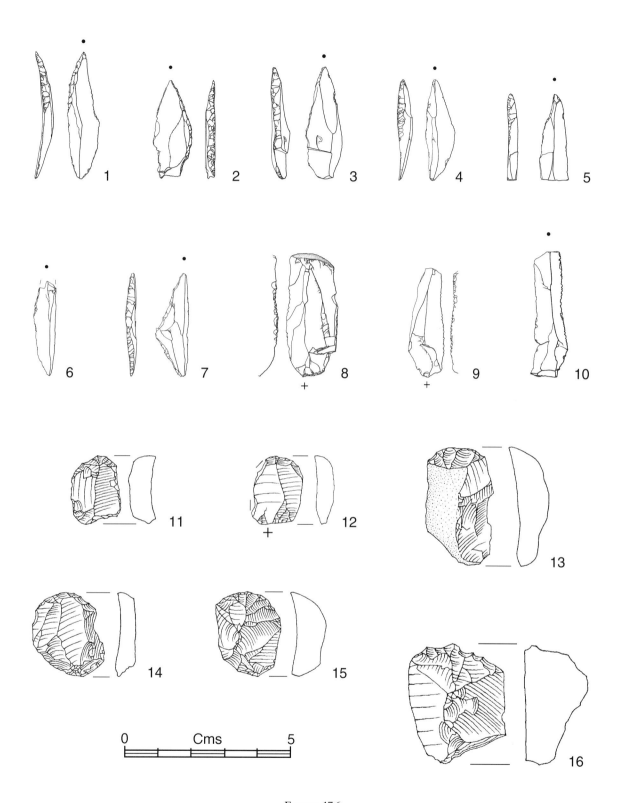

FIGURE 17.6

Burry Holms Early Mesolithic finds: 1–6 obliquely blunted points; 7 large isosceles triangle; 8–10 microdenticulates; 11–16 scrapers.

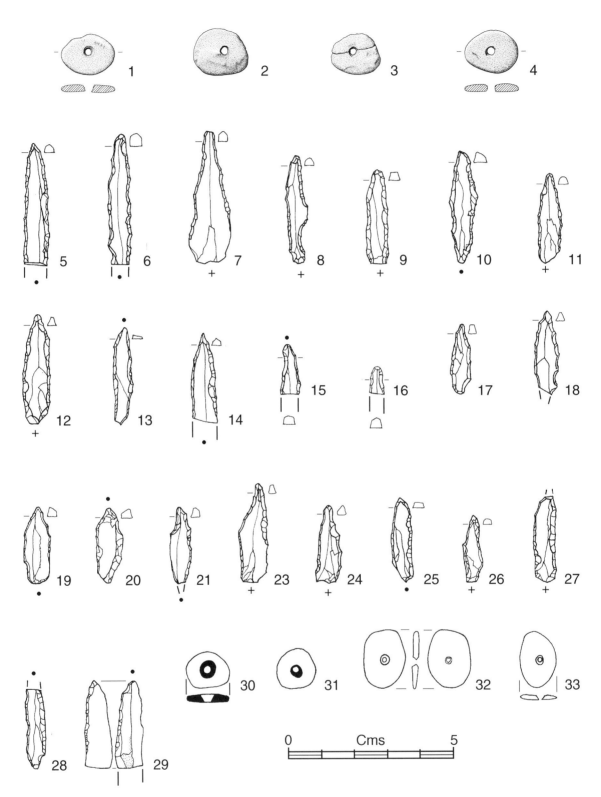

FIGURE 17.7

Early Mesolithic beads and *mèches de foret*: 1–4 The Nab Head shale beads; 5–29 The Nab Head *mèches de foret*; 30 bead from Linney Burrows; 31 bead from Freshwater East; 32 bead from Palmerston Farm; 33 bead from Waun Fignen Felen.

earliest and latest lithic assemblages, perhaps innovated from Continental sources from *c*.7950–8250 cal BC (Jacobi pers. comm.).

Microdenticulated blades (microdenticulates) are a component only of those assemblages dominated by obliquely backed points, occurring for instance at Burry Holms, Trwyn Du, Rhuddlan, Oakhanger VII (Hants), Marsh Benham (Berks), and Middlezoy (Somerset), where they form a significant component of the assemblages. The microdenticulate is missing from those sites dominated by large triangles such as Star Carr and Flixton (Yorks), Broxbourne 104 (Herts), The Nab Head, and Daylight Rock.

The *mèche de foret* or drill bit is an unusual but distinctive artefact type in some Early Mesolithic assemblages both in Britain and Scandinavia (Clark 1975, 108). Its presence is particularly prominent at The Nab Head Site I, where 44 examples comprise seven per cent of the tool inventory. These specimens are usually blades or bladelets narrowed by abrupt bilateral modification to create a rod-like, or awl-shaped, outline with a near cylindrical section at the distal ends (Fig. 17.7). Their tips are frequently somewhat rounded, as if by abrasion, and a rotational movement during use is indicated both by this and the presence of invasive micro-scaling damage to the ventral surface. *Mèches de foret* are also important constituents of the tool-kit at Daylight Rock (10%) and, notably, at Star Carr (12%). However, those from Star Carr (Clark 1954, 106) and nearby Flixton (Moore 1950) tend to be rather larger than those from The Nab Head.

No less distinct among Early Mesolithic assemblages, including those in Wales, are core axeheads/adzes, although these are often recorded as isolated finds (e.g. 'Castell Pocha', Pencaer; Benton; & Porth-y-Rhaw, Solva (Grimes 1951, 14); St Davids (Jacobi 1980, 146); & Brunt Farm, Dale (Wainwright 1963, 112), all in Pembrokeshire). Excavated examples include a specimen from The Nab Head Site I (David 1990, 156), making a total of four from that site, and two examples from Trwyn Du. Very few of these latter specimens are made of flint, a raw material which seems rarely to have been available in large enough pieces for their manufacture. Here we illustrate a further specimen, a residual find from among medieval features excavated at Newport, Pembrokeshire (Fig. 17.8).

Other lithic tool forms include scrapers, which in the main Welsh collections conform to the very neat end or double-ended types typical of most Early Mesolithic assemblages. Burins are less ubiquitous but are significant, if modest, components of the assemblages from The Nab Head and Daylight Rock.

Raw materials

With a very varied solid geology and having also been traversed by several ice fronts, Wales has a wide range of erratic material accumulated in its drift deposits. There seems little doubt that it was from these, and from beach shingle in particular, that flints and other rock types must have been gathered for tool manufacture at sites both inland, such as Waun Fignen Felen, in the Brecon Beacons, and nearer the coast, as at The Nab Head. However, research has proceeded little beyond such generalizations and all too often raw materials are ascribed to such sources without much consideration of local alternatives such as river gravels and rock outcrops. Current research at Burry Holms, Gower, has so far identified artefacts of two distinct types of flint as well as a black silicified mudstone, a very fine quartzite, and a silicified limestone. These are all believed to have been available locally, and indeed can be collected today eroding out of the local glacial drift deposits (T. Young pers. comm.).

The raw materials used at Waun Fignen Felen include Cretaceous flint, a Cretaceous Greensand chert, and a Carboniferous chert. The flint is assumed to have been collected from the seashore, while the Greensand chert can be found on the 100ft terrace at Abbots Leigh near Bristol (Barton *et al.* 1995), the nearest primary source being Westbury, Wiltshire (S. Howe pers. comm.). Though such areas must have been well within the purview of the occupants of the site, and specimens of Greensand chert may indeed have been imported from south of the Severn Estuary (Barton *et al.* 1995), it is also likely that the majority was collected, with the flint, from Welsh beaches where it is also known to occur. The Carboniferous chert is available locally (Barton *et al.* 1995).

Of the raw materials used at The Nab Head Site I some 99 per cent of the lithic assemblage is of pebble flint presumed to have been introduced onto the contemporary beaches by the erosion of terrestrial glacial deposits, or through the on-shore accumulation of Pleistocene sediments from the Bristol Channel or Celtic and Irish Seas. As may be expected from such a catchment, several colours and textures of flint are represented, as they are on the beaches today. Shades of opaque grey and pale flint with mottling tend to predominate, with rarer translucent black, grey, and yellow pieces. The degree of subsequent patination is also extremely variable. A noticeable feature of the flint assemblage, however, is that patination is more pronounced among those artefacts interpreted as later in the occupation sequence. Such a reversal of the usual correlation of increasing patination with age may perhaps eventually be explained in terms of a change in raw material sources or of evolving soil conditions on the headland. A consideration here is the possible influence of shellfish middens later in the Mesolithic, which, if they once existed on the site, might have provided the calcareous conditions responsible for the observed differential patination.

Apart from flint, there are several types of fine-textured extrusive igneous rock types – tuffs and rhyolites particularly – which fracture conchoidally and may be flaked in much the same way as flint. Most of the 488 non-flint artefacts from Site I are of such material, the primary sources of which are the outcrops of Ordovician volcanic rock now exposed in north Pembrokeshire and, nearer by, on Skomer Island and the Wooltack peninsula. In view of the variety of the Pembrokeshire volcanic rocks and the confusion arising from drift-derived secondary sources, specific petrological identification of this flaked material is unlikely to have any significant archaeological bearing (R. Sanderson pers. comm.). Such raw material can be expected to have been collected from beaches along with flint cobbles, the main attraction being its larger size and suitability for manufacturing tools such as core axeheads/adzes, for which the flint pebbles were rarely bulky enough.

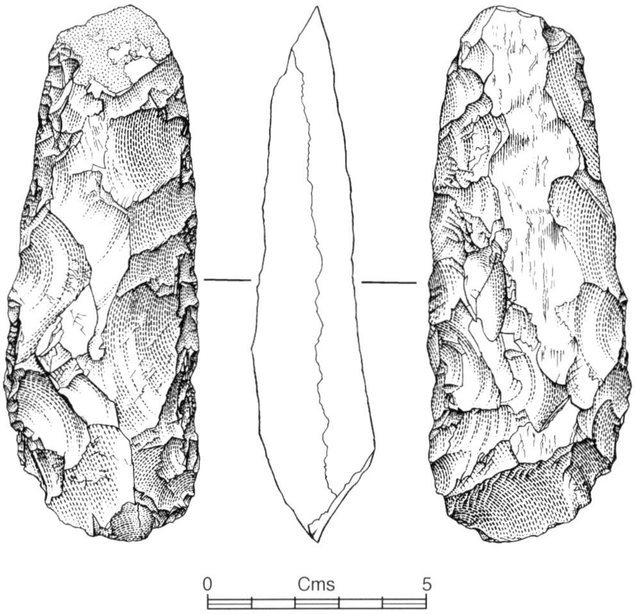

Finally, among the flaked tools and debris found on Site I are small quantities of Cretaceous Greensand chert. This is another component of local beach shingle and, as with the other stone and flint types, its presence on the site reflects nothing more than opportunistic gathering of workable raw material.

At Rhuddlan there are local sources of Carboniferous chert which have been exploited and on which 84 per cent of the lithic assemblage is made. This chert originates from the Carboniferous limestone of the Vale of Clwyd. Berridge (1994) suggests that it was probably collected from scree slopes beneath the limestone cliffs. The other raw materials are flint and rhyolite. Flint comprises 15 per cent of the assemblage and originates as pebbles,

probably collected from local beaches and eroding out of the glacial drift deposits. The worked rhyolite is of Snowdonian origin (Berridge 1994).

Trwyn Du is another site where raw material sources were probably local. Of the 5320 lithic artefacts from the site, only 127 have been ascribed to chert in a recent re-examination of the collection. There is a local chert source and later sites, including Trefignath, Anglesey, have also produced chert artefacts (Smith & Lynch 1987). Also at Trwyn Du are the two core axeheads/adzes made of chert and crystal tuff which are also likely to be of local origin (Clough & Cummins 1988, 246).

We note that primary sources of chert are rather more widespread in Wales than seems to have been appreciated by previous archaeological commentators. Chert occurs within the Carboniferous limestone throughout Wales. A frequently quoted source in north Wales is that of Gronant, in the Prestatyn area, but perhaps without sufficient consideration of other, often more local, sources. Chert can be found outcropping as far west as Anglesey and as far east as Halkyn, near Wrexham. It also occurs in the Namurian

FIGURE 17.8

Early Mesolithic core axehead/adze from Newport, Pembrokeshire.

of NE Wales especially in the Cefn-y-Fedw Sandstone (Wedd & King 1924). Cherts occur in the Carboniferous limestone of south Wales too. While there thus seems to be a definite preference towards use of flint from beach or drift deposits at most sites, the sources of other raw materials needs further research. Certainly, local non-flint materials contribute a more or less significant element to most lithic collections in Wales.

Economy

Very few data are available from Wales with which to speculate how its Early Mesolithic inhabitants may have conformed with models of subsistence activity proposed for elsewhere in Britain and Europe. No sites with adequate organic preservation have been investigated and a detailed knowledge of the available biota

310

is missing. There has also been substantial land-loss over the period concerned. The apparent concentration of findspots near to the present coast must in part be an artificial phenomenon, although some of these sites were close enough for the former coast to be incorporated within a day's walk.

The frequent use of beach pebble flint as a raw material for tools is certainly a recurring indicator of coastal influence. At The Nab Head, for instance, such flint, as well as chert, flakeable volcanic stone, and also the shale used to make beads (see below), can be expected to have been collected during visits to the coast for other purposes (Binford 1979). The small valley on the side of which the site lies would have provided convenient access to a proto-St Brides Bay only a short distance (c.6km) to the NE. The occupants of the site could thus easily have taken advantage of the full range of potential resources from both terrestrial and marine environments. That Early Mesolithic mobility was extensive can be judged by the dispersed findspots of apparently contemporary lithic remains at sites such as Burry Holms, Rhuddlan, Waun Fignen Felen, and Aberystwyth. Certain materials such as shale and Greensand chert were evidently moved from further afield, supporting the assumption of the mobility of human groups at this time (Barton *et al.* 1995).

While mobility may be assumed, its temporal and spatial characteristics remain unknown. No seasonal indicators are yet available, nor any clear evidence of the targets or means of subsistence. The locations, size, and content of the lithic scatters only provide clues. Welsh evidence does not contradict the basic model (Mellars 1976) in which larger aggregations of lithic material at lowland, coastal, and riverine sites are contrasted with smaller less diverse scatters that are found inland and on higher ground. Although complicated by the superposition of later occupations at the favoured lowland sites, it is possible that the latter represent longer-term exploitation than inland sites, which may have been more episodic in nature and of a smaller scale. The larger lowland sites may be those with the greatest combined advantages coincident for the greatest part of the year and might imply longer-term residence with a broader and perhaps less specialized range of activities.

Characterization of the range of activities implied above is dependent upon inferences from the lithic tool-kits. At The Nab Head, for instance, the large number of scrapers, and the burins, are indicative of the processing of organic materials such as hides, bone, and antler, and carry the implication that such activities were of a domestic, 'base-camp', nature. The procurement of game is suggested by the presence of microliths (although the function of these solely as hunting armatures is not proven: Finlayson & Mithen 1997). A relatively long

duration of the occupation at the site is perhaps most strongly hinted at by the evidence for manufacture of core axeheads/adzes, and beads. It has been argued that core axeheads/adzes were made here for use elsewhere, and it could be suggested that the accumulation of several types of lithic raw materials might also be seen as an index of duration of use of the site. The manufacture of beads is a rare and specialized activity for which the site can be singled out. The speculation that these held value as tokens of status, perhaps even passing into an exchange system, suggests that The Nab Head might even have been prominent within a regional site hierarchy. Occupation of other sites in Pembrokeshire with similar tool-kits, namely Palmerston Farm, Penpant, and Daylight Rock, might possibly have been of shorter duration.

While sharing a comparable topographic and near-coastal location to these lowland sites, the lithic assemblage from Burry Holms, also dominated by microliths and scrapers, is distinguished by the inclusion of microdenticulates. Beads and *mèches de foret* are also absent here. In the north, the sites at Rhuddlan, where the preferred location was sandy and riverine, are suggestive of the exploitation of a wide range of fish, plants, and mammals (Manley 1981). In general, the attraction of riverine locations includes fishing, transport, and access to lithic and other raw materials.

The best documented upland site is at Waun Fignen Felen where it has been observed that no processing tools are present (Barton *et al.* 1995). The locations around a lake edge would have been ideal for hunting waterfowl and other game. The sites here, with their small amounts of debitage, seem to be consistent with single knapping events associated mainly with the production of microliths and other tools for immediate use (Barton *et al.* 1995).

Traces of any upland activity elsewhere in Wales are very slight and evidence for anthropogenic effects on upland vegetation at this time is equivocal (Barton *et al.* 1995; Smith & Cloutman 1988). Occupation is indicated by broad-blade microliths from Gop Cave, Denbigh-shire, and at Brenig, on the Denbigh Moors, where four large obliquely backed points and the fragment of a large triangle have been dismissed as statistically insignificant among an assemblage dominated by Later Mesolithic activity (Healey 1993). However, an Early Mesolithic presence here is perhaps lent greater credibility now that similar microlith types have also been recognized among the lithic collection from the neighbouring site of Llyn Aled Isaf.

If Wales is therefore particularly deficient in evidence for the subsistence strategies of its Early Mesolithic inhabitants, there remains one striking component of the artefact collections which deserves more prolonged comment – the apparently non-utilitarian items.

Beads, figurines, and engraved pebbles

The stone beads are worthy of particular note. These are abundant at The Nab Head Site I, where almost 700 are recorded, all (with one exception of Old Red Sandstone) made of small discs of a water-smoothed blue-grey shale, still found today on the local beaches. The beads are usually oval in shape, occasionally with rounded sub-angular perimeters, and are typically *c.*2–3mm thick. With few exceptions, they are perforated by a central hole, U-shaped in section, and drilled from only one face. The presence of partially drilled beads and bead 'blanks' – or unworked discs of shale – clearly suggests that the site was a production centre. This impression is confirmed by the many flint *mèches de forets* whose rounded tips fit neatly within the bead perforations (Fig. 17.7).

Experimentation using replica *mèches de foret* has demonstrated that two people can make approximately 100 beads in an hour using a bow- or pump-drill, although without such mechanical assistance the process is much slower and more laborious. Given the ease with which they can be made and the quantities of *mèches de foret* discarded at the site (at least 75), it would not be surprising if the extant beads from The Nab Head represent only a small fraction of a potentially prodigious quantity of such items, many of which may have been lost to erosion and careless excavation. The surface condition of the flint drill-bits found at The Nab Head has so far precluded microwear study. In his examination of examples of such tools from both Star Carr and Mount Sandel, Dumont has suggested that they were used on bone, wood, hide, and unidentified materials. Potential hafting traces were found on two of the Mount Sandel tools, and for most instances of use-wear, a boring and rotary motion was indicated (Dumont 1983; 1985).

There are many potential uses for beads, but here it is possible only to speculate. They are unlikely to have had any practical role and were possibly of aesthetic, 'psychic' (*sensu* Clark 1975), or status value. In all probability they may have been worn about the person as adornment for both the living and the dead, although there is no supporting evidence for burials at the site. They may be strung in several ways, not least edge-to-edge, forming elaborate designs incorporated into garments, hair, or extraneous decoration on personal items, tools, weapons, or cult objects. The presence of so many *mèches de foret* at the site hint that shale may not have been the only material so treated. Soil conditions have not favoured the preservation of shell, bone, antler, fossil or walrus ivory, teeth, leather, or wood, all of which could be decorated or pierced using the same basic instrument. It is signifi-cant that no stone beads were found at Daylight Rock (van Nèdervelde pers. comm.) where *mèches de foret* are

an important element of the tool-kit (10% of all tools and fragments).

The very substantial number of beads recorded from The Nab Head sets the site apart from its apparent con-temporaries both in Britain and further afield. However, a number of other sites in Britain have produced similar beads. Excavations at Waun Fignen Felen, Site 6, uncovered one complete example and two fragments made of spotted mudstone associated with Early Mesolithic artefacts (Barton *et al.* 1995; Berridge 1981). At Freshwater East, Pembrokeshire, a shale bead like those from The Nab Head was found eroding from a coastal section with lithic artefacts of Early Mesolithic appearance (Leach 1933; Jacobi 1980, fig. 4.5). Surface finds have been made from Linney Burrows and Palmerston Farm, Pembrokeshire (Fig. 17.7), in both cases associated with lithic collections containing Mesolithic artefacts. In England beads have also been found at sites including Star Carr (Clark 1954, 167) where 27 beads of Lias shale were recovered, while at Rushy Brow (Lancs) four shale bead fragments were found within sediment samples collected from a site with broad-blade microliths (Howard-Davis 1996) which are indistinguishable in terms of size and outline from those at Star Carr. Single beads have also been found with Mesolithic artefacts at three additional sites: Staple Crag (Co. Durham), has produced a sub-oval ?shale bead, centrally pierced from one face (Coggins *et al.* 1989, fig. 3, no. 35); at Manton Warren Area 5 (South Humberside) a bead of grey-brown shale was a surface find with both Early Mesolithic large triangles and Later Mesolithic tools (Jacobi pers. comm.); and at Thatcham Site VI (Berks), where a fragment of a small perforated oval pebble of siliceous limestone was found with Early Mesolithic artefacts (Jacobi pers. comm.). In sum, this listing is strongly suggestive of the association of such stone beads with presumed Early Mesolithic flintwork. The recent find of a bead from Chapel Cave, near Malham (Yorks), has unspecific Mesolithic associations (Donahue & Lovis 2000) and therefore there are no instances where such beads can be demonstrated to be associated only with Later Mesolithic narrow-blade material.

As the *mèches de foret* from Star Carr are mostly too large to have drilled the beads from that site, The Nab Head is at present the only site where actual manufacture of beads may be suggested. The presence of individual beads on the four remaining Welsh sites may imply that these objects, in addition to a possible ornamental role, also played a part in a system of exchange; indeed it has been determined that the beads at Waun Fignen Felen may have a Pembrokeshire origin (Barton *et al.* 1995). The mobility of human groups at this time was surely great enough to account for one or more such groups leaving similar material traces at different and sometimes widely separated locations.

Reference to the beads at The Nab Head would not be complete without a mention of the now well-known 'figurine', 'phallus', or 'amulet' (Fig. 17.9) found by the Revd J. P. Gordon-Williams in about 1925, associated with at least nine beads (Gordon-Williams 1925; 1926). The carving appears to be made out of shale similar to that of the beads. It is now a very dark grey in colour with a texture and appearance not unlike graphite, presumably owing to persistent handling, not least since its discovery. The finder's reference to an original coating of 'soapy substance' is particularly curious and both the longevity of the site and its soil conditions belie his suggestion that the object retained an original deposit of fat or clay in which it had been stored in a bag alongside the 'necklace'.

Microscopic examination shows some slight modern damage and extensive but faint signs of the original sculpting. Narrow incised grooves define the Y-shaped central area, while the 'testes' appear to have been modelled by abrasion, leaving a faceted surface with very faint directional striations overlain in places by more random scratches. The 'shaft' has striations parallel to its axis, but this, like most of the dorsal surface, is much muted and smoothed by soft attrition or polishing. The ventral surface is flat and seems to be largely unmodified.

What is at first glance clearly a phallic representation could, with a little conceptual licence, become a symbol of the two sexes very subtly blended into a single bisexual object. Such stylization and economy of expression, but limited to one sex or the other and particularly associated with the 'Venuses', is common in Upper Palaeolithic figurines from throughout Europe (Leroi-Gourhan 1968). Examples of intentional bisexual representations, however, are unusual in the European Palaeolithic. Breuil (1955) compared The Nab Head piece with a figure from Trasimeno, Italy, and another from Weinberg, Mauern, Germany, but neither parallel is very satisfactory (Delporte 1979, figs 64 & 79).

In support of the feminine aspect of the Welsh piece is its profile, which is reminiscent of the stylized engravings of women found at several late Magdalenian sites such as Lalinde, France, or Gonnersdorf, Germany. Although stylized anthropomorphic figures engraved or drilled on bone or antler occur within the Early Holocene (Clark 1975, 155), figurines 'in the round' do not reappear until the early Neolithic cultures of parts of the eastern Mediterranean. The Nab Head specimen would consequently seem to be entirely isolated from any meaningful comparative studies.

It may be stated here, for the record, that it was the opinion of Professor W. F. Grimes (pers. comm.) that Gordon-Williams's scruples may not have allayed

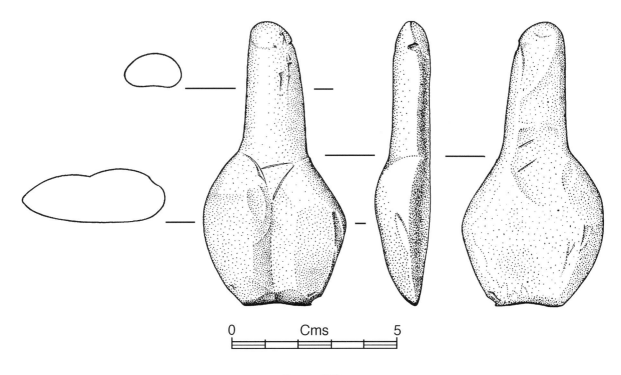

FIGURE 17.9
Early Mesolithic artwork: The Nab Head figurine.

a temptation to invent such an important discovery. Grimes knew the clergyman well, but this suggestion is based only on a personal assessment of his character, rather than on any specific indications or intimations of forgery. A motive might be found in the intense rivalry between local amateur collectors at this time.

In conclusion, therefore, it is perhaps more realistic to view The Nab Head object as simply a phallus, perhaps an amulet, without any convenient parallel. If genuine, its association seems most likely to be with the beads, also of shale, found with it and which have been attributed, with much of the flintwork, to the Early Mesolithic use of the site.

Jacobi (1980) has speculated that a further item from The Nab Head collection may be important. It is a rounded sliver of shale with a groove apparently incised into its broader end, parallel to the long axis (Gordon-Williams 1926, 93). Oriented vertically with the groove at the bottom, this piece might be interpreted as a stylized Venus figurine (Jacobi 1980, 159). Its surface is unfortunately too weathered even to be sure if it has in fact been artificially modified.

Other non-utilitarian lithic artefacts from Wales include the six engraved pebbles found during excavations at Rhuddlan (Fig. 17.10; Berridge 1994). Although five of these were from residual contexts, one was excavated from the shallow hollow on Site M which contained an Early Mesolithic assemblage and from which the insecure ^{14}C determination of 7680–7380 cal BC (BM-822) was obtained (see above). Technical similarities among all six engraved pebbles suggest that they may all be Mesolithic. The striations were compared with experimentally produced marks on pebbles and results showed a match between the original striations and those made using replica flint or chert artefacts (Roberts 1994). More recently, comparable engraved pebbles have been discovered at Trevose Head, Cornwall, and while these are surface finds among a collection with both an Early Mesolithic and a later prehistoric component, the similarities with the Rhuddlan specimens are striking (P. Berridge pers. comm.).

These very singular finds are the only tangible evidence for a 'psychic' or social dimension to the Early Mesolithic in Wales. Unfortunately, there is minimal surviving evidence for human burial at this time, although this certainly seems to have taken place in caves, as evidenced by burials from Gough's Cave and Aveline's Hole, both near Cheddar. The latter cave, for which tantalizingly few records remain (Davies 1921; 1922), seems to have been the site of a collective burial of as many as 70 individuals (Schulting & Wysocki 2002), from some of which ^{14}C determinations overlap with those from the earliest Welsh sites. The single but largely complete individual from Gough's Cave could also have been a contemporary of the inhabitants of Daylight Rock and The Nab Head, with a ^{14}C determination of 8550–7970 cal BC (OxA-814: Gowlett *et al.* 1986). No human material of this antiquity has yet been identified from Wales, the earliest determination being that for a human ulna of 8240–7600 cal BC (OxA-4024; Hedges *et al.* 1996) from The Worms Head Cave, Gower, just three miles south of Burry Holms. The series of determinations from Caldey Island (Schulting 1998, 178; Schulting & Richards 2002, 1014) all fall later than the earliest secure dates for the Later Mesolithic.

Later Mesolithic Wales

The definition of a Late or Later Mesolithic in Britain has its origin in the recognition of distinct lithic assemblages which date no earlier than *c.*7950 cal BC. In particular, after this time there is a marked change in the composition of the microlithic component, the limited range of relatively broad and large early microlith shapes being succeeded by a suite of more various and smaller narrow-blade or 'geometric' types. Especially common among the latter are narrow elongated scalene triangles, straight- and convex-backed bladelets, lanceolates, and less commonly, four-sided, and 'micro-*petit tranchet*' forms, among others. The non-microlithic tool-kit that accompanies such items includes less refined scrapers than previously, and various retouched flakes and blades; burins and microdenticulates are also known to occur and can be difficult to distinguish from those in earlier assemblages. Core axeheads/adzes seem to disappear in some areas, such as northern England, but continue to be found in later contexts in parts of southern England. *Mèches de foret* appear to be absent from micro-triangle assemblages. Alongside such changes in the tool inventory, some parts of the country also saw a change in the types of raw material exploited (Pitts & Jacobi 1979).

In Wales, among the 296 recorded Mesolithic findspots (Jacobi 1980; Wymer 1977), there are many more sites with the later narrow-blade types than there are with a solely earlier broad-blade assemblage. Collections from the former sites are mainly characterized by the presence of scalene micro-triangles, 'rods', and various points of lanceolate outline. These are often associated with burins, denticulates, notched, nosed, and truncated pieces, and choppers. A recurring feature in the lithic inventory of coastally located sites are pebble tools, usually elongated beach pebbles with bevelled ends.

The distribution of the narrow-blade findspots in Wales (Fig. 17.11) is biased by the constraints of

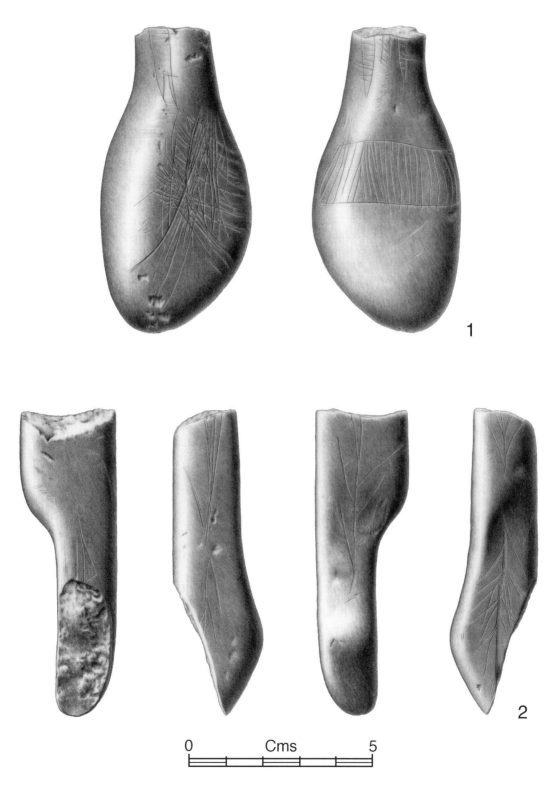

FIGURE 17.10
Early Mesolithic artwork: Rhuddlan decorated pebbles.

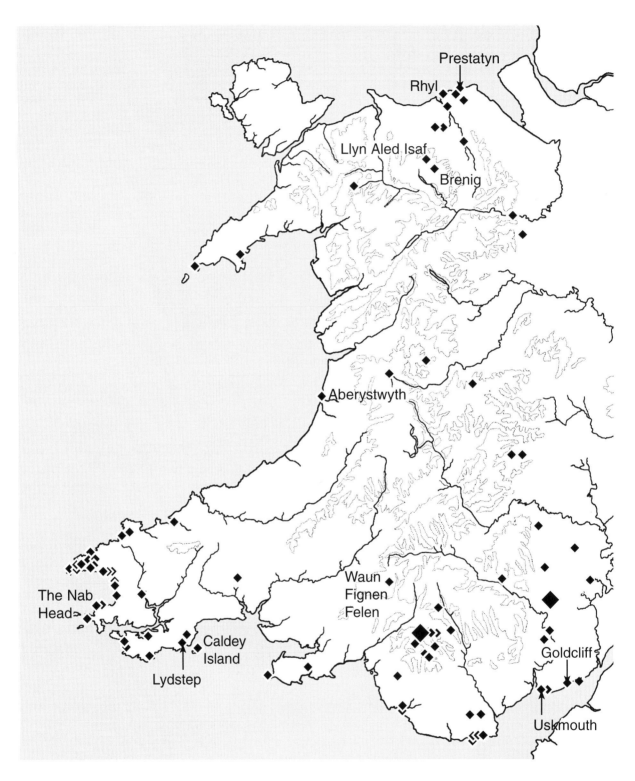

FIGURE 17.11
Distribution map of Later Mesolithic findspots in Wales.

surface cover and concentrated local collecting, with the consequent clustering of sites on the coasts of south and west Wales (David 1990) and in the Glamorgan uplands (Stanton 1984). Within these areas work at The Nab Head Site II and more recently at Ogmore-by-Sea, Bridgend, and Goldcliff, Newport, has added to our knowledge of the period. Outside these areas only three sites – Prestatyn (Clark 1938; 1939), Brenig (Lynch 1993), and The Hendre, Rhuddlan (Manley & Healey 1982), all in Denbighshire – have received any detailed treatment; systematic exploration or documentation of other sites has been minimal.

Chronology
The ^{14}C record for this period in Wales continues to be patchy, as for the Early Mesolithic, but there are a growing number of findspots for which determinations can be applied directly to the material culture they are supposedly dating (Fig. 17.12).

The first of these, chronologically, is at Prestatyn. A section, excavated here during construction work in the town, was recorded by Mr F. Gilbert Smith in 1926 (*ms.* at the British Museum). Smith recorded the stratigraphy in detail and identified a distinct archaeological horizon within it. The lithic assemblage comprises narrow scalene triangles, small obliquely backed and straight-backed bladelets, and an isosceles micro-triangle. As well as microliths there are retouched flakes and convex scrapers (Clark 1938; 1939; Smith 1926). Two hazelnut shells were submitted for dating with results of 8200–7540 cal BC (OxA-2268) and 8200–7580 cal BC (OxA-2269). These dates appear to push the narrow-blade lithic assemblage very early in the chronological sequence for both Britain and the Continent. At Duvensee, in Germany, for instance, the latest date obtained for an Early Mesolithic microlith assemblage (living-site 6) is 8270–7600 cal BC (KL-1112), while an assemblage of narrow scalene triangles and obliquely backed bladelets, very similar to those from Prestatyn, is recorded from living-site 13 and dated to *c.*7700 cal BC (Bokelmann 1985; Willkomm 1985). For England, the only relevant determination to precede those from Prestatyn is that for Filpoke Beacon (Co. Durham) of 8270–7540 cal BC (Q-1474; Jacobi 1976).

It is apparent that the Prestatyn narrow-blade material would seem to pre-date the broad-blade type at Trwyn Du and Rhuddlan Site M, while being nearly identical in age to that from Rhuddlan Site E. The doubts already expressed concerning the reliability of these other dates from north Wales would thus seem to be emphasized by the Prestatyn results. With these reservations in mind, it is nevertheless of interest to note that simple obliquely backed points are common to all these

collections, although at Prestatyn they are subsidiary to narrow scalene triangles. The size of obliquely backed points has been shown to diminish with time (Pitts & Jacobi 1979), and one could speculate that an evolution in scalene triangles might also be detectable. The 'narrow' triangles from Prestatyn are, in these terms, both simpler and larger than other narrow-blade microlith assemblages of later date which contain both smaller and more various microlith shapes (Fig. 17.13). With their significant representation of obliquely backed points, the Prestatyn microliths might thus be argued to conform to some kind of technological development sequential with earlier forms. Such theoretical links are less obvious among the non-microlithic component of the tool-kits, although it could be significant that end scrapers are common to both the Prestatyn and Early Mesolithic artefact assemblages.

Such attempts to see typological links spanning the Early to Later Mesolithic technologies may well be unfounded, however, and do not, as yet, take into account important additional factors such as the influence of changing raw materials, nor the needs of different hunting strategies (Myers 1989). More significant, too, may be the differences between the two groupings, rather than the similarities. Core axeheads/adzes and *mèches de foret* are apparently absent from later assemblages, although at Prestatyn it is important to remember that only a very small area was investigated and the resulting collection is probably unrepresentative of the whole. Clearly, more sites, larger artefact assemblages, and closer dating are required before we can begin to explain this transition properly.

Following its apparent inception in the north, the dating of the Welsh Later Mesolithic is provided by ^{14}C determinations mostly obtained from findspots in the south and west. Eleven determinations are now available for human skeletal material from caves. These determinations are joined by others on organic artefacts and food remains from Uskmouth, Splash Point at Rhyl, Goldcliff, and Lydstep.

At The Nab Head Site II four determinations ranging from 7320–3540 cal BC have been obtained. Each is on an individual piece of charcoal, and therefore should not present the problems involved with 'average' dates on bulked samples. At The Nab Head, however, soil profiles are relatively thin, and allowance must be made for the possibility of the mobility of individual charcoal fragments of different ages through the profile, accumulating at the same horizon as the lithic industry. Indeed, the introduction of charcoal from different sources at or near the site must explain the very wide chronological spread of dates obtained. Post-Mesolithic activity on the site also cannot be discounted (David

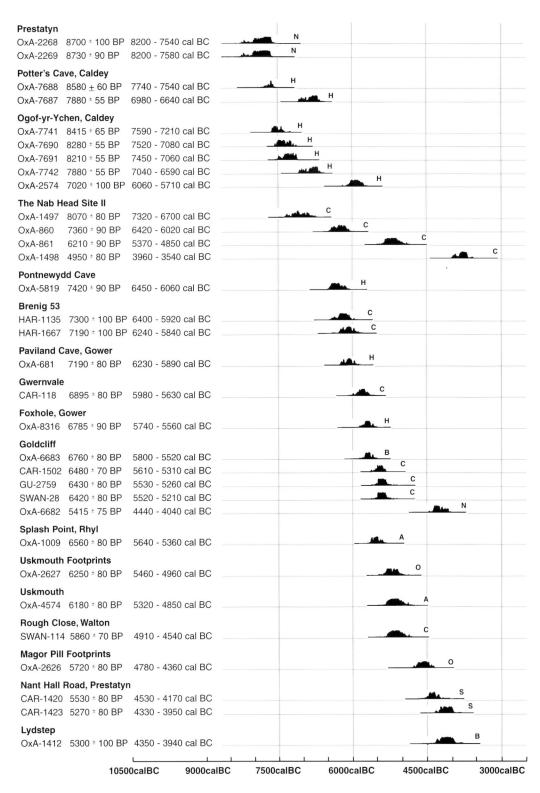

Prestatyn
OxA-2268 8700 ± 100 BP 8200 - 7540 cal BC
OxA-2269 8730 ± 90 BP 8200 - 7580 cal BC

Potter's Cave, Caldey
OxA-7688 8580 ± 60 BP 7740 - 7540 cal BC
OxA-7687 7880 ± 55 BP 6980 - 6640 cal BC

Ogof-yr-Ychen, Caldey
OxA-7741 8415 ± 65 BP 7590 - 7210 cal BC
OxA-7690 8280 ± 55 BP 7520 - 7080 cal BC
OxA-7691 8210 ± 55 BP 7450 - 7060 cal BC
OxA-7742 7880 ± 55 BP 7040 - 6590 cal BC
OxA-2574 7020 ± 100 BP 6060 - 5710 cal BC

The Nab Head Site II
OxA-1497 8070 ± 80 BP 7320 - 6700 cal BC
OxA-860 7360 ± 90 BP 6420 - 6020 cal BC
OxA-861 6210 ± 90 BP 5370 - 4850 cal BC
OxA-1498 4950 ± 80 BP 3960 - 3540 cal BC

Pontnewydd Cave
OxA-5819 7420 ± 90 BP 6450 - 6060 cal BC

Brenig 53
HAR-1135 7300 ± 100 BP 6400 - 5920 cal BC
HAR-1667 7190 ± 100 BP 6240 - 5840 cal BC

Paviland Cave, Gower
OxA-681 7190 ± 80 BP 6230 - 5890 cal BC

Gwernvale
CAR-118 6895 ± 80 BP 5980 - 5630 cal BC

Foxhole, Gower
OxA-8316 6785 ± 90 BP 5740 - 5560 cal BC

Goldcliff
OxA-6683 6760 ± 80 BP 5800 - 5520 cal BC
CAR-1502 6480 ± 70 BP 5610 - 5310 cal BC
GU-2759 6430 ± 80 BP 5530 - 5260 cal BC
SWAN-28 6420 ± 80 BP 5520 - 5210 cal BC
OxA-6682 5415 ± 75 BP 4440 - 4040 cal BC

Splash Point, Rhyl
OxA-1009 6560 ± 80 BP 5640 - 5360 cal BC

Uskmouth Footprints
OxA-2627 6250 ± 80 BP 5460 - 4960 cal BC

Uskmouth
OxA-4574 6180 ± 80 BP 5320 - 4850 cal BC

Rough Close, Walton
SWAN-114 5860 ± 70 BP 4910 - 4540 cal BC

Magor Pill Footprints
OxA-2626 5720 ± 80 BP 4780 - 4360 cal BC

Nant Hall Road, Prestatyn
CAR-1420 5530 ± 80 BP 4530 - 4170 cal BC
CAR-1423 5270 ± 80 BP 4330 - 3950 cal BC

Lydstep
OxA-1412 5300 ± 100 BP 4350 - 3940 cal BC

10500calBC 9000calBC 7500calBC 6000calBC 4500calBC 3000calBC

FIGURE 17.12

The chronological range of radiocarbon determinations for the Welsh Later Mesolithic period. Key: A = artefact; B = animal bone; C = charcoal; H = human bone; N = nutshell; O = organic sediment; S = shell midden.

1990, 237). Despite this possibility the lithic assemblage appears at first sight to be homogenous and to belong, if not to a single event, then to repeated occupations over a relatively brief timespan, perhaps a few generations. However, the AMS determinations indicate activity over at least 3000 years, and such an impression needs careful reconsideration. The range of dating obtained cannot be related to any particular episode of activity on the headland and it is now clear that the area was visited at different times during the Later Mesolithic. Of the other dates for Wales, only those for Prestatyn fall outside the range represented at The Nab Head. The Nab Head appears to be typical of coastal sites where occupation has recurred repetitively, creating a palimpsest of artefact scatters. As evident here, attempts to disentangle the characteristics and dating of the component parts of such aggregations present major methodological problems, especially in dry shallow soils.

From non-coastal sites ^{14}C determinations are few and far between. At Brenig 53, the stratigraphically latest of a group of intercutting bowl-shaped pits contained a microlith, six pieces of debitage, and charcoal (Allen 1993). Radiocarbon determinations from this complex have provided results of 6400–5920 cal BC (HAR-1135) and 6240–5840 cal BC (HAR-1667: Lynch 1993, 30). Over 30 stakeholes were found in rows near the pits but unfortunately cannot certainly be attributed to the Mesolithic phase. At Rough Close in the Walton area of Radnorshire, charcoal from a pit, without artefacts, has provided a result of 4910–4540 cal BC (SWAN-114: Gibson 1999, 11), and at Gwernvale, Monmouthshire, a determination of 5980–5630 cal BC (CAR-118) was obtained from a pit in the landsurface beneath the Neolithic long cairn (Britnell & Savory 1984, 50).

This summary of the dating evidence points to the likelihood that Wales was exploited by 'narrow-blade communities' from c.8000–3750 cal BC. It seems highly probable that this exploitation was continuous, but it is at present a curiosity of the record that all the calibrated dates on human bone fall within the earlier half of this span, that part of it which is nearly bereft of actual cultural remains; apart from the determinations from Prestatyn and two from The Nab Head, all the calibrated dates for the Welsh Later Mesolithic fall later than 6000 cal BC.

The environment
The developing woodland succession of the Early Holocene reached its peak of dense mixed deciduous woodland during the Atlantic phase. The rapid rise in sea level from as low as −15.2m OD in the Early Mesolithic to about −4.64m OD at c.5900 cal BC (Tooley 1978) led to a climate of increasing oceanicity. Wetter and windier

conditions, in combination with warmer summers and milder winters, induced exceptional growth of mixed alder-oak woodlands with elm, and occasional lime and ash, replacing the birch and pine of the preceding Boreal. As with previous periods, there was considerable local diversity in the response of vegetation to the varying constraints of topography and geography. The western 'maritime fringe' experienced exceptionally mild winters, although temperature lapse rates with altitude ensured a significant contrast with adjacent uplands. The wooded landscape of oak-alder-hazel forest was nevertheless very extensive here, although on the most exposed areas only hazel scrub may have survived, leaving oak and alder confined to sheltered valley locations (Donald 1987). Wood peats exposed at intertidal locations around south and west Wales indicate the prevalence of a uniform alder-carr vegetation in less exposed coastal and estuarine areas (Lewis 1992).

Much of the Bristol Channel and Cardigan Bay areas was probably flooded by c.7950 cal BC when sea level was at about −22m, and sea level continued to rise throughout the Later Mesolithic period, reaching about −2m at c. 4850 cal BC (Heyworth & Kidson 1982, fig. 2). In many lowland coastal areas a rising water-table kept pace with sea level, encouraging the upward development of peats supporting woodland carr. Inundation of these woodlands appears to have been spasmodic, dependant on the breaching of offshore barriers during storm surges and/or exceptional tides (Heyworth & Kidson 1982; Lewis 1992).

Inland, in upland areas, an imbalance in water loss led to the initiation of ombrogenous peats as early as c.6450 cal BC in the uplands of south Wales, though it has been argued by Smith (Smith 1984; Smith & Cloutman 1988) that after an initial climatic change at the end of the Boreal period, both the spread of alder and the initiation of upland peats may have been encouraged by environmental damage by man.

The main components of the terrestrial fauna inhabiting the largely forested conditions of the Later Mesolithic had already become well established in the earlier Boreal and Preboreal. Prey species include red and roe deer, wild pig, and wild cattle. Otter and brown bear have been identified in Atlantic-age contexts (Grigson 1981), and it may also be assumed that wolf, beaver, pine marten, badger, hedgehog, mole, common shrew, and the water vole were common throughout the Postglacial (Grigson 1981). Marine mammals recorded from Scottish midden sites, and which may have frequented other parts of the British coast, include common and grey seal, rorqual, and dolphin. Fish species including saithe, cod, haddock, turbot, salmonid, and sturgeon have been identified in Scottish midden sites (Coles

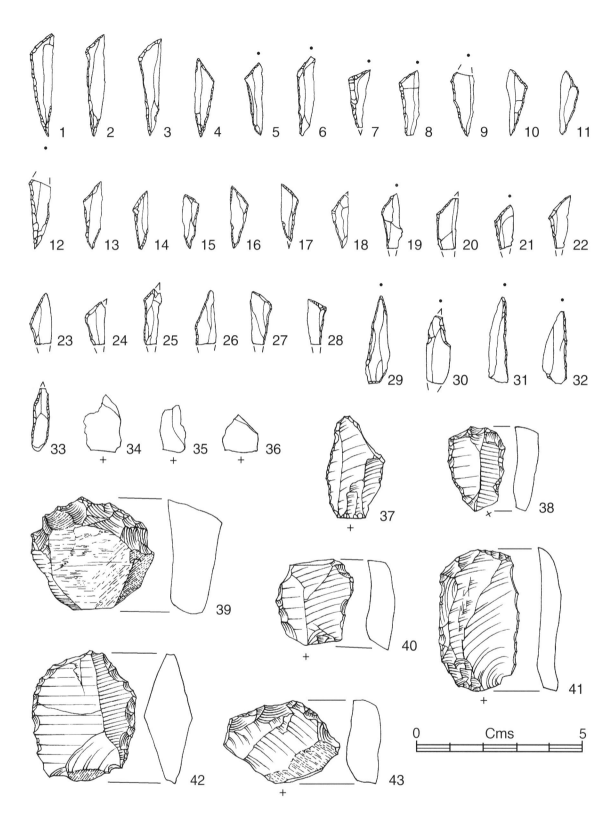

FIGURE 17.13
Prestatyn Later Mesolithic finds: 1–33 microliths; 34–36 microburins; 37–43 scrapers.

1971). At Morton (Fife) some 40 species of shellfish were recognized, including crab. Freshwater fish such as pike and perch may have been confined to the river systems draining into the southern North Sea (Wheeler 1977), while salmonids and eels were probably present throughout the country. Birds are also well represented on northern sites and coastal species are frequently found; wildfowl and woodland birds will have been abundant nearly everywhere.

With such faunal diversity, it is a disappointment that evidence for it, and its exploitation by man, is so limited in Wales. Although it may be a safe probability to assume the presence of many elements within the faunal range pieced together from diverse locations elsewhere in Britain, such instances from Wales are all but missing. Those that there are come from either submerged peat deposits or from a small number of stratified cave sites. At Potter's Cave on Caldey, a fauna including wild cattle, pig, fox, deer (unspecified), and dog has been identified (Lacaille & Grimes 1955, 126). While these animals were apparently associated with unretouched blades and cores of Mesolithic character (Jacobi 1980, 183) it cannot be certain to which part of this period they belong. Much the same comment could be made for the occurrences of faunal and artefact remains at Nanna's Cave and Ogof-yr-Ychen, also on Caldey, and at Cathole, Gower, where Campbell (1977, 120) records faunal remains associated with a Later Mesolithic assemblage. Ogof Carreg Hir, Pembrokeshire (Davies 1978; 1989) produced a Later Mesolithic microlith from 'midden' deposits, possibly of mixed ages, which also included remains of red and roe deer, fox, wolf, bear, and bird bones. At Foel Fawr Cave, Llandovery, ^{14}C determinations on wild cattle bones centre at c.6100 cal BC (BM-1809, BM-1810, BM-1903; Burleigh et al. 1982), but these finds are without archaeological association.

Finds from coastal deposits are often tantalizingly without chronological information. For example, several undiagnostic flint flakes and broken bladelets were recovered with fragmentary remains of red deer, small mammal bones, insects, charcoal, and wood at a height of c.2m above OD at Horton Beach, Gower (M. Davies pers. comm.). Finds of groups of flints are also reported from Amroth, Frainslake, Abermawr, and Newport, all in Pembrokeshire (David 1990, 198; Lewis 1992). At Frainslake there were two flint scatters as well as evidence for 'a windscreen of gorse, birch, hazel and alder ... set in peat ... [with] ... on the north side of this shelter which ran in a gentle curve for 4.5 yards ... an area bearing much charcoal, flint chips ... a large rabattu point ... etc.' (Gordon-Williams 1926, 108; cf. Leach 1918). The associated lithic material which survives is undated, although the presence of bladelet cores and bevelled pebbles implies a Mesolithic attribution (Jacobi 1980, 175). At other sites, finds such as those of wild cattle bones at Whitesands Bay, Pembrokeshire, and at Rumney on the Severn Levels have proved to be of Neolithic and Bronze Age derivation.

Perhaps the most convincing evidence for the association of man and fauna from Wales is the complete pig skeleton discovered on the foreshore at Lydstep Haven, Pembrokeshire, during a temporary exposure of the 'forest bed' in 1916 (Leach 1918). In the woody peat, directly above the neck vertebrae, were two small backed bladelets. Although no lesions are detectable on the surviving skeletal material (S. Payne pers. comm.), it nevertheless seems justifiable to regard the group as representing a hunting loss (Jacobi 1980, 175). The ^{14}C determination of 4350–3940 cal BC (OxA-1412; Hedges et al. 1989) is surprisingly late. However, more recently, excavations of a Later Mesolithic cultural horizon at Goldcliff, in the Severn Levels, have identified the certain exploitation of red deer, roe deer, wild pig, and otter, as well as species of estuarine fish and some birds; wolf was also present (Bell et al. 2000, 48). Tens of thousands of animal prints have been noted in this intertidal area of the Levels, where extensive tracts of Mesolithic landscape can be exposed (Bell et al. 2001).

Artefacts and raw materials
The suite of lithic artefacts which characterize the Welsh Later Mesolithic has been referred to above. As with our discussion of the Early Mesolithic we remain dependant upon the lithic artefacts, in the absence of much else, for the attempted definition of the incidence and lifestyle of the Later Mesolithic population of Wales.

The prevalent raw material is beach pebble flint, supplemented in SW Wales at nearly every findspot by low percentages (<4%) of other stone such as Cretaceous chert or local conchoidally fracturing igneous rock. In north Wales a higher proportion of the assemblages are made of locally available Carboniferous chert, but with beach pebble flint still present at all sites. Small-sized beach pebble flint is, however, an intractable material to work and the abundance of waste almost certainly results from expediency rather than simple wantonness. Use was made of the entire range of raw material available at the time, in contrast to the apparently deliberate selection of the largest pebbles during the preceding Early Mesolithic. It remains to be seen whether or not a rising sea level limited the availability of the latter and, by necessitating the use of smaller raw material, motivated the introduction of a narrow-blade technology – or whether this was a consequence of changing hunting technologies (Myers 1989). There is no geological or geomorphological reasoning to support

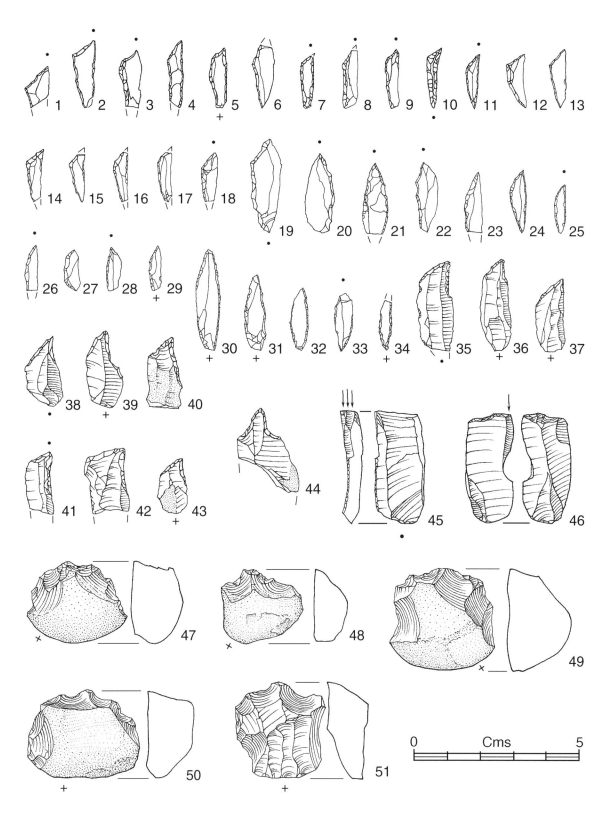

FIGURE 17.14
Cwm Bach, Pembrokeshire, Later Mesolithic finds: 1–34 microliths; 35–44 'becs'; 45–46 burins; 47–51 denticulates.

a significant differential distribution of grades of flint pebble. It seems unlikely, therefore, that the constraints of raw material were, on their own, responsible for the observed innovations in lithic tools.

A highly distinctive accompaniment to narrow-blade microliths are denticulates (Fig. 17.14). These are made on large primary or secondary flakes, often D-shaped in cross-section, and can be identified by steep and coarse retouch around a part of their perimeter, lending them a notched or denticulated outline. An alternative term for these might be 'denticulated scrapers', although their function is not yet understood and their form is often intermediate between scraper and bladelet core.

Less conspicuous, but locally significant, are burins, and a variety of 'end-tools' often taking the form of asymmetrically retouched points ('becs') on flakes or bladelets. Apart from occasional coarsely flaked pebbles ('choppers') there are no diagnostic core tools in these assemblages. Core axeheads/adzes and picks seem to be absent (with the possible exception of two unstratified examples from Goldcliff, not associated with the excavated Later Mesolithic site there: Bell et al. 2000, 46).

This absence of core tools is amply made up, on coastal sites at least, by the presence of large numbers of pebble tools. Predominantly these are the so-called bevelled pebbles, the use of which remains tediously unresolved. We illustrate them here with examples from The Nab Head Site II where 55 complete examples and fragments of many more were excavated (Fig. 17.15). In each case the tool is made from an elongate and usually flattish water-worn pebble probably originating, like the flint, from nearby beaches. In well-preserved examples there is usually a pronounced bevelled edge on either side of one or sometimes both ends. Very often, it is clear that the end of the tool has also been flaked by percussion and then abraded or bevelled. Sometimes there is evidence for pecking or percussion on the flanks of the stone and in one case the end and part of the lateral margin has a distinct polish through use.

Bevelled pebbles – the 'limpet scoops' or 'limpet hammers' of former literature – have been the subject of much discussion ever since their recognition in the 'Obanian' caves and middens of western Scotland (Anderson 1895; 1898; Bishop 1914, 95; Breuil 1922; Cantrill 1915; Clark 1955; Gordon-Williams 1926; Grieve 1883; Jacobi 1980; Lacaille 1954; Mellars 1987; Movius 1942; Reynolds 1983; Roberts 1987). It is not intended to re-state the debate in detail here since attempts to resolve the function of these enigmatic tools are no further advanced than they were at the outset, almost 100 years ago. Experimentation has, however, thrown doubt on their association with limpets or other

shellfish and instead a possible role in hide-working is favoured by Jacobi (1980, 189). Others have proposed a function associated with percussion (Breuil 1922; Roberts 1987; Wickham-Jones & Sharples 1984). There is one factor in particular, however, which links the many findspots upon which bevelled pebbles have been found. They are, without exception, coastal or near-coastal and, more particularly, widely spread along the Atlantic seaboard only on rocky coastlines. Sites on 'soft' shorelines with sandy coasts – such as Ogmore-by-Sea – have not produced such tools. Jacobi (1980, fig. 4.30) has mapped their occurrences on the coasts of Wales and the SW peninsula, and bevelled pebbles are also recorded from Ireland (Movius 1942; Woodman 1978a, 115) and the Isle of Man (Woodman 1978b).

Despite their wide geographical spread along the Atlantic margin, and the common factor of bevelling, there is very considerable variation in the morphology of these tools. Both the width and shape of the bevelled end(s) vary, as do the pebbles on which they are worked. Most of those from west Wales are somewhat less 'shapely' than those on 'Obanian' and some Cornish sites where they can be small, neat, and symmetrical (Lacaille 1954, figs 88 & 94; Smith 1982, fig. 15, no. 77). The slimness of some of the latter is reminiscent of Early Bronze Age 'finger-stones', but the impression is belied by the misshapen and casual nature of many others. Raw material is also variable, with bone and red deer antler bevelled artefacts precisely analogous to their stone counterparts recorded from the calcareous 'Obanian' deposits.

The relationship between size and raw material of bevelled tools from a range of British sites is shown (Fig. 17.16). From this it is clear that tools of all three raw materials (stone, bone, and antler) from the 'Obanian' middens are distinguished by their overall smallness and relatively narrow bevelled ends (Reynolds 1983). Within this group, the stone bevelled pebbles are predominantly larger than their bone and antler counterparts, yet none approach the dimensions of the bevelled pebbles from Cornish and Welsh sites and Alderney (Channel Islands). Such variation may in part be explained by the selection imposed by geology upon the availability of suitable pebble-blanks. However, as small stone pebbles could be argued to have been more or less equally available to 'Obanian' and Welsh Mesolithic groups, but unused by the latter, some genuine functional or cultural difference would appear to have existed in the use of these tools between the two areas.

As some 33 per cent of the bevelled implements from midden sites on Oronsay are of bone or antler (Reynolds 1983), it must remain speculative whether tools of these materials were also used on the more southerly findspots, where soil conditions are acidic, or even on sites located

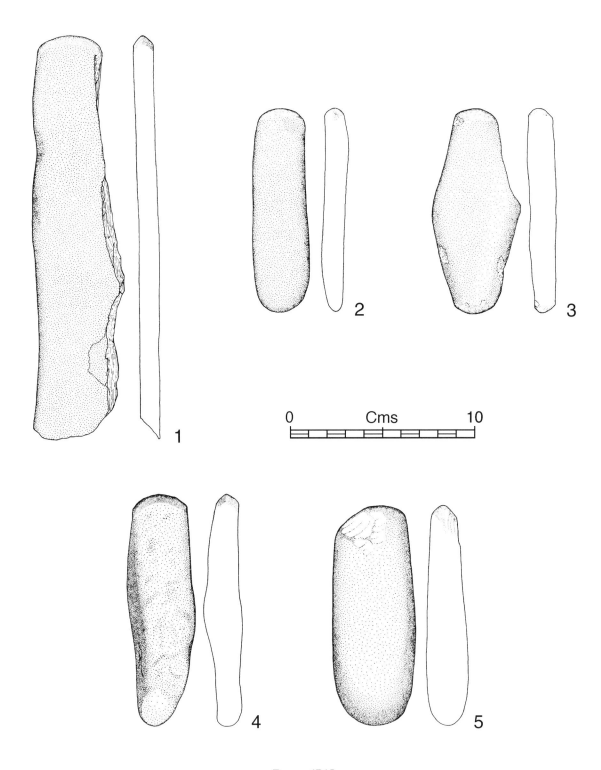

FIGURE 17.15
Later Mesolithic bevelled pebbles: 1–3 The Nab Head Site II; 4–5 Cwm Bach I.

inland. In SW Wales an example of a bevelled tool made of bone is recorded from Nanna's Cave, Caldey (Lacaille & Grimes 1955, fig. 17), and a possible bone implement from Frainslake (David 1990, fig. 5.2, no. 2) may also belong in this same general category. Interestingly, the dimensions of the Nanna's Cave specimen place it within the Scottish group.

While quantities of bevelled pebbles have for long been a familiar feature of coastal findspots, The Nab Head Site II is distinguished by the additional presence of altogether more finished and elaborately modified ground stone tools. These are pecked and ground stone axeheads or adzes, of which three have been recovered, and a single perforated and ground stone disc (Fig. 17.17). No precise analogues for such axeheads have yet been recovered from any excavated British prehistoric context. Most striking about their appearance is their similarity, one to another. All three have a clearly defined symmetrical working-edge ground from both faces. The blade is gently curved, flaring to give a very slight but distinctive 'flange' at either side. The 'trunk' is approximately cylindrical in outline, tapering to a rounded butt. In section it is oval with the faces of the tool locally ground or polished flat. The flanks and much of the overall surface of both axeheads 1 and 3 are pecked, and it may be assumed that axehead 2 also owes its finished shape to a deliberate and thorough modification of its entire surface.

Thin-sections of axeheads 2 and 3 identify their raw material as deriving from medium-grained basic igneous rock belonging to outcrops in west Wales (C. Houlder pers. comm.), erratics from which will have become incorporated in the local drift geology, and subsequently into beach shingle. Axehead 1, the most recent find, appears to be of a similar rock-type. The most plausible explanation for the manufacture of these objects is that they were judiciously selected from beach shingle as suitably shaped, dense, and workable pebble blanks, which were then pecked and ground into their predetermined shape. An unfinished specimen, a surface find from Scalby Moor, Pembrokeshire, now in Tenby Museum, supports this suggestion. The selection of appropriately shaped blanks followed by a minimal surface modification seems also to have been the procedure followed in the manufacture of some maceheads and, later in prehistory, stone axe-hammers (Fenton 1984). This method of selection and manufacture can again be seen as an economical and effective response to the lack of suitable flint raw material in the area. Pecked and ground stone axeheads may also have had some functional superiority over any flaked counterparts.

The other lithic associations from the site would seem to place these axeheads securely within the Later

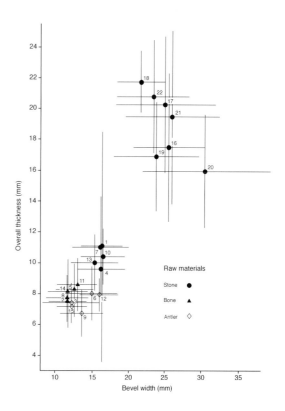

FIGURE 17.16

Plots of the average values (with standard deviations) of thickness and bevel width for samples of bevelled tools of differing raw materials from selected sites in Britain. Key: 1–3 Cnoc Coig, Oronsay; 4–6 Caisteal nan Gillean I, Oronsay; 7–9 Caisteal nan Gillean II, Oronsay; 10–12 Cnoc Sligeach, Oronsay; 13 Priory Midden, Oronsay; 14–15 Risga, Loch Sunart; 16 The Nab Head Site II, Pembrokeshire; 17 Cwm Bach I, Pembrokeshire; 18 Llanunwas, Pembrokeshire; 19 Gwithian, Cornwall; 20 Carn Greeb, Cornwall; 21 Short Point Gulley, Pembrokeshire; 22 Ramaskell, Pembrokeshire.

Mesolithic. Their technological characteristics differ both from those of the bevelled pebbles and the 'finer' Neolithic axeheads to which they bear only some resemblance. Indeed, a preliminary search through records for all finds of Welsh axeheads indicates that a few have significant similarities to those from The Nab Head Site II and could perhaps be their contemporaries. Examples include an axehead in Tenby Museum found 'from a spot near The Nab Head' (Leach 1933) and that from Scalby Moor. The latter is a partially pecked large axehead-shaped sandstone pebble, clearly the beginnings of an axehead-like implement which remains unfinished. From Caron-uwch-clawdd, near Strata Florida, Ceredigion, is a pecked, ground, and polished axehead of quartz-dolerite, perhaps originating from

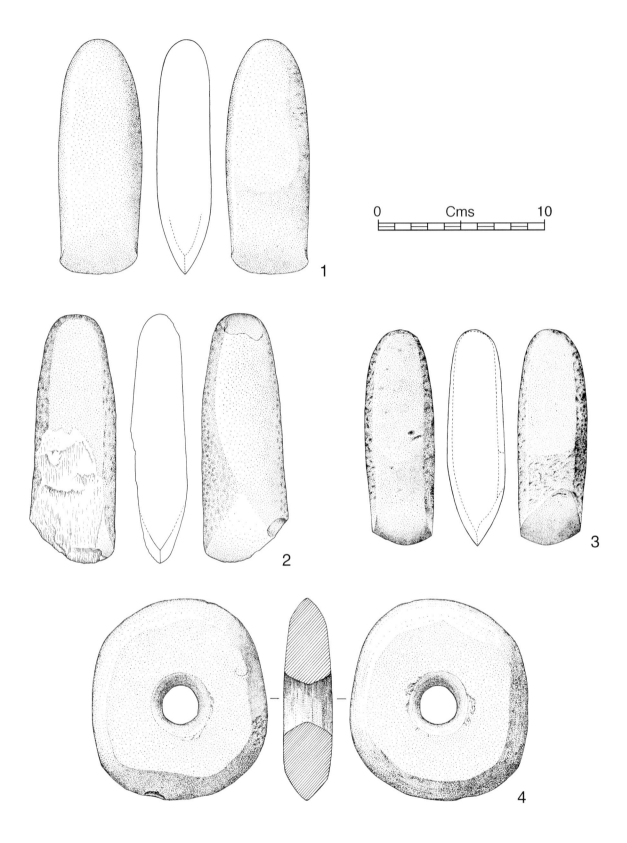

FIGURE 17.17
The Nab Head Site II, ground stone tools: 1–3 pecked and ground stone axeheads; 4 perforated and ground stone disc.

northern Pembrokeshire (Wheeler 1925, fig. 22; Shotton 1972, 90). This dark green axehead has all the features of The Nab Head axes but it is larger and has a 'slicker' polished finish. Its shape and section correspond well with the Mesolithic examples as do the splayed blade and the clear evidence for shaping by pecking. At Stackpole Warren, Pembrokeshire, a fragment of an axehead was excavated from a buried soil in an area (Site A) of intense later prehistoric activity (Benson *et al.* 1990, fig. 40.11). At Brunt Farm, near Dale, Pembrokeshire, two axeheads have been found: one is a naturally-shaped spatulate pebble the broader end of which is axehead-like in profile, although there are no clear traces of manufacture; the second more nearly represents the shape of Neolithic examples and has a smoothed working edge. Most of these examples are isolated and unstratified, all lacking a secure Mesolithic attribution. A rather less speculative example, owing to its apparent association with a Later Mesolithic flint assemblage rather than its morphology, which is atypical, is that which has recently come to light during excavations in 1999 at Ogmore-by-Sea, Bridgend (Aldhouse-Green 2000, fig. 1.10g).

Outside mainland Britain, an immediate comparison with The Nab Head axeheads is prompted by the 'literally thousands' of stone axeheads attributed to the Later Mesolithic of NE Ireland. None of these Irish axeheads is exactly like those from Site II at The Nab Head (P. Woodman pers. comm.). Although they are mostly made from pebbles, as are those from Wales, they do not exhibit the same controlled overall surface modification. The Irish examples are for the most part sharpened pebbles which retain much of their natural surface and, despite a very wide morphological range, do not show any preference for the splayed edges, which are such a deliberate and distinctive feature of The Nab Head pieces. Mainland Britain is perhaps rather exceptional in not having clear evidence for the use of stone axeheads in the Mesolithic. One ground stone axehead recorded from Cambwell, Scotland, while resembling those from The Nab Head, is an isolated find without a secure Mesolithic context (Saville 1994). The Danish 'stump-butted' pecked and ground stone axeheads of the Later Mesolithic Kongemose phase (Clark 1975, fig. 46) are like those from Wales but without the 'flanges', as are the stone axeheads of the succeeding mid-late Ertebølle phases. Pecked stone axeheads feature earlier than this and were already in use in late Boreal times at Agerød I in southern Sweden (Althin 1954) and also feature consistently in the Mesolithic of central Sweden and coastal Bohuslän (Welinder 1977). Pecked and ground 'core adzes', many of which are closely reminiscent of The Nab Head implements, are present on coastal Norwegian sites from the beginning of the middle

Mesolithic at *c.*8250 cal BC (Gjessing 1920; Nygaard 1987; Bruen Olsen & Alsaker 1984).

There are at least two observations to make on the apparent absence, or at least rarity, of stone axeheads from most of the British Mesolithic. Over much of lowland England the more suitable flint raw material was abundant, therefore removing the necessity for a use of less tractable stone. Secondly, within the Later Mesolithic the evidence for axehead manufacture would in any case appear to be confined to southern England and then only to a limited number of sites – Later Mesolithic axeheads were in use at Broomhill (O'Malley & Jacobi 1978); Hermitage Rocks (Jacobi & Tebbutt 1981); Wawcott IV (Froom 1972); and Culverwell (Palmer 1977, 184). The recently reported finds from Goldcliff (Bell *et al.* 2000, 48, figs 4.7 & 4.9) unfortunately lack any stratigraphic context, although the excavators suggested that debitage of tuff from the Mesolithic site might be indicative of contemporary core axehead/adze manufacture.

The other find from the excavation at The Nab Head Site II which sets it apart from other British Later Mesolithic assemblages is that of a perforated and ground stone disc (Fig. 17.17). It is made of extremely fine-grained altered igneous rock (C. Houlder pers. comm.) which has weathered to a light green-brown colour. As with the axeheads and other non-flint raw material at the site, this rock type would have been available on local beaches. The stone has a centrally pecked hour-glass perforation (diameter 22mm), and its entire and nearly circular perimeter (diameter 118 × 109mm) has been ground to an edge, from both faces, presenting an angled 'blade' of between 70° and 90°. Both faces are smooth and probably consist of a natural pebble surface, while the edges clearly preserve the traces of concentric grinding. The implement is scarcely damaged and has no obvious signs of functionally related wear.

Organic artefacts from the Later Mesolithic have been recovered from various findspots on the coast. Most definitive are the two antler mattocks from Splash Point, Rhyl, and Uskmouth, which have respectively provided ^{14}C determinations of 5640–5360 cal BC (OxA-1009; Hedges *et al.* 1988) and 5320–4850 cal BC (OxA-4574; Aldhouse-Green & Housley 1993). The specimen from Splash Point (Fig. 17.18) is made of red deer antler perforated above the trez tine and has been truncated to form a blade parallel to the shaft-hole. The blade is badly damaged but smoothing by apparent use is visible. The specimen from Uskmouth – attributed in a publication error to reindeer (Aldhouse-Green *et al.* 1992, 46) – is now identified as part of the beam of a red deer antler (A. Currant pers. comm.). A perforation at right angles to a tine – of which insufficient survives to enable its closer

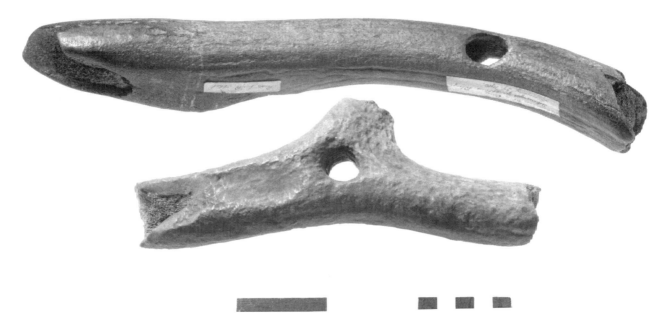

FIGURE 17.18
Antler mattocks from Splash Point, Rhyl (top) and Uskmouth (bottom). Scale in 10 and 50mm divisions.
Photograph: National Museum of Wales.

placement on the original antler – contains what appears to be traces of a hafting adhesive. The mattock does not sit easily into any of the four groups identified by Smith (1989) for the perforation is, unusually, in the same plane as the bevelled, working edge of the tool. The original form of the tool is, however, unclear owing to heavy damage at both ends.

Shaft-hole antler implements are widespread in parts of northern Europe, and in Britain the earliest recorded are those of elk antler, from Star Carr (Clark 1954, 157). Red deer antler examples appear in Later Mesolithic contexts, but have now been dated from all periods up to and including the Iron Age (Hedges *et al.* 1988). The Rhyl specimen – a Type D unbalanced or laterally perforated antler-beam mattock (Smith 1989) has technological similarities to the large group, of mixed chronology, known from the Thames area (Lacaille 1961), but is noticeably different to those from Scottish Obanian and Danish late Ertebølle contexts. This last group, in which the perforation is made through the stump of the trez tine, would appear to date to the very end of the Mesolithic.

There is a marked paucity of artefactual evidence for any social or other dimension to the Later Mesolithic in Wales. So far there is insufficient material available to attempt the sort of stylistic analysis of microlith forms which has lead to the speculative identification of 'social territories' elsewhere (Jacobi 1979). On present evidence, raw materials are too locally derived and non-specific to be used for the reconstruction of territorial extent, or contacts, although the precocious use of ground stone tools (with attendant implications of, for instance, prestige) may anticipate developments in the Neolithic.

Non-utilitarian items are rarer still and there is at present little scope for the exploration of any implications of the occurrence and distribution of decorative items such as beads. A single perforated cowrie shell bead (Fig. 17.19) has been identified with material from Nanna's Cave, Caldey, among the collections of the National Museums & Galleries of Wales. This has two perforations and is identified as *Trivia* cf. *arctica* (I. Killeen pers. comm.). That such beads may be Later Mesolithic is suggested by equivalent specimens found in such a context during recent excavations at King Arthur's Cave and Madawg Rockshelter in the Wye Valley (Barton *et al.* 1997).

Also noted from among the Caldey Island material is a perforated netted dog whelk shell (*Hinia reticulata*) and a perforated winkle (*Littorina obtusata*; identifications by I. Killeen), both of uncertain provenance, but probably from Nanna's Cave, the latter again having their equivalents at Madawg Rockshelter (Barton 1993) and King Arthur's Cave (Barton *et al.* 1997) where, at both sites, they were found in association with the perforated cowrie shells. However, their association with human remains of Early Mesolithic date at Aveline's Hole and of Upper Palaeolithic date at Gough's Cave makes such attributions to the Later Mesolithic ambiguous.

Although burials clearly occur in caves no formal graves or grave goods have yet been encountered; it is unfortunate that, away from areas of limestone geology and intertidal sediments, the soil conditions over much of Wales do not favour organic preservation. Finds of ochre at Prestatyn (Clark 1939) are suggestive of the use of applied colour, for symbolic or aesthetic purposes.

Lifestyle

Any reconstruction of the economy and social organization of the Later Mesolithic inhabitants of Wales is heavily dependent upon examination of the character of lithic artefacts and the distribution of such finds, supplemented occasionally by organic remains and evidence of environmental setting.

With its upland core and lowland coastal margin, past discussion has emphasized the dichotomy between these two zones and the potential they offered for separate but complementary exploitation at differing seasons. Special emphasis has often been placed on the high ecological productivity of the coastal zone, inclusive of abundant marine, littoral, and terrestrial animal and plant resources, as well as lithic raw materials. Certainly, the large number and high incidence of flint scatters on or near to the contemporary coast is extremely compelling evidence for a concentrated exploitation of this zone (Fig. 17.11). Indeed, a more or less intensive exploitation, enhanced no doubt by an advanced technical ability with boats, seems to characterize much of the NW Atlantic seaboard. In contrast, upland sites are pictured as less hospitable, particularly in winter, but offering freshwater resources and ample hunting opportunities, in particular of deer, during the summer months. Flint scatters are locally very abundant on some high-level watersheds, for instance in SE Wales (Stanton 1984), but they tend to be smaller in scale than their lowland counterparts, and can be dominated by artefacts such as microliths, which in such cases are often assumed to indicate hunting activities (e.g. Barton *et al.* 1995). A social dimension to the model is added by the notion that summer upland exploitation allowed for the beneficial dispersal from the larger groups of people that aggregated at coastal locations during other seasons, thereby relieving tensions and encouraging much more extended social connections to develop. It is noted that beach pebble flint was utilized at many upland sites, and may thus be an indicator of the movement of people between the two zones (Jacobi 1980, 195), but otherwise there is little evidence with which to bolster such enticing models as described.

The coastal sites, so predominant and with such suggestive settings, justify further comment, singling out examples from south and west Wales in particular. For instance, fieldwork has identified some 40 of

FIGURE 17.19

Nanna's Cave, Caldey Island: perforated cowrie shell bead.

these on the north Pembrokeshire coast (David 1990, 241–61), in addition to those already documented for the south of the county (e.g. Cantrill 1915; Wainwright 1963). Among the former are some vast aggregations of lithic material, in some cases covering several hectares and giving the impression of repeated revisiting of favoured locations. The scatters are mostly of debitage from the working of beach pebble flint, dominated by bladelet cores and flakes, but characterized by the suite of tool types described earlier. Despite an overall homogeneity among the lithic collections, there are nonetheless some apparent differences in the spectrum of tool types present which imply a degree of variation in the activities taking place at different sites. An exception to the norm of microliths, denticulates, and bevelled pebbles is provided (for instance) by the site at Cwm Bach I, Pembrokeshire, where there are also significant numbers of burins (12% of the retouched component), truncated pieces, and '*becs*', as well as unusual pebble tools such as 'counter-sunk pebbles'. Although such variations between tool-kits can be observed, and may be assumed to relate to varying subsistence activities, the archaeological record is otherwise far too impoverished to determine what such activities may have been. Much speculation has, for example, been expended on inconclusive attempts to explain the repeated occurrence of bevelled pebbles. Ingeniously contrived links between these tools and the exploitation of seals (Jacobi 1980, 189; Movius 1942) remain unconfirmed.

It seems likely, with such an abundance of resources near the coast, that exploitation strategies will also have been combined at particular locations, leading to complex lithic signatures which in many cases have become mixed as the same locations were revisited over extended periods of time, perhaps with changing subsistence targets. Certain categories of site, such as shell middens or seal kills on the contemporary foreshore, may since have disappeared through erosion, inundation, or sedimentation. That many sites were revisited over periods of thousands of years is apparent from palimpsests of chronologically quite distinct tool types, which in some cases extend from the earliest Mesolithic to the Neolithic, as exemplified by the span of ^{14}C determinations at The Nab Head. While it is always tempting to seek economically and geographically deterministic explanations for the particular appeal of such coastal sites, their evident use for such extended timescales invokes other considerations. These include the possible importance of embedded tradition and folk memory, which may lead to certain landmarks and types of site acquiring particular appeal above and beyond the undertaking of any shorter term subsistence objectives (David 1990, 289). Such explanations, and the concept of 'place' in a hypothesized Mesolithic cosmology (Tilley 1994), provoking though they are, are even more elusive of verification than the subsistence strategies that undoubtedly did play a role.

Here we can turn again to those fleeting glimpses of better-preserved Later Mesolithic remains on the present foreshore, rather than the clifftops. As indicated above, these are usually without useful contextual and chronological supporting evidence, but a recent exception has been provided by the excavation of part of a newly discovered site at Goldcliff, on the Severn Levels.

Goldcliff is a projection into the Severn Estuary c.4km east of Newport, which in the Later Mesolithic was once a small wooded island surrounded by marsh, c.3.5m above contemporary sea level (Bell et al. 2000). There is widespread evidence for Mesolithic activity on the island, but excavations have been concentrated near the present-day high-water mark where faunal remains, charcoal, and cultural material were observed in a clearly defined clay layer sealed beneath estuarine clay and peat. A modest excavated lithic collection of 633 pieces included 15 retouched items, among which the only certainly diagnostic Later Mesolithic pieces are three narrow-blade microliths. The debitage, mostly of beach pebble flint, but with some tuff and chert, is predominantly composed of flakes but includes bladelet and bipolar scalar cores. Bevelled pebbles, significantly, are absent. The faunal remains found associated with this material were identified as red and roe deer, pig, otter, wolf, bird (mallard and coot), and five species of small fish (eel, smelt, goby, stickleback, and flatfish). A significant proportion of this and the lithic material are burnt and two per cent of the mammal bones are marked by cuts, with additional evidence for deliberate bone breakage. Radiocarbon determinations (Bell et al. 2000, 59) on a cut deer bone give a result of 5800–5520 cal BC (OxA-6683), and results on three samples of charcoal centre on 5410 cal BC, while a further determination, on hazelnut shell, of 4440–4040 cal BC (OxA-6682), is substantially later and is broadly equivalent to that on the Lydstep pig.

At the time of the main occupation at Goldcliff (estimated to have occurred between c.5600–5200 cal BC) sea level was retreating, and the surrounding vegetation was oak woodland with hazel scrub, the growth of the latter perhaps being encouraged by the human activity. The hunting and fishing potential of such surroundings and of the adjacent estuary is clear (Bell et al. 2000, 61). The anatomical representation, and the burning of bones, suggests that deer may have been processed at the site and cooked there, although some bits may have been taken away. By contrast, pigs were butchered but not burnt, with the choicer joints perhaps being removed elsewhere. Although no definitive evidence for structures, pits, or hearths was found (with the exception of a stakehole), the distributions of burnt bone and lithic materials suggest strongly that different activities were taking place in discrete areas. Seasonal indicators (pig and fish bones) are taken to imply short-term occupation in winter (or early spring).

An unusual addition to the range of evidence emerging from Goldcliff has been the discovery of approximately contemporary human footprints preserved in laminated estuarine silts exposed at low tide at Uskmouth and Magor Pill (Aldhouse-Green et al. 1992) and at Goldcliff (Bell et al. 2001). The first were found in 1986 at Uskmouth, where three trails of prints were subsequently recorded within an estuarine clay overlain by peat, close to the find of the Uskmouth mattock (see above). A ^{14}C determination on the peat provides a terminus ante quem of 5460–4960 cal BC (OxA-2627). Environmental interpretation of the area suggests saltmarsh in the vicinity at the time the footprints were made, with a dry-land environment dominated by mixed deciduous woodland with pine, lime, elm, and hazel. The estuary landscape would have been one of an open environment of intertidal mudflats and salt-marshes gradually being colonized seawards, first by reedswamp and later by carr woodland. The footprints are significant in giving us some tangible evidence of Later Mesolithic people and it is worth noting that the determination for the Uskmouth antler mattock at 5320–4850 cal BC (OxA-4574: Aldhouse-Green & Housley 1993) is remarkably similar to that for the footprints.

At Magor Pill, a little further east from Uskmouth, a further trail of prints was identified crossed by other prints, the extent of which was limited owing to poor preservation. These prints have a *terminus ante quem* of 4780–4360 cal BC (OxA-2626; Aldhouse-Green *et al.* 1992). Further human footprints have also been identified at Goldcliff (Bell *et al.* 2001).

Surprisingly little evidence has yet been forthcoming from Welsh coastal sites for the particular exploitation of any one resource. Given the emphasis upon shellfish at Mesolithic sites further afield (e.g. Bailey 1978; Mellars 1987), and the likely abundance of these along Welsh coasts, it is surprising that middens are not more visible in the archaeological record. Apart from a possible instance from Nanna's Cave, Caldey, (Lacaille & Grimes 1955, 101), the only other relevant evidence may be that from Nant Hall Road, Prestatyn, where a shell midden was found in 1991 during development work (Britnell & Flook 1991). Subsequent work has identified flint and chert artefacts from four shell middens. Two middens of cockle shells appear to be Neolithic in age (Thomas 1992), while ^{14}C determinations from two mussel-shell middens have given results of 4330–3950 cal BC (CAR-1423) and 4530–4170 cal BC (CAR-1420), suggesting a very Late Mesolithic or early Neolithic origin (Thomas 1993). The site and its lithic assemblage are unpublished beyond the brief reports quoted above.

Turning inland and towards the higher ground of the Cambrian Mountains and its valley systems one is faced with a relative vacuum. Much of the area is not suitable for the observation and collection of worked lithic material and it is likely that the current distribution is both very uneven and incomplete. Exceptional concentrations of finds such as those recorded in the Craig-y-Llyn area of the Glamorgan uplands (Savory 1961; 1962; Stanton 1984) must, to some extent, reflect the influence that local collectors can exert on distribution maps. The Glamorgan findspots, located on the upland interfluves drained by the south Wales valleys, mostly at heights exceeding 500m, though predominantly Mesolithic, include both Early and Later components, and lack chronological resolution. A similar cluster of findspots has also been identified in the Black Mountains of Monmouthshire (Olding 2000; Walker forthcoming), while more substantial lithic scatters are recorded on valley side and in valley-bottom locations, for example, in

Usk, Llanmelin Wood, and Troy Meadows, all in Monmouthshire (Walker forthcoming).

Further west, on the Brecon Beacons at the head of the Tawe valley, is Waun Fignen Felen where a number of small scatters of Later Mesolithic material, including microliths, have been studied (Barton *et al.* 1995). These are interpreted as evidence of short-term hunting expeditions to take advantage of the animals and birds also attracted to this shallow upland lake marsh, the surroundings of which may have been deliberately fired to promote grazing.

Other inland sites include Brenig, Llyn Aled Isaf, and Tandderwen in north Wales, all of which have produced substantial lithic assemblages. Brenig 53 has already been referred to above. The collection from Llyn Aled Isaf, only some 7km from Brenig, still awaits publication but is known to include a substantial Later Mesolithic component made on flint and local cherts. There is also the possibility of structural evidence at this site (Jenkins 1990). At Tandderwen, near Denbigh, a site excavated for its early Christian and Bronze Age burials was also found to have a Later Mesolithic assemblage. There are no ^{14}C determinations for this assemblage but the presence of narrow-blade microliths and knapping debitage would suggest a late date (Brassil *et al.* 1991, 70). Recent excavation and earlier fieldwalking in the Walton Basin of Radnorshire has also located quantities of lithic material but only a small proportion seems to be Later Mesolithic (Gibson 1999, 51).

The end of the Mesolithic period

From the evidence partially outlined above it would seem that Wales supported a more or less flourishing Later Mesolithic population exploiting all of the available territory, but with a marked concentration of activity near the contemporary coastline which offered a mild climate, very abundant and various resources, as well as a coastwise ease of communication. Such an optimization has prompted suggestions that hunter-gatherers may have been able to subsist at coastal sites throughout the year and may thus have developed sedentary habits. Whether such stable and economically well-sustained societies were then predisposed towards an early uptake of agricultural practices and Neolithic ideas, or actually had no need of them until much later, is unresolved. The dating evidence from Wales certainly indicates the likelihood of an overlap, even if the social and economic dynamics of the 'transition' remain completely obscure.

The age of the pig from Lydstep Haven, with its incontrovertibly associated microliths, is centred on *c.*4150 cal BC, apparently later than the first documented appearance of distinct Neolithic activity in Wales, at Coygan Camp, Carmarthenshire. If this dating is correct (and caution is necessary on account of the use of preservatives on the specimen; Jacobi pers. comm.), the unfortunate creature may have expired at just the time when indigenous hunters were confronting or adopting the new (or simply different) subsistence methods. One can even conjecture (Lewis 1992) that the pig was a domesticate, in which case it might have been a Neolithic escapee fallen prey to, or poached by, an indigenous hunter.

Further suggestive intermingling of traits so often perceived to be exclusive either to hunting or agricultural communities is provided by the ground stone tools from Mesolithic contexts at The Nab Head. Here stone axeheads with micro-triangle microliths may date from as early as *c.*3750 cal BC, if not substantially earlier. Finds from The Nab Head Site II include a crude leaf-shaped arrowhead, found with bevelled pebbles and micro-triangle microliths. While these objects cannot be guaranteed to be coeval, there is a temptation to muse on the circumstances that might have made them so – perhaps a farmer's ineffective shot at an animal later brought down by hunters? That such speculation might be taken at all seriously is perhaps an indication of the severe shortage of data upon which to construct any more convincing scenarios. Such scenarios should also include consideration of the role played by social pressures and the influence of ideologies on the transition, perhaps even in providing the main impetus for change. The shared coastal locations of Neolithic burial chambers and Mesolithic flint scatters in west Wales seem more than mere coincidence, and, although both types of site remain very poorly dated, it seems probable that there is a degree of chronological overlap (David 1990, 298). It has been suggested (Tilley 1994, 86) that the special significance invested in certain places by indigenous Mesolithic peoples may have extended to the later symbolic placement of ritual megalithic structures.

Conclusion

If the above account has repeatedly stressed the lack of sufficient data to describe the Welsh Mesolithic adequately, then in conclusion we should offer some suggestions for redressing this imbalance. Perhaps the single most pressing need is for new fieldwork, aimed both towards the location of new sites in understudied areas such as the inland core, and also towards the thorough excavation of examples where good organic preservation is assured. Only through the latter process will the chronological, economic, and environmental contexts become adequately defined. Invaluable though lithics have been in building up our existing database, it is now crucial that this information is fleshed out with a

fuller knowledge of the missing organic component and linked authoritatively to an absolute timescale. From this will develop a better comprehension of social dynamics, which could be enhanced by closer study of raw material movements and the future investigation of human remains and burial sites.

As has recently been demonstrated at sites in the Severn Levels, it is just such intertidal and lowland zones that seem most suited to such future research effort. The recognition of the high level of preservation and the great spatial extent of relevant deposits, as well as the vulnerability of these delicate remains to further erosion, lend a special urgency to this objective. Caves, too, will continue to offer promising targets for future excavation, both in lowland and highland areas.

Note

1. Radiocarbon determinations have been calibrated with data from Stuiver *et al.* (1998), using OxCal (v2.18) (Bronk Ramsey 1995). The date ranges have been calculated according to the maximum intercept method (Stuiver and Reimer 1986) and are cited in the text at two sigma (95 per cent confidence). They are quoted in the form recommended by Mook (1986), with the end points rounded outwards to 10 years.

Acknowledgements

We are grateful to Alan Saville for the invitation to present a paper at this conference and for giving us the opportunity to publish some of our work. We both thank Roger Jacobi for all his encouragement and support over the years and for reading this text through in draft. Rick Schulting and Martin Bell have very kindly made some of their unpublished research available to us and permitted us to quote from it in this publication. Thanks are also due to Steve Burrow and Stephen Howe for their help with references, dates, and petrology; and also to Peter Marshall who provided the ^{14}C calibrations. The illustrations are principally the work of Jackie Chadwick, Tony Daly, Andrew David, and Hazel Martingell.

References

Aldhouse-Green, S. 2000. Palaeolithic and Mesolithic Wales. *In* F. Lynch, S. Aldhouse-Green and J.L. Davies (eds), *Prehistoric Wales*, 1–41. Stroud: Sutton Publishing.

Aldhouse-Green, S.H.R. and Housley, R.A. 1993. The Uskmouth antler mattock: a radiocarbon date. *Archaeologia Cambrensis* **142**, 340.

Aldhouse-Green, S.H.R., Whittle, A.W.R., Allen, J.R.L., Caseldine, A.E., Culver, S.J., Day, M.H., Lundquist, J. and Upton, D. 1992. Prehistoric human footprints from the Severn Estuary at Uskmouth and Magor Pill, Gwent, Wales. *Archaeologia Cambrensis* **141**, 14–55.

Allen, D. 1993. Brenig 53: Mesolithic and Neolithic occupation area. *In* F. Lynch, *Excavations in the Brenig Valley: A Mesolithic and Bronze Age Landscape in North Wales*, 17–22. Bangor: Cambrian Archaeological Association (Monograph No. **5**).

Alley, R. B. 2000. The Younger Dryas cold interval as viewed from central Greenland. *Quaternary Science Reviews* **19**, 213–26.

Alley, R.B., Meese, D.A., Shuman, C.A., Gow, A.J., Taylor, K.C., Grootes, P.M., White, J.W.C., Ram, M., Waddington E.D., Mayewski, P.A. and Zielinski, G.A. 1993. Abrupt increase in snow accumulation at the end of the Younger Dryas event. *Nature* **362**, 527–9.

Althin, C.A. 1954. *The Chronology of the Stone Age Settlement of Scania, Sweden. I. The Mesolithic Settlement.* Lund: C.W.K. Gleerups Förlag (Acta Archaeologia Lundensia Series in 4°, No. **1**).

Anderson, J. 1895. Notice of a cave recently discovered at Oban, containing human remains, and a refuse-heap of shells and bones of animals, and stone and bone implements. *Proceedings of the Society of Antiquaries of Scotland* **29** (1894–95), 211–30.

Anderson, J. 1898. Notes on the content of a small cave or rock shelter at Druimvargie, Oban; and of three shell-mounds in Oronsay. *Proceedings of the Society of Antiquaries of Scotland* **32** (1897–98), 298–313.

Bailey, G.N. 1978. Shell middens as indicators of postglacial economies: a territorial perspective. *In* P. Mellars (ed.), *The Early Postglacial Settlement of Northern Europe*, 37–63. London: Duckworth.

Balaam, N., Bell, M., David, A., Levitan, B., McPhail, R., Robinson, M. and Scaife, R. 1987. Prehistoric and Romano-British sites at Westward Ho!, Devon. *In* N.D. Balaam, B. Levitan and V. Straker (eds), *Studies in Palaeoeconomy and Environment in South West England*, 163–264. Oxford: British Archaeological Reports (British Series **181**).

Barton, R.N.E. 1991. Technical innovation and continuity at the end of the Pleistocene in Britain. *In* N. Barton, A.J. Roberts and D.A. Roe (eds), *The Late Glacial in North-West Europe*, 234–45. London: Council for British Archaeology (Research Report **77**).

Barton, R.N.E. 1993. An interim report on the survey and excavations in the Wye Valley 1993. *Proceedings of the University of Bristol Spelaeological Society* **19**(3), 337–46.

Barton, R.N.E., Berridge, P.J., Walker, M.J.C. and Bevins, R.E. 1995. Persistent places in the Mesolithic landscape: an example from the Black Mountain uplands of South Wales. *Proceedings of the Prehistoric Society* **61**, 81–116.

Barton, R.N.E., Price, C. and Proctor, C. 1997. Wye Valley Caves Project: recent investigations at King Arthur's Cave and Madawg Rockshelter. *In* S.G. Lewis and D. Maddy

(eds), *The Quaternary of The South Midlands and the Welsh Marches: Field Guide*, 63–73. London: Quaternary Research Association.

Bell, M., Allen, J.R.L., Nayling, N. and Buckley, S. 2001. Mesolithic to Neolithic coastal environmental change c.6500–3500 cal BC. *Archaeology in the Severn Estuary* **12**, 27–53.

Bell, M., Caseldine, A. and Neumann, H. 2000. *A Prehistoric Intertidal Archaeology in the Welsh Severn Estuary.* York: Council for British Archaeology (Research Report **120**).

Benson, D.G., Evans, J.G. and Williams, G.H. 1990. Excavations at Stackpole Warren, Dyfed. *Proceedings of the Prehistoric Society* **56**, 179–246.

Berridge, P. 1981. Waun Fignen Felen. *Archaeology in Wales* **21**, 20.

Berridge, P. 1994. General discussion of the Mesolithic at Rhuddlan. *In* H. Quinnell and M.P. Blockley, *Excavations at Rhuddlan, Clwyd 1969–73, Mesolithic to Medieval*, 126–31. York: Council for British Archaeology (Research Report **95**).

Binford, L.R. 1979. Organization and formation processes: looking at curated technologies. *Journal of Anthropological Research* **35**(3), 255–73.

Birks, H.J.B. 1989. Holocene isochrome maps and patterns of tree-spreading in the British Isles. *Journal of Biogeography* **16**, 503–40.

Bishop, A.H. 1914. An Oransay shell-mound – a Scottish pre-Neolithic site. *Proceedings of the Society of Antiquaries of Scotland* **48** (1913–14), 52–108.

Bokelmann, K. 1985. Duvensee, Wohnplatz 13. *Offa* **42**, 13–33.

Brassil, K.S., Owen, W.G. and Britnell, W.J. 1991. Prehistoric and early Medieval cemeteries at Tandderwen, near Denbigh, Clwyd. *Archaeological Journal* **148**, 46–97.

Breuil, H. 1922. Observations on the pre-Neolithic industries of Scotland. *Proceedings of the Society of Antiquaries of Scotland* **56** (1921–22), 261–81.

Breuil, H. 1955. Statuette bisexuée dans le microlithique de Nab Head St-Bride's, Pembrokeshire. *Congrès Préhistorique de France: Compte Rendue de la XIVe Session, Strasbourg-Metz 1953*, 183–4. Paris: Société Préhistorique Française.

Britnell, B. and Flook, R. 1991. Nant Hall Road, Prestatyn. *Archaeology in Wales* **31**, 18.

Britnell, W.J. and Savory, H.N. 1984. *Gwernvale and Penywyrlod: Two Neolithic Long Cairns in The Black Mountains of Brecknock.* Bangor: Cambrian Archaeological Association (Monograph No. **2**).

Bronk Ramsey, C. 1995. Radiocarbon calibration and analysis of stratigraphy: the OxCal Program. *Radiocarbon* **37**, 425–30.

Bruen Olsen, A. and Alsaker, S. 1984. Greenstone and diabase utilization in the Stone Age of western Norway: technological and sociocultural aspects of axe and adze production and distribution. *Norwegian Archaeological Review* **17**(2), 71–103.

333

Burleigh, R. Matthews, K. and Ambers, J. 1982. British Museum Natural Radiocarbon Measurements XV, *Radiocarbon* **24**, 262–90.

Burrow, S. 2003. *Catalogue of the Mesolithic and Neolithic Collections in the National Museums & Galleries of Wales.* Cardiff: National Museums & Galleries of Wales.

Campbell, J.B. 1977. *The Upper Palaeolithic of Britain, Vols. I–II.* Oxford: Clarendon Press.

Cantrill, T.C. 1915. Flint chipping floors in south-west Pembrokeshire. *Archaeologia Cambrensis* **70**, 157–210.

Caseldine, A. 1990. *Environmental Archaeology in Wales.* Lampeter: St. David's University College.

Clark, J.G.D. 1932. *The Mesolithic Age in Britain.* Cambridge: Cambridge University Press.

Clark, J.G.D. 1938. Microlithic industries from tufa deposits at Prestatyn, Flintshire, and Blashenwell, Dorset. *Proceedings of the Prehistoric Society* **4**, 330–4.

Clark, J.G.D. 1939. A further note on the tufa deposits at Prestatyn, Flintshire. *Proceedings of the Prehistoric Society* **5**, 201–2.

Clark, J.G.D. 1954. *Star Carr.* Cambridge: Cambridge University Press.

Clark, J.G.D. 1955. Notes on the Obanian with special reference to antler- and bone-work. *Proceedings of the Society of Antiquaries of Scotland* **89** (1955–6), 91–106.

Clark, J.G.D. 1975. *The Earlier Stone Age Settlement of Scandinavia.* Cambridge: Cambridge University Press.

Clough, T.H.McK. and Cummins, W.A. 1988. *Stone Axe Studies Volume 2.* London: Council for British Archaeology (Research Report **67**).

Coggins, D., Laurie, T. and Young, R. 1989. The late Upper Palaeolithic of the northern Pennine Dales in the light of recent fieldwork. *In* C. Bonsall (ed.), *The Mesolithic in Europe*, 164–74. Edinburgh: John Donald.

Coles, J.M. 1971. The early settlement of Scotland: excavations at Morton, Fife. *Proceedings of the Prehistoric Society* **37**(2), 284–366.

Dansgaard, W., Johnsen, S.J., Clausen, H.B., Dahl-Jensen, D., Gundestrup, N.S., Hammer, C.U., Hvidberg, C.S., Steffenson, J.P., Sveinbjornsdottir, A.E., Jouzel, J. and Bond, G. 1993. Evidence for general instability of past climate from a 250-kyr ice-core record. *Nature* **364**, 218–20.

David, A.E.U. 1989. Some aspects of the human presence in west Wales during the Mesolithic. *In* C. Bonsall (ed.), *The Mesolithic in Europe*, 241–53. Edinburgh: John Donald.

David, A.E.U. 1990. *Palaeolithic and Mesolithic Settlement in Wales with Special Reference to Dyfed.* Unpublished PhD thesis, University of Lancaster.

Davies, J.A. 1921. Aveline's Hole, Burrington Coombe. An Upper Palaeolithic station. *Proceedings of the University of Bristol Spelaeological Society* **1**(2), 61–82.

Davies, J.A. 1922. Second report on Aveline's Hole. *Proceedings of the University of Bristol Spelaeological Society* **1**(3), 113–25.

Davies, M. 1978. Ogof Carreg Hir – excavations of 7th March, 1977. *Journal of the Cambrian Caving Council* **4**, 43–5.

Davies, M. 1989. Recent advances in cave archaeology in southwest Wales. *In* T.D. Ford (ed.), *Limestones and Caves of Wales*, 79–91. Cambridge: Cambridge University Press.

Day, S.P. and Mellars, P.A. 1994. 'Absolute' dating of Mesolithic human activity at Star Carr, Yorkshire: new palaeoecological studies and identification of the 9600BP radiocarbon 'plateau'. *Proceedings of the Prehistoric Society* **60**, 417–22.

Delporte, H. 1979. *L'Image de la Femme dans L'Art Prehistorique.* Paris: Picard.

Donahue, R.E. and Lovis, W. 2000. *Yorkshire Dales Hunter-Gatherer Research Project Interim Report 1999.* Bradford: University of Bradford (Bradford Archaeological Sciences Research **8**).

Donald, A.P. 1987. *Aspects of Lateglacial and Postglacial Environments in South-West Wales.* Unpublished PhD thesis, University of Wales, Lampeter.

Dumont, J.V. 1983. An interim report on the Star Carr microwear study. *Oxford Journal of Archaeology* **2**, 127–45.

Dumont, J.V. 1985. A preliminary report on the Mount Sandel microwear study. *In* P.C. Woodman, *Excavations at Mount Sandel 1973–77, County Londonderry*, 61–70. Belfast: HMSO.

Fairbanks, R.G. 1989. A 17,000-year glacio-eustatic sea level record: influence of glacial melting rates on the Younger Dryas event and deep-ocean circulation. *Nature* **342**, 637–42.

Fairbridge, R.W. 1961. Eustatic changes in sea-level. *In* L.H. Ahrens *et al.* (eds), *Physics and Chemistry of the Earth 4.* London: Pergamon Press.

Fenton, M.B. 1984. The nature of the source and the manufacture of Scottish battle-axes and axe-hammers. *Proceedings of the Prehistoric Society* **50**, 217–44.

Finlayson, B. and Mithen, S. 1997. The microwear and morphology of microliths from Gleann Mor. *In* H. Knecht (ed.), *Projectile Technology*, 107–29. New York: Plenum Press.

Froom, F.R. 1972. A Mesolithic site at Wawcott, Kintbury. *Berkshire Archaeological Journal* **66**, 23–44.

Gibson, A. 1999. *The Walton Basin Project: Excavations and Survey in a Prehistoric Landscape 1993–7.* York: Council for British Archaeology (Research Report **118**).

Gillespie, R., Gowlett, J.A.J., Hall, E.T., Hedges, R.E.M. and Perry, C. 1985. Radiocarbon dates from the Oxford AMS system: *Archaeometry* datelist 2. *Archaeometry* **27**(2), 237–46.

Gjessing, H. 1920. *Rogalands Steinalder.* Stavanger: Stavanger Museum.

Godwin, H., Suggate, R.P. and Willis, E.H. 1958. Radiocarbon dating of the eustatic rise in ocean-level. *Nature* **181**, 1518–19.

Gordon-Williams, J.P. 1925. Nabs Head Chipping Floor. *Transactions of the Carmarthenshire Antiquarian Society and Field Club* **18**(46), 80.

Gordon-Williams, J.P. 1926. The Nab Head Chipping Floor. 2. *Archaeologia Cambrensis* **81**, 86–110.

Gowlett, J.A.J., Hedges, R.E.M., Law, I.A. and Perry, C. 1986. Radiocarbon dates from the Oxford AMS system: *Archaeometry* datelist 4. *Archaeometry* **28**(2), 206–21.

Grieve, S. 1883. Notice of the discovery of remains of the Great Auk or Garefowl (*Alca impennis*, L.) on the Island of Oronsay, Argyllshire. *Journal of the Linnean Society, Zoology* **16**, 479–87.

Grigson, C. 1981. Fauna. *In* I. Simmons and M. Tooley (eds), *The Environment in British Prehistory*, 110–24. London: Duckworth.

Grimes, W.F. 1951. *Prehistory of Wales*. Cardiff: National Museum of Wales.

Healey E. 1993. The lithic artefacts of Mesolithic date. *In* F. Lynch, *Excavations in the Brenig Valley: A Mesolithic and Bronze Age Landscape in North Wales*, 22–32. Bangor: Cambrian Archaeological Association (Monograph No. **5**).

Hedges, R.E.M., Housley, R.A., Law, I.A and Perry, C. 1988. Radiocarbon dates from the Oxford AMS system: *Archaeometry* datelist 7. *Archaeometry* **30**(1), 155–64.

Hedges, R.E.M., Housley, R.A., Law, I.A. and Bronk, C.R. 1989. Radiocarbon dates from the Oxford AMS system: *Archaeometry* datelist 9. *Archaeometry* **31**(2), 207–34.

Hedges, R.E.M., Housley, R.A., Pettitt, P.B., Bronk Ramsey, C. and Van Klinken, G.J. 1996. Radiocarbon dates from the Oxford AMS system: *Archaeometry* datelist 21. *Archaeometry* **38**(1), 181–207.

Heyworth, A. and Kidson, C. 1982. Sea-level changes in southwest England and Wales. *Proceedings of the Geologists' Association* **93**(1), 91–111.

Hibbert, F.A. and Switsur, V.R. 1976. Radiocarbon dating of Flandrian pollen zones in Wales and northern England. *New Phytologist* **77**, 793–807.

Howard-Davis, C. 1996. Seeing the sites: survey and excavation on the Anglezarke Uplands, Lancashire. *Proceedings of the Prehistoric Society* **62**, 133–66.

Jacobi, R.M. 1976. Britain inside and outside Mesolithic Europe. *Proceedings of the Prehistoric Society* **42**, 67–84.

Jacobi, R.M. 1978. The Mesolithic of Sussex. *In* P.L. Drewett (ed.), *Archaeology in Sussex to AD 1500*, 15–22. London: Council for British Archaeology (Research Report **29**).

Jacobi, R.M. 1979. Early Flandrian hunters in the South-West. *Devon Archaeological Society Proceedings* **37**, 48–93.

Jacobi, R.M. 1980. The Early Holocene settlement of Wales. *In* J.A. Taylor (ed.), *Culture and Environment in Prehistoric Wales*, 131–206. Oxford: British Archaeological Reports (British Series **76**).

Jacobi, R.M. 1982. Later hunters in Kent: Tasmania and the earliest Neolithic. *In* P.E. Leach (ed.), *Archaeology in Kent to 1500 AD*, 12–24. London: Council for British Archaeology (Research Report **48**).

Jacobi, R. 1984. The Mesolithic of northern East Anglia and contemporary territories. *In* C. Barringer (ed.), *Aspects of East Anglian Pre-History*, 43–76. Norwich: Geo Books.

Jacobi, R.M. 1987. Misanthropic miscellany: musings on British early Flandrian archaeology and other flights of fancy. *In* P. Rowley-Conwy, M. Zvelebil and H.P. Blankholm (eds), *Mesolithic Northwest Europe: Recent Trends*, 163–8. Sheffield: Department of Archaeology and Prehistory, University of Sheffield.

Jacobi, R.M. and Tebbutt, C.F. 1981. A late Mesolithic rock-shelter at High Hurstwood, Sussex. *Sussex Archaeological Collections* **119**, 1–36.

Jenkins, D. 1990. Pedogenesis and archaeology at Aled Isaf. *In* K. Addison, M.J. Edge, and R. Watkins (eds), *North Wales: Field Guide*, 138–40. Coventry: Quaternary Research Association.

Kidson, C. and Heyworth, A. 1973. The Flandrian sea-level rise in the Bristol Channel. *Proceedings of the Ussher Society* **2**, 565–84.

Lacaille, A.D. 1954. *The Stone Age in Scotland*. London: Oxford University Press.

Lacaille, A.D. 1961. Mesolithic facies in Middlesex and London. *Transactions of the London and Middlesex Archaeological Society* **20**(3), 100–150.

Lacaille, A.D. and Grimes, W.F. 1955. The prehistory of Caldey. *Archaeologia Cambrensis* **104**, 85–165.

Lambeck, K. 1996. Glaciation and sea-level change for Ireland and the Irish Sea since late Devensian/Midlandian time. *Journal of the Geological Society, London* **153**, 853–72.

Leach, A.L. 1918. Flint working sites on the submerged land (Submerged Forest) bordering the Pembrokeshire coast. *Proceedings of the Geologists' Association* **29**(2), 46–64.

Leach, A.L. 1933. Stone implements from the Nab Head, St Brides, Pembrokeshire. *Archaeologia Cambrensis* **88**, 229–36.

Leroi-Gourhan, A. 1968. *The Art of Prehistoric Man in Western Europe*. London: Thames & Hudson.

Lewis, M. 1992. *The Prehistory of Coastal SW Wales 7500–3600 BP: an Interdisciplinary Palaeoenvironmental and Archaeological Investigation*. Unpublished PhD thesis, University of Wales, Lampeter.

Lynch, F. 1993. *Excavations in the Brenig Valley: A Mesolithic and Bronze Age Landscape in North Wales*. Bangor: Cambrian Archaeological Association (Monograph No. **5**).

Manley, J. 1981. Rhuddlan and coastal evolution. *Landscape History: Journal of the Society for Landscape Studies* **3**, 1–15.

Manley, J. and Healey, E. 1982. Excavations at Hendre, Rhuddlan: the Mesolithic finds. *Archaeologia Cambrensis* **131**, 18–48.

Mellars, P. 1976. Settlement patterns and industrial variability in the British Mesolithic. *In* G. de G. Sieveking, I.H. Longworth and K.E. Wilson (eds), *Problems in Social and Economic Archaeology*, 375–99. London: Duckworth.

Mellars, P. 1987. *Excavations on Oronsay: Prehistoric Human Ecology on a Small Island*. Edinburgh: Edinburgh University Press.

Mellars, P. and Dark, P. 1998. *Star Carr in Context*. Cambridge: McDonald Institute Monograph.

Mein, A.G. 1996. Trostrey Castle, Trostrey. *Archaeology in Wales* **36**, 64–6.

Mook, W.G. 1986. Business meeting: recommendations/ resolutions adopted by the Twelfth International Radiocarbon Conference. *Radiocarbon* **28**, 799.

Moore, J.W. 1950. Mesolithic sites in the neighbourhood of Flixton, north-east Yorkshire. *Proceedings of the Prehistoric Society* **16**, 101–8.

Moore, P.D. 1972. Studies in the vegetational history of mid-Wales III: early Flandrian pollen data from west Cardiganshire. *New Phytologist* **71**, 947–59.

Movius, H.L. 1942. *The Irish Stone Age*. Cambridge: Cambridge University Press.

Myers, A. 1989. Lithics, risk and change in the Mesolithic. *In* I. Brooks and P. Phillips (eds), *Breaking the Stony Silence*, 131–60. Oxford: British Archaeological Reports (British Series **213**).

Nygaard, S.E. 1987. Socio-economic developments along the south-western coast of Norway between 10,000 and 4,000 BP. *In* P. Rowley-Conwy, M. Zvelebil and H.P. Blankholm (eds), *Mesolithic Northwest Europe: Recent Trends,* 147–54. Sheffield: Department of Archaeology and Prehistory, University of Sheffield.

Olding, F. 2000. *The Prehistoric Landscapes of the Eastern Black Mountains*. Oxford: Archaeopress (British Archaeological Reports, British Series **297**).

O'Malley, M. and Jacobi, R.M. 1978. The excavation of a Mesolithic occupation site at Broomhill, Braishfield, Hampshire. *Rescue Archaeology in Hampshire* **4**, 16–39.

Palmer, S. 1977. *Mesolithic Cultures of Britain*. Poole: Dolphin Press.

Pitts, M. and Jacobi, R.M. 1979. Some aspects of change in flaked stone industries in southern Britain. *Journal of Archaeological Science* **6**, 163–77.

Radley, J. and Mellars, P. 1964. A Mesolithic structure at Deepcar, Yorkshire, England, and the affinities of its associated flint industries. *Proceedings of the Prehistoric Society* **30**, 1–24.

Reynier, M.J. 1998. Early Mesolithic settlement in England and Wales: some preliminary observations. *In* N. Ashton, F. Healy and P. Pettitt (eds), *Stone Age Archaeology: Essays in Honour of John Wymer,* 174–84. Oxford: Oxbow Books (Oxbow Monograph **102**/Lithic Studies Society Occasional Paper **6**).

Reynolds, T.A. 1983. *Form, Function and Technology: a Test Case of Limpet Scoops*. Unpublished BA dissertation, Faculty of Archaeology, University of Cambridge.

Roberts, A. 1987. The later Mesolithic occupation of the Cornish coast at Gwithian: preliminary results. *In* P. Rowley-Conwy, M. Zvelebil and H.P. Blankholm (eds), *Mesolithic Northwest Europe: Recent Trends,* 131–7. Sheffield: Department of Archaeology and Prehistory, University of Sheffield.

Roberts, A. 1994. The scanning electron microscope analysis of the engraved pebbles. *In* H. Quinnell and M.P. Blockley, *Excavations at Rhuddlan, Clwyd 1969–73 Mesolithic to Medieval*, 119–24. York: Council for British Archaeology (Research Report **95**).

Saville, A. 1994. A possible Mesolithic stone axehead from Scotland. *Lithics* **15**, 25–8.

Savory, H.N. 1961. Recent archaeological excavation and discovery in Glamorgan. 1, Prehistoric periods. *Morgannwg* **5**, 76–8.

Savory, H.N. 1962. Recent archaeological excavation and discovery in Glamorgan. 1, Prehistoric periods. *Morgannwg* **6**, 95.

Schulting, R. and Wysocki, M. 2002. The Mesolithic human skeletal collection from Aveline's Hole: a preliminary note. *Proceedings of the University of Bristol Spelaeological Society* **22**(3), 255–68.

Schulting, R.J. 1998. *Slighting the Sea: the Mesolithic–Neolithic Transition in Northwest Europe*. Unpublished PhD thesis, University of Reading.

Schulting, R.J. and Richards, M.J. 2002. Finding the coastal Mesolithic in southwest Britain: AMS dates and stable isotope results on human remains from Caldey Island, south Wales. *Antiquity* **76**, 1011–25.

Shotton, F.W. 1972. The large stone axes ascribed to north-west Pembrokeshire. *In* F. Lynch and C. Burgess (eds), *Prehistoric Man in Wales and The West*, 85–92. Bath: Adams & Dart.

Sieveking, G. de G. 1971. The Kendrick's Cave Mandible. *British Museum Quarterly* **35**, 230–50.

Smith, A.G. 1984. Newferry and the Boreal-Atlantic transition. *New Phytologist* **98**, 35–55.

Smith, A.G. and Cloutman, E.W. 1988. Reconstruction of Holocene vegetation history in three dimensions at Waun-Fignen-Felen, an upland site in South Wales. *Philosophical Transactions of The Royal Society of London* B**322**, 159–219.

Smith, C. 1989. British antler mattocks. *In* C. Bonsall (ed.), *The Mesolithic in Europe*, 272–83. Edinburgh: John Donald.

Smith, C.A. and Lynch, F.M. 1987. *Trefignath and Din Dryfol: The Excavation of Two Megalithic Tombs in Anglesey*. Bangor: Cambrian Archaeological Association (Monograph No. **3**).

Smith, G. 1926. Prehistoric remains at Bryn Newydd, Prestatyn. *Proceedings of the Llandudno, Colwyn Bay and District Field Club* **13**, 62–7.

Smith, G. 1982. The excavation of Mesolithic, Neolithic and Bronze Age settlements at Poldowrian, St Keverne, 1980. *Cornish Archaeology* **21**, 23–62.

Stanton, Y.C. 1984. The Mesolithic period: early Post-glacial hunter-gatherer communities in Glamorgan. *In* H.N. Savory (ed.), *Glamorgan County History, Volume 2, Early Glamorgan*, 33–121. Cardiff: University of Wales Press.

Stuiver, M. and Reimer, P.J. 1986. A computer program for radiocarbon age calculation. *Radiocarbon* **28**, 1022–30.

Stuiver, M., Reimer, P.J., Bard, E., Beck, J.W., Burr, G.S., Hughen, K.A., Kromer, B., McCormac, G., van der Plicht, J. and Spurk, M. 1998. INTCAL98 radiocarbon age calibration, 24,000–0 cal BP. *Radiocarbon* **40**, 1041–83.

Taylor, J.A. 1973. Chronometers and chronicles: a study of palaeoenvironments in west Wales. *Progress in Geography* **5**, 250–334.

Taylor, J.A. 1980. Environmental changes in Wales during the Holocene period. *In* J.A. Taylor (ed.), *Culture and Environment in Prehistoric Wales,* 101–30. Oxford: British Archaeological Reports (British Series **76**).

Ters, M. 1973. Les variations du niveau marin depuis 10,000 ans, le long du littoral Atlantique Français. *In* Comité National Français de l'INQUA, *Le Quaternaire: Geodynamique, Stratigraphie et Environment*, 114–36. Paris: CNRS.

Thomas, D. 1992. Nant Hall Road, Prestatyn. *Archaeology in Wales* **32**, 59.

Thomas, D. 1993. Nant Hall Road, Prestatyn. *Archaeology in Wales* **33**, 50.

Tilley, C., 1994. *A Phenomenology of Landscape.* Oxford: Berg.

Tooley, M.J. 1978. *Sea-level Changes: North-West England During the Flandrian Stage.* Oxford: Clarendon Press.

Verhart, L.B.M. 1988. Mesolithic barbed points and other implements from Europoort, The Netherlands. *Oudheidkundige Mededelingen uit het Rijksmuseum van Oudheden te Leiden* **68**, 145–94.

Wainwright, G.J. 1963. A reinterpretation of the microlithic industries of Wales. *Proceedings of the Prehistoric Society* **29**, 99–132.

Walker, E.A. 2000. Burry Holms, Llangennith, Gower. *Archaeology in Wales* **40**, 88–9.

Walker, E.A. forthcoming. The Mesolithic: the final hunter-gatherer-fisher societies of south-eastern Wales. *In* M. Aldhouse-Green and R. Howell (eds), *Gwent County History Volume I.* Cardiff: University of Wales Press.

Walker, M.J.C. and Harkness, D.D. 1990. Radiocarbon dating the Devensian Lateglacial in Britain: new evidence from Llanilid, South Wales. *Journal of Quaternary Science* **5**, 135–44.

Wedd, C.B. and King, W.B.R. 1924. *The Geology of the Country around Flint, Hawarden and Caergwrle. Memoir of the Geological Survey of Great Britain and Ireland: Explanation of Sheet 108.* London: HMSO.

Welinder, S. 1977. *The Mesolithic Stone Age of Eastern Middle Sweden.* Stockholm (Antikvariskt Arkiv **65**).

West, R.G. 1977. *Pleistocene Geology and Biology* (2nd edn). London: Longman.

Wheeler, A. 1977. The origin and distribution of freshwater fishes in the British Isles. *Journal of Biogeography* **4**, 1–24.

Wheeler, R.E.M. 1925. *Prehistoric and Roman Wales.* Oxford: Clarendon Press.

White, R.B. 1978. Excavations at Trwyn Du, Anglesey, 1974. *Archaeologia Cambrensis*, **127**, 16–39.

Whittle, A. and Wysocki, M. 1998. Parc le Breos Cwm transepted long cairn, Gower, West Glamorgan: date, contents and context. *Proceedings of the Prehistoric Society* **64**, 139–82.

Wickham-Jones, C.R. and Sharples, N. 1984. *An interim report on the excavations at Farm Fields, Kinloch, Rhum, 1984.* Edinburgh: Artefact Research Unit, National Museum of Antiquities (circulated report, unpublished).

Willkomm, von H. 1985. Kernphysikalische untersuchungen. *Offa* **42**, 32–3.

Woodman, P.C. 1978a. *The Mesolithic in Ireland.* Oxford: British Archaeological Reports (British Series **58**).

Woodman, P.C. 1978b. A reappraisal of the Manx Mesolithic. *In* P. Davey (ed.), *Man and Environment in the Isle of Man,* 119–39. Oxford: British Archaeological Reports (British Series **54**).

Wymer, J.J. (ed.). 1977. *Gazetteer of Mesolithic Sites in England and Wales.* London: Council for British Archaeology (Research Report **20**).

Chapter 18

The Mesolithic Period in England:
Current Perspectives and New Research

NICK BARTON and ALISON ROBERTS

This chapter provides a review of recently published research on the Mesolithic period in England. It re-examines the ^{14}C record for the Early and Later Mesolithic, and uses new isotopic studies on human bones to compare dietary behavioural patterns in the two phases. Applying information on lithic raw material use, the paper argues that in the Early Mesolithic people practiced high logistical mobility, possibly accompanied by low residential mobility. This can be contrasted with the Later Mesolithic when people may have made more frequent residential moves and had high logistical mobility but occupied smaller home territories.

Introduction

The purpose of this paper is to review some of the latest developments in the Mesolithic period in England based on the results of published research up to 2001. In broad chronological terms the Mesolithic period extends from *c.*10,000 to 5500 BP. Its beginning corresponded to a sudden and intense climatic warming, an event identified globally with the onset of the present Holocene Interglacial. The timing of the earliest Mesolithic presence in England, therefore, continues to raise specific issues about the nature of the environment during this period, how people adapted to it, and about aspects of continuity with the preceding Upper Palaeolithic period. Such matters have a direct bearing on the question of the first peopling of Scotland, since it is generally believed that the earliest colonizers arrived from the south (Finlayson 1998). As in other regions of Europe the English Mesolithic archaeological record can be divided into distinctive Early and Later phases. Although discussion of these is dealt with within a 'time period' framework, we also address more thematic topics concerning changes in mobility patterns and subsistence behaviour in Postglacial hunter-gatherer societies.

Chronological and environmental considerations

Any discussion of the Early Mesolithic must be set in the wider context of climatic and environmental changes at the Pleistocene-Holocene boundary. In ^{14}C years the beginning of the Holocene is situated at *c.*10,000 BP but this date is not in accord with absolute calendrical records that set the limit closer to 11,600 years ago (Alley *et al.* 1993). One of the main sources of discrepancy is the known periodic variation in atmospheric $^{14}CO_2$ that distorts the ^{14}C record by producing near constant ^{14}C ages or 'plateaux' over short periods of time (Kromer & Becker 1993; Kromer *et al.* 1996; Ashmore this volume). Several of these compressions have been identified in the period covering the Mesolithic and one effect is that samples of greatly varying age produce overlapping results, giving the impression of a close chronological relationship where none exists. Although there is now an accurate calibration curve extending back to 11,800 calendar years ago (Gulliksen *et al.* 1998; Stuiver & van der Plicht 1998), it is still not referred to very widely. In consequence, extra caution is necessary when interpreting the radiocarbon record of this period. For the sake of clarity all ^{14}C dates quoted below are in uncorrected radiocarbon years BP.

As a result of recent work a much clearer picture is beginning to emerge concerning the scale and rapidity of climatic changes at the Pleistocene-Holocene transition. The information comes from a variety of proxy indicators including evidence from ice-core records, fossil beetles, chironomids (non-biting midge larvae), and stable isotopes (Lowe *et al.* 1999). Immediately prior to the Postglacial warming, they reveal a widely documented phase of intense cold (the Younger Dryas Stadial), probably lasting for some 500 ^{14}C years (Alley *et al.* 1993; Björk *et al.* 1998). During this period polar ice would have extended as far south as the SW coast of Ireland (Ruddiman *et al.* 1977) and ground temperatures in England were depressed to an estimated −5°C, with average winter temperatures of −17°C (Atkinson *et al.*

1987). From this low point of extreme cold, the transition to milder conditions seems to have taken place very abruptly. Proxy indicators reveal an extremely sharp rise in mean annual temperatures of about 7°C producing average summer temperatures of 15.8°C (Atkinson *et al.* 1987). Current estimates suggest this change occurred within the space of 20–50 years (Alley *et al.* 1993; Severinghaus *et al.* 1998).

The delay in the botanical response to the initial Holocene climatic warming is well documented in Britain (Bennett & Preece 1998). In a recent reappraisal of the evidence by Mellars and Dark (1998), it has been suggested that the arrival of fully developed birch woodland may have been delayed by up to 300–400 years after the first phase of warming. Except for parts of Yorkshire (Mellars & Dark 1998) and East Anglia (Bennett 1983) where tree birch was present, evidence from other areas of the country suggests that the early Postglacial landscape for a long time remained fairly open. In SE England this is indicated by the occurrence of juniper scrub and rich herbaceous communities from 10,100 BP and lasting until *c.*9800 BP (Bennett & Preece 1998), with a broadly similar pattern inferred for NW England (Godwin *et al.* 1957). Pollen profiles from the upland moors of SW England record the presence of juniper and crowberry communities well into the early Holocene, with birch woodland generally not becoming fully established in the region until *c.*9600–9500 BP, and even later at higher altitudes (Brown 1977; Caseldine & Hatton 1996; Caseldine & Maguire 1986). Some areas of the English Midlands also remained largely treeless until after *c.*9600 BP (Bartley & Morgan 1990). The absence of woodland here may not just have been controlled by climatic factors. For example, there is no evidence for sustained tree growth on the chalk of the Yorkshire Wolds (Bush 1993; Bush & Flenley 1987) and the same may have been true for areas of similar geology in southern England (A. Parker pers. comm.). Thus, the overall picture emerging is of an Early Holocene landscape characterized by open vegetation, consisting mostly of low shrub and herbaceous plant communities with limited or no tree cover.

Despite the rapidity of climatic improvement, faunal records from England show that cold-adapted mammalian species continued to be present well into the Early Holocene. The clearest evidence of this persistence comes from reindeer (*Rangifer tarandus*). According to available AMS ^{14}C determinations on individual specimens this species was present in many parts of the country until about 9700 BP (Fig. 18.1), and possibly even later in Scotland if the isolated date of 8300±90 BP (SRR-2105) from Creag nan Uamh,

Sutherland (Lawson 1984), is accepted at face value. The extinction of reindeer between 9800–9700 BP in Denmark (Aaris-Sørensen 1999), suggests a broadly synchronous event across northern Europe. In England, its survival is probably largely attributable to a continuation of open vegetation conditions in the Preboreal, but other potential contributory factors including thermal tolerance and local presence of upland refugia have also been identified (Coard & Chamberlain 1999). Wild horse (*Equus ferus*), another member of the native Lateglacial fauna, is also known from Early Holocene records, but becomes increasingly rare through time. Its numbers seem to have been affected by the closing of environments and the commensurate reduction of grazing opportunities. Isolated late occurrences of horse have been noted at Flixton II in Yorkshire dating to *c.*9160 BP (P. Rowley-Conwy pers. comm.) and in the Wye Valley, Herefordshire, where a recently excavated specimen from Cavall's Cave has a reported age of 7440±70 BP (OxA-8168).

The time lag in vegetational succession may explain the relatively late arrival of mammalian species more typically indicative of Postglacial conditions (Coard & Chamberlain 1999). In England, a gradual change in the fauna is signalled after 9700 BP (Fig. 18.1) by the appearance of species common to open birch woodland, such as European elk (*Alces alces*), at Star Carr, Yorkshire, and Thatcham III, Berkshire. Other typical woodland indicators like wild cattle (*Bos primigenius*), roe deer (*Capreolus capreolus*), and beaver (*Castor fiber*) also begin to appear after this time, and the development of more closed woodland environments is signified after *c.*9000 BP by the occurrence of northern lynx (*Lynx lynx*), which has been AMS dated to 8930±90 BP (OxA-7143) at Kitley Shelter Cave, Devon (Coard & Chamberlain 1999).

Technology and typology in the Mesolithic

The chronological ordering of the Mesolithic into distinctive 'Early' and 'Later' *facies* is still the most widely accepted method of classification in use today (Jacobi 1973; Mellars 1974). The division is based on well-established typological and technological criteria of lithic artefacts and is also supported by dating evidence which places the Early Mesolithic between *c.*10,000–8500 BP and the Later Mesolithic between *c.*8500–5500 BP (Mithen 1999; Wymer 1991). Despite the continuing usefulness of these categories in a broad sense, in reality the boundaries are imprecise and there appears to be far more complexity than the bi-partite

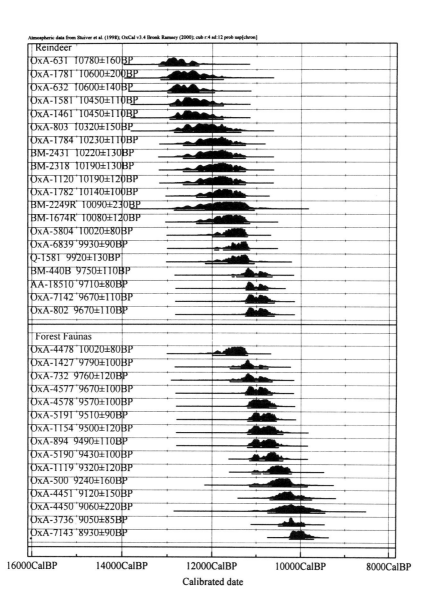

Atmospheric data from Stuiver et al. (1998); OxCal v3.4 Bronk Ramsey (2000); cub r:4 sd:12 prob usp[chron]

Reindeer
OxA-631 10780±160BP
OxA-1781 10600±200BP
OxA-632 10600±140BP
OxA-1581 10450±110BP
OxA-1461 10450±110BP
OxA-803 10320±150BP
OxA-1784 10230±110BP
BM-2431 10220±130BP
BM-2318 10190±130BP
OxA-1120 10190±120BP
OxA-1782 10140±100BP
BM-2249R 10090±230BP
BM-1674R 10080±120BP
OxA-5804 10020±80BP
OxA-6839 9930±90BP
Q-1581 9920±130BP
BM-440B 9750±110BP
AA-18510 9710±80BP
OxA-7142 9670±110BP
OxA-802 9670±110BP

Forest Faunas
OxA-4478 10020±80BP
OxA-1427 9790±100BP
OxA-732 9760±120BP
OxA-4577 9670±100BP
OxA-4578 9570±100BP
OxA-5191 9510±90BP
OxA-1154 9500±120BP
OxA-894 9490±110BP
OxA-5190 9430±100BP
OxA-1119 9320±120BP
OxA-500 9240±160BP
OxA-4451 9120±150BP
OxA-4450 9060±220BP
OxA-3736 9050±85BP
OxA-7143 8930±90BP

16000CalBP   14000CalBP   12000CalBP   10000CalBP   8000CalBP
Calibrated date

FIGURE 18.1

AMS ^{14}C dates for reindeer (*Rangifer tarandus*) and temperate woodland fauna in the Late Pleistocene–Early Holocene. The dates are calibrated according to OxCal 3.4.

division would imply. There is now an increasing need to review some of the terminology for assemblages within each of the categories (Barton 1989). For example, many authorities would now recognize two, if not more, phases of the Early Mesolithic.

Long-blade technology

Evidence for what might be termed an Epipalaeolithic (*sensu* Clark 1980, 39) or Initial Mesolithic technology comes from a number of locations mainly concentrated in southern England and often near good quality flint

sources (Barton 1989; 1998; Cook & Jacobi 1994; Wymer 1976). Lithic assemblages of this kind are characterized by large, well-made blades (> 120mm) and opposed-platform blade cores more than 100mm in length. Among artefacts commonly associated with these assemblages are heavily edge-damaged blades, known as 'bruised blades' or *lames machurées*. The damage on them has been interpreted as a form of use-wear resulting from chopping hard materials such as bone or antler (Barton 1986), or alternatively from the shaping and maintenance of sandstone knapping tools (Fagnart

& Plisson 1997). The assemblages are overwhelmingly dominated by blade debitage products but among the few retouched tools are end scrapers and burins, sometimes on the ends of large flakes or blades, as well as microliths not unlike those found in the Early Mesolithic.

From the point of view of the *chaîne opératoire* the long-blade assemblages are regarded as more 'Upper Palaeolithic-like' than Mesolithic (Barton 1986; 1998; Dumont 1997). This is particularly seen in the various stages of core preparation and reduction, for example in the special use of faceting preparation of striking platforms. It is likely that features such as these have some degree of chronological significance and support the contention that the long-blade technology is allied to the Final Palaeolithic.

The long-blade technology is believed to cover a relatively restricted time-span covering the end of the Youngest Dryas and the initial Holocene. Among the ^{14}C dates published are those from Three Ways Wharf, Uxbridge, Greater London, and Sproughton, Ipswich, Suffolk, while new dating based on OSL (optically stimulated luminescence) has been obtained from Avington VI, Berkshire. The AMS dating at Three Ways Wharf of $10,270 \pm 100$ BP (OxA-1788) and $10,010 \pm 120$ BP (OxA-1902), is on two well-associated horse teeth within a scatter of long and bruised blades (Lewis 1991). The earlier of the two dates falls just prior to the known plateau at 10,000 BP and compares favourably with directly dated reindeer specimens from the Ahrensburgian layer at Stellmoor in Germany (Fischer & Tauber 1986). The lithic technologies at both localities are regarded as broadly comparable (Barton 1989) and it is relevant that the small-stemmed points found at Stellmoor are also present at several British sites, including Avington VI (Barton 1997a; Barton & Froom 1986). Further confidence in this chronological interpretation is provided by a sequence of three OSL dates from the site of Avington VI that gave a minimum value of *c.*10,300 years ago for sediments enclosing the long-blade assemblage (Barton *et al.* 1998).

While some of the long-blade dating evidence appears to fall within the final part of the Younger Dryas, indications from the site of Sproughton suggest that the same technology may also have persisted into the initial Holocene. The Sproughton industry was recovered from above an infilled channel of the River Gipping. A comprehensive series of ^{14}C dates on wood exists for the channel with an age of 9888 ± 120 BP (HAR-259) attributed to the uppermost sample (Rose 1976; Wymer 1976), just beneath the deposits containing the long blades and thus providing a maximum age for the industry.

Some further evidence for chronological ordering within the long-blade technology may be detectable based on nuances in the styles of microliths in these assemblages. Of particular note, in this respect, are the simple oblique points with a markedly concave truncation and showing additional retouch at the base present at Uxbridge (Lewis 1991, fig. 23.10) and recognized at the newly discovered site of Launde in Leicestershire (L. Cooper pers. comm.). Here, striking parallels can be seen among microliths from the Epi-Ahrensburgian sites of Oudehaske and Gramsbergen I in The Netherlands (Johansen & Stapert 1998, fig. 69), and may imply the existence of geographically extensive social networks stretching from eastern Britain into the northern Netherlands, possibly over a relatively brief period of the latest Glacial.

The Preboreal Early Mesolithic phase (10,000–9000 BP)

Flint assemblages combining simple microlith forms (oblique points and broad triangles) with a range of other equipment including end scrapers, microdenticulates, burins, awls (*mèches de foret*), and bifacially flaked axeheads or adzes can be defined unequivocally as Early Mesolithic. The appearance of axeheads and adzes in these toolkits does not seem to be fortuitous and provides further anecdotal evidence for human adaptation to an increasingly wooded environment (cf. Childe 1931).

Within the English Early Mesolithic two typologically discrete groupings have been identified (Jacobi 1976; Radley & Mellars 1964). They are represented on the one hand by 'Star Carr type' assemblages in which the microliths are dominated by broad oblique points, isosceles triangles, and trapezoids, and, on the other hand, by 'Deepcar type' assemblages in which the microliths are typified by more slender oblique points with a rarity of isosceles triangles and trapezoids (Fig. 18.2; cf. Reynier 1997). There is no clear agreement concerning the significance of the two groupings.

A recent reassessment of the evidence proposed that the Star Carr type assemblages were generally older than those of the Deepcar group, though with some degree of chronological overlap (Reynier 1998). Reynier also suggested differing distribution patterns for the two assemblage groups, with Star Carr assemblages being concentrated in northern and western Britain in both upland and lowland river valley locations, whereas Deepcar assemblages are found throughout the country but predominantly in lowland river-valley locations (Fig. 18.3). If the artefacts are representative of separate social groupings then this may indicate different settlement strategies (Reynier 1998, 178) or perhaps contemporary use of the landscape by human groups occupying very similar geographic ranges (Mellars & Dark 1998, 240). Alternatively, they may simply indicate functional

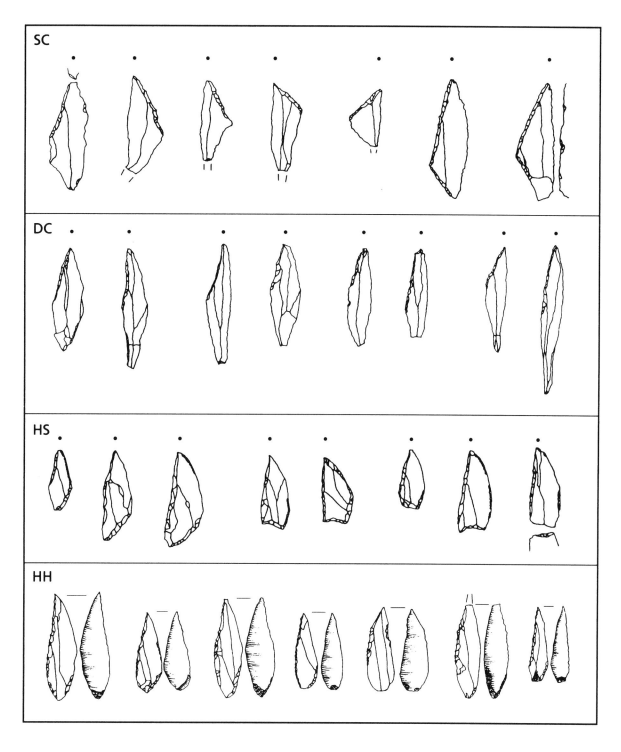

FIGURE 18.2

Selected Early Mesolithic microlith forms from English sites. SC: 'Star Carr type' from Broxbourne 104, Hertfordshire (top row); DC: 'Deepcar type' from Marsh Benham, Berkshire (top middle row); HS: 'Horsham type' from Longmoor 1, Hampshire (lower middle row, with Horsham points fourth to eighth from left); and HH: 'Honey Hill type' from Two Mile Bottom, Suffolk (bottom row, all inverse basally retouched points). (After Reynier 1997, figs 2–5; scale approx. actual size)

FIGURE 18.3

Distribution of main 'Star Carr type' (open circles) and 'Deepcar type' (closed circles) assemblages in England and Wales (after Reynier 1997, fig. 1, with additions).

variation within one major grouping. Unfortunately there is no way of resolving the question at present given the paucity of dates available for the Early Mesolithic assemblages and the difficulties presented by the plateau around 9500–9600 BP. Nevertheless, it may be no coincidence that the broad oblique microlith forms in Star Carr type assemblages are prefigured in the initial Holocene long-blade assemblages, and this may argue in favour of a slightly earlier chronological development.

As has already been stated, one of the major challenges currently facing archaeologists studying the Mesolithic period is to begin to establish a reliable chronology for the Early Mesolithic (Jacobi 1994). So far the oldest acknowledged dates for this period are those from Star Carr. Recently published information suggests that Mesolithic human activity in the area around the site probably began a little after 9700 BP (Dark 1998; 2000). Slightly later dates, including one on a birch resin 'cake' of 9350±90 BP (OxA-2343; Roberts et al. 1998), suggest that the occupation horizon revealed during the 1950s excavations may have occurred between 9400–9100 BP (Mellars & Dark 1998, 211). At Thatcham III potentially much older occupation traces

have been uncovered (Churchill 1962; Wymer 1962), though the dating evidence is unfortunately ambiguous (Barton 1991). The site is nonetheless worthy of interest because it includes rare examples of hearth structures (Wymer 1962). Two hearths have yielded ^{14}C dates of 10,365±170 BP (Q-659) and 10,030±170 BP (Q-658) respectively on bulked charcoal and, if taken at face value, may suggest that human activity began at the site in the Lateglacial. While there is no way of determining which, if any, of the lithic artefacts might belong to this phase, it can be noted that a new AMS date of 9200±90 BP (OxA-2848) has also been obtained from site III (Roberts et al. 1998). The date is from resin adhering to a struck flake found within the main occupation horizon in Layer 4 and thus provides an incontrovertible link with the Early Mesolithic assemblage from the same layer.

The Boreal Early Mesolithic phase (9000–8500 BP)
Occupying a slightly later chronological position than the Star Carr and Deepcar assemblages, and arguably part of an innovation process that began c.9000 BP, is another set of Early Mesolithic assemblages distributed mainly in southern England. They include the 'Horsham' (Clark 1934) and 'Honey Hill' (Saville 1981a; 1981b) assemblage types, each defined by the presence of distinctive basally retouched microlith forms (Fig. 18.2). The groupings have recently been re-examined by Reynier (1997). The type fossil for the Horsham group is the hollow-based point, but oblique forms still continue to be marginally the more common microlith form in assemblages of this kind. The oblique forms have been shown to be significantly shorter than those in the Preboreal (Reynier 1994). In the Honey Hill group the most characteristic microlith is the inverse basally retouched backed point, though here again small oblique points usually predominate. The two groupings appear to occupy non-overlapping geographical distributions (Fig. 18.4). Whereas the Horsham group is mainly confined to SE England, the Honey Hill group appears most frequently in the Midlands and East Anglia (Reynier 1997). It may be possible to identify a long-blade facies in the latter group, if the microlith components present at the King's Site, Suffolk, do indeed form part of a homogeneous assemblage as has been suggested recently (R. Jacobi pers. comm.).

So far there is only very limited dating evidence for the Boreal assemblages. Two dates from Longmoor Inclosure I, Hampshire, of 8930±100 BP (OxA-376) and 8760±110 BP (OxA-377; Gillespie et al. 1985), currently offer the most reliable estimates for the age of the Horsham group. Other evidence in support of a later 'Horsham' phase in the Early Mesolithic is provided in Rankine's observation that a few of the Horsham points at Oakhanger were recovered in a stratigraphically higher position than the main Early Mesolithic assemblage (Rankine *et al.* 1960). There are presently no dates available for the Honey Hill group, nor any evidence that the group overlapped chronologically with the Horsham assemblages. Some indication of the late persistence of the Honey Hill group is given by two dates of just over 8000 ^{14}C years old from Ballacregga, Glen Wyllin, Isle of Man, for an assemblage containing inversely basally retouched backed points (S. McCartan pers. comm. and this volume).

It is clear from this brief summary that the Boreal phase of the Early Mesolithic is in need of further detailed assessment and study. Apart from new excavation, one potentially useful line of enquiry would be a re-examination of the geographical spread of the microlith types making up the Horsham and Honey Hill assemblages, and to identify further stylistic or regional groupings. The currently available evidence indicates the occurrence of a range of basally retouched microlith types outside the main Horsham and Honey Hill areas. For example, inverse basally retouched microlithic points are known from the Isle of Man (Clark 1935) and from findspots in north Devon and Cornwall as far SW as Trevose Head. Variants of hollow-based forms occur in north and east Devon (Berridge 1985; Rosenfeld 1969), the Isle of Man (Woodman 1987), and south Wales (Wainwright 1963). Such a distribution, if signifying mutually overlapping annual ranges or hunting territories, may hint at a growth in population and with it the possibility of increased competition for resources.

On the other hand it may be no coincidence that the appearance of these microlith types after *c.*9000 BP corresponded with the major phase of deciduous forest expansion across most of the country (Bell & Walker 1992). If the developing woodland led to a greater fragmentation and isolation of communities then it is in just such a period that we might expect to see the emergence of more pronounced regional diversity in microlith styles. It is also worth keeping in mind Reynier's (1997) suggestion that the emergence of basally modified points at this time might indicate that changes were being made to traditional hafting arrangements.

The Later Mesolithic phase (8500–5500 BP)

The occurrence of lithic assemblages dominated by small geometric microlith forms is a defining characteristic of the Later Mesolithic. In England such assemblages begin to appear after *c.*8500 BP but it is difficult to see whether this was a further consequence of changes initiated in the Boreal Early Mesolithic or

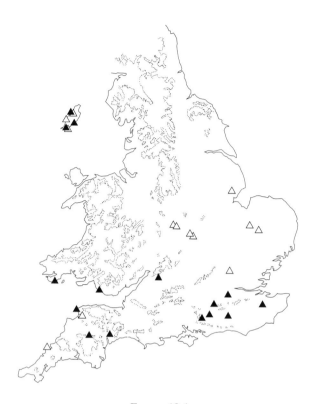

FIGURE 18.4

Distribution of findspots with hollow-based points ('Horsham type' and related variants; closed triangles) and basally inverse retouched points ('Honey Hill type' and related variants; open triangles) in England and Wales (after Reynier 1997, fig. 1, with additions).

indicative of a sharp break with existing traditions. Although Jacobi (1976) has made the point that the divergence of the English Later Mesolithic from the European technologies was linked to the opening of the English Channel, newer evidence suggests that Britain did not become a true island until *c.*7000 ^{14}C BP (Funnell 1995). It therefore seems unlikely that the development of the Later Mesolithic in England was in complete isolation from the rest of Europe.

Despite the wealth of findspots that can be attributed on typological grounds to the Later Mesolithic, the number of well-dated assemblages in England remains disappointingly sparse. To complicate matters many of the published ^{14}C dates (e.g. Smith 1992) have uncertain associations or are on bulked charcoal samples and should be treated with caution or discarded. Among the smaller sample of acceptable dates are AMS determinations on humanly modified items and on wood charcoal from sealed contexts, such as pits, which may contain lithic artefacts. A good example of the former is the AMS dating programme on bone and antler artefacts (Tolan-

Smith & Bonsall 1998), but few of the specimens are from contexts firmly associated with lithic artefacts. As with other parts of the Mesolithic chronology, difficulties in interpretation are compounded during this period by the existence of further compressions in the radiocarbon record, including those at 8750 BP and 8250 BP (Kromer & Becker 1993).

Among the oldest reliably dated English sites with geometric microliths is Site B101 Tolpitts Lane, Hertfordshire, which contained straight-backed pieces and small scalene triangles. Here, charcoal fragments collected from a shallow depression with lithic artefacts yielded an age determination of 8260±120 BP (Q-1147; Switsur & Jacobi 1979). Potentially of similar or slightly earlier age is the assemblage from a pit infill at Broom Hill, Hampshire. This deposit contained 33 microliths of Later Mesolithic types including small oblique points, curved backed pieces, straight-backed bladelets, and narrow scalene triangles. In this case the assemblage was sandwiched by a charcoal date of 7830±120 BP (Q-1460) from the 'top' of the pit infill, and a series of three dates from the base of the pit: 8540±150 BP (Q-1192); 8315±150 BP (Q-1383); and 8515±150 BP (Q-1528) (O'Malley & Jacobi 1978).

Another well-contexted early date for a Later Mesolithic assemblage comes from a presumed composite arrowhead from Seamer Carr, Yorkshire. The age determination of 8210±150 BP (HAR-6498) on a fragment of crushed poplar or willow wood, probably the shaft, provides a secure date on a group of 16 microliths, made up of 15 straight backed forms and one broken 'point' (David 1998).

Within the broad definition of geometric microliths are a range of tiny forms described as microscalene triangles, microtranchets, microrhomboids, and microlunates. Assemblages that contain these microlith forms are also usually associated with 'rods' (narrow straight pieces with backing along both edges, cf. Jacobi 1984). Dating evidence for these assemblages is still extremely poor, but they do not seem to occur much before 7000 BP. At Three Holes Cave, Devon, recent excavations near the entrance of the cave have produced a well-stratified Later Mesolithic assemblage consisting of microscalene triangles and rods. AMS dates on associated smashed red deer bones show that the site was occupied during the early Atlantic chronozone (6330±75 BP, OxA-4491; 6120±75 BP, OxA-4492; Roberts 1996). Palaeoenvironmental analyses from the site indicate that during this period the local environment was one of dense woodland and temperatures were warmer than those of today.

Broadly comparable dates for the occurrence of microscalene triangles have been obtained from Misbourne,

Wiltshire, on associated bovid remains (6190±90 BP, OxA-601; 6100±120 BP, OxA-619; 5970±100 BP, OxA-618; Gowlett et al. 1986; R. Jacobi pers. comm.) and from the site of Madawg Rockshelter, Herefordshire, where the younger of two age determinations on burnt hazelnut charcoal (6655±65 BP, OxA-6082) provides an age for a hearth deposit containing a burnt microscalene triangle (Barton 1997b). Similar dates are also available for assemblages containing microscalene forms in Wales, most notably from the site of Goldcliff in the Severn Estuary where the main Mesolithic context (1202) is well-dated to 6760±80 BP (OxA-6683 on a cut red deer bone), 6430±80 (GU-2759 on charcoal), and 6420±80 (SWAN-28 on charcoal; Barton & Bell 2000; for other examples see David & Walker this volume). Potentially the earliest dated occurrence of this microlith form is from the site of Broxbourne 105, Hertfordshire, excavated in 1972 (Switsur & Jacobi 1979). This site produced refitting debitage products and 42 microliths, including a discrete group of 14 microscalene triangles and a single rod that may be the remains of a composite arrowhead. The date of 7230±150BP (OxA-593) on an associated aurochs's tooth is reliably supported by the results of palaeoenvironmental work on the peat profile at the site (Jacobi 1994).

The relatively sudden appearance of these minute geometric forms close to 7000 BP seems to have been a widespread event and marks a significant innovation in the Later Mesolithic toolkit. No single cause has yet been put forward to explain the introduction of these forms though it might be significant that the changes took place against a background of rapid global climatic cooling c.7300 BP (c.8200 ice core years ago), which saw a decline in annual average temperatures of 6°±2°C and may have lasted for 200 to 300 calendar years (Alley et al. 1997). The pattern of the event in the Greenland ice core is described as being the same as that of the Younger Dryas (i.e. cold, dry, windy, dusty, and low in methane), although at only about half of the amplitude. What effect this cooling and aridity might have had on the environment in Britain is as yet uncertain, but it is worth noting from the ice-core records that elsewhere forest-fire frequency increased 90 per cent during this event (Alley et al. 1997)

Much uncertainty still surrounds the chronology of the very final part of Later Mesolithic activity in England and by implication its relationship with that of the earliest Neolithic. Currently the youngest dated Mesolithic assemblage comes from the site of Stratford's Yard in Buckinghamshire, where a well-stratified lithic collection with a microtranchet component has an age of 5890±100 BP (BM-2404) (Stainton 1989). Another possible example comes from a natural shaft in the chalk at Sixpenny Handley, Dorset, where a long sequence of AMS ^{14}C dates provides a well-bracketed age for a small group of rod-like microliths (probably the remains of a hafted arrow) at between 5355±45 (OxA-8011) and 5275±50 BP (OxA-7987), which underlie a level containing Neolithic artefacts (Allen & Green 1998). The paucity of reliably dated sites for this period belies the fact that where a contextual relationship can be shown to exist between Later Mesolithic and early Neolithic flint assemblages, as for example in buried soils or underlying Neolithic earthworks, the Mesolithic finds often include minute geometric forms (e.g. Saville 1989).

Human skeletal evidence and diet

Leaving aside questions of chronology, considerable research efforts are presently being devoted to studying non-material aspects of human lifestyles in the Mesolithic. An example of this kind is provided by the application of stable isotope analysis to the study of human diet. The method has been used routinely for many years in the Scandinavian Mesolithic (Larsson 1997; Price 1989; Schoeninger et al. 1983; Tauber 1981) but has only recently been extended to include human remains in Britain. The new work is an important by-product of the AMS dating programme at Oxford (Schulting & Richards 2000). During preparation of the human bone for dating the collagen can also be sampled for its δ^{13}C and δ^{15}N values (Richards & Hedges 1999a;

Richards & Mellars 1998; Richards & Schulting 2000). The basis of the method is fairly simple – by calculating the δ^{13}C values (the ratio of ^{12}C and ^{13}C) of the bone collagen it is possible to determine the main source of protein in the diet over the last 5–15 years of an individual's lifetime (Richards & Hedges 1999b). Using this technique the relative proportion of marine or terrestrial foods in the diet can often be estimated. For example, a human bone collagen δ^{13}C content of –11 or –12‰ would indicate an over-whelmingly (> 95 per cent) seafood diet, while at the other extreme, an almost totally land-based diet (> 95 per cent) would be shown by values of –20 to –21‰. Useful supplementary information on food intake is provided by the δ^{15}N values, which can be used to determine the relative contributions of plant versus animal protein in the diet (Richards & Mellars 1998).

Isotopic analysis of Mesolithic human material from England (Table 18.1) so far includes samples from the sites of Thatcham III in Berkshire, Aveline's Hole and Totty Pot in Somerset, Breakwater Quarry in Devon, and Staythorpe in Nottinghamshire (Richards 2001; Richards & Schulting 2000; Schulting & Richards 2000; M. Richards pers. comm.). Except for Thatcham III and Staythorpe, all the sites are cave locations (Fig. 18.5) and the assumption is that at least some of the remains represent deliberate human interments. The other striking feature is that apart from Breakwater Quarry they are all from inland locations, the most extreme case being Thatcham III that lies at least 80km from the nearest coastline.

TABLE 18.1

Mesolithic human and dog stable isotope values from England (after Richards & Schulting 2000 and Richards 2001).

Site	Lab no.	^{14}C BP	Sample	δ^{13}C‰	δ^{15}N‰
Aveline's Hole	OxA-799	9100±100	*Homo*	−19.3	7.5
Aveline's Hole	OxA-800	8860±100	*Homo*	−19.5	8.0
Aveline's Hole	OxA-1070	8740±100	*Homo*	−18.7	8.7
Totty Pot	BM-2973	8180±70	*Homo*	−20.6	7.0
Thatcham 3	—	—	*Homo*	−21.9	8.4
Thatcham 4	—	—	*Canis*	−19.5	7.5
Breakwater Quarry Cave	OxA-4777	8615±75	*Homo*	−20.2	—
Staythorpe	Beta-144016	6790±40	*Homo*	−20.4	9.3

FIGURE 18.5

Distribution of Mesolithic human remains in England and Wales. Open circle (open air site): 1 – Thatcham III. Open triangles (caves and rockshelters): 2–5 – Gough's Cave, Totty Pot, Badger Hole, Aveline's Hole; 6 – Kent's Cavern; 7 – Breakwater Quarry Cave, Oreston; 8 – Fox Hole; 9 – Worm's Head; 10–12 – Ogof-yr-ychen, Daylight Rock, Potter's Cave; 13 – Pontnewydd Cave.

Although it has not been possible to date all the human material, it is clear from stratigraphic information that the specimen from Thatcham III derives from an Early Mesolithic context (Wymer 1962). Of the dated specimens all are of Preboreal or Boreal Mesolithic age, except for Staythorpe and Totty Pot. The results from the Early Mesolithic are remarkably consistent in showing a high terrestrial protein component to the diet. The humerus recovered from Thatcham III, possibly of an adult female (Newell *et al.* 1979), shows the strongest terrestrial dietary signal of all the samples (−21.9‰). Given the inland position of the site this is not especially surprising, although if anadromous fish, such as salmon, had been eaten this should have been detectable in the isotopic analysis (Richards & Hedges 1999a). This information finds confirmation in the low presence of fish remains recovered at site despite good conditions of preservation (Wymer 1962). Of potential relevance here too is that a bone of dog from the nearby location of Thatcham IV reveals very similar isotopic values to

that of the human bone, no doubt reflecting the closely interactive relationship between the two species during this period.

It is also worth remarking that these results are in agreement with δ^{13}C values obtained on Early Mesolithic human material from elsewhere in NW Europe, including that of −24.1‰ from a cranial specimen recovered in 1994 from near the North Hinder Bank in what is now the southern basin of the North Sea (9640±400BP, UtC-10063; Erdbrink & Tacoma 1997).

These results are in contrast to earlier work which suggested a marine influence in the Early Mesolithic diet based on a study of a juvenile dog vertebra from Seamer Carr (Clutton-Brock & Noe-Nyggard 1990). The strong marine signal in the bone implied that humans and their domesticated dogs were frequent visitors to the coast. This interpretation was subsequently undermined following the publication of results that attributed the low δ^{13}C isotopic values to ingestion by the dog of locally derived foods from the calcareous waters of Lake Pickering (Day 1996). A separate analysis of the dog bone failed to reveal any preserved collagen at all in the original sample (Richards & Schulting 2000). More recently, a δ^{13}C value of −19.0‰ obtained on a dog from the nearby site of Star Carr (Ramsey pers. comm.) would seem to confirm a largely terrestrial protein diet and further weakens the case for intensive exploitation of the marine littoral by humans during the Preboreal. One adjunct of this study that also requires investigation is the relevance of the very early ^{14}C date on an isolated bone of domestic dog from Seamer Carr of 9940±100 BP (OxA-1030; Hedges *et al.* 1987). Although apparently earlier than any of the Mesolithic dates in the area, it would be of interest to establish whether or not the age could have been amplified, for example by fractionation linked to a high marine dietary intake. If this were so, it could theoretically reduce the ^{14}C age of the sample by as much as 400 years (Stuiver & Braziunas 1993), thereby bringing it much closer into line with the occupation dates for Star Carr.

Very similar dietary signals have been obtained from the other late Preboreal and Boreal Mesolithic human samples. If Aveline's Hole is representative, it shows that most of the dietary protein of the inhabitants of the Mendips was obtained from land-based animal sources. The δ^{15}N values indicate that meat consumption was relatively high in Mesolithic humans, sharing a similar trophic level to carnivores such as northern lynx (*Lynx lynx*) (Richards & Schulting 2000). One unexpected result, however, is the high dietary intake of terrestrial animal protein shown by the Breakwater Quarry individual. Despite the position of the site, which would have been within a few kilometres of the Boreal shoreline, the $\delta^{13}C$ value on the dated bone implies a non-marine food diet. If not simply representing the food preferences of one individual or a change in diet in the latter stages of life, it implies that even in near coastal situations greater emphasis was placed on hunting and consuming land mammals rather than marine foods.

Out of the existing sample, isotopic information on the human diet in the Later Mesolithic is restricted to just two examples in England – from Totty Pot, in the Mendips, and Staythorpe, Nottinghamshire (Richards 2001) – both inland locations. The isolated femur of an adult female from Staythorpe comes from a palaeochannel in the Trent Valley, whereas the find from Totty Pot seems to be part of a deliberate burial. Both finds, however, do confirm the underlying pattern already established for the Early Mesolithic of the major part played in the diet by land-based mammals. Paradoxically, they also provide an interesting contrast with Later Mesolithic human remains from coastal locations outside England, which for the first time reflect a strong marine influence in the diet. Such sites, along the Atlantic western seaboard, include examples from the Inner Hebrides of Scotland (Richards & Mellars 1998), west Wales (Richards & Schulting 2000; R. Schulting pers. comm.), and from western Ireland (Woodman et al. 1999).

Some of the clearest marine signatures (>80%) are found in human remains from Caldey Island, Wales (Richards & Schulting 2000), which are broadly contemporary with the Totty Pot individual. Schulting has suggested that the most likely marine source of protein for this population came from sea mammals, such as seals (ibid.; Schulting pers. comm.). The Caldey evidence is particularly significant because it could imply a year-round focus of activities at the coast. Apart from specialized seal hunting and trapping during the late winter and early spring – when species such as grey seal (Halichoerus grypus) are found in large colonies and are at their most abundant (Grigson 1989) – the high proportion could also indicate storage of meat and blubber for consumption during the other months.

A further intriguing aspect of the dietary data in the Later Mesolithic is the degree of variability that it displays where evidence is preserved within the coastal zone. A case in point is the southern coastline of Wales where results from Caldey Island reveal markedly different dietary signatures from those of the nearby Gower Coast (David & Walker this volume). Unlike the Caldey individuals, the human remains from Worm's Head and Fox Hole indicate a significant intake of protein derived from terrestrial sources. Whether or not this can be attributed to the economic practices

of separate social groupings and/or the proximity and nature of the contemporary coastline is of course difficult to interpret on present evidence. Some indication that contemporary Later Mesolithic groups were following distinctive inland and coastal exploitation patterns is, however, suggested by isotopic evidence from western Ireland (Woodman et al. 1999). Here, isotopic differences have been noted between individuals from the inland location of Killuragh Cave (terrestrial signal) and from the coastal site of Ferriter's Cove in the Dingle Peninsula (marine signal). Some of the implications of these observations will be explored in the section on raw materials and human mobility patterns below.

Raw materials, mobility, and social territories

Studies of lithic raw materials are highly informative in reconstructing past mobility patterns, and this is especially true of the Mesolithic of northern and western England where a range of distinctive lithic types was used and can be accurately provenanced. Local sources may be defined as those occurring within the immediate vicinity of the site, non-local or exotic sources are by inference located outside this area but the distances involved may vary considerably. So far a number of studies have highlighted the long-distance importation of lithic materials into areas where the local sources were either scarce or of unpredictable quality (Jacobi 1978; Mellars & Dark 1998; Spikins 1996). In the Early Mesolithic this was no doubt partly in response to the continued emphasis on high-quality blade production that necessitated the selective procurement of suitable fine-grained rocks. The pattern of raw material extraction may indicate the range over which people moved during the annual cycle.

Some of the most detailed information on the use of raw materials in the Early Mesolithic comes from northern England where attention has been focused on Star Carr and lithic assemblages of related type. Clark (1972), in his seminal work *Star Carr: a Case Study in Bioarchaeology*, introduced the idea that Mesolithic hunter-gatherers operated within distinct winter and summer ranges as part of an extensive annual hunting territory. The potential scale of this territory could be measured against raw material distances, on the one hand between a site in the Pennines and a source near Star Carr, and on the other by the occurrence of artefacts in a distinctive white flint at various Pennine sites, which could only have originated from the north Lincolnshire Wolds, 80km away. Indeed, in some cases, the white flint artefacts occur in the same frequencies (80–99%) as on the sites immediately adjacent to the flint sources. Long-distance links between individual findspots have also been described by Jacobi (1978), who noted precise parallels between the microlith forms found at Star Carr and those from the upland sites of Pointed Stone 2 and 3, situated 40km to the NW on the North York Moors. This theme has also recently been addressed by Mellars and Conneler (1998) who have shown that some of the high quality translucent flints at Star Carr must have been transported up to 40km from sources in the NE part of the Vale of Pickering. Evidence for long-distance movement of raw materials does not appear to be confined to this area alone. For example, in NE England flints have been documented in the Wear Valley, which have travelled from at least as far south as Yorkshire (Young 1987), while work in south Wales indicates that flint, chert, and mudstone were moved across distances of over 80km (Barton *et al.* 1995). When viewed in totality these examples would appear to lend weight to the idea of widespread human movements in the landscape during this period.

Additional scope for analysing human mobility patterns is offered through the study of bone stable isotopes. So far the results of preliminary work on Early Mesolithic diets indicate a tendency for the consumption of terrestrial foods with little apparent input from migratory fish species or marine sources. This might be taken to mean that although people were travelling extensively in the landscape they were not spending long periods at the coast. Alternatively, the data sample is small and possibly unrepresentative of the population as a whole. Despite these uncertainties, none of the evidence is inconsistent with the idea that Early Mesolithic foragers occupied fairly extensive annual territories, whether solely inland (cf. Donahue & Lovis 2000) or including the coastline as argued by others (Clutton-Brock & Noe-Nygaard 1990).

In the case of Star Carr, the presence of pieces of amber and beads of Liassic Shale could be used to infer links with the nearby Preboreal coastline (Clark 1954). Other studies have noted the apparent geographic relationship between Early Mesolithic sites and major river catchments (Barton *et al.* 1995; Reynier 1998). The location of sites along large drainage networks may lend additional support to the coastal-inland mobility model, at least for certain areas of Britain (Barton *et al.* 1995). It is also clear that rivers provided an easier means of access and communication in a landscape increasingly covered by woodland (Reynier 1998; Roberts 1996; 1999). This seems to be in marked contrast to patterns observed in the earlier Mesolithic of west Sweden where studies have suggested only limited levels of human mobility in this period (Nordquist 1995).

Further perspectives on Mesolithic territorial behaviour and mobility patterns have been presented using the ethnographic record of Boreal forest hunter-gatherers (Barton *et al.* 1995; Smith 1992). Modern Boreal environments typically contain a large number of potential food resources, but the biomass is relatively reduced (Goudie 1984) and animal game such as large ungulates are at low density and are either solitary or live in small groups (Winterhalder 1981). Boreal woodlands are also characterized by a marked cyclical variation in the abundance of certain plant and animal species leading to periodic collapses in their numbers (Larsen 1980). Human density is generally at the lower end of the scale (0.01–0.02 persons per km^2) and many hunter-gatherer groups in these environments invest a great deal of effort in mobility (Kelly 1995). The adoption of risk-reducing strategies can be seen, for example, in the Koyukon people of Alaska, who moved frequently and exploited a very wide variety of plant and animal foods to offset the fluctuations in food resource availability (Nelson 1982). Conversely, much lower levels of mobility are sometimes possible, especially where supported by trapping and fishing, and where food surpluses are regularly stored (Holliday 1998). However, there appear to be few parallels for this latter behaviour in Mesolithic England. For example, application of the same simple criteria reveals no evidence for systematic trapping of small animals or the catching of anadromous fish. Equally, despite the records of pits containing charred hazelnut shells there is little to demonstrate the existence of large-scale storage facilities. Thus there is nothing immediately apparent in the archaeological record to suggest low levels of mobility in the settlement system.

Nevertheless, the organization of movement in the Mesolithic still requires greater clarification. It might, for example, repay looking at Binford's (1980) categories of *logistical* mobility (task-specific groups or individuals moving to and from the residential unit) and *residential* mobility (entire group movements from camp to camp), to see if there are any Mesolithic parallels. So far, there is some slight indication that the collection of raw materials was logistically organized, but it might also be the case that both types existed in parallel. Ethnographic evidence cautions us that the two systems are not necessarily mutually incompatible. This is illustrated in certain examples of Boreal forest hunter-gatherers who practice both high logistical and high residential mobility (Kelly 1995).

Conventionally, the transition between the Early and Later Mesolithic is signified not only by changes in material equipment but also by a transformation in economic behaviour. A major factor in this process has been identified as the eustatic rise in global sea levels, which saw a reduction of available landmass and led humans to concentrate more heavily on coastal resources (Rowley-Conwy 1983; Zvelebil & Rowley-Conwy 1986). This is exemplified in many areas on the Atlantic coastline as far south as Portugal (Zvelebil & Rowley-Conwy 1986), and in Scandinavia by the occurrence of massive shell middens marking major residential 'base-camps' (Andersen 1987 and this volume; Larsson 1990). The intensification of activities in the coastal zone has also been linked to increased sedentism in Late Mesolithic societies, an observation further strengthened by the contemporary appearance of large planned cemeteries (Zvelebil & Rowley-Conwy 1986). During the same period inland areas may have become marginalized or even largely depopulated (Larsson 1983), prompting speculation that Mesolithic groups had ceased to move residentially. Despite the attractive simplicity of this model, its application as an article of faith has recently been challenged (Woodman *et al.* 1999). For example, based on isotopic evidence on dog bones, Larsson (1997) has suggested a greater degree of diversity in economic practices, with some groups located semi-permanently at the coast while others operated further inland. One of the implications of this new interpretation is that the two zones were exploited independently by different human groups (Larsson 1997). The sedentary hunter-gatherer model has also been heavily criticized by Woodman in relation to southern Ireland, where ecological conditions were not the same as in Scandinavia (Woodman *et al.* 1999).

In England, there is as yet no convincing evidence for sedentary behaviour in the Late Mesolithic period. Shell middens mark a number of coastal occupations in the SW of the country (Jacobi 1979), but none so far is on the same size or scale as the Scandinavian examples. Where major accumulations with lithic artefacts do exist, as in the case of Culverwell, Portland, Dorset (Palmer 1999), the middens are fairly thin and scattered over a wide area and could indicate seasonal or short-term use rather than the presence of more permanent base-camp settlements. The range of available dates for Culverwell is consistent with the view that the site was occupied intermittently for a period of up to a millennium (Palmer 1999, 91–3).

There is currently no suggestion of any open-air burials or large cemeteries in Mesolithic England. It has to be accepted, however, that this could be due to the vagaries of the archaeological record. It is conceivable, for example, that some features formerly discounted as tree-throw hollows or storage pits (though probably not those with charred hazelnut shells) could be the only remains of former burials. The recent discovery of Mesolithic pit-graves in parts of NW Europe not previously known for burials should at least alert us to

the possibility. For example, single inhumations in pits sometimes resting or propped against large blocks of sandstone are now known from the Late Mesolithic of the Eure-et-Loir region of northern France (Verjux & Dubois 1997), while multiple human remains of Boreal age have been excavated from a large pit at Chaussée-Tirancourt in the Somme Valley (Ducrocq 1997). The submergence of the Mesolithic coastline is another factor that would have reduced the archaeological visibility of such sites.

Notwithstanding the lack of open-air burials, there is some evidence to suggest that human remains were deliberately interred in caves. These include most notably the inhumation at Gough's Cave of 'Cheddar Man', a complete adult male individual (Stringer 1985) buried in a side fissure and probably originally one of several burials in this part of the cave (Jacobi pers. comm.). A more important cemetery must have existed at the nearby site of Aveline's Hole, on the north side of Mendip, where '50 perfect skeletons' were discovered lying parallel to one another in 1805 (Jacobi 1987; Tratman 1977). Unfortunately these and virtually all the remains of a further 20 individuals, including two found in 1924 with red ochre and beads made of pig and red deer incisors (Mithen 1999), were destroyed during the Second World War. Of the other dated Mesolithic human remains from caves in England, only those at Totty Pot are likely to represent a deliberate burial. In all of these cases, the human remains are significantly earlier than the major cemetery evidence in NW Europe, which generally dates to after 6500 BP (Mithen 1999). Table 18.2 lists the dates currently available for human remains of Mesolithic age in England.

An overall reduction in the size and quality of raw materials has been widely signalled in the Later Mesolithic record (Pitts & Jacobi 1979). This change has been attributed to a number of possible causative factors that need not have been mutually exclusive. Reasons put forward have included the exhaustion of good-quality raw materials, decreasing visibility of sources in the landscape, higher population levels, and/or significant changes in mobility patterns (Mithen 1999). Although it is difficult at present to eliminate any of these explanations, it seems clear that smaller-size material became more commonly used and was collected from a variety of both local and non-local sources. Evidence for formal contacts between the coast and the interior are well documented during this period. The presence of lithic artefacts made of materials of demonstrably coastal origin at inland locations in northern and SW England illustrates this point particularly well.

Moreover, in western England a distinctive pattern has emerged of Late Mesolithic sites situated along the

TABLE 18.2
List of dated human remains from the English Mesolithic. Key to references: 1 – Gowlett *et al.* 1986; 2 – Barker *et al.* 1971; 3 – Hedges *et al.* 1989; 4 – Tratman 1977; 5 – Hedges *et al.* 1987; 6 – Richards & Schulting 2000; 7 – Richards 2001.

Site	County	Lab no.	^{14}C date	Human bone	Reference
Gough's Cave	Somerset	OxA-814	9100±110	talus	1
Gough's Cave	Somerset	BM-525	9080±150	tibia	2
Badger Hole	Somerset	OxA-1459	9360±100	mandible	3
Badger Hole	Somerset	OxA-679	9060±130	mandible (juv.)	1
Aveline's Hole	Somerset	BM-471	9144±110	femur	2
Aveline's Hole	Somerset	Q-1458	9090±110	post-crania	4
Aveline's Hole	Somerset	OxA-799	9100±100	humerus	1
Aveline's Hole	Somerset	OxA-800	8860±100	humerus	1
Aveline's Hole	Somerset	OxA-1070	8740±100	humerus	5
Breakwater Quarry Cave	Devon	OxA-4777	8615±75	unspecified	6
Kent's Cavern	Devon	OxA-1786	8070±90	maxilla	3
Totty Pot	Somerset	BM-2973	8180±70	humerus	
Staythorpe	Nottinghamshire	Beta-144016	6790±40	femur	7

major river networks and on headlands overlooking estuaries (Berridge & Roberts 1986; Roberts 1987). In the Torbryan Valley, Devon, for example, a number of cave sites have been investigated which lie within the middle catchment of the River Dart, about 20km inland from the coast. One of these sites, at Three Holes Cave, contains a small collection of artefacts with microscalene triangles with associated dates on red-deer bones of 6330±75 BP (OxA-4491) and 6120±75 BP (OxA-4492; Roberts 1996). Apart from the flints that are made on beach cobbles, other coastal imports include a sandstone 'abrader', with an adhering marine worm cast, and numerous perforated shell beads of European cowrie (*Trivia monarcha*) and periwinkle (*Littorina* sp.), as well as a modified example of dentalium (*Dentalium* sp.). The perforations would have allowed the stringing together or sewing of these objects onto items of clothing or other materials.

The existence of longer-distance contacts are also indicated by striking similarities in microlith types found at Three Holes Cave and at sites in the upper reaches of the Dart system on the eastern slopes of Dartmoor (Roberts 1996 and in preparation). The assemblages contain beach-derived flint and chert, whose closest direct sources lie over 35–40km away on the south coast of Devon. A very similar pattern can be recognized in north Devon. Here, the distribution of greensand chert and specific microlith types appears to be developed along the river catchments draining northwards off Dartmoor, and may demonstrate the existence of independent social networks focusing on the north coast of Devon.

The importance of rivers as means of communication and for transporting raw materials may also explain the presence of coastally imported items at several Late Mesolithic cave and rockshelter sites in the Wye Valley, on the English-Welsh border in Herefordshire. The sites lie about 25km upstream from the confluence of the River Wye and the Severn estuary (Barton *et al.* 1997). Finds of imported flint and perforated cowrie shells have been recorded at Madawg Shelter where the younger of two dates from associated hearth deposits gave an age of 6655 ± 65 BP (OxA-6082). Perforated shells of identical type as well as imported periwinkle beads have been recorded at the nearby site of King Arthur's Cave (Barton 1997b). On the basis of the small size of the occupations at Madawg shelter and outside the entrance of King Arthur's Cave we would expect that larger residential units, if they existed at all, would have been situated further downstream and closer to the estuary. There is some circumstantial evidence that the use of inland locations at this time may have been of an ephemeral and possibly seasonal nature. Such a view is consistent with the recorded presence of a charred sloe/blackthorn stone (*Prunus spinosa*) and burnt hazelnut shells in the hearth at Madawg shelter (Barton 1997b), indicating perhaps a late summer or autumn occupation of this site.

Conclusions

In the light of the foregoing discussion, we would suggest that while there are detectable differences in the patterns of human mobility in the Early and Later Mesolithic phases the contrasts between them should not be unduly exaggerated. The results of new isotopic studies on human bone plus the lithic raw material data do not contradict the widely accepted model of high logistical mobility in early Postglacial hunter-gatherer groups. Whether this was accompanied by low residential mobility, as might be predicted by Binford's (1980) *collector* paradigm, however, remains unclear. The extensive territories of the Early Mesolithic no doubt included both inland and coastal zones. But there is so far little evidence for major exploitation of marine resources or a reliance on migrating fish species, at least on the isotopic evidence. On the other hand, given the loss of the original coastline, the lack of any positive proof in this respect need not be surprising. In the Later Mesolithic the evidence for systematic coastal-inland contacts increases and access to the interior was clearly facilitated by movements along rivers. It is possible that the lower reaches of river basins were the main focus of residential activity, as this enabled maximum access to richly varied estuarine wetland and coastal habitats. Besides offering a diversity of plant foods (Zvelebil 1994), one added advantage may have been the slightly earlier growth of ungulate browse in these environments (Coles 1998).

Nevertheless, the results of recent work in coastal south Wales (Barton & Bell 2000; Bell *et al.* 2000) and SW Ireland (Woodman *et al.* 1999) warn us that we may not expect to find major residential units in such places, especially if the population density remained relatively low. Instead a case could logically be made for frequent residential moves, albeit localized within a particular setting (e.g. estuarine), and in combination with longer-distance forays by individuals along the main river networks (i.e. high logistical mobility). As in the Scandinavian Late Mesolithic, the latter could be taken to imply the existence of mutually exclusive resource systems but in this case with overlapping geographic ranges. This might also help explain differences between apparently contemporary Mesolithic groups in south Wales; the Caldey Island humans with a preferentially marine diet and the nearby Gower group who exploited foods from predominantly inland environments.

Acknowledgements

Thanks are due to the organizers of the conference for inviting this paper and especially to Alan Saville for his forbearance in editing the proceedings. The figures were produced with the help of Robert Pomfret and Gerry Black, Oxford Brookes University. Michael Richards is thanked for his comments on an earlier version of this paper, as is Rick Schulting for allowing us access to their unpublished isotopic data.

References

Aaris-Sørensen, K. 1999. *Danmarks Forhistoriske Dryeverdin.* Københaven: Gyldendal.

Allen, M.J. and Green, M. 1998. The Fir Tree Field Shaft; the date and archaeological and palaeo-environmental potential of a chalk swallowhole feature. *Proceedings of the Dorset Natural History and Archaeological Society* **120**, 25–37.

Alley, R.B., Meese, D.A., Shuman, C.A., Gow, A.J., Taylor, K.C., Grootes, P.M., White, J.W.C., Ram, M., Waddington, E.D., Mayewski, P.A. and Zielinski, G.A. 1993. Abrupt increase in snow accumulation at the end of the Younger Dryas. *Nature* **362**, 527–9.

Alley, R.B., Mayewski, P.A., Sowers, T., Stuiver, M., Taylor, K.C. and Clark, P.U. 1997. Holocene climatic instability: a prominent, widespread event 8200 yr ago. *Geology* **25**, 483–6.

Andersen, 1987. Tybrind Vig: A submerged Ertebølle Settlement in Denmark. *In* J.M. Coles and A.J. Lawson (eds), *European Wetlands in Prehistory,* 253–89. Oxford: Oxford University Press.

Atkinson, T.C., Briffa, K.R. and Coope, G.R. 1987. Seasonal temperatures in Britain during the past 22,000 years reconstructed using beetle remains. *Nature* **325**, 587–92.

Barker, H., Burleigh, R. and Meeks, N. 1971. British Museum natural radiocarbon measurements VII. *Radiocarbon* **13**, 157–88.

Bartley, D.D. and Morgan, A.V. 1990. The palynological record of the King's Pool, Stafford, England. *New Phytologist* **77**, 177–94.

Barton, R.N.E. 1986. Experiments with long blades from Sproughton, near Ipswich, Suffolk. *In* D.A. Roe (ed.), *Studies in the Upper Palaeolithic of Britain and Northwest Europe*, 129–41. Oxford: British Archaeological Reports (International Series **296**).

Barton, R.N.E. 1989. Long blade technology in southern Britain. *In* C. Bonsall (ed.), *The Mesolithic in Europe*, 264–71. Edinburgh: John Donald.

Barton, R.N.E. 1991. Technological innovation and continuity at the end of the Pleistocene in Britain. *In* N. Barton, A.J. Roberts and D.A. Roe (eds), *The Late Glacial in North-West Europe*, 234–45. York: Council for British Archaeology (Research Report **77**).

Barton, R.N.E. 1997a. *Stone Age Britain*. London: Batsford/English Heritage.

Barton, R.N.E. 1997b. Fifth interim report on the survey and excavations in the Wye Valley, 1997, and new AMS radiocarbon dating results from Madawg Rockshelter. *Proceedings of the University of Bristol Spelaeological Society* **21**(3), 99–108.

Barton, R.N.E. 1998. Long blade technology and the question of British Late Pleistocene-Early Holocene lithic assemblages. *In* N. Ashton, F. Healy and P. Pettitt (eds), *Stone Age Archaeology: Essays in Honour of John Wymer*, 158–64. Oxford: Oxbow (Oxbow Monograph **102**/Lithic Studies Society Occasional Paper **6**).

Barton, R.N.E. and Bell, M. 2000. Mesolithic site conclusions. *In* M. Bell, A. Caseldine and H. Neumann (eds), *Prehistoric Intertidal Archaeology in the Welsh Severn Estuary*. 58–63. York: Council for British Archaeology (Research Report **120**).

Barton, R.N.E. and Froom, F.R. 1986. The long blade assemblage from Avington VI, Berkshire. *In* S.N. Collcutt (ed.), The *Palaeolithic of Britain and its Nearest Neighbours: Recent Trends*, 80–4. Sheffield: Department of Archaeology and Prehistory, University of Sheffield.

Barton, R.N.E., Berridge, P.J., Walker, M.J.C. and Bevins, R.E. 1995. Persistent places in the Mesolithic landscape: an example from the Black Mountain uplands of South Wales. *Proceedings of the Prehistoric Society* **61**, 81–116.

Barton, R.N.E., Price, C. and Proctor, C. 1997. The Wye Valley Caves Project: recent investigations at King Arthur's Cave and Madawg rockshelter. *In* S.G. Lewis and D. Maddy (eds*), The Quaternary of the South Midlands and the Welsh Marches: Field Guide*, 63–75. London: Quaternary Research Association.

Barton, R.N.E., Antoine, P., Dumont, S., Hall, S and Munaut, A.V. 1998. New optically stimulated luminescence (OSL) dates from a Late-Glacial site in the Kennet Valley at Avington VI, Berkshire, UK. *Quaternary Newsletter* **85**, 21–31.

Bell, M. and Walker, M.J.C. 1992. *Late Quaternary Environmental Change: Physical and Human Perspectives*. Harlow: Longman Scientific and Technical.

Bell, M., Caseldine, A. and Neumann, H. (eds), 2000. *Prehistoric Intertidal Archaeology in the Welsh Severn Estuary*. York: Council for British Archaeology (Research Report **120**).

Bennett, K.D. 1983. Devensian Late-glacial and Flandrian vegetational history at Hockham Mere, Norfolk, England. *New Phytologist* **95**, 457–87.

Bennett, K.D. and Preece, R.C. 1998. Palaeobotany. *In* R.C. Preece and D.R. Bridgland (eds), *Late Quaternary Environmental Change in North-West Europe. Excavations at Holywell Coombe, South-East England*, 121–48. London: Chapman & Hall.

Berridge, P.J. 1985. Mesolithic sites in the Yarty Valley. *Proceedings of the Devon Archaeological Society* **34**, 1–21.

Berridge, P. and Roberts, A. 1986. The Mesolithic period in Cornwall. *Cornish Archaeology* **25**, 7–34.

Björk, S., Walker, M.J.C., Cwynar, L., Johnsen, S.J., Knudsen, K.L., Lowe, J.J., Wohlfarth, B. and INTIMATE Members. 1998. An event stratigraphy for the last termination in the North Atlantic based on the Greenland Ice Core record: a proposal by the INTIMATE group. *Journal of Quaternary Science* **13**, 283–92.

Binford, L. 1980. Willow smoke and dog's tails: hunter-gatherer settlement systems and archaeological site formation. *American Antiquity* **45**, 4–20.

Brown, A.P. 1977. Late-Devensian and Flandrian vegetational history of Bodmin Moor, Cornwall. *Philosophical Transactions of the Royal Society of London* **B276**, 251–320.

Bush, M.B. 1993. An 11,400 year palaeoecological history of a British chalk grassland. *Journal of Vegetation Science* **4**, 47–66.

Bush, M.B. and Flenley, J.R. 1987. The age of the British chalk grassland. *Nature* **329**, 434–6.

Caseldine, C. and Hatton, J. 1996. Vegetation history of Dartmoor – Holocene development and the impact of human activity. *In* D.J. Charman, R.M. Newnham and D.G. Croot (eds), *Devon and East Cornwall Field Guide*, 48–61. London: Quaternary Research Association.

Caseldine, C.J. and Maguire, D.J. 1986. Late glacial/early Flandrian vegetation change on northern Dartmoor, south west England. *Journal of Biogeography*. **13**, 255–64.

Childe, V.G. 1931. The forest cultures of northern Europe: a study in evolution and diffusion. *Journal of the Royal Anthropological Institute* **61**, 325–48.

Churchill, D.M. 1962. The stratigraphy of the Mesolithic sites III and V at Thatcham, Berkshire, England. *Proceedings of the Prehistoric Society* **28**, 362–70.

Clark, J.G.D. 1934. The classification a microlithic culture: the Tardenoisian of Horsham. *Archaeological Journal* **90**, 52–77.

Clark, J.D.G. 1935. The prehistory of the Isle of Man. *Proceedings of the Prehistoric Society* **1**, 70–92.

354

Clark, J.G.D. 1954. *Star Carr.* Cambridge: Cambridge University Press.

Clark, J.G.D. 1972. *Star Carr: a Case Study in Bioarchaeology.* Reading (MA): Addison-Wesley (Addison Module in Anthropology **10**).

Clark, J.G.D. 1980. *Mesolithic Prelude.* Edinburgh: Edinburgh University Press.

Clutton-Brock, J. and Noe-Nygaard, N. 1990. New osteological and C-isotope evidence on Mesolithic dogs: companions to hunters and fishers at Star Carr, Seamer Carr and Kongemose. *Journal of Archaeological Science* **17**, 643–53.

Coard, R. and Chamberlain, A.T. 1999. The nature and timing of faunal change in the British Isles across the Pleistocene/Holocene transition. *The Holocene* **9**(3), 372–6.

Coles, B.J. 1998. Doggerland: a speculative survey. *Proceedings of the Prehistoric Society* **64**, 45–81.

Cook, J. and Jacobi, R. 1994. A reindeer antler or 'Lyngby' axe from Northamptonshire and its context in the British Late Glacial. *Proceedings of the Prehistoric Society* **60**, 75–84.

Dark, P. 1998. Radiocarbon-dating of the lake-edge deposits. *In* P. Mellars and P. Dark, *Star Carr in context,* 125–46. Cambridge: McDonald Institute Monograph.

Dark, P. 2000. Revised 'absolute' dating of the early Mesolithic site of Star Carr, North Yorkshire, in the light of changes in the early Holocene tree-ring chronology. *Antiquity* **74**, 304–7.

David, A. 1998. Two assemblages of later Mesolithic microliths from Seamer Carr, North Yorkshire: fact and fancy. *In* N. Ashton, F. Healy and P. Pettitt (eds), *Stone Age Archaeology: Essays in Honour of John Wymer,* 196–204. Oxford: Oxbow (Oxbow Monograph **102**/Lithic Studies Society Occasional Paper **6**).

Day, S.P. 1996. Dogs, deer and diet at Star Carr: a reconsideration of C-isotope evidence from early Mesolithic dog remains from the Vale of Pickering, Yorkshire, England. *Journal of Archaeological Science* **23**, 783–7.

Donahue, R.E. and Lovis, W.A. 2000. *Yorkshire Dales Hunter-Gatherer Research Project. Interim Report 1999.* University of Bradford.

Ducrocq, T. 1997. Contribution à la connaissance du Mésolithique du basin de la Somme. *In* J.-P. Fagnart and A. Thévenin (eds), *Le Tardiglaciaire en Europe du Nord-Ouest,* 107–21. Paris: Éditions du CTHS.

Dumont, S. 1997. Nouvelles recherches sur la transition tardiglaciaire-préboréal dans le Sud et l'Est de l'Angleterre. *In* J.-P. Fagnart and A. Thévenin (eds), *Le Tardiglaciaire en Europe du Nord-Ouest,* 517–27. Paris: CTHS.

Erdbrink, D.P.B. and Tacoma, J. 1997. Une calotte humaine datée au 14C du basin sud de la mer du Nord. *L'Anthropologie* **100**, 541–5.

Fagnart, J.-P. and Plisson, H. 1997. Fonction des pièces mâchurées du Paléolithique final du bassin de la Somme: caractères tracéologiques et donnés contextuelles. *In* J.-P. Fagnart and A. Thévenin (eds), *Le Tardiglaciaire en Europe du Nord-Ouest,* 95–106. Paris: Éditions du CTHS.

Finlayson, B. 1998. *Wild Harvesters. The First People of Scotland.* Edinburgh: Canongate/Historic Scotland.

Fischer, A. and Tauber, H. 1986. New C-14 datings of Late Upper Palaeolithic cultures from Northwestern Europe. *Journal of Danish Archaeology* **5**, 7–13.

Funnell, B.M. 1995. Global sea-level and the (pen-)insularity of late Cenozoic Britain. *In* R.C. Preece (ed.), *Island Britain: a Quaternary Perspective,* 3–13. London: Geological Society.

Gillespie, R., Gowlett, J.A.J., Hall, E.T., Hedges, R.E.M. and Perry, C. 1985. Radiocarbon dates from the Oxford AMS system: *Archaeometry* datelist 2. *Archaeometry* **27**, 237–46.

Godwin, H., Walker, D. and Willis, E.H. 1957. Radiocarbon dating and Post-glacial vegetational history: Scaleby Moss. *Proceedings of the Royal Society of London* **B147**, 352–66.

Goudie, A. 1984. *The Nature of the Environment.* Oxford: Blackwell.

Gowlett, J.A.J., Hedges, R.E.M., Law, I.A. and Perry, C. 1986. Radiocarbon dates from the Oxford AMS system: *Archaeometry* Datelist 4. *Archaeometry* **28**, 206–21.

Grigson, C. 1989. Bird-foraging patterns in the Mesolithic. *In* C. Bonsall (ed.), *The Mesolithic in Europe,* 60–72. Edinburgh: John Donald.

Gulliksen, S., Birks, H.H., Possnert, G. and Mangerud, J. 1998. The calendar age of the Younger Dryas-Holocene transition at Kråkenes, western Norway. *The Holocene* **8**, 249–59.

Hedges, R.E.M., Housley, R.A., Law, I.A. and Bronk, C.R. 1987. Radiocarbon dates from the Oxford AMS system: *Archaeometry* datelist 6. *Archaeometry* **29,** 289–306.

Hedges, R.E.M., Housley, R.A., Law, I.A. and Bronk, C.R. 1989. Radiocarbon dates from the Oxford AMS system: *Archaeometry* datelist 9. *Archaeometry* **31**, 207–34.

Holliday, T.W. 1998. The ecological context of trapping among recent hunter-gatherers: implications for subsistence in terminal Pleistocene Europe. *Current Anthropology* **39**(5), 711–20.

Jacobi, R.M. 1973. Aspects of the Mesolithic Age in Great Britain. *In* S.K. Kozłowski (ed.), *The Mesolithic in Europe,* 237–66. Warsaw: Warsaw University Press.

Jacobi, R.M. 1976. Britain inside and outside Mesolithic Europe. *Proceedings of the Prehistoric Society* **42**, 67–84.

Jacobi, R.M. 1978. Northern England in the eighth millennium BC: an essay. *In* P. Mellars (ed.), *The Early Postglacial Settlement of Northern Europe: an Ecological Perspective,* 295–332. London: Duckworth.

Jacobi, R.M. 1979. Early Flandrian hunters of the south-west. *Proceedings of the Devon Archaeological Society* **37**, 48–93.

Jacobi, R.M. 1984. The Mesolithic of northern East Anglia and contemporary territories. *In* C. Baringer (ed.), *Aspects of East Anglian Pre-history*, 43–76. Norwich: Geo Books.

Jacobi, R.M. 1987. Misanthropic miscellany: musings on British Early Flandrian archaeology and other flights of fancy. *In* P. Rowley-Conwy, M. Zvelebil and H.P. Blankholm (eds), *Mesolithic Northwest Europe: Recent Trends*, 163–8. Sheffield: Department of Archaeology and Prehistory, University of Sheffield.

Jacobi, R.M. 1994. Mesolithic radiocarbon dates: a first review of some recent dates. *In* N. Ashton and A. David (eds), *Stories in Stone,* 192–8. London: Lithic Studies Society (Occasional Paper **4**).

Johansen, L. and Stapert, D. 1998. Two 'Epi-Ahrensburgian' sites in the northern Netherlands: Oudehaske (Friesland) and Gramsbergen (Overijssel). *Palaeohistoria* **39/40** (1997/1998), 1–87.

Kelly, R.L. 1995. *The Foraging Spectrum: Diversity in Hunter-Gatherer Lifeways.* Washington: Smithsonian Institution Press.

Kromer, B. and Becker, B. 1993. German oak and pine ¹⁴C calibration 7200–9400 BC. *Radiocarbon* **35**, 125–7.

Kromer, B., Ambers, J., Baillie, M.G.L., Damon, P.E., Hesshaimer, V., Hofmann, J., Jöris, O., Levin, I., Manning, S.W., McCormac, F.G., Van der Plicht, J., Spurk, M., Stuiver, M. and Weninger, B. 1996. Report: summary of the workshop 'aspects of high-precision radiocarbon calibration'. *Radiocarbon* **38**, 607–10.

Larsen, J.A. 1980. *The Boreal Ecosystem.* London: Academic Press.

Larsson, L. 1983. *Ageröd V. An Atlantic Bog site in Central Scania.* Lund: Almquist & Wicksell International (Acta Archaeologica Lundensia, Series in 8°, No. **12**).

Larsson, L. 1990. The Mesolithic of southern Scandinavia. *Journal of World Prehistory* **4**(3), 257–309.

Larsson, L. 1997. Coastal settlement during the Mesolithic and Neolithic periods in the southernmost part of Sweden. *In* D. Król (ed.), *The Built Environment of Coast Areas during the Stone Age*, 12–21. Gdansk: Regional Centre for Studies and Preservation of the Built Environment.

Lawson, T.J. 1984. Reindeer in the Scottish Quaternary. *Quaternary Newsletter* **42**, 1–7.

Lewis, J. 1991. A late Glacial and early Postglacial site at Three Ways Wharf, Uxbridge, London: interim report. *In* N. Barton, A.J. Roberts and D.A. Roe (eds), *The Late Glacial in North-West Europe,* 246–55. York: Council for British Archaeology (Research Report **77**).

Lowe, J.J., Birks, H.H., Brooks, S.J., Coope, G.R., Harkness, D.D., Mayle, F.E., Sheldrick, C., Turney, C.S.M. and Walker, M.J.C. 1999. The chronology of palaeoenvironmental changes during the Last Glacial-Holocene transition: towards an event stratigraphy for the British Isles. *Journal of the Geological Society, London* **156**, 397–410.

Mellars, P.M. 1974. The Palaeolithic and Mesolithic. *In* C. Renfrew (ed.), *British Prehistory*, 41–99. London: Duckworth.

Mellars, P. and Conneler, C. 1998. Lithic assemblages. *In* P. Mellars and P. Dark, *Star Carr in Context*, 83–98. Cambridge: McDonald Institute Monograph.

Mellars, P. and Dark, P. 1998. *Star Carr in Context: New Archaeological and Palaeoecological Investigations at the Early Mesolithic Site of Star Carr, North Yorkshire.* Cambridge: McDonald Institute Monograph.

Mithen, S. 1999. Hunter-gatherers of the Mesolithic. *In* J. Hunter and I. Ralston (eds), *The Archaeology of Britain*, 35–58. London: Routledge.

Nelson, R.K. 1982. A conservation ethic and environment: the Kuyukon of Alaska. In N.M. Williams and E.S. Hunn (eds), *Resource Managers: North American and Australian Hunter-Gatherers*, 211–28. Boulder: Westview Press.

Newell, R.R., Constandse-Westermann, T.S. and Meikeljohn, C. 1979. The skeletal remains of Mesolithic man in western Europe: an evaluative catalogue. *Journal of Human Evolution* **8**(1), 1–228.

Nordquist, B. 1995. The Mesolithic settlements of the west coast of Sweden – with special emphasis on chronology and topography of coastal settlements. *In* A. Fischer (ed.), *Man and the Sea in the Mesolithic*, 185–96. Oxford: Oxbow (Oxbow Monograph **53**).

O'Malley, M. and Jacobi, R.M. 1978. The excavation of a Mesolithic occupation site at Broom Hill, Braishfield, Hampshire, 1971–1973. *Rescue Archaeology in Hampshire* **4**, 16–38.

Palmer, S. 1999. *Culverwell Mesolithic Habitation Site, Isle of Portland, Dorset: Excavation and Research Studies.* Oxford: British Archaeological Reports (British Series **287**).

Pitts, M. and Jacobi, R.M. 1979. Some aspects of change in flaked stone industries of the Mesolithic and Neolithic in southern Britain. *Journal of Archaeological Science* **6**, 163–77.

Price, T.D. 1989. The reconstruction of Mesolithic diets. *In* C. Bonsall (ed.), *The Mesolithic in Europe*, 48–59. Edinburgh: John Donald.

Radley, J. and Mellars, P.A. 1964. A Mesolithic structure at Deepcar, Yorkshire, England, and the affinities of its associated flint industries. *Proceedings of the Prehistoric Society* **30**, 1–24.

Rankine, W.F., Rankine, W.M. and Dimbleby, G.W. 1960. Further excavations at a Mesolithic site at Oakhanger, Selbourne, Hants. *Proceedings of the Prehistoric Society* **26**, 246–62.

Reynier, M. 1994. A stylistic analysis of ten early Mesolithic sites in south east England. *In* N. Ashton and A. David (eds), *Stories in Stone*, 199–205. London: Lithic Studies Society (Occasional Paper **4**).

Reynier, M.J. 1997. Radiocarbon dating of early Mesolithic stone technologies from Great Britain. *In* J.-P. Fagnart and A. Thévenin (eds), *Le Tardiglaciaire en Europe du Nord-Ouest*, 529–42. Paris: CTHS.

Reynier, M.J. 1998. Early Mesolithic settlement in England and Wales: some preliminary observations. *In* N. Ashton, F. Healy and P. Pettitt (eds), *Stone Age Archaeology: Essays in Honour of John Wymer*, 174–84. Oxford: Oxbow (Oxbow Monograph **102**/Lithic Studies Society Occasional Paper **6**).

Richards, M. 2001. Stable isotope analysis of human bone. *In* G. Davies (ed.), *Interim Statement on the Archaeological Works at Staythorpe Power Station (ARCUS 438f)*. Unpublished report by ARCUS, University of Sheffield.

Richards, M.P. and Hedges, R.E.M. 1999a. Stable isotope evidence for similarities in the types of marine foods used by Late Mesolithic humans at sites along the Atlantic coast of Europe. *Journal of Archaeological Science* **26**, 717–22.

Richards, M.P. and Hedges, R.E.M. 1999b. A Neolithic revolution? New evidence of diet in the British Neolithic. *Antiquity* **73**, 891–7.

Richards, M.P. and Mellars, P.A. 1998. Stable isotopes and the seasonality of the Oronsay middens. *Antiquity* **72**, 178–84.

Richards, M.P. and Schulting, R.J. 2000. Charactérisation de la subsistance pendant le mésolithique britannique. Nouvelles informations d'après l'analyse des isotopes stables. *Les Nouvelles de l'Archeologie* **80**, 20–26.

Roberts, A. J. 1987. Late Mesolithic occupation of the Cornish coast at Gwithian: preliminary results. *In* P. Rowley-Conwy, M. Zvelebil and H.P. Blankholm (eds), *Mesolithic Northwest Europe: Recent Trends*, 131–8. Sheffield: Department of Archaeology and Prehistory, University of Sheffield.

Roberts, A. 1996. Evidence for late Pleistocene and early Holocene human activity and environmental change from the Torbryan Valley, south Devon. In D.J. Charman, R.M. Newnham and D.G. Croot (eds), *Devon and East Cornwall Field Guide*, 168–204. London: Quaternary Research Association.

Roberts, A. 1999. Late Upper Palaeolithic and Mesolithic hunting-gathering communities. *In* R. Kain and W. Ravenhill (eds), *Historical Atlas of South-West England*, 47–50. Exeter: University of Exeter Press.

Roberts, A.J., Barton, R.N.E. and Evans, J. 1998. Early Mesolithic mastic: radiocarbon dating and analysis of organic residues. In N. Ashton, F. Healy and P. Pettitt (eds), *Stone Age Archaeology: Essays in Honour of John Wymer*, 185–92. Oxford: Oxbow (Oxbow Monograph **102**/Lithic Studies Society Occasional Paper **6**).

Rose, J. 1976. The date of the buried channel deposits at Sproughton. *In* J.J. Wymer, A long blade industry from Sproughton, Suffolk. *East Anglian Archaeology* **3**, 11–15.

Rosenfeld, A. 1969. Palaeolithic and Mesolithic. *In* F. Barlow (ed.), *Exeter and its Region*, 129–36. Exeter: University of Exeter Press.

Rowley-Conwy, P. 1983. Sedentary hunters: the Ertebølle. *In* G.N. Bailey (ed.), *Hunter-Gatherer Economy in Prehistory: a European Perspective*. 111–26. Cambridge: Cambridge University Press.

Ruddiman, W.F., Sancetta, C.D. and McIntyre, A. 1977. Glacial/Interglacial response rate of subpolar North Atlantic waters to climatic change: the record in ocean sediments. *Philosophical Transactions of the Royal Society of London* **B280**, 119–42.

Saville, A. 1981a. Mesolithic industries in Central England: an exploratory investigation using microlith typology. *Archaeological Journal* **138**, 49–71.

Saville, A. 1981b. Honey Hill, Elkington: a Northamptonshire Mesolithic site. *Northamptonshire Archaeology* **16**, 1–13.

Saville, A. 1989. A Mesolithic flint assemblage from Hazelton, Gloucestershire, England and its implications. *In* C. Bonsall (ed.), *The Mesolithic in Europe*, 258–63. Edinburgh: John Donald.

Schoeninger, M., DeNiro, M. and Tauber, H. 1983. Stable nitrogen isotope ratios of bone collagen reflect marine and terrestrial components of prehistoric human diet. *Science* **220**, 1381–3.

Schulting, R.J. and Richards, M.P. 2000. The use of stable isotopes in studies of subsistence and seasonality in the British Mesolithic. *In* R. Young (ed.), *Mesolithic Lifeways: Current Research from Britain and Ireland*, 55–65. Leicester: University of Leicester (Leicester Archaeology Monographs **7**).

Severinghaus, J.P., Sowers, T., Brook, E.J., Alley, R.B. and Bender, M.L. 1998. Timing of abrupt climatic change at the end of the Younger Dryas interval from thermally fractionated gases in polar ice. *Nature* **391**, 141–6.

Smith, C. 1992. *Late Stone Age Hunters of the British Isles*. London: Routledge.

Spikins, P. 1996. Rivers, boundaries and change: a hypothesis of changing settlement patterns in the Mesolithic of Northern England. *In* T. Pollard and A. Morrison (eds), *The Early Prehistory of Scotland*, 87–107. Edinburgh: Edinburgh University Press.

Stainton, B. 1989. Excavation of an early prehistoric site at Stratford's Yard, Chesham. *Records of Buckinghamshire* **31**, 49–74.

Stringer, C.B. 1985. The hominid remains from Gough's Cave. *Proceedings of the University of Bristol Spelaeological Society* **17**(2), 145–52.

Stuiver, M and Brazunias, T. 1993. Modelling atmospheric ^{14}C influences and ^{14}C ages of marine samples to 10,000 BC. *Radiocarbon* **35**(1), 137–90.

Stuiver, M. and van der Plicht, J. (eds). 1998. INTCAL98. *Radiocarbon* **40**, 1098–164.

Switsur, V.R. and Jacobi, R.M. 1979. A radiocarbon chronology for the early postglacial stone industries of England and Wales. *In* R. Berger and H.E. Suess (eds), *Radiocarbon Dating. Proceedings of the Ninth International Conference, Los Angeles and La Jolla 1976*, 41–68. Berkeley: University of California Press.

Tauber, H. 1981. ^{13}C evidence for dietary habits of prehistoric man in Denmark. *Nature* **292**, 332–3.

Tolan-Smith, C. and Bonsall, C. 1998. Stone Age studies in the British Isles: the impact of accelerator dating. In *Actes du Colloque «¹⁴C et Archéologie», Lyon, 1998*, 249–57. Paris (Memoires de la Société Préhistorique Francaise **26**).

Tratman, E.K. 1977. A further radiocarbon date on human bone material from Aveline's Hole, Burrington Combe, Mendip. *Proceedings of the University of Bristol Spelaeological Society* **14**(3), 261–2.

Verjux, C. and Dubois, J.-P. 1997. Rites funéraires Mésolithiques originaux à Auneau (Eure-et-Loir). *In* J.-P. Fagnart and A. Thévenin (eds), *Le Tardiglaciaire en Europe du Nord-Ouest*, 265–77. Paris: CTHS.

Wainwright, G.J. 1963. A reinterpretation of the microlithic industries of Wales. *Proceedings of the Prehistoric Society* **29**, 99–132.

Winterhalder, B. 1981. Foraging strategies in the Boreal Forest: an analysis of Cree hunting and gathering. *In* B. Winterhalder and E. Alden Smith (eds), *Hunter-Gatherer Foraging Strategies: Ethnographic and Archeological Analyses,* 66–98. Chicago: University of Chicago Press.

Woodman, P.C. 1987. The impact of resource availability on lithic industrial traditions in prehistoric Ireland. *In* P. Rowley-Conwy, M. Zvelebil and H.P. Blankholm (eds),

Mesolithic Northwest Europe: Recent Trends, 138–46. Sheffield: Department of Archaeology and Prehistory, University of Sheffield.

Woodman, P.C., Anderson, E. and Finlay, N. 1999. *Excavations at Ferriter's Cove, 1983–95: Last Foragers, First Farmers in the Dingle Peninsula*. Bray: Wordwell.

Wymer, J.J. 1962. Excavations of the Maglemosian sites at Thatcham, Berkshire, England. *Proceedings of the Prehistoric Society* **28**, 329–61.

Wymer, J.J. 1976. A long blade industry from Sproughton, Suffolk. *East Anglian Archaeology* **3**, 1–15.

Wymer, J. 1991. *Mesolithic Britain*. Princes Risborough: Shire Publications.

Young, R. 1987. *Lithics and Subsistence in the North-East of England*. Oxford: British Archaeological Reports (British Series **161**).

Zvelebil, M. 1994. Plant use in the Mesolithic and its role in the transition to farming. *Proceedings of the Prehistoric Society* **60**, 13–37.

Zvelebil, M. and Rowley-Conwy, P. 1986. Foragers and Farmers in Atlantic Europe. *In* M. Zvelebil (ed.), *Hunters in Transition: Mesolithic Societies of Temperate Eurasia and their Transition to Farming*, 67–94. Cambridge: Cambridge University Press.

Chapter 19

Conference Discussion Session: Saturday Afternoon, 6 September 1999
The Mesolithic Period in NW Europe and Britain: Regional Aspects: Session 2

CHAIR: STEVEN MITHEN

[The speakers in this session were Peter Woodman, Elizabeth Walker, Sinéad McCartan
and Nick Barton]

ZOFIA SULGOSTOWSKA	It is only a remark. We have more and more evidence that during the Mesolithic stone polishing was evident: from Ireland, from Finland, and from Olenii Ostrov [Russia] in Mesolithic graves. And I see [a confusion], as Professor Woodman suggested in the morning, [in the terminology]. [If polishing is no longer a determinant of] the Younger Stone Age [we need better characterization of what] stone technology is typical of the Neolithic.
PETER WOODMAN	Well, if we expand that, I mean that was one of the reasons why I drew attention to the Norwegian evidence, which would suggest, certainly from 8000 BP, that at Bømlo and perhaps Flora on the west coast there is very extensive axe production and polishing taking place. If you look at middle Sweden there are very, very significant numbers of Mesolithic ground stone axes as well. If you go further afield, if you look at Australia 20,000 years ago, they have ground stone axes. So that really the bottom line is that ground stone artefacts are not a type fossil of the shift from an Older Stone Age to a Younger Stone Age. We even have some up in north Norway, so unlike pottery it is not a type fossil for a change.
FRANCES HEALY	On a different topic, Nick Barton was absolutely right to say that we should be looking for stratified sequences when trying to tussle with what happened in the fifth and fourth millennia, but these are extremely hard to find and I wonder if one of the reasons isn't lurking in the distinctly Late Mesolithic dates which Elizabeth [Walker] quoted from the intertidal zone at Newport. Are we looking at a period where a great deal of settlement was coastal and is now largely inaccessible?
NICK BARTON	I can just say, hear hear! I think too perhaps we haven't necessarily been looking hard enough in the right sort of places and that really what one needs to do is to try and find locations … admittedly something like a doline in the middle of a field [on] Martin Green's farm [in Dorset] is not going turn up all the time [and] is not necessarily going to answer our questions, but I think one has to keep an open mind and perhaps look in areas where we haven't looked in any great detail before, so I could just echo your sentiments.
CLIVE BONSALL	I wonder if I could just ask for a point of clarification from Nick [Barton]? The doline site – you mentioned a date of 5250 for the Neolithic level, what was the date on?
NICK BARTON	So far as I know it was a date on charcoal within a hearth.
CLIVE BONSALL	Do we know what the charcoal was?

NICK BARTON

I would have to go and have a look at the original report, but if need be I'll send you a copy or give you a reference.

CLIVE BONSALL

But it was a charcoal date?

NICK BARTON

Am I right Paul [Pettitt]? Do you recall? Clive's question – I don't know if you remember in detail any of the samples from the Fir Tree Field shaft in Dorset? [No] OK, I think it is best cleared up later then, sorry. [Editor's note: see Allen & Green (1998)]

PATRICK ASHMORE

We have all been talking quite a lot about coastality so I was particularly interested in the very important point, which Nick [Barton] made, about the fact that proximity to a coast doesn't imply, necessarily, reliance on marine resources, and I wondered what views the other panel members had on this?

SINÉAD MCCARTAN

In terms of the Isle of Man, I think, given its size and locality and the distribution so far … I think marine resources were obviously very important, but an awful lot of sites are in juxtaposition with other resources such as the rivers. Or where you are finding sites in the valleys, they are quite close to large wetland areas as well, where there was potential for wild fowling and so forth. I think my situation, the Manx situation, is slightly different than Wales and Ireland, so I'll pass to Ireland!

PETER WOODMAN

OK, well, like many regions of course we have lost our Early Mesolithic coastal zone. This has been an issue that I can remember people like Lars [Larsson] addressing many years ago, as to what role did the coast have in the period before say 7000 BP, when you have [subsequently] lost that coastline. My feeling was that by and large we still don't seem to have that many good indications of settlement out on the coast suggesting any very intensive use of marine resources in the Early Mesolithic. Again the trouble with Mount Sandel, which is the only site that we can really infer from, where there's any organic preservation on the coast (and it's not great even at that), is that primarily they're using the migratory fish species that are moving in and out of the River Bann system, namely salmon and eels, and that the open-sea fish are extremely rare, by I think it's a factor of, maybe, a 100th in comparison to the others. Namely we have bass and we have flounders and that's all. So that, even though they were within a few kilometres of where the sea was – and actually Rick Battarbee has shown it's quite possible that there was a saline wedge coming up the Bann estuary at that stage – they seem to have been using hardly any pure marine resources. In fact the sea bass – it's something like one or two vertebrae – and yet they were obviously [available] a few miles away.

STEVEN MITHEN

One of the themes that Peter [Woodman] mentioned was about regional variation and Sinéad [McCartan] spoke about isolationism and the developments in the Isle of Man. I'm always struck that when we look at any ethnographically documented hunter-gatherers, and those we can find living in Boreal environments or reliant on coastal exploitation, these people are typically covering vast areas. And I've tried imposing either fairly complex, like [North American] NW Coast, or very simple like Tierra del Fuego, hunter-gatherers on Scotland. They are covering areas from the tip of the Western Isles right down to the Isle of Man and I wondered whether if we're still in our Mesolithic studies making a fundamental error on this scale of movement and we're thinking about the Isle of Man as if it can be a distinct area but really it's just part of a vast area that's being covered, and we're making a big error in how we conceive of the scale of exploitation.

SINÉAD MCCARTAN

No, I think you are right. I think the whole question of insular development as a factor of isolation is just one scenario really. I think it's quite naïve to think that there wasn't quite a lot of movement along … or contact with other groups, and my preference …

360

STEVEN MITHEN

I didn't mean necessarily with other groups. I mean individual groups moving [within] really extensive areas, as we have regularly documented ethnographically, and whether the sequence we're seeing in the Isle of Man and Ireland and Wales, [whether] we are really dealing with parts of individual groups exploiting these vast areas.

SINÉAD MCCARTAN

Possibly!

PETER WOODMAN

Although again with the Manx material you do have this factor of these local distinctive characteristics in the typology, and I know it sounds awfully subjective but a lot of these tanged points that occur in the broad-blade assemblage, or whatever you want to call it in the Isle of Man, they just wouldn't be found on an Irish site. They are very different. But I think that there are two levels. One of them, I was actually quite surprised to see for example this extremely high density of $\delta^{13}C$ of -13.8 for the samples from the Dingle Peninsula, suggesting that they are using primarily that peninsula and adjacent coastal areas, set against slightly further inland a $\delta^{13}C$ of -21 or -22 at more or less the same date. And it actually pulled me up short and I thought, yes, I was always inclined, like you, to go along with the model that they covered very big areas – the movement of those materials in the north-east of Ireland right from the centre right through to the coast, where you are talking about certainly a hundred miles across not particularly easy territory, they didn't even necessarily always have the advantage of good river communications to go in those directions – that was the model I was living with. And yet here at the other end of Ireland it seemed to be very different. But I wonder; one area that I have always tried to draw analogies from are the Saami communities of the Arctic – that's not the reason why I went to work there by the way! – but the Russians have some very interesting maps of the Kola Peninsula and the territories aren't always very large. The Kola Peninsula is roughly about the same size as Ireland, though it doesn't look like it when you see it on the maps, and you would have maybe, I would say from traditional ethnographic sources, 20 to 30 territories on that. But then the interesting thing is that of course, you can get the exotics that can be moved over huge distances as part of exchange, of necessary mating networks, and all the rest of it and that's actually where you begin to get things like highly exotic, in the Stone Age up there, you get highly exotic slate being moved over very large distances. You'll even find southern Scandinavian square-sided axes in the far north, and actually that's where I would see some of this new evidence of very early domesticates perhaps fitting in at that level. It's a very tiny percentage that you are seeing, which is only really the exotics, but the territories are maybe not that large.

STEVEN MITHEN

So you can pick your analogy and …

PETER WOODMAN

Yes, whichever one you want!

ROGER JACOBI

Just coming back to the discussion of mobility and how far people are wandering in the English Mesolithic; obviously Nick [Barton] has talked about Wales and the Wye Valley. Just thinking of Yorkshire and Lincolnshire sites, there's obviously a source of flint in the Humber Estuary and the Doncaster area and that is used, as Paul Mellars obviously knows probably better than any of us, up on the southern Pennines. It's also turning up on the Clevelands and just recently, going through the collection from Lackford Heath in west Suffolk there's the exactly same white flint turning up as microliths, which are being introduced to the site. And then again looking at north Lincolnshire, everyone has probably heard of Horsham points, which are mainly found in Hampshire, Surrey, and Sussex, well they're turning up in north Lincolnshire. And Midlands-type inverse basally retouched points are turning up in North Yorkshire, just as isolated examples, and Nick [Barton] was telling me over lunch of Midlands-type inverse basally retouched points turning up in north Cornwall. So there really is a lot of disparate evidence to suggest that in the English Mesolithic, people, perhaps occasionally, are moving over enormous distances.

PETER WOODMAN
Actually we have chert moving over significant distances from the inland of Ireland to the exterior, but again, rather like Roger [Jacobi] says, it's the one piece that you say, Good Lord!, look at that!

PAUL MELLARS
[Question to Nick Barton] In relation to those dates for that cluster of rod-like microliths, either you or Roger [Jacobi] might be best to answer, is it now generally true that most of the late dates for microlithic industries in Britain are of rod-like microliths, rather than triangular? Could one make a case for saying that the final stage of the Mesolithic in England is a rod-dominated stage or, … you would know the dates better than I would. What does Roger think?

NICK BARTON
Roger [Jacobi] probably has a better idea than I do, but …

PAUL MELLARS
I know there are a lot of dates, like [that from] Rocher Moss [Pennines], of similar very late date and there are quite a few others that I vaguely recall, but I thought you might have them at your fingertips.

ROGER JACOBI
I'm really very unhappy about the Pennine dates Paul [Mellars]. Firstly the Rocher Moss South sample really was a very disparate scatter of charcoal fragments at the top of a mineral soil sealed by much later peat so [there] really wasn't a good control. There is – I've got letters from Roy Switsur talking about this – a problem with Dunford Bridge [Pennines], about which Dunford site the samples actually came from …

PAUL MELLARS
No, that was one of Jeff Radley's sites. I don't think there is any doubt about which site it came from, I didn't think so …

ROGER JACOBI
I'll copy the letter to you. There is a problem. Again you have the same problem anyway [of samples] in a very mineral soil. I am struck with one group of really well-contexted rod material from northern England made of this eastern British speckled grey flint. It's the group from Seamer Carr [North Yorkshire], it's an arrowhead group – Andrew David has published it – that has got dates of 8000 years ago …

PAUL MELLARS
That's very significant …

ROGER JACOBI
I must admit that I prefer that dating to [the dates from] either Dunford Bridge B or Rocher Moss South. I must admit I have begun to think of a lot of the rod material as being earlier in the Late Mesolithic rather than later.

PAUL MELLARS
That's what triggered off my thinking but just finally, conversely, do we have good evidence that typical scalene microlith triangle industries continue as late as that? Does anybody know what the latest good dates are for scalene triangles?

NICK BARTON
I think the problem is that we haven't got very well contexted sites, but certainly even micro-scalene triangles continue quite a long way on and in the Wye Valley I think we have got dates about 6000 BP.

ROGER JACOBI
There are dates expected from March Hill … I haven't seen any publications of Penny Spikins's results.

CHANTAL CONNELLER
Penny Spikins has got a very late date for a rod site [March Hill Top] of 5200 BP, and a scalene triangle site [March Hill Carr] of 5800 BP.

CLIVE BONSALL

Just on this topic of scalene triangles, the evidence such as it is from the Cumbrian coast and from western Scotland would suggest that they do go on in those areas after 6000 BP and in west of Scotland down to at least 5300 BP.

STEVEN MITHEN

Do we have some questions other than about microliths?

PAUL PETTITT

Is it fair to return to mobility?

STEVEN MITHEN

Yes that's fine, that's good!

PAUL PETTITT

I'm worried really about how reliable we think our proxy indicators of mobility are and I could suggest, for example, that an elaborately decorated spear tipped with a Horsham point and imbued with social values is exactly the sort of thing you want to swap for coastal resources or whatever, and we know that shells are exactly the sort of thing that fly around in a landscape! I wonder what the speakers or Steve [Mithen], or anybody, think of an alternative scenario in which we have relatively low levels of sedentism, such as we may have on the Isle of Man, as we saw on Oronsay, supported by an elaborate exchange system which ultimately would provide the mechanism by which Neolithic items, even Peter's [Woodman] cows could begin circulating around the landscape!

SINÉAD MCCARTAN

One of the strange things about the Manx assemblage is that you are not getting material brought in from elsewhere so that there doesn't appear to be an apparent exchange of say raw materials [nor] I think, vice versa, anything going out. And this is one of the questions, was the island actually isolated? Were groups on the island isolated at all or did they maintain contacts elsewhere? I don't know …

PETER WOODMAN

Yes, I would agree with Sinéad about the Isle of Man and again we're back with the Irish situation, where in terms of [items] going out there is this extraordinary lack, given all the high-quality material in Antrim, of good-quality flint going out in the Mesolithic. But actually in the Neolithic, the three biggest hordes of Irish flint in the Neolithic period come from Scotland, not from Ireland. But I was wondering, are we inclined, just to take Paul's [Pettitt] point of over-imbuing, [of] giving far too great an importance to the lithics? In other words, there wasn't any value in sending a few Bann flakes across the Irish Sea to the Mull of Kintyre, where quite frankly they had a perfectly adequate technology with what they had and they maybe regarded theirs as superior. Whereas if you look at communities that were highly mobile – I was actually thinking of the best analogy I could come up with [which] was the Australian one, where John Mulvaney has shown in many instances items coming from the Indian Ocean travelling right into the centre of Australia and other items coming from the Pacific coast travelling into the centre of Australia as well. He has one very famous diagram that shows [items] travelling with these mobile communities over very, very considerable distances of an order of magnitude we haven't even been talking about, so it can happen.

STEVEN MITHEN

I wonder if Elizabeth [Walker] might want to comment about the shale beads from Nab Head? Do you see them being produced for exchange and [over] what sort of distance are we finding them?

ELIZABETH WALKER

Well, all the sites from which the shale beads have actually been found have been fairly local to Pembrokeshire. The beads at Waun Fignen Felen I believe are of a local material, they're from mudstone rather than shale. So, I don't feel there's really sufficient evidence to say that there was movement to any broader scale than within the immediate vicinity there.

NICK BARTON

The other thing I think maybe you need to factor into this is the general idea of population levels, if we can speculate on that. I just get the impression, certainly in the Early Mesolithic, we are looking at relatively low population density and I don't know [whether] it would have been high enough for these sort of rather crowded territories with exchange of materials in say SW Britain at 6000 or 7000 years ago? I just don't see it myself. I think the more parsimonious explanation is that we know they had canoes, at least not [on the basis of actual finds] in England but certainly in other parts of Europe, and I can see them simply moving up and down river valleys. And this is the simplest explanation for the materials finding their way up river valleys. I'm quite happy to see a major base camp on Dartmoor and in fact they're just going to the seaside for their holidays! But basing evidence of trade on this sort of evidence is a little bit dodgy I agree, so your [Paul Pettitt's] point is well taken.

ALAN SAVILLE

Just to pick up on a point that Sinéad [McCartan] made there. I thought, when I was looking at the slides she was showing this afternoon of the raw material that was being used for the Late Mesolithic material on Man, that it did look very distinctively Antrim, in opposition to the Early Mesolithic material, which didn't.

SINÉAD MCCARTAN

There's a very good source of Antrim-like flint on the NW coast of the Isle of Man, presumably originally from the same [geological] source, so what you are getting is maybe on a slightly smaller scale than the Irish material, but you are just getting that technology almost, not fully replicated, but in a slightly smaller fashion. The size of nodules [is] quite substantial on the Isle of Man and, in terms of mobility, the mobility might be down the river valleys, up and down river valleys, but again you've got an island situation where there's no Mesolithic site really greater than two kilometres from the sea and that's about as far as you get it.

WILLIAM DUNLOP

Could I just return to this connection between north Antrim and Scotland? We have heard about the flint from north Antrim finding its way right down to the middle of Ireland, and yet if you are in north Antrim and look across to the Mull of Kintyre, it is so close it's just across the road and yet the influence does not seem to have extended to Scotland. Now I presume that Scotland was populated at this time and I presume that there were means for transport, boats to cross the sea, and yet it seems to me that there's almost no influence which has come either way between Scotland and that north-eastern part of Ireland. Is there any good reason for this? Now apart from the fact we are depending on this thing of flint, the lithics, you would have thought that something, [that] there would have been some sort of exchange in some way which could have been identified?

PETER WOODMAN

Well, what I suggested, I think actually way back in 1981 or 1982, was that we have to look for social explanations – that the most intriguing thing about the Irish Later Mesolithic is the fact that it did develop in an entirely different direction from what was happening on the adjacent island, namely Britain, which incidentally was also doing its own thing, which often tends to be forgotten here, in comparison to mainland Europe. So we had two groupings with their own priorities as to how their technology should develop and there were probably more social reasons rather than any other reasons why there was no apparent uptake by adjacent communities when ideas were ... I mean contact was obviously there, but they were just sociologically distinct and they just didn't see any reason to pick up those technologies. And I think actually if I could pass that back to Sinéad, [what] intrigues me is that the Isle of Man is not as close as Scotland is and yet we obviously have a different scenario.

SINÉAD MCCARTAN

Well, as you probably know Billy [William Dunlop], we now have Later Mesolithic stuff on Rathlin Island, which is very close to Islay and particularly close to the Mull of

364

Kintyre. And it is one of the things that has struck me, and I don't know how you explain it, that at the same time that you have the Larnian material, the Late Mesolithic material, on Rathlin, on Islay they're using a microlithic tradition and although there are [possible] social reasons, I'm not quite sure how you would explain that.

WILLIAM DUNLOP

I knew an old boy during the 1930s, he was knocking ninety [years of age] at the time, and he told me that when he was young they used to row across from the Ards peninsula, from Ballywater over to Wigtownshire, to chase the girls in Scotland. Did this not happen then?

SINÉAD MCCARTAN

I'm sure it did! There's also historical records of people leaving Ballycastle early in the morning, going to the fairs in Campbeltown and back again [to] Ballycastle for tea time, so I'm sure ...

STEVEN MITHEN

There's got to be two issues here, whether there is contact of people moving between these areas ...

SINÉAD MCCARTAN

... and identifying that contact ...

STEVEN MITHEN

... and secondly whether they're actually adopting and sharing material culture. They could be doing one without the other.

PETER WOODMAN

If you actually look at what is happening in the Neolithic – and we shouldn't forget about it! – the interesting thing is that the porcellanite axes are moving into parts of Argyll but they are not moving into Galloway. So we are seeing [different] forms of territoriality there in the Mesolithic and in the Neolithic.

SINÉAD MCCARTAN

And also with Professor Simpson's work on the pitchstone – we are seeing stuff coming in, certainly the pitchstone coming in from Scotland, onto some of the major Neolithic sites.

STEVE MITHEN

I wonder whether any of our Scandinavian colleagues could comment, because is it not right that we see these strong social boundaries in material culture in the Later Mesolithic in Scandinavia over very short distances? Lars [Larsson], I was wondering really whether you think the British situation looks peculiar from the point of view of southern Scandinavia or whether it ...

LARS LARSSON

Well, I can give you one example. It's a situation [at] about 8000 years BP and there are two datings. One from the Strait of the Öresund, the strait between Sweden and Denmark, and it was a skull that had been found on the bottom of the sea and it gave good evidence of marine resources. [From] the same [period] there have been two graves found about 40km inland, or maybe 30km, but it's not that far away, and they indicate ... terrestrial resources. So [within] just 40km you find one population, maybe a population that was related to the coastal area, and then one for the inland, so this is the situation just based on two datings.

STEVEN MITHEN

You have very strong boundaries between these?

LARS LARSSON

Yes, it seems to be. And there are other dates, for example of dogs, during the Late Mesolithic I think, that indicate something that's similar.

TORBEN BALLIN

If you look at the situation in southern Norway and for example compare the material culture of western Norway with that of the south coast then you have a very strict border,

365

a wee bit south of Stavanger, where you see some raw materials on one side almost not crossing [to the other side]. Once in a while you might find the odd exotic bit, like an arrowhead for example in rhyolite, but there's a quite distinct border, where [distributions stop] and it looks as if there wasn't any contact, but then you have the exotica ….

STEVEN MITHEN   So there is some sort of contact?

TORBEN BALLIN   Yes, but even here, you don't even have, for example, an Irish Sea in between, it's the same landmass but a very distinct border and we have axe types that stop quite distinctly there, like the Nøstvet axes of the Late Mesolithic that don't go any further than to that border.

PETER WOODMAN   Actually that's one of the intriguing things of the Bømla and Flora axe quarries. They're not that far apart on the ground, but one of them exchanges northwards and the other exchanges southwards along the west coast. [This] has been used occasionally by people to infer two very different territories on the west coast.

NICK BARTON   If I can just pick up on the question of territoriality, I don't know if people are familiar here with the work of Oliver Kayser in southern Brittany where he seems to have different microlith groups, typologically distinct groupings that appear all to be more or less contemporary but occupy different river-valley catchments, parallel to one another on the south Brittany coastline. So it is possible, if you want then to play that particular game of looking at style and microliths and linking that with territories, that there seems to be a very good example, at least in southern Brittany. And of course there's Peter Gendel's work – in Belgium wasn't it? – where he saw stylistic differences between the spatial distribution of artefacts, of microlith shapes, and argued for distinct territories accordingly. So there are examples.

PAUL MELLARS   If I can ask Steve [Mithen], is that the kind of thing you're doing, in the Southern Hebrides Project, are you looking at micro-stylistic differences?

STEVEN MITHEN   Yes, we have done, but in those assemblages we are really looking at varying frequencies of microlith types, and I don't think we have got as dramatic contrasts there around which to build distinct social entities and social groups. I think it's a continuous pattern of variation and the scale there is still pretty small; we are not dealing with areas of more than perhaps 20km or something like that.

PAUL MELLARS   But if you zoomed in on something very specific, like the precise morphology of say the scalene triangles – the size or the way the different edges are retouched? I mean there might just be some information in that.

STEVEN MITHEN   Yes, we can break our collection of sites up into two very interesting groups in terms of frequencies of microlithic types where there are some very high frequencies of scalene triangles and some with very high frequencies of backed blades such as you find in all sorts of parts of the world, and we speculate as to how they might be interpreted. I happen to think we are dealing with individual families with particular traditions, which are being passed through particular lines. It seems to me that the dilemma we have in Mesolithic studies is that we can see so much of a material culture [which] is suggesting we have these social boundaries, social patterns, but we don't have any independent sort of data to investigate those. We always end up in rather circular arguments. I don't know if you think that's the case?

SINÉAD MCCARTAN   I think it's certainly the case with the Manx stuff – you are always going to debate whether the variation is due to chronology, function, or whatever, social or whatever, but

I'm hoping in the next couple of years that problem will be re-addressed and certainly [we will be] tightening up the chronological framework and until we can do that, and the same is really [true] for Wales as well, without that strict chronological framework we are having something of a circular argument.

SØREN ANDERSEN

Just a short remark or comment to this talk on territories. If we turn back to the very well investigated south Scandinavian area, we can see there is a very clear trend through time from territories defined by armatures covering up to 100,000km^2 down to the Late Mesolithic where similar territories [are] just between 500 and 1000km^2. That's a clear trend through time so when you are talking about all this you must also cope with the chronology – you can't just fling up a lot of balls in the air and say this is this and this is that – you must [link] it exactly to chronology and as soon as you don't have any chronology [then] I think this is just some fantasy talk.

ALAN SAVILLE

Following on from that, it is one thing talking about distinctions in terms of stylistic variations between microliths when you are looking at what is essentially the same technology, it's rather different when you are looking at two apparently completely different technologies in the divide between Ireland and Scotland, where you seem to have a microlithic technology going on in Islay or elsewhere and a non-microlithic one in Ireland. And – at the risk of annoying Peter [Woodman] again, as I know I usually do at conferences by saying this! – part of the problem may lie in the fact that we have so few dates for microlithic sites from the north of Ireland. I mean how many dated sites are there?

PETER WOODMAN

There are four sites with dates between 9000 and 8000 BP which have microliths and then we have about 8 or 10 sites at a later date after 7500 BP throughout Ireland which don't have any microliths on them. Not only do [they] not have any microliths, but instead of having a soft-hammer, controlled percussion technology, [they] have a hard-hammer uncontrolled technology, and those sites are found in flint rich areas, they are found in the interior of Ireland, they are found in areas where they are using other raw materials – that's deliberately why I showed [in my talk] that site from Mayo where they were using quartz – they're using rhyolites in the SE, they're using other materials in the SW. So that in reality, the idea that somehow we have managed to inconveniently miss microliths is I think totally untenable from the period after 8000 BP. And actually of course we have now this new site in the south in Killuragh Cave, which again has microliths associated with dates of around about 8000 BP. The bottom line is, don't transfer your paradigm into our world!

GRAEME WARREN

It was going back to the idea that there were territories or broad regions and that the reasons for these might be partly social. What I thought was an interesting implication of that is that these things have some chronological duration; these are resolved over quite long time spans, which I thought had interesting implications again for the processes of social reproduction. And I wondered if anyone would like to comment about that?

NICK BARTON

It's difficult to say. For example, [in the case of] the cowrie shells, it would be very nice to see that they all could be fitted into a period which overlaps neatly with the Obanian and you could see some scheme whereby people were moving right up and down the west coast. But I think, in a way echoing what Søren [Andersen] says, we really do need some decent chronological controls and I hate to always have to use that as a defence, but I don't think we necessarily have the chronological controls.

PETER WOODMAN

The business about stylistic variation. I must say that in Ireland we have never really been able to pick up territoriality on the basis of stylistic differences and the one thing that really shook me was within the Mount Sandel assemblage – and it's buried there in the excavation report and I'm not trying to sell that because as far as I know that book has sold out! – but within that we had a number of pits at Mount Sandel with burnt microliths and burnt hazelnuts in them and the interesting thing was that they were very finite groups. And what I found fascinating was that we had very different-looking scalene triangles in different pits, all within roughly the same comparatively short chronological horizon. And my suspicion is that if we had had those in a different context we would either have arranged them chronologically, or if they had been found in different sites we would have been talking about stylistic variation and territoriality. It seemed to me that this was actually at the individual level rather than anything else.

PUBLICATIONS REFERRED TO, OR WHICH CONTAIN AMPLIFICATION OF POINTS RAISED, IN THIS DISCUSSION SESSION:

Allen, M.J. and Green, M. 1998. The Fir Tree Field Shaft; the date and archaeological and palaeo-environmental potential of a chalk swallowhole feature. *Proceedings of the Dorset Natural History and Archaeological Society* **120**, 25–38.

David, A. 1998. Two assemblages of later Mesolithic microliths from Seamer Carr, North Yorkshire: fact and fancy. *In* N. Ashton, F. Healy and P. Pettitt (eds), *Stone Age Archaeology: Essays in Honour of John Wymer*, 196–204. Oxford: Oxbow Books (Lithic Studies Society Occasional Paper **6**/Oxbow Monograph **102**).

Gendel, P.A. 1984. *Mesolithic Social Territories in Northwestern Europe*. Oxford: British Archaeological Reports (International Series **218**).

Gouletquer, P., Kayser, O., Le Goffic, M. and Marchand, G. 1997. Éléments pour une esquisse géographique du Mésolithique de la Bretagne occidentale. *In* J.-P. Fagnart and A. Thévenin (eds), *Le Tardiglaciaire en Europe du Nord-Ouest*, 293–307. Paris: CTHS.

Saville, A. 1999. A cache of flint axeheads and other flint artefacts from Auchenhoan, near Campbeltown, Kintyre, Scotland. *Proceedings of the Prehistoric Society* **65**, 83–123.

Simpson, D. and Meighan, I. 1999. Pitchstone – a new trading material in Neolithic Ireland. *Archaeology Ireland* **48**, 26–30.

Spikins, P. 1999. *Mesolithic Northern England: Environment, Population and Settlement*. Oxford: British Archaeological Reports (British Series **283**).

Spikins, P. 2002. *Prehistoric People of the Pennines*. Leeds: West Yorkshire Archaeology Service.

Spikins, P., Conneller, C., Ayestaran, H. and Scaife, B. 2002. GIS based interpolation applied to distinguishing occupation phases of early prehistoric sites. *Journal of Archaeological Science* **29**, 1235–45.

Switsur, V.R. and Jacobi, R.M. 1975. Radiocarbon dates for the Pennine Mesolithic. *Nature* **256**, 32–4.

Woodman, P.C. 1985. *Excavations at Mount Sandel 1973–77, County Londonderry*. Belfast: HMSO.

Woodman, P.C., Anderson, E. and Finlay, N. 1999. *Excavations at Ferriter's Cove, 1983–95: Last Foragers, First Farmers in the Dingle Peninsula*. Bray: Wordwell.

Section 5

NORTHERN EUROPE

Chapter 20

The Mesolithic Period in Southern Scandinavia:
with Special Reference to Burials and Cemeteries

LARS LARSSON

Burials and cemeteries have become a very important element in the study of the Mesolithic period in southern Scandinavia. Through these, mortuary practices as well as other aspects of the world view and social relations may be examined in a way that was not previously possible. During recent years a number of Late Mesolithic cemeteries have been found in SW Scandinavia. Cemeteries seem to be a recurrent phenomenon at Late Mesolithic sites.

This contribution is based on the information about the cemeteries found at Skateholm in Scania, southernmost Sweden. Although excavated several years ago they can be used as a basis for the presentation and interpretation of burials and mortuary practice in the Mesolithic period. At Skateholm a combination of settlement and interrelated cemetery has been excavated at two sites and the traces of at least one additional site with settlement remains and graves were documented within the confines of an ancient bay. The study of the Skateholm material has produced indications which point to a complicated burial ritual. This concerns not only the interred individuals, but also a whole range of activities from the moment it was realized that the individual was dying up to the act of refilling the grave. Some comparisons are made with cemeteries in western as well as eastern Europe.

Introduction

Already in connection with the investigation of the eponymous site of Ertebølle (Fig. 20.1) in northern Jutland during the 1890s, clear evidence of burials was found (Madsen *et al.* 1900, 77–80). At the Late Mesolithic settlement site of Blocksbjerg in eastern Denmark, the stratigraphic circumstances convinced the excavator that the graves really had been dug before the deposition of the occupation layer and thus belonged to the first phase of settlement (Westerby 1927, 28–9). Further graves were documented in both Denmark and Sweden, but these were isolated burials, which were

classified more or less as Mesolithic curiosities of no real significance for deepening our knowledge of the conceptual world and the traces this left in mortuary practices. Uncertainty about the age of certain categories of finds, as in the case of a grave discovered at Barum in NE Scania in 1940, also meant that such discoveries led to heated debates about their age, whether Mesolithic or Neolithic (Althin 1951; Lidén 1942; Rydbeck 1945).

Mesolithic cemeteries – a focus of attention

The study of the Mesolithic period in southern Scandinavia has mainly been based on the results of settlement investigations, primarily of sites adjacent to the sea or a lake (Larsson 1990b). Excavations concentrated on the settlement areas close to the ancient shorelines and on their refuse layers, where the possibility of finding artefacts not only of mineral materials, but also of organic materials, was greatest. Only minor areas were thus investigated.

Research during recent years has been geared to obtaining an overall picture of the infrastructure of the settlements, in an attempt to identify different areas of activity. One approach has involved the excavation of sectors of sites which were previously considered not to be worth the effort. This applies in the majority of cases – where the sites are situated on slopes – to the upslope areas with few finds.

Interest in the upper slopes of the settlement areas derived from the results of the excavation conducted at the Henriksholm/Bøgebakken site at Vedbæk, on the Danish coast of the Öresund strait (Figs 20.1 & 20.4). The settlement at Henriksholm had been investigated in stages ever since the 1920s. It was located on the lower part of a south-facing slope (Albrethsen & Brinch Petersen 1977). Shortly after the final planned excavation in 1975, construction work was carried out on the upper reaches of the slope – at Bøgebakken – where graves of Mesolithic age were found. Altogether 18 graves were investigated (Figs 20.2 & 20.3). There were strong indications that the cemetery had originally been more extensive as sections adjacent to the research area had previously been disturbed by road building.

It was by pure chance that the cemetery at Bøgebakken was found. The question was then whether the Henriksholm/Bøgebakken phenomenon was anything other than unique. It would be possible, by the simple expedient of broadening the scope of the excavated area, to establish whether constructions existed not only in the form of graves, but also in the form of a range of other features which might equally contribute to our knowledge of the infrastructure of a Mesolithic society.

The investigation of the cemetery at Bøgebakken attracted considerable attention, yet this discovery should not really have provoked the surprise it did. Although not in the immediate vicinity, in other parts of NE and western Europe there is clear evidence of Mesolithic burials in true cemeteries. In the latter area, cemeteries had already been found in and below shell middens at Téviec and Hoëdic on the southern shore of Brittany during the 1930s (Péquart & Péquart 1954; Péquart et al. 1937; Schulting 1996). Graves with antlers and cenotaphs are evident as well as the use of fire in the mortuary practice. Further to the south a cemetery with more than 30 graves was found below a shell midden at Moita do Sebastião, central Portugal, during excavations

in the 1950s (Roche 1960). The large cemetery with 141 distinct graves at Olenii Ostrov in Karelia was excavated in the 1930s (Gurina 1956); however, it was not until much later that its Mesolithic affinity was finally accepted (Price & Jacobs 1990).

The Skateholm project – the research area

It is now more than 20 years since the sites at Skateholm, southernmost Sweden, were discovered. Several new sites with graves and cemeteries have been found but Skateholm is still the area which gives the best and most varied examples of how grave customs and mortuary practice are related to Late Mesolithic society (Larsson 1984; 1988b; 1989a; 1989c).

The object of the Skateholm project was to study the Late Mesolithic settlement around an ancient lagoon on the southern coast of Scania, which is the southernmost county in Sweden (Fig. 20.1). The lagoon was formed as a result of transgressions during the Late Atlantic and early Sub-Boreal (Gaillard et al. 1988; Lemdahl & Göransson 1988). The area which was the object of archaeological investigation and research comprises flat, low-lying terrain and was subject to changes in

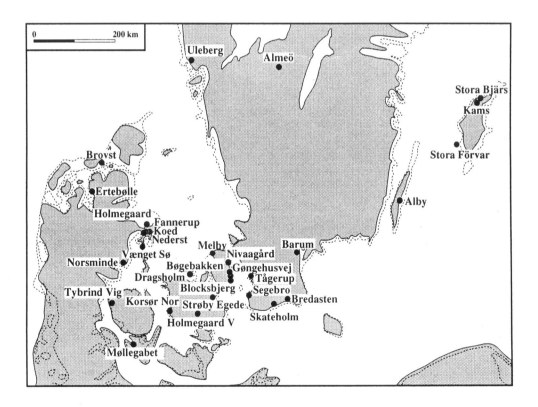

FIGURE 20.1
Southern Scandinavia showing the location of sites with Late Mesolithic graves or cemeteries.

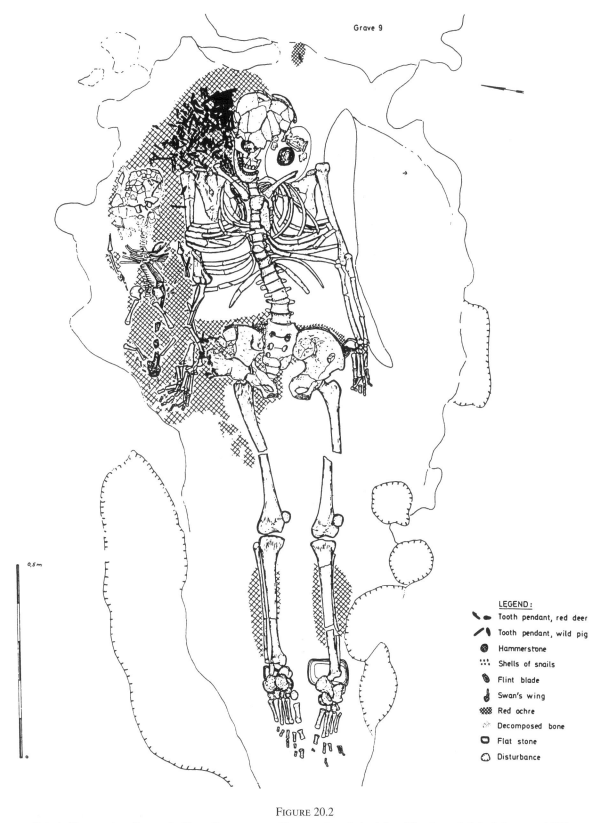

Grave 9

LEGEND:

Tooth pendant, red deer
Tooth pendant, wild pig
Hammerstone
Shells of snails
Flint blade
Swan's wing
Red ochre
Decomposed bone
Flat stone
Disturbance

0,5 m

FIGURE 20.2

Bøgebakken, eastern Denmark. Grave 8: a woman with a new-born baby (after Albrethsen & Brinch Petersen 1977).

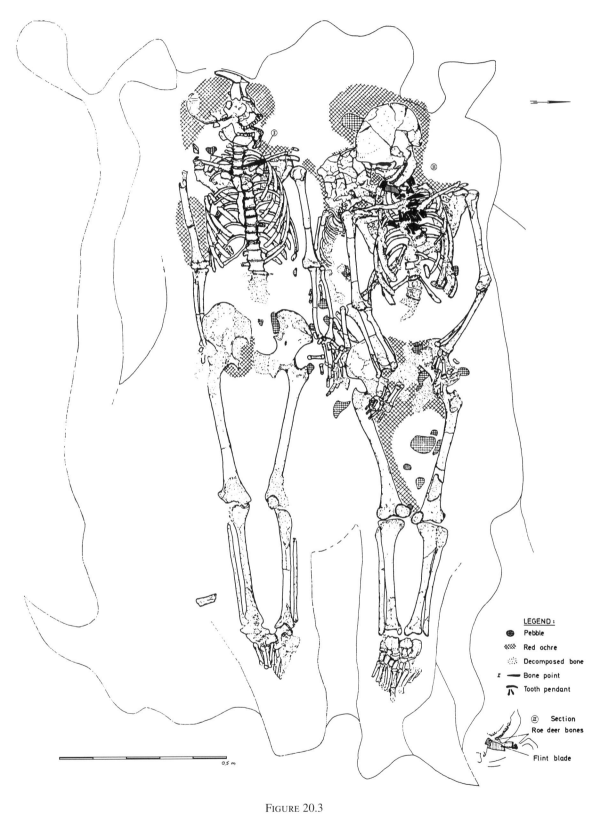

LEGEND:

● Pebble
▨ Red ochre
⣿ Decomposed bone
I ── Bone point
⋔ Tooth pendant

Ⅱ Section
Roe deer bones

Flint blade

FIGURE 20.3
Bøgebakken, eastern Denmark. Grave 19: triple grave with two adults and a child (after Albrethsen & Brinch Petersen 1977).

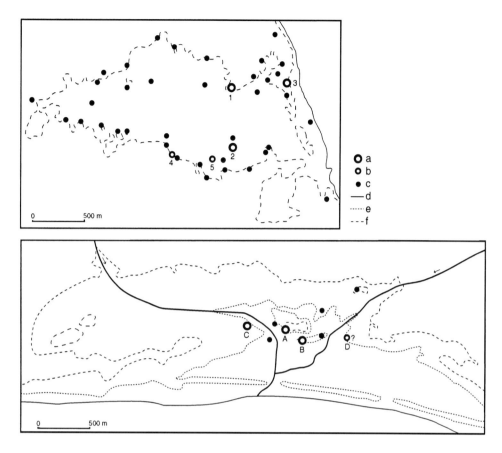

FIGURE 20.4

The relationship of land and sea during stages of the Late Mesolithic period, with the location of settlement sites, graves, and cemeteries within the lagoon at Vedbæk, eastern Denmark (top) and Skateholm, southern Sweden (bottom). Key: 1: Henriksholm–Bøgebakken; 2: Vedbæk Boldbaner; 3: Gøngehusvej; 4: Maglemosegård; 5: Vænget Nord; A: Skateholm I; B: Skateholm II; C: Skateholm III; D: Skateholm IX; a: settlement with cemetery; b: settlement with grave; c: settlement; d: present sea level; e: 3m above sea level; f: 5m above sea level.

the relationship between land and water during the Late Mesolithic and Neolithic oceanic transgressions and regressions. At its greatest extent during the latest part of the Mesolithic and the early Neolithic periods, the lagoon was almost 4km long and c.1km wide, more or less parallel to the present coastline (Fig. 20.4).

The excavations covered the upper part of the settlement areas in order to look for graves and other features. A combination of occupation layer and interrelated cemetery was identified on two sites, Skateholm I and Skateholm II.

The oldest of the main sites, known as Skateholm II, is situated on the westernmost part of the southern slope of a raised area. During an early part of the Late Mesolithic period, this raised area was a long and narrow island in the shallow lagoon (Fig. 20.4). Twenty-two graves were found. As its highest point was situated at only

c.3m above the present-day sea level, the site became completely submerged during a later phase of the Late Mesolithic. The site was abandoned at c.6000 BP.

Considerable quantities of settlement remains in the form of flint artefacts and bones were found at Skateholm I, which was situated on the southernmost side of a slope (Fig. 20.4). When the water level was +3m Skateholm I was situated on a small spur of a roughly rectangular-shaped island. Altogether 65 graves have been excavated at Skateholm I, which is dated to a more recent part of the Late Mesolithic than Skateholm II (c.6000–5500 BP). Skateholm I was also affected by the rising sea, as attested by the absence of refuse layers, which have been completely washed away.

Several other Mesolithic sites were found around the perimeter of the ancient shoreline, and one – Skateholm III – was discovered only 300m west of Skateholm I (Fig.

20.4). At Skateholm III skeletons are known to have been found in the course of gravel extraction during the 1930s. Several graves were recognized but just one was excavated. A ^{14}C date of 5850 ± 90 BP (Lu-2156) for the skeleton indicates that the cemetery at Skateholm III was somewhat younger than Skateholm I.

The research at Skateholm was concentrated mainly on the Skateholm I and Skateholm II sites. Studies of the changes in sea level indicate that these sites were on small islands at the time of their settlement, and that the inhabitants were forced to leave them and move to higher ground after a few centuries. The Skateholm III site was located on the easternmost part of a long and narrow headland of sand. All three sites feature settlement remains as well as interrelated cemeteries. The sites were found within the compass of an area no greater than 500m across.

Yet another site – Skateholm IX, situated in the eastern part of the lagoon – is of interest in this perspective (Fig. 20.4). The site is large and of about the same age as Skateholm I. However, due to restrictions by the landowner, the extent of the excavated area had to be limited. Parts of a pit with human bones have been excavated, indicating the existence of a grave and presumably a cemetery.

The results of the investigations at Skateholm served as confirmation that the cemetery which had been investigated at Bøgebakken in eastern Zealand was not a unique find.

Southern Scandinavian cemeteries

Since the excavation of the Skateholm sites and cemeteries, several other combinations of settlements and graves have been excavated. For most of these sites the topographical setting in a local as well as in a regional perspective is similar. Instead of just excavating the area in relation to the sea shore, parts of the site situated further away from the previous shore have become the main target of investigation. The discovery of graves can be attributed to the fact that the archaeologists had been made aware that graves might be found there as well as other features of importance for the study of Mesolithic societies, such as pits, hearths, and houses.

Cemeteries and graves in their local and regional settings

The location of the Skateholm sites at the shore or on islands in former lagoons is a characteristic of sites with graves.

The cemetery at Bøgebakken was located in a former lagoon, now the Maglemose bog, close to Vedbæk on the eastern shore of Zealand. At other locations close

to the shores of the prehistoric lagoon graves have been discovered, such as the Vedbæk Boldbaner site with a couple of graves, which was found in the 1940s (Mathiassen 1946). On other sites, such as Vænget Nor (Brinch Petersen 1989b; Juel Jensen & Brinch Petersen 1985) and Maglemosegård (Brinch Petersen 1979), only single graves were found within occupation sites which were totally excavated (Fig. 20.4). At Skateholm, spurs and banks of sand protected the entrance to the lagoon. A concentration of modern country cottages along the shoreline have hampered surveys for other sites at Skateholm. Sites with graves were found, however, on the sand banks or spurs which protected the lagoon at Vedbæk from direct exposure to the sea. One example is the site of Gøngehusvej 7 (Fig. 20.4), with a cemetery including several graves (Brinch Petersen 1990; Brinch Petersen et al. 1993).

Within one and the same lagoon several sites with one or several graves may be found. In some cases clear chronological differences occur; however, the chronological differences between sites may be so small that more than one cemetery could have existed contemporaneously within a lagoon.

The reason why concentrations of sites with graves are still limited to Skateholm and Vedbæk has more to do with the intensity of survey and excavation in those locations rather than with any prehistoric conditions. That places of similar potential exist along the coasts of southern Scandinavia is evident from the situation along the coasts of the Öresund strait on which Vedbæk is situated (Fig. 20.5).

The bog at Nivå is another prehistoric lagoon to the north of Vedbæk on the same side of the Öresund, with a further example at Klampenborg, a little to the south of Vedbæk. At Nivågård, the south-easternmost site with a shell midden, a grave has been excavated (Jensen & Hansen 1999; Kannegaard Nielsen & Brinch Petersen 1993); at Klampenborg, at least one grave was found on the Blocksbjerg site (Westerby 1927); and at Strøby Egede further south along the Zealand shoreline, parts of a cemetery were implied by two graves, one of them containing eight individuals (Brinch Petersen 1988a).

In 1998 a rescue excavation of a site at Tågerup, situated in a lagoon on the Swedish shore of the Öresund opposite Vedbæk, revealed at least five graves (Karsten & Knarrström 2003). Circumstances did not allow the excavation team to search for the total extent of the cemetery, which means that the cemetery could have been larger. This site was actually one of a small number, including Skateholm, which was picked out in the late 1970s as being of special interest for a research project about the Late Mesolithic of southernmost Sweden.

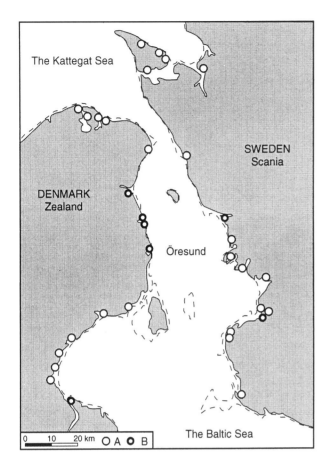

FIGURE 20.5
The strait of Öresund at 5m above sea level, with settlement sites and cemeteries. Key: A: main settlement site; B: settlement with cemetery.

About 20km east of Skateholm on the southern coast of southernmost Sweden there is another prehistoric lagoon, the Öja-Hagestads Mosse bog. Mesolithic sites have been found on islands as well as on the sand banks protecting the lagoon. Just two of the sites have been extensively excavated (Larsson 1986). In one of these – Bredasten (Fig. 20.1) – a small pit with a dog skeleton was found within an area delimited by a shallow trench. This might be interpreted as a dog grave.

Due to the tilting of southern Denmark since the Lateglacial, sites have been submerged. Graves now in a submerged position but formerly situated around lagoons have been found at two locations, Tybrind Vig (Andersen 1985) and Møllegabet II (Grøn & Skaarup 1991), south of Funen (Fig. 20.6). Graves from Korsør Nor on the western shore of Zealand (Fig. 20.1) were found somewhat below the present sea level (Norling-Christensen & Bröste 1945).

In conjunction with the shell middens in eastern Jutland (Fig. 20.1), not only single graves have been identified, but also cemeteries such as Nederst and Koed (Brinch Petersen 1988b; 1989a; Hougaard Rasmussen 1989). If one adds the graves from Melby in northern Zealand (Lund Hansen *et al.* 1972) and Dragsholm (Brinch Petersen 1974) on the northern shore of the same island (Fig. 20.7), the finds in Denmark are considerable. Most of them have been found close to lagoons or places with a high biomass production.

This is also true for the location of sites in Sweden with single graves, such as Barum in NE Scania (Gejvall 1970) and Uleberg (Wigforss 1968) on the west coast (Fig. 20.1). On the island of Gotland in the Baltic Sea, graves have been found at two sites, Kams and Stora Bjärs (Arwidsson 1949; 1979; Larsson 1982a).

Graves and cemeteries

Graves or cemeteries seem be a recurrent phenomenon at Late Mesolithic sites (a cemetery is defined as a site with more than two persons interred). Double graves do occur as well as graves with a larger number of interred. At Gøngehusvej 7 a pit held the cremated bones of five individuals, young as well as old (Brinch Petersen & Meiklejohn 2003). At Strøby Egede, eastern Denmark, a grave was excavated with eight persons, newborn as well as old (Brinch Petersen 1988a). Four interred, all probably male, were placed in one direction, while four of female sex were placed in the other direction in the pit.

A question is whether there might be a distinction between settlement sites with cemeteries and others with single graves. Single graves from large sites where there has only been limited excavation might very well indicate cemeteries, but finds of single graves within extensively excavated sites such as Maglemosegård show that one or just a couple of interments could be made within a site.

In the case of Mesolithic sites in Portugal, no relationship between the size of the occupation area and the number of graves seems to exist. Large sites include a small number of graves and vice versa (Gonzales Morales & Morais Arnaud 1990; Larsson 1996; Morais Arnaud 1989). In southern Scandinavia, however, only large sites seem to include numerous graves.

There are indications that members of the same society were buried in different cemeteries, depending on their age or sex. One such indication is the distribution of ages – predominantly among the males – at Skateholm I and Skateholm II (Persson & Persson 1988). At Skateholm I there are few in the *adultus* group and many in the *maturus* group, and vice versa at Skateholm II. The female distribution is less clear between the two

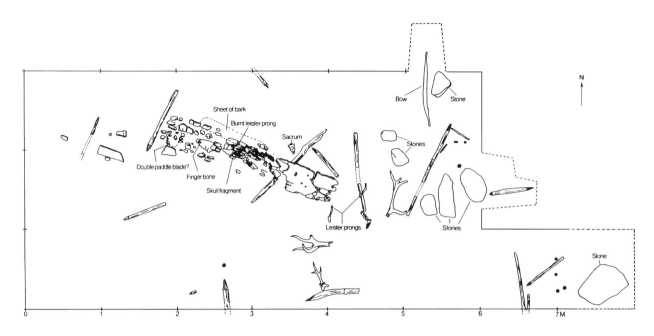

FIGURE 20.6

Grave from the submerged site Møllegabet II south of Funen. The deceased was placed in the stern of a canoe which was wrapped in bark and placed below sea level (after Grøn & Skaarup 1991).

cemeteries. However, there is a great deal to contradict the possible existence of a synchronous relationship between the cemeteries.

On sites such as Skateholm I–II and Bøgebakken, the distribution of graves supports the hypothesis that they were arranged in areas well known – for perhaps centuries – to hold interments. The positioning of the graves within the cemetery almost certainly has a special meaning. Different groupings can be discerned by simply examining the distribution of the graves within Skateholm I. It must be said, however, that the picture is not complete; several graves have suffered severe damage as a result of modern cultivation. Some graves may have been totally destroyed in that process. Age, sex, and the quantity of grave goods vary within the same group. Both odontological and osteological investigations suggest, however, the existence of a close genetic connection between certain individuals in the same grouping (Alexandersen 1988; Persson & Persson 1988). The same family or related members may thus have their special place within the same area of the cemetery.

Examples of graves overlapping older ones are few in number. Therefore, graves could have been visible above the surface. A stone or a post may have marked the grave, or in some cases a stone setting. The latter is known from Mesolithic graves in northern Sweden, where ploughing has not disturbed the surface as it has in the fully tilled landscape of southern Scandinavia (Liedgren 1993).

The relation of graves and shell middens in southern Scandinavia is so far unclear. Graves of Mesolithic age have certainly been found at middens and at one site, Neders in eastern Jutland, seven graves in total were excavated (Johansen 1993). Most of the graves were found between heaps of shells. At large shell middens, such as Ertebølle (Andersen & Johansen 1986) and Bjørnsholm (Andersen 1991), skeletons have been found, but it is not possible to determine whether they represent single graves or parts of cemeteries, as the new excavations have been rather limited in scope.

The interred

Hardly any other period of prehistory can provide such a variety of mortuary practices as the Late Mesolithic. At Skateholm significant variation in the placing of the interred has been found. Three main categories of body positions can be identified: supine, seated, and crouching (Figs 20.8–10). Many variations of these categories occur. The crouching position, for example, ranges from a position in which the extremities are only slightly angled, to an extremely contorted position, which must denote that the deceased person was tightly trussed and bound hand and foot. In most graves of southernmost Scandinavia the interred are placed in a supine position, less frequently in a crouching posture.

The Skateholm cemeteries provided several expressions of contemporary mortuary practice. Some of these have not been found anywhere else, but subsequent finds have produced indications which confirm complicated burial rituals. These involve not only the interred individuals, but also the whole range of activities from the moment it was realized that the individual was dying up to the act of refilling the grave. Although this insight is in itself nothing new, few investigations have provided so many examples of so many diverse activities, which clearly point to such complex mortuary practices. The dying individual appears to have eaten a 'last supper' with a particular content, evidence of which is provided by the fish bones found in the area of the stomach (Jonsson 1986a; 1986b). The positioning of the deceased in the grave and the composition of the grave goods followed a particular pattern. The rituals included the deposition not only of objects such as tools and ornaments but also skeletal parts of animals, such as jawbones of marten, metatarsals of red deer, and a hoof from a roe deer. Food for the 'journey', including fish, was also placed in the grave.

For most graves no traces of any covering of the body are visible. In same cases, however, organic remains or traces of containers have been recognized. The deceased were wrapped in a skin or in bark. At the site of Gøngehusvej 7, children were buried on a large wooden plate (Fig. 20.11; Brinch Petersen 1990).

Judging from the dark colouration caused by some kind of wooden cover, the stern of a dugout canoe was used as a coffin in a grave at Skateholm II. At the submerged site of Møllegabet II, on western Funen (Fig. 20.6), the deceased person was placed in the stern of a canoe which was itself wrapped in bark and placed below sea level close to the settlement (Grøn & Skaarup 1991; Skaarup 1995). Wrapping the dead in bark seems to have been rather common.

Cremation of the body does occur. At Skateholm I both of the two cremation graves were combinations with wooden constructions. In one case the bones were placed in small pits inside the construction and in postholes belonging to it. Cremation graves have been found at sites related to the bog at Vedbæk, eastern Zealand (Kannegaard Nielsen & Brinch Petersen 1993).

Grave goods

Various activities took place in connection with the infilling of the grave. Food was eaten, and the leftovers were thrown into the fill. Even objects such as tools and ornaments were placed in the grave-pit, apparently casually, although these are often objects of the same type that appear as grave goods directly related to the interred individual. Traces of wooden structures raised over the grave-pit were found at Skateholm. These had been burnt down prior to the infilling of the grave. No

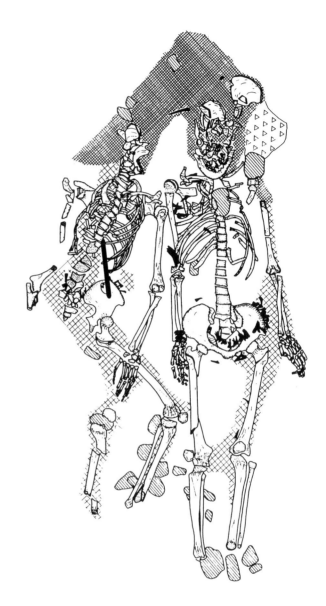

FIGURE 20.7

Dragsholm, eastern Denmark. A double grave with two women (after Brinch Petersen 1974). Areas with cross-hatching mark the distribution of red ochre.

similar constructions have been found at any other Mesolithic site so far. However, wooden constructions above graves in the long barrows of the early Neolithic period might reflect a continuation of this practice (Rudebeck 2002), especially as they were sometimes set on fire, just like those at Skateholm.

The contents of the filling of the grave-pits differ considerably between graves, but also in relation to different parts of one and the same filling. This might mean that the infilling operation was deliberately divided

FIGURE 20.8

Skateholm II, southern Sweden. Grave X with two adult males, one in a sitting, the other in a supine, position. A dog was found in the grave infill just above the human skeletons.

into several stages with different types of soils being used.

It is possible to learn a good deal from what remains and, indeed, from what does not. For example, a hand or a foot or, in one case, a lower arm and a thigh bone may be missing from an otherwise well-preserved skeleton (Nilsson Stutz 2003). This may mean that these parts were deliberately removed, and that the deceased individual also had a concrete symbolic function, even if only in partial form, in the land of the living.

The composition of the grave goods follows a more distinctive pattern than the body positions. Tools such as knives and axes are typically found with men, while women have ornaments such as belt decorations made of animal teeth. In addition, various combinations of animal bones were sewn on to clothing. Antler bases are also found buried in a small number of graves. Red ochre is common in most graves; more often than not this covers only limited parts of the deceased, such as the head and the hip area. It may be noted that certain elements of these Late Mesolithic burial customs recur more generally. One of them is the widely distributed custom of depositing the antlers of red deer in the grave (Fig. 20.9; Albrethsen & Brinch Petersen 1977; Péquart & Péquart 1954; Péquart *et al.* 1937).

Clear indications exist, with regard to the number and distribution of the grave goods, that the question is primarily one of contemporary world view, which appears to have been considerably more complex than a simple expression of the status of the deceased person in a society which is subdivided by class. Several facts provide evidence of this situation, such as that a number of children were accorded grave goods which are not compatible with their ages. A two-year-old child received two knife blades at Skateholm II and at Nederst a five-year-old child was buried with several different objects. These were tools which the children could hardly apply to any practical use in daily life.

Several sources of error may of course exist in an evaluation of the grave goods in terms of both quality and quantity. Objects occur in the fill immediately above the deceased and it is not always certain whether an object was intended as a grave good. In all probability there is a hidden gradation in respect of the relationship of the objects to the dead. Certain objects may already have been acquired at birth in the form of a family or clan attribute, such as a totem exemplified by a skeletal part of a particular animal. Other objects were probably acquired at various times during the person's lifetime. The sum of the personal possessions of the interred individual may thus reasonably be expressed in terms of the number and quality of the grave goods bestowed on the deceased person. Graves without grave goods are common, as are graves with a small number of artefacts, while just a small number of graves contain many objects.

There are similarities but marked differences as well between the mortuary practice of Skateholm and the Danish cemeteries (Larsson 1989b). The variations in body posture exemplified at Skateholm cannot be seen on either side of the Öresund strait, less than 80km away, or in other Mesolithic cemeteries in present-day Denmark (Fig. 20.1). That the interred in Mesolithic graves on the Swedish east and west coast, but not in Denmark, are placed in a sitting position is of special interest. This could indicate that the societies in the western and eastern parts of southern Scandinavia had different mortuary practices based on different network structures.

Dog graves

An interesting aspect is the variation in the treatment of dogs in the burial ritual (Larsson 1989b; 1990a; 1995b). At Skateholm the first substantial evidence for dog graves was found (Fig. 20.12). If these graves are to be ranked in any way, then at the top of the scale is an individually interred dog at Skateholm II, upon which a number of grave goods were bestowed. A red deer antler was laid along its spine, and three flint blades were placed in the hip region, in the same fashion as such objects appear in male graves. A decorated antler hammer was placed on the chest of the dog. Here we have two categories of grave goods, antlers and blades, which are reminiscent of human graves, with the latter especially associated with male graves. On the other hand, the antler hammer is without parallel in terms of grave goods.

Another factor which is similar to those encountered in human graves is the strewing of red ochre over the dog's corpse. All of this reflects a symbolism which appears to apply to humans and dogs alike, in spite of the fact that not one of the eight canine graves at Skateholm I can be related spatially to a human grave. They in fact appear to have been regarded as 'different' in that six of the canine graves lie within a delimited area. There may have been a boundary between the two species, in the sense that one was seen to be something apart from the other.

Before the excavation of the dog graves at Skateholm, graves for dogs were potentially indicated at two other Scanian sites. At Segebro it was speculated that the well-preserved canine bones could be interpreted as the remains of dog graves (Lepiksaar 1982). At another site in central Scania, a part of a skeleton was found back in the 1930s (Dahr 1937). At Bredasten, like the

FIGURE 20.9

Skateholm II, southern Sweden. Grave XI with a young male in a supine position. Deer antlers were placed across the feet end of the grave.

Skateholm sites located within the context of an ancient lagoon and just 25km from Skateholm, a construction measuring 3.5m × 4.5m was encountered, delimited by a ditch (Larsson 1986). The skeleton of a puppy was found within this enclosure, buried in a shallow pit (Jonsson 1986a). This construction may constitute some kind of grave.

In the analyses of the bones from Mesolithic sites of southern Scandinavia, references are made to finds

FIGURE 20.10

Skateholm I, southern Sweden. Grave 47 with a young man and an infant on the man's right side (arrow). Three stone axeheads and a stone were placed between the thighs of the young man.

of tubular bones and crania of dogs in the Danish Late Mesolithic sites, such as Dyrholmen and Vedbæk Boldbaner, supporting the assumption that the ritual interment of dogs was a commonly practised element in Late Mesolithic burial custom (Aaris Sørensen 1977, 172; Degerbøl 1933, 539). Finds from other sites in northern Europe dated to the Early Mesolithic, such as Star Carr, may indicate the same habit (Clutton-Brock & Noe-Nygaard 1990, 643–6).

Within the context of the Early Mesolithic site of Almeö at Hornborgarsjön lake, central Sweden (Fig. 20.1), there is also evidence pertaining to the presence of canine graves (Arnesson-Westerdahl 1983; 1985). Here, at least three finds of dog can be classified as ritual interments. A fourth may also be interpreted as a grave. One of the finds comprised the skeletal remains of a dog, some parts being burnt, others completely free from damage by fire. Thus, the corpse appears to have been subjected to certain rites involving fire, without this ritual earning the title of actual cremation. Three flints were found in one concentration of canine bones; another dog was almost certainly strewn with red ochre.

In a cemetery at Nederst on east Jutland, six dogs in total were found within the context of an area containing human graves (Johansen 1993). On one of them a hearth was placed on top of the grave, similar to the circumstances of a dog grave at Skateholm I.

A cemetery with five graves on a sand ridge at Vedbæk was combined with an intact skeleton of a dog, most likely the evidence of a grave (Brinch Petersen 1990, 28).

Structures of special importance for mortuary practice
A rectangular structure measuring 4m × 4m, which differed in shape and composition from all other features,

was encountered inside the cemetery at Skateholm II (Larsson 1988a). Its outer limits were demarcated by a belt of sand-mixed red ochre on all sides, enclosing an area of soot-admixed sand. A thin layer of red ochre lay beneath the latter in one half of this structure, where posthole stains were also recognized. The unique aspect in the context of Skateholm is the exaggerated application of red ochre in such large amounts over so great an area of the structure. Occurrences of this substance are otherwise only known within the graves. The distribution of flints and human bones in the concentrations found inside the area of red ochre suggests deliberate depositions. Some of the bones were also found to be conjoined, indicating that musculature and sinews were intact at the time of deposition. The structure had a special ritual function associated in one way or another with mortuary practice.

Another structure inside the cemetery at Skateholm II was found close to a grave. It was a pit, oval in shape and of normal grave size (Fig. 20.13). No traces of human remains were found, however, although the pit contained three red deer antlers. The finds in this feature can be compared to those found in certain graves in the same cemetery. Either it is the remains of a grave, from which the traces of the interred individual have been removed for some reason or another, or it is an example of the cenotaph phenomenon referred to in other reports of Mesolithic cemeteries (Albrethsen & Brinch Petersen 1977; Péquart & Péquart 1954; Péquart *et al.* 1937).

One grave at Skateholm I consisted of a pit, *c.*2m in diameter and more than 1m deep. A small amount of cremated human bone was found at the outer edge of the pit. The shape of the feature corresponds to a huge posthole. One cannot avoid drawing parallels with the mortuary poles of the North American Pacific coast (Malin 1986). These poles had a cavity in which the cremated bones of chiefs were placed. A similar mortuary practice is known from northern Australia. That huge poles might have been of ritual significance is suggested by the large postholes found close to Stonehenge and dated to between 9200 and 8100 BP (Allen 1995).

Burial customs from different perspectives

The Skateholm graves provide the opportunity to observe an important temporal perspective, since the dynamics in the relationship between tradition and innovation in burial customs can be examined. The crouching position, for example, is virtually unknown in the older cemetery at Skateholm II, whereas almost two-fifths of the individuals interred at Skateholm I, the younger cemetery, were placed in this position. The number placed in the supine position was halved at Skateholm I. The custom of depositing red deer antlers in the grave is, on the contrary, quite unknown at Skateholm I, whereas it is a common feature at Skateholm II.

The number and quality of the grave goods gradually diminishes between the two chronological phases represented by the two cemeteries. However, the many variations in the position of the interred individuals become more accentuated in the younger cemetery. This illustrates how the mortuary practice goes through a process of change during this period of prehistory.

It cannot be clearly established whether the large sites such as Skateholm I and II are to be regarded as having been permanently inhabited or seasonally occupied (Rowley-Conwy 1998). In the time range indicated by the radiometric datings, the number of graves is far too small even to include a family group. Since it must probably be assumed that the dead were also dealt with in other ways, which have not left any traces in the locations investigated, the number of inhabitants may have been very much larger than a family group. Such an interpretation is supported by the large amount of waste material at these sites.

In a study of mortuary practices among hunter-gatherers it has been claimed that true cemeteries do not exist (Knutsson 1995). The Skateholm cemeteries are regarded by Knutsson as adjuncts to repeated settlements which were deserted when a member died and was buried. The small number of overlapping graves and the structure of the graves are two of several indications of the unlikelihood of this hypothesis. The ethnographic records concerning hunter-gatherers stem from regions which are peripheral, not only to present settlement, but most likely to the settlement of hunter-gatherers with a complex social structure. The records of such societies date to an early colonization stage by individuals from

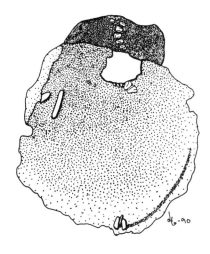

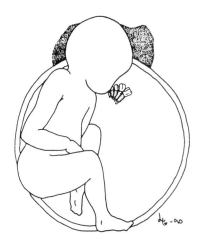

FIGURE 20.11

Reconstructed grave from Gøngehusvej 7, eastern Denmark, with a child placed on a wooden plate (after Brinch Petersen 1990).

European communities when notes were few and there was limited interest in, and special knowledge of, the existing inhabitants.

Another observation in contrast to the hypothesis of several settlement intervals is the experiment in which the reaction of wild boars to buried meat has been observed (Rausing 1991). All meat buried in pits with a depth of 0.6–1.0m was dug up and consumed by wild boars less than three weeks after being deposited. Wild boar was a frequent animal, especially in areas close to the flooded beaches which would have occurred close to previously settled areas (Jonsson 1988). If graves were left unattended there should be many examples of graves more or less destroyed by wild boars – but there are not!

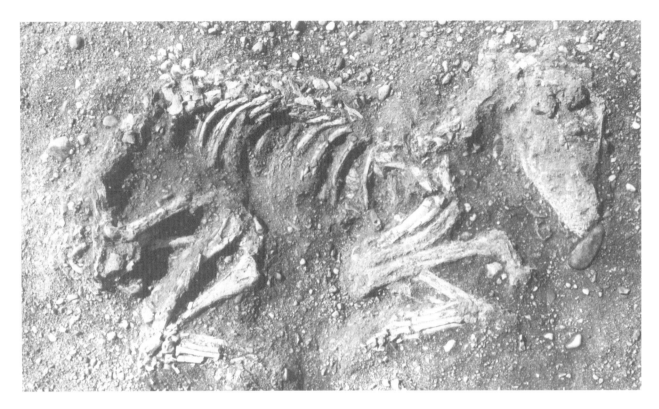

FIGURE 20.12
Skateholm I, southern Sweden. Grave 23, one of the total of eight dog graves documented at this site.

Graves during the Mesolithic

The Mesolithic of southern Scandinavia is divided into three cultural stages: the Maglemose culture, the Kongemose culture, and the Ertebølle culture. The relevant chronology is shown in Fig. 20.14. Almost nothing is known about the mortuary practice of the Maglemose culture. Just as in the later part of the Mesolithic period, human bones are found in occupation layers. These might in some cases originate from shallow graves destroyed during later activities. However, the fact that a majority are fragments from skulls and extremities indicates an intentional choice of skeleton parts (Larsson *et al.* 1981). These bones probably had a meaning in activities of ritual importance, but the question is whether they were incorporated in funeral practice as such. It is more plausible that they were linked to rituals involving past generations. Two human skeletons were found close to the Holmegård V site and dated to the late Maglemose culture but information about these possible graves remains incomplete.

As a matter of fact, the earliest Mesolithic graves are the dog graves from Almeö in western Sweden. These are dated to the Preboreal.

At Kams, on the Baltic island of Gotland, two burials in a crouched, sitting position and the remains of a third skeleton have been found (Arwidsson 1949). One of the crouched inhumations was dated to 8050±75 BP (Lu-1983; Larsson 1982a). Another grave with a male in a crouched position has been dated to 7970±80 BP (Ua-10426; Lindqvist & Possnert 1999). The cave of Stora Förvar on a small island off Gotland was excavated in the 19th century (Lindqvist & Possnert 1999). Analyses of bones from a part of the excavation there have recovered several bones from a small child as well as bones from nine other individuals. Accelerator datings indicate a time range from 8555±135 (Ua-3132) to 8220±95 BP (Ua-3788).

Except for the graves at Tågerup, in the southernmost part of Sweden, graves are lacking from the early part of the Kongemose culture *c.*8000–7000 BP. Graves, mainly containing cremation burials, are known from slightly later (7000–6500 BP), while most graves have been dated to either a very late part of the Kongemose culture or the early Ertebølle culture (6500–6000 BP). Graves do exist from the late part of the Ertebølle culture but the number is much smaller than from the early part of the culture (Price

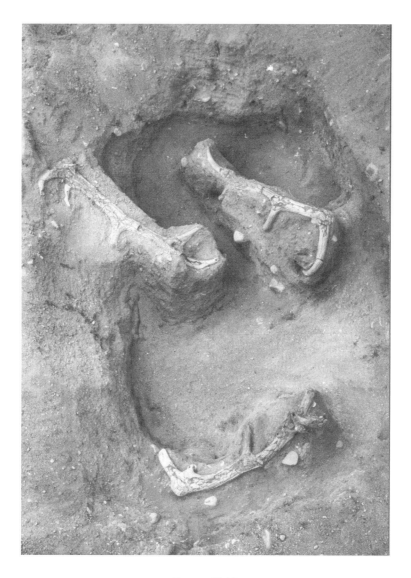

FIGURE 20.13
Structure 8, Skateholm II, southern Sweden. A pit containing three red deer antlers;
an example of the cenotaph phenomenon?

1999). During the same period the transgressions were at their highest, which might have caused intensive destruction of sites and graves. Whether the decrease in the number of graves and cemeteries known is due to these natural causes or the effect of social changes remains an open question.

The coast and the inland

All Mesolithic cemeteries are found close to the sea and so there is a question as to whether cemeteries ever existed inland within southern Scandinavia. The only

known graves from the interior are those for dogs at the site of Almeö, close to the Hornborgarsjön lake in western Sweden, dating to the Preboreal. In that case one must bear in mind that the site is located as much as 100km from the former sea.

The absence of Early Mesolithic graves might indicate that the cemeteries were located close to the sea, since the Early Mesolithic coast was submerged already during the late Boreal and early Atlantic periods. We know of some submerged sites located in the same setting as those from the Late Mesolithic, but excavations have so far been of very limited extent (Larsson 1999). Elsewhere in Europe inland graves and cemeteries are

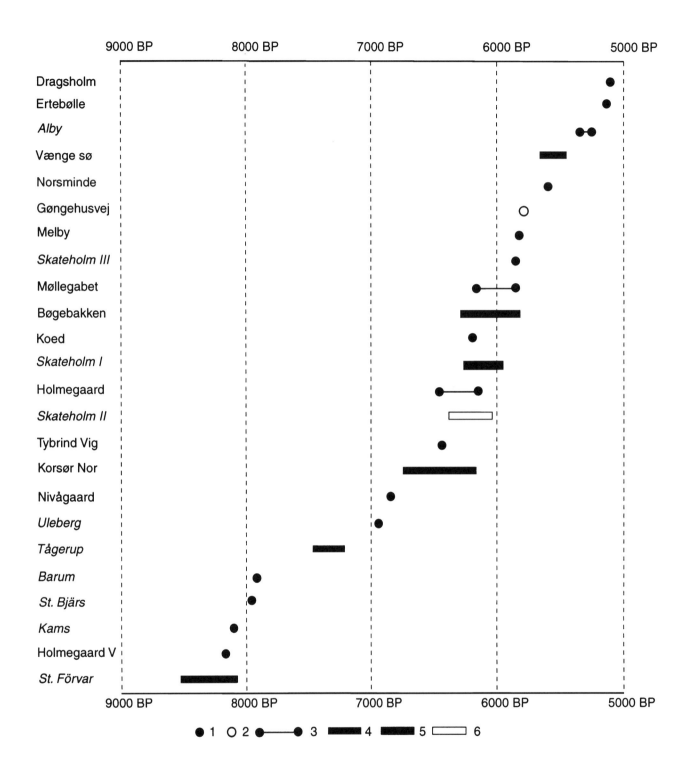

FIGURE 20.14

The chronology of graves and cemeteries of southern Scandinavia according to uncalibrated BP ^{14}C determinations. Key: 1: grave dated by sample from the interred; 2: grave dated by charcoal in direct connection with the interred; 3: grave dated by two samples from the interred; 4: cemetery with two or more dates of the interred; 5: two or more dates of fragmentary skeletons which might have belonged to a cemetery; 6: dates from a settlement with a cemetery. (Swedish sites in italic.)

well known from the Early Mesolithic phase (Newell *et al.* 1979). Such cemeteries are also known from the Baltic area (Zagorski 1987).

The division into inland and coastal zones has been discussed in connection with the relation of seasonal moves and exchange systems (Andersen 1995; Larsson 1980). In such cases the coastal zone has been considered to have extended between 10 and 15km from the seashore. A zone 15–30km from the shore has been regarded as an area which was exploited by the coastal settlers, while areas further from the shore might have been used by a separate population. Some researchers have argued for an interior population using sites as close as 15km to the shore (Noe-Nygaard 1988; 1995, 261–3).

Cemeteries could very well exist in the interior, for instance, some 30km from the coast. That graves have not been found may be due to several factors. The area classifiable as the interior within southern Scandinavia is of limited extent; only areas in central Jutland and the central part of southern Sweden could be considered. Another factor is that very few large Mesolithic settlements, which do exist in the interior, have been intensively excavated. That the interior is mainly covered by soils which do not preserve organic material is yet another complication. However, Mesolithic graves should be identifiable even in such soils by traces of the grave-pits and especially by the presence of red ochre. Among the graves at Skateholm I, for instance, 65 per cent included red ochre. In just one case so far, however, Segebro on the Scanian coast of the Öresund strait, have burials been indicated by red ochre and artefacts in pits within the highest sector of the site (Larsson 1982b, 31).

Mesolithic cemeteries in a wider geographic perspective

In western Europe cemeteries are found in and below shell middens, as at Téviec and Hoëdic on the southern shore of Brittany (Péquart & Péquart 1954; Péquart *et al.* 1937; Schulting 1996). Graves with antlers and also cenotaphs are evident, as well as the use of fire in mortuary practice. Further to the south several, if not most, shell middens have cemeteries of varying sizes (Larsson 1995a; 1996). Within some areas, such as the settlement along the River Sado in southern Portugal, most shell middens, small as well as large, include a cemetery. However, there does not seem to be any relationship between the number of graves and the size of the shell middens.

New studies and radiometric datings of previously investigated cemeteries provide valuable perspectives on the Mesolithic cemeteries along the east coast of the Baltic and neighbouring areas. According to radiocarbon dates, the large cemetery with 141 graves at Olenii Ostrov in Karelia (O'Shea & Zvelebil 1984) was used during the period 7700–7300 BP (Price & Jacobs 1990). A grave within a cemetery at Spiginas in northern Lithuania has been dated to 7470 ± 60 BP (GIN-5571; Butrimas 1989).

The cemetery at Zvejnieki is situated close to the shore of Lake Burtnieki in northern Latvia. The cemetery was excavated in the period 1964–71 by Zagorski (1974). Two main concentrations of graves were found. Zvejnieki is the largest cemetery in northern Europe, consisting of 315 graves, and according to the artefacts the site was used as a burial ground as well as a settlement from the Late Mesolithic until the Late Neolithic period (Zagorski 1987). Important skeletal material was also gathered (Denisova 1975). The earliest date for a burial at Zvejnieki is 8240 ± 70 BP (Ua-3634; Zagorska 1997; Zagorska & Larsson 1994). However, most of the Mesolithic graves are dated to the period *c.*6800–5200 BP.

This would suggest that the cemeteries at Olenii Ostrov and Spiginas are partly contemporary with the burials in Zvejnieki. The ^{14}C results show that we have a considerable quantity of grave material dating from the sixth and fifth millennia throughout northern Europe. This provides us with an excellent basis for a future comparative study of the burial practices of northern European hunter-gatherer societies.

The great variety of positions of the interred at Skateholm in comparison with other cemeteries where there are almost no differences in the burial position might be due to its location in the SE part of the Scandinavian peninsula. Influences from eastern Europe, with for instance a variety of burial positions in the Olenii Ostrov cemetery in Karelia, as well as examples of the sitting position, such as at Janisławice in Poland, might have had a greater impact in this part of southern Scandinavia (Tomaszewski & Willis 1993).

Why cemeteries?

Another crucial question is why cemeteries were founded at all. In a way I think that the basic reasons coincide with why monuments were built during the Neolithic period. To use the terminology of nuclear physics, we get the impression that a 'critical mass' is necessary if a need to build monuments is to arise. Unlike nuclear physics, however, it is not a question of the accumulation of one component, but rather of a mixture of several different components. One of the ingredients is the geographical conditions. This is obvious from the fact that Mesolithic cemeteries as well as megalithic tombs are completely absent in certain regions. Mostly they are concentrated in areas with an ecologically varied zonation. Another ingredient is population density, which should not be confused with population growth, although there is often a certain association. A third ingredient is the scope of contact with other social groups. Further ingredients are the shaping of traditions as regards the social structure and hence the structure of the conceptual world and the composition of the economic base.

This does not mean that exactly the same mixture was necessary on every occasion for the 'critical mass' to arise. Nor should this be taken as evidence that the custom of establishing cemeteries arose independently in several different areas. It is most likely that they had a common origin. On the other hand, we must reckon with different combinations and varying significance of the above variables for the custom to have been adopted. Some general ideas may have existed, but we should not therefore ignore the conditions and conceptions that were specific to each region.

If a comparison is made between the south of Scandinavia and the north of Continental Europe concerning mortuary practice during the late Atlantic phase, a number of interesting factors will emerge; these should not be ignored. One such factor concerns the relationship between a significant variation in burial practices in southern Scandinavia and the comparatively homogeneous burial practice of contemporaneous societies in adjacent parts of Europe (Veit 1993). These societies, which are often perceived as complex, usually have a comparatively limited number of forms of expression in their burial practices. The forms of expression seem to differ according to whether the manifestation of complexity is social or ritual.

It is also necessary to point out that we are concerned here with a contrast between an inland agricultural society and a coastal fishing society. One factor which is perhaps of critical significance within the social organization that manifests itself in the burial practice is the changed relationship between land and water.

A rise in sea level in the order of +20m occurred during the late Boreal and early Atlantic phases. In parts of southern Scandinavian about two-thirds of the landscape disappeared beneath the water. This must not necessarily be regarded as ecologically critical for the hunter-gatherer societies. New, abundant fishing environments are formed just as quickly as old ones disappear. The social aspect should be far more interesting to study. These changes were so drastic that their effects must have been clearly identifiable in the landscape. Being forced to change one's physical map from one generation to the next probably also had consequences for the

mental map. Fishing above a shallow bank on which previous generations were known to have lived must have produced a significant effect on peoples' conceptual world. The stresses were thus of both a physical and a mental nature.

Is it possible in the case of Skateholm II, for example, that no one living there knew that the cemetery would become submerged within one or two generations? The need to have the deceased close by the place inhabited by the living was greater than the need to preserve the graves from physical changes for the foreseeable future.

Perhaps we are dealing with a form of territorial marking here, which might be aimed less obviously against other societies and more against the changeability of nature, which threatens the social and mental situation of mankind. Could it be that the establishment of cemeteries quite simply represents an attempt to halt changing nature; an attempt to bring about a status quo? This idea may well be seen as a totally subjective observation, but I believe that greater consideration must be given in future analyses to the mental relationship between people and the landscape, in order to fully appreciate Late Mesolithic societies.

No graves in Scotland?

Graves and cemeteries are present along the entire west European coast from Denmark to Portugal. But so far the record of Mesolithic graves in the British Isles is scarce. Some human remains appear in contexts which seem to belong to destroyed graves (Smith 1992, 137). In other cases the find circumstances of disarticulated bones hints at a certain role in ritual practices involving remains of ancestors equivalent to the behaviour at sites in southern Scandinavia (Meiklejohn & Denston 1987, 297–9). The absence of Mesolithic graves could be a reality due to the circumstance that the mortuary practice accepted by the local society manifests itself in the deposition of parts of skeletons within special sites. Other funerary rites could have involved deposition of the body outside the site in a way that did not leave any traces. But the information from Aveline's Hole in Somerset, where two of the skeletons were tinged with red ochre, is an important marker of a mortuary practice similar to that practised on continental Europe.

If such mortuary rituals were practised elsewhere in Britain, why have burials not been found in Scotland? The reason might be the same as that which for a long time made burials an unusual feature in south Scandinavian archaeology – the excavation trenches were not positioned within sectors of the sites where a burial ground was likely to appear. Excavation has to be extended to areas outside the centre of a site and to areas where preservation is poor not only for organic refuse but for occupation layers as well. The finding of burials in south Scandinavian shell middens seems to be much more accidental due to the limited extent of excavation. The largest cemeteries are not found in this type of refuse deposit anyway. The most favourable landscape to investigate would be a lagoon or deep bay for a long time favoured as a protected water basin, preferably with a mixture of fresh, brackish, and salt water and an irregular shoreline which provides the potential for headlands and islands to form as a consequence of changing sea level. This might also mean that burials and cemeteries have been submerged as well as covered by layers caused by transgression. It is not an easy task, but worth trying, as this article has tried to show.

References

Aaris Sørensen K. 1977. Vedbæk-jægeren og hans hunde. *In* E. Brinch Petersen, J. Jønsson, P. Vang Petersen and K. Aaris-Sørensen. *I marken og i museerne. Vedbækprojektet.* Søllerødbogen **1977**, 170–76.

Albrethsen, S.E. & Brinch Petersen, E. 1977. Excavation of a Mesolithic cemetery at Vedbæk, Denmark. *Acta Archaeologica* **47**, 1–28.

Alexandersen, V. 1988. Description of the human dentitions from the Late Mesolithic Grave-Field at Skateholm, Southern Sweden. *In* L. Larsson (ed.), *The Skateholm Project. I. Man and Environment,* 106–63. Lund: Almqvist & Wiksell International (Regiae Societatis Humaniorum Litterarum Lundensis **LXXIX**).

Allen, M.J. 1995. Before Stonehenge: Mesolithic human activity in a wildwood landscape. *In* R.M.J. Cleal, K.E. Walker and R. Montague (eds), *Stonehenge in Its Landscape: Twentieth-Century Excavations,* 470–3. London: English Heritage (Archaeological Report **10**).

Althin, C.-A. 1951. Bäckaskogs-och Lummelundagravarnas ålder. *Fornvännen* **46**, 360–4.

Andersen, S.H. 1985. Tybrind Vig. A preliminary report on a submerged Ertebølle settlement on the west coast of Fyn. *Journal of Danish Archaeology* **4**, 52–69.

Andersen, S.H. 1991. Bjørnsholm. A stratified Køkkenmødding on the central Limfjord, north Jutland. *Journal of Danish Archaeology* **10**, 59–96.

Andersen, S.H. 1995. Ringkloster. Ertebølle trappers and wild boar hunters in eastern Jutland. *Journal of Danish Archaeology* **12** (1994–1995), 13–59.

Andersen, S.H. and Johansen, E. 1986. Ertebølle revisited. *Journal of Danish Archaeology* **5**, 31–61.

Arnesson-Westerdahl, A. 1983. Mesolitiskt hundfynd vid Hornborgasjön. Värdefulla fauna- och domestikationshistoriska fynd. *Fauna och flora* **78**, 71–2.

Arnesson-Westerdahl, A. 1985. Djuren vid Hornborgarsjön för 9 000 år sedan. *Sveriges Natur* **1985**, no.3, 40–43.

Arwidsson, G. 1949. Stenåldersfynden från Kams i Lummelunda. *Gotländskt Arkiv* **1948–49**, 147–67.

Arwidsson, G. 1979. Stenåldersmannen från Stora Bjärs i Stenkyrka. *Arkeologi på Gotland,* 17–23. Visby: Barry Press Förlag.

Brinch Petersen, E. 1974. Gravene ved Dragsholm. Fra jægere til bønder fra 6000 år siden. *Nationalmuseets Arbejdsmark* **1974**, 112–20.

Brinch Petersen, E. 1979. Udgravningerne i sommaren 1978. *In* E. Brinch Petersen, V. Alexandersen, P. Vang Petersen, and C. Christiansen (eds), Vedbækprojektet. Ny og gammel forskning. *Søllerødbogen* **1979**, 21–9.

Brinch Petersen, E. 1988a. Ein mesolithisches Grab mit acht Personen von Strøby Egede, Seeland. *Archäologisches Korrespondenzblatt* **18**(2), 121–5.

Brinch Petersen, E. 1988b. Late Palaeolithic and Mesolithic. *Arkæologiske Udgravninger i Danmark* **1987**, 79–81.

Brinch Petersen, E. 1989a. Late Palaeolithic and Mesolithic. *Arkæologiske Udgravninger i Danmark* **1988**, 73–5.

Brinch Petersen, E. 1989b. Vænget Nord: excavation, documentation and interpretation of a Mesolithic Site at Vedbæk, Denmark. *In* C. Bonsall (ed.), *The Mesolithic in Europe,* 325–30. Edinburgh: John Donald.

Brinch Petersen, E. 1990. Nye graver fra Jægerstenalderen. Strøby Egede og Vedbæk. *Nationalmuseets Arbejdsmark* **1990**, 19–33.

Brinch Petersen, E. and Meiklejohn, C. 2003. Three cremations and a funeral: aspects of burial practice in Mesolithic Vedbæk. *In* L. Larsson, H. Kindgren, K. Knutsson, D. Loeffler and A. Åkerlund (eds), *Mesolithic on the Move: Papers presented at the Sixth International Conference on the Mesolithic in Europe, Stockholm 2000,* 485–93. Oxford: Oxbow Books.

Brinch Petersen, E., Alexandersen, V. and Meiklejohn, C. 1993. Vedbæk, graven midt i byen. *Nationalmuseets Arbejdsmark* **1993**, 61–9.

Butrimas, A. 1989. Mesolithic graves from Spiginas, Lithuania. *Mesolithic Miscellany* **10**(2), 10–11.

Clutton-Bock J. and Noe-Nygaard, N. 1990. New osteological and C-isotope evidence on Mesolithic dogs: companions to hunters and fishers at Star Carr, Seamer Carr and Kongemose. *Journal of Archaeological Science* **17**, 643–53.

Dahr, E. 1937. *Studien über Hunde aus primitiven Steinzeitkulturen in Nordeuropa.* Lunds Universitets Årsskrift, N.F. Avd 2. Bd. **32**, Nr. 4. Lund.

Degerbøl, M. 1933. *Danmarks Pattedyr i Fortiden i Sammenligning med recente Former.* København: Munksgaard (Videnskabelige Meddelelser fra Dansk naturhistorisk Forening i København **96**).

Denisova, R.Ya. 1975. *Antropologiya Drevnikh Baltov.* Riga: Zinatne.

Gaillard, M.-J., Göransson, H., Håkansson, H. and Lemdahl, G. 1988. The palaeoenvironment at Skateholm-Järavallen (Southern Sweden) during Atlantic and Early Subboreal time on the basis of pollen-, macrofossil-, and insect-analyses. *In* L. Larsson (ed.), *The Skateholm Project. I. Man and Environment,* 52–5. Lund: Almqvist & Wiksell International (Societatis Humaniorum Litterarum Lundensis **LXXIX**).

Gejvall, N.-G. 1970. The fisherman from Barum – mother of several children! Palaeo-anatomic finds in the skeleton from Bäckaskog. *Fornvännen* **65**, 281–9.

Gonzalez Morales, M.R. and Morais Arnaud, J.E. 1990. Recent research on the Mesolithic in the Iberian Peninsula: problems and perspectives. *In* P.M. Vermeersch and P. Van Peer (eds), *Contributions to the Mesolithic in Europe,* 451–61. Leuven: Leuven University Press.

Grøn, O. & Skaarup, J. 1991. Møllegabet II – a submerged Mesolithic site and a "boat burial" from Ærø. *Journal of Danish Archaeology* **10**, 38–50.

Gurina, N. 1956. *Olneostrovski mogilnik.* Moskva (Materialy i issledovaniya po arkheologgi SSSR **47**).

Hougaard Rasmussen, G. 1989. Okkergrave fra ældre stenalder på Djursland. *Kuml* **1988–89**, 31–41.

Jensen, O.L. & Hansen, K.M. 1999. Barnegraven fra Nivågård. *Hørsholm Egns Museum Årbog* **1998**, 7–21.

Johansen, E. 1993. Late Paleolithic and Mesolithic. *Arkæologiske Udgravninger i Danmark* **1992**, 109–13.

Jonsson, L. 1986a. Animal bones from Bredasten – preliminary results. *In* M. Larsson, Bredasten – an early Ertebølle Site with a dwelling structure in south Scania. *Papers of the Archaeological Institute of Lund* **6** (1985–1986), 50–51.

Jonsson, L. 1986b. Fish remains in Late Mesolithic human graves at Skateholm, Scania, south Sweden. *In* D.C. Brinkhuizen and A.T. Clason (eds), *Fish and Archaeology: Studies in Osteometry, Taphonomy, Seasonality and Fishing Methods,* 62–79. Oxford: British Archaeological Reports (International Series **S294**).

Jonsson, L. 1988. The vertebrate faunal remains from the Late Atlantic settlement Skateholm in Scania, south Sweden. *In* L. Larsson. (ed.), *The Skateholm Project. I. Man and Environment,* 56–88. Lund: Almqvist & Wiksell International (Societatis Humaniorum Litterarum Lundensis **LXXIX**).

Juel Jensen, H. and Brinch Petersen, E. 1985. A functional study of lithics from Vænget Nord, a Mesolithic site at Vedbæk, N.E. Sjælland. *Journal of Danish Archaeology* **4**, 40–51.

Kannegaard Nielsen, E. and Brinch Petersen, E. 1993. Burials, people and dogs. *In* S. Hvass and B. Storgaard (eds), *Digging into the Past,* 76–81. København: The Royal Society of Northern Antiquaries/Jutland Archaeological Society.

Karsten, P. and Knarrström, B. 2003. *The Tågerup Excavations.* Stockholm: National Heritage Board.

Knutsson, H. 1995. *Slutvandrat? Aspekter på övergången från rörlig till bofast tillvaro.* Uppsala: Societas Archaeologica Upsaliensis (*Aun* **20**).

Larsson, L. 1980. Some aspects of the Kongemose Culture of Southern Sweden. *Papers of the Archaeological Institute University of Lund* **4** (1979–1980), 5–22.

Larsson, L. 1982a. De äldsta gutarna. *Gotländskt Arkiv* **54**, 7–14.

Larsson, L. 1982b. *Segebro. En Tidigatlantisk Boplats vid Sege ås Mynning.* Malmö: Malmö museum (Malmöfynd **4**).

Larsson, L. 1984. The Skateholm Project. A Late Mesolithic settlement and cemetery complex at a south Swedish bay. *Papers of the Archaeological Institute University of Lund* **5** (1983–1984), 5–38.

Larsson, L. 1988a. A construction for ceremonial activities from the Late Mesolithic. *Papers of the Archaeological Institute of Lund* **7** (1987–1988), 5–18.

Larsson, L. 1988b. The Skateholm Project. Late Mesolithic settlement at a south Swedish lagoon. *In* L. Larsson (ed.), *The Skateholm Project. I. Man and Environment,* 9–19. Lund: Almqvist & Wiksell International (Societatis Humaniorum Litterarum Lundensis **LXXIX**).

Larsson, L. 1989a. Big dog and poor man. Mortuary practices in Mesolithic societies of southern Sweden. *In* T.B. Larsson and H. Lundmark (eds), *Approaches to Swedish Prehistory. A Spectrum of Problems and Perspectives in Contemporary Research,* 211–23. Oxford: British Archaeological Reports (International Series **S500**).

Larsson, L. 1989b Ethnicity and traditions in Mesolithic mortuary practices of southern Scandinavia. *In* S. J. Shennan (ed.), *Archaeological Approaches to Cultural Identity,* 210–18. London: Unwin Hyman.

Larsson, L. 1989c. Late Mesolithic settlements and cemeteries at Skateholm, southern Sweden. *In* C. Bonsall (ed.), *The Mesolithic in Europe,* 367–78. Edinburgh: John Donald.

Larsson, L. 1990a. Dogs in fraction – symbols in action. *In* P.M. Vermeersch and P. van Peer (eds), *Contributions to the Mesolithic in Europe,* 153–60. Leuven: Leuven University Press.

Larsson, L. 1990b The Mesolithic of southern Scandinavia. *Journal of World Prehistory* **4**(3), 257–309.

Larsson, L. 1993. The Skateholm Project: Late Mesolithic coastal settlement in southern Sweden. *In* P. Bogucki (ed.), *Case Studies in European Prehistory,* 31–62. Ann Arbor: CRC.

Larsson, L. 1995a. Man and sea in southern Scandinavia during the Late Mesolithic. The role of cemeteries in the view of society. *In* A. Fischer (ed.), *Man and Sea in the Mesolithic,* 95–104. Oxford: Oxbow Books (Oxbow Monograph **53**).

Larsson, L. 1995b. Pratiques mortuaires et sépultures de chiens dans les sociétés mésolithiques de Scandinavie méridionale. *L'Anthropologie* **98**(4) (1994), 562–75.

Larsson, L. 1996. Late Atlantic settlement in southern Portugal. Results of an excavation of a Mesolithic shell midden by the River Sado. *Current Swedish Archaeology* **4**, 123–39.

Larsson, L. 1999. Submarine settlement remains on the bottom of the Öresund Strait, southern Scandinavia. *In* A. Thevénin (ed.), *L'Europe des derniers chasseurs: Épipaléolithique et Mésolithique,* 327–34. Paris: CTHS.

Larsson, L., Meiklejohn, C. and Newell, R.R. 1981. Human skeletal material from the Mesolithic site of Ageröd I:HC, Scania, southern Sweden. *Fornvännen* **76**, 161–8.

Larsson, M. 1986. Bredasten – an early Ertebølle Site with a dwelling structure in south Scania. *Papers of the Archaeological Institute of Lund* **6** (1985–1986), 5–49.

Lemdahl, G. and Göransson, H. 1988. Geological investigations at Skateholm, southern Sweden. *In* L. Larsson (ed.), *The Skateholm Project. I. Man and Environment,* 20–6. Lund: Almqvist & Wiksell International (Societatis Humaniorum Litterarum Lundensis **LXXIX**).

Lepiksaar J. 1982. Djurrester från den tidigatlantiska boplatsen vid Segebro nära Malmö i Skåne (Sydsverige). *In* L. Larsson, *Segebro. En Tidigatlantisk Boplats vid Sege ås Mynning,* 105–28. Malmö: Malmö museer (Malmöfynd **4**).

Lidén, O. 1942. *De flinteggade benspetsarnas nordiska kulturfas.* Lund: Gleerup (Kungl. Humanistiska Vetenskapssamfundet i Lund **XXXIII**).

Liedgren, L. 1993. Rödockragravar från stenåldern. *Populär Arkeologi* **1993** (2), 28–9.

Lindqvist, C. and Possnert, G. 1999. The first seal hunter families on Gotland. On the Mesolithic occupation in the Stora Förvar Cave. *Current Swedish Archaeology* **7**, 65–87.

Lund Hansen, U., Vagn Nielsen, O. and Alexandersen, V. 1972. A Mesolithic grave from Melby in Zealand, Denmark. *Acta Archaeologica* **43**, 239–49.

Madsen, A.P., Müller, S., Neergaard, C., Petersen, C.G.J., Rostrup, E., Steenstrup, K.J.V and Winge, H. 1900. *Affaldsdynger fra Stenalderen i Danmark Undersøgte for Nationalmuseet.* København: Reitzel.

Malin, E. 1986. *Totem Poles of the Pacific Northwest Coast.* Portland: Timber Press.

Mathiassen. T. 1946. En boplads fra ældre stenalder ved Vedbæk Boldbaner. *Søllerødbogen* **1946**, 19–35.

Meiklejohn, C. and Denston, C. B. 1987. The human skeletal material. *In* P. Mellars, *Excavation on Oronsay: Prehistoric Human Ecology on a Small Island,* 290–300. Edinburgh: Edinburgh University Press.

Morais Arnaud, J.E. 1989. The Mesolithic communities of the Sado Valley, Portugal, in their ecological setting. *In* C. Bonsall (ed.), *The Mesolithic in Europe,* 614–31. Edinburgh: John Donald.

Newell, R.R., Constandse-Westermann, T.S. and Meiklejohn, C. 1979. The skeletal remains of Mesolithic man in Western Europe: an evaluative catalogue. *Journal of Human Evolution* **8**, 1–228.

Nilsson Stutz, L. 2003. *Embodied Rituals and Ritualized Bodies: Tracing Ritual Practices in Late Mesolithic Burials.* Lund: Almqvist & Wiksell International (*Acta Archaeologica Lundensia* **46**).

Noe-Nygaard, N. 1988. Delta ^{13}C-values of dog bone reveal the nature of changes in man's food resources at the Mesolithic–Neolithic transition, Denmark. *Chemical Geolog, Isotope Geoscience Section* **73**, 87–96.

Noe-Nygaard, N. 1995. *Ecological, Sedimentary, and Geochemical Evolution of the Late-glacial to Postglacial Åmose Lacustrine Basin, Denmark.* Oslo: Scandinavian University Press (Fossils & Strata **37**).

Norling-Christensen, H. and Bröste, K. 1945. Skeletgraven fra Korsør Nor. *Fra Nationalmuseets Arbejdsmark* **1945**, 5–17.

O'Shea, J. and Zvelebil, M. 1984. Oleneostrovski mogilnik: reconstructing the social and economic organization of prehistoric foragers in northern Russia. *Journal of Anthropological Archaeology* **3**, 1–40.

Péquart, M. and Péquart, St-J. 1954 *Hoëdic. Deuxième Station-Nécropole du Mésolithique Côtier Armoricain.* Anvers: de Sikkel.

Péquart, M., Péquart, St-J., Boule, M. and Vallois, H. 1937. *Téviec. Station-Nécropole Mésolithique du Morbihan.* Paris (Archives de l'Institut de Paléontologie Humaine, Mémoire **18**).

Persson, O. and Persson, E. 1988. Anthropological report concerning the interred Mesolithic populations from Skateholm, southern Sweden. Excavation season 1983–4. *In* L. Larsson (ed.), *The Skateholm Project. I. Man and Environment,* 89–105. Lund: Lund University Press (Societatis Humaniorum Litterarum Lundensis **LXXIX**).

Price, T. D. 1999. Human population in Europe during the Mesolithic. *In* E. Cziesla, T. Kersting and S. Pratsch (eds), *Den Bogen spannen … Festschrift für Bernhard Gramsch,* 185–95. Weissbach: Beirer & Behran.

Price, T.D. and Jacobs, K. 1990. Olenii Ostrov: first radiocarbon dates from a major Mesolithic cemetery in Karelia, USSR. *Antiquity* **64**, 849–53.

Rausing, G. 1991. Bears, boars and burials. *Fornvännen* **86**, 73–7.

Roche, J. 1960. *Le Gisment Mésolithique de Moita do Sebastião (Muge – Portugal) Archéologie.* Lisboa: Instituto de Alta Cultura.

Rowley-Conwy, P. 1998. Cemeteries, seasonality and complexity in the Ertebølle of southern Scandinavia. *In* M. Zvelebil, L. Domańska and R. Dennell (eds), *Harvesting the Sea, Farming the Forest. The Emergence of Neolithic Societies in the Baltic Region,* 193–202. Sheffield: Sheffield Academic Press.

Rudebeck, E. 2002. Likt och olikt i sydskandinaviska långhögar. *In* L. Larsson (ed.), *Monumentala Gravformer i det Äldsta Bondesamhället,* 119–46. Lund: University of Lund, Department of Archaeology and Ancient History (Report Series **83**).

Rydbeck, O. 1945. Skelettgraven i Bäckaskog (sittande hukläge) och dess ålder. *Meddelanden från Lunds universitets historiska museum* **1945**, 1–44.

Schulting, R.J. 1996. Antlers, bone pins and flint blades: the Mesolithic cemeteries of Téviec and Hoëdic, Brittany. *Antiquity* **70**, 335–50.

Skaarup, J. 1995. Stone-Age burials in boats. *In* C. Crumlin-Pedersen and O.B. Munch Thye (eds), *The Ship as Symbol in Prehistoric and Medieval Scandinavia,* 51–8. København: Nationalmuseet (Studies in Archaeology & History **1**).

Smith, C. 1992. *Late Stone Age Hunters of the British Isles.* London: Routledge.

Tomaszewski, A. J. and Willis, R. 1993. Tool-kits and burial rites: the case of Janisławice Mesolithic grave. *Proceedings of the Prehistoric Society* **59**, 105–12.

Veit, U. 1993. Burials within settlements of the Linearbandkeramik and Stichbandkeramik cultures of central Europe. On the social construction of death in early Neolithic society. *Journal of European Archaeology* **1**: 107–40.

Westerby, E. 1927. *Stenaldersboplader ved Klampenborg. Nogle Bidrag til Studiet af den Mesolitiske Periode.* København.

Wigforss, J. 1968. Gamla vänner daterade. *Fynd meddelanden* **1968**, no. 1, 4.

Zagorska, I. 1997. The first radiocarbon datings from Zvejnieki Stone Age burial ground, Latvia. *Finska Fornminnesföreningen Iskos* **11**, 42–6.

Zagorska, I. and Larsson, L. 1994. New data on the chronology of the Zvejnieki Stone Age cemetery. *Mesolithic Miscellany* **15**(2), 3–10.

Zagorski, F. 1974. Zvejnieku akmens laikmeta kapulauka apbedijumu tipologija un chronologija. *Arheologija un etnografija* **XI**, 7–24.

Zagorski, F. 1987. *Zvejnieku akmens laikmeta kapulauks.* Riga: Zinatne.

Chapter 21

Danish Shell Middens Reviewed

SØREN H. ANDERSEN

Shell middens in Denmark have been a focus of inter-disciplinary study for almost 150 years. This research has made a major contribution to our understanding of Late Mesolithic society and economy. Much information has been gained about pre-midden horizons, about associated settlements, about the formation process of the middens, and about continuity of shell-midden use from the Mesolithic into the Neolithic period. These aspects are reviewed here in detail, but some questions remain unanswered and ensure that shell-midden research will continue.

Introduction

Today, just over one hundred years after the publication of the results of the major investigation of the shell midden at Ertebølle in NW Jutland (Madsen *et al.* 1900), there is good reason to pause and review the situation. This is a suitable time to raise questions of relevance to this research, to seek to identify ways of answering those questions, and to try to set out guidelines for the next few years of research into the Danish prehistoric refuse heaps.

Shell middens (Danish *Køkkenmøddinger* – strictly 'kitchen middens') have been the object of intensive research for almost 150 years (Andersen 2000). This is in part because they are very 'visible' and therefore attracted attention from even the early days of archaeology, and also because they gave rise to many finds of well-preserved faunal remains; this led to the establishment of a tradition of fruitful cross-disciplinary research cooperation between archaeology and the natural sciences, a tradition which is still alive and which is a distinguishing feature of Danish Mesolithic research. In relation to most other types of early prehistoric settlements, the shell middens offer a number of evident advantages associated with the remains of fauna, the types of deposits, and the rapid tempo of deposit; together these factors result in unusually good opportunities for the study of 'snap-shot' evidence and of the organization of the settlement in plan, over and above what can be deduced from vertical stratigraphic analysis. In addition there is a particular group of middens, known as 'stratified shell heaps', which is still the best source for studies of the transition from the Mesolithic to the Neolithic periods and thus also for evidence about the very earliest Neolithic living conditions.

Since the nineteenth century, research into the Danish shell middens has gone through a number of stages. From excavations aiming at collecting artefacts to chronological and typological investigations, through excavations of parts of refuse heaps and then investigations of entire large ones, to today's regional projects dealing with settlement systems – as most recently seen implemented at Norsminde Fjord in eastern Jutland (Andersen 1976; 1989) and the former Bjørnsholm Fjord at Limfjorden (Andersen 1991, 61).

Excavation techniques have also undergone changes over the last 100–150 years, but the most decisive difference is the change from excavating sections and small areas of large refuse heaps – particularly in order to study their stratigraphy and chronology – to total excavation of small- and medium-size heaps, for example at Norsminde (Andersen 1989) and Brovst (Andersen 1969), in addition to Egsminde and Siggård in the former Bjørnsholm Fjord (Note 1). In these cases it was not only complete refuse heaps, but also the areas below and around the shell layers that were investigated. For instance, some 900m² of the Visborg shell midden, on Mariager Fjord, have been investigated in this way (Andersen 1999) (Note 2).

The new research strategy is combined with questions which are linked to the nature of the settlement, and to the arrangement and use of the site. It is the settlement plan and dwelling-structure, and the function of the refuse heap in the contemporary settlement system as a whole, which have been the main focus of attention in the last 10–20 years.

Together with the altered excavation methods there are also new dating techniques – chiefly ^{14}C – which have produced many new and important results, for instance the age of the earliest shell heaps and the chronology of the occurrence of the shell middens, in addition to a clear insight into the pace of the accumulation of deposits within the structures and their period of use (Andersen 1995). Today we know that some of the largest shell middens, such as Ertebølle and Bjørnsholm, were in use for up to 1000 years, and this is evidence of a very stable settlement system and a corresponding constancy in the natural surroundings, primarily the resources of the maritime environment (Andersen 1995, 62). The new dates have also shown that other major shell middens, for example Meilgård, were created in the course of a much shorter time-span – in that case about 400–500 years (Note 3).

Apart from the culture-history aspects of these dates, they also provide a reason for the scale of productivity of the 'Atlantic oyster banks'. In 1922 the marine biologist C.G.J. Petersen (1922) reached the conclusion that Meilgård had been used during about 1200 years on the basis of modern oyster production in the Limfjord, but the above-mentioned dating results show that the shell midden was accumulated in about half that time. We thus have new information which supports our theory that the Atlantic Ocean must actually have had a far higher degree of biological productivity than the sea has today. The investigations of recent years have also shown that the 'kitchen-midden concept' of earlier times does not cover a uniform find-group, but includes shell-heaps of different size, age, and function (see below). In addition there are regional differences between the Jutland, western Danish, and Zealand, eastern Danish, shell middens (Fig. 21.1) (Note 4).

Finally, there is also a growing recognition of the possibility of using ethnographic information (descriptions and pictures) with major significance for the interpretation of the Danish shell middens.

A question which has been the subject of analysis has of course been: are the shell middens settlements? Are they in fact *the* settlements? In the case of the overwhelming majority the answer has to be 'yes'. The shell middens all contain a mixture of remains of meals, ordinary refuse, and workshop-areas, with artefacts and structures which are associated with a settlement: fireplaces of two main types, fire-pits, extensive layers of ash, fishbone-remains, 'butchery areas', working areas for the manufacture of flint tools and weapons, postholes and pits, in addition to a few graves. Also there is refuse such as broken pieces of tools and weapons.

The only element which is still absent are well-defined remains of dwellings in association with the shell middens, but it seems that these are also gradually beginning to appear in excavations of the areas under the shell-layers, as at Lollikhuse (Sørensen 1993), Åle (Note 5), and Vænge Sø in eastern Jutland (Fig. 21.2). In addition there are many finds of postholes and stakeholes

in the shell layers, though so far it has not proved possible to establish from these occurrences any meaningful pattern on the surface of a settlement site.

However, in spite of finds of more structures in recent years which are interpreted as remains of dwellings, we are still in the situation where we cannot yet present a generally accepted 'model' for the house type of the Ertebølle culture, nor for where the settlement would be located in relation to the shell heap.

In the most recent analysis of the Ertebølle shell midden, the conclusion was that shell middens were a type of coastal settlement where the population carried on a large number of everyday activities on the surface of the shell heap, but the dwelling spaces were situated outside the shell heap, either behind it or in some other situation where the traces gradually came to be covered by later shell layers (Andersen & Johansen 1986, 59). Thus the questions remained: where did the people live, and was the shell midden the whole settlement area, or only a part of it?

Many of the investigations of recent years have therefore been directed towards resolving these issues, and an account of the provisional results is given in this article. The excavations have primarily been directed at the area under and around the shell heaps, rather than concentrating on the shell heaps themselves.

'Pre-midden layers'

It has become apparent from the shell midden excavations that in many cases there are 'pre-midden layers' with plentiful finds *underneath* the shell middens. The layers which rest directly on the old ground surface contain large quantities of charcoal and ash and are rich in worked flint, shell patches, cooking stones, and animal bones. In the layers there are also settlement-related structures such as stone-built fireplaces, areas for making flint tools, areas with red ochre, and in some cases traces of dwellings, as at Lollikhuse on Roskilde Fjord (Sørensen 1993) and Åle in the former Bjørnsholm Fjord (Note 5). At Norsminde a grave with a skeleton was also found in a layer of this type under the shell midden (Andersen 1989, 27–8), and several of the graves from Nederst belong to the pre-midden layer at that site (Kannegård 1990). It should be noted that stone-built fireplaces are a particularly typical form of structure in these layers. At Ertebølle, in the 'old' excavation, two such fireplaces were found (Madsen *et al.* 1900, 25–6), and in the new reappraisal excavation one more appeared (Fig. 21.3).

In some situations it can be difficult to distinguish between the 'pre-midden layer' and the 'old' humus

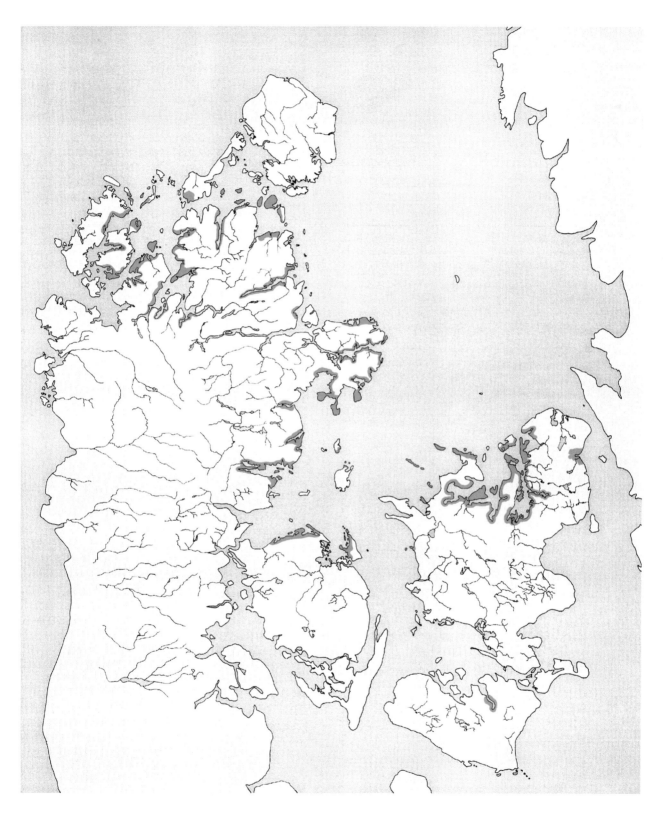

FIGURE 21.1
The occurrence of Stone Age shell middens in Denmark (shaded). (Drawn by E. Rasmussen)

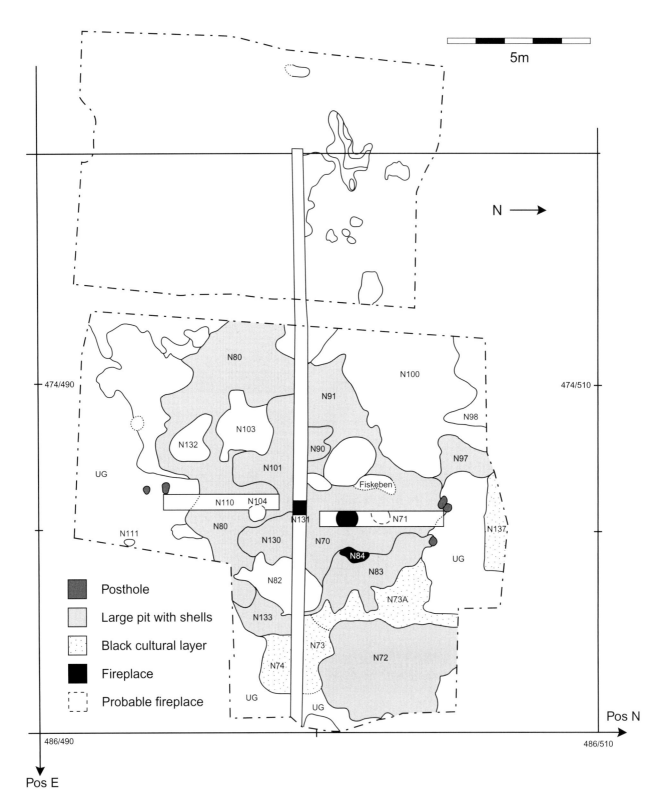

5m

N —→

474/490

474/510

N80

N100

N91

N98

N103

N132

N90

N97

UG

N101

Fiskeben

N110   N104

N131   N71

N137

N111

N80

N70

UG

N130

N84

N82

N83

N73A

N133

N74

N73

N72

UG

UG

Posthole

Large pit with shells

Black cultural layer

Fireplace

Probable fireplace

Pos N

486/490

486/510

Pos E

FIGURE 21.2

Vænge Sø III midden. A sub-rectangular depression below the midden is most probably the remains of a house structure partially dug into the subsoil. In the centre is a group of fireplaces and some postholes were recorded along the edges. (Drawn by E. Rasmussen)

surface, and this is particularly true in situations where the layer only contains a little charcoal and few artefacts. The difficulties are further compounded by the fact that these 'pre-midden layers' do not occur under all shell middens, and rarely under the whole of a shell midden, and because they are not equally plentiful in objects and structures across their whole surface; there was, for example, a layer of this type under part of the Meilgård refuse-heap (Andersen 1960, 28 – where a fireplace is mentioned), but only under a small part of it, and at Visborg the 'pre-midden layer' was only substantial and rich in finds along the prehistoric shore-line. Provisional observations suggest that these culture layers in general are both smaller and more limited in extent than the covering shell-layers.

At Ertebølle the 'pre-midden layer' was up to 0.1m in depth and held an abundance of artefacts. In addition to worked flint and animal bones, there were also many 'cooking stones' in the deposit (Fig. 21.3). The depth of the layer and its contents of artefacts and structures show that it either represents one long-term period of occupation of the site or several short-term ones. Layers of this type with settlement structures and artefacts are the earliest *in situ* evidence of dwelling on the site, and thus represent settlement activity *before* the shell heaps were deposited and brought about a 'sealing off' of these culture layers.

The 'pre-midden layers' have been scientifically dated in only a few cases. At Ertebølle the layer was dated to 4690–4620 cal BC (K-4366; Andersen & Johansen 1986, 49); at Norsminde the dating was 4780–4750 cal BC (K-5199; Andersen 1989, 26–8); and at Bjørnsholm the dating covered *c.*4700–4600 cal BC (K-5070 & 5071). In most cases the layers are dated by their artefact content (by typology), or there are *ante quem* datings of the shell heaps above them. The ^{14}C dates support the archaeological/stratigraphic datings, however, and all indicate the early Ertebølle period, 5400–4600 cal BC, which also accords well with the fact that there are only rare occurrences of pottery in layers of this type. In no case is the 'pre-midden layer' dated to the late or very late Ertebølle culture (4300–4000 cal BC).

The lack of maritime mollusc-shells in the layers shows that the 'pre-midden layers' represent a different type of settlement from the shell middens, and that they correspond to the 'ordinary Ertebølle coastal settlements' (without shell middens) (Andersen 1995, 48–9).

It should be stressed that so far it has been impossible to determine whether in some cases there may have been small local shell heaps associated with the 'pre-midden layers'. It could for instance be considered feasible that the layers were the expression of a type of settlement in which the huts/houses were all the time situated beside

a shell heap, but were later covered by the shell layer as a result of the gradual horizontal growth of the settlement along the coast (Andersen & Johansen 1986, 59). Chronological investigations of the 'pre-midden layers' indicate, however, that they were relatively rapidly covered over, and that there does not seem to be any internal horizontal/chronological difference between the different areas of the layer.

Taken as a whole, our current observations suggest that *c.*4800–4600 cal BC a change took place in the form of settlement and pattern of subsistence, including a change in the scale and significance of collecting maritime molluscs, and this resulted in the beginnings and fast accumulation of shell middens at some of the coastal settlements. The number of shell middens increased in the following centuries, and this culminated in the period *c.*4600–4000 cal BC (Fig. 21.4; Andersen 1992, 74, fig. 4a).

During the same period an increase in 'natural shell banks' can also be seen (Andersen 1992, 74; 1995, fig. 9a), and these centuries are also characterized by a constant rise in the sea level of the Atlantic Ocean (Christensen 1998, 15 & fig. 5), which must have caused an erosion of the coastal areas and thus also a considerable rise in mineral levels in the sea. Even though there is still doubt about this, it is tempting to see a connection between these observations. The explanation for the incipient and steadily more extensive depositing of maritime shells at some coastal settlements and the increasing number of shell middens from this time may owe their origins to the maritime biotope and the shell banks from this time becoming so productive that more comprehensive collection of molluscs was possible. This would mean that the increase in frequency of the shell middens at the end of the Atlantic period was a direct function of increased marine productivity in the sea during those centuries (Fig. 21.4).

Settlements behind the shell middens?

Another aspect that has featured in the debates of recent years on shell middens is the question of exactly where the settlements were situated.

In connection with the revised investigation at Ertebølle, discussion took place as to whether the dwellings could either have been placed behind the shell heap or at the side of it (Andersen & Johansen 1986, 59). Could there possibly be traces of settlement behind the shell middens? Has there been an actual settlement situated there, and does the shell midden in that case simply represent refuse heaped up on the shore in front of the dwellings themselves? In order to throw more

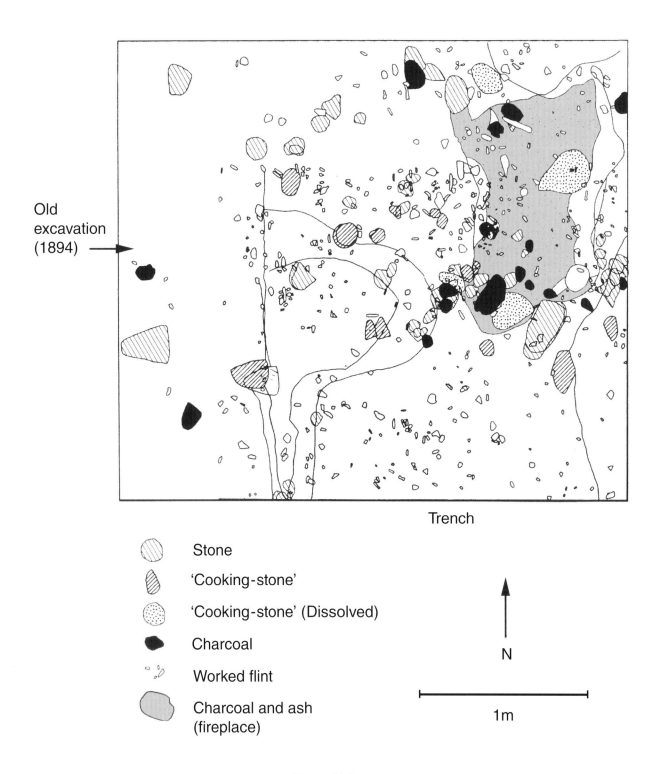

Old excavation (1894) →

Trench

- (Stone) Stone
- ('Cooking-stone') 'Cooking-stone'
- ('Cooking-stone' Dissolved) 'Cooking-stone' (Dissolved)
- (Charcoal) Charcoal
- (Worked flint) Worked flint
- (Charcoal and ash fireplace) Charcoal and ash (fireplace)

N

1m

FIGURE 21.3

Plan of part of the 'pre-midden layer' under the Ertebølle midden. The horizon has been ^{14}C-dated to the older Ertebølle period (*c*.4700 cal BC). (Drawn by E. Rasmussen)

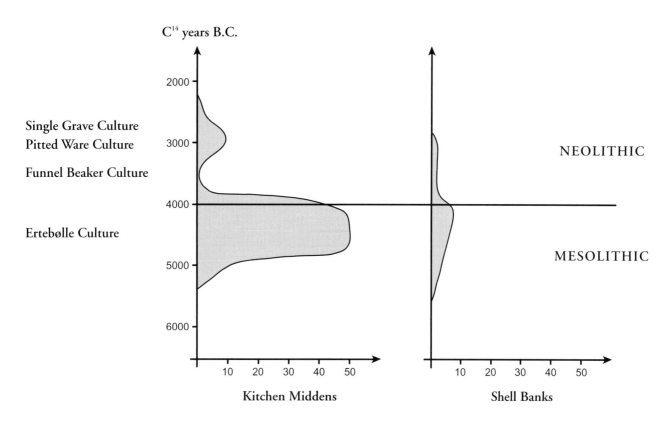

FIGURE 21.4

Numerical frequencies of shell middens and 'natural' shell banks in Denmark. The two phenomena seem to follow the same course.
(Drawn by E. Rasmussen)

light on this question further large surface investigations of the areas behind and below the shell layer have been carried out at Ertebølle and a number of other places.

Before the analysis of the above questions is taken further, attention must be drawn to the fact that a number of shell middens have been covered by the sea, which may well have washed away small or large parts of the upper culture layers, and in other situations culture layers may have been ploughed away. This is of course true not only of the shell layer itself, but also of the more unprotected layers around and behind the shell middens.

In all cases of small- or medium-sized shell middens only sparse finds have been encountered in the area behind the shell middens. As a rule there is a congruent distribution of shell layers and flint refuse, tools, animal bones, and so on. In cases such as Norsminde, where the shell midden has been well-protected by later earth layers, this must indicate that there was no large-scale nor long-term settlement activity *behind* that shell midden (Note 6).

The circumstances are different, however, in the cases of the large shell middens, where the settlement activity

has lasted over a period of *c.*1000 years, as at Ertebølle and Bjørnsholm (Andersen 1991; Andersen & Johansen 1986), or about 500 years, as at Meilgård (Liversage 1992, fig. 83). At each of these sites a large area behind the shell heap has been uncovered, either in the form of extensive horizontal stripping, as at Ertebølle and Bjørnsholm, or by means of trenches and trial-holes as at Meilgård (Andersen 1960, 29; Andersen 1991, 64 & fig. 3; Andersen & Johansen 1986, 35–9 & figs 4–5).

At Meilgård, where in all 64m² were investigated, a stone-set fireplace was observed, as well as numerous deposition horizons, flint waste, flint tools of late Ertebølle type, and small patches (<1m in diameter) of thin, localized shell layers in an area *c.*40m × 50m behind the shell midden itself; the artefacts found formed a 'culture layer', which could be split into several smaller circular concentrations, measuring *c.*3–4m × 3–4m (Andersen 1960, 29). These observations provide evidence that the area behind the shell heap was used for settlement activities. Behind the Ertebølle heap three large fields with a combined total area of *c.*1000m² were excavated (Andersen & Johansen 1986, fig. 4), and at Bjørnsholm an area of *c.*800m² immedi-

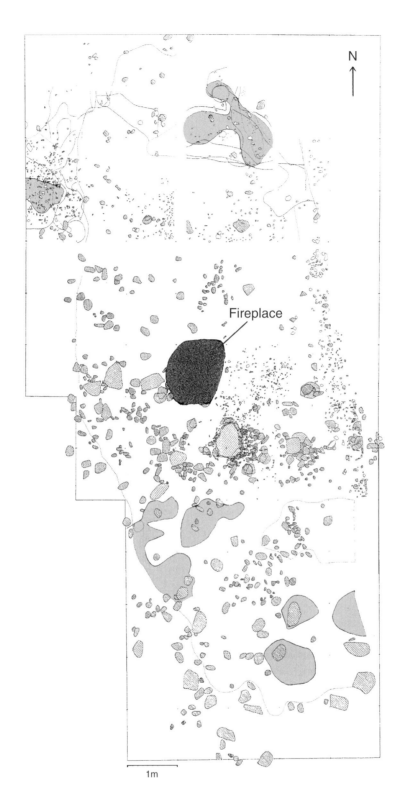

FIGURE 21.5

Sub-rectangular area to the rear of the Ertebølle midden characterized by a central fireplace and a big stone surrounded by numerous pieces of flint debris. The stone has functioned as a 'sitting stone' during flint knapping. The periphery of the area is characterized by a ring of shallow pits (shaded). (Drawn by E. Rasmussen)

ately behind the thickest part of the shell midden (which is protected) was investigated (Andersen 1991, fig. 3).

At all three sites artefacts from the Ertebølle culture were found behind the shell heaps (on the landward side), but distributed over areas of very varied extent and with variable density. Since the shell middens are often situated on sand, normally only flint is preserved, but in rare cases, as at Meilgård and Bjørnsholm, finds of pottery and bone-remains have also been made in those layers. At Norsminde worked flint was found, with a stone-built fireplace behind the shell heap, and similarly a fireplace was found behind the Åle shell midden in the former Bjørnsholm Fjord (Andersen 1991, fig. 3) (Note 5). Behind the shell heap at Holmegård on Djursland there were also several stone-built fireplaces (Note 7).

At both Ertebølle and Bjørnsholm there were *in situ* layers with frequent occurrences of worked flint and flint implements of mid and late Ertebølle types; at Ertebølle the densest find concentration covered an area c.15m×6m, but worked flint and a few pot-shaped pits were also found in an area measuring c.30m×50m. Within this the largest flint concentration included a suspected workshop area with a 'sitting-stone' surrounded by an oblong fan-shaped distribution (c.8m×5m) of flint spalls, waste, and unfinished or rejected implements. In the centre of this area was a roughly circular fireplace (1.2m diameter), and around the periphery of the concentration there was a 'ring' of flat-bottomed oval or irregular pits measuring c.2m×4m (Andersen & Johansen 1986, fig. 5). The overall impression received from this area is that there has been an organized settlement structure (Fig. 21.5).

At Bjørnsholm artefacts were also found behind the shell heap, and the largest concentration measured c.10m×20m and was c.0.2m thick. This represents several settlement phases, which is also confirmed by the fact that within this area several small and slightly diffuse sub-concentrations of worked flint could be distinguished together with 'patches' of mussel shells, cooking stones, a few animal bones and potsherds, postholes, and small pits. The small artefact-concentrations measured c.3–4m×3–4m (Andersen 1991, 65).

Both at Ertebølle and Bjørnsholm the areas behind the shell heaps are today cultivated fields, and even if the artefacts theoretically might have been moved by agricultural activity, the *in situ* layers at these sites as well as the results of the distribution analysis of the partially ploughed up settlement of Bro in NW Funen (Andersen 1972, 14–18), show that the occurrence of flint at Ertebølle and Bjørnsholm must closely correspond to the extent of the area where there were settlement activities behind the shell middens in the Ertebølle period. The artefacts in the culture layers date those layers as contemporary with the main settlements in the actual

shell midden, which in most cases means that they belong to the mid or late Ertebølle culture (4600–4000 cal BC).

At the moment we have to conclude that behind the large shell middens (on the landward side) there are areas with worked flint and tools, fireplaces, pits, and possible postholes over a distance of up to c.40m from the shell heap. The finds show that these areas can be divided up into smaller 'patches' measuring c.3–4m×3–4m. Both 'working areas' and fireplaces have been identified, but no indisputable traces of dwellings or graves have been found in those areas so far. An observation such as this may reflect real conditions – that there never were dwellings or graves in the area behind the shell heaps, which seems to be supported by the sites where the area was rapidly covered after the Ertebølle period – but the absence of such structures may also be the result of some of these areas having been removed by ploughing and erosion (e.g. signs of marine erosion of the area behind the Ertebølle heap; Andersen & Johansen 1986, 42).

It looks as if the horizontal extent and the thickness of these layers, as well as the intensity of finds, are to some extent a function of the length of use of the shell middens. However, the culture layers behind the shell heaps are of a lesser extent and contain fewer finds than the shell middens themselves, and at the same time the number of structural settlement features – in particular fireplaces, but also pits, and so on – is considerably smaller than in the heaps. With the exception of Ertebølle there are no traces of an 'organization' of finds and structures, and no indications either, in particular in relation to fireplaces, that these are situated in special areas or create stratigraphic contexts, such as is the case in the actual shell middens (Andersen & Johansen 1986, fig. 12). Thus culture layers from the Ertebølle period have been identified in all the cases where recent excavations have been undertaken over large areas behind the shell heaps (and these culture layers are of a larger extent than previously supposed), but we can still not at present establish whether the dwellings were situated behind the shell heaps.

The conclusion is that there *were* activities taking place behind the shell middens, but that they were of a (slightly) different kind and took up a smaller physical area than those in or on the shell heaps. It is interesting to note that the small 'flint patches' which have been found, for instance behind the Bjørnsholm and Meilgård heaps, have the same size as the smallest shell mound which has been distinguished within the shell middens themselves (see below).

How do the 'pre-midden' layers relate, then, to the finds behind the shell heaps? Are they the same layer, which originally covered both the area under the shell midden and that behind it, or are these two independent phenomena? Where it has been possible to investigate this question it looks as if there are actually two separate phenomena. At Ertebølle there was no stratigraphic connection between the culture layer below the shell midden (the pre-midden layer) and the finds behind the heap, and the same is true of Bjørnsholm and Meilgård, where the pre-midden layer was also clearly earlier than the finds behind the heap itself.

Settlement in front of the shell middens?

In a few cases archaeological excavations have also been carried out in the area in front of the shell middens (i.e. on the side towards the sea). In certain of these cases blackish-grey sand layers with charcoal content and a large proportion of fire-damaged cooking stones were noted, as at Flynderhage and Norslund (Andersen & Malmros 1965, 37). But in most cases the area in front of the middens is highly vulnerable to the proximity of the sea, with erosion and disturbance of layers as a consequence. This is certainly true at Ertebølle and Bjørnsholm (Andersen & Johansen 1986, 42). In the cases where the deposition environment has been undisturbed, it is often possible to find 'refuse layers' rich in artefacts and with particularly good preservation conditions for organic remains at the foot of the shell midden and in front of it, for example at Flynderhage in Norsminde Fjord.

At Meilgård scattered flint artefacts were found at the base of the shell midden, but it was not possible to discern an actual culture layer or other traces of settlement (Andersen 1960, 28–9). At Visborg, where the observation conditions were ideal, the distribution of artefacts and settlement structures could clearly be seen to be concentrated in the direction towards the prehistoric coastline, which in this case must evidently have functioned as the most important area of the settlement surface.

In conclusion we have to state, however, that there still have not been enough systematic excavations to enable us to draw firm conclusions concerning the possible existence of dwelling-structures in the areas in front of the shell middens.

The shell middens were 'organized'

If one tries to imagine that the whole surface of the large shell middens was in use at the same time, this seems improbable. On the contrary, it looks as if the activities have changed focus from time to time, and the surface

has mostly been uneven. In spite of this the new investigations show with great clarity that the shell middens had an internal 'organization' which was maintained throughout long periods of time; for example there are in the heaps discernible areas in which shells were deposited and others where there were fireplaces and workshop areas (Andersen & Johansen 1986, 45–8).

The fireplaces merit special attention on account of the fact that ethnographic literature and illustrations show that fireplaces in hunter-gatherer settlements are either very close to the dwellings or actually within them; they thus attract our interest because of our need to find the missing house structures.

At the same time the new investigations show that around the fireplaces in the shell heaps extensive ash layers can be found, with scattered 'cooking stones' and destroyed implements and tools, in addition to potsherds and charred animal bones – in particular fish bones from food-preparation. Also there are layers of flint waste and special 'anvil-stones' which show that primary working of flint (as well as the repair of weapons and tools) was a frequent activity in addition to food-preparation (Fig. 21.6). The distribution of bones and bone-splinters around the fireplaces corresponds closely to the observations Binford (1983, 153) has made in connection with modern hunter-gatherer groups, concerning the 'drop and toss zones'. All these observations show that the fireplaces were really centres for a whole range of settlement activities.

The shell middens are not homogeneous entities. It is well-known that the Mesolithic shell middens in Denmark consist of a mixture of oysters, cockles, mussels, and periwinkles, normally with oysters as the completely dominant species. Since these types of shellfish do not require the same environmental conditions – for instance cockles live at some depth down in the seabed and have to be dug up, while oysters are found attached to the seabed and in banks – it is evident that when the types are regularly found in the shell middens in defined small mounds or as layers consisting of one particular type (the so-called 'meal-heaps'), this is confirmation that the collection, preparation, and waste depositing, at least in a number of situations, if not always, was specific to the type of shellfish. The fact that the different types did not necessarily require the same preparation may also have resulted in type-specific collection and preparation. The heaps and layers which consist of one type are as a rule also wholly or almost entirely lacking other culture remains.

Since it is clearly a fact, however, that mixed shellfish remains are found in large areas of the shell-midden layers, this may mean that the food-collecting covered several species, or, more probably, that the meal-refuse

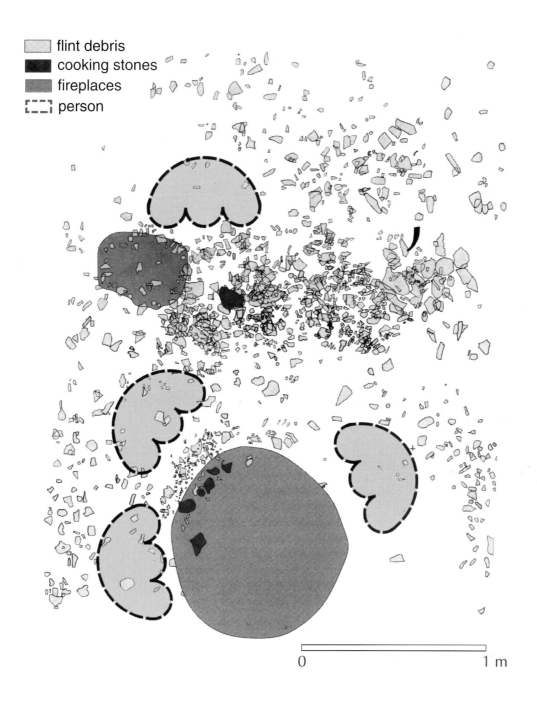

flint debris
cooking stones
fireplaces
person

0   1 m

FIGURE 21.6

Two circular fireplaces (shaded) in the Visborg shell midden surrounded by flint waste. Large flakes at the periphery reveal areas of initial knapping, while smaller chips closer to the fireplaces indicate areas of retouching and resharpening. The 'empty' areas probably indicate where the flint-knappers sat (dashed outline). In amongst the flint, was a red deer antler tine (black) used for flint percussion. (Drawn by E. Rasmussen)

(the shells) was thrown out each time at the same place and thus became mixed, or that a repeated clearing-up of the midden's surface was carried out, resulting in a mixing of the contents of the refuse mounds. It is also possible that the mixing is the result of a 'levelling out' because the surface had lain open for a long time. 'Clearing out' can also be observed both in the form of shell-depositing in defined areas (as at Ertebølle) and in the mixing of

FIGURE 21.7

Plan of the fully excavated Egsminde shell midden with two parallel series of fireplaces along the prehistoric beach.
(Drawn by E. Rasmussen)

artefacts and shells on the settlement surface itself. An indication counter to consequential clearing up, however, is the fact that the areas around the fireplaces very often clearly reflect 'functional and workshop areas' with traces of food-preparation and tool production.

Another new and interesting result of the horizontal excavations of shell middens in recent years is the identification of an internal structure which seems to follow the prehistoric coastline. At several sites, for example Norsminde, Siggård, and Egsminde, the fireplaces were regularly distributed along the shore. At Egsminde they were situated in two parallel rows along the prehistoric shoreline with a distance of c.2–3m between the rows and c.5–6m between the fireplaces (Fig. 21.7). Under the Siggård midden there were four fireplaces – with a distance between them of c.6–8m – which made up a row along the shore (Fig. 21.8).

Fixed structures such as these have so far only been found in these three places, but this may be because these are relatively small shell heaps and they are among the

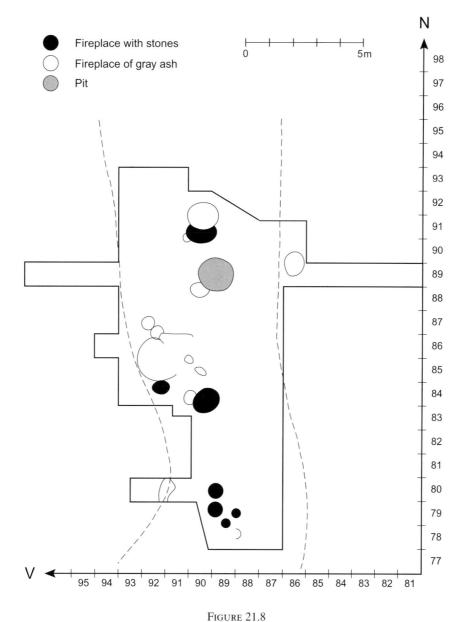

FIGURE 21.8

Plan of the Siggård midden with fireplaces, pits, etc. (Drawn by E. Rasmussen)

few that have been totally excavated. The regularity in the internal structure of these shell middens probably indicates that the fireplaces were in use at the same time, and that they therefore more probably represent one camp than a series of camps along the shore throughout a certain period. In that case there must have been several fireplaces in use at the same time, and we thus have traces at these sites of social units consisting of about four to five 'households'. The above evidence shows that the shell middens were not exclusively random refuse-mounds, but should rather be perceived as a kind of 'construction' in the landscape.

Are the shell middens distinguishable from the other contemporary coastal settlements by any feature other than the collection of shellfish?

A distinct difference between the shell middens and the 'ordinary' coastal settlements is that mussels and other shellfish were not only eaten down at the shore (which may have happened everywhere), but in some situations they were brought from the shell banks to certain coastal settlements (the shell middens). Shellfish were a year-round or a seasonal source of food which brought to certain locations (the shell middens) an extra and stable resource which was not available at other coastal sites. Furthermore, because of the size and visibility of the shell middens, it is possible to think that they may have functioned as territorial landmarks, as particularly significant sites in the settlement territory.

Our investigations show that the collection of shellfish was regular and of significance for the population, but that this activity took place on a larger scale in some periods than in others. The ^{14}C dating of the Ertebølle heap, for instance, shows that in spite of its very long period of use the collection of shellfish was particularly marked in the centuries 4600–4400 cal BC.

The smallest unit in the shell middens

While it has been clear for a long time that the large shell middens were composed of a number of smaller heaps, there has been great uncertainty about the size of 'the smallest unit' (Andersen & Johansen 1986, 45). The small units have now been defined not just by analysis of the large shell middens, as for example at Ertebølle (Andersen & Johansen 1986, fig. 11), but also by means of the excavation of a number of small shell heaps. In recent years attention has to a large degree been directed towards 'separating out' small units within the shell middens; these small units can be recognized in that – in contrast to the surrounding shell material – they either consist of one single type, or are distinguished by a particular structure or colour which makes them distinct from the surrounding layers. They cannot have lain exposed to the surface for a long time, because in that case they would have 'flattened out' and become mixed with the surrounding shell material. Units such as this are c.0.05–0.5m thick and have a very limited horizontal extent. At Dyngby the smallest unit measured c.6m×6m; at Brovst (layer 4) from c.4m×4m to 7m×7m; (layer 8) c.7m×7m; and (layer 11) c.4m×4m and 5m×5m; at Siggård the unit measured c.5m×8m. These dimensions correspond to the observations at Norsminde, where it was possible to discern individual shell heaps which measured 3–4m×3–4m. Similarly, the 'splitting up' into stratigraphic units in the Ertebølle heap shows that it consists of shell heaps which measure no more than c.2–7m×2–7m (Andersen & Johansen 1986, fig. 11).

During the investigation of the settlement at Lystrup just north of Århus (Andersen 1994, 7–36), several small shell heaps were also observed outside the 'coherent' shell-midden layer, which is ^{14}C-dated to c.5300–4900 cal BC and thus is one of the earliest shell heaps (Andersen 1994, 16). Here four small distinct oval-shaped 'shell patches' were found; two of them were beside large embedded stones which presumably had

functioned as 'tables' or seats (Fig. 21.9). The shell heaps consisted of an upper thin layer of oyster shells resting on shell-fragments of cockles, mussels, and periwinkles. The oyster layer measured c.2m×3.5m and 3m×6m (N-S/E-W), while the thickness of the layer was c.30–100mm. Around the big stones the shells lay in a border c.0.4–1.1m wide and c.30–100mm thick. These shell patches contained a very varied number of fish bones (in three cases a large quantity), but only a few large animal bones; the quantity of flint refuse was small in all shell patches. At the largest shell patch most of the flint refuse was found outside the shell layer, and just north of the shell heap there was a concentration of 'cooking stones'. These examples are illustrative of the smallest type of 'kitchen midden'. It is interesting to note that these small heaps have the same dimensions as the previously mentioned 'flint patches' behind the Bjørnsholm and Meilgård shell middens, and that they similarly correspond in extent to the two flint concentrations at the settlement of Rønbjerg Strandvolde ('ordinary coastal settlement'), which respectively measured 6m in diameter and c.6m×8–10m (Skousen 1998, fig. 14). The diameter of these small shell heaps (c.6m) also corresponds very closely to the shell-covered area around the fireplaces at Norsminde (Andersen 1989, fig. 8b), Siggård, and Egsminde.

It looks, therefore, as if the shell middens were created out of small units of an average size of c.6m across. This size is closely related to the extent of distribution of worked flint at the smallest locations *without* shell layers.

A special type of shell heap is the 'small shell midden' placed around a central fireplace. This is known from Brovst (layers 4 and 11), and also from Dyngby. The structure suggests that these are the traces of small 'organized' units (short occupation).

There are, however, even smaller *ad hoc* occurrences which must almost be considered as remains of single meals. These are known from several excavations in recent years, for instance from the small shell midden at Dyngby in eastern Jutland (Note 8). The midden there was situated on a layer of natural chalk deposited by running water at the foot of a slope (then the shore). Mixed up with the chalk – and thus earlier than the shell heap itself – were a few shells of oysters and cockles in addition to some pieces of flint waste. The finds did not form a layer and must be interpreted as traces of repeated but very short-term occupation during which meals were eaten and the remains (collected mussel shells) and worked flint were thrown away. This type of find, which has also been observed at other sites in this area, probably shows the simplest form of shell midden and can be called a 'meal patch' (i.e. shore occupation of

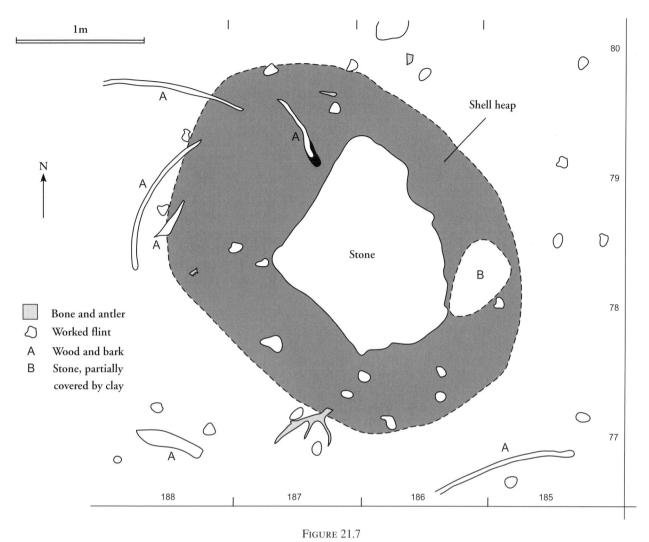

1m

80

Shell heap

79

N

Stone

B

78

Bone and antler
Worked flint
A Wood and bark
B Stone, partially
covered by clay

77

188 187 186 185

FIGURE 21.7
Plan of the fully excavated Egsminde shell midden with two parallel series of fireplaces along the prehistoric beach.

such a brief or intermittent duration that no actual shell midden was formed). Furthermore, these small patches can be differentiated from the large shell middens by the fact that they do not include settlement structures.

In conclusion the small shell middens must represent 'episodes'; traces of single activities which sometimes, but not always, consisted of the collection and consumption of food, and the depositing of the remains of one type of shellfish, but which were also regularly characterized by the deposition of all kinds of different refuse lying around a fireplace. Whether the small heaps therefore also (always) reflect a single occupation is much more difficult to determine (Andersen & Johansen 1986, 45; cf. Binford 1982, 16).

The overall total of small shell heaps such as this in medium and large shell middens cannot be calculated accurately, since so far in almost all cases figures are

only based on estimates from profile sections. In smaller shell middens, where it has been possible to individually differentiate small patches in plan, no similar calculations have yet been made.

'Stratified shell middens'

In addition to what has already been mentioned there are a number of particular questions associated with what are known as 'stratified shell heaps', such as Norsminde (Andersen 1989) and Bjørnsholm (Andersen 1991).

This group of shell middens is the most important source of information about the process of change from the Mesolithic to the Neolithic period in southern Scandinavia. In addition it is one of the most important sources available for the study of the earliest Neolithic living conditions and possibly seasonal settlement. The most important settlement element associated with these locations is that they demonstrate continuity of location from late Mesolithic to early Neolithic times.

There was previously a view that these locations constituted a special, and not particularly common, group of shell middens and that this was mainly a feature of large shell middens. The intensive and long-term regional investigations carried out in recent years, as at the former Bjørnsholm Fjord, in addition to a review of all excavations of Danish shell middens, shows with complete unanimity that the stratified shell middens are the rule and not the exception. In the Bjørnsholm area, at least 50 per cent of the shell heaps are stratified, and at Norsminde fjord the figure is about 80 per cent. Similar conditions apparently apply in the rest of the country, where known shell middens such as Kolind, Sebber, Havnø, Åmølle, Gjessinggård, and Nederst (Mathiassen *et al.* 1942, 37–46 & 56–60), Meilgård (Andersen 1960), Langø (Broholm 1928), and numerous others are *all* stratified. In addition, it has become evident that it is not only the large structures that are stratified; this find-group also includes many small shell middens such as Egsminde and Lundgård in the Bjørnsholm Fjord. (Note 9). The picture is so uniform that the absence of early Neolithic layers from some shell middens is more likely to be the result of secondary erosion and/or plough damage than an actual absence of early Neolithic occupation of the site.

The conclusion is therefore that we must change our previous view, and that there apparently has been continuity of location in general along the Danish coasts; not just at the transition between the Mesolithic and Neolithic periods, but also during the initial 200–300 years of the Neolithic period itself.

From this it also follows that the actual transition from the Mesolithic to the Neolithic periods can best be studied at the coastal settlement sites, which is not really so remarkable, since at that time either the whole, or at least the majority, of the Late Mesolithic population lived at the coast, and the social network was linear (along the coast). It must have been through precisely such networks that technological and ideological impulses – as well as innovations in living conditions – were transmitted.

The difficulty, in several cases, of identifying the actual 'transition phase' at several of the well-known stratified coastal settlement sites has been caused by a number of factors. It is evident that geological conditions such as movement of the shoreline and erosion of the find-layers from the transition phase in some areas may be the explanation for the absence of settlement layers from that time, but there are also a number of archaeological-stratigraphical reasons for experiencing extreme difficulty in identifying layers from the transition between the Ertebølle culture and the Funnel Beaker culture at *c.*3950 cal BC. Firstly, the actual 'typological transition phase' was apparently of short duration, and this automatically means that the stratigraphic evidence will be of limited extent and depth, resulting in its 'archaeological visibility' being low. Moreover, refuse deposition on the shell middens did not take place at exactly the same place all the time, but on the contrary changed location at regular intervals; the chances of finding a shell heap with a diameter of 3–4m from the transition phase in a randomly placed 1m-wide section through the shell midden – not to mention managing to extract and date material from precisely such a single episode – are very, very small. The ongoing study of the Norsminde shell midden shows that at several places in the shell layer small segments with a diameter of 3–4m can be identified as being from the transition phase, and that as it happened these layers were not 'hit' by the profile surveys so far published (Andersen 1989, fig. 4).

Precisely because both Norsminde and Visborg have been totally excavated it has been possible to document continual use of those sites from Mesolithic to Neolithic times. This result could perhaps also have been reached by means of a traditional 'section excavation', but this would have depended on where the section in question was placed in relation to the respective refuse heaps from different time-phases; here the advantage of large-scale uncovering of the surfaces – horizontal excavation – really makes itself felt.

The precondition for this surprising continuity of location is of course that the basic economic conditions remained unchanged in the transition phase and on into the early part of the Neolithic period. It has been documented that the situation of the settlements in the Late Mesolithic period was chiefly determined by access to good fishing and sea hunting (Andersen 1995, 48). Since settlements did not change position in fjords and bays from the Mesolithic to the Neolithic periods, and new early Neolithic coastal sites were not established, but on the contrary the settlements remained in use on the same sites ('stratified shell middens'), the conclusion must be that there was continuity of basic economic conditions throughout the Late Mesolithic and the beginning of the early Neolithic periods. This is confirmed by the available lists of fauna, which show a very large coincidence of species (compare, for example, the species lists from Norsminde and Bjørnsholm: Møhl & Rowley-Conwy in Andersen 1989, 39–40; Bratlund 1991, 97–104). A complete comparison between the fauna lists is made more difficult by the fact that the bone remains in the early Neolithic layer, which, as the latest horizon, is situated uppermost, have been more exposed to destruction by rain and the percolation of groundwater than the deeper and thicker Ertebølle layer. This is particularly significant in relation to small, more fragile bones such as those of birds and fish.

The Late Mesolithic locations also maintained their social position in the early part of the Neolithic period. This is evident in that the locations which were the major ones in the Ertebølle culture continued to be the largest in the early Funnel Beaker culture, and we also find rich graves and exotica at those sites (e.g. Bjørnsholm: Andersen 1995, 62 & fig. 25; Andersen & Johansen 1990). The graves in particular, but also the size of the settlements, show that these coastal sites had a high degree of economic and social significance for the population and society (Andersen & Johansen 1990, 54 & 92).

At several stratified locations descriptions have been given of how there is a clear change between early layers dominated by oysters (Ertebølle culture) and later layers dominated by cockles (Funnel Beaker culture), for example at Norsminde. In this connection it should be noted, however, that even though this shift in the predominant type of shellfish can be seen in the shell middens, there are also oysters in the early Neolithic layer series, and in significant quantities in the very earliest Neolithic layer, where oysters form up to 10–30 per cent (e.g. at Norsminde: Andersen 1989, fig. 23). During the recent excavations at Visborg a shift of this type has been observed, but at that site it apparently occurs slightly later than at Norsminde and Bjørnsholm. At Visborg the actual transition layer between the Mesolithic and Neolithic periods is dominated by oysters. The difference may be because maritime conditions changed later in Mariager Fjord than for instance at Norsminde, possibly because it is larger and more directly open towards Kattegat, which would mean that there would be access for fresh seawater, rich in nourishment, for a longer time than in the smaller fjords, which rapidly became cut off by accumulated coastal banks.

Other types of shell heap

A description has been given above of a group of small shell heaps, which can best be characterized as 'meal heaps', as well as the stratified shell heaps. In Denmark, however, there are also other types of shell heap. These are shell heaps which consist virtually exclusively of shells, with very few artefacts. Examples of such heaps are known from Holmegård and Tronhøjen (Note 10), but the Fårevejle shell midden in NW Zealand should also be considered part of this group (Madsen *et al.* 1900, 112–22).

Very particular attention should be accorded to the 'natural' shell banks or beds in which artefacts have often been found, chiefly harpoons and flint tools, but also structures used for fishing, such as fishing-barriers. The shell banks with artefacts occur around the whole country and have been described at Kolindsund, Lammefjorden, Roskilde Fjord, and Stavns Fjord on Samsø (Troels Smith 1995, 63 & fig. 4).

Conclusion

Now, a good hundred years after the first major shell midden investigations, we have made noticeable progress in research into these conspicuous and interesting cultural remains from Mesolithic times (Andersen 2000).

Today we know that the shell middens are a special variant of the Ertebølle culture's coastal settlements, and that they demonstrate continuity of location throughout long periods – in some places up to about 1000 years – and that this continuity continues for some time into the Neolithic period. In many cases there are settlement traces under the shell middens which date from the period before 4700 cal BC; these are known as pre-midden layers, and represent a settlement form different from the shell middens. At about 4700 cal BC the deposits change in character, and the shell middens begin to accumulate in a series of coastal locations, probably as an expression of an increase in the quantity and size of the natural shell beds. From the same time the number and size of the shell middens increases considerably.

The new excavations have shown that the area behind the shell middens was part of the total settlement area, possibly the place where the dwellings were situated, while the shell middens were the spot where the everyday activities took place around the fireplaces. The shell middens thus did not form the whole settlement, but only part of it. In several cases it has been possible to observe a form of internal organization – a 'settlement structure' – where the fireplaces in particular are placed with regular intervals between them (at Norsminde and Egsminde) and in specific settlement areas, which is an indication that several fireplaces were used at the same time, and that the social unit included several households. Other areas were used for workshop activities and dumping of food-waste. The shell middens are built up out of small shell patches, and the new excavations show that the smallest unit has an average size of *c*.6m diameter. These small patches, which in some cases lie deposited around a central fireplace, are traces of short-term occupation, and can best be described as 'meal heaps' or '*ad hoc* patches'.

The organization of the settlements was linear and followed the prehistoric coastlines, where the shell middens are found together with and among the coastal settlements without shells. Another characteristic feature of settlements in the defined fjord systems is that one settlement area is significantly larger than all the others, and often so large that in length, breadth, and total volume it is larger than all the others together.

The traces of houses are still few and disparate, but it seems to be possible to discern a house-form in which the floor is partially dug down below surface level; sunken floor levels of this type have now been found in several cases under protective layers of shells.

In spite of clear progress in research into the Danish shell middens we still lack clear answers to questions such as: where did people live, and how did they dispose of refuse; how much of the shell heap was in use at the same time; how and how often did they change living-places on the shell heap; and what factors contributing to decomposition (taphonomic conditions) have affected the shell heaps since they were deposited, and to what extent? In addition to ordinary deterioration (erosion and subsidence), marine erosion has to be reckoned as the most important factor in this process. To this one must add 'human' elements such as levelling of the surface of the shell heaps; in heaps subjected to this the layers may appear horizontal or almost horizontal.

If in future we are to be able to answer some of the questions raised in this paper, we must develop new excavation methods which are directed more towards analyses of the settlement areas and their layout – that is methods of a more 'three-dimensional' kind.

Notes

1. Egsminde, Siggård, and Lundgård. All unpublished. Moesgård Museum ref. nos. 3822, 3378, 3380. These sites were excavated in the context of a joint research project conducted by Aalborg Historiske Museum (Erik Johansen) and Aarhus University (Søren H. Andersen).
2. Visborg, see Andersen (1999). Moesgård Museum, ref. no. 3933.
3. Unpublished excavation by the author in the 1970s and subsequent ^{14}C-datings of stratigraphic series through the shell heap. Cf. Moesgård Museum, ref. no. 1700. See Liversage (1992).
4. The drawings accompanying this chapter have kindly been prepared by Ea Rasmussen.
5. Åle. Unpublished. Moesgård Museum, ref. no. 3251.

6. These layers should not be confused with the early Neolithic settlement layers which are also found behind some Danish shell middens, for example at Bjørnsholm (Andersen & Johansen 1990, 50–54, figs 4 & 17).
7. Holmegård. Unpublished. Moesgård Museum, ref. no. 1532.
8. Dyngby. Unpublished. Moesgård Museum, ref. no. 3754. Saksild parish, Hads district, Århus.
9. Egsminde and Lundgård. See Note 1.
10. Tronhøjen. Unpublished. Moesgård Museum, ref. no. 1963.

References

Andersen, H.H. 1960. Køkkenmøddingen ved Mejlgård. *Kuml* **1960**, 26–35.

Andersen, S.H. 1969. Brovst. En kystboplads fra ældre stenalder (Brovst, a coastal settlement from the Mesolithic). *Kuml* **1969**, 67–90.

Andersen, S.H. 1972. Bro. En senglacial boplads på Fyn (Bro, a late glacial settlement of northern Funen). *Kuml* **1972**, 6–60.

Andersen, S.H. 1976. Et østjysk fjordsystems bebyggelse i stenalderen; Norsminde Fjord undersøgelsen. *In* H. Thrane (ed.), *Bebyggelsesarkæologi*, 18–62. Odense: Odense University (Skrifter fra Institut for Historie og Samfundsvidenskab **17**).

Andersen, S.H. 1989. Norsminde: a "køkkenmødding" with Late Mesolithic and Early Neolithic occupation. *Journal of Danish Archaeology* **8**, 13–40.

Andersen, S.H. 1991. Bjørnsholm: a stratified køkkenmødding on the central Limfjord, North Jutland. *Journal of Danish Archaeology* **10**, 59–96.

Andersen, S.H. 1992. Marin udnyttelse af Limfjorden i stenalderen. In *Limfjordsprojektet. Rapport nr.4: Limfjordsfiskeri i fortid og nutid*, 65–96. Århus.

Andersen, S.H. 1994. Ertebøllebåde fra Lystrup (Ertebølle canoes from Lystrup). *Kuml* **1993–94**, 7–38.

Andersen, S.H. 1995. Coastal adaption and marine exploitation in Late Mesolithic Denmark – with special emphasis on the Limfjord region. *In* A. Fischer (ed.), *Man and Sea in the Mesolithic*, 41–66. Oxford: Oxbow Books (Oxbow Monograph **53**).

Andersen, S.H. 1999. Fjorden i oldtiden. *Geologi – Nyt fra GEUS, Temanummer Mariager Fjord* (December 1999), 10–11. København.

Andersen, S.H. 2000. 'Køkkenmøddinger' (shell middens) in Denmark: a survey. *Proceedings of the Prehistoric Society* **66**, 361–84.

Andersen, S.H. and Johansen, E. 1986. Ertebølle revisited. *Journal of Danish Archaeology* **5**, 31–61.

Andersen, S.H. and Johansen, E. 1990. An early Neolithic grave at Bjørnsholm, north Jutland. *Journal of Danish Archaeology* **9**, 38–58.

Andersen, S.H. and Malmros, C. 1965. Norslund. En kystboplads fra ældre stenalder (Norslund. A coastal settlement from the Old Stone Age). *Kuml* **1965**, 35–114.

Binford, L.R. 1982. The archaeology of place. *Journal of Anthropological Archaeology* **1**(1), 5–31.

Binford, L.R. 1983. *In Pursuit of the Past: Decoding the Archaeological Record*. London: Thames & Hudson.

Bratlund, B. 1991. The bone remains of mammals and birds from the Bjørnsholm shell-mound. *Journal of Danish Archaeology* **10**, 97–104.

Broholm, H.C. 1928. Langøfundet. En Boplads fra den ældre Stenalder paa Fyn. *Aarbøger for nordisk Oldkyndighed og Historie* **1928**, 129–90.

Christensen, C. 1998. Miljøet omkring Spodsbjergbopladsen – samt et bidrag til fastlæggelse af submarine kystlinier i det sydlige Danmark. *In* H. Sørensen (ed.), *Spodsbjerg – en yngre stenalderboplads på Langeland*, 7–28. Rudkøbing.

Kannegaard, E. 1990. 'Nederst'. *Arkæologiske udgravninger i Danmark 1989* **268**, 165. (Rigsantikvarens Arkæologiske Sekretariat: København).

Liversage, D. 1992. *Barkær: Long Barrows and Settlements*. København: Akademisk Forlag (Arkæologiske Studier vol. **IX**).

Madsen, A.P., Müller, S, Neergaard, C., Petersen, C.G.J., Rostrup, E., Steenstrup, K.J.V. and Winge, H. 1900. *Affaldsdynger fra Stenalderen i Danmark undersøgte for Nationalmuseet*. København: Reitzel.

Mathiassen, Th., Degerbøl, M. and Troels-Smith, J. 1942. *Dyrholmen. En Stenalderboplads paa Djursland*. København: Det Kongelige Danske Videnskabernes Selskab (Arkæologisk-Kunsthistoriske Skrifter Bd.**I**, Nr.1).

Petersen, C.G.J. 1922. Om Tidsbestemmelse og Ernæringsforhold i den ældre Stenalder i Danmark. *Det Kongelige Danske Videnskabernes Selskab, Biologiske Meddelelser* **3**/9, 1–20.

Skousen, H. 1998. Rønbjerg Strandvolde – en kystboplads ved Limfjorden (Rønbjerg Strandvolde – a coastal settlement by the Limfjord). *Kuml* **1997–98**, 29–73.

Sørensen, S.A. 1993. Lollikhuse – a dwelling site under a kitchen midden. *Journal of Danish Archaeology* **11** (1992–93), 19–29.

Troels-Smith, J. 1995. Claudi-kiler, østersbanker og tidevand. *In* H. Hansen and B. Aaby (eds), *Stavns Fjord – et natur- og kulturhistorisk forskningsområde på Samsø*, 59–67. København.

Chapter 22

The Mesolithic Period in Southern Norway:
Material Culture and Chronology

TORBEN BJARKE BALLIN

This chapter puts forward a revised view of the hunter-gatherer Stone Age of southern Norway, which includes a slight adjustment, and combination, of existing chronologies, and a presentation of the material culture associated with the region's Mesolithic phases. The chronology here is based on examination and comparison of a large number of lithic assemblages from east, west, and south Norway, and the methodology incorporates typological studies, technological attribute analyses, and raw material analyses. It is demonstrated that typological, technological, and raw material attributes can be equally diagnostic (chronologically and regionally) and, apart from familiarizing the anglophone archaeological community with the material culture of southern Norway, it is also the author's aim to present a methodology of relevance to the existing Mesolithic chronology of Scotland.

Introduction

In this chapter the author presents a 'new' framework for the Stone Age of southern Norway. This framework is primarily a fusion and co-ordination of existing regional chronologies (Bjerck 1986; Mikkelsen 1975b), which subdivides the Mesolithic phases into earlier and later sections. The basis of this chronological division is typological (diagnostic types), emphasizing microliths and arrowheads, supplemented by analyses of technology (mainly blade technology) and raw material preference.

The work presented here is based on Ballin (1999a), with the Farsund Project forming its point of departure. This project was carried out from 1992 to 1994 under the auspices of Oslo University's Collection of Antiquities ('Universitetets Oldsaksamling'). In connection with industrial development at Farsund on Lista, SW Norway, an area of *c.*110,000m² was surveyed, and 36 sites, mainly from the Stone Age, were recorded and excavated. The sites cover all phases from the second half of the middle Mesolithic to the end of the middle Neolithic, and for the first time a coherent picture of the Stone Age of south

Norway could be presented. Generally all archaeological activity in southern Norway has concentrated on the evidence from east and west Norway.

The finds from the Farsund Project were discussed in a monograph (Ballin & Lass Jensen 1995), and the University's Collection of Antiquities allocated means for further research into this material (The Farsund Research Project). As part of this research, the Stone Age of southern Norway was divided into three regions (east, west, and south Norway) as well as into a sequence of phases, with the lithic material from the three regions compared phase by phase. Within the period middle Mesolithic to middle Neolithic (the chronological span of the Farsund Project) comparison was based on selected museum collections (16 site assemblages) (Fig. 22.1), whereas early Mesolithic and late Neolithic finds were investigated via archaeological literature. Based on this analysis a chronological framework (Fig. 22.2) for the Stone Age of southern Norway was put forward as well as outlines of the associated territorial structure. In the Farsund Research Project the Stone Age material of southern Norway was also compared with contemporary finds from the adjacent regions of western Sweden and southern Scandinavia, but not northern Norway, as the phases succeeding the northern Komsa Culture are poorly understood.

Geographical concepts

In the author's thesis the boundary between southern and northern Norway is defined by the location of Stad on the Norwegian west coast (Fig. 22.1). By this means, southern Norway consists of the counties of Østfold, Akershus, Vestfold, Hedmark, Oppland, Buskerud, Telemark, Aust-Agder, Vest-Agder, Rogaland, and Hordaland, as well as Sogn and Fjordane. The region of east Norway is defined as Østfold, Akershus, Vestfold, and Telemark, west Norway as Hordaland and Sogn and Fjordane, and south Norway is defined as Aust-Agder and Vest-Agder. Of the two adjacent regions, southern Scandinavia is defined as Denmark and Scania (southernmost Sweden), whereas western Sweden is defined as the counties of Bohuslän, Västergötland, and northern Halland.

FIGURE 22.1

The counties of southern Norway and the sites analysed in Ballin (1999a).

To reduce the possibility of mixing regional and economic aspects it was decided to select sites from only one ecological zone: the coastal zone. A settlement was classified as coastal if the sea of the time was part of the site's catchment area (radius 10km; Higgs & Vita-Finzi 1972, 28) and thereby an integral part of the economic strategy at the site.

The Mesolithic/Neolithic transition in southern Norway

In Mikkelsen's chronological framework for the Mesolithic of east Norway he dated the Mesolithic/ Neolithic transition to c.5000 BP (Mikkelsen 1975b, 31), whereas this phenomenon today is dated to c.5200 BP (Ballin 1999a; Bergsvik 1995, 115; Bruen Olsen 1992, 124; Nærøy 1994, 19). A phase displacement of only 200 years may seem insignificant, but in this case it causes problems as to the exact position of Mikkelsen's phase 4. Does this phase constitute the last phase of the

Mesolithic (as stated by Mikkelsen), or is it the first Neolithic phase (Fig. 22.2)?

Before this problem can be addressed, the content of the two chronological concepts, Mesolithic and Neolithic, must be defined. Recently the case of the Norwegian Mesolithic/Neolithic transition has been discussed by Prescott (1996), who lists a series of different interpretations. For instance, the concepts of Mesolithic and Neolithic can be seen as different chronological periods, evolutionary steps, economies, modes of production, or different combinations of cultural phenomena (Prescott 1996, 77).

If 'Neolithic' is defined as an economy or a mode of production, it has traditionally been seen as the Stone Age period in which the hunter-gatherer economy was replaced by agriculture. Based on this definition, Prescott (1996, 79) argues convincingly for the absence of a Neolithic period in Norway, and he calls attention to weaknesses attached to the preserved indicators (bone, seeds, coprolites, pollen, and pottery) for a Norwegian Neolithic. Referring to Zvelebil

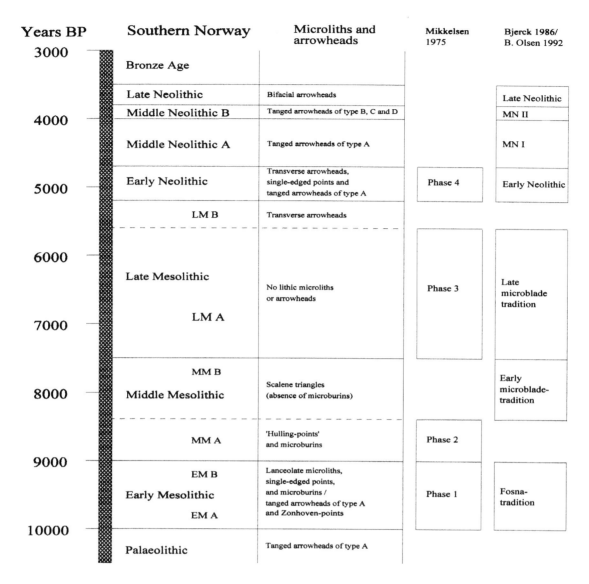

FIGURE 22.2

Chronological framework for the Stone Age of southern Norway. The framework is correlated with the primary diagnostic types, the microliths and arrowheads, as well as with the most accepted regional phase systems (Bjerck 1986; Bruen Olsen 1992; Mikkelsen 1975b).

and Rowley-Conwy's staged model concerning the introduction of a Neolithic economy in any given area (availability–substitution–consolidation; Zvelebil & Rowley-Conwy 1984), Prescott suggests that the early Neolithic (EN) and the early middle Neolithic (MN A) constitute an availability phase, in which agriculture is acknowledged but not introduced, whereas the late middle Neolithic (MN B) possibly constitutes a short substitution phase, in which agriculture is being introduced and during which the hunter-gatherer economy is replaced by the new economy. In the late

Neolithic the agricultural economy is consolidated, but Prescott (1996, 84) considers this phase to be the dawn of the coming Metal Age rather than an actual Stone Age phase (cf. Bakka & Kaland 1971).

According to Prescott (1996, 83), there is a possibility that east Norway may have been properly Neolithic during the EN and MN A, which he finds expressed in a larger import of Neolithic artefacts (e.g. ground flint axeheads from the Funnel-beaker Culture) and ideology (e.g. megalithic graves). The two(!) megalithic graves can be dated to the beginning of MN A (Østmo 1982;

1984), whereas the EN artefacts of east Norway are very poorly dated.

The application of the Neolithic concept in southern Norway must be seen in its context of research history, as it is mainly based on artefactual parallels between the larger lithic artefacts in southern Norway and the Neolithic of southern Scandinavia (the Funnel-beaker Culture). The Neolithic phases of southern Norway mentioned above are primarily expressions of differences within the local material culture, and only to a minor degree do they say anything about the economy or ideology of the phases in question.

Economically the late Mesolithic and the EN of southern Norway may be seen as a continuum. The Mesolithic/Neolithic transition is defined by the introduction (import?) of 'Neolithic' types such as ground flint axeheads, battle-axes, and pottery. As these types are rarely found on EN settlement sites, researchers have chosen to use the introduction of tanged arrowheads and cylindrical core technology as the main indicators of the transition. In west Norway this event coincides with the introduction of rhyolite in blade production. The introduction of tanged arrowheads and cylindrical (opposed platform) technology is dated to c.5200 BP (Bruen Olsen 1992, 93).

Research history of the chronology of southern Norway

During the first 30 years of this century the two classical Mesolithic phases of southern Norway were established. The Nøstvet Culture was recognized in 1904 due to Hansen's observations from the county of Østfold in east Norway (Hansen 1904), and the Fosna Culture was recognized in 1924 through Nummedal's description of finds from the county of Møre and Trøndelag in central Norway (Nummedal 1924; 1929). However, opinions as to the relations between the two cultures have differed strongly. It has been claimed that the Fosna Culture is older than the Nøstvet Culture (e.g. Gjessing 1945), that they are contemporaneous (Freundt 1948), and that the two Mesolithic cultures were contemporaneous with parts of the Neolithic (Hagen 1967). During the inter-war period and immediately after the Second World War it was common to regard Mesolithic and Neolithic cultures as contemporary ('cultural dualism'), which we know today they were not.

In the 1960–70s a large number of Stone Age sites were investigated in east Norway. Many of those are today regarded as chronological type-sites, such as the early Mesolithic site of Rørmyr II, Østfold County (Skar & Coulson 1985), the middle Mesolithic site of Tørkop,

Østfold County (Ballin 1999c), and the late Mesolithic site of Frebergsvik, Vestfold County (Mikkelsen 1975a). Based on more recent material from the county of Østfold, Mikkelsen (1975b) put forward a chronological framework for east Norway in which, by means of artefact combinations, shoreline dating, and radiocarbon dates, he subdivided the Mesolithic material from east Norway into four phases. Phases 1 and 3 corresponded to the Fosna Culture and the Nøstvet Culture, phase 2 constituted a transitional phase represented by the presence of 'hulling-points' (Note 1; Fig. 22.2), and phase 4 was a final Mesolithic phase characterized by the contemporary presence of transverse arrowheads, single-edged points, and plain tanged arrowheads (type A) ('Late flint-point using groups').

Based on a re-evaluation of the shoreline conditions in Østfold and a comparison of material from east Norway, and also on more recent finds from Denmark and west Sweden, Lindblom suggested an adjustment of Mikkelsen's dates for the four phases, but not for their content (Lindblom 1984, 53). The changes suggested by Lindblom were considerable, and the new dates of the phases are largely identical to the dates suggested by this author (Ballin 1999a). However, Mikkelsen's phases are still widely used as a chronological scheme for the Mesolithic period in east Norway.

Gjessing maintained that the typical Nøstvet Culture was exclusively a cultural entity of east Norway (Gjessing 1945, 78), but not until the 1980s was it established unequivocally that the main diagnostic type of this culture, the Nøstvet axehead, is absent in west Norway (Alsaker 1987, 101; Indrelid 1978, 151). Primarily in the light of stone axehead studies from west Norway, Bruen Olsen and Alsaker proposed a chronological framework with three Mesolithic phases and two Neolithic phases. The Mesolithic phases were designated the early, middle, and late Mesolithic, with the early and late Mesolithic corresponding to the Fosna Culture and the Nøstvet Culture, whereas the Neolithic phases were named Neolithic I and II, corresponding to the early/middle Neolithic and the late Neolithic respectively (Bruen Olsen & Alsaker 1984, 87). According to Bruen Olsen and Alsaker stone axeheads were introduced in the middle Mesolithic. The dates of this chronological system correspond well with the dates of the author's chronological framework for southern Norway (Ballin 1999a).

In 1978 Indrelid renamed the west Norwegian variant of the Nøstvet Culture the Late Mesolithic Microblade Tradition, as microblades are characteristic of this phase, whereas Nøstvet axeheads are absent in west Norway (Indrelid 1978, 151). This proposal was taken up by Bjerck (1983), who put forward a three-phase chronological framework for the Mesolithic of west Norway, naming the Fosna phase the Flint-using Tradition ('Flintplasstraditionen'), the Nøstvet phase was called the Late Microblade Tradition, and the so far unnoticed transitional phase was called the Early Microblade Tradition (Bjerck 1983; 1986) (Note 2). The dates of Bjerck's and Bruen Olsen and Alsaker's frameworks correspond well with each other. Apart from typological differences, an important element in Bjerck's chronology was technological differences between the phases demonstrated through attribute analyses of the blade material.

In 1989 Nygaard proposed a chronological framework for the Mesolithic of west Norway in which this period was subdivided into four phases (Fosna I/II and Nøstvet I/II; Nygaard 1989; 1990). Nygaard's phases were defined by artefact assemblages associated with socio-economic conditions, but her chronology was never widely accepted. In connection with the Farsund Project in south Norway it was considered which chronological framework to use during the excavations and the post-excavation work – Mikkelsen's (1975b), Bjerck's (1986), or Nygaard's (1990) – and the three chronologies were tested on the excavated assemblages. Nygaard's phases were too weakly defined, and very often assemblages could be referred to more than one of her phases, whereas the assemblages could be unequivocally referred to one or the other of Mikkelsen's or Bjerck's phases. In Ballin (1999a), Mikkelsen's and Bjerck's regional chronologies were unified in one single chronological framework for the Mesolithic of southern Norway (Fig. 22.2).

General methodology

The basis of all archaeological research is the ability to date archaeological finds with a reasonable degree of precision. Within Stone Age research it is not always necessary to obtain an absolute date for the finds, but regardless of whether one wants to investigate the cultural development of a region (diachronous comparison), or one wants to analyse, for example, technological, economical, or social differences between two separate regions (synchronous comparison), it is absolutely necessary to assess whether the assemblages that are being compared are contemporary or of a different age. Relative dates of the finds are crucial.

In Stone Age contexts the most common methods applied in relative dating are ^{14}C analysis (which also gives an absolute date), shoreline displacement dating, and stratigraphy, but in many cases only one, or maybe none, of these methods will be applicable. Often ^{14}C analysis must be ruled out due to the lack of organic

material in a secure context, whereas shoreline displacement dating may be impossible because of a relatively static shoreline, or maybe the settlement in question was not coastal. Stratigraphic observations may be irrelevant for a number of reasons, but in Norway almost all archaeologically relevant stratigraphy has been blurred by podsolization (Note 3).

Frequently the archaeologist studying the Stone Age will be faced with a situation in which only analyses of the site assemblage may produce a relative date, and due to the unfortunate influence of many soil types on organic matter, only lithic material will have survived. In these cases a relative date can best be obtained by analyses of typology, technology, or raw-materials.

Typology
Typology is the study of artefact similarity, and within a given category (arrowheads, scrapers, etc.) artefacts can be divided into types. Traditionally, typological dating was carried out with reference to a number of type series starting with simpler types that were followed by more sophisticated types, but today typological dating means dating based on similarities with artefacts dated in other ways, such as find combinations, stratigraphy, or ^{14}C analysis (Rasmussen 1979, 184; Voss 1985, 253).

The central concept within typological dating is the diagnostic artefact, that is, a type associated with certain archaeological cultures, cultural groups, or techno-complexes. The concept may be subdivided into three categories (Note 4), namely: 1) types with a practically universal distribution in time and space (e.g. the end scraper); 2) types occurring in certain periods (the Mesolithic or Neolithic) or more than one phase (e.g. core axes); and 3) types occurring exclusively in a single phase or sub-phase and thereby defining it (e.g. scalene triangles). It is suggested that artefact types of category 3 are termed primary diagnostic types and artefacts of category 2 secondary diagnostic types (the diagnostic types of southern Norway are shown in Fig. 22.3).

However, to be able to date a type it must be unequivocally defined in relation to other types; a typological apparatus or classification system must be constructed. It has been discussed by which premises a typological classification system ought to be built (Hayden 1984; Hill & Evans 1972), but in general terms classification systems are constructed to solve certain archaeological problems (e.g. chronology). Within Stone Age research they are practically always morphological, as a consistent functional classification would have to be based on the application of use-wear analysis. This is often not possible because of surface alterations of the lithic raw material.

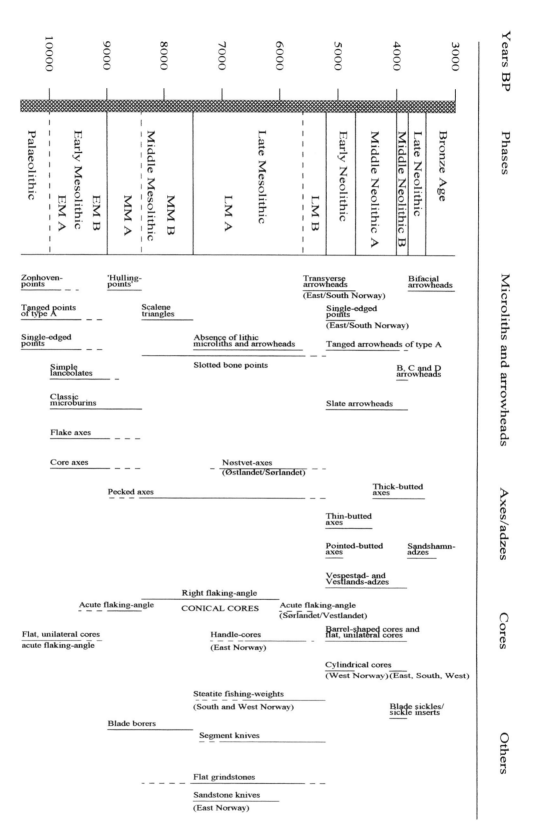

FIGURE 22.3

The diagnostic artefact types of southern Norway and their chronological occurrence.

418

In spite of the fact that a classification system has to be conditioned by a problem – it is not absolute – it is an advantage to have a relatively fixed classification system to support discussions in which lithic artefact types are central. The basic type definitions ought to be fixed, thus preventing misunderstandings (e.g. the definition of the blade concept as $L \geq 2W$). This classification system should be geographically limited to a region with mutual typological and technological traditions, like the northern parts of Norway, Sweden, and Finland (the Slate Complex), southern Norway/western Sweden, southern Scandinavia, or Great Britain.

The necessity of this geographical delimitation may be exemplified by the microblade concept. This concept is defined differently in southern Norway/western Sweden and southern Scandinavia, with the microblade being defined as a blade with a maximum width of 8mm in the former region, and in the latter region it is defined as a blade with a maximum width of 10mm. The two different definitions are based on different raw material situations in the two regions. In southern Scandinavia there is an abundance of high-quality flint in large nodules, whereas flint in southern Norway/western Sweden occurs more sporadically and in smaller pieces. In southern Norway/western Sweden it is possible to operate with a rule of thumb saying that blade populations with an average width of c.8mm are middle Mesolithic, populations with an average width less than 8mm are late Mesolithic, and populations with an average width larger than 8mm are either early Mesolithic or Neolithic (cf. Fig. 22.4).

A lithic classification system should be hierarchical to make it possible to add new classes or sub-classes as the need for more detail arises. The upper level of the system must be tripartite, consisting of the classes: debitage (chips, flakes, blades, and indeterminate fragments), cores, and tools. By-products (microburins, burin spalls, axe sharpening flakes, etc.) may be regarded as an independent class, but generally it will be more practical to place the individual by-products with the tools they are complementary to (microburins with microliths, burin spalls with burins, etc.). The second level is made up by main categories, which in the tool class will be the main tool types (axeheads, arrowheads, microliths, scrapers, etc.), whereas the third level consists of different types of the main tool groups (e.g. for scrapers: circular scrapers, end-scrapers, double-scrapers, side-scrapers, shaft-scrapers, etc.). Below this level a fourth and fifth level may be added if it is of relevance to the archaeological problem under investigation.

A proper and complete lithic classification system has never been put forward in southern Scandinavia, as archaeologists have generally been content with classification systems covering one phase or sub-phase

(Blankholm et al. 1967; Brinch Petersen 1966; Skaarup 1979), detailed classification of individual artefact categories (Lomborg 1973; Nielsen 1977a; 1977b), or general but subjective lists of definitions for laymen as well as archaeologists (Glob 1952; Mathiassen 1948; Müller 1888; Rud 1979; Vang Petersen 1993). The situation in southern Norway/western Sweden has been the reverse, with a tendency to put forward general, hierarchical classification systems for lithic artefacts with less focus on detail (Andersson et al. 1978; Ballin 1996; Helskog et al. 1976; Indrelid 1990). The classification systems of southern Norway are probably the direct result of the excavation of very large amounts of lithic artefacts in connection with the industrial development of the last 30 years (e.g. the Farsund Project: c.640,000 artefacts) combined with a legal obligation to excavate all affected monuments and settlements and classify and catalogue the resulting finds.

In connection with the relative dating of lithic assemblages the typological approach may prove insufficient if, for example, an assemblage contains few or no diagnostic types at all (cores or tools). In this situation one will have to proceed to a technological assessment of the finds, and in many cases this approach will be just as reliable for relative dating as the typological method.

Technological profiles

Methodological background

Detailed attribute analysis of blade material has been applied for more than 25 years (Sollberger & Patterson 1976). The method was developed in close relationship to experimental flint-knapping, with the general aim of giving a detailed description of the technology behind the primary production of individual Stone Age cultures or phases. This description could then be used as a means of relative dating.

Attribute analysis of blade material is seen in two different versions, with one version being restricted to metric attributes (Andersen 1982; 1983; Bjerck 1983; 1986; Bjerck & Ringstad 1985), whereas the other version combines metric and descriptive attributes (Hartz 1987; Madsen 1992; Sollberger & Patterson 1976). The metric attributes usually include the dimensions of the blades and their platform remnants as well as the flaking angle, whereas the descriptive attributes encompass the different types of platform edge preparation and platform preparation (core preparation/core rejuvenation).

The metric form of analysis is obviously the least time-consuming, whereas the combined form, due to the higher number of attributes, gives a more detailed

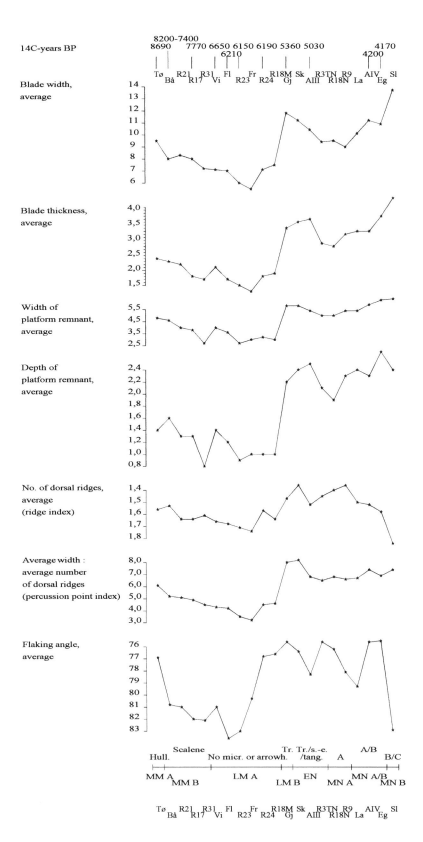

FIGURE 22.4

Blade attributes – sequence diagram. The rhyolite blades of Austvik III are excluded.

technological profile. The two versions of attribute analysis have different levels of costs and different degrees of applicability. If one compares finds from chronologically neighbouring cultures or phases (e.g. the early and middle Mesolithic of southern Norway) the metric form is practical and unproblematic, as the course of development unequivocally goes from big towards small, from coarse towards fine (Bjerck 1983; 1986; Bjerck & Ringstad 1985; Nærøy 1994). Metric attribute analysis becomes problematic when one compares finds separated by a larger time-span (e.g. the early and late Mesolithic of southern Norway), as the course of development may have fluctuated resulting in identical metrical attributes in early and late blade populations. In this case, an analysis of the descriptive attributes of the populations will almost certainly make it possible to distinguish between the two.

Methodology

The approach here is primarily based on the method of Madsen (1992) as presented in his article on blade technology in the Danish Late Palaeolithic. The method is combined metric-descriptive, and Madsen's method has been adjusted to make it more generally applicable.

The metric attributes involved are the width and thickness of the blades, the width and depth of the platform remnants, flaking angle, and number of dorsal ridges. The descriptive attributes are forms of platform-edge/platform-surface preparation, cortex, type of bulb of percussion, size of bulbar scar, and cone characteristics. The length of the blades was not selected as an attribute, as only between 10–40 per cent of the investigated blade assemblages are intact (Note 5). In this type of analysis, only intact blades and proximal ends are examined.

Dimensions. The blade definition follows Helskog *et al.* (1976) (Note 6), and the blades and the platform remnants are measured in mm to one decimal. For all populations an average value has been calculated for the metric attributes, as well as average values for the width:thickness of the blades (W:T ratio) (Note 7), and the width:depth of the platform remnants (W:D ratio) (Note 8). A point of percussion index is calculated by dividing the average width of any blade population by the average number of dorsal ridges. The point of percussion index is a measure of the distance between the individual points of percussion in a blade series, that is the points on which the pressure-flaker was positioned to detach the individual blade. Generally only unretouched blades were included as only they have their original dimensions intact, but in cases of very small populations, it has, for statistical reasons, been considered appropriate to include blades with minute lateral retouch. The retouch

of these blades is discrete, and the width values are only slightly affected.

The flaking angle. This has been measured without decimals, and contrary to Bjerck (1983; 1986), who measures this attribute between platform remnant and ventral side, the author has chosen to follow Sollberger and Patterson (1976, 518) and measure the angle between platform remnant and dorsal side: 'For these measurements, approximately 20–25 per cent of the dorsal surface, proximal end of the blade is used, and any bevel at the striking platform is ignored'. By measuring the ventral angle a measure is achieved of the actual result of the applied technology (which, to some extent, is due to chance: flaws in the raw-material, technological idiosyncracies, etc.), whereas measuring the angle with the carefully prepared dorsal side will provide a measure of the intentions or mental template of the flintknapper. An additional factor is that it may be difficult to measure the angle of the platform remnant/ventral side on very curved blades. The two practices result in almost identical results; the ventral angles are however slightly less acute.

Number of dorsal ridges. Due to the chosen blade definition, a blade will always have at least one dorsal ridge (Helskog *et al.* 1976, 14). An average value (the ridge index) is calculated for the individual blade populations. As discussed in Ballin (1995b, 34), the ridge index seems to be a fairly accurate measure of the technical quality of the populations; a high ridge index means a high degree of regularity. In Ballin (1999a) a scale of regularity was created based on the ridge index: 1) 1.00–1.45 irregular blades; 2) 1.46–1.55 regular blades; 3) 1.56–1.65 very regular blades; and 4) 1.66– >elegant blades.

Degree of cortex cover. This is indicated as presence/absence. Barton's (1988, 115) more detailed indications (1: <10 per cent, 2: 11–50 per cent, 3: 51–90 per cent, 4: >90 per cent) were considered but ruled out as an unwarranted level of detail.

Bulb of percussion. In this article, three types of bulbs are distinguished: 1) pronounced bulb; 2) neither bulb nor lip; and 3) pronounced lip. A pronounced bulb indicates direct technique, a lip indicates indirect technique, whereas the absence of both is an intermediate form.

Bulbar scar. In this work, bulbar scars are indicated as presence/absence. A bulbar scar is a thin flake detached from the surface of the bulb of percussion. Usually it will be very small (a few mm² or less) and it is generally interpreted as an indicator of direct technique. However, Zimmermann (1987, 193) disputes this, and it must be stressed that bulbar scars are not valid as indicators of direct technique *per se* but only in a statistical sense; the

TABLE 22.1
Blade attributes – technological profiles

Profile	Delimitation	Average width	Average thickness	Average width of platform remnant	Average depth of platform remnant	W:T ratio	W:D ratio	Average flaking angle	Ridge index\regularity	Percussion point index	Edge preparation	Platform preparation	Crested blades	Core types
1	MM A	9.5	2.4	4.8	1.4	4,0	3,4	77	1.56 (very regular blades)	6.1	Abrasion	Facetting	Unilateral	Conical cores
2	MM B (- Early LM A?)	7,2–8,3	1,7–2,3	2,7–4,5	0,8–1,6	3,4–4,4	2,8–3,4	81-82	1,53–1,64 (very regular blades)	4,5–5,2	Abrasion	Facetting	Unilateral	Conical cores
3	LM A (c.6,200 BP - South/West)	6,0–6,6	1,5–1,8	2,7–3,6	0,9–1,3	3,7–4,0	2,8–3,0	80-83	1,59–1,71 (very regular – elegant blades)	3,5–4,2	None-coarse trimm.	Fine facetting	Unilateral	Conical microblade cores
4	Middle-Later LM A (East Norway)	5.5	1.3	3.0	1.0	4.2	3,0	80	1.74 (elegant blades)	3.2	Fine trimming	Facetting	Unilateral	Handle-cores
5	Middle-Later LM A (South/West)	7,1–7,5	1,8–1,9	3,0–3,2	1.0	3,9–4,0	3,0–3,2	77	1,57–1,64 (very regular blades)	4,5–4,6	Fine trimming	None	Unilateral	Conical microblade cores
6	LM B-MN A	9,0–11,8	2,9–3,6	5,0–6,0	1,9–2,6	2,8–3,5	2,3–2,6	76-78	1,36–1,49 (irregular blades)	6,5–8,2	None-coarse trimm.	Coarse facetting	Bilateral	Barrel-shaped cores
7	EN (West Norway)	10.3	4.2	6.2	2.8	2.5	2.2	80	1.50 (regular blades)	6.7	None-coarse trimm.	Coarse facetting	Unilateral	Slender cylindrical cores
8	MN B	10,1–13,7	3,3–4,4	5,4–6,4	2,4–2,7	2,9–3,1	2,3–2,7	75-83	1,50–1,84 (regular – elegant blades)	6,7–7,4	Fine trimming	Facetting	Bilateral	Slender cylindrical cores

more, and the larger, bulbar scars there are in a blade population, the more 'violent' (i.e. direct) technique has been involved.

Cone characteristics. On blades with a pronounced bulb or neither bulb nor lip it is assessed whether any of the following attributes may be present in connection with the point of percussion: 1) a circular scar of percussion (on the platform); 2) a circular scar of percussion continued in a pronounced ventral cone; and 3) an actual bulbar detachment. Where a bulbar scar is a minor flake detached *on* the bulb of percussion, a bulbar detachment is a detachment *of* the bulb of percussion. In both cases the result will be small, bi-convex *éraillure*-flakes; the more pronounced *éraillure*-flakes originate from bulbar detachments. The three cone characteristics are all unequivocal indicators of direct technique.

Preparation system. In the analysis of the assemblages from Southern Norway seven attributes are distinguished. Preparation of the platform edge: 1) no dorsal preparation; 2) trimming; and 3) abrasion; preparation of the platform surface: 4) cortex-covered platform remnant; 5) no platform preparation; 6) faceted platform remnant (≤3 facets); and 7) finely faceted platform remnant (>3 facets). Abrasion of the platform edge may appear as a slight polish of the 'horns' or projections between the dorsal flake scars as well as rounding of the entire platform edge. The polish must be distinct to be labelled abrasion, as gloss may appear naturally after deposition in sand (Keeley 1980). These attributes and their combinations are chronologically highly significant (Fig. 22.5; Table 22.1).

Raw material preference
Generally only flint has been exploited in east and south Norway, and the use of raw material preference as a diagnostic element has primarily been a topic in the

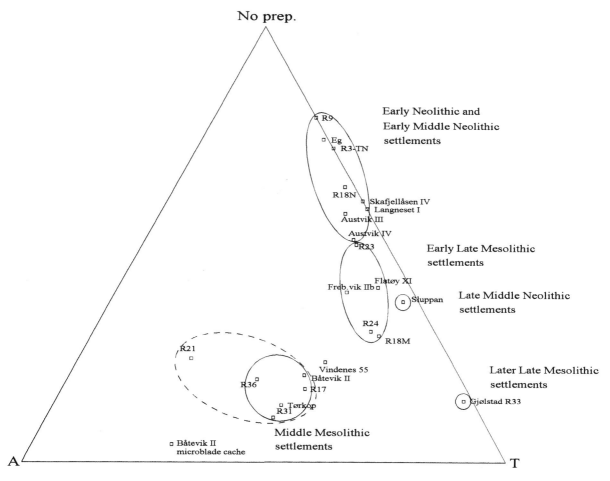

FIGURE 22.5
Grouping of sites from the Stone Age of southern Norway by the platform preparation system for flakes/blades. Key: No prep. = no preparation of the platform edge; A = abrasion; T = trimming.

Stone Age research of west Norway. With relevance to this region a table has been constructed showing the raw materials utilized in the Mesolithic and Neolithic (Table 22.2). Total dominance is defined as >85 per cent of an assemblage, dominance as 41–85 per cent, frequent appearance as 11–40 per cent, and appearance as 1–10 per cent (Bruen Olsen 1992, 84).

When using the presence of raw materials as a chronological indicator it is important to assess whether the context of the raw materials expresses style or function, with style being '… formal variation in material culture that transmits information about personal and social identity' (Wiessner 1983, 256). If the decision to use or not use a specific raw material is only due to the presence or absence of that material the context is functional, whereas the preference of a raw material with a weak presence or the discrimination of a raw material with a strong presence represents a stylistic context (transmission of social information, generally relating to group identification). An example of the former is the use of local raw materials in the Norwegian High Mountains (an adaptation to the absence of flint), whereas an example of the latter is the preference of specific raw materials in the local axehead production of west Norway, with the proportion of these raw materials (diabase/greenstone) not reflecting the local raw material

situation (Bruen Olsen & Alsaker 1984, 96). Raw material preference expressing function ought to result in a gradually declining fall-off curve (Renfrew 1977, 73) reflecting the presence of the material in question, whereas raw material preference expressing style should result in a marked drop in frequency at the border of the specific group's territory (Hodder 1979, 447).

The Stone Age chronology of southern Norway

The chronological framework

The basic element of the Stone Age chronology of southern Norway is the chronological framework. This framework (Fig. 22.2) is a system based on phases with each phase being defined by exclusive presence of armature types (microliths/arrowheads) or combinations of armatures. All other diagnostic types, sub-types, technological profiles, and raw material preferences will refer to this framework.

Fig. 22.2 is composed of four columns. The column furthest to the left shows the phases and sub-phases (or chronozones), followed by a column showing the primary diagnostic types of these phases: microliths and arrowheads. The two columns to the right show

TABLE 22.2
Raw-material chronology for West Norway (Bruen Olsen 1992, 84).

	Total dominance	Dominance	Frequent appearance	Appearance	Absence
EM	Flint			Quartz White quartzite Blue mylonite	Div. stone Rhyolite Slate
MM		Flint	Quartz White quartzite	Blue mylonite Rock crystal Div. stone	Rhyolite Slate
LM		Flint Quartz White quartzite	Blue mylonite Rock crystal	Yellow mylonite Green mylonite Div. stone	Rhyolite Slate
EN		Rhyolite Div. mylonite	Flint Quartz Div. quartzite Slate	Div. stone	
MN		Quartz Div. quartzite	Flint Slate	Rhyolite Div. mylonite Div. stone	

Mikkelsen's and Bjerck's/Bruen Olsen's regional phases as boxes parallel to the phases to which they correspond (Ballin 1999a; Bjerck 1986; Bruen Olsen 1992; Mikkelsen 1975b).

The early Mesolithic has been subdivided with reference to the division proposed for the Myrvatn sites, SW Norway (Bang-Andersen 1990). This is based on fluctuations in the arrowhead/microlith ratio, but the exact boundary between the two sub-phases must await future scrutiny of the early Mesolithic. The middle Mesolithic has been subdivided with reference to the author's analyses of the finds from Tørkop in east Norway (Østfold County), Lundevågen R21/22 in south Norway (Vest-Agder County), and Båtevik II (Sogn and Fjordane County) in west Norway (Ballin 1995a; 1995b; 1997a; 1999a; 1999b; 1999c; Ballin & Lass Jensen 1995) as well as ¹⁴C-dated contexts with 'hulling-points' and scalene triangles. The following sites have also been important to the understanding of the middle Mesolithic of southern Norway: Foldsjøen 4A, Sørtrøndelag County (Skar 1989); Dysvikja, Møre and Romsdal County (Bjerck 1983, 49); Lundevågen R17, Vest-Agder County (Ballin & Lass Jensen 1995, 36); and Vinterbro, Akershus County (Jaksland 2001).

The subdivision of the late Mesolithic is primarily based on the settlement Gjølstad R33, Akershus County (Berg 1995, 82), at which transverse arrowheads are the only armature type. The ¹⁴C-dates of c.5350 BP (supported by the dates of the Svevollen sites, Hedmark County; Fuglestvedt 1995, 99) displace Mikkelsen's phase 4 into the early Neolithic (Fig. 22.2). None of the sites used by Mikkelsen to support his phase 4 were ¹⁴C-dated (Mikkelsen 1975b, 23), and the Torsrød settlement, Vestfold County (Østmo 1976), used to consolidate this phase, has so many closely situated hearths that the finds are likely to represent an accumulation of remains from more than one visit to the site. A diagram showing the diagnostic types of southern Norway is illustrated as Fig. 22.3.

Mesolithic phases in southern Norway

The early Mesolithic (EM: 10,000–9000 BP): Norway and western Sweden (a characteristic assemblage is shown in Fig. 22.6)

Typology: diagnostic types
Zonhoven-points (replaced approximately mid-EM). Small tanged arrowheads (type A), which may have had the proximal end removed by bilateral microburin technique (Ballin 1997b). Single-edged points with the tip in the proximal end. This end may have been removed by unilateral microburin technique. EM single-edged points very often have a marked elbow on the longest, convex retouched side. EN points have the tip in the distal end, they are never made using the microburin technique, and the longest retouched side is always regularly convex. Plain lanceolates and segments made in microburin technique. Microburins: unilateral microburins from the production of single-edged points, lanceolates, and segments; and bilateral microburins from the production of tanged arrowheads (Ballin 1997b). Flake and core axeheads in flint. Flat, unilateral cores with an acute flaking angle. These opposed-platform cores are larger as well as coarser than the unilateral, opposed-platform cores from EN and MN A.

Typology: absence
Borers and stone axeheads.

Technology
The blades of the EM are coarse macroblades with an acute flaking angle. With reference to Bjerck (1983; 1986) it may be assumed that the flaking angle in EM was slightly more acute (c.70–78°) than in the other acute-angle phases, SM A and the Neolithic (76–78°). In the beginning of the EM blades were produced on flat, unilateral cores, but by the end of this phase the first conical blade cores appeared. Bipolar technology is known.

Raw material preference
Flint is totally dominant.

Comments
As mentioned above, it may be possible to subdivide the EM based on the fluctuating microlith/arrowhead ratio, and it will probably be possible to define several technological profiles within the phase. This chronological unit corresponds to the traditional Fosna Phase, Mikkelsen's phase 1 (Mikkelsen 1975b, 27) and Bjerck's Flint-using Tradition (Bjerck 1986, 107).

The early middle Mesolithic (MM A: 9000–8400 BP): southern Norway and western Sweden (a characteristic assemblage is shown in Fig. 22.7)

Typology: diagnostic types
Lanceolates (small numbers); 'Hulling-points'; microburins; core axeheads in flint; pecked stone axeheads; conical blade and microblade cores with acute flaking angles; unilateral crested blades; blade borers; core borers.

425

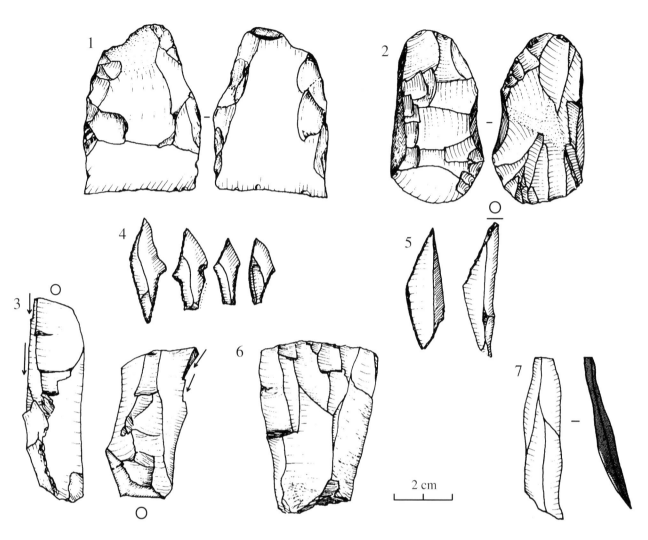

FIGURE 22.6

Typical early Mesolithic assemblage (Bjerck 1995, 136). Key: 1 flake adze; 2 core adze; 3 burins; 4 single-edged points; 5 lanceolate microliths; 6 unifacial blade core; and 7 blade.

Typology: absence

Flat, unilateral cores have been replaced. Tanged arrow-heads and single-edged points have been replaced.

Typology: frequencies

Generally, there is very little armature in the middle Mesolithic – approximately 15 per cent in contrast to 0 per cent in LM A and 35–40 per cent in LM B and the Neolithic.

Technology

The blade technology in MM A is a macroblade technology, and in Ballin (1999a) it is defined as profile 1:

average blade width: 9.5mm; average flaking angle: 77°; ridge index (regularity): 1.56 (very regular blades); platform edge preparation: abrasion; platform surface preparation: faceting; technique: indirect. In the middle Mesolithic bipolar cores make up 45–65 per cent of bipolar cores + platform cores.

Raw material preference

On Foldsjøen 4A, Tørkop, and the contemporary west Swedish sites, flint is totally dominant.

Comments

This chronological unit corresponds to Mikkelsen's phase 2 (Mikkelsen 1975b, 28).

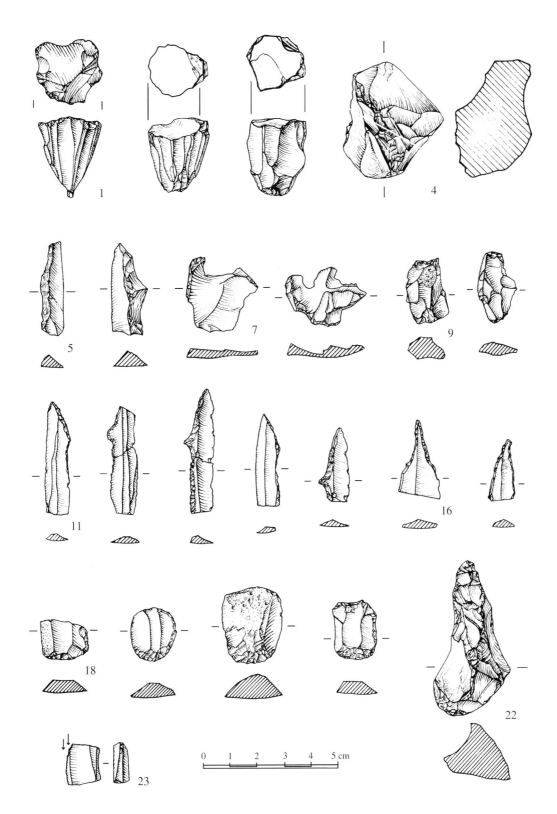

FIGURE 22.7

Typical middle Mesolithic (MM A) assemblage – Tørkop (Ballin 1999a). Key: 1–3 conical cores; 4 irregular core; 5–6 unilateral crested blades; 7–8 platform rejuvenation flakes; 9–10 bipolar cores; 11–15 'hulling points'; 16–17 blade borers; 18–21 flake and blade scrapers; 22 core borer; and 23 burin.

The late middle Mesolithic (MM B: 8400–7500 BP): southern Norway (and probably western Sweden) (a characteristic assemblage is shown in Fig. 22.8)

Typology: diagnostic types
Scalene triangles for insertion in slotted bone points (cf. Larsson 1978, 69); pecked stone axeheads; conical blade and microblade cores with a steep flaking angle; unilateral crested blades; and blade borers.

Typology: absence
'Hulling-points' have been replaced; microburins are absent, as the Norwegian scalene triangles are not produced applying microburin technique; core and flake axeheads have been replaced.

Typology: frequencies
Generally, there is very little armature in the middle Mesolithic: *c.*15 per cent in contrast to 0 per cent in LM A and 35–40 per cent in LM B and the Neolithic.

Technology
The blade technology develops during MM B from a combined blade/microblade technology with blades and microblades comprising a metric continuum to a proper microblade technology. This technology is in Ballin (1999a) defined as profile 2: average blade width: 7.2–8.3mm; average flaking angle: 81–82°; ridge index (regularity): 1.53–1.64 (very regular blades); platform edge preparation: abrasion; platform surface preparation: faceting; technique: indirect. In the middle Mesolithic bipolar cores make up 45–65 per cent of bipolar cores+platform cores.

Raw material preference
In east and south Norway flint is totally dominant, whereas a greater variation develops in west Norway. For example, at Båtevik II *c.*80 per cent of the assemblage is flint, and *c.*15 per cent quartzite, with five per cent in other raw materials.

Comments
The position of the scalene triangles in western Sweden is not yet fully understood, so it is with caution the region has been included in this chronological unit. In MM B the classical dichotomy east/south Norway and west Norway starts to develop, in the beginning as a difference in raw material preference. This chronological unit corresponds to Bjerck's Early Microblade Tradition (Bjerck 1986, 107–10).

The early late Mesolithic 1 (LM A1: 7500–5600 BP): south Norway and west Norway

Typology: diagnostic types
Conical microblade cores, in the period *c.*7500–6200 BP with a steep flaking angle, later with an acute flaking angle. Unilateral crested blades. Pecked and ground stone axeheads (west Norway) and Nøstvet axeheads (flaked stone axeheads) (south Norway). Small steatite fishing weights.

Typology: absence
Scalene triangles have disappeared; there are no lithic armature types in LM A. Conical macroblade cores have been replaced. Nøstvet axeheads are absent in west Norway and ground stone axeheads are absent outside west Norway. Sandstone knives are absent.

Typology: frequencies
The period MM A–LM A is characterized by many borers: 20–30 per cent in contrast to 0–10 per cent in the following phases. Stone axeheads are frequent, and amount to *c.*8 per cent in contrast to 0–2 per cent in all other phases. As a consequence of the abundant stone axeheads many fragments of flat grindstones are seen.

Technology
The blade technology in LM A is a microblade technology, which in west and south Norway develops from profile 2 (MM B) through profile 3 (*c.*6200 BP) to profile 5 (later LM A) (Ballin 1999a). Profile 3: average blade width: 6.0–6.6mm; average flaking angle: 80–83°; ridge index (regularity): 1.59–1.71 (very regular – elegant blades); platform edge preparation: none – coarse trimming; platform surface preparation: fine faceting; technique: indirect. Profile 5: average blade width: 7.1–7.5mm; average flaking angle: 77°; ridge index (regularity): 1.57–1.64 (very regular blades); platform edge preparation: fine trimming; platform surface preparation: none; technique: indirect. In LM A bipolar cores make up 65–85 per cent of bipolar cores+platform cores.

Raw material preference
During the LM A of west Norway raw material preference develops from high flint proportions (Vindenes: 71.3 per cent) to lower flint proportions (Flatøy XI: 45.0 per cent). The raw materials replacing flint are primarily quartz or quartzite, with fine-grained, light quartzite being the most common (Vindenes: 27.1% and Flatøy XI: 48.0%). In the assemblage of Flatøy XI, six per cent rock-crystal is seen as well. In Nordhordland, as well as Sogn and Fjordane, mylonite is common. In the tool

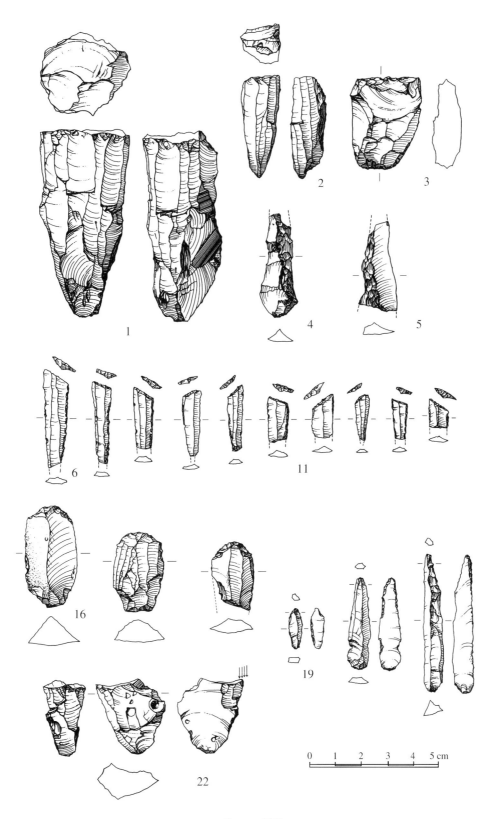

FIGURE 22.8

Typical middle Mesolithic (MM B) assemblage – Lundevågen R21/22 (Ballin 1999a). Key: 1–2 conical cores; 3 bipolar core; 4–5 unilateral crested blades; 6–15 scalene triangles; 16–18 flake and blade scrapers; 19–21 blade borers; and 22 burin.

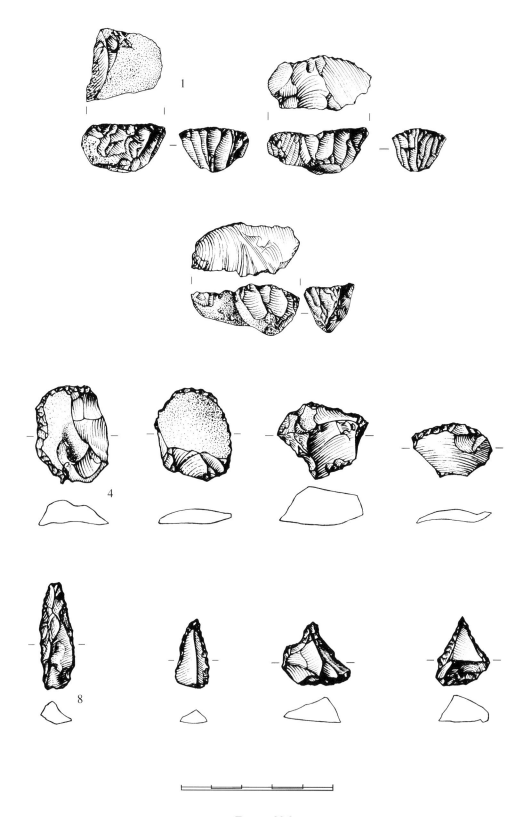

FIGURE 22.9

Typical late Mesolithic (LM A) assemblage – Frebergsvik (Ballin 1999a). Key: 1–3 handle-cores; 4–7 flake scrapers; 8–11 flake borers.
Frebergsvik is located in east Norway; in west and south Norway the handle-cores would be replaced by conical microblade cores.
Scale in cms.

group stone is common due to the many late Mesolithic stone axeheads.

Comments

In this phase south Norway occupies a position between the distinctly different assemblages of east and west Norway. This is exemplified through the presence of conical cores (absence of handle-cores) and small steatite fishing weights as in west Norway, whereas the stone axeheads are primarily pecked stone and Nøstvet axeheads as in east Norway; the pointed-butted ground stone axehead of west Norway does not appear east of Lista (SW Norway). In its raw material preference south Norway affiliates with flint-dominated east Norway. This chronological unit corresponds to Bjerck's Late Microblade Tradition (Bjerck 1986, 110).

The early late Mesolithic 2 (LM A2: 7200–5600 BP): east Norway and western Sweden (a characteristic assemblage is shown in Fig. 22.9)

Typology: diagnostic types
Handle-cores; unilateral crested blades; pecked stone axeheads; Nøstvet axeheads; segment knives; large fishing weights in hard stone; and sandstone knives.

Typology: absence
Scalene triangles have disappeared; there are no lithic armature types in LM A. Conical macroblade cores have been replaced. Sandstone knives are absent in Western Sweden.

Typology: frequencies
See above – LM A1.

Technology
The blade technology is in LM A a microblade technology, and in east Norway it is defined as profile 4 (Ballin 1999a): average blade width 5.5mm; average flaking angle 80°; ridge index (regularity): 1.74 (elegant blades); platform edge preparation: fine trimming; platform surface preparation: faceting; technique: indirect. In LM A bipolar cores make up 65–85 per cent of bipolar cores + platform cores.

Raw material preference
In east Norway and western Sweden LM A is totally dominated by flint (Frebergsvik IIb/IV) at 96.4 per cent, supplemented by a small amount of stone (axehead production). In east Norway the dominating axehead material is diabase, whereas in western Sweden it is

greenstone in the coastal region (Bohuslän) and diabase in the inland (Västergötland).

Comments

Several of the more significant elements of this chronological unit are weakly dated in east Norway, for example the handle-core and the Nøstvet axehead, but with reference to dates from western Sweden it may be assumed that the handle-core was not introduced prior to *c.*7200 BP (Larsson 1990, 281), leaving a technological hiatus in the beginning of the late Mesolithic of east Norway (*c.*7500–7200 BP). In western Sweden Nøstvet axeheads are called Lihult axeheads. In this region there are also flint core axes present. This chronological unit corresponds to Mikkelsen's phase 3 (Mikkelsen 1975b, 29).

The later late Mesolithic (LM B: 5600–5200 BP): east Norway, south Norway and western Sweden (a characteristic assemblage is shown in Fig. 22.10)

Typology: diagnostic types
Transverse arrowheads; preforms of transverse arrowheads (truncated proximal ends of flakes); unilateral/bilateral crested blades; Nøstvet axeheads; and segment knives.

Typology: absence
Sandstone knives are absent.

Typology: frequencies
During the LM B, regular microblade cores are gradually replaced by irregular macroblade cores.

Technology
The blade technology in LM B develops from a microblade technology (profiles 4 and 5, cf. above) to a macroblade technology (profile 6) (Ballin 1999a). The type site for this phase, Gjølstad R33, belongs to the later part of the phase (profile 6) and it has the following attributes: average blade width: 11.8 mm; average flaking angle: 76°; ridge index (regularity): 1.47 (regular blades – later Neolithic sites belonging to this profile are decidedly irregular); platform edge preparation: fine trimming; platform surface preparation: coarse faceting; technique: indirect technique dominates but it is supplemented by direct technique. In the assemblage from Gjølstad R33 there is a very low percentage of bipolar cores (13% of bipolar cores + platform cores). In all other assemblages analysed by the author there are more than 45 per cent of bipolar cores. This frequency is supported by the finds

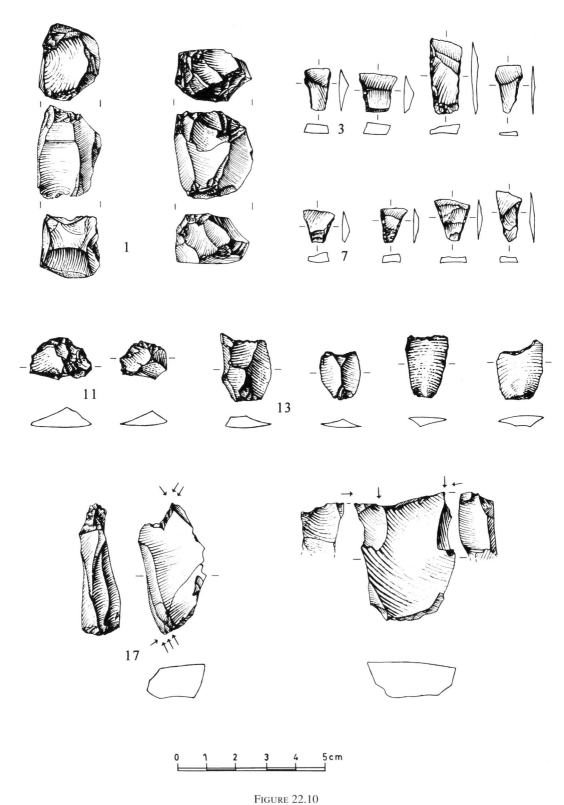

FIGURE 22.10

Typical late Mesolithic (LM B) assemblage – Gjølstad R33 (Ballin 1999a). Key: 1–2 barrel-shaped opposed-platform cores; 3–10 transverse arrowheads; 11–12 flake scrapers; 13–16 rough-outs for transverse arrowheads (proximal ends of flakes); and 17–18 burins (17 shows how a plunging burin spall has split the tool diagonally).

from the Halden Project (Inge Lindblom pers. comm.), and it must be considered diagnostic to the phase.

Raw material preference
In east Norway, south Norway, and western Sweden, raw material preference is totally dominated by the use of flint (Gjølstad R33: *c*.99 per cent). In west Norway transverse arrowheads are extremely rare, and this region is probably not part of this chronological unit.

Comments
Core axeheads are present in western Sweden, and possibly flake axeheads are introduced here during LM B. The Lihult axehead (i.e. Nøstvet axehead) is replaced by the south Scandinavian Limhamn axehead (a flaked-and-ground axehead type).

The relevance of Norwegian chronology to Scottish Mesolithic research

This discussion can be subdivided into two parts, that is, the question of direct relevance (i.e. whether it may be possible to prove any direct contact between the two regions), and methodological relevance.

Direct relevance
Direct contact between southern Norway and Scotland has not yet been demonstrated, but the possibility of this contact has been discussed in papers on either side of the North Sea (Bjerck 1995; Wickham-Jones 1994, 50). The hypothesis about direct contact is primarily based on the eustatic situation in the Preboreal with vast quantities of water being stored in the polar caps, thus draining the North Sea Basin. This drained area is frequently referred to as the North Sea Continent. Southern Norway and the North Sea Continent were separated by a narrow channel ('Norskerenna'), and even though the boat types of that time were simple (hide boats or log boats), it would have been possible to cross this barrier.

The early Mesolithic of southern Norway is relatively well documented, and any analysis of possible contact between the two regions would have to focus on typological and technological attributes. Typologically this phase is characterized by plain tanged arrowheads, Zonhoven points, single-edged points, lanceolates, and microburins, as well as core and flake axeheads. Stone axeheads and borers are absent. Technologically the phase is characterized by simple macroblade technology based on flat, unilateral opposed-platform cores which around the transition EM/MM A are replaced by large conical cores with acute flaking angles (70–78°). Bipolar technology is known but not as frequently applied as in the later Mesolithic phases.

The Early Mesolithic of Scotland is still fairly weakly documented, and the question of contact can therefore not be dealt with yet. However, any contact would have to have occurred before the transition EM/MM A, as the MM A of southern Norway is characterized by the presence of 'hulling-point' microliths, whereas the contemporary microlith type in Scotland is the isosceles triangle, as in southern Scandinavia and Europe in general. In MM B scalene triangles are introduced in southern Norway, but they are produced without the application of microburin technique, whereas scalene triangles are made using the microburin technique in Scotland as well as in southern Scandinavia and Europe.

A test of a possible contact between the two regions would have to concentrate on diagnostic types such as plain tanged arrowheads, single-edged points, and flake axeheads as well as attribute analysis of early Mesolithic blade populations on either side of the North Sea. Attribute analysis of early Mesolithic blade populations has not been undertaken by the author, as the early Mesolithic was not covered by the archaeological finds of south Norway (the Farsund Project).

Methodological relevance
At present the question of direct contact between southern Norway and Scotland is unclarified, and the relevance of the Mesolithic chronology of southern Norway to Mesolithic research in Scotland lies primarily in the methodological field. In the chronological work concerning the British Mesolithic, two issues especially have been addressed, namely the changing microlith types and the average width of the blades. For the moment chronological research seems to be in a cul-de-sac. It is the author's opinion that this situation may be changed by tightening definitions (a more comprehensive and stringent conceptual framework) and an increased degree of detail in the typological and technological fields.

In the typological field a proper and all-encompassing lithic classification system should be constructed, so that definitions of all types and sub-types are unequivocal. For example, the British definition of the microlith is slightly 'flimsy', and different morphological and functional types can be gathered under this concept, with significant repercussions in the discussion of cultural history. For instance, it is frequently discussed whether Mesolithic groups may have survived into the Neolithic period, largely based on discussion of whether microliths were produced in the Neolithic (e.g. Pollard 1997, 100).

The author suggests that the definition of the chronologically important microlith is adjusted to:

> due to their small sizes, microliths are lithic artefacts manufactured to form part of composite tools, either

as points or as edges/barbs; they generally conform to a restricted number of forms or sub-types, shaped by blunting retouch, and they are in most cases made on bladelets; the tips of the microliths were manufactured by removing usually the proximal end, and this process was commonly carried out in microburin technique.

Following this definition, transverse arrowheads are not microliths, as they were not produced on bladelets but on blades or flakes, and they were never produced in microburin technique; they are, as the name implies, arrowheads. In the same way, backed bladelets (sometimes called 'rods') are not microliths either, as they have not had the proximal end removed; artefacts classified as 'rod fragments' may just as well derive from other artefact types such as small borers or drill tips. The scalene triangles of southern Norway are probably the only 'microliths' in Europe produced without ever applying the microburin technique.

With the above definition, the British microliths can be restricted to the Mesolithic period, and the microlithic sub-types may be used in the construction of a proper chronological framework for the British/Scottish Mesolithic. But the typological work must be expanded to encompass other, potentially diagnostic, artefact categories (see above, Fig. 22.3).

Technological work should concentrate around attribute analysis of blades from relatively small settlements, which distribution analysis (horizontal stratigraphy) has rendered probable that they are chronologically 'clean'. Blade samples from 'clean' sites will have a homogenous appearance, and in addition to defining technological profiles of type sites, the approach may help in deselecting sites that are of no value to chronological research. For example, a curve diagram of the widths of blades from a chronologically 'clean' site will normally take the shape of a regular bell, whereas a mixed site may show a curve with more than one peak (Note 9). In the same way a point diagram of a 'clean' site will normally show a single dense cluster, whereas a mixed site may show more than one cluster (Fig. 22.11).

It is highly likely that many of the classic Scottish and English Mesolithic settlements represent finds accumulated over several phases, and it is an important secondary task for technological analysis to separate 'clean' sites from mixed sites – perhaps combined with comprehensive distribution analysis (horizontal stratigraphy) – as many Mesolithic sites have a weakly developed vertical stratigraphy.

It is the author's hope that increased use of detailed typo-technological attribute analysis of Scottish Mesolithic assemblages will allow further sub-division of the Scottish Mesolithic period. A more detailed chronological framework would be a practical tool for analysts investigating the Scottish Mesolithic.

Notes

1. 'Hulling-point' is a Scandinavian term for a large lanceolate with a barb retouched on one lateral side approximately one third from the tip (Ballin 1999c). The side with the barb is usually fully retouched, and the opposite side unretouched. Some pieces have basal retouch. Most 'hulling-points' are made by microburin technique.

2. The term 'Early Microblade Tradition' has been criticized by the author (Ballin 1999a) as this phase is equally characterized by blades and microblades, in contrast to the Late Microblade Tradition during which only microblades were produced (see below).

3. Over thousands of years most minerals (and thereby colours, textures, etc.) have been washed out of the Norwegian soil, forming more or less compact layers of iron pan. Due to this geological process, Mesolithic sites with intact layering, or features such as postholes, are rarely found.

4. The tri-partite sub-division of diagnostic artefacts is based on the Scandinavian chronological terminology: the Mesolithic, Neolithic, Bronze Age, and Iron Age are referred to as periods – sub-divisions within these periods are referred to as phases (e.g. the Norwegian middle Mesolithic) or sub-phases (e.g. the Norwegian middle Mesolithic A). In the present paper, the terms 'period' and 'phase' or 'sub-phase' are used according to Scandinavian terminology.

5. As a control of this assumption, Lundevågen R21/22 was chosen for testing, and the total blade material and the intact blades (12 per cent) were compared. This examination showed that the intact blades were simpler at all levels. The intact blades were broader and thicker, and they had fewer dorsal ridges, more cortex, more acute angles of percussion, more direct-percussion indicators, and simpler preparation of platform edge and surface. Based on these results, it must be assumed that the intact blades were also the shortest.

6. 'The length-width ratio is $\geq 2:1$. For more than $\frac{2}{3}$ of their length the sides of the artefact are approximately rectilinear. One or more ridges run parallel to the sides.'

7. The smaller the W:T ratio, the thicker the blade (relatively).

8. The smaller the W:D ratio, the plumper the platform remnant (relatively).

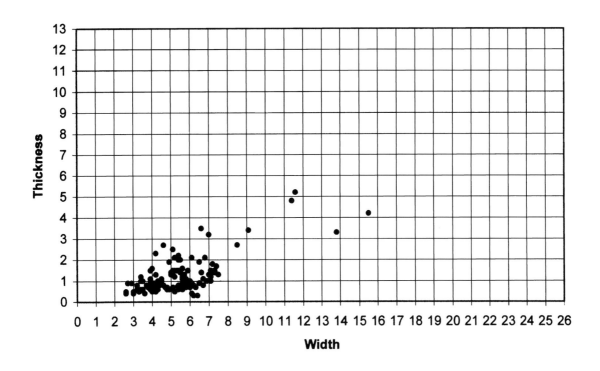

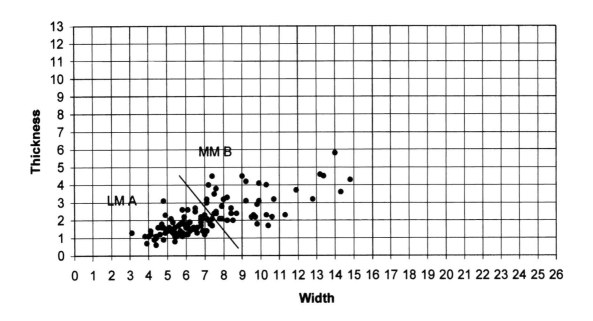

FIGURE 22.11

Examples of width:thickness ratios for chronologically 'clean' and mixed sites. Upper: Frebergsvik IIb/IV. W:T ratio for a chronologically 'clean' site (LM A); lower: Vindenes 55. W:T ratio for a mixed site (MM B/LM A).

9. At present, the fluctuation of blade dimensions through time is an insufficiently explained fact based on observations of blade populations from chronologically 'clean' sites (Andersen 1982; Ballin 1995a; 1999a). As demonstrated here, this fact forms an important tool in analysis of site chronology. Andersen (1982) suggests that the fluctuation of Danish blade dimensions may represent adaptation to changes in microlith and arrowhead size and typology. The present author suggests that the explanation of the fluctuating Norwegian blade dimensions may represent adaptation to changes in microlith and arrowhead typology combined with changing raw material availability (e.g. continuously decreasing flint resources, increasing use of local raw materials, and increasing import of Danish flint in the second half of the Neolithic). The general use in Britain (Mellars 1974) of the terms 'broad blade assemblages' (Early) and 'narrow blade assemblages' (Later) indicates that gradual fluctuation of blade dimensions is a phenomenon in Britain as well.

References

Alsaker, S. 1987. *Bømlo. Steinalderens Råstoffsentrum på Sørvestlandet.* Bergen: Universitetet i Bergen (Arkeologiske avhandlinger fra Historisk Museum **4**).

Andersen, K. 1982. Mesolitiske flækker fra Åmosen. *Aarbøger for Nordisk Oldkyndighed og Historie* **1982**, 5–18.

Andersen, K. 1983. *Stenalderbebyggelsen i den vestsjællandske Åmose.* København: Fredningsstyrelsen.

Andersson, S., Rex-Svensson, K. and Wigforss, J. 1978. Sorteringsschema för flinta. *Fynd rapporter* **1978**, 217–52.

Bakka, E. and Kaland, P.E. 1971. Early farming in Hordaland, western Norway. Problems and approaches in archaeology and pollen analysis. *Norwegian Archaeological Review* **4**(2), 1–35.

Ballin, T.B. 1995a. Beskrivelse og analyse af skævtrekanterne fra Farsund. *Universitetets Oldsaksamling Årbok* **1993/1994**, 79–90.

Ballin, T.B. 1995b. Teknologiske profiler. Datering af stenalderbopladser ved attributanalyse. *Universitetets Oldsaksamling Årbok* **1993/1994**, 25–46.

Ballin, T.B. 1996. *Klassifikationssystem for stenartefakter.* Oslo: Universitetets Oldsaksamling, Varia **36**.

Ballin, T.B. 1997a. Mikroflækkerne på Båtevik II. Reflektioner omkring et depotfund. *Universitetets Oldsaksamling Årbok* **1995/1996**, 15–30.

Ballin, T.B. 1997b. Mikroliter. Diskussion af et begreb. *Universitetets Oldsaksamling Årbok* **1995/1996**, 7–13.

Ballin, T.B. 1999a. *Kronologiske og Regionale Forhold i Sydnorsk Stenalder. En Analyse med Udgangspunkt i Bopladserne ved Lundevågen (Farsundprosjektet).* Unpublished PhD thesis, Institute of Prehistoric Archaeology, Aarhus University.

Ballin, T.B. 1999b. The Middle Mesolithic in Southern Norway. *In* J. Boaz (ed.), *The Mesolithic of Central Scandinavia*, 203–16. Oslo: Universitetets Oldsaksamlings Skrifter, Ny rekke **22**.

Ballin, T.B. 1999c. The artefactual material. Blade technology. Distribution analysis. Dating. Chronological and geographical distribution of 'Hulling-points'. *In* E. Mikkelsen, T.B. Ballin and A.K. Hufthammer, Tørkop. A Boreal settlement in south-eastern Norway. *Acta Archaeologica* **70**, 29–43.

Ballin, T.B. and Lass Jensen, O. 1995. *Farsundprosjektet – stenalderbopladser på Lista.* Oslo: Universitetets Oldsaksamling, Varia **29**.

Bang-Andersen, S. 1990. The Myrvatn Group, a Preboreal find-complex in southwest Norway. *In* P.M. Vermeersch and P. Van Peer (eds), *Contributions to the Mesolithic in Europe*, 215–26. Leuven: Leuven University Press.

Barton, C.M. 1988. *Lithic Variability and Middle Paleolithic Behaviour: New Evidence from the Iberian Peninsula.* Oxford: British Archaeological Reports (International Series **S408**).

Berg, E. 1995. *Dobbeltspor/E6-prosjektet. Steinalderlokaliteter fra senmesolittisk tid i Vestby, Akershus.* Oslo: Universitetets Oldsaksamling, Varia **32**.

Bergsvik, K.A. 1995. Bosetningsmønstre på kysten av Nordhordland i steinalder. En geografisk analyse. *In* K.A. Bergsvik, S. Nygaard and A.J. Nærøy (eds), *Steinalderkonferansen i Bergen 1993*, 111–30. Bergen: Arkeologiske Skrifter **8**, Arkeologisk Institutt, Universitetet i Bergen.

Bjerck, H.B. 1983. *Kronologisk og geografisk fordeling av mesolitiske element i Vest- og Midt-Norge.* Upubliceret magistergradsafhandling. Historisk Museum, Universitetet i Bergen.

Bjerck, H.B. 1986. The Fosna-Nøstvet problem. A consideration of archaeological units and chronozones in the south Norwegian Mesolithic period. *Norwegian Archaeological Review* **19**(2), 103–21.

Bjerck, H.B. 1995. The North Sea Continent and the pioneer settlement of Norway. *In* A. Fischer (ed.), *Man and Sea in the Mesolithic*, 131–44. Oxford: Oxbow Books (Oxbow Monograph **53**).

Bjerck, H.B. and Ringstad, B. 1985. *De kulturhistoriske undersøkelsene på Tjernagel, Sveio.* Bergen: Historisk Museum, Universitetet i Bergen (Arkeologiske Rapporter **9**).

Blankholm, R., Blankholm, E. and Andersen, S.H. 1967. Stallerupholm. Et bidrag til belysning af Maglemosekulturen i Østjylland. *Kuml* **1967**, 61–115.

Brinch Petersen, E. 1966. Klosterlund – Sønder Hadsund – Bøllund. Les trois sites principaux du Maglémosien ancien en Jutland. Essai de typologie et de chronologie. *Acta Archaeologica* **37**, 77–185.

Bruen Olsen, A. 1992. *Kotedalen – en boplass gjennom 5000 år. Bind 1. Fangstbosetning og tidlig jordbruk i Vestnorsk steinalder: nye funn og nye perspektiver.* Bergen.

Bruen Olsen, A. and Alsaker, S. 1984. Greenstone and diabase utilization in the Stone Age of western Norway: technological and sociocultural aspects of axe and adze production and distribution. *Norwegian Archaeological Review* **17**(2), 71–103.

Freundt, E.A. 1948. Komsa – Fosna – Sandarna. Problems of the Scandinavian Mesolithicum. *Acta Archaeologica* **19**, 1–68.

Fuglestvedt, I. 1995. Svevollen – spor av senmesolittisk bosetning i lavlandets indre skogssone. *In* K.A. Bergsvik, S. Nygaard and A.J. Nærøy (eds), *Steinalderkonferansen i Bergen 1993*, 95–110. Bergen: Arkeologiske Skrifter **8**, Arkeologisk Institutt, Universitetet i Bergen.

Gjessing, G. 1945. *Norges Steinalder.* Oslo: Norsk Arkeologisk Selskap.

Glob, P.V. 1952. *Danske Oldsager II: Yngre Stenalder.* København: Gyldendalske Boghandel, Nordisk Forlag.

Hagen, A. 1967. *Norges Oldtid.* Oslo: J.W. Cappelens Forlag.

Hansen, A.M. 1904. *Landnåm i Norge. En Utsigt over Bosætningens Historie.* Kristiania: W.C. Fabritius & Sønner A/S.

Hartz, S. 1987. Neue spätpaläolitische Fundplätze bei Ahrenshöft, Kreis Nordfriesland. *Offa* **44**, 5–52.

Hayden, B. 1984. Are emic types relevant to archaeology? *Ethnohistory* **31**(2), 79–92.

Helskog, K., Indrelid, S. and Mikkelsen, E. 1976. Morfologisk klassifisering av slåtte steinartefakter. *Universitetets Oldsaksamling Årbok* **1972/1974**, 9–52.

Higgs, E.S. and Vita-Finzi, C. 1972. Prehistoric economies: a territorial approach. *In* E.S. Higgs (ed.), *Papers in Economic Prehistory*, 27–36. Cambridge: Cambridge University Press.

Hill, J.N. and Evans, R.K. 1972. A model for classification and typology. *In* D.L. Clarke (ed.), *Models in Archaeology*, 231–73. London: Methuen.

Hodder, I. 1979. Economic and social stress and material culture patterning. *American Antiquity* **44**(3), 446–54.

Indrelid, S. 1978. Mesolithic economy and settlement patterns in Norway. *In* P. Mellars (ed.), *The Early Postglacial Settlement of Northern Europe*, 147–76. London: Duckworth.

Indrelid, S. 1990. *Katalogiseringsnøkkel for steinartefakter fra steinalder og bronsealder. Foreløpig utkast til første del.* Bergen: Historisk Museum, Universitetet i Bergen.

Jaksland, L. 2001. *Vinterbrolokalitetene – en kronologisk sekvens fra mellom- og senmesolitikum i Ås, Akershus.* Oslo: Universitetets Oldsaksamling, Varia **52**.

Keeley, L. H. 1980. *Experimental Determination of Stone Tool Uses. A Microwear Analysis.* Chicago: University of Chicago Press.

Larsson, L. 1978. *Ageröd I:B – Ageröd I:D. A Study of Early Atlantic Settlement in Scania.* Lund (Acta Archaeologica Lundensia, Series in 4°, **12**).

Larsson, L. 1990. The Mesolithic of southern Scandinavia. *Journal of World Prehistory* **4**(3), 257–309.

Lindblom, I. 1984. Former for økologisk tilpasning i mesolitikum, Østfold. *Universitetets Oldsaksamling Årbok* **1982/1983**, 43–86.

Lomborg, E. 1973. *Die Flintdolche Dänemarks. Studien über Chronologie und Kulturbeziehungen des südskandinavischen Spätneolitikums.* København: H.J. Lynge og Søn (Nordiske Fortidsminder, Serie B – in quarto, Bind **1**).

Madsen, B. 1992. Hamburgkulturens flintteknologi i Jels. *In* J. Holm and F. Rieck, *Istidsjægere ved Jelssøerne*, 93–131. Haderslev (Skrifter fra Museumsrådet for Sønderjyllands Amt **5**).

Mathiassen, T. 1948. *Danske Oldsager I: Ældre Stenalder.* København: Gyldendalske Boghandel, Nordisk Forlag.

Mellars, P.A. 1974. The Palaeolithic and Mesolithic. *In* C. Renfrew (ed.), *British Prehistory: a New Outline*, 41–99. London: Duckworth.

Mikkelsen, E. 1975a. *Frebergsvik. Et mesolitisk boplassområde ved Oslofjorden.* Oslo: Universitetets Oldsaksamlings Skrifter, Ny rekke **1**.

Mikkelsen, E. 1975b. Mesolithic in South-eastern Norway. *Norwegian Archaeological Review* **8**(1), 19–35.

Müller, S. 1888. *Ordning af Danmarks Oldsager, I. Stenalderen.* København.

Nærøy, A.J. 1994. *Troll-prosjektet. Arkeologiske undersøkelser på Kollsnes, Øygarden k., Hordaland, 1989–1992.* Bergen: Arkeologiske Rapporter **19**.

Nielsen, P.O. 1977a. Die Flintbeile der frühen Trichterbecherkultur in Dänemark. *Acta Archaeologica* **48**, 61–138.

Nielsen, P.O. 1977b. De tyknakkede flintøksers kronologi. *Aarbøger for Nordisk Oldkyndighed og Historie* **1977**, 5–71.

Nummedal, A. 1924. Om flintpladsene. *Norsk Geologisk Tidsskrift* **7** (1922–23), 89–141.

Nummedal, A. 1929. Et steinaldersfunn i Ski. *Norsk Geologisk Tidsskrift* **10**, 474–81.

Nygaard, S. 1989. The Stone Age of northern Scandinavia: a review. *Journal of World Prehistory* **3**(1), 71–116.

Nygaard, S. 1990. Mesolithic western Norway. *In* P.M. Vermeersch and P. Van Peer (eds), *Contributions to the Mesolithic in Europe*, 227–37. Leuven: Leuven University Press.

Pollard, T. 1997. Excavation of a Neolithic settlement and ritual complex at Beckton Farm, Lockerbie, Dumfries & Galloway. *Proceedings of the Society of Antiquaries of Scotland* **127**, 69–121.

Prescott, C. 1996. Was there *really* a Neolithic in Norway? *Antiquity* **70**, 77–87.

Rasmussen, B. 1979. *Arkæologi. Gads Fagleksikon.* København: G.E.C. Gad.

Renfrew, C. 1977. Alternative models for exchange and spatial distribution. *In* T.K. Earle and J.E. Ericson (eds), *Exchange Systems in Prehistory*, 71–90. New York: Academic Press.

Rud, M. (ed.) 1979. *Jeg ser på Oldsager. Danske Oldsager i Tekst og Billeder.* København: Politikens Forlag.

Skaarup, J. 1979. *Flaadet. En tidlig Maglemoseboplads på Langeland.* Rudkøbing: Meddelelser fra Langelands Museum.

Skar, B. 1989. Foldsjøen 4A, en stenalderboplads i zonen mellem kyst og fjeld. *Viking* **52**, 7–21.

Skar, B. and Coulson, S. 1985. The early Mesolithic site Rørmyr II. A re-examination of one of the Høgnipen Sites, SE Norway. *Acta Archaeologica* **56**, 167–83.

Sollberger, J.B. and Patterson, L.W. 1976. Prismatic blade replication. *American Antiquity* **41**(4), 517–31.

Vang Petersen, P. 1993. *Flint fra Danmarks Oldtid.* København: Høst & Søn.

Voss, O. 1985. Typologi. *In* L. Hedeager and K. Kristansen (eds), *Arkæologi Leksikon*, 253–4. København: Politikens Danmarkshistorie.

Wickham-Jones, C.R. 1994. *Scotland's First Settlers.* London: Batsford/Historic Scotland.

Wiessner, P. 1983. Style and social information in Kalahari San projectile points. *American Antiquity* **48**(2), 253–76.

Zimmermann, A. 1987. Some aspects of the formation of flint assemblages. *Archaeologia Interregionalis* **1987**, 187–201.

Zvelebil, M. and Rowley-Conwy, P. 1984. Transition to farming in northern Europe: a hunter-gatherer perspective. *Norwegian Archaeological Review* **17**(2), 104–24.

Østmo, E. 1976. Torsrød. En senmesolittisk kystboplass i Vestfold. *Universitetets Oldsaksamling Årbok* **1972/1974**, 41–52.

Østmo, E. 1982. Megalittgraven på Skjeltorp i Skjeberg. *Viking* **46**, 5–35.

Østmo, E. 1984. En dysse på Holtenes i Hurum. Nytt lys over østnorsk traktbegerkultur. *Viking* **48**, 70–82.

Chapter 23

The Mesolithic Period in Poland as Seen From the Perspective of Peat-Bog Sites

ZOFIA SULGOSTOWSKA

Research on peat-bog sites, intensified during the last 15 years, has provided new data about the Late Pleistocene and Early Holocene environment, and about the behaviour of Mesolithic human groups and their relations to Palaeolithic and Neolithic societies. Excavations at Witów, Całowanie, Pobiel, Chwalim, Dudka, Łajty, Tłokowo, Miłuki, and Pławienko have revealed well-preserved organic remains which make possible the reconstruction of Mesolithic chronology, economy (hunting, fishing, and plant gathering), and transport, as well as burial rites and art. As a result of these investigations, reconstruction of the Polish Mesolithic in its European context has been significantly enhanced.

Introduction

Archaeological research problems are much the same around the globe. Field archaeologists working on the Mesolithic period hope to find sites with excellently preserved remains, to excavate them properly, to extract all possible information using diverse methods, and to publish them in a clear way. In my opinion the peat-bog sites are in this regard among the most desirable and informative. Investigating them is a relatively recent part of the Polish Mesolithic research tradition, as shown in summary fashion in Table 23.1.

During the 1920–30s, though several Final Palaeolithic sandy sites were excavated and a relevant Polish terminology was coined by Krukowski (1939), only a single Mesolithic site was excavated and French terminology, accepted for the Stone Age, was used for this period. It was not until after the Second World War that archaeological field work flourished. Professor Stefan Krukowski and his school (comprising almost all the authors of the main publications cited here) started excavations at Rydno, a hematite mine and flint processing complex (where excavations are still in progress), and also in the Vistula Valley. The name of Krukowski is well known due to the term *microburin de Krukowski*, but few know him as the creator in the 1930s

of a dynamic technological system of lithic artefact processing (see Lech & Partyka 1992), which would now be known as *chaîne opératoire*.

The results from this early fieldwork formed a base from which to establish a new taxonomic division of the Polish Mesolithic, related to other units used elsewhere in Europe but with local names. This was undertaken largely by two charming ladies, Hanna Więckowska and Maria Marczak (1965) from my own Institute of Archaeology and Ethnology, and by Stefan Kozłowski (1967) at Warsaw University. It was a time of intense – mainly typological – discussions. The weak point was chronology. The first ^{14}C measurements, accompanying environmental reconstruction of the Final Pleistocene and Early Holocene sites, were possible at the beginning of the 1970s with the recovery of suitable samples from multi-season excavations at Całowanie and Witów, where sandy deposits were in contact with organic sediments.

Results of Polish Mesolithic research were presented at the First International Symposium on the 'Mesolithic in Europe' organized in 1973 by Stefan Kozłowski in Warsaw, at which an important paper 'The Late Mesolithic: an example of multi-aspectual analysis of open air sites from sandy lowlands', was read and subsequently published by Schild *et al.* (1975). The research in this paper represented a major achievement because all possible analyses had been carried out: spatial analysis with refitting; investigation of the raw material economy; study of stone processing and functional analysis using use-wear; chronological assessment with a few ^{14}C dates; and the application of indirect data to the economy. However, this publication also showed the limits of sandy sites as the archaeological basis for prehistoric reconstruction.

Polish peat-bog sites

The tradition of excavating Mesolithic peat sites is now 40 years old. It started with sites known from earlier surface collections such as Całowanie, Witów, Pobiel,

TABLE 23.1

Chart summarizing the history of research on the Mesolithic period in Poland. During the period 1955–99 some 125 Mesolithic sites have been excavated.

FIELD WORK		MAIN PUBLICATIONS
XIX century (second half) Beginning of collecting from surface of sites		
1920	1926	**Kozłowski Leon** L'époque mésolithique en Pologne. L'Anthropologie.
	1928	**Antoniewicz Włodzimienz** Środkowa epoka kamienia (Mezolit) [w:] Archeologia Polski.
Excavation at Ostrowo near Gdańsk - Józef Kostrzewski	1929	**Kostrzewski Józef** Nouvelles fouilles et découvertes en Poméranie Polonaise. Revue Anthropologique.
1930	1939	Od mezolitu do okresu wędrówek ludów, [w:] Prahistoria Ziem Polskich.
1950 **Large scale rescue excavations** **(Professor Stefan Krukowski & his school)** – Vistula Valley – dam and water retainers construction – Rydno – hematite mine and flint workshops area (1956 – continued by Romuald Schild, Halina Królik, Jacek Tomaszewski) **Peat-bog sites** **Witów** (1955–1964) Maria & Waldemar Chmielewski		
1960 **Całowanie** (1963–69, 1983, 1991) Romuald Schild	1967	**Więckowska Hanna, Marczak Maria** Próba podziału kulturowego mezolitu Mazowsza.
Pobiel (1967–1985) Zbigniew Bagniewski	1967	**Kozłowski Stefan K.** Niektóre uwagi o polskim mezolicie (na marginesie referatu H. Więckowskiej i M.Marczak).
1970 **Systematic recording of surface sites** continued	1972	Pradzieje ziem polskich od IX do V tysiąclecia p.n.e. Warszawa.
	1973	**International Symposium „The Mesolithic in Europe"**
	1975	**Więckowska Hanna** Społeczności łowiecko-rybackie wczesnego holocenu, [w:] Prahistoria Ziem Polskich.
Chwalim (1975–1979) Michał Kobusiewicz	1975	**Kozłowski Stefan K., Kozłowski Janusz K.** Epoka kamienia na ziemiach polskich.
	1975	**Schild Romuald, Marczak Maria, Królik Halina** Późny mezolit. Próba wieloaspektowej analizy stanowisk piaskowych.
1980 **Northern Poland**	1981	**Cyrek Krzysztof** Uzyskiwanie i użytkowanie surowców krzemiennych w mezolicie dorzeczy Wisły i górnej Warty.
	1983	**Bagniewski Zbigniew** Mezolityczne społeczności myśliwsko-rybackie południowej części Pojezierza Kaszubskiego.
	1985	**Schild Romuald, Królik Halina, Marczak Maria** Kopalnia krzemienia czekoladowego w Tomaszowie.
Dudka (1986 – continued) Witold Gumiński & Jan Fiedorczuk	1985	**Więckowska Hanna** Osadnictwo późnopaleolityczne i mezolityczne nad dolną Narwią.
Łajty (1989 – continued) Zofia Sulgostowska	1989	**Kozłowski Stefan K.** Mesolithic in Poland. A new Approach.
1990 **Tłokowo** (1992–1998) Romuald Schild	1993	**Kobusiewicz Michał, Kabaciński Jacek** Chwalim. Subboreal hunter-gatherers of the Polish Plain.
Miłuki (1992 – continued) Jerzy Brzozowski & Jerzy Siemaszko	1996	**Schild Romuald** Radiochronology of the Early Mesolithic in Poland.
Pławienko (1993 – continued) Zbigniew Bagniewski	1997	**Galiński Tadeusz** Mezolit Europy.

440

and Chwalim. In the 1970s a new national project entitled 'Systematic Recording of Surface Sites' was begun. Polish territory was divided into 7km × 3km areas and all surface sites from the Stone Age to the 17th century AD were plotted onto maps at 1:25,000 scale. The example of NE Poland demonstrates the significance of the results. This was previously an archaeologically barren area with only a few stray finds of bone and antler objects, found during peat cutting. There were no lithic artefacts associated with these objects, which were dated palynologically (by the German scientist Hugo Gross (1939); this territory belonged to Germany at that time).

It was the ambition of Dr Elżbieta Kempisty, my late colleague, and I to find a Stone Age peat-bog site in this area. During systematic surface investigations started

FIGURE 23.1

Location of excavated Mesolithic peat-bog sites. Key: a – human remains; b – faunal remains; FP – Final Palaeolithic; M – Mesolithic; N – Neolithic; H – Hallstatt period. Całowanie, voi. Mazowieckie (FP+M), R. Schild excavations 1963–91; Chwalim, voi. Wielkopolskie (FP+M+N), M. Kobusiewicz excavations 1975–9; Dudka, voi. Warmińsko-Mazurskie (FP+M+N), W. Gumiński and J.Fiedorczuk excavations 1986-onwards; Łajty, voi. Warmińsko-Mazurskie (FP+M+H), Z. Sulgostowska excavations 1989–onwards; Miłuki, voi. Warmińsko-Mazurskie (M), J. Brzozowski and J. Siemaszko excavations 1992–onwards; Pobiel 10, voi. Dolnośląskie (M), Z. Bagniewski excavations 1967–85; Pławienko, voi. Zachodniopomorskie (M), Z. Bagniewski excavations 1993-onwards; Tłokowo, voi. Warmińsko-Mazurskie (M), R. Schild excavations 1992–8; Witów, voi. Łódzkie (FP+M), M. and W. Chmielewski excavations 1955–64.

441

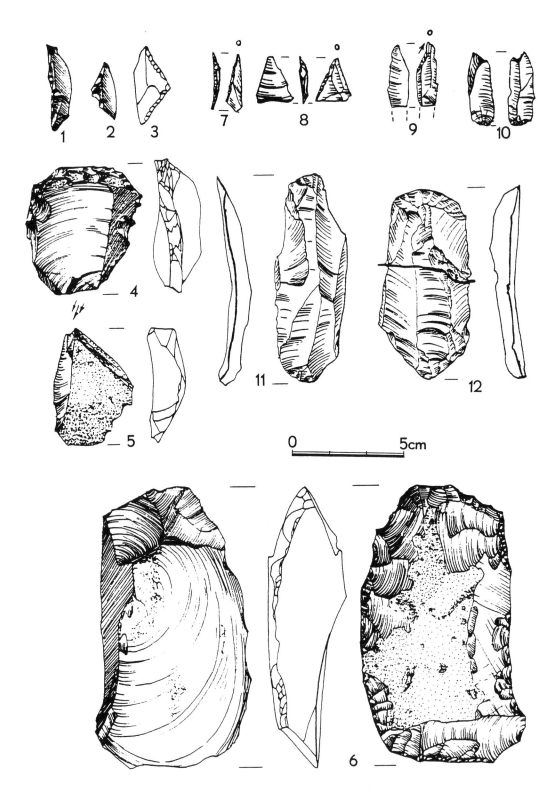

FIGURE 23.2

Lithic artefact inventory of the Early Mesolithic Narvian cycle (= Komornica culture). Chwalim: 1–3 microliths, 4 end scraper, 5 burin, 6 flake axehead (after Kobusiewicz & Kabaciński 1993); Łajty: 7–9 microliths, 10 microburin, 11 blade, 12 end scraper.

in the 1980s many new sites were recorded (Kempisty & Sulgostowska 1986). In view of the predominantly pastural landuse, it was only by searching the upcast from molehills that enabled us to find the site of Dudka, and by the inspection of drainage channels we located flint chips and burnt bones on a small island – the Łajty site. Another site, Tłokowo, was recorded by a farmer digging a well for water for his cattle.

The most promising sites, Dudka (Gumiński & Fiedorczuk 1989) and Łajty (Sulgostowska 1996), were excavated. The map (Fig. 23.1) shows the location of the sites discussed, which have not all received the same level of investigation. In the region of the Masurian lakeland, Warmińsko-Mazurskie voivodeship, four Mesolithic peat sites have been excavated during the last 13 years from a 3000km² area.

In Poland as a whole, 125 Mesolithic sites have been excavated in the period 1955–99, but peat sites constitute less than 10 per cent of these, and since not all of these have been published, information about the results of the excavations is not widely known. Nevertheless, these excavations are very important and are underpinning new syntheses of the Polish Mesolithic period. Multi-disciplinary research has provided new data about the Late Pleistocene and Early Holocene environment and the subsistence strategies of Mesolithic human groups. Because of the precise chronology obtained, the hypothesis about the refugial character of some regions has been revised and the relations between Late Mesolithic groups and Neolithic farmers have been established.

Finds from the peat sites corroborate the general subdivisions of the Polish Mesolithic, formed on the basis of lithic artefacts recovered from open-air sandy sites, the two main units of which are as follows. The Narvian cycle (= the Komornica culture), typical of the Early Mesolithic (Preboreal and Boreal), related to the Duvense or Maglemose tradition *sensu largo* – with a characteristic lithic technology of blades and double-platform cores and artefact inventories including end scrapers, burins, perforators, and blade insets – is known from the sites of Pobiel and Chwalim in central Poland and from Łajty in NE Poland (Fig. 23.2). Because of the peat sites, our knowledge about antler, bone, and wood processing has been greatly enlarged. Diverse types of harpoons, axeheads, points, arrowheads, chisels, daggers, hafts, and fish hooks were recorded at the sites of Chwalim, Pobiel, Dudka, and Tłokowo. The subsequent Vistulian cycle (= the Janisławice culture) from the Atlantic period is not yet represented by homogenous assemblages from any peat sites.

Economy

I shall focus on new data concerning the economy. Gatherer activity is confirmed by plant macrofossils recovered as charred remains in samples taken from Całowanie, Łajty, and Tłokowo, analysed by Kubiak-Martens (1998), which show that 20 different plants were gathered and prepared for consumption by grinding and probably by cooking. Among them are tubers of arrowhead (*Sagittaria sagittifolia*) at Całowanie and Łajty, and rhizomes of knotgrass/'bistort' (*Polygonum* sp.) at Całowanie and Łajty, of horsetail (*Equisetum* sp.) at Łajty, and of reedmace (*Typha* sp.) at Tłokowo. Also represented are seeds of bogbean (*Menyantes trifoliate*) at Całowanie and Łajty; and stinging nettle (*Urtica dioica*) at Tłokowo, flowerheads of the Valerianaceae family at Łajty, and fruits – wild strawberry (*Fragaria vesca/viridis*) at Całowanie and Łajty, and ?blackberry (*Rubus* sp.) at Łajty – were apparently gathered.

The animal-bone remains at most sites are very often highly fragmented and burnt. It seems that after having been burned they were crushed, ground, or pulverised to produce powder. This may have been consumed in order to supplement the calcium level in the Mesolithic diet, which was probably too low to cover the natural demand for this element. Hence the hypothesis that, for Mesolithic people, animal bones were a supplementary source of calcium (Lasota-Moskalewska *et al.* 1997).

It is impossible to establish the proportion of plants to meat in the Mesolithic diet, but the number of mammal bones from all the sites, as well as flint arrowheads, suggest that hunting was an important part of subsistence strategy. Table 23.2 shows the faunal remains and, because of the very diverse numbers of elements (at Dudka 772; at Pobiel 474; and less than 50 at Chwalim, Tłokowo, and Łajty), the percentages have been omitted. The dominant species were ruminants; mainly red deer, but wild boar was also important. Territorial diversities, either between the regions of NE or western Poland, or between peat sites and sandy sites, cannot be observed from these remains. The unique instance, outside of the peat sites, for faunal reconstruction in the Atlantic period is provided by the burial goods from Janisławice, comprising red deer, roe deer, aurochs, wild boar, beaver, and Mustelidae (Lasota-Moskalewska *et al.* 1985). Among fish remains, pike, which was speared during the spawning period in spring, is dominant in NE Poland (at Dudka and Tłokowo). The Mesolithic diet was also enriched by fowl, birds' eggs, and turtles at Pobiel (Bagniewski 1990) and Dudka (Gumiński 1995).

When we compare faunal remains from Polish sites with those from Latvia, Estonia, and northern Russia, where the predominance of elk is evident, it is unclear

TABLE 23.2
Faunal remains (game and fish) from Polish Mesolithic sites.

	Site	Dudka	Łajty	Tłokowo	Chwalim	Pobiel
PREBOREAL & BOREAL	Mammals	red deer wild boar roe deer elk ruminants horse wolf/dog otter/marten	red deer roe deer wild boar horse	roe deer red deer wild boar otter	red deer aurochs (European bison) elk	red deer wild boar beaver aurochs horse roe deer fox elk otter
	Fish	pike perch wels	—	pike	—	tench
ATLANTIC	Mammals	red deer ruminants elk wild boar wolf/dog roe deer	—	—	—	wild boar red deer aurochs beaver roe deer elk horse fox otter
	Fish	pike perch wels	—	—	—	—
Reference		Gumiński 1995	Sulgostowska 1996	Schild *et al.* 2003	Kobusiewicz & Kabacinski 1993	Bagniewski 1990

whether this was an effect of environmental determinism or the cultural tradition of the Kunda culture – the main East European Early Mesolithic unit. It is worth underlining that NE Poland is a territory where Maglemose and Duvensee traditions, named locally the Narvian-Komornician and Kunda cultures, had a very typical and efficient flint processing technology, in the Kunda culture using the pressure-flaking technique for producing excellent blades. Blade insets were an important part of the Kunda flint tool-kit, as shown by those in the Tłokowo bone point (Fig. 23.3), but also tanged points are recorded at Miłuki.

To summarize the economy, one can say that it demonstrates a complex exploitation of the environment, including land and water resources, with plant-gathering as an integral part of the subsistence strategy of the pre-agrarian groups. Sites were located near rivers, as at Całowanie, Chwalim, and Pobiel, or on lake margins. Water transport is confirmed by the wooden dugout at Dudka (Gumiński 1995) and by the oar blade from Pławienko (Bagniewski 1995). Wooden platform construction at Dudka and Tłokowo (Schild *et al.* 2003) suggests a well-organized society. Sites were occupied seasonally and Miłuki is the only site where a dwelling structure is reported (Brzozowski & Siemaszko 1996).

Burial practices

Mesolithic single graves and the unique Boreal cemetery at Mszano (Marciniak 1993) are located in sandy areas, though human remains were also found at Pobiel (two fragments of skull – apparently from the same infant).

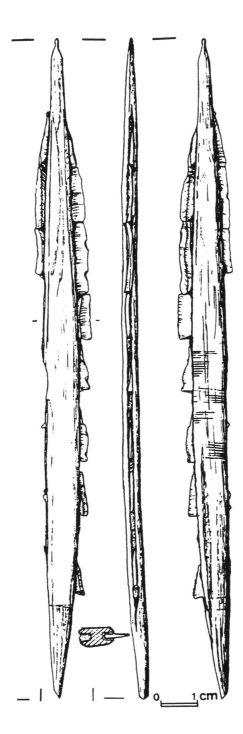

Figure 23.3
Tłokowo, voi. Warmińsko-Mazurskie. Bone point with flint insets
(after Sulgostowska & Hoffmann 1993; see also Sulgostowska
1996, fig. 5).

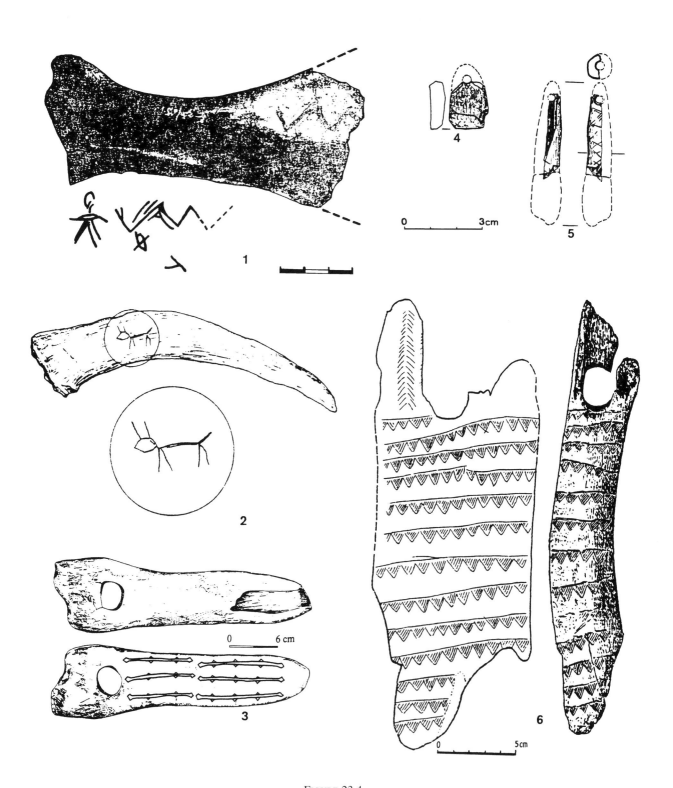

FIGURE 23.4

Antler, bone, and amber decorated objects: 1–2 Pobiel 10 bone and antler (after Bagniewski 1990); 3 Trudna bone 'hoe' (after Domańska 1974); 4–5 amber and bone pendants Dudka (after Fiedorczuk 1995); 6 Pułtusk red deer antler 'mattock' (after Sulgostowska & Polak 1983).

According to Bagniewski (1990) the child was probably drowned in the nearby river. A new hypothesis was presented by the excavator of Dudka (Gumiński 1999), who suggested that the fragmentation and dispersal of human bones, with a surplus of calottes and teeth over long bones, reflects a two-stage burial rite in which finally the skull was crushed and the rest of the skeleton burnt. At Dudka, among 270 fragments of human bones, only six (belonging to four individuals) are from Mesolithic strata. According to Gumiński (pers. comm.) the most recent excavation seasons at Dudka revealed graves with skeletons in a sitting position, probably of Boreal date.

Art

Decorated antler and bone objects continue to be found, both as stray finds or during systematic excavations (as at Pobiel, Trudna, and Pułtusk), as well as tooth and amber pendants (at Dudka). Anthropomorphic, zoomorphic, and geometric ornaments can of course be found from the Atlantic Ocean to Siberia and the perforated artefact from Pułtusk (Fig. 23.4, 6), decorated all over with pendant triangles, is an example of the *horror vacui* style associated with Maglemose art *sensu largo* (Sulgostowska & Polak 1983).

Palaeolithic–Mesolithic–Neolithic relations

Peat sites have a key role in discussions of what exactly we mean by the concepts of Palaeolithic, Mesolithic, and Neolithic culture in the Terminal Pleistocene to Early Holocene phases. With the ^{14}C dates now available, most of them from sealed peat sites, it is evident that at the very beginning of the Preboreal, Final Palaeolithic tanged points of the Mazovian/Swiderian tradition were still present. The Mesolithic Narvian tradition, beginning *c.*9600 BP in western Poland (at Chwalim), seems to begin perhaps *c.*150 ^{14}C years later in central Poland (at Całowanie), and *c.*300 ^{14}C years later in NE Poland (at Łajty). Chronological aspects of Palaeolithic–Mesolithic relations have been discussed by Schild (1996) and Sulgostowska (1999), and ^{14}C measurements for the Polish Mesolithic are summarized in Schild (1998).

The problem is how long the Mesolithic way of life continued. The initial dispersal of agriculture seems to be limited to some areas with fertile soils in southern and central Poland, Silesia, the Kraków region, and Kujawy. The Linear Pottery settlement at Strachów, Silesia (Kulczycka-Leciejewiczowa 1997), has produced very early ^{14}C measurements: 6535 ± 110 BP (Bln–1789); 6250 ± 110 BP (Bln–1790b); and 6160 ± 50 BP (Bln–

1788). However, sealed Sub-Boreal layers from the peat-sites of Chwalim (central Poland) and Dudka (NE Poland) suggest examples of a conservative, Mesolithic-style economy; some pottery was present, but together with animal remains indicating that big-game hunting, fishing, fowling, and turtle-collecting were still the basis of the economy. Similarly at Dudka (Gumiński 1998), in the period 2200–1800 BC, domestic animals (sheep/goat and dog) constituted less than 10 per cent of the fauna. At Chwalim (Kobusiewicz & Kabaciński 1993) domestic animals were also absent in the upper layer dated from 4630 ± 70 BP (Gd–1176) to 4280 ± 45 BP (Bln–2019). The environmental evidence indicates that both sites were visited repeatedly in spring or early summer (March–June). The lithic artefacts from Chwalim and Dudka, however, are not related to any from Late Mesolithic inventories (Schild 1998).

For this phenomenon of hunter-gatherers with pottery the terms 'Subneolithic' (Wiślanski 1979) and 'Paraneolithic' (Kempisty 1981) have been proposed. Nevertheless, using data from open sandy sites to demonstrate ostensibly unlikely cross-cultural associations in Polish prehistory, such as between Bronze Age pottery and Mesolithic lithic artefacts, is dangerous. The perils of dating open-air sandy sites have been discussed many times (e.g. Schild 1998) and it must be the case that the stratification of peat-bog sites, occupied from the Final Palaeolithic to the Hallstatt period, is the key to solving such problems.

Conclusion

The peat sites excavated and still being excavated in Poland will be the subject of more detailed studies in future, but thanks to them we have been able to draw closer to Mesolithic societies, which were both conservative and innovative, with a complex economy, social organization, arts and crafts, and complicated burial rites.

I have had the honour and pleasure to present the results of research on the Mesolithic peat-bog sites from various regions of Poland. I believe that peat-bog sites are the future of prehistoric research.

References

Antoniewicz, W. 1928. *Archeologia Polski. Zarys czasów przed-historycznych i wczesnośredniowiecznych ziem Polski.* Warszawa.

Bagniewski, Z. 1983. Mezolityczne społeczności myśliwsko-rybackie południowej części Pojezierza kaszubskiego. *Studia Archeologiczne* **12**, 1–141.

Bagniewski, Z. 1990. Obozowisko mezolityczne z doliny Baryczy. Pobiel 10, woj. leszczyńskie. *Studia Archeologiczne* **19**, 3–218.

Bagniewski, Z. 1995. Obozowisko kultury Oldesloe na terenie Pojezierza Dobiegniewskiego. *Śląskie Sprawozdania Archeologiczne* **36**, 85–105.

Brzozowski, J. and Siemaszko, J. 1996. Dolnomezolityczne obozowisko kultury kundajskiej w Miłukach, stanowisko 4, w świetle datowań dendrochronologicznych i radiowęglowych. *Zeszyty Naukowe Politechniki Śląskiej* (Seria: Matematyka-Fizyka **80**, Geochronometria **14**), 229–38.

Cyrek, K. 1981. Uzyskiwanie i użytkowanie surowców krzemiennych w mezolicie dorzecza Wisły i górnej Warty. *Prace i Materiały Muzeum Archeologicznego i Etnograficznego w Łodzi, Seria archeologiczna* **28**, 5–108.

Domańska, L. 1974. Motyka kościana z Trudnej, pow. Złotów. *Koszalińskie Zeszyty Muzealne* **3** (1973), 25–9.

Fiedorczuk, J. 1995. Mesolithic finds at Dudka 1, Great Masurian lakeland, and their chronological-taxonomic relations. *Przegląd Archeologiczny* **43**, 47–59.

Galiński, T. 1997. *Mezolit Europy*. Szczecin.

Gross, H. 1939. Moorgeologische Untersuchung der vorgeschichtlichen Dörfer im Zedmar-Bruch, Prussia. *Sitzungsberichte der Altertumsgesellschaft* **33**, 100–15.

Gumiński, W. 1995. Environment, economy and habitation during the Mesolithic at Dudka, Great Masurian lakeland, NE Poland. *Przegląd Archeologiczny* **43**, 5–46.

Gumiński, W. 1998. The peat-bog site Dudka, Masurian lakeland: an example of conservative ecomomy. *In* M. Zvelebil, L. Domańska and R. Dennell (eds), *Harvesting the Sea, Farming the Forest. The Emergence of Neolithic Societies in the Baltic Region*, 103–9. Sheffield: Sheffield Academic Press.

Gumiński, W. 1999. Scattered human bones on a prehistoric camp site, Dudka, NE Poland, an indication of a peculiar burial rite. *Symposium International Préhistoire: Pratiques Mortuaires. Mort: Paléolithique-Mésolithique-Néolithique, 12–16 Septembre 1999. Pré-Actes* (pages unnumbered). Leuven.

Gumiński, W. and Fiedorczuk, J. 1989. Dudka 1: a Stone Age peat-bog site in north-eastern Poland. *Acta Archaeologica* **60**, 51–70.

Kempisty, E. 1981. Review of T. Wiślański, *Krąg Ludów Subneolitycznych w Polsce. Archeologia Polski* **26**(2), 436–44.

Kempisty, E. and Sulgostowska, Z. 1986. Badania rozpoznawcze wokół torfowiska Łąki Staświńskie, woj. Suwałki. *Sprawozdania Archeologiczne* **38**, 57–76.

Kobusiewicz, M. and Kabaciński, J. 1993. *Chwalim: Subboreal Hunter-Gatherers of the Polish Plain*. Poznań: Institute of Archaeology and Ethnology, Polish Academy of Sciences.

Kostrzewski, J. 1929. Nouvelles fouilles et découvertes en Poméranie polonaise. *Revue Anthropologique* **39**, 383–97.

Kostrzewski, J. 1939. Od mezolitu do wędrówek ludów. *In* J. Kostrzewski (ed.), *Prahistoria Ziem Polskich, z.1, Encyklopedia Polska* PAU **4**, 118–359. Kraków: Akademii Umiejętności.

Kozłowski, J.K. and Kozłowski, S.K. 1975. *Epoka Kamienia na Ziemiach Polskich*. Warszawa: Państwowe Wydawnictwo Naukowe.

Kozłowski, L. 1926. L'époque mésolithique en Pologne. *L'Anthropologie* **36**, 47–74.

Kozłowski, S.K. 1967. Niektóre uwagi o polskim mezolicie (na marginesie referatu H. Więckowskiej i M. Marczak). *Materiały do prahistorii plejstocenu i wczesnego holocenu Polski*, 33–51. Warszawa-Wrocław: Ossolinium.

Kozłowski, S.K. 1972. *Pradzieje ziem Polskich od IX do V Tysiąclecia p.n.e.* Warszawa: Państwowe Wydawnictwo Naukowe.

Kozłowski, S.K. 1989. *Mesolithic in Poland: a New Approach*. Warszawa: Wydawnictwa Uniwersytetu Warszawskiego.

Krukowski, S. 1939. Paleolit. *In* J. Kostrzewski (ed.), *Prahistoria Ziem Polskich, z.1, Encyklopedia Polski* PAU **4**, 1–117. Kraków: Akademii Umiejętności.

Kubiak-Martens, L. 1998. Botanical Component of Hunter-Gatherer Subsistence Strategies in Temperate Europe during the Late Glacial and Early Holocene (Evidence from Selected Archaeological Sites). Unpublished PhD thesis, Poznań University.

Kulczycka-Leciejewiczowa A. 1997. *Strachów – Osiedle Neolitycznych Rolników na Śląsku*. Wrocław: Instytut Archeologii i Etnologii PAN.

Lasota-Moskalewska, A., Kobryń, H. and Świeżyński, K. 1985. Zabytki pochodzenia zwierzęcego z grobu mezolitycznego w Janisławicach, woj. skierniewickie. *Archeologia Polski* **30**(2), 287–309.

Lasota-Moskalewska, A., Kobryń, H., Sulgostowska, Z., Siemaszko, J. and Brzozowski, J. 1997. Animal bones as a source of calcium for Mesolithic man. *Przegląd Archeologiczny* **45**, 25–32.

Lech, J. and Partyka, J. 1992. *Prof. Stefan Krukowski (1890–1982): Działalność Archeologiczna i jej Znaczenie dla Nauki Polskiej*. Ojców: Ojcowski Park Narodowy, Prace i Materiały Muzeum im Prof. Władysława Szafera.

Marciniak, M. 1993. Mesolithic burial and dwelling structure from the Boreal period excavated at Mszano site 14, Toruń district, Poland: preliminary report. *Mesolithic Miscellany* **14**, 7–11.

Schild, R. 1996. Radiochronology of the Early Mesolithic in Poland. *In* L. Larsson (ed.), *The Earliest Settlement of Scandinavia and its Relationship with Neighbouring Areas*, 285–95. Stockholm: Almquist and Wiksell International (=*Acta Archaeologica Lundensia*, series in 8°, No. **24**).

Schild, R. 1998. The perils of dating open-air sandy sites of the North European Plain. *In* M. Zvelebil, L. Domańska and R. Dennell (eds), *Harvesting the Sea, Farming the Forest. The Emergence of Neolithic Societies in the Baltic Region*, 71–6. Sheffield: Sheffield Academic Press.

448

Schild, R., Marczak, M. and Królik, H. 1975. *Późny Mezolit. Próba Wieloaspektowej Analizy Otwartych Stanowisk Piaskowych*. Wrocław-Warszawa: Ossolineum.

Schild, R., Krolik, H. and Marczak, M. 1985. *Kopalnia Krzemienia Czekoladowego w Tomaszowie*. Warszawa-Wrocław: Ossolineum.

Schild, R., Tobolski, K., Kubiak-Martens, L., Bratlund, B., Eicher, U., Calderoni, G., Makowiecki, D., Pazdur, A. & M.M., Schweingruber, F.H., Van Neer, W., Winiarska-Kabacińska, M. and Żurek, S. 2003. Harvesting pike at Tłokowo. *In* L. Larsson et al. (eds), *Mesolithic on the Move: Papers Presented at the Sixth International Conference on the Mesolithic in Europe, Stockholm 2000*, 149–55. Oxford: Oxbow Books.

Sulgostowska, Z. 1996. The earliest Mesolithic settlement of north-eastern Poland. *In* L. Larsson (ed.), *The Earliest Settlement of Scandinavia and its Relationship with Neigbouring Areas*, 297–304. Stockholm: Almquist and Wiksell International (=*Acta Archaeologica Lundensia*, Series in 8°, No. **24**).

Sulgostowska, Z. 1999. Final Palaeolithic/Early Mesolithic relations in the eastern Subbalticum Basin. *Proceedings of the XIII Congress UISPP. Vol. III*, 9–16.

Sulgostowska, Z. and Hoffmann, M. 1993. Kościane ostrze mezolityczne z wkładkami krzemiennymi z Tłokowa, woj. Olsztyńskie – aspekt technologiczny. *Archeologia Polski* **38**, 75–88.

Sulgostowska, Z. and Polak, Z. 1983. Ornamentowana motyka rogowa z Narwi pod Pułtuskiem, woj. Ciechanowskie (A decorated horn mattock-head from the Narew River near Pułtusk, Ciechanów voivodeship). *Wiadomości Archeologiczne* **49** (2), 191–6.

Więckowska, H. 1975. Społeczności łowiecko-rybackie wczesnego holocenu. *In* W. Chmielewski and W. Hensel (eds), *Prahistoria Ziem Polskich, Vol. I. Paleolit i Mezolit*, 339–438. Warszawa-Wrocław-Kraków-Gdańsk: Ossolineum.

Więckowska, H. 1985. *Osadnictwo póznopaleolityczne i mezolityczne nad dolną Narwią*. Warszawa-Wrocław: Ossolineum.

Więckowska, H. and Marczak, M. 1965. Próba podziału kulturowego mezolitu Mazowsza. *In* W. Chmielewski (ed.), *Materiały do Prahistorii Polski w Plejstocenie i wczesnym Holocenie*, 9–45. Warszawa-Wrocław.

Wiślański, T. 1979. Krąg ludów subneolitycznych w Polsce. *In* W. Hensel and T. Wiślański (eds), *Prahistoria Ziem Polskich, Vol. II, Neolit*, 319–36. Wrocław-Warszawa.

Chapter 24

Conference Discussion Session: Saturday Morning, 6 September 1999
The Mesolithic Period in NW Europe and Britain: Regional Aspects: Session 1

CHAIR: PETER WOODMAN

[The first two speakers in this session were Torben Ballin and Lars Larsson]

PETER WOODMAN

We have had two very different types of papers [exhibiting] different priorities. Norwegian archaeology has a different set of priorities entirely from parts of southern Scandinavia, so you have an opportunity to question people about very different aspects of the Mesolithic of these regions. I must admit that working in north Norway I'm foregoing my temptation to actually get into typological discussion with Torben [Ballin] but if I could abuse my role as Chair for this morning by asking two short questions. The first one is: you said very coyly at the beginning of your lecture, that the Neolithic of course in many parts of southern Norway really still retained a Mesolithic economy. Do you think that rather like those of us working in the northern parts of Norway you would be better using the terms Older Stone Age and Younger Stone Age and ignoring the Mesolithic/Neolithic division, with all the meaning it tends to bring with it?

TORBEN BALLIN

Well, I think what I would suggest is that we keep the terminology we have, because if we start changing the terminology and start referring [to] sites we have formerly referred to as Neolithic and start calling them Mesolithic, we ...

PETER WOODMAN

I said maybe instead of calling them anything we use the term Younger Stone Age, which is what happens more in the north of Norway, and it doesn't carry with it all that baggage that the term Neolithic carries.

TORBEN BALLIN

Yes, I think that would not be a problem and it might be a good idea, because my research suggests that in southern Norway we don't see proper Neolithic economy until we get to about the end of the middle Neolithic, which is close to the very end of the Neolithic, so it is all a bit confusing. So maybe it would be a solution.

PETER WOODMAN

The other short question was: do you actually believe that the axe production, the polished stone axe production at Bømlo and Flora, really goes back to 9000 BP? I noticed on your diagram that it was dotted as you moved from 8000 to 9000. Do you really think polished stone axe production goes back to 9000? I have serious doubts.

TORBEN BALLIN

Well, I know that Asle Bruen Olsen and Sigmund Alsaker suggest that, but I'm well aware that we can't prove any stone axe production until we get to about the middle of what I call the middle Mesolithic, so it is still an open question.

PETER WOODMAN

But it is interesting that from then on there is this major production, these two major [axehead] production sites on the west coast.

TORBEN BALLIN   Yes, which carry on well into the Neolithic.

PAUL MELLARS   I have a question for Lars [Larsson]. Why do you think you have all these Mesolithic cemeteries in Scandinavia and we can't find them in Britain?

LARS LARSSON   Well, I don't really know, but I would say that you might have been looking in the wrong place! We discussed that together with Søren [Andersen] at breakfast and he said, 'Well it took a hundred years for the Scandinavian archaeologists to find them', so you have time!

PAUL MELLARS   So the next question is: where should we be looking for them that we are not looking now?

LARS LARSSON   Well, I don't know where you are looking for sites as such, but I think that if you look in the western part of Europe ... I have been working a bit in Portugal, for example, and I think you should look at lagoons, sites that would have been lagoons during the Late Mesolithic. And I would think that there might be possibilities to find submerged sites too. You mentioned that yourself yesterday, that there are a lot of sites that have been destroyed by the rise of the sea, but there might be good protection too, as for example Søren Andersen found in southern Fyn and at other sites where graves might exist. And I don't know if you have [made] the same mistakes as in Scandinavia where you have excavated an area too close to the former sea shore? You should perhaps excavate further up from the concentration of the settlement or the debitage.

NICK BARTON   I was wondering as well Lars [Larsson] whether you wanted to mention the fact that, according to our discussion this morning, that [Professor] Louwe Kooijmans is now finding Mesolithic burials [in the Netherlands] and of course there are Mesolithic burials from France that have recently been published as well, so I think they are around.

LARS LARSSON   Yes. In the example from the Netherlands they had, I think, to dig through something like four metres of peat down to the settlement, so it takes a lot of effort and a lot of money.

JANE MURRAY   Equally, however, I was very interested in your demonstration of regional variation, so that one does have to take on board the possibility of regional variation being something completely different.

LARS LARSSON   Well, I didn't really understand if that was a question or just a statement.

JANE MURRAY   A suggestion that one doesn't need to think there have to be burials waiting to be found, given that you have such variations in burial custom from one side of the strait from Sweden to Denmark, you can have a completely different set-up once you have crossed the North Sea.

LARS LARSSON   It could be, as I showed you [in my talk there are ethnographically attested instances of] burial in water or in the trees, but I don't think so. There should have been contacts. If you find graves along the North Atlantic coast from Norway down to Portugal, why not in the British Isles?

PETER WOODMAN   If I could maybe just pick up on Lars's [Larsson] point about where people have looked? I think I remember about a year or two years before the discovery of the Vedbæk cemetery, Eric Brinch Petersen carried out an excavation – I'm not sure if Lars remembers this – [there was] this fixation [with] excavating areas with good quality organic preservation down in low-lying areas where you were going to find all the animal bones, you were going to find the amber, you were going to find decorated bone objects. It's a very strong temptation and that's actually what there was [in this case] – a preliminary trial excavation carried out in the area they thought was important at Vedbæk Bøgebakken – and of course when the builders for the school turned up they weren't interested in building a school in a bog! They wanted to build on the top of the ridge and as soon as they went in, human remains started to come up on the top of this ridge. So it is often that we have had priorities in what we wanted – we wanted to repeat Star Carr and we have wanted to find those sorts of environments – but it is often the adjacent regions that will produce the burials.

ROGER JACOBI

Talking about the apparent absence of cemeteries in Britain, can I put in a plug for Aveline's Hole on the north side of Mendip, where there are watercolours made in the 1820s which show the cave to be full of skeletons? A count was made in the 1930s of the ear bones which were still in the University of Bristol Spelaeological Museum at that time and the total came to over 50 individuals being represented by burials. We do have a series of very coherent British Museum and Oxford radiocarbon dates which put the site at the Preboreal to early Boreal transition, so clearly in that case I think we do have at least one British Mesolithic cemetery site.

CLIVE BONSALL

I think part of the answer to Paul's [Mellars] question is that in Scotland and Britain generally we invest an awful lot of time and effort investigating shell middens and lithic scatters and I think probably what we are doing a lot of the time is we are just investigating the rubbish dumps of these sites, and in order to find the areas where people were actually living and where they were burying their dead I think we have to look beyond, we have to look outside these areas of immediate archaeological interest. Could I just follow up with a question for Lars [Larsson]? Your wooden constructions associated with burials; were they built right on top of the grave pits or were they built immediately adjacent?

LARS LARSSON

They were built on the top of the grave pit, and the reason why we can identify them is that there are partly burnt [timbers] or big pieces of charcoal – that could be combined to [reconstruct] trunks – in the filling of the grave, just when the filling-in has started. They have just put some sand on the interred and then they fired the structure. But there are posts that might just indicate a sort of marking of the grave as well. Adding to that there are several indications that there are fires being lit in the filling or just adjacent to the pit and the charcoal and [associated] material were deposited in the grave.

PETER WOODMAN

You mentioned that there were structures on top of some graves from northern Sweden?

LARS LARSSON

Yes, there have been some graves found from the same period in northern Sweden and there you have the stone setting, the layers of stone covering the grave – probably a marking or perhaps a protection from animals. These are [found] in excellent conditions where nothing has changed for the last 6000 years, so you have the area intact and you can see the stone settings, and there seem to be different shapes of stone settings as well, above the Mesolithic graves.

PAUL MELLARS

I think one of the critical questions about these graves and cemeteries you have got in south Scandinavia is whether or not [they are] reflecting a different kind of social system. I mean some people have associated cemeteries of that kind with either sedentary, large, almost village-like settlements, or as a reflection of territoriality. So one of the interesting questions is whether there is something in the ecology and demography of your areas which led to these high population densities, these sedentary or semi-sedentary occupations on the coast and reflecting territoriality that we are not getting in Britain. That's what I was really driving at, whether there's a kind of social complexity, as Peter Rowley-Conwy and others have argued, due to particularly high population densities perhaps [in turn] due to particularly productive ecological environments in south Scandinavia that we are not getting in Britain.

LARS LARSSON

Well, this is one of the maps I showed you and if you look at the sites shown with a thick ring ... The thin rings are the sites without graves, but those with the thick rings [are sites with graves in] environments with a lagoon at the Late Mesolithic, or a river mouth, or delta structure, something like that, with a high bio-mass production. And as we can see from the preserved remains of bones you have, for example at Skateholm, almost 90 species identified; so there's a variety, just as you mentioned yesterday. If something goes wrong then there's always something else to concentrate on; if fishing is bad for a season then you have hunting or fowling or something like that. I think that is very important, and [there is] territoriality probably because these areas must have attracted people, according to the large amount of debris and artefacts. I heard from my student – she has been working on 1300 transverse arrowheads and the excavated material on one of the sites was 1.8 tonnes of flint, so if it was a small family group then they have produced a lot of material. I think it is more like some families living on a site for maybe centuries. Another thing is, could it also be a sort of territorial marking against the change of the landscape because, at least at Skateholm and some other sites, you had a rather rapid change of the relation between land and water, and could it be a sort of marking against the rising of the sea level? Sort of trying to keep water down! Well, I know it's a crazy idea but there might be something to it!

PAUL MELLARS

Almost a sort of religious idea?

LARS LARSSON

Yes, something like that.

STEVEN MITHEN

On this question of the nature of the society we are dealing with, I'm always intrigued and amazed by the diversity of burial customs and practices, as one sees even within the different cemeteries of Skateholm. It always strikes me that this looks like we are dealing much more with family groups with their own particular burial practices that they are able to continue, and I'm almost surprised that you haven't got that over-arching, larger social, strong society that one would imagine would go with a complex society that we are talking about. So it strikes me there's always a slight conflict where the big cemetery, the settlement, suggests what Peter [Rowley-Conwy] and others would describe as a complex hunter-gatherer society, but this high degree of variability and diversity implies that individual families have got a high degree of independence from that. I wonder if you could comment on this almost paradox we have here?

LARS LARSSON

Yes, but Skateholm is a bit different from the other ones. If you look, for example, on the Danish sites there is not that variation. And there is this question that might be solved by doing DNA analysis. We have more or less the concentrations within Skateholm I, with 65 graves, where you can do something about it and it turns out that within each concentration, according at least to the study of the jaws and teeth, there seem to be related persons, [who] are genetically closely related. There also seems within such concentrations to be a variety of mortuary practice, so you can't say just one concentration has one kind of burial practice and the other concentration has another one, no.

STEVEN MITHEN

So why is Skateholm so different from the other cemeteries?

LARS LARSSON	I have been thinking about that for almost 20 years and I don't have any good answer! I thought that the new graves, the new cemeteries that have been excavated, should show something similar but they haven't, not really.
PETER WOODMAN	OK, I think we have had quite a number of interesting points. I think actually Steven [Mithen] has a very good point. I was just wondering, if we look at this in a slightly broader sense, we tend to be over-impressed by what we have found in the last 20 years because we didn't have these cemeteries before, but if you look actually at places like Olenii Ostrov, which even with what survives – and we tend to forget that a large chunk of that cemetery was gone by the time the excavations took place – there we're talking in hundreds, not in tens. If we look at some of the Russian or Ukrainian, I think it now is, evidence on the rivers there, we are talking about hundreds. Seen from that perspective the cemeteries in Western Europe are actually quite small and I think that Lars [Larsson] also made a very important point that maybe we were still inclined to look almost too much for simple economic ecological relationships or increasing populations. He did make the point and we shouldn't forget it that it's a mix of a number of different elements. And for example with Olenii Ostrov, it's on a tiny island in the middle of Lake Onega, and it's highly probable that it was an area where there was exchange between regions, at least with what we can see [from] what survives in the record. High-quality flint [from one region] coming in contact [at Lake Onega] with [artefacts from] another region, and the suggestion there is that the complexity is more to do with exchange, not to do with population densities. So I think we are probably just at the beginning of this.

[The final two speakers in this session were Søren Andersen and Zofia Sulgostowska]

PETER WOODMAN	OK, two more perspectives on the Mesolithic of areas adjacent to Scotland. Again we can see that there is diversity in approaches and priorities.
DEREK SIMPSON	Question for Professor Andersen. In view of the very low calorific value of shellfish, is it not likely that a high percentage of [shellfish in] these middens were used indirectly as bait rather than directly ingested by human beings?
SØREN ANDERSEN	Yes, why not? That is an idea which has been proposed several times and I'm very open for that.
STEVEN BIRCH	It's interesting that obviously on a lot of your [Danish] midden sites you are getting a lot of oyster shell remains, whereas on the Scottish sites you have a predominance of limpets. Obviously oysters you would think are more suitable for human consumption, whereas the limpets could have been for bait for fishing rather than for consumption.
SØREN ANDERSEN	Yes, but we don't have limpets in the Danish area.
PETER WOODMAN	There's no such thing as a large rock in Denmark actually, to attach them to!
UNIDENTIFIED MEMBER OF THE AUDIENCE	Following on from this limpet thing, or oysters and shells. Is it possible that they're actually a more cultural object, the equivalent of the 'pot noodle' if you like, not taken for their calorific value but more for their value in society. I mean, you get this whole thing of conspicuous consumption. Although the oysters are being used and eaten, the calorific content is low, but their social meaning could be fairly high … you get that as well.

SØREN ANDERSEN

Yes, I can answer that in a way by saying that in some areas of Australia the middens are used as territorial markers, so that's a social aspect associated with the middens, but I would rather turn the question around and say I don't think the meaning of collecting shellfish is a question of getting food, it is rather a question of getting minerals. Because minerals are much more essential for humans than calories. These guys have been fishing tonnes of fish, so these few calories from the shellfish are no use. So either they were just [eaten] to change the diet sometimes or it is more for the mineral input. I am much more in favour of the last aspect than the first one.

PETER WOODMAN

It is also true that by and large the shells tend to reflect the environment. In other words in places like Denmark or Strangford Loch in Ireland, you get oysters on that sort of soft muddy coastline, whereas in many parts of Scotland such as [where] Paul [Mellars] [has] worked on Oronsay, we've got these rocky shores where you get predominantly limpets. In fact, maybe one of the things we don't spend enough time [on] is looking at the atypical or non-typical discovery of shells which may well have got more significant social functions.

PATRICK ASHMORE

[Question to Dr Sulgostowska] Do you get structures outwith the settlement sites in your peat bogs, for instance trackways?

ZOFIA SULGOSTOWSKA

I think [there] is only one structure [known so far], at Miłuki, and it was a dwelling – but it is not yet fully published so you know I can't tell you [much about it]. But I think that mostly these peat sites are seasonal sites so [there perhaps] was no reason to put much work into such construction. As [the settlement location is] almost always a sandy island, and the people prefer to settle on the higher points with the sandy soil, [there is a lack of preservation of structural remains as] only in the areas near the water are [such organic] remains well preserved. I hope that probably we shall find some – such as at the Danish sites of Tybrind Vig or Ulkestrup – but it is the beginning of our [work on the] peat sites.

DAPHNE LORIMER

Could you say a little about the mineral content of shellfish as opposed to ordinary fish. What is it that they have got that is so special, what minerals?

SØREN ANDERSEN

I don't dare to give you details … but I think it's zinc and calcium … that's all the minerals I know!

PAUL HUMPHREYS

Is there any evidence for shellfish being transported to inland sites or are shells always consumed basically at the site of their collection?

SØREN ANDERSEN

Yes, there is a significant difference there between the Mesolithic and the Neolithic behaviour because from the Mesolithic period you always find the shells on the coast, on the beach so to say, but in the Neolithic you can find sites 400m, 500m, 1km from the coastline. So the attitude to shellfish changed in some way from the Mesolithic to the Neolithic, but don't ask me what that means!

CAROLINE WICKHAM-JONES

You were talking about – it is another shell midden related question I'm afraid – you were talking about the difference, if I understood it, between the Mesolithic and Neolithic shell middens; that you were getting a predominance of oyster in the Mesolithic and cockles in the Neolithic. Are you then saying that in the Mesolithic shell middens were exploited at different times of the year to the Neolithic, or is there an environmental change that's making them swing from one to another?

456

Discussion

Søren Andersen	At the moment we are doing very careful analyses of microfauna, the foraminifera, in the sediments which very clearly indicate changes in the salinity and also in the temperature of the water, so I think that the changes in the composition of the middens is a direct reflection of the marine environment. If you saw some of the graphs [I showed] … you didn't see a complete [disappearance] of oysters, just a decrease.
Peter Woodman	Is there any evidence in some of those middens of a discontinuity between the oyster and the cockle in the radiocarbon dates?
Søren Andersen	Quite the contrary. This change seems to have been very fast, and very abrupt, and what is interesting in a south Scandinavian situation is that this change is contemporary with the introduction of agriculture, at least it is contemporary with the change from the late Mesolithic Ertebølle to the early Neolithic Funnel Beaker Culture in this area, but I'm not saying that these things have anything to do with each other.
Rob Young	[A question for Dr Sulgostowska] Do your peat sites show any pollen evidence for land clearance, for interference with vegetation?
Zofia Sulgostowska	Yes, but only in the upper parts [of the peat sites], so it is [related to the] introduction of agriculture; [it] is connected with Funnel Beaker Culture in this north-eastern [part of] Poland. So it was a really quite remote part, but in central Poland … [there are Mesolithic sites with pollen evidence] and I can give references to the published palynological data.
Alan Saville	Another question for Zofia [Sulgostowska]. I wondered, you said – about the technique of prospection for finding the peat bog sites – that basically you are searching in the drainage ditches, where they are available, to find evidence in the cuttings. But I was wondering about the prospection technique thereafter? How you are expanding outwards from that, how you are deciding where to do your excavations and possibly locate further sites or the extent of sites?
Zofia Sulgostowska	We do try to check all these works but also sometimes it is by chance – it is moles which help us. [The surface] is covered by grass and sometimes you see [in the molehills] in such sandy deposits [that] you can find pottery. So it was the case in Dudka. I found first from [molehills] the pottery and then we have a test pit, small one, one by one metre … we prefer the small test pits. Really it is hard work. There is no tradition of peat cutting in Poland – [many] Danish sites were found during peat cutting – [but in Poland] we have the use of charcoal and wood [for burning, rather than peat].
Paul Mellars	A lot of these questions are raising the issue of why people actually eat shellfish, which in many ways is one of the critical questions. Now I suppose from our perspective it's not difficult to say why people eat oysters because we find them attractive and we can understand that anybody living near oyster beds would eat [oysters] as an attractive part of the food supply simply for variety. But when you come on to question as to why people eat vast numbers of limpets then it is perceptually difficult for us to understand. And that is a great question on Oronsay. I could give various reasons why I'm sure that the limpets were not bait, they were being eaten, and I think historically it's very significant that exploitation of limpets in particular is associated with times of scarcity. And we know that in the 19th century people were doing that when there were no other foods, so I do think the idea of limpets as a kind of stress or starvation resource is the one that fits the bill best. What we desperately needed on Oronsay and some of these other sites is seasonality data on the limpets to find out whether they're exploiting the limpets at the same time as they were fishing and what I suspect, and this is one thing we have never

457

done. If you could do that I'm sure you would find that they were exploiting the limpets at precisely the times they weren't fishing. That is probably the late winter and spring, because that's the time when you can't get the saithe and my hypothesis, which is highly testable if we can get good seasonality data out of the limpets, is that it's that starvation period of the year – they were probably doing a second run round the sites to harvest the limpets. So I'm sure it was food supply and I'm sure it was in the case of limpets a great stress resource, but it is the '$64,000-question' about these shell middens, why they eat shellfish at all.

PETER WOODMAN   Or 64,000 limpets in some cases! I think that's the problem, it's just a huge number.

PAUL MELLARS   A million!

GORDON MACLACHLAN   Question for Dr Zofia [Sulgostowska]. I noticed in several sites the presence of dog bones. Were they being used as food or, relative to the previous lecture, were they used in a higher status?

ZOFIA SULGOSTOWSKA   Dogs were [found] only at Dudka and I think that the new discovery by Witold Gumiński shows that probably it was the same ritual as in Skateholm – the [dog bones] were [from] burials of dogs, or dogs were put in the grave pit – but this is recent research and it is not published so I would like only to mention it. [Dog burial] is a tradition also in northern Russia – as at the Popovo cemetery. So the whole of northern Europe has this tradition, but in Popova dogs were [also] used [for] meat as part of the diet.

SØREN ANDERSEN   I don't know if I can make a short comment to that from the Danish Mesolithic. We have many, many sites with well-preserved faunal remains and from all the sites we have many, many dog bones with clear cutting marks from skinning, both across the nose and across the legs – so the dogs have been eaten very frequently, maybe always, I don't know. But it's the normal case to find dog bones scattered in the dumps or in the middens and very, very often with cut-marks from skinning.

PUBLICATIONS REFERRED TO, OR WHICH CONTAIN AMPLIFICATION OF POINTS RAISED, IN THIS DISCUSSION SESSION:

Bergsvik, K.A. and Olsen, A.B. 2003. Traffic in stone adzes in Mesolithic western Norway. *In* L. Larsson, H. Kindgren, K. Knutsson, D. Loeffler and A. Åkerlund (eds), *Mesolithic on the Move. Papers Presented at the Sixth International Conference on the Mesolithic in Europe, Stockholm 2000*, 395–404. Oxford: Oxbow Books.

Larsson, L. 2003. Land, water and symbolic aspects of the Mesolithic in southern Scandinavia. *Before Farming 2003/4* **3**, 1–13.

Louwe Kooijmans, L.P. 2003. The Hardinxweld sites in the Rhine/Meuse delta, The Netherlands, 5500–4500 cal BC. *In* L. Larsson, H. Kindgren, K. Knutsson, D. Loeffler and A. Åkerlund (eds), *Mesolithic on the Move. Papers Presented at the Sixth International Conference on the Mesolithic in Europe, Stockholm 2000*, 608–24. Oxford: Oxbow Books.

Milner, N. 2002. Oysters, cockles and kitchenmiddens: changing practices at the Mesolithic/Neolithic transition. *In* P. Miracle and N. Milner (eds), *Consuming Passions and Patterns of Consumption*, 89–96. Cambridge: McDonald Institute Monograph.

Price, T.D. and Brown, J.A. (eds). 1985. *Prehistoric Hunter-Gatherers: the Emergence of Cultural Complexity*. London: Academic Press.

Rowley-Conwy, P. 1983. Sedentary hunters: the Ertebølle example. *In* G. Bailey (ed.), *Hunter-Gatherer Economy in Prehistory: a European Perspective*, 111–30. Cambridge: Cambridge University Press.

Schulting, R. and Wysocki, M. 2002. The Mesolithic human skeletal collection from Aveline's Hole: a preliminary note. *Proceedings of the University of Bristol Spelaeological Society* **22**(3), 255–68.